Soviet and Post-Soviet Politics and Society (SPPS) Vol. 207
ISSN 1614-3515

General Editor: Andreas Umland,
Stockholm Centre for Eastern European Studies, andreas.umland@ui.se

Commissioning Editor: Max Jakob Horstmann,
London, mjh@ibidem.eu

EDITORIAL COMMITTEE*

DOMESTIC & COMPARATIVE POLITICS
Prof. **Ellen Bos**, *Andrássy University of Budapest*
Dr. **Gergana Dimova**, *Florida State University*
Prof. **Heiko Pleines**, *University of Bremen*
Dr. **Sarah Whitmore**, *Oxford Brookes University*
Dr. **Harald Wydra**, *University of Cambridge*

SOCIETY, CLASS & ETHNICITY
Col. **David Glantz**, *"Journal of Slavic Military Studies"*
Dr. **Marlène Laruelle**, *George Washington University*
Dr. **Stephen Shulman**, *Southern Illinois University*
Prof. **Stefan Troebst**, *University of Leipzig*

POLITICAL ECONOMY & PUBLIC POLICY
Prof. **Andreas Goldthau**, *University of Erfurt*
Dr. **Robert Kravchuk**, *University of North Carolina*
Dr. **David Lane**, *University of Cambridge*
Dr. **Carol Leonard**, *University of Oxford*
Dr. **Maria Popova**, *McGill University, Montreal*

FOREIGN POLICY & INTERNATIONAL AFFAIRS
Dr. **Peter Duncan**, *University College London*
Prof. **Andreas Heinemann-Grüder**, *University of Bonn*
Prof. **Gerhard Mangott**, *University of Innsbruck*
Dr. **Diana Schmidt-Pfister**, *University of Konstanz*
Dr. **Lisbeth Tarlow**, *Harvard University, Cambridge*
Dr. **Christian Wipperfürth**, *N-Ost Network, Berlin*
Dr. **William Zimmerman**, *University of Michigan*

HISTORY, CULTURE & THOUGHT
Dr. **Catherine Andreyev**, *University of Oxford*
Prof. **Mark Bassin**, *Södertörn University*
Prof. **Karsten Brüggemann**, *Tallinn University*
Prof. **Alexander Etkind**, *Central European University*
Prof. **Gasan Gusejnov**, *Free University of Berlin*
Prof. **Leonid Luks**, *Catholic University of Eichstaett*
Dr. **Olga Malinova**, *Russian Academy of Sciences*
Dr. **Richard Mole**, *University College London*
Prof. **Andrei Rogatchevski**, *University of Tromsø*
Dr. **Mark Tauger**, *West Virginia University*

ADVISORY BOARD*

Prof. **Dominique Arel**, *University of Ottawa*
Prof. **Jörg Baberowski**, *Humboldt University of Berlin*
Prof. **Margarita Balmaceda**, *Seton Hall University*
Dr. **John Barber**, *University of Cambridge*
Prof. **Timm Beichelt**, *European University Viadrina*
Dr. **Katrin Boeckh**, *University of Munich*
Prof. em. **Archie Brown**, *University of Oxford*
Dr. **Vyacheslav Bryukhovetsky**, *Kyiv-Mohyla Academy*
Prof. **Timothy Colton**, *Harvard University, Cambridge*
Prof. **Paul D'Anieri**, *University of California*
Dr. **Heike Dörrenbächer**, *Friedrich Naumann Foundation*
Dr. **John Dunlop**, *Hoover Institution, Stanford, California*
Dr. **Sabine Fischer**, *SWP, Berlin*
Dr. **Geir Flikke**, *NUPI, Oslo*
Prof. **David Galbreath**, *University of Aberdeen*
Prof. **Frank Golczewski**, *University of Hamburg*
Dr. **Nikolas Gvosdev**, *Naval War College, Newport, RI*
Prof. **Mark von Hagen**, *Arizona State University*
Prof. **Guido Hausmann**, *University of Regensburg*
Prof. **Dale Herspring**, *Kansas State University*
Dr. **Stefani Hoffman**, *Hebrew University of Jerusalem*
Prof. em. **Andrzej Korbonski**, *University of California*
Dr. **Iris Kempe**, *"Caucasus Analytical Digest"*
Prof. **Herbert Küpper**, *Institut für Ostrecht Regensburg*
Prof. **Rainer Lindner**, *University of Konstanz*

Dr. **Luke March**, *University of Edinburgh*
Prof. **Michael McFaul**, *Stanford University, Palo Alto*
Prof. **Birgit Menzel**, *University of Mainz-Germersheim*
Dr. **Alex Pravda**, *University of Oxford*
Dr. **Erik van Ree**, *University of Amsterdam*
Dr. **Joachim Rogall**, *Robert Bosch Foundation Stuttgart*
Prof. **Peter Rutland**, *Wesleyan University, Middletown*
Prof. **Gwendolyn Sasse**, *University of Oxford*
Prof. **Jutta Scherrer**, *EHESS, Paris*
Prof. **Robert Service**, *University of Oxford*
Mr. **James Sherr**, *RIIA Chatham House London*
Dr. **Oxana Shevel**, *Tufts University, Medford*
Prof. **Eberhard Schneider**, *University of Siegen*
Prof. **Olexander Shnyrkov**, *Shevchenko University, Kyiv*
Prof. **Hans-Henning Schröder**, *SWP, Berlin*
Prof. **Yuri Shapoval**, *Ukrainian Academy of Sciences*
Dr. **Lisa Sundstrom**, *University of British Columbia*
Dr. **Philip Walters**, *"Religion, State and Society"*, *Oxford*
Prof. **Zenon Wasyliw**, *Ithaca College, New York State*
Dr. **Lucan Way**, *University of Toronto*
Dr. **Markus Wehner**, *"Frankfurter Allgemeine Zeitung"*
Dr. **Ѧ**
Prof.
Prof.

* While the Editorial Committee and Advisory Board support the General
for publication, responsibility for remaining errors and misinterpretation

Soviet and Post-Soviet Politics and Society (SPPS)
ISSN 1614-3515

Founded in 2004 and refereed since 2007, SPPS makes available affordable English-, German-, and Russian-language studies on the history of the countries of the former Soviet bloc from the late Tsarist period to today. It publishes between 5 and 20 volumes per year and focuses on issues in transitions to and from democracy such as economic crisis, identity formation, civil society development, and constitutional reform in CEE and the NIS. SPPS also aims to highlight so far understudied themes in East European studies such as right-wing radicalism, religious life, higher education, or human rights protection. The authors and titles of all previously published volumes are listed at the end of this book. For a full description of the series and reviews of its books, see www.ibidem-verlag.de/red/spps.

Editorial correspondence & manuscripts should be sent to: Dr. Andreas Umland, Department of Political Science, Kyiv-Mohyla Academy, vul. Voloska 8/5, UA-04070 Kyiv, UKRAINE; andreas.umland@cantab.net

Business correspondence & review copy requests should be sent to: *ibidem* Press, Leuschnerstr. 40, 30457 Hannover, Germany; tel.: +49 511 2622200; fax: +49 511 2622201; spps@ibidem.eu.

Authors, reviewers, referees, and editors for (as well as all other persons sympathetic to) SPPS are invited to join its networks at www.facebook.com/group.php?gid=52638198614 www.linkedin.com/groups?about=&gid=103012 www.xing.com/net/spps-ibidem-verlag/

Recent Volumes

198 Oksana Kim
The Development and Challenges of Russian Corporate Governance I
The Roles and Functions of Boards of Directors
With a foreword by Sheila M. Puffer
ISBN 978-3-8382-1287-6

199 Thomas D. Grant
International Law and the Post-Soviet Space I
Essays on Chechnya and the Baltic States
With a foreword by Stephen M. Schwebel
ISBN 978-3-8382-1279-1

200 Thomas D. Grant
International Law and the Post-Soviet Space II
Essays on Ukraine, Intervention, and Non-Proliferation
ISBN 978-3-8382-1280-7

201 Slavomír Michálek, Michal Štefansky
The Age of Fear
The Cold War and Its Influence on Czecho-slovakia 1945–1968
ISBN 978-3-8382-1285-2

202 Iulia-Sabina Joja
Romania's Strategic Culture 1990–2014
Continuity and Change in a Post-Communist Country's Evolution of National Interests and Security Policies
With a foreword by Heiko Biehl
ISBN 978-3-8382-1286-9

203 Andrei Rogatchevski, Yngvar B. Steinholt, Arve Hansen, David-Emil Wickström
War of Songs
Popular Music and Recent Russia-Ukraine Relations
With a foreword by Artemy Troitsky
ISBN 978-3-8382-1173-2

204 Maria Lipman (Ed.)
Russian Voices on Post-Crimea Russia
An Almanac of Counterpoint Essays from 2015–2018
ISBN 978-3-8382-1251-7

205 Ksenia Maksimovtsova
Language Conflicts in Contemporary Estonia, Latvia, and Ukraine
A Comparative Exploration of Discourses in Post-Soviet Russian-Language Digital Media
With a foreword by Ammon Cheskin
ISBN 978-3-8382-1282-1

206 Michal Vít
The EU's Impact on Identity Formation in East-Central Europe between 2004 and 2013
Perceptions of the Nation and Europe in Political Parties of the Czech Republic, Poland, and Slovakia
With a foreword by Andrea Pető
ISBN 978-3-8382-1275-3

Per A. Rudling

TARNISHED HEROES

The Organization of Ukrainian Nationalists in the
Memory Politics of Post-Soviet Ukraine

Bibliographic information published by the Deutsche Nationalbibliothek
Die Deutsche Nationalbibliothek lists this publication in the Deutsche Nationalbibliografie; detailed bibliographic data are available in the Internet at http://dnb.d-nb.de.

Bibliografische Information der Deutschen Nationalbibliothek
Die Deutsche Nationalbibliothek verzeichnet diese Publikation in der Deutschen Nationalbibliografie; detaillierte bibliografische Daten sind im Internet über http://dnb.d-nb.de abrufbar.

Cover picture: ID 106956509 © Palinchak | Dreamstime.com

ISBN-13: 978-3-8382-0999-9
© *ibidem*-Verlag, Hannover • Stuttgart 2024
All rights reserved.

No part of this publication may be reproduced, stored in or introduced into a retrieval system, or transmitted, in any form, or by any means (electronic, mechanical, photocopying, recording or otherwise) without the prior written permission of the publisher. Any person who commits any unauthorized act in relation to this publication may be liable to criminal prosecution and civil claims for damages.

Alle Rechte vorbehalten. Das Werk einschließlich aller seiner Teile ist urheberrechtlich geschützt. Jede Verwertung außerhalb der engen Grenzen des Urheberrechtsgesetzes ist ohne Zustimmung des Verlages unzulässig und strafbar. Dies gilt insbesondere für Vervielfältigungen, Übersetzungen, Mikroverfilmungen und elektronische Speicherformen sowie die Einspeicherung und Verarbeitung in elektronischen Systemen.

Printed in the United States of America

In the memory of Jeffrey Burds (1958-2024)

For the Ukrainian defenders of freedom, democracy and
the right to self-determination

Contents

Acknowledgements 9

A Note on Transliteration and Place Names 13

Table of Figures 15

Introduction 17

1. Imagining Ukraine. Imperialism, Federalism, and Nationalism in a Borderland, 1848-1923 23

2. Nation Formation in a Stateless Nation. The Shaping of Modern Ukraine, 1922-1991 51

3. Managing Memory in Post-Soviet Ukraine. From "Scientific Marxism-Leninism" to the Ukrainian Institute of National Memory, 1991–2019 81

4. "Not Quite Klaus Barbie, but in That Category". Mykola Lebed', the CIA, and the Airbrushing of the Past 133

5. The Cult of Roman Shukhevych in Ukraine. Myth Making with Complications 165

6. Yushchenko's Fascist. The Bandera Cult in Ukraine and Canada 207

7. Eugenics and Racial Anthropology in the Ukrainian Radical Nationalist Tradition 255

8. "Saving the OUN from a Collaborationist and Possibly Fascist Fate". On the Genealogy of the Discourse on the OUN's "Non-Fascism" 297

9. "Benderites," UkroNazis and *Rashizm*. Studying the Historical Ukrainian Far Right in Times of Disinformation and Hybrid Warfare 333

Archival References 385

Bibliography 387

Index 455

Acknowledgements

The research for this book has been conducted within the research project, "Ukrainian Long-Distance Nationalism in the Cold War: A Transnational History," which has been generously funded at the Department of History, Lund University by the Knut and Alice Wallenberg Foundation, research grant 2019.0151. The foundation's generosity constitutes a sustained commitment to Ukrainian studies in Lund. I am also much indebted to the Marcus and Amalia Wallenberg Foundation and the MSCA4Ukraine Consortium for their support for displaced Ukrainian scholars, a generosity which has greatly contributed to the development of a dynamic research environment. Funding from the European Union, for the research project "Facing the Past: Public History for a Stronger Europe," HORIZON-WIDERA-2021-ACCESSS-03-01-Twinning Grant agreement 101079466 has underwritten new academic networks between the universities of, Lund University, Potsdam, Luxembourg and Vilnius. The author wishes to express his gratitude to the Swedish Institute, for obtaining a Baltic Sea Region Thematic Partnership Grant, and to Mikhail Tiahly at the Ukrainian Center for Holocaust Studies in Kyiv for hosting me. Funding from Inga och John Hains Stiftelse för Vetenskaplig Humanistisk Forskning, the LMK foundation and the Einar Hansens Allhemsstiftelse have underwritten our work and strengthened our research environment. I am very grateful for their generosity.

The author has benefited from discussions and feedback from colleagues and friends; the collaboration with Mark Bassin, Joachim Ekman, Florence Frölich, Vit Kysilka, Tora Lane, Ninna Mörner and Irina Sandomirskaja at the Center for Baltic and East European Studies at Södertörn University College was helpful in the conceptualization of this work. Roman Dubasevych at the Lehrstuhl für Ukrainische Kulturwissenschaft, Alexander Drost at the Interdisciplinary Center for Baltic Sear Research (IFZO) at the University of Greifswald as well as the newly established Center for Modern European Studies (CEMES) Öresund Network of Lund University, Malmö University and the University of Copenhagen have all provided arenas for networking and discussing drafts of chapters. In Lund, our doctoral candidates Sebastian Graf, Christian Kofoed Hansen, postdoctoral fellows Milosz J. Cordes, Ernest Gyidel, Odeta Rudling, visiting scholars Aniela Radiecka and Francesco Zavatti have benefited from the ability to work and interact with our MAW-funded Ukrainian professors Denys Kiryukhin, Heorhii Kas'ianov and Liubov' Kuplevats'ka as well as our visiting professors Jan Grabowski and Joanna B. Michlic. Our visiting faculty members have been integral to the research environment which made this work possible. Per-Arne Bodin has been an exemplary mentor within the Wallenberg Academy Fellow program. At the Royal Swedish Academy of Sciences Cecilia Herbst, Julia Holmvik and Gunilla Hallersjö have been extraordinarily helpful and supportive. Here in Lund, Wallenberg Scholar Marianne Gullberg has been very generous with her time, feedback, and encouragement.

Thanks are due to Andreas Umland, whose enthusiastic encouragement played no small role for the appearance of this volume. From a Kyiv under Russian bombardment, Andreas solicited constructive and very helpful comments by multiple anonymous reviewers. Input and feedback by Julie Fedor and Yuliya Yurchuk have improved the text. Jana Dävers and Valerie Lange have been very helpful as the manuscript was turned into a book. My student helpers Augustas Alekna and Ebba Sahlén have assisted with formatting, Sune Bechmann Pedersen, Erik Bodensten, Henrik Brändén, Nadav Davidovitch, Moritz Epple, Kristian Gerner, Eleonora Narvselius, Tomas Sniegon, Marius Turda and Barbara Törnquist-Plewa, Rakefet Zalashik have read and commented texts. Thanks are due also to Mykola Afanansiev, Jeffrey Burds, Marko Carynnyk, Krzysztof Janiga, David Marples, Jared McBride, John-Paul Himka, Oleksandr Melnyk, Grzegorz Rossoliński-Liebe, and Wiesław Tokarczuk for generously sharing materials, time and constructive criticism. At the National University of Singapore, where sections of this books were authored, Peter Borschberg and Brian P. Farrell were exemplary colleagues, whose experience, kindness and support were invaluable for the new administrator of the European Studies Program, navigating a new academic environment and academic culture. In Lund, Kristian Gerner, Klas-Göran Karlsson, Wiebke Kolbe, Christine Malm, Mikael Ottosson, Barbara Törnquist-Plewa, Henrik Rosengren, Lina Sturefelt, Ulf Zander, Johan Östling and Joachim Östlund eased the process of re-integration into Swedish academia.

The patience, understanding, and unwavering support of my wife Odeta—who pursued her own research on Lithuanian nationalism while commuting between the continents—is extraordinary. So is the kind and selfless support by *močiutė* Rita Mikstienė, without whose loving dedication and commitment to her grandchildren Gunnar *Augustelis*, Gustav, and Oskar the managing of the life puzzle while alternating between Oslo, Vienna, Singapore, Karlstad, and Lund would not have been manageable. I wish I had the words I need to express my heartfelt gratitude.

A Note on Transliteration and Place Names

Throughout this book Ukrainian terms and name forms for Ukrainian places and persons are used. In accordance with the publishers guidelines, the transliterations follow the modified Library of Congress system of transliteration from the Cyrillic. Russian and Ukrainian я is transliterated as "ia," (except initial Я: "Ya," eg. Yaroslav) Russian e as "e," (except initial E, "Ye," eg. Yeltsin), Ukrainian є as "ie" (except initial Є, "Ye," eg. Yendyk) Russian and Ukrainian ю as "iu," (except initial Ю, given as "Yu" eg. Yukhnovs'kyi). Ukrainian ї is transliterated as "i". Russian and Ukrainian soft sign, ь, as ', Russian hard sign, ъ, Ukrainian apostrophe ' as ", eg. V"iatrovych. Ukrainian names already transliterated in non-Ukrainian printed sources appear as they do in the sources, eg Serhy, Ostriitchouk, Kubijovyč.

Ukrainian name forms and terms are used, i.e. Kyiv, L'viv, Odesa. As many place names have undergone multiple changes over the past century contemporary names are provided next to historical ones. All translations are my own unless otherwise noted.

Table of Figures

Figure 1.1 "Map of Ukraine." A 1919 postcard visualizing the nationalist imagination of a Ukraine, from the Sian and Danube rivers in the west to the Caucasus and Caspian Sea in the East. https://en.wikipedia.org/wiki/Ukraine_after_ the_Russian_Revolution#/media/File:Map_of_Ukraine_ (postcard_1919).jpg (Accessed September 17, 2018) 44

Figure 3.1. "May 8—The Day of Memory and Reconciliation. VICTORS OVER NAZISM. UPA soldier Stepan Petrash and Red Army officer Ivan Zaluzhnyi." Propaganda poster from the Ukrainian Institute of National Memory, 2017. https://old.uinp.gov.ua/news/do-dnya-pamya ti-i-primirennya-ukraina-zgaduvatime-svii-vnesok-v- peremogu-nad-agresorom (accessed 25 May 2021) 118

Figure 4.1. Joe Conason "To Catch a Nazi," *The Village Voice*, 11 February 1986... 147

Figure 4.2. German Wanted Poster of Mykola Lebed' (October, 1941). The Mykola Lebed' Archive at the Harvard Ukrainian Research Institute, Cambridge, MA 154

Figure 6.1. Philatelic "all-inclusive" memory. Multi-totalitarian cover, on which postal stamps with red star, red banner and the ribbon of St. George on the occasion of the 60th anniversary in the Great Patriotic War (2005) share space with stamps with the emblem and red-and-black banner of the OUN(b) paying tribute to Shukhevych (2007) and Bandera (2009) on the centennials of their births. In the author's private collection.. 231

Figure 7.1. Dr. Rostislav Yendyk, Anthropological Map of Ukraine, delineating the various Ukrainian racial groups: Nordic, Sub-Nordic, Dinaric, Armenoid, Mediterranean, Sub-Laponoid, Paleo-Asiatic, Laponoid, and Central Asiatic. Yendyk, *Vstup do rasovoi budovy* (1949), 440............ 289

Figure 7.2. "Epicanthic fold." Yendyk, *Vstup do rasovoi budovy Ukrainy* (1949), 59... 290

Figure 7.3. "Nordic Race," from Yendyk, *Vstup do rasovoi budovy Ukrainy* (1949), 57... 290

Figure 7.4. "Nasal forms of whites (1), yellows (2), and blacks (3)" Yendyk, *Vstup do rasovoi budovy Ukrainy*, 59...................... 293

Figure 8.1. The death of Ante Pavelić as announced in the OUN(b)'s *ABN Correspondence* XI, no. 2 (March-April 1960): 13. 314

Figure 9.1. Courtesy of website *Hoaxlines*. "Stories about 'Ukrainian Nazis' were rare before 2014 when they surged at the moment when Russia's plans faltered," *Hoaxlines*, 3 August 2022, https://hackmd.io/@Hoaxlines/aug-3-2022 (accessed 7 August 2022) 359

Figure 9.2. Russian propaganda poster, "Russia's Borders are Endless" 2020. https://uk.wikipedia.org/wiki/Рашизм#/media/Файл:Границі_Росії_ніде_не_закінчуються.jpg (accessed 25 October 2022) 363

Introduction

Following the 2014 popular uprising against the corrupt government of Viktor Yanukovych (b. 1950, president 2010-2014) and the subsequent Russian invasion, journalist Anne Applebaum (b. 1964) argued "Nationalism is exactly what Ukraine needs." The argument for nationalism, she admitted, is not easily made: "you can't really make 'the case' for nationalism; you can only inculcate it, teach it to your children, cultivate it at public events. If you do so, nationalism can in turn inspire you so that you try to improve your country, to help it live up to the image you want it to have....Ukrainians need more of this kind of inspiration, not less ... They need more occasions when they can shout, 'Slava Ukraini—Heroyam Slava'—'Glory to Ukraine, Glory to its Heroes,' which was, yes, the slogan of the controversial Ukrainian Revolutionary Army [sic!] in the 1940s, but has been adopted to a new context."[1] Whereas Applebaum acknowledged its problematic history, she welcomed the appropriation of the symbolism of the Organization of Ukrainian Nationalists (OUN) by a young, aspiring democracy. In this approach, Appelbaum is not alone; between 2005 and 2010, and 2014-2019 the promotion of the legacy of the OUN and UPA was official Ukrainian policy. President Viktor Yushchenko (b. 1954, president 2005-2010) posthumously designated its leaders official heroes of Ukraine; under Petro Poroshenko (b. 1965, president 2014-2019) they were formally rehabilitated. In 2015 "disrespect" for them was outlawed.

Across the region, there is an increasing gulf widening between new research findings in the academic discipline of history and claims advanced by governmental agencies of "national memory"—as a rule nurturing narratives of self-victimization and identity construction by maintaining and reproducing traumas of the past. This book seeks to address this gulf. The status as a vic-

---

1   Anne Applebaum, "Nationalism Is Exactly What Ukraine Needs," *AnneApplebaum*, May 12, 2014, https://www.anneapplebaum.com/2014/05/12/nationalism-is-exactly-what-ukraine-needs/ (Accessed May 18, 2014).

tim nation is politically attracted in that it serves the aim of obtaining a "moral alibi" by dislodging agency and responsibility in past atrocities, communist as well as nationalist. Moreover, this narration is often invoked to justify wrongdoings by the ingroup as defensive actions.[2] At the heart of this inquiry lies a set of deeper questions: is it possible to decouple history and memory? What are the stakes and liabilities of doing so?

The study starts with a background on the origins of Ukrainian nationalism and its development in the Habsburg and Russian Empires. Chapter one chronicles the emergence of modern Ukrainian nationalism from its emergence, in the mid-19th century until the end of World War I, the division of Ukrainian-speaking lands and the establishment of the Soviet Union in 1922-23. Chapter two provides the context and background to how the frustration born out of the failure to establish a Ukrainian nation-state in 1918-1919 came to shape Ukrainian nationalism during the following decades. The crisis of democracy, rise of authoritarianism, fascism and Stalinism fueled a process of radicalization. In Soviet Ukraine, policies aimed at "rooting" Soviet rule by stimulating Ukrainian national consciousness and cultural autonomy were replaced, from 1928, by hyper-centralization, purges, and terror. Collectivization of agriculture was carried out at an utterly brutal pace, resulting in a massive famine devastating much of rural Ukraine. Purges, at the end of the 1930s paralyzed society and stifled political initiative. In Western Ukraine, part of the increasingly authoritarian Second Polish republic, a violent Ukrainian extreme right movement gained notoriety over the 1930s. The Soviet occupation of Western Ukraine destroyed the fabric of Western Ukrainian society; the German occupation in 1941 triggered new waves of mass violence, and marked the beginning of the Holocaust. During the period of extreme political violence, also constituted the peak of Ukrainian Nationalist violence; OUN

---

2   Florence Fröhlich, "Victimhood and Building Identities on Past Suffering," in Ninna Mörner, ed. *Constructions and Instrumentalization of the Past: A Comparative Study on Memory Management in the Region (=CBEES State of the Region Report, 2020)* (Huddinge: Center for Baltic and East European Studies, 2020), 23-36, here: 25.

terror against political rivals and ethnic minorities culminated in 1941-44. Uniting most of the Ukrainian ethnographic territories, post-war Ukrainian SSR (RSR in Ukrainian), "the Second Soviet Republic," came to play a key role in the Soviet Union.

The third chapter is a study of the crystallization of post-Soviet narrations of the past, and, the emergence of government agencies aimed at shaping "national memory." Specific attention is placed on the institutional framework behind the *Geschichtspolitik* conducted since this became a governmental priority from 2005.

The narration promoted by the newly established governmental agencies of memory management were not new. Chapters four, five, and six, problematize, respectively, the edifyingly patriotic narration the OUN, in emigration and, from 1990, in Ukraine. Structured around three of its wartime leaders—Mykola Lebed' (1909 or 1910-1998), Roman Shukhevych (1907-1950) and Stepan Bandera (1909-1959) they inquire strategies of patriotic disavowal, deflection, and denial. If Bandera led the radical faction that split the OUN in 1940-41, Lebed' served as its acting leader from August 1941 to May, 1943, when he was replaced by Shukhevych, who led the organization until the fall of 1944, the climax of which its campaign of ethnic violence.

Long venerated in the Ukrainian diaspora, these men were rehabilitated after 2005, with the latter two assigned central roles in modern Ukrainian history. As the ideological orientation of these men diverged sharply from liberal democratic norms, significant efforts were invested in re-casting the new national heroes as appropriate symbols for the young state. Problematic aspects of OUN ideology were misrepresented, involvement in mass atrocities denied, covered up, or legitimized. The airbrushing, practiced in emigration during the Cold War became government policy under Yushchenko. The main lines of argumentation of the denialist discourse were well established by the 1980s; new inquiry into Ukrainian Nationalist collaboration in the Holocaust was met with a well-rehearsed, coordinated apologia. As we will see, the emotional arguments that followed Yushchenko's designation of Shukevych and Bandera as Heroes of Ukraine in 2007 and 2010 mirrored those in the Ukrainian diaspora press following the exposure of Lebed' by a New York paper a quarter-century earlier.

While there now is a significant body of literature on the role of the OUN in anti-Jewish and anti-Polish violence, other aspects of OUN ideology remain understudied. Chapter seven is a study of racial and eugenic thought in the Ukrainian ultra-nationalist tradition. These currents in OUN thought are closely associated with yet another war-time leader, rehabilitated by Yushchenko; Bandera's deputy, the self-proclaimed 1941 OUN "Prime Minister" Yaroslav Stets'ko (1912-1986).

The post-1945 historiography of the OUN offers specific difficulties; unlike the situation in former Axis powers, where the institutional framework and continuity was broken, the Ukrainian far right continued its activities in emigration, first from Germany, then from Canada and the US. In exile, the OUN(b) leaders were in a position not only to shape the narration of the war, integrated into various institutional framework, many of which covertly or overtly funded by their new host countries. For nearly half a century, Lebed' was actively involved in promoting a sanitized, heroic legacy of himself and the organizations he led. Funded covertly by the U.S. government for over four decades, Lebed' and the revisionist splinter group of the OUN that he managed, engaged in a systematic white-washing the inconvenient aspects of his own, and the OUN's past. During the Cold War the émigré Nationalists found new roles for themselves as "the West's most faithful allies." Sponsorship came from from several state actors; Lebed's group mostly from the U.S., Bandera and Stets'ko from Franco's Spain and Chang Kai-Shek's Taiwan. From 1971, all three wings of the OUN benefited from Canadian multicultural funding. For a number of reasons, including strategic interest and reasons of geopolitics, the historiography was significantly distorted; to the systematic distortions by émigré Nationalists during the Cold War yet another layer of distortion was added following the repatriation to Ukraine of these narratives after 1991.

What is the proper nomenclature and taxonomy to be used to categorize OUN(b) ideology? During the Cold War, diaspora scholarship developed a rigid taxonomy which precluded the existence of Ukrainian fascism, denied the very existence of anti-Semitic organizations, ruling out, a priori, phenomena, observed in the rest of Europe, such as collaboration. Diaspora activists developed a coded language which served as an ideological underpinning to their discourse of disavowal and denial, further complicating a candid engagement with local agency in wartime ethnic violence. A candid engagement with this "undigested" past was not facilitated by the establishment of an government agencies of memory management. In 2006, a Ukrainian Institute of National Memory was established, staffed with activists from the OUN(b)'s own front organizations. In 2015, another complicating factor was added, a set of memory laws were enacted, explicitly designated in order to "protect" the edifyingly patriotic narration and outlaw "disrespect" for the OUN(b) and UPA. Chapter eight seeks to contextualize the genealogy of the discourse of the OUN's "non-fascism" and "non-collaboration," hegemonic in the Ukrainian diaspora, re-patriated to Ukraine proper after 1990.

Memory cultures of disavowal and memory laws have hampered understanding and complicated processes of reconciliation between Ukraine, Poland, and Israel. If there is any beneficiary from this, it is the Russian Federation. Its use of systematic dissemination of disinformation further complicates addressing the dark past. Ill-advised memory policies under Volodymyr Zelenskyi's (b. 1978, president 2019-) predecessors are weaponized as the basis for a relentless barrage of disinformation in an attempt to discredit the Ukrainian state project as "Nazi," "genocidal," and "satanist." The Russian Federation's shrill misrepresentations goes beyond merely falsification of history. Its systematic distortion forms the ideological underpinning for the Russian Federation's policy of revenge and neo-imperial expansion. This issue has become something more than merely an academic discussion of how to engage a troubled historical past; these issues are directly connected to contemporary politics, and has come to form the basis for large scale warfare in Europe. Following the full-scale Russian military assault on Ukraine, the long overdue critical engagement with a difficult past, suppressed by multiple actors—Soviet censors, émigré Nationalists, memory laws and governmental memory managers—already difficult in an era of fake news and information warfare has been rendered all but impossible. Even raising these issues has become a liability, which inevitably lead to accusations of "promoting the Kremlin's narrative," "neo-Soviet historiography," or "Ukrainophobia," and denunciations to deans, head of departments, and vice chancellors.

Is it even possible to discuss these matters in times of war? Should the difficulty chapters of the past even be problematized? Answering these questions in the affirmative, this study concludes with a post-script, written during the 2022 full-scale Russian invasion of Ukraine. It argues that the Organization of Ukrainian Nationalists, its militias and paramilitaries need to be problematized, deconstructed, and scrutinized. As symbols for a liberal, democratic and pluralistic society they are tarnished heroes. As Ukraine starts membership negotiations with the European Union, the author hopes that this book would help facilitate critical and candid discussions on the past.

1. Imagining Ukraine
Imperialism, Federalism, and Nationalism in a Borderland, 1848-1923

Borderlands invite us to reflect on the legacies of empire and nation, on identity and belonging, on various forms of social organization. Most textbooks in Ukrainian history takes a departure in the name of the country. "Ukraine means borderland," Orest Subtelny (1941-2016) starts his influential *Ukraine: A History*.[3] In the introduction to *Ukraine: Birth of a Modern Nation*, Serhii Yekelchyk (b. 1966) similarly stresses how being a borderland "between the open plains and the protective forests, Eastern and Western Christianity," and "the oppressive Russian Empire and its more democratic European neighbors" has defined much of Ukrainian history.[4] The borders of these parts of Europe have been volatile; stronger states have regarded weak neighbors as a vacuum which would be filled by others if our state does not act first. From Silesia to Crimea and the Caucasus, the lands have seen enormous changes of borders; states like Poland, Prussia, and Lithuania have appeared and vanished whereas historical regions like Galicia, Bessarabia, Silesia, Transcarpathia and Transnistria re-configured within liquid boundaries.[5]

Over the 20th century, Ukraine, with its fertile soil was subjected to an unparalleled rearrangement of borders. Its vast size, the absence of clear geographic boundaries, divergent historical experiences and ethnolinguistic diversity of this land complicated and delayed the formation of a joint Ukrainian nation state. Indeed, as Taras Kuzio (b. 1958) notes, "Competition between mu-

---

3   Orest Subtelny, *Ukraine: A History*, 4th ed. (Toronto: University of Toronto Press, 2009), 3.
4   Serhy Yekelchyk, *Ukraine: Birth of a Modern Nation* (Oxford: Oxford University Press, 2007), 4.
5   Alexander V. Prusin, *The Lands Between: Conflict in the East European Borderlands, 1870-1992* (Oxford: Oxford University Press, 2010), 1-10; Timothy Snyder, *The Reconstruction of Nations: Poland, Ukraine, Lithuania, Belarus, 1569-1999* (New Haven: Yale University Press, 2003), 15-51.

tually exclusive and multiple identities is a product not only of different historical legacies but also of the lack of territorial unity of that was to constitute the imagined community of 'Ukraine.'"[6]

Nation and Empire

Historically, Europeans and Asians have lived longer under imperial rule than under any other forms of historical organization.[7] In fact, imperialism and its consequences—empire and colonies—have been central forces of all civilizations from the beginnings of recorded history. Due to the diversity of space of empires, there is no scholarly consensus in regard to the defining characteristics of an empire.[8]

Today, the term itself is emotive, often associated with notions of oppression, arrogance, and exploitation. This is, however, a relatively recent state of affairs. Until World War one, many politicians were proud to call themselves imperialists, and the term denoted positive connotations, and possession of empire was regarded as a source of pride, not least among members of the expanding middle class.[9]

Historians of empire Jack Fairey (b. 1970) and Brian P. Farrell (b. 1960) note how "Empires were fundamental drivers of the process of globalization because they consolidated large areas." Fairey and Farrell argue that "as empires moved toward each other, they increasingly sought to reconcile, one way or another, their mutually overlapping claims and interests. The modern concept of an 'international order' should more accurately be seen as an order built primarily by empires, not by nation-states. Finally, imperial governance was itself reshaped by globalization; empires

---

6 Taras Kuzio, *Ukraine: Democratization, Corruption, and the New Russian Imperialism* (Santa Barbara, CA: Praeger Security International 2015), 2.
7 Jack Fairey and Brian P. Farrell, "Series Introduction: Reordering an Imperial Modern Asia," in Idem., *Empire in Asia: A New Global History. Volume 1. From Chinggisid to Qing* (London: Bloomsbury Academic, 2018), 1-8, here: 1.
8 Fairey and Farrell, "Series Introduction," 4.
9 Eric J. Hobsbawm, *The Age of Empire, 1875-1914* (London: Cardinal, 1989), 60, 70-73.

become more and more alike through processes of influence, imitation, and assimilation."[10]

Also critics of imperialism such as Homi Bhabha (b. 1949) Derek Walcott (1930-2017) and Robert J. C. Young (b. 1950) note the positive energies released by intercultural contacts and hybridity in colonial settings.[11] One, somewhat paradoxical consequence of these processes was the global spread of nationalism. Historian of empire Christopher Bayly (1945-2015) noted how "Imperialism and nationalism were part of the same phenomenon...The rise of exclusive nationalisms, grasping and using the powers of the new and more interventionist state, was the critical force propelling both the new imperialism and the hardening of the boundaries between majority and assumed 'ethnic' populations across the world." Bayly stresses the interaction between the two: "Imperialism and nationalism reacted on each other to redivide the world and its people."[12]

Nationalism

If 'empire' is an emotive word, no less so is 'nationalism.' Its legacy in the 20th century is often associated with antagonism and conflict, including some of the most violent episodes in recorded human history. Like empires and imperialism, nationalism manifests itself in a multitude of shapes and forms; its romantic legacy includes the desire to provide an area for popular representation and democratic governance. Johann Gottfried Herder (1744-1803) contented in 1784 that "The most natural state, is, therefore, one nation, an extended family with one national character...Nothing, therefore, is more manifestly contrary to the purposes of political government than the unnatural enlargement of states, the wild

---

10 Fairey and Farrell, "Series Introduction," 6-7.
11 On postcolonialism in post-Soviet Ukraine see Roman Dubasevych, *Zwischen kulturellem Gedächtnis, Mythos und Nostalgie: Die Erinnerung an die Habsburgermonarchie in der ukrainischen Kultur der Gegenwart* (Vienna: Böhlau, 2017), 229ff, on hybridity in the Ukrainian literature see Yuliya Ilchuk, *Nikolai Gogol: Performing Hybrid Identity* (Toronto: University of Toronto Press, 2021).
12 Christopher A. Bayly, *The Birth of the Modern World 1780-1914: Global Connections and Comparisons* (Oxford: Blackwell, 2004), here: 242-243.

mixing of various peoples and nationalities under one scepter. The scepter of humanity is much too weak and small to allow the grafting of preposterous parts; glued together they turn into a fragile machine ... devoid of internal life, and its components would be lacking in sympathy vis a vis one another."[13]

Herder wrote these words on the eve of the French revolution and died shortly before the Napoleonic occupation of Germany. Though no supporter of antagonistic nationalism, Herder's ideas shaped the romantic idea, to cite Elie Kedourie's (1926-1992) that, "that humanity is naturally divided into nations, that nations are known by certain characteristics that can be ascertained, and that the only legitimate type of government is self-government."[14]

Indeed, the idea that the people is sovereign is a shared raison d'être of nationalism and democracy; romantic nationalism during the *Vormärz* era was associated with radical and liberal calls for democratic reform and were driving forces behind the "spring of nations" of 1848 where liberals and nationalists (though this was not always the case among Slavs and Germans) fought side by side for constitutional reform and national independence.[15]

In the Anglo-Saxon tradition a similar argument was articulated, on a liberal basis, in order to provide representation, participation and good governance. In his *Considerations on Representative Government*, published in 1861, John Stuart Mill (1806-1873) argued that "Free institutions are next to impossible in a country

---

13   Johann Gottfried Herder, *Ideen zur Philosophie der Geschichte der Menschheit*, Zweiter Teil, Neuntes Buch, Band I. (Berlin and Weimar: Aufbau-Verlag, 1965), 368.
14   Godfried van Benthem van den Bergh, "Herder and the Idea of a Nation," *Human Figurations: Long-term perspectives on the human condition*, Vol. 1, issue 1 (May 2018), https://quod.lib.umich.edu/h/humfig/11217607.0007.103/--herder-and-the-idea-of-a-nation?rgn=main;view=fulltext (Accessed September 17, 2021); Elie Kedourie, *Nationalism*. 4th, expanded edition (Cambridge, MA: Blackwell, 1993), 9.
15   Hobsbawm, *Age of Empire*, 143; George Rudé, *Debate on Europe, 1815-1850* (New York: Harper & Row, 1972), 98. On the revolution of 1848 in Galicia, see Kai Struve, *Bauern und Nation in Galizien: Über Zuhörigkeit und soziale Emanzipation im 19. Jahrhundert*, (Göttingen: Vandenhoeck & Ruprecht, 2005), 85-105.

made up of different nationalities. Among a people without fellow-feeling, especially if they read and speak different languages, the united public opinion, necessary to the working of representative government, cannot exist."[16] Therefore, he contended, "It is in general a necessary condition of free institutions that the boundaries of governments should coincide in the main with those of nationalities."[17] Mill equated "free institutions" with "national" institutions, depicting the homogenous "nation-state" a "necessary condition of free institutions." The opposite position was articulated by Lord Acton (1834-1902) — also, on the basis of liberalism. Acton argued that "The combination of different nations in one State is as necessary a condition of civilized life as the combination of men in society...Where political and national boundaries coincide, society ceases to advance, and nations relapse into a condition corresponding to that of men who renounce intercourse with fellow men."[18] To Acton, "multi-national" states, such as the Britain and the Austro-Hungarian empire, who encompassed several distinct nationalities without oppressing them constituted ideal forms of government; in such modern empires—"nations" would remain internally homogenous, while the multiethnic framework would help maintain checks and balances and prevent despotism.

The aim here is not to assess whether it is Mills or Acton that is right; nor to evaluate the merits and demerits of empires or multinational polities or nation-states as such; this discussion has continued to this day, inconclusively.

British political scientist Margaret Canovan (1939-2018) argued that nationhood is a necessary precondition of liberal democratic welfare states, as these require both statehood and political communities.[19] Israeli philosopher Yoram Hazony (b. 1964) links

---

16 John Stuart Mill, "Considerations on Representative Government," in idem., *On Liberty and Other Essays*, ed. John Gray (Oxford: Oxford University Press, 1991), 428.
17 John Stuart Mill, "Consideration on Representative Government," 430.
18 John Emerich Edward Dalberg-Acton, *The History of Freedom and Other Essays* (London: Macmillan, 1907), 290.
19 Margaret Canovan, *Nation and Political Theory* (Cheltenham: Edward Elgar, 1996).

nationalism to virtues, pointing at how citizens of nation states tend to reject civil war and are raised to be considerate to all fellow countrymen and not only to the own tribe. Hazony argues that nationalism thus fosters reluctance against wars of aggression against other nation states, something he, in turn links to a third virtue: the appreciation of collective freedom and self-determination. According to Hazony, nationalism fosters "a measure of humility with respect to the wisdom and achievements of the nations," based upon the realization that also other nation states have their traditions and institutions. Only in competition with others do we learn which ones to emulate, and which to reject. Last but not least, the members of the nation state, ideally, do see themselves not as rivals but "family members"- something which strengthens support for individual freedoms and rights. Following Herder, Hazony argues that "nationalism, alone among the political dispositions ... offers a consistent counterweight to this fanaticism of the universal, establishing the diversity of independent order, and the tolerance and appreciation of such diversity as a virtue in the individual."[20]

By placing citizenship and statehood as a point of departure, Historian Timothy Snyder (b. 1969) identifies state destruction, the abandonment of enlightenment-based concept of statehood and citizenship as a necessary prerequisite that enabled the Holocaust.[21] Hitler, "did not believe in sovereignty as such and could imagine state destruction as the proper end of the war just as easily as he could see it as the proper beginning."[22] Therefore, Snyder argues, Hitler was no German nationalist, aiming for an enlarged German state, but rather, "a zoological anarchist."[23] Snyder lands in a position akin to Hazony, arguing that "Zionists of all orienta-

---

[20] Yoram Hazony, *The Virtue of Nationalism* (New York: Basic Books, 2018), quotes at 231 and 233.
[21] Timothy Snyder, *Black Earth: The Holocaust as History and Warning* (New York: Tim Duggan Books, 2015)
[22] Snyder, *Black Earth*, 241.
[23] Snyder, *Black Earth*, 241.

tions were correct to believe that statehood was crucial to future national existence."[24]

Similar analyses are often commonly encountered among Ukrainian observers, who often connect the 1918-1919 failure to obtain statehood to "the genocide of the Ukrainian people," the Soviet famine of 1932-33. Nationalism, and its end product, statehood, the argument goes, is not only a necessary precondition for democratic societal organization, but ultimately a safeguard against physical annihilation.

Nationalism with Upper and Lower *n*

Not all nationalisms are, however, peaceful and democratic facilitators of welfare states, solidarity, and harmonious co-existence. As Kedourie noted, it is "a misunderstanding to ask whether nationalism is politics of the right or the left. It is neither."[25] For the purpose of studying Ukrainian nationalism, Kedourie's words are helpful, as the discussions are laden with considerable terminological confusion. The most prominent Ukrainian far right group of the 20th century, the radical wing of the Organization of Ukrainian Nationalism, the followers of Stepan Bandera, known as OUN(b), referred to its ideology, simply, as Ukrainian Nationalism. With its totalitarianism, anti-Semitism, voluntarism, corporativism, cult of violence, *Führerprinzip* and raised arm salute, their strand of nationalism can be placed squarely in the fascist tradition.[26]

---

24 Snyder, *Black Earth*, 334.
25 Kedourie, *Nationalism*, 4th ed., 84
26 On the discussions regarding the categorization of the OUN, see Andreas Umland, "Der ukrainische Nationalismus zwischen Stereotyp und Wirklichkeit: Zu einigen Komplikationen bei der Interpretation von befreiungs- vs. ultranationalistischen Tendenzen in der modernen Ukraine," *Ukraine-Analysen* 107 (2012): 9; Idem., and Yuliya Yurchuk, "Introduction: Diverging Evaluations of the OUN(b)'s Ideology and Activities during World War II" 137-145; John-Paul Himka, "OUN and Fascism, Definitions and Blood," 166-175 and Omer Bartov, "Fascism in Practice and Contemporary Politics," 176-184, in *Journal of Soviet and Post-Soviet Politics and Society*, Vol. 7, No. 2 (2021). On Ukrainian ultra-nationalism in the interwar era, see Oleksandr Zaitsev, *Ukrains'kyi intehral'nyi natsionalizm (1920-1930-ti roky): Narysy intelektual'noi istorii* (Kyiv: Krytyka, 2013).

Focusing on the OUN and the UPA on the basis of original research this book seeks to problematize their utilization as symbols and role models of an emerging democracy, an aspiring member of the Euro-Atlantic community. In order to make a distinction between the more generic nationalist aim — the political commitment to Ukrainian statehood — and the totalitarian ideology of Dmytro Dontsov (1883-1973), Yaroslav Stets'ko and Mykhailo Kolodzins'kyi (1902-1939), this book marks this distinction by referring to the latter with capital N, as Ukrainian Nationalism.

Ukrainian Nationalism in European Context

When Russian nationalism, in the 19th century started to conceptualize the nation in ethno-linguistic terms, the Ukrainians were not (unlike, for instance, the Finns and the Poles) excluded from the national community based on a pedigree of Kievan Rus'. Official doctrine regarded "Little Russians" — as they were known in the Russian Empire — and Belorussians as branches of the Russian nation, and integral to the Russian empire, which regarded itself as the inheritor of the traditions of Kyivan (or Kievan) Rus'.[27] When the first Ukrainian grammar, *The Grammar of the Little Russian Dialect*, appeared in 1818, its author Oleksii Pavlovs'kyi (1772-1822) treated it as a dialect of the Russian language.[28]

Romantic notions of essentialism and particularism started to emerge in the late 18th centuries, notably. Herder developed his notions of a *Volksgeist* working in Livonia, travelling among the Slavic and Baltic peoples, whose local traditions made a strong impression on him. In 1769, the young Herder projected his romantic nationalist notions onto the local populations, for whom he envisioned a glorious future: "one day the spirit of civilization will visit them! Ukraine will become a new Greece; the beautiful heav-

---

27 Barbara Törnquist-Plewa, "Ukraina — en territoriell och politik eller en språklig och etnisk gemenskap?," *Historisk Tidsskrift*, no. 4 (1996): 494–547, here: 510.
28 Al. Pavlovs'kyi, *Grammatika malorossiiskago narechia, ili Grammaticheskoe pokazanie sushchesvenneishikh otlichii, otdalivshikh Malorossiiskoe narechie ot chistago Rossiiskago iazyka, soprovozhdaemoe raznyi po semu predmetu zamechaniiami i sochineniiami* (St. Petersburg: Tipografiia V. Plavil'shchikova, 1818).

en of this people, their merry existence, their musical nature, their fruitful land, and so on, will one day awaken; out of so many little wild peoples, as the Greeks were also once, a mannered nation will come to be; their borders will stretch out to the Black Sea and from there through the world. Hungary, these nations, and an area of Poland and Russia will be participants in this new civilization; from the northeast, the spirit will go over Europe, which lies in sleep, and make it subservient to this spirit."[29]

Modern nationalism arrived late to Ukraine. For its emergence, popularization, and dissemination the influence of the poet Taras Shevchenko (1814-61) can hardly be underestimated. His poetry rejuvenated the Ukrainian language, his promotion of folklore had a tremendous influence on the early stages of Ukrainian national mobilization and contributed to the imagination of Ukrainians as a distinct community. His contemporary Mykola Kostomarov (1817-85) began referring to Ukrainians and Russians as two different nationalities.[30] This nascent Ukrainian nationalism was met with repression from the imperial Russian authorities; from the forced "re-integration" of the Greek Catholic Church with the Russian Orthodox Church in 1839, to formal restrictions on the use of the Ukrainian language in 1863 and 1876.[31]

No one understood the potential of history for the purpose of nationalist mobilization better than Mykhailo Hrushevs'kyi (1866-1934). Having left the Russian empire for the Austro-Hungarian one in 1894, the Kholm (Chełm) native wrote *History of Ukraine-*

---

[29] Johann Gottfried Herder, "Journal meiner Reise im Jahr 1769" in *Johann Gottfried von Herder's Lebensbild. Sein chronologisch-geordneter Briefwechsel, verbunden mit den hierhergehörigen Mittheilungen aus seinem ungedruckten Nachlasse, und mit den nöthigen Belegen aus seinen und seiner Zeitgenossen Schriften herausgegeben von seinem Sohne Dr. Emil Gottfried von Herder, königl. Bayer. Regierungsrath. Zweiter Band*, in Emil Gottfrid von Herder (ed.) (Erlangen: Verlag von Theodor Bläsing, 1846), 155-334 here: 242-243

[30] Serhii Plokhy, *Ukraine & Russia: Representations of the Past* (Toronto: University of Toronto Press, 2008), 7; Thomas M. Prymak, *Mykola Kostomarov: A Biography* (Toronto: University of Toronto Press, 1995).

[31] Faith Hillis, *Children of Rus': Right-Bank Ukraine and the Invention of a Russian Nation* (Ithaca: Cornell University Press, 2013), 87-113; Theodore R. Weeks, "The 'End' of the Uniate Church in Russia: The 'Vozsoedinenie' of 1875," *Jahrbücher für Geschichte Osteuropas*, Bd. 44, H. 1 (1996): 28-40.

Rus' (*Istoriia Ukrainy-Rus'*), published in ten massive volumes between 1898 and 1936. Hrushevs'kyi claimed the legacy of the medieval Rus' state for Ukraine. He combined his role as "national" historian with political activism, serving briefly as head of the *Rada* of the Ukrainian People's Republic in 1918.[32]

The early Ukrainian nationalists faced a number of issues to be addressed. What constituted Ukraine? Who should be included in this incipient nation? What are its geographical boundaries? The pioneers of Ukrainian nationalism faced a situation similar to those faced by other stateless groups. Similar to the German case a century earlier, Ukrainian nationalism was articulated as an answer to the national question in rivalry with federalist options. In his 1796 *Grundriss des Völker- und Weltbürgerrechts*, penned in the midst of the Revolutionary Wars with France, Johann Gottlieb Fichte (1762-1814) envisioned a league of free and politically autonomous nations to cooperate within the framework of a league of nations. Following the Battle of Jena, in his 1807-1808 *Reden an die deutsche Nation* of 1807-1808, Fichte positioned himself as a German nationalist.[33] Fichte's *Reden* was, however, an elite project. Neither when originally delivered, nor when printed in 1809 did they generate much popular interest.[34] A more effective popularizer of the ideas of an ethno-linguistically defined nation was the historian, poet, and political activist Ernst Moritz Arndt (1769-1860). In his 1813 poem "What is the German fatherland? (*"Was ist des Deutschen Vaterland?"*) Arndt called for a nation united on the basis of common language, a fatherland to extend "As far as the German tongue sounds/And sings songs to God in heaven!" (*So*

---

[32] Plokhy, *Ukraine & Russia*, 80; Thomas M. Prymak, *Mykhailo Hrushevsky: The Politics of National Culture* (Toronto: University of Toronto Press, 1987); Lukasz Adamski, *Nacjonalista postępowy: Mychajło Hruszewski i jego poglądy na Polskę i Polaków* (Warsaw: Wydawnictwo Naukowe PWN, 2011).

[33] Rune Johansson, "Ideér om Europa—Europa som idé: Europeiskt enhets- och samarbetstänkande," in Sven Tägil (ed.) *Europa—historiens återkomst* (Hedemora: Gidlunds bokförlag, 1993), 48–110, here: 72.

[34] Sten Dahlstedt and Sven-Erik Liedman, *Nationalismens logik: Nationella identiteter i England, Frankrike och Tyskland decennierna kring sekelskiftet 1900* (Stockholm: Natur och kultur, 1996), 28.

weit die deutsche Zunge klingt/ Und Gott im Himmel Lieder singt!)[35] August Heinrich Hoffman von Fallersleben's (1798-1874) *Deutschlandlied* of 1841 specified the borders of the imagined ethnolinguistic community more precisely: "From the Meuse to the Neman, From the Adige to the Belt" (*Von der Maas bis an die Memel, Von der Etsch bis an den Belt*).

The Appeal of Federalism

The situation in the Habsburg, later Austro-Hungarian empire differed sharply from that of the Russian empire. Due to the particular political circumstances following the revolution of 1848 and the *Ausgleich* of 1867, the Galician Ukrainians, or Ruthenians, as they were known, were recognized as a separate nation already before they had completed their process of nation formation.[36] They had their own representatives in the Austrian diet and were allowed to develop their cultural institutions.[37] There was no consensus among the Ruthenian activists about who they were; were they Russians, a separate east Slavic nation, or did they constitute a common nation along with the "Little Russians" in the Russian empire?[38] As, by the turn of the 20th century, Ukrainian nationalism in Austrian Galicia reached the stage of a mass movement,

---

35 Sigrid Nieberle, "'Und Gott im Himmel Lieder singt'· Zur prekären Rezeption von Ernst Moritz Arndt Des Deutschen Vaterland," in Walter Erhart, Arne Koch (eds.), *Ernst Moritz Arndt (1769-1860): Deutscher Nationalismus – Europa -Transatlantische Perspektiven* (Berlin: De Gruyter, 2007), 121-136. Arndt inspired Galician Ukrainian nationalists, who translated his poetry into Ukrainian. Ernst Morits [Moritz] Arndt, "Pisnia pro bat'kivshchynu 1812 z nimets'koi vyzvol'noi poezii," trans. S. Hordyns'kyi, in Stepan Volynets' *"Za narod": Kalendar na 1943 rik* (L'viv: Ukrains'ke vydavnytstvo, n.d.[1942]), 57.
36 On the Ukrainian nationalist mobilization in Galicia, see John-Paul Himka, *Galician Villagers and the Ukrainian National Movement in the Nineteenth Century* (Edmonton: Canadian Institute of Ukrainian Studies, 1988); idem. *Religion and Nationality in Western Ukraine: The Greek Catholic Church and the Ruthenian National Movement in Galicia, 1870-1900* (Montreal: McGill-Queen's University Press, 1998); Andriy Zayarnyuk, *Framing the Ukrainian Peasantry in Habsburg Galicia, 1846-1914* (Edmonton: Canadian Institute of Ukrainian Studies Press, 2013).
37 Törnquist-Plewa, "Ukraina," 521.
38 Struve, *Bauern und Nation in Galizien*, 435-436.

these were questions that called for an answer.[39] Galician Ukrainian nationalism was contradictory; on the one hand so strong was the loyalty of the Galician Ukrainians to the Habsburg crown that they were often referred to as the "Tyroleans of the East."[40] Yet, towards the end of the century, Ukrainian nationalism underwent a process of radicalization.[41] If the lenient, and relative liberal conditions offered by Habsburg imperial rule provided the framework, rivalry with the Polish minority stimulated the radicalization and determined the form of Galician Ukrainian nationalism. Generations of political development separate from, and radically different from the conditions in Russian Ukraine, separate religious foundations and distinct local dialects could very well have paved the wave for the development of a separate nationality. Yet, historian Barbara Törnquist-Plewa (b. 1960) suggests that the inferiority complex and lack of confidence of the Ruthenian elite, combined with fears of Polish domination strongly influenced the Ruthenian elite not to move in that direction and to declare itself a separate nation.[42] Separatism was not on their agenda; the maximalist demand was the division of the *Kronland* into a Polish and Ruthenian part.[43] Perceptive contemporary observers noted that such a development was in the making. In 1907, the prominent Austrian Marxist Otto Bauer (1881-1938) noted in regard to the emerging Galician Ukrainian national consciousness that "it is certain that also the Ruthenians are about to embark on a path which the Czech already have behind themselves, and the Slovenians have already entered. The *Volksschule*, military service, general suffrage, newspapers and national assemblies expose the Ruthenian masses to the same cultural influences. The excitement

---

39   Andreas Kappeler, *Kleine Geschichte der Ukraine*, (Munich: Verlag C. H. Beck, 2000), 139; Larry Wolff, *The Idea of Galicia: History and Fantasy in Habsburg Political Culture* (Stanford: Stanford University Press, 2010).
40   Paul Robert Magocsi, *The Roots of Ukrainian Nationalism: Galicia as Ukraine's Piedmont* (Toronto: University of Toronto Press, 2002), 65-72.
41   Kerstin S. Jobst, *Geschichte der Ukraine* (Stuttgart: Reclam, 2015), 154-155.
42   Törnquist-Plewa, "Ukraina," 521.
43   Jobst, *Geschichte der Ukraine*, 158-159.

that the Russian revolution [of 1905] brought forth in the broad Ukrainian masses also finds its reverberation in East Galicia."[44]

Bauer believed that the national conflicts that threatened the very existence of the Austro-Hungarian Empire could be transcended in what he envisioned as a socialist *Vereinigten Staaten von Gross-Österreich*.[45] A *Nationalitätenstaat*, or federation of nationalities, he reasoned would be superior to nation states and reflected the assumption that size equated power.[46] The federalist option had significant traction among the Ruthenians of the Habsburg monarchy, who sought, in the first hand, the democratization and federalization of the empire. At the turn of the century, these sorts of ideas started to reach Ukrainian-speakers to the east of the Zbruch, who started to envision similar federalist concepts for the transformation of the Russian Empire.[47]

The political preconditions for the development of Ukrainian nationalism, in the realms of the Russian Empire could hardly have been more different. In Austrian Galicia, the Habsburg authorities offered highly advantageous political conditions for Ukrainian national mobilization beyond that what the budding national movement in the impoverished East Galician countryside was able to meet. By sharp contrast, the Russian empire, the most autocratic state in Europe, Ukrainian national consciousness was limited and the social basis for an effective nationalist mobilization largely lacking. Whether it manifested itself in federalist or separatist forms, the tsarist authorities cracked down on all Ukrainian national activism as subversive and inadmissible.[48]

---

44   Otto Bauer "Die Nationalitätenfrage und die Sozialdemokratie," in *Marx-Studien: Blätter für Theorie und Politik des wissenschaftlichen Sozialismus*, Vol. 2, ed. Max Adler and Rudolf Hilferding (Vienna: Ignaz Brand, 1907), 238.
45   Benedict Anderson, "Introduction" in Gopal Balakrishnan, ed., *Mapping the Nation* (London: Verso, 1996), 1-16, here: 3. On Bauer's concepts, see Olena P. Pal'ko, *Natsional'ne pytannia v teoriiakh avstromarksyzmu* (Kyiv: NAN Ukrainy, 2022), 130-145.
46   Dieter Langewiesche, *Der Gewaltsame Lehrer* (Munich: C.H. Beck, 2019), 270-271.
47   Frank Golczewski, *Deutsche und Ukrainer 1914-1939* (Paderborn: Ferdinand Schöningh, 2010), 289.
48   Kuzio, *Ukraine: Democratization, Corruption, and the New Russian Imperialism* 14.

However, before the revolutionary upheaval of 1917 and subsequent state collapse, one cannot speak of an irridentist movement.[49] Moreover, Ukrainian nationalism was contested. In terms of identity, in right-bank Ukraine it had a powerful competitor in the rivalling Russian nationalist project, a powerful competitor to the embryonic Ukrainian nationalist project.[50]

In his 1895 *Ukraina Irredenta* (*Ukraina uiarmlena*), the Galician social democratic politician Yuliian Bachyns'kyi (1870-1940) called for a "Free, great, and politically independent Ukraine, indivisible from the Sian to the Caucasus!"[51] In 1903 the call resonated in the Russian empire as Mykola Mikhnovs'kyi (1873-1924) called for "An Independent Ukraine—from the river Sian to the Caucasus."[52]

The Russian empire did not break up as a result of nationalist activism. Historian Joshua Sanborn (b. 1969) sees the collapse of the Russian Empire as a process of decolonization, triggered by the Great War which culminated "in the apocalyptic death spiral of the Russian Civil War,"[53] a process of disintegration through the combined impact of imperial challenge, state failure and social disaster, resulting in war lordism, paramilitarization of society through a process in which "decolonization necessarily entails state failure."[54] Still, in the period immediately following the abdication of the tsar, the dominant trend in the western borderlands of the former Russian empire was towards federalism—a "maximalist" aim at this point was national autonomy within a demo-

---

49 Jobst, *Geschichte der Ukraine*, 123.
50 Hillis, *Children of Rus'*; Klimentii Fedevich, *Za Viru, Tsaria i kobziaria: Malorosiis'ki monarkisti i ukrains'kyi natsional'nyi rukh (1905-1917 roki)*, per. z. ros. Katerina Demchuk (Kyiv: Krityka, 2017).
51 Yuliian Bachyns'kyi, *Ukraina irredenta*. Trete vydanie. (Berlin: Vydavnytstvo ukrains'koi molodi, 1924), online version, no page numbers https://zbruc.eu/node/54638 (Accessed October 10, 2022).
52 Mykola Mikhnovs'kyi, *Samostiina Ukraina* (Kyiv: Diokor, 2002), 6.
53 Joshua A. Sanborn, *Imperial Apocalypse: The Great War & the Destruction of the Russian Empire* (Oxford: Oxford University Press, 2014), 243.
54 Joshua Sanborn, "War of Decolonization: The Russian Empire in the Great War," in Eric Lohr, Vera Tolz, Alexander Semyonov, and Mark von Hagen (eds.) *The Empire and Nationalism at War*, (Bloomington, IN: Slavica Publishers, 2014), 49-71, here: 55-57; Sanborn, *Imperial Apocalypse*, 243, 6.

cratic Russian federation.⁵⁵ "[F]rom Crimea to Turkestan and from Chechnya to Estonia," Sanborn notes, "the message from these self-appointed nationalist groups was the same: no more empire, but federation rather than independence."⁵⁶ Political activists, who in subsequent decades would occupy key roles in the Ukrainian People's Republic, among them Dmytro Doroshenko (1882-1951) and Volodymyr Vynnychenko (1880-1951) saw national and class consciousness as interlinked phenomena. Such activists attempted to reconcile socialist and federalist position in pursuit of Ukrainian autonomy in federation with Russia.⁵⁷

A Parade of Ukrainian Independences

War and revolution energized Ukrainian national consciousness, tilting the balance from federalism towards separatism.⁵⁸ The emergence, or, rather re-emergence of coordinating centers, councils, *rada* in Ukrainian (*soviet*, in Russian) sprung from the same impetus of the workers' councils during the revolution of 1905. The collapse of the Russian empire stimulated autonomist currents across the region. In the Ukrainian case, three stages can be identified in the 1917-1918 movement towards independence, each accompanied by manifestos, so-called *Universals* — the name the Cossacks had used for their decrees. The first of these was a quest for autonomy within a federation following the abdication of the tsar in the February Revolution of 1917. Issued on June 23, 1917, it proclaimed the establishment of a government, the Central *Rada* (council), representing various loosely organized agrarian socialist, autonomist, left-leaning and liberal groups claiming to represent all Ukrainian territory. This phase lasted from March to November 1917. Following the Bolsheviks' seizure of power, the

---

55 Jobst, *Geschichte der Ukraine*, 167.
56 Sanborn, *Imperial Apocalypse*, 213.
57 Golczewski, *Deutsche und Ukrainer*, 463. On Doroshenko, see Thomas M. Prymak, "Dmytro Doroshenko: A Ukrainian Émigré Historian of the Interwar Period," *Harvard Ukrainian Studies*, vol. 25, no. 1-2 (2001): 31-56. On Vynnychenko, see Mykola Soroka, *Faces of Displacement: The Writings of Volodymyr Vynnychenko* (Montreal and Kingston: McGill-Queen's University Press, 2012).
58 Langewiesche, *Der Gewaltsame Lehrer*, 270-271.

Central Rada issued its Third *Universal* on November 20, 1917, in which it declared Ukraine an autonomous unit in a proposed future democratic federation, claiming authority over nine majority-Ukrainian *guberniias*.[59]

Unable to assert themselves in the councils in central Ukraine, as they had in the key cities of the empire, such as Petrograd and Moscow, the Bolsheviks initiated parallel processes or setting up their own councils, mirroring, and rivalling that of the Central Rada.[60] In order to root their hold on power in Ukraine on December 11-12/24-25, 1917 the Bolsheviks gathered the First All-Ukrainian Congress of Councils, or *Radas* (*Pershyi Vseukrains'kyi z"izd Rad*) in Kharkiv, which declared the establishment of the Ukrainian People's Republic of Councils (*Ukrains'ka Narodna Respublika Rad*, UNRR) "in close alliance with" the Russian republic of councils (or *soviets*). After the Bolsheviks' dispersal of the Constituent Assembly on January 6/19 2018, federation ceased to be a viable option to the Central Rada, which on January 9/22, 1918 issued its Fourth *Universal*, in which it cut all ties with the Bolsheviks, renaming itself the Ukrainian People's Republic (*Ukrains'ka Narodna Respublika*, UNR), "an independent, subordinated to none, free, sovereign state of the Ukrainian Nation."[61] Popular support for the UNR was similarly limited.[62] Two rival-

---

[59] Andrew Wilson, *Ukrainian Nationalism in the 1990s: A Minority Faith* (Cambridge: Cambridge University Press, 1997), 12.

[60] Of the 8,202,063 votes cast in the eight Ukrainian *guberniias* the joint list of Ukrainian and Russian SRs received 67.8 per cent. Carrying 10.0 per cent of the votes the Bolsheviks were a distant second. They performed strongly in the emerging industrial cities of eastern Ukraine; 59 per cent of the votes in Kam'ians'ke, 47.9 in Luhans'k, 47 in Yuzivka (today: Donets'k), and 27.9 in Kharkiv. Jurij Borys, *The Russian Communist Party and the Sovietization of Ukraine: A Study in the Communist Doctrine of the Self-Determination of Nations* (Stockholm: Norstedts, 1960), 157-161; Richard Pipes, *The Russian Revolution* (New York: Vintage Books, 1990), 541-542; Sanborn, *Imperial Apocalypse*, 229; Wilson, *Ukrainian Nationalism in the 1990s*, 40.

[61] Sanborn, *Imperial Apocalypse*, 231; Wilson, *Ukrainian Nationalism in the 1990s*, 12; Mark von Hagen, *War in a European Borderland: Occupations and Occupation Plans in Galicia and Ukraine 1914-1918* (Seattle: University of Washington Press, 2007), 88; Borys, *The Russian Communist Party*, 120.

[62] Stephen L. Guthier, "The Popular Basis of Ukrainian Nationalism in 1917," *Slavic Review*, vol. 38, no. 1 (March 1979): 30-47; Jobst, *Geschichte der Ukraine*, 168.

ling political bodies, both rereferring to themselves in terms of *Radas*—the Ukrainian *People's* and Ukrainian *Socialist*, based in central and eastern parts of the land now stood against one another. They would be followed by several more such short-lived polities.

Since 1916, Imperial Germany made use of the strategic establishment of *Saisonstaaten*. In December 1916 it had established a Kingdom of Poland, in September 1917 a Council of Lithuania. In the Land *Ober Ost*—the German-occupied territories to the northeast of Prussia—it stimulated the development of a Belarusian national consciousness.[63] By the spring of 1918, Finland, having declared independence in December 1917, was evolving towards a German protectorate; a monarchy was declared in May 1918, with Kaiser Wilhelm's brother-in-law Friedrich Karl of Hesse (1868-1940) elected king in October 1918.[64] In September 1918, it announced the formation of the United Baltic Duchy of Estonia, Livonia, and Courland.

The Bolsheviks demonstrated similarly significant skill applying the nationalities' principle strategically—declaring, dissolving, and re-arranging short-lived republics of councils rather unsentimentally, in accordance with the needs of the constantly changing geopolitical situation: in the following weeks, the Bolsheviks declared yet another three republics of councils in Ukraine. On 17/30 January 1918, after having expelled the UNR troops from the Kherson and Bessarabia *guberniias* the Bolsheviks declared the establishment of the Odesan Republic of Councils, (*Odes'ka Radians'ka Respublika, ORR*). On January 30/February 12, 1918, it was followed by the Donetsk and Kryvoi Rih Republic of Councils (*Donets'ko-Kryvoriz'ka Radianska Republika*, DKRR), and

---

[63] Dorota Michaluk and Per Anders Rudling, "From the Grand Duchy of Lithuania to the Belarusian Democratic Republic: The Idea of Belarusian Statehood during the German Occupation of Belarusian Lands, 1915-1919," *The Journal of Belarusian Studies*, vol. 7, no. 2 (2014): 3-36, here: 9-11.
[64] Juhani Paasivirta, *Finland år 1918 och relationerna till utlandet*, trans. Henrik von Bonsdorff (Helsinki: Tiden, 1962), 224-225,

the Socialist Republic of Councils of Taurida (*Radians'ka Sotsialistycha Respublika Tavrydy*) on March 18, 1918.[65]

Bolshevik revolts in several Ukrainian cities rapidly undermined the position of the UNR Rada, which was now desperately seeking foreign aid. As they evacuated Kyiv from the advancing Red Army the UNR Rada, over the protest of the Bolsheviks', signed a peace treaty with the Central Powers in Brest-Litovsk on the night of February 8-9, 1918, enlisting their support.[66] The treaty contained a provision to facilitate their military intervention on behalf of the all but powerless UNR Rada against the Bolsheviks.[67] The Bolsheviks, themselves divided on whether to sign a separate peace with the Central Powers, sought to delay the signing of a final treaty. On February 18, as the talks with the Bolsheviks stalled, the Germans and Austro-Hungarians broke the armistice with the Bolsheviks, launching Operation *Faustschlag*, a massive onslaught of 53 divisions, was a strength of 450,000 men. The Central Powers captured Zhytomyr on 24 February and Kyiv on March 2. The Central Powers received virtually no resistance.

Through the Brest-Litovsk treaty of March 3, 1918, Lenin's government now recognized, *de jure*, the independence of the UNR as a puppet state in the German orbit.[68] Now, the ad hoc Ukrainian republics, set up by the Bolsheviks disintegrated. Following its expulsion of the Bolsheviks by the Germans, the Odesa Republic of Councils ceased its existence on March 13, 1918, merely a month after its declaration. The DKRR was incorporated into yet another ad hoc "independent" republic of councils (Ukrainian: *radians'ka*, Russian: *sovetskaia*, Soviet) republic, declared on the March 17-19, 1918 Second all-Ukrainian Congress of Councils, or *Radas* in the city of Katerynoslav (today Dnipro). Also this polity existed only on paper, as the territories to which it laid claim was already under the control of the Central Powers; the republic was

---

65 The Gregorian calendar was implemented by the Bolsheviks on February 14, 1918 by dropping the Julian dates of 1-13 February, 1918 which thus do not exist in Soviet history.
66 Törnquist-Plewa, "Ukraina," 526.
67 Chernev, "Ukrainization and its Contradictions," 170.
68 Borys, *The Russian Communist Party*, 282.

formally dissolved the following month with little ado.[69] By May 8, 1918 the Germans controlled all Ukrainian lands up to Rostov-na-Donu in the Kuban.[70]

Even though the treaty, concluded on February 9 between the Central Powers and the UNR Rada meant that the former legally recognized the independence of the UNR, Berlin and Vienna regarded it as little more than a "cloak," totally subordinated to the occupying forces.[71] Dominated by Socialist Revolutionaries, SRs, the all but powerless UNR Rada sought to pursue agrarian socialist Ukrainian national culture.[72] Having little interest in agrarian socialism, on April 29, 1918 the German authorities dissolved the Rada, replacing it with a conservative royal dictatorship under Pavlo Skoropads'kyi (1873-1945). The new polity referred to itself as the Ukrainian State (*Ukrains'ka derzhava*), or the Hetmanate, as Skoropads'kyi took the title as *hetman* — that is, chieftain or monarch — while his polity, somewhat confusingly, referred to itself as an "independent republic."[73] The Hetmanate pursued policies of nationalization, and did so with active German support. Like in other areas under its control, the German

---

69   Borys, *The Russian Communist Party*, 138.
70   Golczewski, *Deutsche und Ukrainer*, 193; Peter Borowsky, "Germany's Ukrainian Policy during World War I and the Revolution of 1918-1919," in Hans-Joachim Torke and John-Paul Himka (eds.) *German-Ukrainian Relations in Historical Perspective* (Edmonton: Canadian Institute of Ukrainian Studies Press, 1994), 84-94, here: 86; Sanborn, *Imperial Apocalypse*, 240; Pavlo Hai-Nyzhnyk, "Vizyt Het'mana Pavla Skoropads'koho do Nimechchyny u konteksti politychnoho zhyttia Ukrainy 1918 roku," *Ukraina dyplomatychna: Naukovyi shchorichnyk*, vyp. XV (2014): 605-615, here: 605.
71   Golczewski, *Deutsche und Ukrainer*, 194; Borislav Chernev, "Ukrainization and Its Contradictions in the Context of the Brest-Litovsk System," in Lohr, Tolz, Semyonov, and von Hagen (eds.) *The Empire and Nationalism at War*, 163-188, here: 169; Peter Lieb and Wolfram Dornik, "The Ukrainian Policy of the Central Powers during the First World War," in Wolfram Dornik, Georgiy Kasianov, Hannes Leidinger, Peter Lieb, Alexei Miller, Bogdan Musial, Vasyl Rasevych (eds.), *The Emergence of Ukraine: Self-Determination, Occupation, and War in Ukraine, 1917-1922*, trans. Gus Fagan (Edmonton: Canadian Institute of Ukrainian Studies Press, 2015), 37-75, here: 65.
72   Boris Chernev, *Twilight of Empire: The Brest-Litovsk Conference and the Remaking of East-Central Europe, 1917-1918* (Toronto: University of Toronto Press, 2017), 139.
73   Golczewski, *Deutsche und Ukrainer*, 264-265; Chernev, *Twilight of Empire*, 7; von Hagen, *War in a European Borderland*, 88.

occupation authorities made strategic use of nationalities policies, opening schools, theatres, newspapers, with the aim of stimulating local national consciousness in order to counterbalance Russian and Polish claims to disputed borderlands.[74] Impatient with what he regarded as insufficient progress of the nationalizing policies, Kaiser Wilhelm II in June 1918 personally ordered Skoropads'kyi to Ukrainianize his central government.[75] Along with the policies of nationalization and Ukrainization, the Skoropads'kyi regime nurtured grandiose plans for Ukraine; it envisioned the electrification of the country through the construction of hydroelectric dams on the Dnipro, Dnister and Buh and the construction of a canal and lock system that would connect the river systems from the Black to the Baltic Seas. It planned industries for the construction of heavy machinery, textile, chemical and military production, movie production and to bring about land reforms.[76] As Skoropads'kyi's foreign minister Doroshenko echoed Bachyns'kyi and Mikhovs'kyi's calls for an independent Ukraine from the Sian to the Caucasus.[77]

State Collapse and War Lordism

The collapse of the Central Powers again had dramatic consequences for the Ukrainian lands. The armistice of November 11, 1918 annulled the Brest-Litovsk Treaty. Three days later Skoropads'kyi fled Kyiv. As his regime disintegrated, the hetman sought to retain his power by seeking a treaty of federation with the "White" Russian forces, effectively depriving him of any remaining support from the Ukrainian conservative forces.[78] On December 14, 1918, a group of five men, claiming to represent the UNR, launched a counter-coup against the crumbling Skoro-

---

74 Michaluk and Rudling, "From the Grand Duchy of Lithuania,"10-11.
75 Chernev, *Twilight of Empire*, 148.
76 Hai-Nyzhnyk, "Vizyt Het'mana Pavla Skoropads'koho," 610-611.
77 Jobst, *Geschichte der Ukraine*, 173.
78 Pavlo Hai-Nyzhnyk, "Derzhavnyi perevorot 29 kvitnia 1918 r: prychyny ta perebi zakhoplennia vlady P. Skorodads'kym," *Ukrains'kyi istrychnyi zhurnal*, no. 4 (2011): 132-164, here: 164.

pads'ky regime.[79] Invoking a terminology reminiscent the French Thermidorian reaction these men referred to themselves as the Directory.[80] Vynnychenko, its first chairman, was soon replaced by Symon Petliura (1879-1926) as leader.

In the Ukrainian lands of East Galicia—where the nationalization process, by and large had been completed in the first decades of the 20th century nationalist activists sought to fill the void left behind the collapsed Austro-Hungarian empire. Here, a group of activists declared the establishment of the so-called West Ukrainian People's Republic (*Zakhidnoukrains'ka Narodna Respublika*, ZUNR) on November 1, 1918.[81] During its twelve weeks of existence this short-lived *Saisonstaat* pursued a moderate policy, dominated by Greek Catholic, liberal, and socialist currents.[82] At this point the issue whether the Ukrainian-speakers of the former Habsburg and Romanov empires constitute one or two nations was still not fully settled and the emergence of two separate Ukrainian states out of the ruins of the empires realistic possibility.

---

[79] Rudolf A. Mark, "Symon Petliura und die UNR: Vom Sturz des Hetmans Skoropadskyj bis zum Exil in Polen," *Forschungen zur osteuropäischen Geschichte* 40 (1988): 7-228.

[80] Borowsky, "Germany's Ukrainian Policy," 91, Kappeler, *Kleine Geschichte der Ukraine*, 173. The Directory soon shrunk in size to three, before and in 1920 to one person; the Directory ceased to be a collective body as all the powers of the waning UNR were concentrated in the hands of Petliura as acting dictator.

[81] Vasyl Rasevych, "The Western Ukrainian People's Republic of 1918-1919," in Dornik, *et al.* (eds.), *The Emergence of Ukraine*, 132-154; George O. Liber, *Total Wars and the Making of Modern Ukraine, 1914-1954* (Toronto: University of Toronto Press, 2016), 81-86; Törnquist-Plewa,"Ukraine," 523.

[82] John Armstrong, *Ukrainian Nationalism*. 2nd ed. (New York: Columbia University Press, 1963), 18-19.

Figure 1.1 "Map of Ukraine." A 1919 postcard visualizing the nationalist imagination of a Ukraine, from the Sian and Danube rivers in the west to the Caucasus and Caspian Sea in the East.
https://en.wikipedia.org/wiki/Ukraine_after_the_Russian_Revolution#/media/File:Map_of_Ukraine_(postcard_1919).jpg (Accessed September 17, 2018)

On the symbolic date of January 22, 1919, the re-constituted UNR and the ZUNR, crumbling in the face of the Polish eastward expansion, declared the formal merger of the two *Saisonstaaten* into one. While largely symbolic, this date remains a powerful fiction in the nationalists' imagination, as the Day of Unification of Ukrainian Lands.[83] The Directory sent a joint delegation to Versailles in the hope of being able to participate at the peace conference, for which it had prepared maps of "La République Ukraïnienne," claiming an enormous landmass from Białowieża (Ukr: Biloveza), parts of the Lubelszczyzna and Nowy Sacz (Ukr. Novyi Sonch) in the west to the Crimea and the Kuban and the Caspian Sea in the east.[84] At Versailles, the Directory's emissaries

---

83 Jobst, *Geschichte der Ukraine*, 175; Golczewski, *Deutsche und Ukrainer*, 383. Markiian Shvets', *Sviatkove Vidznachennia Dniv Nezalezhnostu i Zluky Zemel Ukrainy 22 sichnia 1918 i 1919 rokiv: Vshanuvannia Ukrians'kykh Veteraniv* (Toronto: Ukrainian Canadian Congress, 2007). https://diasporiana.org.ua/wp-content/uploads/books/13151/file.pdf (Accessed October 2, 2023)

84 For a facsimile of the map, see Dmytro Shurkhalo, "Paryz'ka myrna konferentsiia 1919 roku: na mapi Ukrainy buly Krym i Kuban," *Radio Svoboda*, April

competed ineffectively for the attention of the Big Three. Scores of nationalist activists amassed on the Paris peace conference to argue their cases; from Åland islanders to Belarusians and Kurds. The plotters behind the Directory was seen as a group of adventurers representing few but themselves. The Directory effectively lacked control over the territories to which it laid claims. Its army was in shambles.[85] Claims for recognition were not strengthened by the waves of anti-Semitic violence carried out by its followers. Over one thousand anti-Jewish riots and military actions, commonly referred to as pogroms riveted Volhynia and Podolia in the first three months of 1919.[86] Equating Jews with communism, Petliura's troops carried out massive pogroms, killing upwards of 50,000 Jews.[87] News of the particularly brutal pogroms in Ovruch, Zhytomyr and Proskuriv (today Khmel'nyts'kyi) shocked the world. The February 15, 1919 Proskuriv pogrom alone claimed the lives of between 800 and 1,500 people.[88]

The retreating Petliurites moved their ad hoc "capital" from Vinnytsia to Proskuriv, Rivne and Kamianets'-Podil's'kyi before

---

30, 2017, https://www.radiosvoboda.org/a/28457626.html (Accessed December 22, 2019)

[85] Historian Fritz Fischer (1908-1999) noted how the Directory "failed to raise an army deserving the name," describing Petliura's soldiers as a total force of 2,000 men "in 'theatrical costumes' with no military value." Fritz Fischer, *Germany's Aims in the First World War* (New York: W.W. Norton & Company, 1967), 536.

[86] 167 of these pogroms are analyzed in detail by Jeffrey Veidlinger, *In the Midst of Civilized Europe: The Pogroms of 1918-1921 and the Onset of the Holocaust* (New York: Metropolitan Books, 2021). See also Eugene M. Avrutin and Elisssa Bemporad, eds., *Pogroms: A Documentary History* (Oxford: Oxford University Press, 2021); Elissa Bemporad, *Legacy of Blood: Jews, Pogroms, and Ritual Murder in the Lands of the Soviets* (New York: Oxford University Press, 2019), 14-34; Victoria Khiterer, *Jewish Pogroms in Kiev during the Russian Civil War, 1918-1920* (Lewiston: The Edwin Mellen Press, 2015) and Lidia B. Miliakova, ed., *Kniga pogromov: Pogromy na Ukraine, v Belorussii i evropeiskoi chasti Rossii v period grazhdanskoi voiny, 1918-1922 gg. Sbornik dokumentov* (Moscow: ROSSPEN, 2007).

[87] Christopher Gilley, "Beyond Petliura: The Ukrainian national movement and the 1919 pogroms," *East European Jewish Affairs*, vol 47, no. 1 (2017): 45-61, here: 45-46, and 56.

[88] Gilley, "Beyond Petliura," 46-47; idem., "Was Symon Petliura 'an anti-Semite who massacred Jews during a time of war'?," *Open Democracy*, 13 February 2019.

splitting into two groups, one of which established a government in Stanislaviv (today Ivano-Frankivs'k).[89] In the east, the Bolsheviks returned, restoring control over Kharkiv on January 3, Kyiv on February 4.[90] On March 10, 1919, a new Soviet Ukrainian polity, with its capital in Kharkiv, the Ukrainian Soviet Socialist Republic (*Ukrains'ka Radians'ka Sotsialistychna Respublika*, URSR) was declared. By the spring most of eastern Ukraine was under Bolshevik control.

On May 19, 1919, the newly restored Poland launched an offensive into Ukraine. This new challenge sharply divided the Ukrainian nationalists; the UNR — or rather, what remained of it — signed an armistice with Poland while the ZUNR, from June 1919 under the dictatorship of Ievhen Petrushevych (1863-1940) launched a desperate attack on the Poles.[91] The two "people's republics" had divergent conceptualizations of the enemy; the UNR regarded Russia an existential threat, whereas ZUNR, in their fight against Poland sought recognition from Russia.

The white, anti-Bolshevik movement had significant support in Ukraine. On May 16, 1918, the Don Cossacks had proclaimed the so-called Don Republic, which soon merged with the forces of Anton Denikin (1872-1947). In the second half of 1919 the white forces were advancing. In August, 1919, they captured Kyiv, and Denikin's and Petliura's troops were exchanging fire on the Khreshchatyk, the main street in Kyiv.[92] By September 1919 the white forces pushed the Bolsheviks out of Dnipro Ukraine.[93] In November-December 1919 the Galician army Denikin's white forces whereas the UNR signed an agreement with Poland; this

---

89   Golczewski, *Deutsche und Ukrainer*, 383-384; Georgiy Kasianov, "Ukraine between Revolution, Independence, and Foreign Dominance," in Dornik *et al.* (eds.), *The Emergence of Ukraine*, 76-131, here: 117-118.
90   Borys, *The Russian Communist Party*, 145.
91   Borys, *The Russian Communist Party*, 145; Golczewski, *Deutsche und Ukrainer*, 384.
92   Golczewski, *Deutsche und Ukrainer*, 385.
93   Arvid Fredborg, *Storbritannien och den ryska frågan 1918–1920: Studier i de anglo-ryska relationerna från vapenstilleståndet den 11 november 1918 till den begynnande avspänningen i januari och februari 1920 mellan Storbritannien och Sovjetryssland* (Stockholm: Norstedt & Söner, 1951), 202–205.

resulted in deep mutual bitterness and a full split between the ZUNR and UNR.[94]

Others, still, sketched alternative plans; In May, 1919, the troops of Ukrainian war lord Nykyfor Hryhor"ev (1884-1919), who had fought alongside the Bolsheviks now turned against them. Pogroms now shook the southern Ukrainian territories under the control of his troops; anarchy pure reigned the Ukrainian countryside.[95] Others, were still contemplating ways of cooperating with the Bolsheviks; this included Vynnychenko, the head of the original UNR Rada, who did not recognize Petliura and the Directory. Not yet entirely disillusioned with the Bolsheviks, Vynnychenko instead sought to establish a Ukrainian national dictatorship of laborers, federated with, or in a military alliance with the Russian SFSR and Bela Kun's Socialist Federative Republic of Councils in Hungary.[96]

With the silent support of the Entente, Poland set up a civilian administration in East Galicia in July, 1919. Józef Piłsudski (1867-1935) paid lip service to a Polish-led federation of Ukrainians, Belarusians and Lithuanians. The Polish leadership was, however, split, with the followers of Roman Dmowski's (1864-1939) National Democrats preferring a smaller, but ethnically homogenous Polish nation-state. Piłsudski's attitude towards federation was cautious; he would not discuss a federation, he admitted in private, "without a revolver in my pocket."[97]

---

[94] Shurkhalo, "Paryz'ka myrna konferentsiia 1919 roku."
[95] Kappeler, *Kleine Geschichte der Ukraine*, 177.
[96] Arthur E. Adams, *Bolsheviks in the Ukraine: The Second Campaign, 1918-1919* (New Haven: Yale University Press, 1963), 79-81; Alexander J. Motyl, *The Turn to the Right: The Ideological Origins and Development of Ukrainian Nationalism, 1919-1929* (Boulder, CO: East European Monographs, 1980), 54. The Hungarian word for "councils," *tanácsköztársaság*, is, the English language literature mistranslated as the "Hungarian Soviet Republic."
[97] Anna M. Cienciala and Titus Komarnicki, *From Versailles to Locarno: Keys to Polish Foreign Policy, 1919-1925* (Lawrence: University Press of Kansas, 1984), 122.

In April 1920, Polish forces launched an offensive, capturing Kyiv on May 7, 1920.[98] On April 21, 1920, Poland recognized Petliura's Directory as the government of Ukraine between the river Zbruch and Dnipro. Two weeks later it officially recognized Ukraine an independent state, calling upon other countries to follow its example.[99] Kyiv would not be held for long; in two Soviet counter-offenses, launched on May 24 and June 3, the Polish forces were pushed back. On July 15, 1920, as Soviet troops entered East Galicia a Galician Socialist Republic of Councils (*Halyts'ka Sotsialistychna Radians'ka Respublika*) was proclaimed in Kyiv(!), again in order to legitimize, root and consolidate Bolshevik control over the west Ukrainian borderlands. Yet, this time it was the Bolsheviks that had overstretched. In mid-August the Red Army troops were routed by Warsaw, and forced to retreat. On September 21, 1920, as the Polish troops re-established control over East Galicia the Galician SRR ceased to exist.[100]

* * *

The final year of the devastating world war resulted in state failure, social collapse, anarchy, and civil war.[101] The Ukrainians in the Russian Empire were far from done with their national mobi-

---

[98] Bruski, *Between Prometheism and Realpolitik*, 34; Adam Zamoyski, *Warszawa 1920: Lenins misslyckade erövring av Europa*, trans. Andreas Wadensjö, (Stockholm, Dialogos förlag, 2008), 49–64.

[99] Carl Reuterskiöld, "Polen erkänner Ukraina som självständig stat," Nr. 339, Berlin, May 15 1920; Carl Herngren, Telegram from the Royal Swedish Legation in London. May 28, 1921, "Statsformer och konstitutioner samt frågor om erkännande av nya stater." Folder "Ukraina 1920-," The National Archives of Sweden, Stockholm, Riksarkivet Marieberg (hereafter: RA Marieberg), SE/RA/221/2210.03.1/HP895A; Ivan Lisevych, "Politychni aspekty ukrains'ko-pol's'koho soiuzu 1920 r.," in Zbigniew Karpus, Waldemar Rezmer, and Emilian Wiszka (eds.), *Polska i Ukraina: Sojusz 1920 roku i jego następstwa* (Toruń: Wydawnictwo Uniwersytetu Mikołaja Kopernika, 1997), 81-99; Michael Palij, *The Ukrainian-Polish Defensive Alliance, 1919-1921: An Aspect of the Ukrainian Revolution* (Edmonton: Canadian Institute of Ukrainian Studies Press, 1995), 70-76.

[100] Kasianov, "Ukraine between Revolution," 77.

[101] Sanborn, "War of Decolonization: The Russian Empire in the Great War," 49-71.

lization when the revolution reached them.[102] Paradoxically—or perhaps partially as a consequence of this, in the period between December 1917 and June 1920 no less than ten Ukrainian states were proclaimed.[103] The city of Kyiv passed hands no less than fourteen times;[104] Ukraine had no less than fifteen aspiring regimes in three years.[105] Peace arrived only in March, 1921, with the Treaty of Riga, which divided the Ukrainian ethnic territories between Poland and the Ukrainian RSR. Ukraine was devastated by nearly seven years of exhausting warfare in which regional rivals played the "Ukrainian card" with various degrees of success. The peace treaty signed in Riga was highly unsatisfactorily to most Ukrainian parties.[106] In the Ukrainian RSR, Riga did not end the tribulations. In, 1921-23, a massive famine swept the Volga and Ural regions of the Russian SFSR; it also affected parts of the Ukrainian RSR.[107] Its consequences were amplified by international political isolation and the Bolsheviks' reckless economic policies of War Communism, which, when abandoned, were followed by hyperinflation in the Ukrainian RSR in 1922 and 1923.[108]

Federalism ceased to be a viable option as the continental European empires collapsed and were replaced by ethnic nation states. This breakdown of the European political order Arno May-

---

102 Törnquist-Plewa, "Ukraina," 526.
103 In addition, no less than 120 local "peasant republics" were proclaimed locally during the Ukrainian revolution. Kasianov, "Ukraine between Revolution," 77, 113.
104 Alexei I. Miller, "The Role of the First World War in the Competition between Ukrainian and All-Russian Nationalism," in Lohr, Tolz, Semyonov and von Hagen (eds.), *The Empire and Nationalism at War*, 73-89, here: 87.
105 Zamoyski, *Warszawa 1920*, 54.
106 The historiography diverges in the assessment of the Piłsudski-Petliura pact. See, for instance, Jan Jacek Bruski, *Between Prometheism and Realpolitik: Poland and Soviet Ukraine*, (Krakow: Jagiellonian University Press, 2016), 33 and Palij, *The Ukrainian-Polish Defensive Alliance*, 199.
107 Kazuo Nakai, "Soviet Agricultural Policies in the Ukraine and the 1921-1922 Famine," *Harvard Ukrainian Studies*, vol. 6, no. 1 (March 1982): 43-61; Borys, *The Russian Communist Party*, 280.
108 However, since Ukraine had all but ceased to be a monetized economy, the impact of hyperinflation was less severe than other European countries. Alec Nove, *An Economic History of the USSR* (London: Penguin Books, 1989), 54-55.

er (b. 1926) referred to as "the great ungluing."[109] This process was, however, incomplete and inconsistent. Some of the Habsburg successor states, such as Poland and Czechoslovakia, set up, supposedly, in accordance with Wilsonian principles of national self-determination—were not, other than on paper, nation-states.[110] While Yugoslavia and the USSR would both come to have significant longevity, they were authoritarian dictatorships held together by force—and their disintegration resulted in renewed war and ethnic cleansing.[111]

Violent Breaks

Historian Dieter Langewische (b. 1943) identifies four types of development for the appearance of new nation states: unification without separation; unification and separation; separation and state creation through the destruction of empires. He notes that the sharper the break between present and past, the more violent the subsequent war and violence.[112] The events of 1914-21 constituted the greatest upheaval and ruptures in modern European history.[113] In Ukraine, this heralded a period of social experimentation and utterly brutal transformation that would last a generation. The thirty years between 1914 and 1945 would alter Ukrainian society in its foundations—socially, economically, politically, ethnically and demographically. The extent of the political violence has few parallels in in history.[114]

---

109 Arno J. Mayer, *Wilson vs Lenin: Political Origins of the New Diplomacy, 1917-1918* (New York: Meridan Books, 1964).
110 On the complex and contradictory attempts to forge a Czechoslovak nationality, see Mary Heimann, *Czechoslovakia: The State that Failed* (New Haven: Yale University Press, 2009), 64-69; Ingmar Karlsson, *Det omaka paret: Tjeckernas och slovakernas historia* (Lund: Historiska media, 2019), 77-78.
111 Langewiesche, *Der Gewaltsame Lehrer*, 271; 334-336.
112 Langewiesche, *Der Gewaltsame Lehrer*, 278-279.
113 Max Engman, "Tillbaka till framtiden eller framåt till det förflutna? Imperieupplösningar förr och nu," in idem. (ed.) *När imperier faller: Studier kring riksuppläsningar och nya stater*, (Stockholm: Atlantis, 1994), 8.
114 Liber, *Total Wars*, 5.

2. Nation Formation in a Stateless Nation
The Shaping of Modern Ukraine, 1922-1991

Well aware of the challenges and opportunities posed by nationalism the Bolsheviks wrestled with the issue of how to turn an empire into a federation. They paid close attention not only to how the Germans, but also the young Polish and Lithuanian polities made strategic use of nationalism. The "great ungluing" offered new possibilities. Following his announcement of his fourteen points on January 8, 1918, US president Woodrow Wilson stressed that "Self-determination' is not a mere phrase; it is an imperative principle of action."[115] Wilson in turn, historian Joshua Sanborn (b. 1969) argues, "borrowed the slogan of the self-determination of nations from Eastern Europeans rather than the other way around."[116] The Bolsheviks were impressed by Woodrow Wilson's appropriation of the formula of self-determination as an instrument to weaken the Central Powers.[117] Terry Martin (b.1962) sees Lenin and Wilson as *the* two great proponents of the right to self-determination. Borrowing a contemporary term, Martin argued that "Lenin and Stalin... were, if you will Affirmative Action nationalists."[118]

Yuri Slezkine (b. 1956) similarly stresses the centrality of the nationalities' issue to the Bolsheviks' management of their polity, arguing that "Soviet nationality policy was devised and carried out by nationalists. Lenin's acceptance of the reality of nations and 'national rights' was one of the most uncompromising positions he ever took."[119] Lenin did, however, make a distinction between

---

115 "President Wilson's Address to Congress, Analyzing German and Austrian Peace Utterances," February 11, 1918, http://www.gwpda.org/1918/wilpea ce.html (Accessed April 15, 2019)
116 Sanborn, *Imperial Apocalypse*, 3.
117 Jörg Fisch, *A History of the Self-Determination of Peoples: The Domestication of an Illusion* (Cambridge: Cambridge University Press, 2015), 121.
118 Terry Martin, *The Affirmative Action Empire: Nations and Nationalism in the Soviet Union, 1923-1939* (Ithaca, NY: Cornell University Press, 2001), 341-342.
119 Yuri Slezkine, "The USSR as a Communal Apartment: or How a Socialist State Promoted Ethnic Particularlism," *Slavic Review*, vol. 53, no. 2 (1994): 203.

self-determination and separatism: "The right of nations to self-determination...must under no circumstances be confused with the expediency of a given nation's secession," he had declared already in 1913.[120] Stalin, in a 1920 letter to Lenin presented confederation as a transition step in which different nations are brought into a single political unit. Stalin, the commissar of nationalities argued that a federated republic, the RSFSR, as appropriate for nationalities who had been part of the old Russian empire, but not for nationalities with experience of independence, for which he argued for the establishment of separate Soviet republics—though he noted that the difference in regard to federal relations within the RSFSR and between the RSFSR and other Soviet relations were all but non-existent.[121] Alas, the policies sought to disarm "nationalism by granting what were called the 'forms' of nationhood." Soviet nationality policy was "a strategy designed to avoid perception of empire," at the same time as it "decidedly rejected the model of the nation state."[122] Ukrainian national institutions; a government, communist party, a capital, and administration were set up in accordance with Stalin's dictum "national in form, proletarian in content."[123]

Out of the dozen or so *Saisonstaaten* declared in Ukraine between 1917 and 1919 one polity—the Ukrainian RSR—would come to have an enduring impact. Best characterized as a protostate, this republic was technically independent until the Treaty on the Creation of the Union of Soviet Socialist Republics which came into effect on July 6, 1923, when it became a founding member of the USSR.[124]

---

120 Fisch, *A History of the Self-Determination*, 120.
121 Stalin to Lenin, June 12, 1920, V. I. Lenin, *Polnoe sobranie sochinenii, Tom 41. Mai-noiabr 1920* (Moscow: Gosizpolit, 1981), 513, cited in Ronald Grigor Suny, *The Revenge of the Past: Nationalism, Revolution and the Collapse of the Soviet Union* (Stanford, CA: Stanford University Press, 1993), 178, n. 13.
122 Martin, *Affirmative Action Empire*, 15, 18.
123 J.V. Stalin, "The Political Tasks of the University of the Peoples of the East," in *Works*, Volume 7, (Moscow: Foreign Languages Publishing House, 1954), 135-154, here: 138.
124 Borys, *The Russian Communist Party*, 282-323. The entry of Ukrainian into the USSR was reported to all powers with which the USSR had diplomatic relations, without any objections. Sign. "P.M.," Kungliga Utrikesdepartementet,

NATION FORMATION IN A STATELESS NATION 53

Up until Gorbachev's *Perestroika*, nationalism and nationalities problems in the Soviet Union generated rather limited academic interest.[125] During the Cold War, the Soviet Union was often depicted as a "breaker" or "killer" of nations.[126] However, "nation building" and "nation destroying" do not have to be mutually exclusive. Walker Connor (1926-2017) noted how nation building also entails "nation destroying."[127] Soviet modernity entailed both.[128] The opening of the archives allowed scholars to gain a new understanding of the complex and often contradictory Soviet nationality policies. In recent decades focus has increasingly shifted to the role of the Soviet regime as a *maker* of nations.[129] Strategic nationalization policies have generated considerable interest, with some recent works attempting to understand modern Ukrainian nationalism as products of geopolitical rivalries during World War I and Soviet nationalities polices of the 1920s.[130]

Bolshevik policies over time yielded sharply divergent results in different parts of the Soviet Union: the Soviet experience

---

October 12, 1925. Gr. HP, Avd. 12, Euk. HP 12, RA Marieberg, SE/RA/221/2210.03.1/HP895A.

125 Exceptions included Walker Connor, *The National Question in Marxist-Leninist Theory and Strategy* (Princeton: Princeton University Press, 1984); Erwin Oberländer, *Sowjetpatriotismus und Geschichte: Dokumentation* (Cologne: Verlag Wissenschaft und Politik, 1967); Lowell Tillett, *The Great Friendship: Soviet Historians on the Non-Russian Nationalities* (Chapel Hill: University of North Carolina Press, 1969).

126 Robert Conquest, *The Nation Killers: The Soviet Deportation of Nationalities* (London: Macmillan, 1970); idem., *Stalin: Breaker of Nations* (New York: Penguin Random House, 1991); Walter Kolarz, *Russia and her Colonies* (Hamden, CT: Archon Books, 1967)

127 Walker Connor, "Nation-Building or Nation-Destroying?," *World Politics* vol. 24, no. 3 (April 1972): 332-336.

128 Suny and Martin, "Introduction," in idem., (eds.) *A State of Nations*, 6.

129 Martin, *Affirmative Action Empire*; Suny, *The Revenge of the Past*; Francine Hirsch, "Toward and Empire of Nations: Border-Making in the Formation of Soviet National Identities," *The Russian Review* 59 (April 2000), 201-226.

130 Miller, "The Role of the First World War," 89; Chernev, "Ukrainization and Its Contradictions," 188; Timothy Snyder, *Sketches from a Secret War: A Polish Artist's Mission to Liberate Soviet Ukraine* (New Haven: Yale University Press, 2005). On the analogous situation in neighboring Belorussia, see Alena Marková, *The Path to a Soviet Nation: The Policy of Belarusization* (Paderborn: Schöningh, 2022); Per Anders Rudling, *The Rise and Fall of Belarusian Nationalism, 1906-1931* (Pittsburgh: Pittsburgh University Press, 2014).

largely dislodged Circassian and Turkestani nationalism whereas it produced Kazakh, Uzbek, and Turkmen identities. Circassians were organized into several autonomous republics under different names embarking on nationalizing policies codifying local dialects codified and developed into separate literary languages.[131] A similar pattern could be observed in Central Asia, where tribal groups were organized into Soviet nationalities and, later, separate Soviet republics. In Turkestan, through a process which historian Francine Hirsch (b. 1967) refers to as double assimilation, "the clans, tribes and *narodnosti*" of the former Russian Empire took on Soviet national identities as they were integrated into the Soviet Union.[132] Hirsch argues that "the national-territorial delimitation ... should not be dismissed as a devious strategy of 'divide and rule'... but instead be understood as a manifestation of the Soviet regime's attempt to define a new (and presumably non-imperialistic) model of colonization."[133] She suggests that "Soviet nationalities policy was indeed a variation of Western colonial policy," but contends that "for Soviet policymakers, colonization and 'making nations' went hand in hand."[134]

The appearance of a Belarusian nationality has been described as a result of often arbitrary decisions by Soviet bureaucrats.[135] Indeed, Soviet nationalities policies vis-a-vis the two largest Soviet nationalities, Ukrainians and Russians, alternated between suppression and stimulation. Ronald Grigor Suny (b. 1940) argues how "the processes set in motion by *korenizatsiia* continued until, by the 1960s, most of the republics had become more na-

---

131 Lidia S. Zhigunova and Raymond C. Taras, "Under the Holy Tree: Circassian activism, indigenous cosmologies and decolonizing practices," in Christofer Berglund, Katrine Gotfredsen, Jean Hudson and Bo Petersson (eds.) *Language and Society in the Caucasus: Understanding the Past, Navigating the Present* (Lund: Universus Academic Press, 2021), 190-213, here: 191, n. 1.
132 Francine Hirsch, *Empire of Nations: Ethnographic knowledge and the Making of the Soviet Union* (Ithaca: Cornell University Press, 2005), 186.
133 Hirsch, "Toward an Empire of Nations," 202.
134 Hirsch, "Toward an Empire of Nations," 201, 203.
135 Kristian Gerner, "Ryssland: Statsbildning som historiskt problem," in *Ryssland: ett annat Europa: Historia och samhälle under 1000 år*, ed. Birgitta Furuhagen (Stockholm: Utbildningsradion, 1995), 277.

tional in character, not only demographically, but politically and culturally as well."[136]

As the Ukrainian RSR became the basis for Ukrainian statehood, modernity arrived in Ukraine in Soviet form. The Soviet regime sought to take charge of the processes of nation formation in areas were local populations appeared to lack national consciousness, coalescing peasantry into socialist nationalities, Ukrainianized the institutions and promoted Ukrainians into positions of authority in the republic.[137]

Suny applied the neologism "affirmative action" to describe these, often contradictory Soviet nationalities policies, whereas his colleague Terry Martin refers to the anti-imperial state the Bolsheviks self-consciously attempted to create as an "affirmative action empire."[138] Other terms have been suggested; Taras Kuzio introduced the term "federal colonialism" to address the "state- and in some cases nation-building for non-Russians [that] took place at both the republican and all-union level."[139] The diverging terminologies reflect diverging assessments of often contradictory policies and processes.

Over its 73 years of existence, the policies of the Soviet system differed in intensity and brutality. The end of seven years of armed conflict in 1921 was followed by seven years with a semblance of normalcy. During the cultural and economic liberalization of the so-called New Economic Policy (*Nova ekonomichna polityka*, NEP) of 1921-1928 Soviet Ukraine saw a significant economic recovery, accompanied by a cultural renaissance. The Ukrainian language and culture was promoted by national communists such as Mykola Skrypnyk (1872-1933) and Oleksandr Shums'kyi (1890-

---

136 Suny, *The Revenge of the Past*, 109.
137 Hirsch, *Empire of Nations*, 5-8.
138 Suny, *Revenge of the Past*, 109; Ronald Grigor Suny and Terry Martin, "Introduction", in idem,. *A State of Nations: Empire and Nation-Making in the Age of Lenin and Stalin* (Oxford: Oxford University Press, 2001), 3-20, here: 8.
139 Taras Kuzio, *Theoretical and Comparative Perspectives on Nationalism: New Directions in Cross-Cultural and Post-Communist Studies.* (Stuttgart: ibidem-Verlag, 2007), 101.

1946).[140] Literature and film flourished with writers such as Mykola Khvylovyi (1893-1933) and film maker Oleksandr Dovzhenko (1894-1956) as representatives of a new wave of Ukrainian culture.[141] Ukrainian primary and secondary schools were opened on a mass scale; theatres, newspapers, journals and publishing houses popularized and distributed Ukrainian culture and literature in unprecedented numbers.[142] The joint policies of indigenization and Ukrainianization exercised considerable attraction on Ukrainians beyond the Soviet borders. Dozens of nationalist émigrés — the most prominent being Hrushevs'kyi himself — returned from emigration, raising the prestige of the Kharkiv regime while contributing to the consolidation of Soviet rule in Ukraine.[143] By the second half of the 1920s, this development increasingly worried the central authorities in Moscow. Under the slogan "Away from Moscow!" (*Het' vid Moskvy!*) Khvyloyi and other national communists sought to utilize these policies to advance their own agendas, pushing the Ukrainization further than the central government in Moscow was prepared to accept.[144]

---

140 James Mace, *Communism and the Dilemmas of National Liberation: National Communism in Soviet Ukraine, 1918-1933* (Cambridge, MA: HURI Harvard, 1983), 86-119 and 192-231.

141 Olena Palko, *Making Ukraine Soviet: Literature and Cultural Politics under Lenin and Stalin* (London: Bloomsbury Academic Press, 2022); Alexander Kratochvil, *Mykola Chvyl'ovyj: Eine Studie zu Leben und Werk* (=*Slavistische Beiträge*, Bd. 379) (Munich: Verlag Otta Sagner, 1999); Mykola Khvylovyi, Myroslav Shkandrij, and George S.N. Luckyj, *The Cultural Renaissance in Ukraine: Polemical Pamphlets 1925-26* (Edmonton: The Canadian Institute of Ukrainian Studies Press, 1986); Oleh S. Ilnytzkyj, *Ukrainian Futurism, 1914-1930* (Cambridge, MA: Harvard Ukrainian Research Institute, 1998); George O. Liber, *Alexander Dovzhenko: A Life in Soviet Film* (London: British Film Institute, 2000).ge

142 Matthew Pauly, *Breaking the Tongue: Language, Education, and Power in Soviet Ukraine, 1923-1934* (Toronto: University of Toronto Press, 2014); Mayhill C. Fowler, *Beau Monde on Empire's Edge: State and Stage in Soviet Ukraine* (Toronto: University of Toronto Press, 2017).

143 Christopher Gilley, *The 'Change of Signposts' in the Ukrainian emigration: A Contribution to the History of Sovietophilism in the 1920s.* (Stuttgart: ibidem Verlag, 2014); Martin, *Affirmative Action Empire*, 222-224.

144 Mace, *Communism and the Dilemmas of National Liberation*, 106.

West of the Zbruch

In emigration, the UNR activists were ineffective in winning support for their cause. By 1919-20, the international community had lost virtually all interest in the squabbling émigré groups. To German policy makers, the Ukrainian issue all but disappeared during the immediate post-Versailles years.[145] British diplomats refused to receive the exiles jockeying for recognition; after consulting with Danish and British foreign ministries, in May, 1921 the Swedish foreign ministry stated, unequivocally that "Ukraine does not to exist as a state."[146]

The new Polish constitution defined Poland as a nation-state of the Polish nation.[147] However, as national minorities constituted over 35 per cent of its population, the Second Polish republic was neither a nation-state, nor a federation.[148] In addition, during the early years of its existence, the restored republic was weakened by a polarized and fractured political landscape. Former autonomists and federalists, who, in the late imperial era had sought decentralization turned into centralists of the new nationalizing states, now rejected analogous claims from their own minorities. The role of the state had grown significantly during and after World War I. There was a general trend towards administrative centralization, reinforced by a general move towards authoritarianism from the

---

145 Golczewski, *Deutsche und Ukrainer*, 361.
146 "Currently, Ukraine is regarded as non-existent. [Ukraina anses för närvarande ej existera]" Erik Palmstierna, Ciphered telegram from the Royal Swedish Legation in London. May 28, 1921, HP. 12, Eli. No. 10:b, RA Marieberg, SE/RA/221/2210.03.1/HP895A.
147 Jerzy Borzęcki, *The Soviet-Polish Peace of 1921 and the Creation of Interwar Europe* (New Haven: Yale University Press, 2008), 279.
148 Arthur Sehn, "Etniska minoriteter i Polen i svenska diplomatrapporter 1918–1939: Del 1," *Acta Sueco-Polonica* Nr. 2 (Uppsala: Seminariet i Polens kultur och historia vid Uppsala universitet, 1994): 23–51, here: 27; Alexander J. Motyl, "Thinking About Empire," in Karen Barkey and Mark von Hagen (eds.) *After Empire: Multiethnic Societies and Nation-Building. The Soviet Union and the Russian, Ottoman, and Habsburg Empires* (Boulder, CO: Westview Press, 1997), 21.

mid-1920s onwards.[149] "It is the state which makes the nation and not the nation the state," Piłsudski argued.[150]

Nationalist groups committed to alternative national projects than that pursued by the Polish authorities faced mounting obstacles. Still, a number of democratic Ukrainian political parties were active in interwar Poland, the most significant of which was the Ukrainian National Democratic Alliance (*Ukrains'ke natsional'no-demokratychne ob"ednannia*, UNDO) which sought Ukrainian autonomy, self-governance and cooperation with the Polish authorities within the legal framework of the state. The influence of the UNDO and other Ukrainian parties was limited, and declined further after Jozef Piłsudski's May, 1926 coup d'état turned Poland into an authoritarian, corporativist dictatorship.[151]

The leading Ukrainian far-right group, the Ukrainian Military Organization (*Ukrains'ka Viiskova Orhanizatsiia*, UVO), was, to a significant degree, a veterans' organization. Like many of his contemporaries, its leader Evhen Konovalets' (1891-1938) regarded Petliura's alliance with Poland as treason.[152] An "orientation on Poland, any kind of hopes for its help in our liberation struggle, is absurd," Konovalets stated.[153] He refused to acknowledge defeat in the war and was emboldened by Polish losses on the battlefield against the Soviets. "We have not been defeated!" Konovalets' thundered at its founding congress in Prague in August 1920. "The war is not over! We, the Ukrainian Military Organization, are continuing it….Victory lies before us!'"[154] Bitterly disappointed with the 1921 Treaty of Riga, which required Poland to intern their former Ukrainian allies of the Ukrainian People's Republic, Konovalets' group refused to lay down their weapons.[155] Infuriat-

---

149 Engman, "Tillbaka till framtiden," 15.
150 Hobsbawm, *Age of Empire*, 148.
151 On the coup, see Snyder, *Sketches from a Secret War*, 23-30.
152 Kai Struve, *Deutsche Herrschaft, ukrainischer Nationalismus, antijüdische Gewalt: Der Sommer 1941 in der Westukraine* (Berlin: DeGruyter, 2015), 81.
153 Motyl, *The Turn to the Right*, 103.
154 Trevor Erlacher, "The Furies of Nationalism: Dmytro Dontsov, the Ukrainian Idea, and Europe's Twentieth Century," (Ph.D. Dissertation, University of North Carolina at Chapel Hill, 2017), 208-209.
155 Snyder, *Sketches from a Secret War*, 12.

ed with the unresolved border dispute over the Wilno/Vilnius region, Lithuania funded the militants of the UVO.[156] The rise of revisionist powers in the 1920s and 30s offered new prospectives to the increasingly radical Ukrainian right.[157]

Over the next two decades, Konovalets' group relied on increasingly brutal political violence to achieve Ukrainian independence.[158] In 1929, the UVO became the main impetus for the establishment of the Organization of Ukrainian Nationalists (*Orhanizatsiia Ukrains'kykh Natsionalistiv*, OUN), which came to define the Ukrainian far right in the 1930s, 40s, and in the postwar emigration.[159]

Stalinist Modernization and Terror

Following Piłsudski's return to power in 1926, Ukrainization had played out its role as a foreign policy tool to weaken Poland. As Terry Martin observed, "Once it became clear to the Soviet leadership that cross-border ethnic ties could not be exploited to undermine neighboring countries, but instead had the opposite potential, their response was the ethnic cleansing of the Soviet borderlands and, ultimately, ethnic terror throughout the Soviet Union."[160]

---

156 On the Polish-Lithuanian conflict, see Dangiras Maciulis and Darius Staliunas, *Lithuanian Nationalism and the Vilnius Question, 1883-1940* (Marburg: Verlag Herder-Institut, 2015), 63-149.
157 Gábor Lagzi, "The Ukrainian National Movement in Inter-War Poland—the Case of the Organization of Ukrainian Nationalists (OUN)," *Regio— Minorities, Politics, Society*, No. 1 (2004): 194-206.
158 On the UVO, see Golczewski, *Deutsche und Ukrainer*, 431-457; 547-613; Zaitsev, *Ukrains'kyi integral'nyi natsionalizm*, 241-261; Motyl, *The Turn to The Right*, 105-128.
159 The OUN, founded in 1929, was the most significant interwar Ukrainian fascist organization. It split in 1940 into two wings: one more conservative under Andrii Mel'nyk (1890–1964), known as OUN(m), and a more radical under Stepan Bandera, OUN(b). A second split of the OUN(b) in 1954 led to the appearance of the OUN-Abroad (*OUN zakordonnyi*, OUNz) under Lev Rebet (1912-1957) and Zinovyi Matla (1910-1993). On the history of the OUN, see Franziska Bruder, *"Den ukrainischen Staat erkämpfen oder sterben!": Die Organisation Ukrainischer Nationalisten (OUN) 1929-1948* (Berlin: Metropol, 2007).
160 Martin, *Affirmative Action Empire*, 342.

East of the river Zbruch, Stalin's consolidation of power after 1927 meant a brutal change of the political course: a massive industrialization was launched, accompanied by a brutal collectivization of the agriculture, conducted under slogans such as 'crush the *kurkuls* (i.e. the landowning peasants, Ru: *kulak*) as a class."[161] The strategically important Ukrainian republic was subject to a campaign of a particularly brutally enforced collectivization aimed at transforming the border republic into a "fortress of socialism."[162] Ukrainians were very well represented among the victims. They were also found among the activists who enforced the collectivization, grain requisition and terror.[163] During the height of the terror, the number of Ukrainians in leading positions of the punitive organs increased threefold, to reach roughly their proportion of the population.[164]

If the Kazakh ASSR—then part of the Russian SFSR—saw the highest percentage of excess mortality during the collectivization, in absolute numbers the Ukrainian SSR suffered the greatest population loss in what arguably constituted the Soviet regime's greatest crime against its own people.[165] The most authoritative

---

161 Michal Reiman, *The Birth of Stalinism: The USSR on the Eve of the 'Second Revolution'* (Bloomington and Indianapolis: Indiana University Press, 1987); Olga Velikanova, *Popular Perceptions of Soviet Politics in the 1920s: Disenchantment of the Dreamers*, (London: Palgrave Macmillan, 2013).
162 Martin, *Affirmative Action Empire*, 328.
163 There has been little research conducted on local perpetrators. A partial exception is Daria Mattingly, "'Idle, Drunk, and Good-for-Nothing': The Cultural Memory of Holodomor Rank-and-File Perpetrators," in Małgorzata Głowacka-Grajper and Anna Wylegała (eds.) *The Burden of Memory: History, Memory and Identity in Contemporary Ukraine* (Bloomington, IN: Indiana University Press, 2020), 19-54.
164 The percentage of ethnic Ukrainians among the ranking cadres of the NKVD more than tripled during the terror, from 5.45 to 12.42 per cent between 1936 and 1939, to reach 16.86 on January 1, 1940. According to the 1937 and 1939 censuses Ukrainians constituted 16.33 and 16.47 per cent of the Soviet population. See N. V. Petrov and K. V. Sorokin, *Kto rukovodil NKVD 1934-1941: Spravochnik* (Moscow: Zveniia, 1999), 495.
165 In the Kazakh ASSR between 1.2 and 1.5 million people died of starvation between 1929 and 1933, and the ethnic Kazakh population was reduced by 50 per cent. R.W. Davies and Stephen G. Wheatcroft, *The Years of Hunger: Soviet Agriculture, 1931-1933* (New York: Palgrave Macmillan, 2004), 412. On the Kazakh famine, see Sarah Cameron, *The Hungry Steppe: Famine, Violence, and the Making of Soviet Kazakhstan* (Ithaca, NY: Cornell University Press, 2018).

NATION FORMATION IN A STATELESS NATION 61

studies of the republic's demographic losses during the 1932-33 famine estimate an excess mortality of at least 2.6 million people.[166] In desperation prominent leaders of the republic, among them Skrypnyk and Khvylovyi, committed suicide in the summer of 1933.[167] There was substantial peasant resistance, opposition, even local rebellions against the collectivization.

The collectivization was accompanied by political terror and purges, peaking in the Great Terror of 1937-38, during which 267,579 people were arrested and 122,237 executed in the Ukrainian SSR.[168] By the late 1930s the purges acquired increasingly ethnic characteristics, with Poles and Germans being among its primary targets.[169] At the same time, the Ukrainianization of the republic continued during the terror, increasing the Ukrainian participation in the regime.[170]

---

[166] An international research team led by Jacques Vallin estimated excess population losses of 2.6 million and a birth deficit of 1.1 million in the Ukrainian SSR, and an out-migration of 0.9 million out of the republic. Jacques Vallin, France Meslé, Serguei Adamets, and Serhii Pyrozhkov, "A New Estimate of Ukrainian Population Losses during the Crises of the 1930s and 1940s," *Population Studies* 56, no. 3 (2002): 249-264. A Ukrainian team of researchers, led by Ella Libanova estimated the excess mortality to 3.6 million and the birth deficit to 1.1 million. See Oleh Wolowyna, "The Famine-Genocide of 1932-1933: Estimation of Losses and Demographic Impact," in Bohdan Klid and Alexander Motyl (eds.), *The Holodomor Reader: a Sourcebook on the Famine of 1932-1933 in Ukraine*, (Edmonton: Canadian Institute of Ukrainian Studies, 2012), 59 64, here: 62.

[167] Marco Carynnyk, "A Bit of Blood-stained Batting. Kharkiv, Saturday, 13 May 1933," *Krytyka*, year XIX, Issue 1-2 (207-208), (May 2015): 35-39.

[168] Ivan Bilas, *Represyvno-karal'na systema v Ukraini, 1917-1953: suspil'no-politychnyi ta istoriko-pravovyi analiz. Tom I* (Kyiv: Lybid, 1994), 379. In the entire USSR, 681,692 people were shot in 1937-38 alone, and a total of 799,455 over the entire period 1921-1953. J. Arch Getty, Gábor Rittersporn, Viktor Zemskov, "Victims of the Soviet Penal System in the Pre-War Years: A First Approach on the Basis of Archival Evidence," *American Historical Review*, vol. 98, no. 4 (1993): 1017-1049, here: 1022. On the terror in the Ukrainian SSR, see Lynne Viola, *Stalinist Perpetrators on Trial: Scenes from the Great Terror in Soviet Ukraine* (Oxford: Oxford University Press, 2017).

[169] Martin, *Affirmative Action Empire*, 335-341; Kate Brown, *A Biography of No Place: From Ethnic Borderland to Soviet Heartland* (Cambridge, MA: Harvard University Press, 2003), 118-152.

[170] Amir Weiner, *Making Sense of War: The Second World War and the Fate of the Bolshevik Revolution,* (Princeton: Princeton University Press, 2001), 335.

Massive capital investment was allocated to the republic as it was subjected to a break-neck industrialization, in which massive industrial plants were set up in the eastern part of the republic — turning Dnipropetrovs'k (today Dnipro), Zaporizhzhia, Luhans'ke/Voroshylovhrad (today Luhans'k) and Stalino (today Donets'k) into key Soviet industrial centers.[171] Once established, the rural population adapted to the collective farm system, which, over time, gained significant acceptance.[172]

The new wave of research into Soviet nationalities polices has been slow to reach Ukraine, and its impact has been limited.[173] Soviet rule tends to be externalized and depicted as "Russian," rarely problematizing Ukrainian agency, proprietorship and co-responsibility.[174]

Occupation, Mass Violence, Ethnic Cleansing

Following the German-Soviet partition of Poland, the territory of the Ukrainian SSR was significantly expanded. The Stalinist terror now concentrated to the newly annexed Western borderlands. Hundreds of thousands of people were deported, tens of thou-

---

171 Hiroaki Kuromia, *Freedom and Terror in the Donbas: A Ukrainian-Russian Borderland, 1870s-1990s* (Cambridge: Cambridge University Press, 2002), 151-200.

172 Lynne Viola, *Contending with Stalinism* (Ithaca: Cornell University Press, 2002); Mark Tauger, "Soviet Peasants and Collectivization, 1930-1939: Resistance and Adaptation," *The Journal of Peasant Studies*, vol. 31, nos. 3-4 (2004): 427-456.

173 For instance, when Terry Martin's book appeared in Russian translation well over a decade after the original appeared in English, it was rather coldly received by Ukrainian historians, who dismissed it as an attempt to rehabilitate the image of the "evil empire" into a positive, affirmative action ditto. See, for instance, Oleksandr Rubl'ov and Larysa Iakubova in their review "Pro 'imperiio pozytyvnoi dii' Teri Martyna," *Historians.in.ua*, August 1, 2013, http://www.historians.in.ua/index.php/en/dyskusiya/796-oleksandr-rublov-larysay akubovapro-imperiiu-pozytyvnoi-dii-teri-martyna (Accessed September 28, 2021); Kuzio, *Ukraine: Democratization, Corruption, and the New Russian Imperialism*, 164.

174 See, for instance, Valentyna Kharkun, "Reconstructing the past: narratives of Soviet occupation in Ukrainian museums," *Canadian Slavonic Papers*, vol. 63, no. 1-2 (2021): 148-167; Yuliya Yurchuk, "Historians as Activists: History Writing in Times of War: The Case of Ukraine in 2014-2018," *Nationalities Papers*, vol. 49, no. 4 (2021): 691-709, here: 693, 699-700.

sands shot.[175] Ethnic Poles were again particularly affected. Another group singled out for repression were former members of the Communist Party of Western Ukraine, dissolved by the *Comintern* in 1938.[176]

The Stalinist regime's use of political violence, albeit unprecedented, was eclipsed in scope by the brutalities of Operation Barbarossa. What Adolf Hitler referred to as "a war of racial extermination" constituted a systematic attempt to colonize and fundamentally alter the demography of Ukraine.[177] *Generalplan Ost*, drafted by Heinrich Himmler's *Reichssicherheitshauptamt* (RSHA) in the months prior to the German attack on the Soviet Union, envisioned the killing or expulsion of 30 million people, including 65 per cent of the Ukrainians. Local Slavic and Jewish inhabitants were to be replaced with mainly "Germanic" colonists from western and northern Europe.[178]

The German invasion of the Soviet Union was accompanied by a massive wave of pogroms of at least 58 localities across Western Ukraine, in the areas where the OUN(b) had continued its underground activities during the Soviet occupation. Historian

---

175 Jan T. Gross, *Revolution from Abroad: The Soviet Conquest of Poland's Western Ukraine and Western Belorussia* (Princeton, NJ: Princeton University Press, 2002); Stanisław Ciesielski, Grzegorz Hryciuk and Aleksander Srebakowski, *Masowe deportacje ludności w Związku Radzieckim* (Toruń: Wyd. Adam Marszałek, 2003); Stanisław Ciesielski, Wojchiech Materski and Andrzej Paczkowski, *Represje sowieckie wobec Polaków i obywateli polskich*, Wyd. II (Warsaw: Ośrodek Karta, 2002).
176 Borys Lewytzkyj, *Die Sowjetukraine 1944-1963* (Cologne: Kiepenhauer & Witsch, 1964), 28.
177 On the German policies, see Karel C. Berkhoff, *Harvest of Despair: Life and Death in Ukraine Under Nazi Rule* (Cambridge, MA: The Belknap Press of Harvard University Press, 2004); Wendy Lower, *Nazi Empire-Building and the Holocaust in Ukraine* (Chapel Hill: University of North Carolina Press, 2005), and Alex J. Kay, *Exploitation, Resettlement, Mass Murder: Political and Economic Planning for German Occupation Police in the Soviet Union, 1940-1942* (New York: Berghahn Books, 2006).
178 Stephen G. Fritz, *Ostkrieg: Hitler's War of Extermination in the East* (Lexington, KY: University Press of Kentucky, 2011); Czesław Madajczyk, "Vom 'Generalplan Ost' zum Generalsiedlungsplan," in Mechthild Rössler and Sabine Schleiermacher (eds.), *Der 'Generalplan Ost': Hauptlinien der nationalsozialistischen Planungs- und Vernichtungspolitik* (Berlin: Akademie-Verlag, 1993), 96-117.

Kai Struve (b. 1966), author of the most authoritative study of the pogroms, estimates that between 7,295 and 11,309 Jews were murdered in the violence launched by local Ukrainian Nationalist militias.[179] The violence was triggered by a conflation of factors: on the eve of Barbarossa, the OUN(b) had drafted a blueprint for a nationalist uprising which entailed mass violence against Jews and pro-Soviet elements; Reinhard Heydrich (1904-1942) expressed his support for so-called "self-cleansing actions." The retreating Soviets left a carnage behind them, as the NKVD executed several thousand prison inmates as they evacuated their facilities during the final days of June, 1941. Equating Jews with communism, militia groups set up by the OUN(b), attacked the civilian Jewish population, holding it collectively responsible for Soviet atrocities.[180]

Radicalized by the experiences by the German and Soviet occupations, the Galician Ukrainian nationalists pursued various paths to accomplish their Ukrainian national project. On the eve of Barbarossa Volodymyr Kubiiovych (1900-1985) the top Ukrainian collaborator in the Generalgouvernement called for "Lebensraum" in order to preserve the "purity of the Ukrainian race" from the Lemko region to the Caspian Sea.[181] The OUN(b) organized

---

179 Struve, *Deutsche Herrschaft*, 671.
180 John-Paul Himka, *Ukrainian Nationalists and the Holocaust: OUN and UPA's Participation in the Destruction of Ukrainian Jewry, 1941-1944* (Stuttgart: ibidem Press, 2021); Jeffrey S. Kopstein and Jason Wittenberg, *Intimate Violence: Anti-Jewish Pogroms on the Eve of the Holocaust* (Ithaca: Cornell University Press, 2018), 84-113; Witold Mędykowski, *W cieniu gigantów: pogromy 1941 r. W byłej sowieckiej strefie okupacyjnej: kontekst historyczny, społeczny i kulturowy* (Warsaw: Instytut Studiów Politycznych Polskiej Akademii Nauk, 2012), 241-277; Andrzej A. Zięba (ed.), *OUN, UPA, i zagłada żydów* (Krakow: Księgarnia akademicka, 2016).
181 Wolodymyr Kubijovytsch and Tymitsch Omeltschenka, "Denkschrift betreffend die Bedeutung der Ukraine für die Neuordnung Europas," Krakow-Berlin 11. Juni 1941, pp. 7-8. Volodymyr Kubijovych Fonds, Library and Archives Canada (hereafter: LAC), Ottawa, ON, MG 31, D 203, Vol. 26, Folder 15, See, also the April 14, 1941 OUN(m) memorandum in Volodymyr Kosyk (ed.), *Ukraina v Druhii svitovii viini u dokumentakh: Zbirnyk nimets'kykh arkhivnykh materialiv*, T. 1 (L'viv: Instytut ukrainoznavstva im. I. Krypiakievycha NAN Ukrainy), 17-21, here: 17. On Kubiiovych, see Paweł Markiewicz, *Unlikely Allies: Nazi German and Ukrainian Nationalist Collaboration in the General Government During World War II* (West Lafayette, IN: Purdue University

"marching groups" (*pokhidne hrupy*) who followed the German troops eastward through Ukraine for the purpose of carrying out a Ukrainian "national revolution," setting up nationalist militias and local OUN chapters.[182]

The radical message resounded in the songs of the OUN(b) paramilitaries: "We'll create through steel and blood, and ardor/ a State from the Danube to the Caucasus/We are knights, who solemnly cast a curse—For [our] death we'll punish you by death!"[183]

Crossing the former Polish-Soviet border at the Zbruch river, the marching groups were dismayed by the lack of national consciousness among the central and eastern Ukrainians. In right-bank Ukraine these Galicians were referred to as "westerners"; in the Donbas their dialect was mistaken for Polish. Historian Amir Weiner (b. 1961) notes "an unbridgeable gap between these two Ukrainian populations, which ran along educational, cultural, and, most likely, class lines as well."[184] If the OUN activists regarded Donbas and Taganrog parts of their imagined community and claimed them for their state project, local residents of these territories rejected the Galician Ukrainian nationalists' claim of a shared identity, in favor of regional, geographic identities. Ukrainian-speaking residents in the Taganrog area objected to being addressed as Ukrainians, insisting that "the Ukrainians" lived to the west of the border.[185]

Irrespective of the OUN's aims, the German authorities split up the vast Ukrainian speaking lands into several administrative

---

Press, 2022) and Ernest Gyidel, "The Ukrainian Legal Press of the General Government: The Case of *Krakivski Visti*, 1940-1944," (Ph.D. dissertation, University of Alberta, 2019), 242.

182 On the OUN(b) marching groups, see Andriy Usach, "The 'Eastern Action' of the OUN(b) and the Anti-Jewish Violence in the Summer of 1941: The Cases of Smotrych and Kupryn," *Euxeinos*, vol. 9, no. 27 (2019): 63-84.

183 "Zdvyvhnem z zaliza, z krovy, i z zavziattia/Derzhavu vid Dunaitsia do Kavkaz /My lytsari, shcho skynemo proklattia -/Za smert' my smertiu pokaraem vas!" In Ie. Shtendera and Petro P. I. Potichnyi (eds.), *Litopys Ukrains'koi Povstans'koi Armii, Tom 25, Pisni UPA: Zibrav i zredaktovav Zenonvii Lavryshyn. Peredmova anhliis'koiu movoiu* (Toronto and L'viv: Vydavnytstvo Litopys UPA, 1996), 24.

184 Weiner, *Making Sense of War*, 331-332.

185 Weiner, *Making Sense of War*, 332.

units separated by sealed borders. The bulk of Ukraine was reorganized as the *Reichskommissariat* Ukraine, under *Reichskommissar* Erich Koch (1896-1986) in Rivne, whereas its easternmost parts remained under military administration.[186] Its westernmost lands were incorporated into the *Genernalgouvernement*, whereas a large part of southeastern Ukraine, occupied by Romania, was reorganized as the Transnistria Governorate.[187]

The wartime experiences of the local Ukrainian population differed significantly from region to region. In Galicia, talented Ukrainian students were awarded scholarship to study at German universities, whereas in the *Reichskommissariat* Ukrainians were prevented from anything beyond a four-year primary school education.[188] In all areas of Ukraine the Jewish population was subjected to a systematic genocide. Western Ukraine was particularly affected. For instance, 98.5 per cent of the Volhynian Jews were murdered.[189] The low rate of survival is partially explained by the activities of local nationalist forces and attitudes of large sections of the local population.[190] About 1.6 million Jews were murdered in Ukraine, with the total war losses being estimated to 6,850,000 — a staggering 5,200,000 of which being civilians.[191] With-

---

186 On Koch, see Davyd Marplz [David R. Marples], "'Zabutyi' voennyi zlochynets'," *Diialoh: Za demokratiiu i sotsiializm v samostiinii Ukraini* vol. 10 (1984): 44-50.
187 On Transnistria, see Vladimir Solonari, *Purifying the Nation: Population Exchange in Nazi-Allied Romania* (Baltimore, MD: The Johns Hopkins University Press, 2010), 168-210.
188 Taras Kurylo, "'The Biggest Calamity that Overshadowed All Other Calamities': Recruitment of Ukrainians 'Eastern Workers' for the War Economy of the Third Reich, 1941-1945," (Ph.D. Dissertation, University of Alberta, 2009), 5.
189 On the Holocaust in Volhynia, see Shmuel Spector, *The Holocaust of the Volhynian Jews, 1941-1944* (Jerusalem: Yad Vashem, 1990), 356-358; Jeffrey Burds, *The Holocaust in Rovno: the massacre at Sosenki Forest, November 1941* (Basingstoke: Palgrave Macmillan, 2014); Jared Graham McBride, "'A Sea of Blood and Tears': Ethnic Diversity and Mass Violence in Nazi-Occupied Volhynia, Ukraine, 1941-1944," (Ph.D. Dissertation, UCLA, 2014), 97-413.
190 Weiner, *Making Sense of War*, 270-271.
191 Alexander Kruglov, "Jewish Losses in Ukraine, 1941-1944," in Ray Brandon and Wendy Lower (eds.), *The Shoah in Ukraine: History, Testimony, Memorialization* (Bloomington: Indiana University Press, 2008), 272-290; Vadim Erklikhman, "Poteri narodonaseleniia v XX veke: spravochnik," *Radio Free Eu-*

in the larger conflict of the Soviet-German war, the Ukrainian Insurgent Army (*Ukrains'ka Povstans'ka Armiia*, UPA), a paramilitary formation led by the radical Bandera wing of the OUN launched a campaign of mass violence against the Polish minority in Volhynia and East Galicia, claiming the lives of over 90,000 Poles.[192]

The various regions of Ukraine perceived the return of the Red Army in 1944 differently; if eastern Ukraine tended to perceive the return of the Red Army as a liberation, the western part of the republic generally regarded it a re-occupation. In Galicia and the Carpathians, the OUN and UPA continued armed resistance into the late 1940s.[193]

On November 26, 1944 the Ukrainian SSR was enlarged with Transcarpathia, which had been occupied by the Red Army the previous month.[194] In 1950 there were some minor adjustments of the border between Poland and the Ukrainian SSR, whereas the last, and final enlargement of the Ukrainian SSR took place in 1954, as Crimea was transferred from the RSFSR, formally in order to commemorate the tercentennial of the Pereiaslavl treaty.

The Soviet Core

The death of Stalin in 1953 brought significant changes for the republic. Policies were liberalized, repressions eased. Collective

---

rope/Radio Liberty, http://www.rferl.mobi/a/soviet-war-dead/26999777.html (Accessed May 15, 2015)

192 Ewa Siemaszko, "Stan badań nad ludobójstwem dokonanym na ludności polskiej przez Organizację Nacjonalistów Ukraińskich i Ukraińską Powstańczą Armię," in Bogusław Paź (ed.), *Prawda historyczna a prawda polityczna w badaniach naukowych: Ludobójstwa na Kresach południowo-wschodniej Polski w latach 1939-1946* (Wrocław: Wydawnictwo Uniwersytetu Wrocławskiego), 319-344, here: 341. The OUN(b) and UPA killed 30,676 local residents between 1944 and 1956 alone. Serhiy Kudelia, "Choosing Violence in Irregular Wars: The Case of Anti-Soviet Insurgency in Western Ukraine," *East European Politics and Societies*, vol. 27, no. 1 (February 2013): 149-181, here: 171-172.

193 The most detailed study of the UPA is Grzegorz Motyka, *Ukraińska partyzantka 1942-1960 Działalność Organizacji Ukraińskich Nacjonalistów i Ukraińskiej Powstańczej Armii* (Warszawa: Instytut Studiów Politycznych PAN. Oficyna wydawnicza Rytm, 2006).

194 Lewytzkyj, *Die Sowjetukraine 1944-1963*, 25.

reprisals aimed at entire ethnic groups were halted. The overt Russian chauvinism of the late Stalin came to an end, whereas the Russificatory pressure was increased.[195] Further capital investments were made into the republic's infrastructure, strengthening the role of the Donetsk coal basin and the military-industrial complex around Dnipropetrovs'k as key Soviet industrial centers. The 1950s and 1960s was an era of relative stability and economic growth, during which most Ukrainians experienced considerable improvement in their standards of living. The number of newly built apartments increased dramatically; refrigerators, telephones, laundry machines, and other commodities became increasingly commonplace.[196]

As part of the Soviet core, "the second Soviet republic," exercised a significant, if not disproportional influence on Soviet politics, particularly in the post-Stalin era.[197] Nikita Khrushchev (1894-1971) self-identified as an ethnic Russian but was raised in the Donbas. He rose to the top echelons of Soviet power as first secretary of the KP(b)U, and the republic remained an important power base for him as Soviet leader. The heavily industrialized area around Dnipropetrovs'k, (today Dnipro) came to supply a considerable part of the Soviet leadership, the most prominent being Leonid Brezhnev (1906-1982) who toppled his former mentor Khrushchev in 1964.[198] A native of its neighboring city of Kamians'ke (1936-2016 Dniprodzerzhyns'k), Brezhnev identified as a

---

[195] Ronald Grigor Suny and Terry Martin, "Introduction," in idem., (eds.) *A State of Nations*, 16.

[196] Yurii Latysh, "Volodymyr Shcherbyts'kyi: liudyna ta ii epokha," *Spil'ne: zhurnal sotsial'noi krytyky*, August 10, 2017, https://commons.com.ua/en/volodimir-sherbickij/ (Accessed July 2, 2018)

[197] The term was popularized through Yaroslav Bilinsky, *The Second Soviet Republic: The Ukraine after World War II* (New Brunswick, NJ: Rutgers University Press, 1964).

[198] Michael Tatu, *Power in the Kremlin: From Khrushchev to Kosygin* (New York: The Viking Press, 1974), 399-423; Kenneth C. Farmer, *Ukrainian Nationalism in the Post-Stalin Era: Myth, Symbols and Ideology in Soviet Nationalities Policy* (The Hague: Martinus Nijhoff Publishers, 1980), 214; Susanne Schattenberg, *Leonid Breschnew: Staatsmann und Schauspieler im Schatten Stalins. Eine Biographie* (Cologne: Böhlau, 2017); Leonid Ilich Brezhnev, *Rabochie i dnevnikovye zapisi: V 3-kh tomakh* (Moscow: Istoricheskaia literatura, 2016).

Ukrainian until the early 1950s.[199] Dnipropetrovs'k was also the power base of his right-hand man in the republic, the long-term first secretary of the Ukrainian Communist Party, Volodymyr Shcherbyts'kyi (1918-1990). Historian Andrii Portnov (b. 1979) refers to the Brezhnev era as a 'golden age' of Dnipropetrovs'k and the city itself as "the unofficial capital of the Brezhhev stagnation."[200] Under Brezhnev, the Ukrainian representation in the top Soviet leadership was particularly significant; between 1965 and 1977, not only the General Secretary of the CPSU, but also the Soviet head of state, the Poltava native Mykola Pidhornyi (Ru: Nikolai Podgornyi, 1903-1983) were from Ukraine. When Kosygin was retired in 1980, the Kharkiv native Mykola Tikhonov (Ru: Nikolai Tikhonov, 1905-1997) succeeded him as Soviet Premier.[201] A 1973 CIA analysis noted that Ukrainian and Soviet identities coexisted quite comfortably, but also identified underlying dissatisfaction. Ukrainians, it noted "occupy high posts in the Party, the government, and the intelligentsia, and while most support the regime at least outwardly, there is a significant minority which does not."[202] Ethnic Ukrainization continued unabetted as the state and party apparatus continued to promote ethnic Ukrainians, whose share of the party apparatus kept rising; in 1979, 88 per cent of the Politburo members of the Ukrainian SSR and 92 per cent of the regional party secretaries were ethnic Ukrainians.[203] The heavy Ukrainian presence at the Soviet echelon did not end with the death of Brezhnev. Konstantin Chernenko (1911-1985)

---

199 A. N. Artizov, N. G. Tomilinaia (eds.), *Brezhnev k 109-letiiu so dnia rozhdeniia: Katalog istoriko-dokumental'noi vystavki* (Moscow: Kuchkovo pole, 2016), 70.
200 Andriy Portnov, "The Heart of Ukraine?: Dnipropetrovsk and the Ukrainian Revolution," in Andrew Wilson, *what does Ukraine think?* (=*European Council on Foreign Relations*, vol. 133), (Berlin: The European Council on Foreign Relations, n.d.), 62-70, here: 63.
201 John Löwenhardt, *The Soviet Politburo*, trans. Dymphna Clark (Edinburgh: Canongate, 1982), 131-132.
202 [redacted], C/SBOP/PO, "SECRET MEMORANDUM FOR C/SA/B2, SUBJECT: QRDYMANIC Project Renewal Comment," 8 May 1973, National Archives Records Administration (hereafter: NARA), College Park, MD, QRPLUMB, Vol. 2, Box 59, RC 230/86/26/01,
203 Ben Fowkes, "The National Question in the Soviet Union under Leonid Brezhnev: Policy and Response," in Edwin Bacon and Mark Sandle (eds.), *Brezhnev Reconsidered*, (Houndmills: Palgrave Macmillan, 2002), 68-89, 75.

was born into a Russified Ukrainian family in Western Siberia. Mikhail Gorbachev's (1931-2022) mother was Ukrainian, as was his wife Raisa (Titarenko) (1932-1999).[204] The prominent Ukrainian presence in the Soviet echelons notwithstanding, linguistic Russification continued unabetted, though its results varied across the republic; if Eastern Ukrainians increasingly adopted the Russian language as the preferred vehicle for everyday communication, Western Ukrainians urbanized without doing so.[205]

Anti-Soviet Nationalist Dissent and Soviet Patriotism

Under Stalin's successors, the state remained authoritarian and repressive. In the 1960s and 70s, Ukraine had one of the largest dissident movements in the USSR, with about 1,000 people in and out of trouble with the authorities.[206] The dissidents varied in focus and orientation; many were sincere communists, animated by genuine patriotism, and critical of the capitalist West.[207] As historian Simone Bellezza (b. 1978) notes, "The Ukrainian *shistdesiatnyky*, in fact, did not think of themselves as dissenters, but as the best product of Ukrainian Soviet culture."[208] The national question was one cause of dissident activity and non-Russians were overrepresented among the dissenters; according to one study of 802 Brezhnev-era dissidents, only 36 were ethnic Russians.[209] At the same time, it was a Ukrainian Communist Par-

---

204 Richard Sakwa, *Frontline Ukraine: Crisis in the Borderlands*, (London: I.B. Tauris, 2014), 22-23.
205 Roman Szporluk, "West Ukraine and West Belorussia," *Soviet Studies*, vol. 31, no. 1 (1979): 76-98.
206 Andrew Wilson, "Ukrainian Politics since Independence," in Agnieszka Pikulicka-Wilczewski and Richard Sakwa (eds.), *Ukraine and Russia: People, Politics, Propaganda and Perspectives*, (Bristol: E-International Relations Publishing, 2015), 104.
207 Simone Attilio Bellezza, "Making Soviet Ukraine Ukrainian: The Debate on Ukrainian Statehood in the Journal *Suchasnist'* (1961-1971)," *Nationalities Papers* 47:3 (2019): 379-393, here: 385.
208 Bellezza, "Making Soviet Ukraine Ukrainian," 387.
209 Kuzio, *Theoretical and Comparative Perspectives on Nationalism*, 104; Borys Lewytzkyj, *Politische Opposition in der Sowjetunion 1960-1972: Analyse und Dokumentation*. (Munich: Deutscher Taschenbuch Verlag, 1972), lists 185 Ukrainian dissidents.

ty with a record number of ethnic Ukrainians which in 1972 carried out an extensive campaign against "bourgeois nationalists."[210] The scope and scale of the repressions had changed significantly since Stalin's death, as had the methods of coercion; the KGB relied on blackmail, hazing, and punitive psychiatry as tools of political coercion and control.[211] The authorities regarded incarceration as a last resort. In the entire Soviet Union, between 1971 and 1975 the authorities imprisoned 893 people on political grounds, between 1976-1980 347, which meant an average number of political arrests of 26 per 100,000,000 residents. When Mikhail Gorbachev initiated his twin policies of *Perebudova* and *Hlasnist'* (Ru: *Perestroika* and *Glasnost'*) in 1987 there were around 750 documented political prisoners in the Soviet Union.[212]

By the mid-1970s economic growth had slowed down considerably and the gap in standard of living between Soviet Ukraine and the Western world widened. Attempts at raising the morale at the workplace during the Andropov interregnum did not have desired results.[213] Ukraine did not obtain independence through a "national uprising" against Moscow, as envisioned by some émigré militants; rather, a wave of change reached Ukraine from the center in Moscow. The Soviet system was not sufficiently competitive. Its lack of transparency, its hypercentralization and bureacratization became increasingly apparent as the western world entered the post-industrial era.[214] The Chernobyl disaster of April 1986 exposed acute enviromental problems which had been

---

210 Mark Beissinger, "Ethnicity, the Personnel Weapon, and Neo-Imperial Integration: Ukraine and RSFSR Provincial Party Officials Compared," *Studies in Comparative Communism*, XXI, no. 1 (Spring, 1988): 76 and 84.
211 Alexaner Podrabinek, *Punitive Medicine* (Ann Arbor: Karoma Publishers, 1980); Rebecca Reich, *State of Madness: Psychiatry, Literature, and Dissent After Stalin* (DeKalb: Northern Illinois University Press, 2018).
212 Robert C. Tucker, *Political Culture and Leadership in Soviet Russia: From Lenin to Gorbachev* (New York: W.W. Norton, 1987), 186.
213 Zhores A. Medvedev, *Andropov: An Insider's Account of Power and Politics Within the Kremlin* (New York: Penguin Books, 1984), 127-160; Roi Medvedev, *Neizvestnyi Andropov* (Rostov-na-Donu: Izd-vo Feniks, 1999), 383-428.
214 David R. Marples, *The Social Impact of the Chernobyl Disaster* (Edmonton: The University of Alberta Press, 1988).

apparent for decades, and served as a catalyst for political mobilization in the republic.[215]

In early 1989, the Popular Movement of Ukraine, known as *Rukh*, was established as a moderately nationalist organization to support and advance Gorbachev's perestroika and to promote Ukrainian sovereignty.[216] Rukh was centered in western Ukraine, particularly in Galicia. To the east of the Zbruch, there was much resistance to change; under Shcherbytskyi the modus operandi of the Brezhnev era largely continued. With Shcherbytskyi's departure in September 1989 national communism started to take hold, also in the Ukrainian Communist Party.[217]

Beyond Western Ukraine, the attitude towards separatism was cautious. Similar to 1917, many reformers in 1990-1991 envisioned federalism and autonomy. The term used was "sovereignty" — precedence of Ukrainian law over union legislation — rather than independence. In March, 1991, 71.48% of Ukrainian voters voted to remain in a reformed Union of Sovereign States (Ukr. *Soiuz Suvernnykh Derzhav*) with Russia, Belarus, and another six republics.[218] Until the failed August 1991 coup in Moscow, Ukrainian separatism remained a minority faith.[219]

When independence arrived, it did so unexpectedly, as the result of a failed coup attempt in Moscow. For two days Leonid Kravchuk (1934-2022, president 1991-1994) who, as Chairman of the Verkhovna Rada was the Ukrainian RSR's nominal head of state, neither condemned nor approved the coup. He broke his silence only following calls for his resignation. Only when the coup failed did he resign from his party positons, and only on

---

215 David R. Marples, *Ukraine under Perestroika: Ecology, Economics and the Workers' Revolt* (Edmonton: The University of Alberta Press, 1991), 173-174.
216 Alexander Burakovskiy, "In Search of a Liberal Polity: The Rukh Council of Nationalities, the Jewish question, and Ukrainian Independence," *East European Jewish Affairs*, vol. 45, no. 1 (2015): 109-131.
217 Taras Kuzio, *Ukraine: Perestroika to Independence*. Second edition. (Houndmills, Basingstoke: Palgrave MacMillan, 2000), 216; Marples, *Ukraine under Perestroika*, 158-159.
218 Andrew G. Beniuk, "The Referendum: On the Road to Ukraine's Independence," (MA Thesis, University of Alberta, 1993).
219 Andrew Wilson, "Ukrainian Nationalism: A Minority Faith," *Slavonic and East European Review*, vol. 73, no. 2 (April 1995), here: 282-288, here: 282-283.

August 27 from the party itself—though in his official biography he pre-dated his resignation to August 19.[220] The former communist ideologue, though he had reinvented himself as a blue and yellow patriot was still awkward as a symbolic founding father of the new state. Despite his commitment to new, nationalizing discourses, he was also a living reminder, not only of the Soviet origins of the new state, and of the prominent role of Ukrainians in the Soviet system. As the demands for a new, edifyingly patriotic narration increased after 2004, new heroes were increasingly sought elsewhere.

Colonialism and Nationalism, Center and Periphery

What is a colony, what is a colonizer? The issue lies at the very heart of the controversies regarding historical memory in contemporary Ukraine. Historian Klas-Göran Karlsson (b. 1955) notes that "Colonies are territories that are organized and exploited in order to satisfy the needs of the motherlands and not that of the colonies."[221] Whether Ukraine should be regarded as core or periphery—i.e. an "exploiter" or "exploited" determines much of the interpretive framework in the discussions of contemporary Ukrainian history. Scholarly analyses of the Ukrainian role in the Soviet enterprise include interpretations of them as both colonizers and colonized, core and center. Ukrainian diaspora analysts, many of which with a family background in Galicia, tend to regard Ukraine—also its industrial east as an imperial periphery. From scholars socialized into that milieu we find unequivocal claims that "the Soviet Union was a Russian empire and the Russian Federation is its successor,"[222] whereas the Ukrainian RSR can

---

220 Bohdan Harasymiw, "Kravchuk, Leonid," *Internet Encyclopedia of Ukraine/Enstyklopediia Ukrainy v Internet*, n.d., but updated 2020, http://www.encyclopediaofukraine.com/display.asp?linkpath=pages%5CK%5CR%5CKravchukLeonid.htm (Accessed July 22, 2020).
221 Klas-Göran Karlsson, *Folkmord: Historien om ett brott mot mänskligheten* (Lund: Historiska Media, 2021), 92.
222 Ksenya Kiebuzinski and Alexander Motyl, "Introduction," in idem. (eds.), *The Great Ukrainian Prison Massacre of 1941: A Sourcebook* (Amsterdam: Amsterdam University Press, 2017), 28.

be portrayed as a "Soviet colony."[223] Taras Kuzio argues that L'viv lies on the "fault line of rival projects of nation building and imperial dominance."[224]

Such analyses do not fully accommodate the hybridity of identities, nor that the fact that Soviet policies varied significantly over the decades.[225] Under Lenin, the Bolsheviks were uncompromising in their rejection of imperialism and colonialism, also practicing anti-colonialism domestically. As they regarded the settlement of Slavic peoples to the Siberian and Kazakh territories a form of colonization of eastern peoples, in the 1920s they closed these areas to emigration from the overpopulated European territories.[226] The Stalinist revolution brought a partial reversal of the Bolshevik policies of the early Soviet era. Kate Brown (b. 1965) notes how the "Soviet state gradually inherited the tsarist role of the civilizing 'Russian big brother' to the primitive nomad."[227] Brown invites reflection on a complex, transformative process in which Ukrainians figured in the role of colonizers and colonized. "The colonized deportees of the Ukrainian hinterland thus were recast as colonizers; their presence on the steppe...amounted to a fortress wall of agricultural settlement, a bulwark against 'primitive' nomadism."[228]

Historian Patryk Babiracki (b. 1978) understands Eastern Europe as an imperial periphery, militarily subordinated to the Sovi-

---

[223] Taras Kuzio, "State and Institutions in Ukraine: A Theoretical and Comparative Introduction," in Taras Kuzio, Robert S. Kravchuk, and Paul D'Anieri (eds.), *State and Institution Building in Ukraine*, (New York: St. Martin's Press, 1999), 1-23, here: 3, 10.

[224] Kuzio, *Ukraine: Democratization, Corruption, and the New Russian Imperialism*, 29. These were not mutually exclusive projects. Rather, both contributed to shaping and conditioning the process of nationalization which continued during the Soviet era. Tarik Cyril Amar, *The Paradox of Ukrainian Lviv: A Borderland City between Stalinists, Nazis, and Nationalists* (Ithaca: Cornell University Press, 2017).

[225] An important study on hybridity of identities in the Ukrainian case is Ilchuk, *Nikolai Gogol*.

[226] Brown, *A Biography of No Place*, 90.

[227] Brown, *A Biography of No Place*, 177.

[228] Brown, *A Biography of No Place*, 189

et center.[229] Aspects of this analysis also applied to the "Soviet West" — the Baltic republics and the areas absorbed into Soviet Ukraine in 1939-44. In Galicia, like in the Baltics, Soviet rule was never fully rooted and accepted; these lands were sometimes referred to as the "Soviet Abroad," or even "Our Abroad."[230]

The situation was quite different east of the Zbruch, that is, in the Ukrainian RSR, located within the Soviet borders of 1922. If anti-Soviet nationalism constituted a minority faith, a considerably more powerful current among Soviet Ukrainian citizens was Soviet patriotism. Fueled by social mobility, historical myths about East Slavic brotherhood and a common origin, Soviet Ukrainian patriotism constituted a political capital that Ukrainians mobilized to assert their place in Soviet society.[231] Soviet modernity strengthened the identification of non-Russian nationalities with their respective republics as their homelands, the borders of which they increasingly regarded as sacrosanct.[232] For the most part, a Ukrainian ethnic identity did not stand in contradiction to a Soviet one. The doctrine of "Friendship of nations" came to constitute, in the words of Terry Martin, the Soviet imagined community.[233]

Imperial and Anti-Imperial Choices

As we have seen, the Ukrainian nationalist tradition has taken democratic, liberal, conservative, socialist, and fascist forms. It has appeared in federalist, separatist and imperialist shapes. Its adherents could — somewhat confusingly — subscribe to two, supposedly irreconcilable positions simultaneously. In the Ukrainian

---

229 Patryk Babiracki, "Interfacing the Soviet Bloc: Recent Literature and New Paradigms," *Ab Imperio* 4 (2011): 376-407.
230 On Galicia's "Western Otherness," see William Jay Risch, *The Ukrainian West: Culture and the Fate of Empire in Soviet Lviv* (Cambridge, MA: Harvard University Press, 2011), 2-11, 82-115.
231 Zbigniew Wojnowski, *The Near Abroad: Socialist Eastern Europe and Soviet Patriotism in Ukraine, 1956-1985* (Toronto: University of Toronto Press, 2017), 13-14, 18; Amar, *The Paradox of Ukrainian Lviv*, 13. On Soviet patriotism, see Oberländer, *Sowjetpatriotismus und Geschichte*.
232 Kuzio, *Theoretical and Comparative Perspectives on Nationalism*, 101.
233 Martin, *The Affirmative Action Empire*; Tillett, *The Great Friendship*.

discourse nationalism is often juxtaposed with imperialism as mutually exclusive. Nationalism is given credence by being casted as "the anti-imperial choice."[234] Such a reductive narration does not allow for the complexity of a situation, where "imperial" and "national" Ukrainian identities often co-existed, overlapped and informed one another. Ukrainian history does not lack nationally conscious activists who remained loyal to imperial centers. We can recall the political leaders of the Galician "Tiroleans of the East," who, in the years after 1848 combined budding Ukrainian national activism with loyalty to the Kaiser.[235] In the 20th century, Ukrainians who opted for the "imperial choice" included figures such as Mykola Pidhornyi, who reconciled Soviet Ukrainian patriotism with his vocation as head of state of the Soviet Union.[236] Conversely, adherents of the supposedly "anti-imperial choice" of Ukrainian nationalism included figures such as Mykola Mikhnovs'kyi who sought to establish a greater Ukraine, "from the Danube to the Caspian Sea." Key OUN ideologues, now routinely cast as "anti-colonial" include people like Mykhailo Kolodzins'kyi and Yurii Lypa (1900-1944) who reconciled *Blut-und-Boden* Ukrainian ethnonationalism with the advocating of Ukrainian imperial

---

234 See, for instance, Yohanan Petrovsky-Shtern, *The Anti-Imperial Choice: The Making of the Ukrainian Jew* (New Haven: Yale University Press, 2009); Iana Prymachenko, "Antykolonial'nyi dyskurs OUN/UPA v suchasnomu ukrains'komu kontektsi borot'by za evropeis'ku identychnist'," *Ukrains'kyi istorychnyi zbirnyk*, vyp. 17 (2014): 328-338.

235 One of the more prominent exponents of this was Greek Catholic L'viv bishop Hryhoryi Iakhymovych (1792-1863), head of the Supreme Ruthenian Council of 1848. Kappeler, *Kleine Geschichte der Ukraine*, 122; Paul Robert Magocsi, *A History of Ukraine: The Land and Its Peoples*. Second, Revised and Expanded Edition (Toronto: University of Toronto Press, 2012), 435.

236 Their self-proclaimed commitment to "anti-imperialism" notwithstanding, the nationally conscious Ukrainian Petro Shelest (1908-1996), first secretary of the Ukrainian Communist Party and Mykola Pidhornyi counted among the most vehement proponents of Soviet military intervention in Czechoslovakia in 1968, an intervention, paradoxically justified with references to combatting the "counterrevolution in Czechoslovakia as a creature of world imperialism." *K sobytiiam v Chekhoslovakii: Fakty, dokumenty, svidetel'stva pressy i ochevidtsev* (Moscow: Press-gruppa sovetskikh zhurnalistov, 1968), 95. Mark Kramer, "Ukraine and the Soviet-Czechoslovak Crisis of 1968 (part 2): New Evidence from the Ukrainian Archives." *Cold War International History Project Bulletin*, Issue 14/15 (2004): 273-276, here: 273-275.

expansion into Central Asia, Siberia, and the far east.[237] Ukrainian identities, whether "imperial" or "anti-imperial," were reconcilable with commitment to projects both national and imperial at the same time.

In some regards the role of Ukrainians in the Soviet Union resembled that of the Scots in the British Empire; an integral component of the imperial core, Ukrainians had a strong influence in the top Soviet echelons of power and took an active part in the Russification of the Baltic republics, Caucasus and Central Asia. Not unlike the union treaty between Scotland and England in 1707, the 1654 Pereiaslav Council united Ukrainian lands with Muscovy through dynastic arrangements between its elites.[238] Through processes of cultural and linguistic assimilation Scots and Ukrainians became part of imperial cores, and their presence at the center amplified their influence globally.[239] This did not, of course, preclude dissonances and conflict. As modern nationalism emerged, in Ukraine and Scotland ethno-national identities competed and co-existed with "imperial" dittos, producing hybrid and paradoxical identities, defying and complicating binary conceptual frameworks. Literary scholar Yuliya Ilchuk (b. 1974) notes in her work on Ukrainian hybridity how "when the Russian Empire emerged as a subject of global history by exerting its power and control over Poland, Ukraine, and the Baltic provinces, Fin-

---

[237] Mykhailo Kolodzins'kyi, *Voenna doktryna ukrains'kykh natsionalistiv* (Kyiv: Tsentr Natsional'noho Vidrodzhennia, 2019); Yurii Lypa, *Pryznachennia Ukrainy* (L'viv: Khortitsia, 1938). See also Marek Wojnar, *Imperium ukraińskie: Źrodła idei i jej miejsce w myśli politycznej ukraińskiego pierwszej połowy XX wieku* (Warsaw: Arcana, 2023).

[238] On the historiography of Pereiaslav, see John Basarab, *Pereiaslav 1654: A Historiographical Study* (Edmonton: Canadian Institute of Ukrainian Studies, University of Alberta, 1982).

[239] As historian Murray Pittock (b. 1962) put it, "Scots enjoyed...projection and self-promoting soft power across the globe, supported by...the infrastructure of the British Empire. The quid pro quo for this liberty—the liberty to control colonial place, position and opportunity in their own interests and (to be frank) against the interests of other subjects of the United Kingdom—was the expectation of loyalty to the Crown and the Union, which was almost always forthcoming." On the Scots in the British empire, see Murray Pittock, *Scotland: The Global History 1603 to the Present* (New Haven: Yale University Press, 2022), 313.

land, and Bessarabia, it colonized these territories and people in the name of the European civilizational project. Much in this ambition of Russia had, and still has, depended on Ukraine's presence and participation in the imperial project."[240]

Much like William Gladstone and Arthur Balfour were able to reconcile their Scottish identity with a super-national—and imperial—British one,[241] Ukrainian politicians like Shelest, Pidhornyi, and Kravchuk embraced identities which were *both* Soviet and Ukrainian.[242] The Soviet project did not exclude Ukrainians. On the contrary, it allotted them a central, indeed disproportional role in the 'all-union,' or 'imperial' project, facilitating a patriotism, which was both Soviet and Ukrainian, reinforced in juxtaposition to the satellite states of the "near abroad." Far from being mutually exclusive, Ukrainian and Soviet identities often overlapped: "To be Soviet meant to be Ukrainian and to be Ukrainian meant to be Soviet,"[243] historian Zbigniew Wojnowski (b. 1983) notes. "A geographically and ethnically defined Soviet patriotism created spaces for citizens to cultivate social capital," Wojnowski continues, something that "was a very effective means of political mobilization."[244] Migration, bilingualism and multi-ethnic landscapes produced hybrid identities which transcended and defied essentialist categorizations. "Ukrainian language, history, and literature turned into positive markers of Sovietness," Wojnowski argues; "Citizens," he notes, "mobilized Ukrainian identities to highlight their belonging in the wider Soviet community."[245] Therefore, "Ukrainian ethnic identities, albeit only when refractured through the prism of Russo-Ukrainian friendship,

---

240 Ilchuk, *Performing Hybridity*, 8.
241 Richard J. Finlay, "The rise and fall of popular imperialism in Scotland, 1850-1950," *Scottish Geographical Society*, Vol. 113, no. 1 (1997): 13-21.
242 Shelest, Kenneth Farmer argues, "invoked elements of the myth of national moral patrimony, adding to his power-base the nationalist intelligentsia, in order to strengthen his position *in the Ukraine.*" Farmer, *Ukrainian Nationalism in the Post-Stalin Era*, 214.
243 Wojnowski, *Near Abroad*, 18.
244 Wojnowski, *Near Abroad*, 20, 25.
245 Wojnowski, *Near Abroad*, 14.

were a key source of legitimacy for the post-Stalinist Soviet state."[246]

As we will see, replacing the Soviet imagined community of "the Great Friendship," of which Ukraine was a constituent member, with a new, national identity would constitute a daunting task. In 1990, east of the Zbruch Ukrainian national self-consciousness was limited. As the post-Soviet economy plummeted, Ukrainians would grow increasingly skeptical of the benefits of independence.[247]

---

246   Wojnowski, *Near Abroad*, 11.
247   Wilson, "Ukrainian Nationalism: A Minority Faith," 282-283.

3. Managing Memory in Post-Soviet Ukraine From "Scientific Marxism-Leninism" to the Ukrainian Institute of National Memory, 1991–2019*

Introduction

From 2006, Ukraine has seen a renaissance for institutes, agencies, and laws to police the production of memory, and to set the bounds of permissible historical discourses. In particular, the presidencies of Viktor Yushchenko and Petro Poroshenko were periods of intense instrumentalization of the recent past. The preference to rely on government agencies to police, manage, and control history writing in Ukraine is not new, but has deep Soviet roots. This chapter aims at outlining some of the major aspects of these currents against the background of a Soviet legacy still discernible in the strongly politicized field of history. Who were the memory actors driving these processes? What were the main rivaling historical memories, and how were they structured? What was the role of interventions by right-wing overseas diaspora groups? The chapter is organized chronologically, covering the period from the attainment of independence in 1991 through to the dismissal of Volodymyr V"iatrovych as head of the Ukrainian Institute of National Memory in 2019.

Independence

After the failed coup attempt against Gorbachev in August 1991 – which was initially supported by Leonid Kravchuk and the Soviet Ukrainian leadership – Ukraine swiftly, and unexpectedly, declared independence. The declaration was followed by a referendum held on 1 December 1991, which yielded a result diametrically opposite to that of the referendum held only eight months earli-

---

*   A previous version of this chapter was published in the *Journal of Soviet and Post-Soviet Politics and Society*, vol. 7, no. 2 (2021): 85-134.

er. If, in March 1991, 70.16% of the votes had been cast to preserve the USSR "as a renewed federation of equal, sovereign republics," now 92.3% of the votes cast answered the question "Do you support the Act of Declaration of Independence of Ukraine?" in the affirmative.[248] Whether the voters had viable alternatives to choose between, and what a "no" vote really meant at a time when the Soviet Union had de facto ceased to function, may be of less relevance than the very fact that the declaration of independence was affirmed by a referendum. This set Ukraine apart from not only Belarus, whose declaration of independence was not subject to a referendum, but also the RSFSR, the only former Soviet republic *not* to declare independence.[249] Regardless of its provenance, the referendum result provides compelling evidence to counter the claims of those, not least in the current leadership of the Russian Federation, who seek to call the legitimacy of Ukrainian statehood into question.

From "Scientific Marxism-Leninism" to "Scientific" Nationalism

Given the far-reaching implications of the dissolution of the USSR and the Soviet bloc, the transformation went remarkably smoothly and is testimony to the restraint and flexibility of the late Soviet elites. Indeed, some objected that these elites were *too* flexible, with many former apparatchiks retaining their power and privilege after the collapse. A point in case is the biography of Leonid Kravchuk, the first president of independent Ukraine. As secretary for ideology and director of the Department of Propaganda and Agitation of the Central Committee of the Communist Party of Ukraine under Volodomyr Shcherbyts'kyi (1918–90), Kravchuk had played a central role in the cultural *Gleichschaltuung* and linguistic Russification of the republic.[250]

---

248 Beniuk, "The Referendum," 14–17.
249 Taras Kuzio, *Theoretical and Comparative Perspectives on Nationalism*, 104.
250 On Kravchuk's ideological campaign against nationalism, see Vladimir Khanin (ed.), *Documents on Ukrainian Jewish Identity and Emigration, 1944–1990* (Portland, OR: Frank Cass, 2003), 293–95. On Shcherbyts'kyi, see Yurii Latysh

Polish former dissident Adam Michnik (b. 1946) argued, paraphrasing Lenin, that "authoritarian ethnic nationalism is the ultimate stage of communism."[251] Michnik illustrated this with Serbia, but there are ample of cases to illustrate his thesis. In the case of Ukraine, the collapse of the Soviet party-state destroyed Kravchuk's power base in the Ukrainian Communist Party, but he retained his ties to the media, which he used to mobilize support.[252] The erstwhile communist ideologue changed skin smoothly and seemingly effortlessly from a "scientific Marxist-Leninist" into a Ukrainian nationalist. A popular joke had it that Kravchuk did not need an umbrella, as he could slip between the raindrops without getting wet.[253] Of course, Kravchuk was not alone. Many of the people in authority during the final years of Soviet rule retained their power and influence, now under a new, blue-and-yellow varnish.[254]

Under Kravchuk, huge state handouts to maintain the loyalties of regional elites drove hyperinflation and helped establish the basis for what political scientist Andrew Wilson (b. 1961) refers to as a new "parasitic rentier class."[255] Wilson argues that "Kravchuk remained wedded to a very Soviet style of politics—clientelism, government as compromise between elites, divide and rule, the *kompromat* of opponents and ... viewing ... state [and] political parties ... as a battleground for personal or group interests."[256] Instead of a stable democracy emerged a system which

---

(ed.), *Shcherbyts'kyi: Zhyttia prysviachene Ukraini* (Kyiv: Vydavnychyi Dim ADEF-Ukraina, 2018); and Yurii Shapoval and Oleksandr Iabubets', *Sluzhytel' zalezhnosty: Volodomyr Shcherbyts'kyi za obstavyn chasu* (Kyiv: Krytyka, 2021).

251 Adam Michnik, "Forum for the Future of Democracy 2010 Keynote speech," *Council of Europe*, https://www.coe.int/t/dgap/forum-democracy/Activities/Forum%20sessions/2010/Speeches/Text%20Michnik%20for%20proceedings_EN_061210%20fin.asp (accessed January 17, 2024)

252 Lucan Way, *Pluralism by Default: Weak Autocrats and the Rise of Competitive Politics* (Baltrimore, MD: Johns Hopkins University Press, 2015), 50.

253 Kuzio, *Ukraine: Democratization, Corruption, and the New Russian Imperialism*, 50.

254 Georgii Kas'ianov, *Ukraina i sosedi: Istoricheskaia politika. 1987-2018* (n.p.: NLO, 2019), 126–29.

255 Andrew Wilson, *The Ukrainians: Unexpected Nation*, 4th ed. (New Haven: Yale University Press, 2015), 257.

256 Wilson, *The Ukrainians*, 183.

historian Philipp Ther (b. 1967) characterizes as "oligarchic-neoliberal."[257]

Following independence, "national" symbolism increased in value as a political and social currency. The new state sought to draw legitimacy from two competing traditions of statehood. In a ceremony in the Verkhovna Rada on 22 August 1992, the former secretary for ideology received the symbolic credentials of the final president-in-exile of the Ukrainian People's Republic, OUN(m) leader Mykola Plav″iuk (1927–2012).[258] This ritual reconciliation between the former Communist ideologue and a nationalist who, during the final phase of World War II had served in German uniform is illustrative for the paradoxes of the post-Ukrainian historical memory. From the outset reconciliation was prioritized above critical engagement with the multi-totalitarian past as two rival authoritarian traditions—Soviet Ukrainian and anti-Soviet Ukrainian nationalism—came to form the basis for a new nationalizing mythology which University of Vienna historian Matthias Kaltenbrunner (b. 1984) has called an "all-inclusive" historical narration.[259]

The immediate post-Soviet years brought a sharp and traumatic decline in living standards for ordinary Ukrainians. The post-communist governments all but entirely lacked knowledge of how a market economy works, and the early 1990s was a period of graft, theft, and the institutionalization of massive corruption. In this process, members of the former *nomenklatura* pocketed enormous wealth while ordinary people experienced a sharp drop in disposable income, birth rate, and life expectancy. In 1993, infla-

---

[257] Philipp Ther, *Die neue Ordnung auf dem alten Kontinent: Eine Geschichte des neoliberalen Europas* (Berlin: Suhrkamp Verlag, 2014), 35.

[258] Kuzio, *Ukraine: Democratization, Corruption, and the New Russian Imperialism*, 177. In late 1944 or early 1945 Plav″iuk joined an SS-organized Ukrainian armed force, consisting largely of former *Schutzmänner*, or auxiliary policemen. During the final days of the war it started to refer to itself as the "Second Ukrainian Division of the Ukrainian National Army." The same formulation was later used in the émigré literature. On Plav″iuk's biography, see Matthias Kaltenbrunner, *Das global vernetzte Dorf: Eine Migrationsgeschichte* (Frankfurt a.M.: Campus Verlag, 2017), 463–73.

[259] Kaltenbrunner, *Das global vernetzte Dorf*, 369–73.

tion was, according to different estimates, 5,371 or 10,200 per cent. GDP per capita between 1990 and 1998 dropped from USD 5,499 to USD 750.[260] Apartments went unheated during the winter of 1996-97, and in many cities power and running water was limited to a couple of hours in the morning and evening.[261] The process of dismantling the Soviet legacy in Ukraine was considerably slower than among its western neighbors; with the exception of western Ukraine, Soviet names of cities, streets, and buildings were retained, and memorials largely left intact.

Chronological Imperialism and *Zakonomirnist'*

Historian Dieter Langewische (b. 1943) notes in regard to the violent transition to modernity how "Voluntarism, as a will to the future, in which one forces history in a new direction, was not only the program of revolutionaries. It was a general attitude in the 19th century."[262] From around the year 1800, in the German-speaking world the word *history* is referred to in the collective singular; it is no longer seen as a collection of histories, from which one can learn for the future. Rather, history becomes something singular and unique.[263]

The rewriting of history is thus often due not to new sources, but rather new perspectives on history—in turn depending on changed political situations.[264] Karl Marx argued that "The changes in the economic foundation lead, sooner or later, to the transformation of the whole, immense, superstructure." According to Marx, these changes included changes to ideology, that is, "the legal, political, religious, artistic, or philosophic ...forms in which

---

260 Wilson, *The Ukrainians*, 253–56. If, in 1990, the GDP per capita in Poland and Ukraine was roughly equal, in 2004 Polish GDP per capita was five times, and in 2012 three times that of Ukraine; D. Kuberska and S. Figiel, "The Competitiveness of Ukraine and Poland," *Socioeconomic Research Bulletin* 3 (50) (2013): 72–78, here: 77; and Grigory Ioffe, *Reassessing Lukashenka: Belarus in Cultural and Geopolitical Context* (New York: Palgrave Macmillan, 2014), 21–51, in particular 26, 29.
261 Ther, *Die neue Ordnung*, 103.
262 Langewiesche, *Der Gewaltsame Lehrer*, 402.
263 Langewiesche, *Der Gewaltsame Lehrer*, 402.
264 Langewiesche, *Der Gewaltsame Lehrer*, 403.

men become conscious of this conflict and fight it out."[265] Italian Marxist Antonio Gramsci (1891–1937) similarly argued that the dominant groups in society establish their position by deliberately shaping the perceptions, values, norms, and attitudes in society, thereby enabling internalization of their cultural hegemony. Through education, churches, and mass media they establish a hegemony and define the limits of what can be expressed in the public sphere, and what may not.[266]

In 1931, another Marxist, Iosif Stalin, bluntly stated that what mattered in history writing was not the sources, but rather "correct attitude."[267] Soviet attempts to control and put in order the past were very far-reaching; Soviet historians approached history from the vantage point of holding keys that allowed a correct and objective view of the past. The Soviet temporal and political space constituted a self-evident and unproblematic framework even for the most distant past. From the vantage point of 2021, the schematic dogmatism of volume one of *The History of the USSR: From Ancient Times to the Year 1861: Primitive Communism, Slave Economy and Feudalism*, published in 1961, is curious reading.[268] This volume illustrates a phenomenon historian Göran B. Nilsson (b. 1934) refers to as "chronological imperialism," or "temporal parochialism" — that is, the projection of contemporary conditions back onto the past.[269] Soviet history writing claimed to be partisan and objective at the same time, and official ideology did not see any contradiction between the two. "The Marxist-Leninist historical science is partisan. This loyalty to party doctrine [Ukr: *partiinist'*] corresponds to true science," as it "excludes any falsification and white

---

265 Karl Marx, "A Contribution to the Critique of Political Economy — Preface" in Karl Marx and Friedrich Engels, *Collected Works*, vol. 29 (Moscow: Progress Publishers, 1987), 261–66, here: 263.
266 Antonio Gramsci, *En kollektiv intellektuell: Urval och inledning av René Coeckelberghs*, trans. Stig Herlitz (Staffanstorp: Cavefors, 1967), 235–46.
267 Andrei Zubov, *Istoriia Rossii: XX vek, 1894–1939* (Moscow: Astrel, 2009), 933.
268 M. W. Netschkina *et al.*, *Geschichte der UdSSR, Band I: Von den ältesten Zeiten bis zum Jahre 1861. Urgesellschaft, Sklavenhalterordnung und Feudalismus. Erster Halbband* Trans. Arno Specht (Berlin: VEB Deutscher Verlag der Wissenschaften, 1961).
269 Göran B. Nilsson, *Den lycklige humanisten: tio offensiva essäer* (Stockholm: Carlssons, 1990), 71.

washing, but also any discrimination in history," the introduction to *History of the USSR* explained.[270] The simple premise of this dialectic foundation was the postulate that the interests of the party converged with those of the Soviet people and thereby with the actual or objective path of historical development.[271] Klas-Göran Karlsson observes that the authoritarian ideological uses of history share joint characteristics and features, "based," as they are,

> upon long and sweeping historical trajectories, which constitute a set chronological frame of references with a "before" and "after," at the same time as its temporal perspectives often appear as pre-determined. They start in a gloomy or, conversely, paradisical distant past, reach a moment when the progress, shaped by struggle between different forces, hangs in the balance. Around the corner, when the struggle has been decided in "our" favor, a future paradise awaits us.[272]

In the Soviet rendition, Ukrainian history was identified with the "struggle" (*zmahannia*) of the Ukrainian people for "reunification" with the Great Russian people, which, Soviet historians insisted, followed Lenin's "law-governed nature of social development" on the basis of "their language, their geographic location, their character and history.'"[273] This rendition of history depicted the expansion of the Russian empire into the territory which today constitutes Ukraine as a progressive, teleological development in which "[t]he Ukrainian people was liberated not only from national and religious suppression of the Polish state, but also from the threat of Turkish enslavement—and thus preserved as a nation."[274] This process was portrayed as national,

---

270 L. W. Tscherepnin and B. A. Rybakow, "Einleitung," in Netschkina *et al.*, *Geschichte der UdSSR, Band I, Erster Halbband*, 1–7, here: 3.
271 Klas-Göran Karlsson, *Historia som vapen: Historiebruk och Sovjetunionens upplösning 1985–1995* (Stockholm: Bokförlaget Natur och Kultur, 1999), 72.
272 Klas-Göran Karlsson, *Folkmord: Historien om ett brott mot mänskligheten* (Lund: Historiska Media, 2021), 81.
273 A. A. Nowosselski, "Die Ukraine und Belorussland im 17. Jh.", in M. W. Netschkina *et al.*, *Geschichte der UdSSR, Band I: Von den ältesten Zeiten bis zum Jahre 1861. Urgesellschaft, Sklavenhalterordnung und Feudalismus. Zweiter Halbband*, trans. Arno Specht (Berlin: VEB Deutscher Verlag der Wissenschaften, 1962), 389–403, here: 394.
274 Nowosselski, "Die Ukraine und Belorussland im 17. Jh.", 400.

social, and cultural emancipation: "The reunification of Ukraine and Belorussia with Russia, along with Lithuania and Moldavia created the preconditions under which Ukrainian, Belorussian, Moldavian and Lithuanian culture could develop."[275]

The Ukrainian Diaspora

The Ukrainian lands changed hands several times during the twentieth century, resulting in competing narratives of Ukrainian history. In emigration the Soviet Ukrainian narrative was challenged by what historian Johan Dietsch (b. 1976) refers to as "another Ukrainian historical culture."[276]

The westward advance of the Red Army triggered a wave of refugees from Ukraine, not least from the areas annexed by the USSR in 1939/40. Of the 220,000–250,000 Ukrainian Displaced Persons (DPs) in Western Europe in 1945–50, 25,000, or 12–15 per cent of the adult population, was politically active, some 8–10,000 in Ukrainian party politics. Of these the OUN(b), with over 5,000 members in Western Europe, was by far the largest political group, whereas the OUN(m), with 1,200–1,500 members, was a distant second.[277] In all, around 150,000 of the Ukrainians displaced during the war would remain in Western countries.[278] An

---

275 S. S. Dmitrijew, "Die russische Kultur und die Kultur der Völker des Russischen Reiches in der ersten Hälfte des 19. Jh.," in Netschkina *et al.*, *Geschichte der UdSSR, Band I. Zweiter Halbband*, 825–66, here: 854. On the use of history in post-war Soviet Ukraine, see Amir Weiner, *Making Sense of War: The Second World War and the Fate of the Bolshevik Revolution* (Princeton: Princeton University Press, 2001); and Serhy Yekelchyk, *Stalin's Empire of Memory: Russian-Ukrainian Relations in the Soviet Historical Imagination* (Toronto: University of Toronto Press, 2014).

276 Johan Dietsch, *Making Sense of Suffering: Holocaust and Holodomor in Ukrainian Historical Culture* (Lund: Department of History, Lund University, 2006), 111–46.

277 Vasyl Markus, "Political Parties in the DP Camps," in Wsevolod W. Isajiw, Yury Boshyk, and Roman Senkus (eds.), *The Refugee Experience: Ukrainian Displaced Persons after World War II* (Edmonton: The Canadian Institute of Ukrainian Studies, University of Alberta, 1992), 115, 118–19.

278 Nick Baron, "Remaking Soviet Society: The Filtration of Returnees from Nazi Germany, 1944–49," in Peter Gatrell and Nick Baron (eds.), *Warlands: Population Resettlement and State Reconstruction in the Soviet-East European Borderlands, 1945–50* (Palgrave Macmillan, 2009), 89–116, here: 96; Kim Salomon, *Refugees in the Cold War: Toward a New International Refugee Regime in the Early*

elitist organization, the OUN was organized as vanguard along Leninist principles, and its influence was considerably greater than its formal membership. US intelligence estimated that up to 80 percent of all Ukrainian DPs from Galicia were loyal to Bandera.[279] As unreconstructed totalitarians, the OUN(b) soon became unacceptable as a partner to the Americans, who instead supported one of its small offshoots. US intelligence initiated a long-term collaboration with the Foreign Representation of the Ukrainian Supreme Liberation Council (*Zakordonne predstavnytstvo Ukrains'koi Holovnoi Vyzvol'noi Rady*, zpUHVR) a small group which had split off from the OUN(b) in 1948. Under the cryptonym AERODYNAMIC Mykola Lebed' operated a highly successful CIA front organization, the Prolog Research and Publishing Corporation in New York, publisher of the journal *Suchasnist'* in Munich.[280] The more conservative OUN(m) slowly moderated over the following decades, integrating, in 1947, with the Ukrainian National Council (*Ukrains'ka Natsaional'na Rada*, UNR), a government in exile claiming to represent the state tradition of the UNR.[281]

The Ukrainian emigration was mainly concentrated in Canada, the US, Great Britain, and Australia. To a significant degree the post-war Ukrainian emigration consisted of people from Galicia.

Postwar Era (Lund: Lund University Press, 1991), 70–73; Tommie Sjöberg, *The Powers and the Persecuted: The Refugee Problem and the Intergovernmental Committee on Refugees* (Lund: Lund University Press, 1991), 178–79; and Wolfgang Jacobmeyer, "The 'Displaced Persons' in West Germany, 1945-1951," in *The Uprooted: Forced Migration as an International Problem in the Post-War Era*, ed. Göran Rystad (Lund: Lund University Press, 1990), 271–88, here: 276–77.

279 Breitman and Goda, *Hitler's Shadow: Nazi War Criminals, U.S. Intelligence, and the Cold War* (Washington, DC: National Archives, 2012), 78; Joe G. Oswald, 1sy Lt. Sig. G, Mil Intel Sec, "HEAD QUARTERS THE UNITED STATES ARMY, Office of the Assistant Chief of Staff, G-2, AFG 403, 24 May 1946, SUBJECT: 'BANDERA' and the Balking Ukraine," TO: Assistant Chief of Staff, G-2, Third United States Army, APO 403, US Army (Attn: Chief, Intelligence Branch)," Mykola Klymyszyn name file, XE184860 Klymyszyn.pdf (page 15 or 28), Army name file, NARA, Washington, DC. Thanks to Jared McBride for sharing this material with the author.

280 See chapter three, and Taras Kuzio, *Ukraine: Democratization, Corruption, and the New Russian Imperialism*, 128.

281 Osyp Barets'kyi et al. (eds.), *Bila knyha: OUN na zlami II i XXI stolit'* (Kyiv: Vydavnytstvo "Kyii," 2006), 50.

The rival strands of historiography developed in the Ukrainian diaspora were, to a significant degree, a spitting image of the Soviet narration in inverted form. Similarly centered around the concept of "struggle" (*zmahannia*) its key agent is not the toiling masses or the East Slavic peoples with their quest for unification, but the Ukrainians and their centuries-long struggle for "national liberation." A narration of suffering and national resistance is constructed around Cossack chieftains such as Bohdan Khmel'nyts'kyi (1595–1657), Ivan Mazepa (1639–1709) and Pylyp Orlyk (1672–1742) of the early modern era, through the Haidamak uprisings in the 18th century, to the "epoch of the liberation struggle," i.e. the Ukrainian People's Republic, to the OUN(b), and the UPA.[282] Self-victimization and valorization of the martyrdom of national heroes, in particular Symon Petliura, Yevhen Konovalets', UPA commander Roman Shukhevych, and Stepan Bandera, are central to this narration, which, with its strong sacral components, leaves little or no space for critical questioning or problematization.[283] This martyrology is interlinked with the assertion that the 1932–33 famine in the Ukrainian SSR — from around 1984 referred to by the neologism *Holodomor* — constituted genocide of the Ukrainian nation.[284]

---

[282] See, for instance, Petro Savaryn, "Kil'ka zauvah do posviachennia khrestapam'iatnyka u nedilliu 31.10.1976," in idem., *Z soboiu vzialy Ukrainu: Vid Ternopillia do Al'berty* (Kyiv: KVITs, 2007), 252–53, here: 253.

[283] Jan-Hinnerk Antons, *Ukrainische Displaced Persons in der Britischen Zone: Lagerleben zwischen nationaler Fixierung und pragmatischen Zukunfts-entwürfen* (Essen: Klartext Verlag, 2014), 265–97; Yuliya Yurchuk, *Reordering of Meaningful Worlds: Memory of the Organization of Ukrainian Nationalists and the Ukrainian Insurgent Army in Post-Soviet Ukraine* (=Stockholm Studies in History 103) (Stockholm: Stockholm University, 2014), 173–74, 203.

[284] Following Heorhii Kas'ianov this study makes a distinction between the 1932–33 famine and its use in discursive strategies, using italics to mark the latter; Heorhii Kas'ianov, *Rozryta mohyla: Holod 1932–1933 rokiv u politytsi, pam'iati ta istorii (1980-ti-2000-ni)* ("Folio," 2018), 6–8. On the diaspora's *Holodomor* discourse, see Rebekah Moore, "'A Crime Against Humanity Arguably Without Parallel in European History': Genocide and the 'Politics' of Victimhood in Western Narratives of the Ukrainian Holodomor," *Australian Journal of Politics and History* 58, no. 3 (September 2012): 367–79.

Poland and Giedroyc: Reconciliation or "Conspiracy of Silence"?

The conflict over memory was not an affair between Soviets and émigrés exclusively. Another component in the rather complex memory landscape was the Polish factor. The Polish state that emerged in 1918 found itself in an adversarial position vis-à-vis its eastern neighbors. Weakening or breaking Russia's influence on Ukraine became an imperative of Polish strategic thought from the 1920s.[285] The idea of strategic collaboration between Poland and its eastern neighbors against Russian rule was not new, but had antecedents dating back to the Decembrist uprising of 1825. The slogan "For Our Freedom and Yours! For Our Common Future!" had been raised by Polish rebels in 1831. Many years later Zbigniew Brzezinski (1928–2017), who served as Jimmy Carter's national security advisor, stressed the key strategic importance of Ukraine for Russian imperialism: "without Ukraine, Russia ceases to be an empire, but with Ukraine suborned and then subjugated, Russia automatically becomes an empire."[286] This was a factor that was immensely significant from the Polish viewpoint, too.

An important influence on the Polish thinking on these issues was Jerzy Giedroyc (1906–2000), a Minsk-born Polish émigré who advocated Polish reconciliation with its eastern neighbors, Ukraine in particular.[287] Covertly funded by the CIA, his Paris-based *Instytut Literackie* worked together with Lebed's circle.[288] From the pages of his influential émigré journal *Kultura*, Giedroyc argued that the Polish emigration ought to accept the geopolitical

---

285 Bruski, *Between Prometheism and Realpolitik.*
286 Zbigniew Brzezinski, "The Premature Partnership," *Foreign Affairs* 73, no. 2 (1994): 67–82, here: 80.
287 Magdalena Semczyszyn and Mariusz Zyalączkowski, *Giedroyc a Ukraina: Ukraińska perspektywa Jerzego Giedroycia i środowiska paryskiego "Kultury"* (Warsaw: IPN, 2014).
288 Alfred A. Reisch, *Hot Books in the Cold War: The CIA-funded Secret Western Book Distribution Program Behind the Iron Curtain* (Budapest: Central European University Press, 2013), 8; and Taras Kuzio, "How America Played a Central Role in Ukraine Becoming Independent," *Kyiv Post*, 11 September 2011, http://www.kyivpost.com/opinion/op-ed/how-america-played-a-central-role-in-ukraine-becom-112603.html (accessed 30 August 2013).

reality of the Curzon Line, as key to reconciliation with its eastern neighbors: "Let the Lithuanians ... enjoy their Vilnius and let the yellow and blue flag fly over L'viv," *Kultura* editorialized in 1952.[289] In Soviet Ukraine and the People's Republic of Poland, the OUN(b) and UPA's anti-Polish massacres could not be openly addressed. Giedroyc had established personal relations with some of the more prominent émigré Ukrainian nationalists already in the interwar period,[290] and the Polish–Ukrainian reconciliation program fostered by Giedroyc and *Kultura* came with a tacit agreement not to mention the "difficult" issues of the past. Critical engagement with the traumatic OUN(b) and UPA massacres was effectively muted through what historian Bogumiła Berdychowska (b. 1964) refers to as a "conspiracy of silence."[291]

In post-socialist Poland the so-called Giedroyc doctrine came to define much of its foreign policy from the early 1990s until 2013–2014 as the country sought to cultivate cordial relations with, and to encourage a pro-Western, or at least anti-Russian line among its eastern neighbors, from Lithuania to Moldova.[292] After joining NATO and the EU, Poland became Ukraine's perhaps most important partner in these fora. During the so-called Orange Revolution of 2004–2005 Polish politicians across the political spectrum openly sided with the protesters and gave the contender, Viktor Yushchenko, their full support. Both the major Polish parties, the conservative Law and Justice Party (*Prawo i Sprawedli-*

---

289 Wojciech Konończuk, "Why Poland Needs a Post-Giedroyc Doctrine towards Ukraine," *New Eastern Europe*, 22 March 2017, http://neweasterneurope.eu /2018/03/22/poland-needs-post-giedroyc-doctrine-towards-ukraine/ (accessed 16 April 2018).
290 Among them the nationalist ideologue Dmytro Dontsov and Pavlo Shandruk (1889–1979), assigned to take over the command of the 14th Ukrainian *Waffen-SS* Division *Galizien* during the final days of the war; Bogumila Berdykhovs'ka [Bogumiła Berdychowska] (ed.), *Ezhy Gedroits' ta ukrains'ka emigratsiia: Lystovannia 1950-1982 rokiv* (Kyiv: Krytyka, 2008), 17–18.
291 Berdykhovs'ka (ed.), *Ezhy Gedroits' ta ukrains'ka emigratsiia*, 36.
292 Timothy Snyder, *The Reconstruction of Nations: Poland, Ukraine, Lithuania, Belarus, 1569–1999* (New Haven: Yale University Press, 2003), 230–31.

wość, PiS) and the center-right Civic Platform (*Platforma Obywatelska*, PO) were romantically pro-Ukrainian.[293]

Pluralism by Default

Ukraine's division between the former Soviet core and periphery, its effective bi-lingualism and political bi-culturalism has defined much of its post-Soviet development. The deep divisions in society and the existence of rivaling, regional post-Soviet economic and political oligarchies have prevented the consolidation of power into one, central, and centralizing authoritarian system. Post-Soviet Ukraine stood out as poorer and more corrupt than the other two East Slavic republics; but at the same time, it was also freer, more transparent, and more pluralistic.[294]

"The factors facilitating pluralism have been deeply intertwined with those that have created dysfunction and corruption in Ukraine,"[295] University of Toronto political scientist Lucan Way (b. 1968) contends:

> Pluralism in "new democracies" is often grounded less in democratic leadership or in emerging civil society and more in the failure of authoritarianism. Dynamic competition frequently emerges because autocrats lack the state capital to steal elections, impose censorship, or repress opposition.[296]

Way refers to this as "pluralism by default." A greater degree of pluralism has been developed where the state capacity is weak and society divided, Way observes: "changes in organizational

---

293 Andrew Wilson, *Ukraine's Orange Revolution* (New Haven: Yale University Press, 2005), 192.
294 Long perceived as Europe's most corrupt country, in 2020, Ukraine was ranked by the Corruption Perceptions Index of Transparency International as the 117th most corrupt country of 180, far below Belarus (63), but ahead or Russia (place 129), which has replaced Ukraine as Europe's most corrupt country; "Corruption Perceptions Index, 2020," *Transparency International*, https://www.transparency.org/en/cpi/2020/index/ukr (accessed 22 June 2021). On the other hand, Ukraine ranks as "Partially Free" by Freedom House "Freedom in the World 2021," alone among the three east Slavic republics; "Ukraine Profile," *Freedom House*, https://freedomhouse.org/country/ukraine/freedom-world/2021 (accessed 22 June 2021).
295 Way, *Pluralism by Default*, 90.
296 Way, *Pluralism by Default*, 260.

capacity best account for shifts in pluralism over time, while national divisions best explain Ukraine's greater pluralism relative to other post-Soviet cases."[297] His colleague Ivan Katchanovski (b. 1967) at the University of Ottawa similarly stresses the role of the western regions in this development: "Results of numerous elections and surveys show that, were it not for the Western regions of Ukraine, this post-Soviet country would most likely have continued to follow Russia's authoritarian path, and pursue a pro-Russian orientation as did the Transnistrian Republic and Belarus."[298]

In 1991, as Ukraine gained independence, historian David Marples (b. 1952) doubted whether Ukraine would retain control over all its territory, noting that "One can dispense with the Crimea, which is unlikely to remain part of a future Ukrainian state and was a Stalinist creation from the first."[299] Marples was certainly not alone in such an assessment: in the 1990s many analysts, including at the CIA, predicted the break-up of Ukraine along ethno-linguistic and regional lines and a Yugoslav-style civil war.[300]

In the southern and eastern parts of the country, the commitment to the cause of independence wavered as Ukraine's economy declined. This was particularly noticeable in the Crimea, where a 1999 poll showed that 71.5 per cent of ethnic Russians and 51.4 per cent Ukrainians polled answered the question "Do you support the Crimea becoming a part of Russia?" in the affirmative.[301]

During the unrest of the "Orange Revolution" a break-up of Ukraine again appeared close, as the Donets'k Oblast' Council declared its intention to unilaterally transform Donets'k oblast' into a republic within Ukraine, modelled on Crimea.[302] On 28 No-

---

297 Way, *Pluralism by Default*, 88.
298 Ivan Katchanovski, *Cleft Countries: Regional Political Divisions and Cultures in Post-Soviet Ukraine and Moldova* (Stuttgart: ibidem-Verlag, 2006), 208.
299 Marples, *Ukraine under Perestroika*, 221.
300 Katchanovski, *Cleft Countries*, 20.
301 Kuzio, *Theoretical and Comparative Perspectives on Nationalism*, 107.
302 "Will Ukraine Split in Wake of Divisive Ballot?," *Poland, Belarus & Ukraine Report, Radio Free Europe/Radio Liberty*, 1 December 2004, vol. 6, no. 44,

vember 2004 over 3,000 delegates from across eastern and southern Ukraine gathered in the mining town Severodonets'k in the Donets'k oblast', where the head of the Donets'k oblast' Rada announced their intention to set up a new state in the form of a federation with the capital in Kharkiv.[303] Andrew Wilson asserts that Ukraine was never on the brink of a civil war, but that the threat of separatism was invoked in order to frighten moderates away from the Maidan. After a compromise was reached the congress dissolved and the planned referendum on local autonomy was scrapped.[304] The disintegration of Ukraine was forestalled, and a peaceful transition of power took place as Yushchenko, after western mediation, succeeded Leonid Kuchma (b. 1938, president 1994-2005) as Ukraine's third president in 2005. Still, analysts, such as the Fund for Peace (FFP), a Washington-based non-profit organization dedicated to conflict prevention and resolution, continued to identify Ukraine as a country at risk of disintegration along with states like Bosnia-Herzegovina, Lebanon, Tanzania, and Uzbekistan.[305]

Core or Periphery?

As the modern history of Ukraine was re-written after 1991 the status of the republic in the USSR became a contentious issue. One interpretation, common among nationally oriented Ukrainians — not least in Western Ukraine and its mainly Galician diaspora — was to regard Ukrainians as colonial subjects, and Ukraine as a territory colonized by "Moscow," or "*moskali*" ("Muscovites," a mildly pejorative term for Russians). According to this interpretation, Moscow and the RSFSR constituted the core, whereas the Soviet republics constituted the periphery.[306] Another, no less

---

https://www.rferl.org/a/1344005.html (accessed 17 November 2018); and Katchanovski, *Cleft Countries*, 20.
303 Andrei Kolesnikov, *Pervyi ukrainskii: Zapisi s perevodoi* (Kyiv: Vagrius, 2005), 298.
304 Wilson, *Ukraine's Orange Revolution*, 145.
305 Katchanovski, *Cleft Countries*, 20, citing "Failed States Index," *Foreign Policy*, no. 149 (July–August 2005): 56–65.
306 Kuzio, *Theoretical and Comparative Perspectives on Nationalism*, 336.

plausible interpretation would be to regard Ukraine as part of the east Slavic core of the union.[307] Similar to Russia and Belarus, a majority of Ukrainians do not regard the period of Soviet rule to be a result of foreign domination.[308] In central and eastern Ukraine, with centuries of joint history as part of the same state, the Russian language remains the de facto language of everyday communication for the vast majority of the urbanites, something reflected in media consumption and flow of information, at least until the Russian invasion of 2014.[309]

Ukrainian memory is, however, divided. Galicia, the heartland of Ukrainian nationalism, had never been under Russian rule.[310] A part of the Habsburg empire until 1918, prior to its partitions in the late 18th century, Galicia had been under Polish rule since the Middle Ages. At the same time, the Ukrainian internal "cultural boundaries" have been fluid. For example, in the 1990s, the northern Sumy and Chernihiv oblasti could be regarded as culturally and linguistically part of the Russian media sphere, voting for parties rooted in Soviet traditions and sharing common historical references with the other two East Slavic republics.[311] Since the turn of the millennium this "boundary" has slowly moved eastwards, as reflected in the growing popularity of political parties which to varying degrees seek to distance Ukraine from Moscow's orbit, a process which has escalated following the Russian invasion in 2014.

---

307 Zbigniew Wojnowski, *The Near Abroad: Socialist Eastern Europe and Soviet Patriotism in Ukraine, 1956–1985* (Toronto: University of Toronto Press, 2017), 14–18.

308 Ioffe, *Reassessing Lukashenka*, 26, citing Yurii Drakakhrust, "Belarus', Raseia, Ukraina: estafeta autaryitaryzmu," *Belarusian Radio Liberty*, 22 August 2010, http://www.svaboda.org/content/transcript/24304775.html (accessed 1 November 2010).

309 Ioffe, *Reassessing Lukashenka*, 18.

310 With the exception of the brief occupations of parts of Galicia by Imperial Russia in 1914–15 and by the Bolsheviks in 1920. See von Hagen, *War in a European Borderland*; and Alexander Victor Prusin, *Nationalizing a Borderland: War, Ethnicity, and Anti-Jewish Violence in East Galicia, 1914–1920* (Tuscaloosa: University of Alabama Press, 2005).

311 Katchanovski, *Cleft Countries*, 71; and Andrew Wilson, *Ukrainian Nationalism in the 1990s: A Minority Faith* (Cambridge: Cambridge University Press, 1997), 138–46.

Holodomor

The collapse of the Soviet Union and the emergence of an independent Ukrainian polity profoundly changed the conditions for the Ukrainian historical establishment. There was now a need for a new official narration—one which legitimized not unification under Muscovy, but Ukrainian statehood. Along with the political elite, much of the intellectual establishment followed the example of Kravchuk. The erstwhile ideologue and Second Secretary of the Ukrainian Communist Party metamorphosed from a "scientific Marxist-Leninist" into blue-and-yellow patriot. Parts of the academic establishment attempted to follow suit, seeking to adopt to the new circumstances.

Yehen Holovakha (b. 1950), head of the Institute of Sociology at the National Academy of Sciences of Ukraine recalls how, when Ukraine became independent and the Communist party banned, "the professors of scientific communism immediately came running and in a few days came up with a program of scientific nationalism."[312] A serious effort was made to install such an integrative ideological "discipline" for all educational institutions, but faced opposition in the Institute of Philosophy and failed to obtain government support at the time.[313]

Kravchuk would become a strong promoter of the genocidal interpretation of Soviet history; arguing that Soviet rule had constituted genocide of the Ukrainian people. Much of the historical establishment underwent a similar transformation, smoothly and seemingly effortlessly morphing into something akin to "scientific" nationalists, trading historical materialism for a narration centered around the claim that the defining feature of Soviet rule was its deliberate attempt to exterminate the Ukrainian nation. In 1986–87 Stanislav Kul'chyts'kyi (b. 1937), perhaps the most prom-

---

312 Yevhen Holovakha, "Sub"iektyvnyi pohliad na ukrains'ku filosofiiu (Rozmova iz Kseniieiu Zborovs'koiu, Aminoiu Kkhelufi ta Vsevolodom Khomoiu)," *Sententiae*, vol. 36, no. 1 (2017): 173-214, here: 193. Thanks to Denys Kiryukhin for bringing this material to the author's attention.
313 Denys Kiryukhin, "The Philosophical Process in Post-Soviet Ukraine," in Mikhail Minakov (ed.), *Philosophy Unchained: Development of Philosophy After the Fall of the Soviet Union* (Stuttgart: ibidem-Verlag, 2022): 301

inent *Holodomor* researcher in Ukraine, led a commission for the Central Committee of the Ukrainian Communist Party to disclose "bourgeois falsifications" with regard to the famine.[314] As the governmental order changed, Kul'chyts'kyi underwent an evolution, a "revolutionary transformation of his world view" (*"svitohliadna revuliutsiia"*), and which led to him becoming one of the most vociferous promoters of the genocide thesis.[315] In his seminal study of the *Holodomor* discourse, historian Heorhyi Kas'ianov (b. 1961) at the Ukrainian Academy of Sciences shows how Kul'chyts'kyi "formed that discourse, academic discourse as well as in the language of politics and ideology,"[316] becoming, in the words of Kas'ianov, "a propagandist of the 'state-building' [*derzhavnyts'koi*] version of national history and defender of the official canon of politics of history."[317]

Still, under Kravchuk and Kuchma, the instrumentalization of history played a rather limited role. Under Kravchuk, a number of laws were passed that made the archives readily accessible to researchers.[318] Kuchma pursued a policy which he referred to as "multi-vector," treating historical memory strategically and rather unsentimentally, emphasizing different parts of memory to differ-

---

314 Still in 1988, in his *The Establishment of the Socialist Order of the Peasantry of the Ukrainian SSR* Kul'chyts'kyi only touched upon 1932–33 once, and then to inform readers that 95–98% of rural children attended school that year— evidence of a great achievement; Kas'ianov, *Rozryta mohyla*, 158, n. 2, citing S. V. Kul'chyts'kyi, S. R. Liakh, and V. I. Marochko, *Stanovlenie osnov sotsionalistich-eskogo uklada zhizni krest'ianstva USSR* (Kyiv: Naukova dumka, 1988), 115.
315 Kas'ianov, *Rozryta mohyla*, 200.
316 Kas'ianov, *Rozryta mohyla*, 212.
317 Kas'ianov, *Rozryta mohyla*, 209.
318 On access to Ukrainian archives, see "Zakon Ukrainy pro Natsional'nyi arkhivnyi fond ta arkhivni ustanovy vid 24.12.1993 No. 3814-XII," http://zakon2.rada.gov.ua/laws/show/3814-12?test=4/UMfPEGznhhCzg.Zio141ZBHI48gs80msh8Ie6; on the laws on state secrets, see "Zakon Ukrainy pro derzhavnu taemnitsiu, document 3855-12, redaktsiia vid 12.06.2015," http://zakon3.rada.gov.ua/laws/show/3855-12?test=4/UMfPEGznhhCzg.Zio141ZBHI48gs80msh8Ie6; and on access to information, see "Zakon Ukrainy pro informatsiiu vid. 02.10.1992, No. 2657-XII," http://zakon2.rada.gov.ua/laws/show/2657-12 (all accessed 28 June 2021).

ent audiences, praising the struggle for independence or invoking Soviet nostalgia, depending on the audience.[319]

Institutes of Memory Production

After Viktor Yushchenko prevailed in the tug of war of the so-called Orange Revolution of 2004–2005 he sought a new historical and political identity for Ukraine. Whereas Kuchma had largely avoided the more difficult historical topics, Yushchenko's presidency marked a sharp departure from this cautious line. He embarked on a project to establish institutions tasked with the political instrumentalization of history, the most important one of which being the Ukrainian Institute of National Memory (*Ukrains'kyi Instytut Natsional'noi Pam'iati*, UINP), established on 31 May 2006 "as a special organ for restoration and preservation of the national memory of the Ukrainian people."[320] The conceptualization was, from the very onset closely associated with radical Nationalist circles, in particular the OUN(b). For over a decade, its activities came to be shaped by the most prominent memory manger in Ukraine, Volodymyr V"iatrovych (b. 1977). Despite his youth, V"iatrovych had significant experience in the field of instrumentalizing history. Since he was twenty V"iatrovych had been a regular contributor to articles on historical topics in the far-right press.[321] His punditry early caught the attention of the diaspora. In 2002 the 25-year-old activist was one of the co-organizers of the Center for the Study of the Liberation Movement (*Tsentr doslidzhen' vyzvol'noho rukhu*, TsDVR) in L'viv,

---

319 Wilson, *Ukrainian Nationalism in the 1990s*, 191–93; and Nikolay Koposov, *Memory Laws, Memory Wars: The Politics of the Past in Europe and Russia* (Cambridge: Cambridge University Press, 2018), 181.
320 Yu. Yekhanurov, "Pro utvorennia Ukrains'koho instytutu natsional'noi pam"iati," Dokument 764-2006-p, https://zakon.rada.gov.ua/laws/show/764-2006-п (accessed 24 June 2019).
321 Volodymyr V"iatrovych, "Heroichnyi reid soten' UPA," *Natsiia i derzhava*, no. 4 (1998): 5; idem., "Taktyka povstan's'kykh reidiv," *Vyzvol'nyi shliakh*, kn. 6 (1999): 685–91.

an OUN(b) façade organization funded with money from the overseas Ukrainian diaspora.[322]

V"iatrovych early demonstrated his significant initiative and organizational ability. An activist in the student protest group *PORA!*, he had gained some prominence during the Orange Revolution of 2004–2005.[323] V"iatrovych refers to his activism to promote the "Ukrainian liberation movement" as "popular science." While he and his aides have formal training as historians, and some of their works have a scholarly apparatus (and are sometimes even co-published with Ukrainian universities) they are not peer reviewed.[324] The works are highly ideological, and fall short of Western academic standards.[325] V"iatrovych's preferred publication venues include the ideological journals of his OUN(b) sponsors, such as *Shliakh peremohy* (*The Path of Victory*) and *Vyzvol'nyi shliakh*, (*The Path of Liberation*) where he affirms a one-dimensional and self-serving narration of the OUN(b)'s history, whitewashing its well-documented participation in the 1941 pogroms and casting its ethnic cleansing of Volhynia and East Galicia in terms of a "second Polish-Ukrainian War" with a supposed "symmetry" in terms of Polish and Ukrainian casualties.[326]

---

322 Sviatoslav Lypovets'kyi, *Orhanizatsiia Ukrains'kykh Natsionalistiv (banderivtsi): Frahmenty diial'nosti ta borot'by* (Kyiv: Ukrains'ka Vydavnycha Spilka, 2010), 84; and "Khaker arkhiviv chekistiv, fihura istorychnoi polityky i ospivuvach UPA: Shcho vidomo pro Volodymyra V"iatrovycha?," *112.ua*, 2 February 2018, https://ua.112.ua/suspilstvo/khaker-arkhiviv-chekistiv-fihura-istoryc hnoi-polityky-i-ospivuvach-upa-shcho-vidomo-pro-volodymyra-viatrovycha -431530.html (accessed 11 October 2018).
323 Christine Emeran, *New Generation Political Activism in Ukraine, 2000–2014* (New York: Routledge, 2017), 65, 80.
324 Gibfried Schenk, *Zwischen Sowjetnostalgie und "Entkommunisierung": Postsowjetische Geschichtspolitik und Erinnerungskultur in der Ukraine* (Erlangen: FAU University Press, 2020), 134.
325 Iryna Vushko, "Historians at War: History, Politics and Memory in Ukraine," *Contemporary European History* 27, no. 1 (2018): 112–24.
326 Per Anders Rudling, "Warfare of War Criminality?: Volodymyr V"iatrovych, Druha pol's'ko-ukrains'ka viina, 1942–1947 (Kyiv: Vydavnychyi Dim 'Kyevo-Mohylians'ka Akademiia, 2011)," *Ab Imperio* 1 (2012): 356–81; here: 374. On the 1941 pogroms, see Struve, *Deutsche Herrschaft*; and Andrzej Zięba (red.), *OUN, UPA i zagłada żydów*. These sorts of chronicles, deliberately ignoring known facts and departing from the established methodology which defines the academic discipline of history while attributing wrongdoings to others,

V"iatrovych collaborates closely with his OUN(b) diaspora sponsors. While financially solvent, and well-connected with the Canadian political elite, the overseas OUN(b) is dominated by aging post-war émigrés largely disconnected from Ukrainian realities. V"iatrovych's talent lies in his ability to skillfully utilize the potential of the new media, communicating with his followers through social media networks. His wife Yaryna Yasynevych (b. 1979), a fellow *PORA!* activist and former aide to an "Orange" member of the Rada, skillfully managed the TsDVR's publishing house. Well-connected to the new political leadership, and with significant funding from overseas diaspora sponsors, V"iatrovych's network came to play a central role in the memory management under Yushchenko.[327] He had a powerful mentor also in SBU director Valentyn Nalivaichenko (b. 1966).

The initiative to set up the TsDVR came from the very top of the OUN(b). On May 20, 2006, OUN(b) leader Andrii Haidamakha (b. 1945, head of the OUN(b) 2001-2009) reported to the society of UPA veterans in the US how "we have called into life a 'Center for the Study of the Liberation Movement' in L'viv. The center will become the most authoritative institution for scientific research and academic elucidation of our history of state-building. It has already become well-known, not only in Ukraine, but in the Baltic

---

be they foreign aggressors, domestic traitors against the noble cause, or produced by latter-day historians without proper hermeneutics, Klas-Göran Karlsson refers to as "tyrannical literature"; Klas-Göran Karlsson, *Europeiska möten med historien: Historiekulturella perspektiv på andra världskriget, förintelsen och den kommunistiska terrorn* (Stockholm: Atlantis, 2010), 358. For a recent illustration of this instrumental use of history, see Jared McBride, "The Many Lives and Afterlives of Khaim Sygal: Borderland Identities and Violence in Wartime Ukraine," *Journal of Genocide Research*, vol. 23, no. 4 (2021): 547-567, here: 455–457.

327 For the English and Polish translations alone of his book *Druha pol's'ko-ukrains'ka viina*, translated into English as *The Gordian Knot* V"iatrovych's sponsors in the Ukrainian–Canadian hard right raised over 50,000 dollars; Mykola Svyntukh-Zaverukha and Mariika Jacyla, "Vydannia 'Druha pol's'ko-ukrains'ka vina' pol'skoio movuiu," *Homin Ukrainy*, 31 March 2013, http://www.homin.ca/news.php/news/11653/group/19 and *The Shevchenko Foundation Annual Report 2015*, p. 32, https://web.archive.org/web/2016 0912145709/http://shevchenkofoundation.com/PDF/2014-2015-Annual-Report.pdf (both accessed 22 June 2021).

states, in Poland and Slovakia. It actively supports the realization of the concept of the President of Ukraine to establish a Ukrainian 'Institute of national memory.'"[328] From the inception of the Ukrainian Institute of National Memory, V"iatrovych's group of activists would occupy central positions in its leadership and management. However, during its first years the institute was led by a former deputy Prime Minister, Ihor Yukhnovs'kyi (b. 1925), who had been Kuchma's former deputy prime minister in 1992-1993. Yukhnovskyi's CV chronicles the all-so-common metamorphosis from communist to nationalist; joining the Communist Party in 1956, Yukhnovs'kyi spent nearly to four decades within its ranks before re-inventing himself as a Ukrainian nationalist as the Soviet Union collapsed. In the early 1990s, he sympathized with the radical right Social Nationalist Party of Ukraine (SNDP) — which in 2004 became the All-Ukrainian Union "Freedom" (*Vseukrains'ke Ob"iednannia Svoboda*).[329] Yukhnovs'kyi has a distinguished career as politician and physicist, but lacks training as a historian. During the first year of Yushchenko's presidency, his administration tasked the archives of the former KGB, (now the Sectoral State Archive of the Security Services of Ukraine (*Haluzevyi derzhavnyi arkhiv Sluzhby Bezpeky Ukrainy*, HDA SBU) with the instrumentalization of history. In 2008 V"iatrovych was appointed director of the HDA SBU in addition to managing the archives of the UINP.

---

328 "No. 77. Lyst holovy provodu OUN Andriia Haidamakhy do holovnoi upravy TV UPA v ZSA 20 travnia 2006 r." In Ihor Homziak and Bohdan Kovalyk, eds., *Al'manakh Tovarystva voivakiv UPA im. hen-khor. Romana Shukheyvcha-'Taras Chuprynynky" v ZSA. Knyha 3, 2001-2015* (New York and L'viv: TV UPA v ZSA, 2018), 175-176.

329 O. Bazhan and O. Loshyts'kyi (eds.), "Stanovlennia Narodnoho rukhu Ukrainy (za dokumentamy Haluzevoho derzhavnoho arkhivu Sluzhby bezpeky Ukrainy)," *Z arkhiviv VUChK, GPU, NKVD, KGB: Naukovyi i dokumental'nyi zhurnal*, no. 2 (33) (2009): 206–326, here: 239, n. 56; and Lilia Kuzik, "Ihor Yukhnovs'kyi: 'Ta derzhava zh mala utvorytysia. I ia vse robyv, shchob vona utvorylas'," *Zaxid.net*, 11 August 2011, https://zaxid.net/igor_yuhno vskiyta_derzhava_zh_mala_utvoritisya_i_ya_vse_robiv_shhob_vona_utvoril as_n1233429 (accessed 30 June 2021).

Legislating *Holodomor*

If the cult of the OUN(b) and UPA constitutes one pillar of the new "national memory" Yushchenko and his legitimizing historians sought to establish, the other is the *Holodomor* discourse — a narration of the 1932–33 famine as genocide of the Ukrainian nation.[330] In November 2006 the Rada narrowly passed legislation that enshrined in law the interpretation that the *Holodomor* was a deliberate genocide aimed at exterminating the Ukrainians, though parliament changed the wording of the law from "Ukrainian nation" (*natsiia*) (the term used in Yushchenko's decree) to "people" (*narid*), thereby replacing the ethnic framing with a political one.[331]

Yushchenko actively sought recognition of the genocidal interpretation of the famine from other states. Most ignored him; the only western countries that heeded his appeal were Canada and Australia, countries with significant, and politically very active Ukrainian diaspora communities. Among the handful of countries that responded to the appeal was Poland, which followed suit and affirmed Yushchenko's narration.[332] During a state visit to Ottawa, Yushchenko reminded his hosts that Ukraine had gained independence six times in the twentieth century and had lost it on five different occasions.[333] Back in Kyiv, he sought to set up a Museum

---

330 Olha Ostriitchouk, *Les Ukrainiens face à leur passé: Vers une meilleure compréhension de clivage Est/Ouest* (Brussels: Peter Lang, 2013), 223–99; and John-Paul Himka, "Interventions: Challenging the Myths of Twentieth-Century Ukrainian History," in *The Convolutions of Historical Politics*, ed. Alexei Miller and Maria Lipman (Budapest: Central European University Press, 2012), 211–38, here: 220.

331 Andrii Portnov, "Memory Wars in Post-Soviet Ukraine (1991–2010)," in *Memory and Theory in Eastern Europe*, eds. Uilleam Blacker, Alexander Etkind, and Julie Fedor (New York: Palgrave Macmillan, 2013), 233–45, here: 244.

332 Per Anders Rudling, "Institutes of Trauma Re-production in a Borderland: Poland, Ukraine, and Lithuania," *CBEES State of the Region Report 2020: Constructions and Instrumentalization of the Past. A Comparative Study on Memory Management in the Region*, ed. Ninna Mörner (Huddinge: CBEES, 2020), 55–68, here: 60.

333 Bohdan S. Kordan, *Strategic Friends: Canada–Ukraine Relations from Independence to the Euromaidan* (Montreal and Kingdton: McGill-Queen's University Press, 2018), 87.

of Soviet Occupation.[334] To Yushchenko, Soviet rule did not only constitute a foreign occupation. It was genocide.

From January 2008 V"iatrovych served as an advisor to SBU director Nalyvaichenko and as a research consultant to the program "Ukraine Remembers, the World Acknowledges." In July 2008 the SBU published a list of 19 people "who provided the organizational-legal basis for the Holodomor-Genocide policies and repressions in Ukraine." Eight of the individuals on the list were of Jewish background, and their ethnicity was underlined by the inclusion in parenthesis of their "real" Ashkenazi names alongside Slavic-sounding names.[335] After V"iatrovych was promoted to director of the HDA SBU in October 2008 the instrumentalization of history intensified. In 2009, the SBU announced the "exact" number of the victims of the "Holodomor-Genocide": 10,063,000 people, of whom, the Ukrainian Security Service declared, 91.2% were ethnic Ukrainians. The SBU had arrived at these "exact" numbers by adding 6,122,000 "unborn" people to the highest scholarly estimates of excess deaths during the 1932–33 famine.[336]

Ruling on *Holodomor*

Voices in the Ukrainian diaspora had long called for Lazar Kaganovich (1893–1991) to be tried *in absentia* for the murder of Ukrainians.[337] The head of the Association of *Holodomor* Researchers in Ukraine (*Asotsiatsiia doslidnykiv holodomoriv v Ukraini*), the former

---

334 "Yushchenko proponue stvoryty v Ukraini Muzei radians'koi okupatsii," *Korrespondent.net*, 2 March 2007, https://ua.korrespondent.net/main/67775/ (accessed 8 March 2007; link no longer active).
335 "Spysok partiinykh i radians'kykh kerivnykiv, kerivnykykh spivrobitnykiv ODPU ta DPU USRR, a takozh dokumentiv, shcho staly orhanizatsiinopravovoiu pidstavoiu dlia povedennia v Ukraini polityky Holodomoru-Henotsydu ta represii," website of the *Sluzhba Bezpeky Ukrainy*, 18 July 2008, http://www.ssu.gov.ua/sbu/control/uk/publish/printable_article?art_id=80407 (accessed 7 August 2008, link no longer active). Thanks to John-Paul Himka for sharing this document with the author.
336 "SBU nazvala ostatochnu kil'kist' zhertv Holodomoru v Ukraini," *TSN.ua*, http://tsn.ua/ukrayina/sbu-nazvala-ostatochnu-kilkist-golodomoru-v-ukra yini.html (accessed 30 October 2011; link no longer active).
337 Dietsch, *Making Sense of Suffering*, 135.

dissident Levko Luk"ianenko (1928–2018), demanded what he referred to as a "Nuremberg 2" process on the crimes of communism.[338] References to Nuremberg were also a prominent feature in V"iatrovych's rhetoric, reinforcing his critique of communism by equating it to Nazism.[339] Once the Verkhovna Rada had legislated the genocidal interpretation into law and the "exact" number of Ukrainian genocide victims had been determined by the Security Service of Ukraine, the matter was now handed over to the courts. In 2010, nineteen years after his death, Kaganovich was put on trial by the Kyiv court of appeals, along with six other long-dead Soviet politicians: Mendel' Khataevich (1893–1937), Yosif Stalin (1878–1953), Viacheslav Molotov (1890–1986), Pavel Postyshev (1887–1939), Stanislav Kosior (1889–1939), Vlas Chubar' (1891–1939), and — two Jews, one Georgian, two Russians, one Pole, and one Ukrainian.[340] On 13 January 2010 the Kyiv court of appeals found the seven dead men guilty of genocide. The court ruled that the men had been motivated by the aim to "crush the Ukrainian national liberation movement and to prevent ... the establishment of an independent Ukrainian State." In its ruling, the court affirmed the highest scholarly estimate as the correct one:

> By creating conditions aimed at the physical annihilation of a part of the Ukrainian people through the Holodomor of 1932–1933 they planned, and consciously organized the genocide of a part of the Ukrainian ethnic group, as a result of which 3,941,000 people were killed.[341]

---

338 Luk"ianenko identified Jews as "organizers of the criminal government," equating the Soviet government with Jews, erroneously identifying also Lenin and Stalin as Jews; Levko Luk"ianenko, *Zlochynna sut' KPRS-KPU: Niurnberh – 2* (Kyiv: MAUP, 2005), 42–44.
339 Sonia Koshkyna, "Volodymyr V"iatrovych: 'Niurnberh' nad komunizmom mozhlyvyi i potribnyi," *Levyi bereg*, 20 May 2016, http://lb.ua/news/2016/05/20/335648_volodimir_vyatrovich_nyurnberg_nad.html (accessed 21 May 2016).
340 The verdict, in its entirety was published as "Ruling in the criminal proceedings over genocide in Ukraine in 1932–1933," *Information Website of the Kharkiv Human Rights Protection Group*, 13 January 2010, http://khpg.org/en/index.php?id=1265217823 (accessed 30 October 2017).
341 "Ruling in the criminal proceedings over genocide in Ukraine in 1932–1933"

Furthermore, it ruled the genocide aimed at exterminating Ukrainians, and, it underlined, not any other group:

> The criminal investigation body has fully and comprehensively established the special intention of Stalin, Molotov, Kaganovich, Postyshev, Kosior, Chubar and Khatayevych—to destroy a part specifically of the Ukrainian (*and not any other*) ethnic group and has objectively proved that this intention applied specifically to a part *of the Ukrainian ethnic group as such*.[342]

Placing a particular stress on ethnicity, and adding a disclaimer for including one ethnic Ukrainian among the perpetrators,[343] the court ruled that,

> It is unqualifiedly proven that Holodomor was planned by the above-mentioned people... as one of the stages of a special operation against a part of the Ukrainian ethnic group as such since it was the Ukrainian nation, and not ethnic minorities, who acted as the bearer of State-creating self-identification by leaving the USSR and establishing an independent Ukrainian State. It is for this reason that the direct target of the Holodomor 1932-1933 was the Ukrainian ethnic group.[344]

Since the guilty were all long since dead, none of the sentences could be carried out. Through this ruling, the court "settled" de jure a historical argument, that the famine constituted *Holodomor*—deliberate genocide, specifically and exclusively aimed at ethnic Ukrainians, and "not any other" ethnic group. A week later, on 20 January 2010, Yushchenko, after having been defeated in the first round of the Ukrainian presidential elections, designated the late Stepan Bandera as Hero of Ukraine, posthumously awarding him the highest award of the Ukrainian state.[345]

---

342 "Ruling in the criminal proceedings over genocide in Ukraine in 1932-1933." Emphasis added.

343 "The participation ... of the ethnic Ukrainian Chubar in no way influences the qualification of the given crime perpetrated by artificially creating in 1932-1933 as genocide since neither domestic criminal legislation nor international criminal law ... depends on the ethnic origin of the criminal. In determining whether there was such a crime it is of no significance whether it was perpetrated by a representative of the so-called titular nation or ethnic minority, Caucasian or Negroid, believer or atheist"; "Ruling in the criminal proceedings over genocide in Ukraine in 1932-1933."

344 "Ruling in the criminal proceedings over genocide in Ukraine in 1932-1933"

345 Grzegorz Rossoliński-Liebe, *Stepan Bandera: The Life and Afterlife of a Ukrainian Nationalist: Fascism, Genocide, and Cult* (Stuttgart: ibidem-Verlag, 2014), 506.

Managing Memory

Given the centrality of the *Holodomor* to the Ukrainian nation-building project, it is rather remarkable how limited, and of how poor quality, the scholarly literature on the famine is.[346] The standard works are pre-archival, and/or intensely ideological. As a result, little of the Ukrainian *Holodomor* literature is integrated into internatinal scholarship. Conversely, important studies in Western languages are either ignored or, if cited, then in Russian or Ukrainian translation.[347] In turn, this is indicative of how Ukrainian higher education and research, to a significant degree, long remained isolated from the international scholarly community. This is particularly noticeable in the field of the humanities, where most researchers lack a command of English and other Western languages, few publish with international peer reviewed journals, and Ukrainian institutions rank very low in international comparisons. Only a handful of Ukrainian universities subscribe to international journals in political science and the humanities. To this picture Taras Kuzio adds "failure to listen to Western advice," "little intellectual input from the West into Ukrainian political programs," and "vacuous populist rhetoric."[348] This parochialism has had direct political consequences, as the government pursued memory policies centered around historical figures perceived as highly controversial in Poland and Israel—not to mention the European Union, which Ukraine has expressed a desire to join. Political scientist Tadeusz A. Olszański (b. 1950) at the Warsaw Center for Eastern Studies, noted how "It seems that Kyiv does not notice or does not understand the significance of the memory

---

346 On the *Holodomor* historiography, see Heorhii Kas'ianov, *Danse macabre: Holod 1932-1933 rokiv u polititsi, masovii svidomosti ta istoriohrafii (1980-ti – pochatok 2000-kh)* (Kyiv: Nash chas, 2010).
347 John-Paul Himka, "Encumbered Memory: The Ukrainian Famine of 1932-33," *Kritika: Explorations in Russian and Eurasian History* 14, no. 2 (Spring 2013): 411-36, here: 413.
348 Kuzio, *Ukraine: Democratization, Corruption, and the New Russian Imperialism,* 164, 165.

of the Holocaust ... in the political discourse that is currently predominant in Europe and the USA."[349]

The "Orange" government did not live up to the high expectations placed on it; Yushchenko's time in power was marred by a slump in the economy and characterized by infighting with Yuliia Tymoshenko (b. 1960), an erstwhile ally. There were few advances in the promised work against the entrenched corruption. Yushchenko's lasting legacy may have been his intense instrumentalization of history.

In 2010, Viktor Yanukovych (b. 1950), who had failed to secure the presidency in 2004, won the presidential elections which the US embassy in Kyiv characterized as "essentially free and fair. None reported systematic fraud that could have undermined the result."[350] In retrospect, the Ukrainian voters' choice to elect Yanukovych may seem puzzling. Yet Yanukovych, a recent study notes, "appeared to be managerial, non-consensual, and [...] had roots in a region where the economy was still functioning."[351] At the same time he was, however, a highly controversial politician—a convicted felon who had served two prison terms, including one for robbery.[352] His government distinguished itself as corrupt, also by Ukrainian standards. As president, Yanukovych resumed an

---

[349] Tadeusz A. Olszański, *The Great Decommunization: Ukraine's Wartime Historical Policy* (=Point of View, No. 65) (Warsaw: Centre for Eastern Studies, 2017), 35–36.

[350] Sign. TEFFT, "Tymoshenko does better than expected but falls short; NGOs declare election free and fair," From: Ukraine Kyiv to Secretary of State, 8 February 2010, https://wikileaks.org/plusd/cables/10KYIV199_a.html (accessed 19 April 2016).

[351] See also Li Bennich-Björkman, Andriy Kashyn, and Sergiy Kurbatov, "The Election of a Kleptocrat: Viktor Ianukovych and the Ukrainian Presidential Elections in 2010," *East/West: Journal of Ukrainian Studies* VI, no. 1 (2019): 91–124, here: 119. On the Party of Regions, see Taras Kuzio, "Rise and Fall of the Party of Regions Political Machine," *Problems of Post-Communism* 62, no. 3 (2015): 174–86; and David R. Marples, "The Yanukovych Election Campaigns in Ukraine, 2004 and 2006: An Analysis," *Journal of Ukrainian Studies*, vol. 35–36 (2010–2011): 265–80.

[352] Ivanna Gorina, "Yanukovychu vozvrashchaiut sudimosti," *Rossiiskaia gazeta*, no. 3819, 13 July 2005, https://rg.ru/2005/07/13/yanukovich.html (accessed 17 November 2018).

authoritarian course akin to the one pursued in Kuchma's second term.

Unlike Yushchenko, Yanukovych showed little interest in the instrumentalization of history. If anything, he sought to return to the "multi-vector" history politics of the Kuchma era, or at least to downplay the divisive memory conflicts stoked under Yushchenko. In a nudge to Yanukovych's Communist allies, Yukhnovs'kyi was replaced by Valerii Soldatenko (b. 1946), a member of the Communist party.[353] At the same time the UINP was transformed into a "scientific-research budgeted institution under the Ukrainian Cabinet of Ministers," and all but disappeared from the political arena.[354] V"iatrovych was dismissed as head of the HDA SBU archives, and replaced by another communist, Ol'ha Ginzburg (b. 1953), a former member of parliament.[355] By court orders, Bandera and Shukhevych were stripped of their posthumous status as Heroes of Ukraine. The instrumentalization of the famine was scaled down. Yanukovych characterized the famine as a tragedy, but objected to its ethnicization. Arguing that many groups in the Soviet Union were subjected to starvation, he rejected what he described as the "incorrect and unjust" narration that the famine constituted "a genocide of a specific people."[356] The Yanukovych government and the Party of Regions sought to brand Ukraine as a pluralistic nation between East and West, where languages and

---

353 Koposov, *Memory Laws*, 190.
354 Serhii Kyrychuk, "'Ya znaiu, chto takoe ukrainskaia revoluiutsiia," *Liva.com.ua*, no date, but summer 2012, http://liva.com.ua/valery-soldatenko.html (accessed 15 July 2013); and "Ukrains'kyi instytut natsional'noi pam"iaty s'ohodni (berezen' 2014 roku)," *Historians.in.ua*, 2 March 2016, http://www.historians.in.ua/index.php/en/institutsiji-istorichnoji-nauki-v-ukrajini/1814-ukrainskyi-instytut-natsionalnoi-pam-iati-sohodni-berezen-2014-roku (accessed 3 March 2016).
355 Egor Smirnov, "Glava Gosudarstvennoi arkhivoi sluzhby Ukrainy Ol'ga Ginzburg: 'Oshchushchaiu sebia khranitelem istorii'," *Versii.com*, 18 January 2012, https://versii.com/news/247764/ (accessed 25 May 2021).
356 Ostriitchouk, *Les Ukrainiens face à leur passé*, 295.

religions co-existed comfortably, stressing the Ukrainian society's cosmopolitanism, diversity, and hybridity.[357]

If the instrumentalization of history decreased under Yanukovych, it did not cease altogether. The Party of Regions and its junior coalition partner, the Communist Party of Ukraine, did not hesitate to exploit divisive episodes of the recent past. In 2011 the Rada passed a controversial flag law which stipulated that the blue-and-yellow Ukrainian national flag be accompanied by a red banner with the hammer and sickle on public buildings during the commemoration of Victory Day, trigging predictably angry protests in L'viv.[358] One of the Party of Region's lawmakers, Vadym Kolesnychenko (b. 1958), stood out as particularly aggressive in his attempts to instrumentalize the past.[359] Compared to V"iatrovych's media-savvy political enthusiasts, Kolesnychenko appeared hopelessly daft and inept at this game. In 2012 and again in 2013, Kolesnychenko stole the work of foreign historians specializing in the Holocaust and ethnic violence in Ukraine, publishing them in poor, unauthorized translations in the name of "The International Anti-Fascist front" with forewords by himself, falsely implying that these researchers endorsed his government's use of history.[360] The divisive potential of "memory" was again utilized, often with an apparent purpose of provoking angry reac-

---

357 Kas'ianov, *Ukraina i sosedi*, 76–78; and Per Ståhlberg and Göran Bolin, "Having a Soul or Choosing a Face? Nation Branding, Identity and Cosmopolitan Imagination," *Social Identities* 22, no. 2 (2016): 274–90, here: 286–87.
358 Roman Dubasevych, "Pryvydy imperii ta demony peryferii," *Zaxid.net*, 23 May 2011, https://zaxid.net/prividi_imperiyi_ta_demoni_periferiyi_n11297 17; "Ukrainian Court Bans Use of Soviet Red Flag," *Radio Free Europe/Radio Liberty*, 17 June 2011, https://www.rferl.org/a/ukraine_court_bans_use_of_soviet_flag/24238302.html (both accessed 18 September 2018).
359 Koposov, *Memory Laws*, 191–92.
360 Vadim Kolesnychenko, ed., *Per Anders Rudling, Timoti Shnaider* [Timothy Snyder], *Gzhegozh Rossolinski-Libe* [Grzegorz Rossoliński-Liebe], "*OUN i UPA: Issledovaniia o sozdanii 'Istoricheskikh' mifiv*": *Sbornik statei* (Kyiv: Zolotye vorota, 2012); Vadim Kolesnychenko, ed., *Anatolii Chaikovskii, Per Anders Rudling, Dzhon-Pol Khimka* [John-Paul Himka], *Sbornik Publikatsii* "*Voina ili voennaia prestupnost'?*" (Kyiv: Zolotye vorota, 2013). Protests by the authors were ignored by the law maker; "Kolesnichenko zovet istorikov v sud," *Ukrainskaia Pravda*, 9 April 2013, https://www.pravda.com.ua/rus/news/2013/04/9/69 87786/ (accessed 21 May 2021).

tions in the western part of the country, which in turn could be utilized to mobilize an aging, mostly eastern and Russophone electoral base. Consistent with this line was also the channeling of considerable amounts of money from the circle around Yanukovych to the far-right party VO Svoboda. That party also received disproportional exposure in state media as well as TV channels owned by pro-Yanukovych oligarchs, in an apparent attempt to make it the main opponent for the presidential elections, scheduled for 2015.[361]

The Second Anti-Yanukovych Revolution

In November 2013, Yanukovych unexpectedly withdrew from a scheduled association agreement with the European Union, triggering a wave of protests. On 16 January 2014, the Verkhovna Rada rushed through ten laws seriously curtailing basic civil liberties, such as freedom of speech and assembly, aimed at ending the protests. Among these "dictatorship laws," were also two laws aimed at legislating memory by criminalizing the glorification of the *Waffen-SS Galizien*, the OUN, and UPA, drafted by Communist party leader Petro Symonenko (b. 1952), with support from Kolesnychenko.[362] This step sharply escalated societal tensions, trigger-

---

[361] Kuzio, *Ukraine: Democratization, Corruption, and the New Russian Imperialism*, 182–83; Anton Shekhovtsov, "The Ukrainian Far Right and the Ukrainian Revolution," *New Europe College Black Sea Link Program Yearbook 2014-2015*, 215–37, here: 219–20; and Serhei Leshchenko, Anton Marchuk, and Sevgil' Musaeva-Borovik, "Rukopisi ne goriat. Chernaia bukhgalteriia Partii regionov: familii, daty, summy," *Ukrains'ka pravda*, 31 May 2016, http://www.pravda.com.ua/cdn/graphics/2016/05/black-pr/index.html (accessed 16 July 2016).

[362] V. Yanukovych, Zakon 729-VII, "Pro vnesennia zminy do Kryminal'noho kodeksu Ukrainy shchodo vidpovidal'nosti za zaperechennia chy vypravdannia zochyniv fashyzmu," *Verkhovna Rada Ukrainy*, 16 January 2014, https://zakon.rada.gov.ua/laws/show/729-18#Text (accessed 24 June 2021); Koposov, *Memory Laws*, 198–99; Winfried Schneider-Deters, *Ukrainische Schicksalsjahre 2013-2019. Band 1: Der Volksaufstand auf dem Majdan im Winter 2013/2014* (Berlin: Berliner Wissenschafts-Verlag, 2021), 277; and Andrew Wilson, *Ukraine Crisis: What it Means for the West* (New Haven: Yale University Press, 2014), 81–82. On the *Waffen-SS Galizien*, see Per Anders Rudling, '"They Defended Ukraine": The 14. Waffen-Grenadier-Division der SS

ing a violent uprising against the regime. Losing his majority in parliament, Yanukovych fled to Russia on 22 February 2014, following a wave of violence which left over a hundred people dead in the capital. The ouster of Yanukovych triggered a Russian invasion, the annexation of the Crimea by the Russian Federation, and the establishment of self-proclaimed "People's Republics" run by local war lords and criminal elements in Luhans'k and Donets'k, who waged a proxy war with Russian support.[363]

With the ousting of Yanukovych and the Russian invasion, memory politics returned to Ukraine with a vengeance. After Yanukovych and his entourage fled to Russia, a transitional government under Oleksandr Turchynov (b. 1964, president 2014) took over. Turchynov occupied the positions of Chairman of the Verkhovna Rada, acting Prime Minister, and President. On 27 February, as Arsenii Yatseniuk (b. 1974) replaced him as acting prime minister, masked soldiers in unmarked uniforms but with modern Russian weapons occupied the parliament and key military bases on Crimea.[364] Yatseniuk's first government consisted of his own populist-conservative *Bat'kivshchyna*, Vitalii Klychko's (b. 1971) centrist *UDAR*, and the far-right *VO Svoboda*.

V"iatrovych 2.0

On 28 March 2014 Deputy Prime Minister Oleksandr Sych (b. 1964) of *VO Svoboda*, issued a decree on re-politicizing the dormant UINP and again assigning it "special status under central organs of the executive branch of power," tasking it with "the

---

(Galizische Nr. 1) Revisited,' *The Journal of Slavic Military Studies* 25, no. 3 (2012): 329–368.

363 On the propaganda offensive, see Sanshiro Hosaka, "Welcome to Surkov's Theater: Russian Political Technology in the Donbas War," *Nationalities Papers* 47, no. 5 (2019): 750–73; and Kimberly Marten, "Russia's Use of Semi-State Security Forces: The Case of the Wagner Group," *Post-Soviet Affairs* 35, no. 3 (2019), 181–204, here: 192–93, 198.

364 Winfried Schneider-Deters, *Ukrainische Schicksalsjahre 2013-2019. Band 2: Die Annexion der Krim und der Krieg im Donbass* (Berlin: Berliner Wissenschafts-Verlag, 2021), 179–95.

MANAGING MEMORY IN POST-SOVIET UKRAINE 113

renewal and retention of national memory."[365] There was again a sharp reversal as the communists Soldatenko and Ginzburg were replaced as directors of the UINP and HDA SBU, by two OUN(b)-affiliated activists, V"iatrovych and Andrii Kohut (b. 1980) of the TsDVR.

The October 2014 elections to the Verkhovna Rada brought a parliament in which the "anti-Maidan" opposition was marginal.[366] As the new parliament gathered in late November 2014 there was now a chance to resume the historical policies thwarted under Yanukovych. The TsDVR team was determined to make maximum use of the situation.

V"iatrovych had a strong backer in the rector of the Kyiv Mohyla Academy, later minister of education, Serhiy Kvit (b. 1965).[367] Another media-savvy TsDVR activist, Ivan Patryliak (b. 1976), would advance to dean of the faculty of history at the Taras Shevchenko University. Through a remarkably quick "march through the institutions," an influential network of radical nationalist memory activists, bridging identity politics, educational policies, and the administration of universities, faculties, and strategic archives, were in a position to exercise a very strong influence on the instrumentalization of memory.[368]

A period of intense instrumentalization of history followed. V"iatrovych was well aware that timing was crucial, and at this moment, and with Yanukovych's former power base paralyzed, there would not be an effective opposition. On 6 April 2015, the Verkhovna Rada rushed through a package of memory laws. Four laws, drafted by V"iatrovych and introduced in the Verkhovna

---

365 Oleksandr Sych, deputy Prime Minister of Ukraine, decree No. 9973/1/1-14, 28 March 2014.
366 The "Opposition Bloc" had a total of 29 out of 424 seats in the Rada that could be filled; The Schneider-Deters, *Ukrainische Schicksalsjahre, Band 1*, 578-579.
367 Kvit has been active in a number of far-right groups, including the Congress of Ukrainian Nationalists (*Konhres ukrains'kykh natsionalistiv*, KUN), Stepan Bandera All-Ukrainian Organization 'Tryzub" (*Tryzub im. Bandery*), and the Right Sector (*Pravyi Sektor*).
368 Andronik Karmeliuk, "Istoriia mizh politykoiu i naukoiu," *Ukrains'kyi pohliad*, 21 June 2019, http://ukrpohliad.org/national-memory/istoriya-mizh-politykoyu-i-naukoyu.html (accessed 9 April 2021).

Rada by Roman Shukhevych's son Yurii (1933-2022), a deputy of the populist nationalist Radical Party of Oleh Liashko (b. 1972), were voted through following a debate in the parliament that lasted but 42 minutes.[369] Two of these pertained to matters of archives and the commemoration of World War II, and did not generate much controversy: law 2540 was intended to increase access to the HDA SBU—but also to centralize the archives under the control of the UINP—something the Union of Archivists of Ukraine opposed. Law 2539 designated 8 May a Day of Memory and Reconciliation—but also contained a provision prohibiting the "falsification" of the history of World War II. The other two laws of the package caused academic historians all the more concern. Law 2558, outlawing communist and Soviet propaganda, effectively banned the Ukrainian Communist Party, whereas law 2538-1 criminalized "disrespect" for the OUN, the UPA, and other far-right groups as "fighters for Ukrainian statehood in the 20th century."[370] The new laws greatly expanded the Ukrainian government's ability to police the representation of recent Ukrainian history, not least its most sensitive aspects pertaining to Ukrainian nationalism and local collaboration in the Holocaust.

The international reactions were sharp. The US Holocaust Memorial Museum expressed its concerns, and an open letter to the Ukrainian government by over 70 historians around the world expressed deep misgivings. The Venice Commission, an advisory body to the Council of Europe, found that the laws violated Euro-

---

369 Georgiy Kasianov, "The Wilson Center, 01/26/2018—What's Past is Prologue: Politics and Historical Memory in Ukraine," lecture at the Kennan Institute, posted 31 January 2018, https://soundcloud.com/the-wilson-center/01262018-whats-past-is-prologue-politics-and-historical-memory-in-ukraine (accessed 31 January 2018), quote at 24:58-29:01.
370 David R. Marples, "Decommunization, Memory Laws, and 'Builders of Ukraine in the 20th Century," *Acta Slavica Iaponica* 39 (2018): 1–22; and Tarik Cyril Amar, "Ukraine's Nationalist 'Decommunization' Laws of Spring 2015: Shielding Perpetrators and Excluding Victims," *Memories at Stake* 9 (Summer-Fall 2019): 99–103. The Communist Party remained one of very few "real" political parties, with mass membership (115,000 members in 2012), and in the 1990s the largest party in the Verkhovna Rada; Way, *Pluralism by Default*, 59.

pean legal standards and requested they be revised and rewritten.[371]

The laws, however, remain in effect, and new laws aimed at policing memory have since been added, notably law 1780-III, which came into force on 1 January 2017 stipulating "specialist reviews" to prevent "propaganda of communist and/or national socialist (Nazi) totalitarian regimes and their symbols." The law has empowered an "expert commission" at the Ukrainian commission for TV and Radio broadcast, chaired by the head of the OUN(m), Bohdan Chervak (b. 1964), with a mandate to censor and prevent the import of books which do not present Ukrainian nationalists in the proper, positive light prescribed by the authorities, and to close down TV stations and ban books which fall short of the ideological requirements.[372] By 2018 the Ukrainian government had obtained a monopoly on memory articulation, with no institutional counterweight to the legislated memory.[373]

The UINP's legitimizing historians also had a far-reaching mandate to rename Ukraine's physical space, something they did at breakneck speed, with limited debate at the local level. The city of Dnipropetrovs'k was renamed by decree, overruling popular preference expressed in a local 2000 referendum to retain the city's name.[374] The situation was similar in other municipalities, renamed with little consideration of local opinion. As of 2015, al-

---

[371] CDL_AD(2015) 041-e, "Joint Interim Opinion on the Law of Ukraine on the condemnation of the communist and national socialist (Nazi) regimes and prohibition of propaganda of their symbols," Venice Commission Opinion No. 823/2015, ODIHR Opinion no. FOE-UKR/230/2014, Adopted by the Venice Commission at its 105th Plenary Session Venice (18–19 December 2015), on the basis of comments by Mr Sergio BARTOLE, Ms Veronika BILKOVA, Ms. Regina KIENER, Ms Hanna SUCHOKA, Mr. Boyko BOEV, Council of Europe: European Commission for Democracy Through Lawa (Venice Commission), OSCE Office for Democratic Institutions and Human Rights (OSCE/ODIHR), http://www.venice.coe.int/webforms/documents/default.aspx?pdf=CDL-AD%282015%29041-e&lang=EN (accessed 15 May 2016).
[372] Rudling, "Institutes of Trauma Re-production," 61.
[373] Anna Kutkina, *Between Lenin and Bandera: Decommunization and Multivocality in (post)Euromaidan Ukraine* (=*Publications of the Faculty of Social Sciences*, 141) (Helsinki: Unigrafia, 2020), 185.
[374] On Dnipopetrovs'k, see Marples, "Decommunization," 6.

ready before the passing of the laws, Ukraine had 100 streets named after Bandera, 46 statues or busts, 14 memorial plaques, and five museums dedicated to his life.[375] In Kyiv, the renaming of *Moskovs'kyi Prospekt* (Moscow Avenue) — an important thoroughfare in the capital where the embassy of the Russian Federation is located — into *Prospekt Bandery* (Bandera Avenue) brought strong international reactions, in particular from Polish and Jewish groups.[376]

V"iatrovych characterizes the entire Soviet period as an "occupation."[377] This narration, developed in the mainly Galician Ukrainian diaspora, and which reduces Ukrainians to little more than passive victims of the actions of a genocidal Soviet "other," has had limited resonance in Ukraine beyond the western part of the country. Such a master narrative may "absolve" Ukrainians from complicity in Soviet political violence, but at the price of removing Ukrainian agency as stakeholders also in the aspects of the Soviet system with significant popular legitimacy, such the Ukrainization and cultural renaissance of the 1920s, the defeat of Nazism in World War II, and educational and scientific achievements in the late Soviet era.[378]

In an apparent attempt to reconcile the mostly Galician narration with more mainstream attitudes that dominated east of the river Zbruch, the agencies of memory production initiated propaganda campaigns, stressing that it was a Ukrainian who raised the Soviet banner over the Reichstag in 1945, emphasizing the disproportionate Ukrainian contributions to the victory over fascism, and seeking to appropriate also establishment figures, such as (the ethnically Russian communist) airplane constructor Oleg Antonov

---

375 Kuzio, *Ukraine: Democratization, Corruption, and the New Russian Imperialism*, 180.
376 Marples, "Decommunization," 8.
377 "Prebyvanie Ukrainy v sostave SSSR — eto okkupatsiia, — V"iatrovich," *tsenzor.net.ua*, 7 January 2018 https://censor.net.ua/news/3043120/prebyvanie_ ukrainy_v_sostave_sssr_eto_okkupatsiya_vyatrovich (accessed 11 January 2018).
378 Christopher Gilley, "Reconciling the Irreconcilable? Left-Wing Ukrainian Nationalism and the Soviet Regime," *Nationalities Papers* 47, no. 3, 341–54, here: 354.

(1906–84) for the anti-Soviet nationalizing discourse.[379] What ensued was a curious and contradictory hybrid narration. Soviet rule was depicted as a genocidal, foreign occupation, in whose achievements the UINP sought a stake for the Ukrainians. UINP propaganda posters disseminated the new narration prescribed by law 2539, "on the commemoration of the victory over Nazism in the Second World War of the years 1939–1945" which designated 8 May a day of "memory and reconciliation." One such UINP poster, prominently disseminated through its media campaigns, unintentionally illustrates the contradictions of the official "all-inclusive" narration. It depicts Red Army officer Ivan Zaluzhnyi (1918–2021),[380] shaking the hand of the UPA insurgent Stepan Petrash (1927-2023).[381] Petrash is dressed in an anachronistic UPA uniform, designed by émigrés during the Cold War. Zaluzhnyi wears a full chest of Soviet medals, prominently displaying otherwise illegal symbols such as red stars, the hammer and sickle, and Iosif Stalin's profile. Against the background of a red-and-black poppy, the handshake between a former UPA insurgent and a veteran of the Soviet occupation regime, is illustrated with the words "VICTORS OVER NAZISM."[382]

---

[379] "The Ukrainian Oleksii Berest under fire set up the Banner of Victory over the Reichstag," UINP Propaganda Poster for the 73rd anniversary of VE Day, on UINP Director Volodymyr V"iatrovych's *Facebook* wall, https://www.faceboo k.com/photo.php?fbid=10211844194239768&set=pcb.10211844199199892&type =3&theater (accessed 29 May 2018).
[380] Ivan Zaluzhnyi (1918–2021) was a decorated Red Army veteran who featured in several propaganda campaigns after his grandson was killed in the war on Donbas in 2014; Yuliya Yurchuk, "Global Symbols Local Meanings: The 'Day of Victory' after Euromaidan," in Timm Beichelt and Susann Worschech (eds.), *Transnational Ukraine? Networks and Ties that Influence contemporary Ukraine* (Stuttgart: ibidem-Verlag, 2017), 89-110, here: 102.
[381] The claims of the UINP propaganda poster notwithstanding, the UPA veteran of the poster did not fight the Nazis. Stepan Petrash, pseudo "Danylko" (1927-2023) joined the UPA in November 1944, six months after the German occupation of Ukraine ended; interview with Stepan Petrash, 22 February 2018, Lokal'na istoriia: Zakhidno-ukrains'kyi tsentr istorychnykh doslidzhen' "Stepan Petrash, strilets' UPA 'Danylo' pro sprobu na misto Halych," User "Lokal'na istoriia," 20 March 2018, *Youtube*, https://www.youtube.com/wa tch?v=ynpl2xWRR-4 (accessed 25 May 2021).
[382] Arsenii Yatseniuk *et al.*, "Proekt Zakonu pro uvichnennia peremohy nad natsyzmom u Druhii svitovii viiny 1939-1945 rokiv," nomer 2539 vid 3 April

118   Tarnished Heroes

Figure 3.1. "May 8—The Day of Memory and Reconciliation. VICTORS OVER NAZISM. UPA soldier Stepan Petrash and Red Army officer Ivan Zaluzhnyi." Propaganda poster from the Ukrainian Institute of National Memory, 2017. https://old.
uinp.gov.ua/news/do-dnya-pamyati-i-primirennya-ukraina-zgaduvatime-svii-vn esok-v-peremogu-nad-agresorom (accessed 25 May 2021).

Two Ukraines—or a House United?

The notion of the existence of "two Ukraines" has become a powerful metaphor to illustrate the divisions between the extremes of Ukraine, that is, the historical East Galicia on the one hand, and the Donbas and Crimea on the other.[383] The concept is primarily associated with Mykola Riabchuk (b. 1953), who identifies an authentic, "aboriginal," and autochthonous Ukrainophone Ukraine in the western part of the country,[384] while maintaining that

---

2015, *Verkhovna Rada Ukrainy*, http://w1.c1.rada.gov.ua/pls/zweb2/webpr oc4_1?pf3511=54649 (accessed 29 June 2021).

383   Joanna Konieczna-Sałamatin, Natalia Otrishchenko, and Tomasz Stryjek, *History. People. Events: Research Report on the Memory of Contemporary Poles and Ukrainians* (Warsaw: Instytut Studiów politycznych Polskiej Akademii Nauk, 2018), 24.

384   Tatjana Hofman, "Cultural Cringe?: Narrative Instrumentalisierungen lokaler Kulturen bei M. Rjabchuk, Ju. Andruchovych und S. Zadan," in Galyna Spodarets and Sabine Stöhr (eds.), *Alles neu macht der Majdan?: Interdiziplinäre*

Ukraine "ends" where the Ukrainian language ends. The territories to the east of the historical Rzeczpospolita, according to Riabchuk, constitute the "Wild Fields," *dyke pole*, part of a quasi-oriental "East Slavonic Ummah."[385] Using stark terminology of colonialism, subjugation, and sexual violence, Riabchuk portrays Ukrainians as a colonial people of aboriginals and creoles; as "Fridays," "slaves," and "rape victims."[386] Alas, in post-Soviet Ukraine two sharply diverging interpretations stand against one another: on the one hand, the notion of Ukraine as the Second Soviet Republic and *secunda inter pares*, a co-organizer and stakeholder in a joint project, and on the other, Ukraine as genocide victim, subjugated by a culturally and civilizationally alien colonialism.[387]

Nationalism and Secessionism

In a linguistically and culturally heterogenous borderland like Ukraine, the ethnonationalist tradition of West Ukraine sometimes clashes with civic, territorial nationalism. The ethnic and civic

---

Perspektiven auf eine Ukraine im Umbruch (Berlin: Wissenschaftlicher Verlag Berlin, 2015), 71–93; Roman Dubasevych, "Majdan-Lyrik: Gibt es eine Poetik der Revolution?," 50–71, here 71, n.28 in Martin Pollak and Stefaniya Ptashnyk (eds.), *Ukraine: Literatur und Kritik* (Salzburg: Otto Müller Verlag, 2016).

385 Oleksandr Vil'chyns'kyi, "Mykola Ribachuk: Iashchirky, iakym shkoda pozbutys' khvosta, pozbuvaiut'sia holovy — Interv'iu," *Zaxid.net*, 9 August 2010, http://zaxid.net/home/showSingleNews.do?mikola_ryabchuk_yashhi rki_yakim_shkhoda_pozbutis_hvosta_pozbuvayutsya_golovi&objectId=1110 717 (accessed 23 October 2011); Mykola Riabchuk, "Emancipation from the East Slavonic Ummah," *New Eastern Europe* 2 (2015), https://www.academia. edu/28580520/Emancipation_from_the_East_Slavonic_ummah._New_Easter n_Europe_no.2_2015 (accessed 18 October 2016). For a critical discussion of these postcolonial rhetorical figures, see Roman Dubasevych, "Die Erinnerung an die Habsburgmonarchie in der ukrainischen Kultur der Gegenwart," (Ph.D. Dissertation, University of Vienna, 2013), 252–53.

386 Mykola Ryabchuk, "The Ukrainian 'Friday' and the Russian 'Robinson': the Uneasy Advent of Postcoloniality," *Canadian-American Slavic Studies* 44 (2010): 7–25; idem., and "Ukraine's Turbulent Past between Hagiography and Demonization," *Raam op Rusland: Podium voor kennis, analyse en debat*, 2 November 2016, http://www.raamoprusland.nl/dossiers/oekraine/311-ukrain e-s-turbulent-past-between-hagiography-and-demonization (accessed 2 November 2016).

387 For a stark example of the latter, see *Russicher Kolonialismus in der Ukraine: Berichte und Dokumente* (Munich: Ukrainischer Verlag, 1962).

versions of Ukrainian nationalism have not always been easily reconcilable. Andrew Wilson observes how "ethno-nationalism has a strong emotive appeal to a minority, who may undermine Ukraine's attempts to construct an open civic state."[388] For much of the 20th century, the civic territorial nationalism has had a powerful rival in the exclusivist authoritarian ethnonationalist tradition of Mykola Mikhnovs'kyi, Dmytro Dontsov, and Yaroslav Stets'ko.[389]

A rift is discernible between, on the one hand, a commitment to an exclusive Ukrainian ethnic nationalism and, on the other, to the territorial integrity of this multi-ethnic polity. The 1939 OUN draft constitution excluded Jews from citizenship in a future state.[390] As the OUN(b) re-affirmed its commitment to exclusive Ukrainian ethno-nationalism in 1968, the OUN(m) started to distance itself from the slogan "Ukraine—for the Ukrainians," fearing that it would risk leading to segregation and inequality of the citizens in a future Ukrainian state.[391] The gulf between the ethnic and civic conceptualizations of Ukrainianness has still not quite been fully bridged. In July 2010, writer Yurii Andrukhovych (b. 1960) publicly raised the issue whether Donets'k and Crimea should remain in Ukraine at all.[392] Neither Donets'k nor Crimea, he argued, feel that they belong to the Ukrainian nation, "because

---

388 Wilson, *Ukrainian Nationalism in the 1990s*, i.
389 On racial thought in the Ukrainian nationalist tradition, see, for instance, Aleksei Bakanov, *"Ni katsapa, ni zhida, ni liakha": Natsional'nyi vopros v ideologii Organizatsii ukrainskikh natsionalistov, 1929–1945 gg.* (Moscow: Algoritm, 2014); Marco Carynnyk, "'Foes of Our Rebirth': Ukrainian Nationalist Discussions about Jews, 1929–1947," *Nationalities Papers* 39, no. 3 (May 2011): 315–52; Grzegorz Rossoliński-Liebe, *The Fascist Kernel of Ukrainian Genocidal Nationalism.* (=*The Carl Beck Papers* 2402) (Pittsburgh: Center for Russian and East European Studies, University of Pittsburgh, 2015). See also chapter six.
390 See Section XI, article 4 of Mykola Stsibors'kyi, "Narys proektu osnovnykh zakoniv (konstitutsii) Ukrains'koi Derzhavy," in *Dokumenty i materialy z istorii Orhanizatsii ukrains'kykh natsionalistiv, tom 7: Dokumenty komisii derzhavnoho planuvannia OUN (KDP OUN)*, O. Kucheruk and Yu. Cherchenko (eds.) (Kyiv: Vydavnytstvo imeni Oleny Telihy, 2002), 8–23, here: 20.
391 Barets'kyi et al. (eds.), *Bila knyha OUN*, 59.
392 This does, however, constitute the view of a vocal minority, whereas proponents of the idea of a "united front" constitute a majority among intellectuals and writers, including, among others, Liuba Yakimchuk, Volodymyr Rafeenko, Olena Stiazhkina, Victoria Amelina.

they are part of the Russian people." Were yet another separatist congress to be called, like the one in Severodonets'k in 2004, the central government ought to welcome their secession.[393] On 14 February 2014, Alexander J. Motyl (b. 1953) joined these voices, cautiously welcoming a secession:

> it may be worth asking whether Ukraine might not be better off without some of its southeastern provinces ... Remove the southeast and Ukraine's treasury experiences an immediate boon; its demographics, energy consumption, and health improve; and its politics automatically become more democratic and less corrupt.[394]

In rather charged language, Motyl characterized these areas as "a rotten slice of Ukraine—a kind of mega Transdnistria."[395] On 22 February 2014, as Kyiv descended into mass violence, Motyl made an about-face, now presenting Ukraine as "a house united," "happily diverse," and the impasse an inter-party disagreement:

> Ukraine's diversity is pretty much on par with that found in just about any country in the world: the United States, Canada, Italy, Germany, Turkey, Brazil, India and so on. Diversity can sometimes spell trouble and it can sometimes mean vitality, but we rarely assume, a priori, that it must lead to ungovernability and partition—except, apparently, in Ukraine, where what is business as usual elsewhere is assumed to be a fatal flaw.[396]

The attitude towards the eastern borderlands of Ukraine vacillates between perceiving them as indispensable territories, integral to a "happily diverse" "house united," and "anti-Ukrainian" and "rotten" lands with which Ukraine could readily dispense. Motyl's inconsistent and contradictory analyses highlight the split between a commitment to two, apparently incompatible, nationalist conceptions. A similar split is discernible also in An-

---

393 Kuzio, *Ukraine: Democratization, Corruption, and the New Russian Imperialism*, 266.
394 Alexander J. Motyl, "Should There Be One Ukraine?," *World Affairs*, 14 February 2014, http://www.worldaffairsjournal.org/blog/alexander-j-motyl/should-there-be-one-ukraine (accessed 23 February 2016).
395 Motyl, "Should There Be One Ukraine?"
396 Alexander J. Motyl, "A House United: Why Analysts Touting Ukraine's East-West Division are Just Plain Wrong," *Foreign Policy*, 22 February 2014, http://foreignpolicy.com/2014/02/22/a-house-united/ (accessed 23 February 2014).

drukhovych's and Riabchuk's writings. Both writers initially supported the military campaign against the separatists, arguing for the issue of secession to be settled in a referendum following a victory by the Ukrainian forces.[397] In 2015, a growing number of observers—including none other than Leonid Kravchuk—raised the question whether the re-integration of Crimea, Donets'k, and Luhans'k would be possible at all.[398] In August 2016, Motyl ended his own ambiguity in favor of secession, calling upon Ukrainians to "move on," and to "stop identifying with lands that are effectively Russian or anti-Ukrainian."[399] Journalist and Maidan activist Dmytro Antoniuk (b. 1976) argues that if representatives from these areas were to "end up in parliament they would take us back to the time when Russian influence dominated Ukraine. That will be the end of this country," he warned. "Those who still live there after years of war have become faithful to Russia and that would mean an enormous step back."[400] Journalist Vitaly Portnikov (b. 1967) similarly argues that the Ukrainian state was organized in accordance with the administrative boundaries of the Soviet era, and not following the boundaries of Ukrainian identity. According to him, Ukraine will survive within the territory where a Ukrainian identity exists.[401]

Lucan Way has aptly noted how:

> The 2014 crisis altered key variables in this analysis that likely affected the future of pluralism ... The exit of Crimea and the Donbas resulted in the departure of a highly Russophile 20 per cent of Ukraine's electorate ... The combination of war and a more unified Ukrainian identity allowed leaders

---

[397] Kuzio, *Ukraine: Democratization, Corruption, and the New Russian Imperialism*, 266.
[398] Schneider-Deters, *Ukrainische Schicksalsjahre. Band 2*, 672–74.
[399] Alexander J. Motyl, "Let It Go: Ukraine's Occupied Donbass Region is a Pointless Burden. It's Time for Kiev to Accept that It's Better Off Without It," *Foreign Policy*, 12 August 2016, http://foreignpolicy.com/2016/08/12/let-it-go-ukraine-russia-donbass/ (accessed 25 September 2016).
[400] Antoniuk cited by Filip Norman, "Svagt fredshopp i krigstrött Ukraina," *Svenska Dagbladet*, 20 April 2020, 14.
[401] Norman, "Svagt fredshopp i krigstrött Ukraina"

to exploit nationalism to unite the population around a common threat, discourage opposition, and justify repression.[402]

The official line from the Ukrainian state is that the disputed territories are Ukrainian and will one day be under Ukrainian government control again. Indeed, from 2014-2015 the government stepped up nationalizing efforts on the Ukrainian territory which remained under the control of the government in Kyiv.

Under Yushchenko and Poroshenko the UINP was dominated by people identifying with the tradition of the OUN(b), seeking to reconcile its ethnonationalist traditions with the demands of administering a large, ethnically diverse state. The rhetoric that emanated from that institute was thus often contradictory. On the one hand, the UINP's L'viv-born director V"iatrovych could insist that Ukraine is "divided not by history, but by the historical myths of Soviet propaganda,"[403] arguing, in line with Soviet tradition, that these people could be re-educated and the "problem" solved through social engineering. The UINP therefore launched "popular-scientific" propaganda campaigns intended to "remove the *Sovok*" — a derogatory term for people rooted in, and shaped by, Soviet identity — from Ukrainians' heads.[404] At the same time, V"iatrovych's deputy, Alina Shpak (b. 1980), another West Ukrainian, from Luts'k, could, in public statements, exclude the residents of Donbas from the Ukrainian community: "What is the Donbas? In the years [19]32-33 they exterminated the peasant population, which traditionally is the carrier of national culture. In its place came the industrialization and the [re]settlement of Donbas. By all kinds of people, only not Ukrainians [*Kym zavhodno, ale*

---

402 Way, *Pluralism by Default*, 91.
403 Halyna Chop, "Volodymyr V"iatrovych: 'Ukraintsiv rozdiliae ne istoriia, a istorychni mify radians'koi propahandy'," *Vysoki zamok*, 17 July 2014, http://wz.lviv.ua/interview/127821 (accessed 1 October 2015); and Koshkyna, "Volodymyr V"iatrovych."
404 "Gud-bai, Lenin. Vladimir V"iatrovych o leninopade, pereimenovanii gorodov i Sovke v golovakh," *Fokus*, 25 May 2016, https://focus.ua/country/349191/ (accessed 26 April 2016).

ne ukraintsiamy]."[405] Similarly, Ukrainian Minister of Culture, Evhen Nyshchuk (b. 1972), from Ivano-Frankivs'k in Galicia, attempted to explain the perceived deficiencies of the easterners in biological-genetic terms, claiming the population of South-eastern Ukraine was unable to accept Ukrainian culture, due to "insufficient genetic purity." "When we speak about the genetics in the Zaporizhzhia and Donbas, these are mixed [*zeveseni*] areas. There is no genetics there, those are consciously mixed [regions].... That was the technology of the Soviet Union," Nyshchuk argued on Ukrainian national TV in November 2016.[406]

At the same time, a generation has now been brought up with the new official history writing, socialized through institutions such as education, the army, memory institutes, and legislation. In 2010, 20 percent of Ukrainians surveyed supported the recognition of OUN and UPA as "fighters for Ukrainian statehood" whereas 60 per cent objected to such a designation. An October 2017 poll showed that the approval had increased to 49 percent approved, whereas only 29 percent objected.[407] Similarly, if 22 percent of Ukrainians surveyed had a positive attitude to the legacy of Stepan Bandera, in 2012, in 2014 this number had increased to 31 percent in 2014, and to 35 per cent in 2016.[408]

---

405 "Chomu Donbas zavzhdy proty?," *Hromadske.volynia.ua*, 29 October 2014, http://hromadske.volyn.ua/chomu-donbas-zavzhdy-proty-2/ (accessed 12 February 2017).

406 "Nyshchuk zaiavyv pro 'vidsutnist' henetyky' na Donbasi," *Korrespondent*, 22 November 2016, http://ua.korrespondent.net/ukraine/events/3777868-nyschuk-zaiavyv-pro-vidsutnist-henetyky-na-donbasi (accessed 30 November 2016). Nyshchuk's claim was strongly criticized, and the minister was compelled to issue an apology the following day; "Ministr Ukrainy i genetika Donbassa," *Donbas Public TV*, 23 November 2016, available online on *Youtube*, https://www.youtube.com/watch?v=KdgSOABnX0o (accessed 30 November 2016).

407 "For the Defender of Ukraine Day," *Sotsiolohichna hrupa Reitinh*, 5 October 2017, http://ratinggroup.ua/en/research/ukraine/ko_dnyu_zaschitnika_uk rainy.html (accessed 10 October 2017); and Vitalii Chervonenko, "Chym zakinchyt'sia 'istorychna kryza' mizh Ukrainoiu ta Pol'shcheiu?," *BBC Ukraina*, 10 November 2017, http://www.bbc.com/ukrainian/features-41934591 (accessed 4 February 2018).

408 A 2016 Ukrainian poll showed that 28 per cent of Ukrainians (not including those living in the occupied territories) regarded Stalin "a wise leader." The support for Stalin is about the same as for Bandera; Liana Novikova,

These polls suggest that the famine offers a greater potential for instrumentalization than do Shukhevych and Bandera. In a November 2013 opinion poll 66 percent of those polled responded that they regard *Holodomor* as a genocide.[409] Following the Russian invasion the number increased to over 75 percent, and higher still in Western Ukraine.[410] V"iatrovych claimed that the approval of the genocide thesis represented proof of the success of official memory politics: "What is important is that 80% of Ukrainians regard the Holodomor a genocide. That testifies to the fact that the more the Ukrainians know their history, the further it dislodges the claim that the Ukrainians are divided by their past."[411] For V"iatrovych, the *Holodomor* discourse unproblematically marries true science and *partiinist'*: it provides "historical knowledge" as well as ideological consciousness: "Holodomor made us a nation."[412]

Memory Conflicts with Poland, Israel, and the EU

Poland remained firmly supportive of Ukraine during the time up to the 2013–2014 protests and the Russian invasion. The years 2013–2016, and the triumph of V"iatrovych and Yasynevych's politics of memory contributed to a polarization in Ukrainian-

---

"Stavlennia ukraintsiv do postaty Stalina," *Kyivs'kyi mizhnarodnyi instytut sotsiolohii*, 4 March 2016, http://kiis.com.ua/?lang=ukr&cat=reports&id=606 &page=1 (accessed 5 March 2016); and Samuel Sokol, "Babi Yar as a Symbol of Holocaust Distortion in Post-Maidan Ukraine," *Israel Journal of Foreign Affairs*, 11, no. 1 (2017): 35–46, here: 41.

409 Olga Andriewsky, "Towards a Decentered History: The Study of the Holodomor and Ukrainian Historiography," *East/West: Journal of Ukrainian Studies*, 2, no. 1 (2015): 18–52, here: 22; and Jaroslaw Martyniuk, "Public Opinion in Ukraine: Attitudes Towards the 1932-33 Holodomor. The Level of Support for the Genocide Thesis among Ukrainians," *Holodomor Studies*, 2, no. 1 (Winter-Spring 2010): 53–61.

410 Konieczna-Sałamatin, Otrishchenko, and Stryjek, *History. People. Events*, 34.

411 Iaroslava Trehubova, "Cherez 82 roky doslidnyky nazvaly kilkist' zhertv Holodomoru," *Radio Svoboda*, 26 November 2015, http://www.radiosvoboda. mobi/a/27390191.html (accessed 30 November 2015).

412 Volodymyr V"iatrovych, "Iak Holodomor zrobyv nas natsieiu," *Holodomor33.org.ua* http://holodomor33.org.ua/volodymyr-vyatrovych-yak-holodo mor-zrobyv-nas-natsijeyu/ (accessed 28 November 2013; link no longer valid as of 14 September 2020).

Polish relations. In October 2015 the conservative Law and Justice Party (*Prawo i Sprawiedliwość*, PiS) returned to power in Poland, this time with an absolute majority in parliament. The low profile kept by Poland was now replaced by increasingly vociferous objections. Already towards the end of Yushchenko's presidency there had been signs that Warsaw's patience was running thin. In 2009 the Sejm had officially characterized the OUN(b) and UPA's massacres as "mass murders, characterized by ethnic cleansing with marks of genocide."[413] In July 2016, the PiS-dominated parliament sharpened the formulation to characterize the massacres as "genocide."[414] At the same time, Israel started to express its concerns openly. In September 2016, during an official visit to Ukraine to mark the 75th anniversary of the Babyn Iar massacre, Israeli president Reuben Rivlin (b. 1939, president 2014-2021) — otherwise known for his cautious and diplomatic style — in a speech in the Verkhovna Rada appealed directly to the Ukrainian legislators to cease propagating the cult of the OUN:[415]

> 1.5 million Jews were killed in the contemporary Ukraine at the time of World War II.... Many of the facilitators of this crime were Ukrainians, and among them the OUN militants stood out... one cannot rehabilitate and glorify anti-Semites. It is not in the political interest to justify or remain silent when we speak about anti-Semitic structures. Countries, sharing racist

---

413 Bronisław Komorowski, "Uchwała Sejmu Rzeczypospolitej Polskiej z dnia 15 lipca 2009 r. w sprawie tragicznego losu Polaków na Kresach Wschodnich," *Sejm of the Republic of Poland official website*, http://orka.sejm.gov.pl/opinie6.nsf/nazwa/2183_u/$file/2183_u.pdf (accessed 18 October 2009).
414 "Senat upamiętnił ofiary rzezi wołyńskiej," *Wiadomości*, 7 July 2016, http://wiadomosci.wp.pl/kat,1342,title,Senat-upamietnil-ofiary-rzezi-wolynskiej,wid,18413272,wiadomosc.html?ticaid=1175d9 (accessed 11 July 2016); and "Uchwała Sejmu Rzeczypospolitej Polskiej z dnia 22 lipca 2016 r. w sprawie oddania hołdu ofiarom ludobójstwa dokonanego przez nacjonalistów ukraińskich na obywaltelach II Rzeczpospolitej Polskiej w latach 1943-1945," *Monitor Polski: Dziennik Urzędowy Rzeczypospolitej Polskiej*, Poz. 726 tom 1 (27 July 2016). On analogous history legislation in Poland, see Jan Grabowski, "The Polish Holocaust Law," *Intersections* vol. 4, no. 1 (2021), 22-25; and Joanna Beata Michlic, "History 'Wars' and the Battle for Truth and National Memory," in Mörner (ed.), *Constructions and Instrumentalization*, 115-38.
415 Per Anders Rudling, "Dispersing the Fog: The OUN and Anti-Jewish Violence in 1941," *Yad Vashem Studies* 44, no. 2 (2016): 227-45, here: 244.

and anti-Semitic attitudes will never become members of the family of the peoples of the world.[416]

In a stark rebuke of the official Ukrainian OUN cult, Rivlin asserted: "we must not be partners in a second crime. We must not play a part in the sin of forgetting or denial."[417] V″iatrovych dismissed all criticism, instead accusing the Israeli president of regurgitating Soviet propaganda—a serious accusation, since law 2558 makes this a crime punishable by up to ten years in prison.[418] In July 2017, the message from the Polish foreign minister Witold Waszczykowski (b. 1957, foreign minister 2015-2018) was blunter, stating directly that Warsaw regarded the end of the state cult of the OUN a condition for Ukraine joining the EU. He declared that "with Bandera Ukraine will not join Europe," and pledged that unless Ukraine ceased the glorification of these groups, Poland would veto a Ukrainian EU membership "as stubbornly as Greece vetoes Macedonia over the name issue."[419] Poland declared V″iatrovych, the author of 2538-1, persona non grata, and barred him from entering the country.[420] In November 2017 the chair of the Polish section of the Polish-Ukrainian Historical Forum, the well-respected historian Waldemar Rezmer (b. 1949) resigned, following which the Polish-Ukrainian historical dialogue all but came to an end.[421] In January 2018 the Polish parliament passed a

---

416 "Prezydent Izrailiu zvynuvatyv OUN u Holokosti," *Radio 24*, 27 September 2016, https://radio24.ua/prezident-izrayilyu-zvinuvativ-oun-u-golokosti_n1 00823 (accessed 28 September 2016), quote at 8:37–10:35.
417 Sam Sokol, "The Tension between Historical Memory and Realpolitik in Israel's Foreign Policy," *Israel Journal of Foreign Affairs*, 12, no. 3 (2019): 311–24, here: 316.
418 Rudling, "Dispersing the Fog," 244.
419 "Waszczykowski dla 'wSieci' o stosunkach polsko-ukraińskich: Nasz przekaz jest bardzo jasny: z Banderą do Europy nie wejdziecie," *wPolityce.pl*, 3 July 2017, http://wpolityce.pl/polityka/347083-waszczykowski-dla-wsieci-o-stos unkach-polsko-ukrainskich-nasz-przekaz-jest-bardzo-jasny-z-bandera-do-eur opy-nie-wejdziecie (accessed 7 July 2017).
420 Grzegorz Osiecki and Zbigniew Parafianowicz, "Czarna lista Waszczykow- skiego. Szef ukraińskiego IPN nie wjedyie do Polski," *Dziennik.pl*, 9 Novem- ber 2017, http://wiadomosci.dziennik.pl/polityka/artykuly/562162,czarna- lista-waszczykowskiego-kto-na-niej-jest-wjazd-do-polski.html (accessed 10 November 2017).
421 Aleksander Szycht, "Co dalej z polsko-ukraińskim dialogiem historycznym?" *Polska Zbrojna*, 22 November 2017, http://www.polska-zbrojna.pl/home/art

law banning the propagation of "Banderism" in Poland, and making it a punishable offense to deny the atrocities of the OUN and UPA.[422] In the spring of 2018, 57 members of the US Congress, from both parties, expressed their deep concern about the cult of the OUN and UPA in Ukraine.[423] A similar statement of concern was issued by the United States Holocaust Memorial Museum.[424]

Largely detached from the international scholarly community, V"iatrovych's networks continued producing myths for domestic use.[425] At a June 2019 conference of the TsDVR Yaryna Yasynevych summoned up her organization's achievements over the past half-decade. She had reasons to be satisfied with the impact her front organization had made in Ukraine:

> There has been a change in the thinking about the tragedy of the Holodomor—80 per cent of people polled recognize the Holodomor a *genocide*, they support the positive slogan *"We remember — we are strong!"* Already 50 per cent of Ukrainians recognize the *soldiers of UPA fighters for Ukrainian independence*, they have received legal recognition, and the hymn of the OUN-UPA became the hymn of the army."[426]

In September 2019, after Poroshenko was voted out of office, V"iatrovych was again dismissed. To date, he continues his

---

icleshow/24148?t=Co-dalej-z-polsko-ukrainskim-dialogiem-historycznym- (accessed 23 November 2017).

422 "Sejm przegłosował ustawę zakazującą propagowania banderyzmu! Kukiz: 'Czekaliśmy od 6 lipca 2016, ale się doczekaliśmy! Nareszcie!'" *W Polityce.pl*, 26 January 2018, https://wpolityce.pl/polityka/378455-sejm-przeglosowal-u stawe-zakazujaca-propagowania-banderyzmu-kukiz-czekalismy-od-6-lipca-2016-ale-sie-doczekalismy-nareszcie (accessed 29 January 2018).

423 "Release: Rep. Khanna Leads Bipartisan Members in Condemning Anti-Semitism in Europe," 25 April 2018, https://khanna.house.gov/media/pre ss-releases/release-rep-khanna-leads-bipartisan-members-condemning-anti-semitism-europe (accessed 22 November 2018).

424 "Museum Expresses Deep Concern about Anti-Romani Violence and Anti-semitism in Ukraine," *United States Holocaust Museum*, 14 May 2018, https://www.ushmm.org/information/press/press-releases/museum-expr esses-deep-concern-about-anti-romani-violence-and-antisemitism-in-ukraine (accessed 17 May 2018).

425 On the concept of history for domestic use, see Andrii Portnov, *Istorii dlia domashn'oho vzhytku: Esei pro pol's'ko-rosiis'ko-ukrains'kyi trykutnyk pam"iati* (Kyiv: Krytyka, 2013).

426 Karmeliuk, "Istoriia mizh politykoiu i naukoiu."

memory activism as a member of the Verkhovna Rada, representing, somewhat discordantly, the "European Solidarity" party.

*   *   *

Under V"iatrovych's leadership, the UINP sought to turn the OUN(b) and the "Ukrainian National Liberation Movement" into the centerpiece of modern Ukrainian history. V"iatrovych came to have a very significant influence on policing the boundaries for how history could be presented, down to aiding the Verkhovna Rada in the drafting of censorship laws to police the history writing in Ukraine. Throughout this process, V"iatrovych regularly invoked his credentials to speak as a scholar and historian. While drafting laws effectively banning the Communist Party and "disrespect" for the OUN(b) and UPA, he did not appear to see the contradiction between *partiinist'* and the commitment to the vocation of a scholar. On the contrary, invoking his credentials to claim to speak "as a historian," he acted with irritation when his political activism was problematized in scholarly fora.[427] International critics were dismissed as informed by Soviet myths or useful idiots of the Kremlin.

In the "national memory" under Yushchenko and Poroshenko the teleological Soviet narration of "struggle" was retained, but filled with a nationalist content, a narration to a significant degree imported from the diaspora. "Such a history," Johan Dietsch notes, "which charter[s] the prehistory of the independent Ukrainian state as a teleological triumph of a primordial Ukrainian nation, a history as a string of pearls starting with Kievan Rus," has "a potential to become as dogmatic as the official history it would replace."[428] The continuity is felt not only in methodology and schematic structure, the neo-positivist claims to an objective "Ukrainian truth" but also in the preference to rely on legislation and government agencies to police history, as mirrored in the

---

427 Vladimir Viatrovich, "Vtoraia pol'sko-ukrainskaia voina i diskussii vokrug nee," *Ab Imperio*, no. 2 (2012): 422–33, here: 431.
428 Dietsch, *Making Sense of Suffering*, 113.

heavy-handed rhetoric of "liquidating historical illiteracy," "uproot the inner Sovok," and instil a Ukrainian "national memory." While the aims and objectives may have changed, the legacy of *"partiinist'"* lingers. As Serhiy Yekelchyk (b. 1966) has aptly noted,

> The overcoming of Soviet historical methodology has not been addressed in Ukrainian historiography for a good reason, namely, that it has not really happened yet. The wholesale restoration of the canon of national history as preserved in the diaspora was accomplished in Ukraine without abandoning Soviet narrative models or conceptualization tools.[429]

L'viv-based historian Yaroslav Hrytsak (b. 1960) notes the potential of national myths to unite, but also their divisive potential, comparing this quality to that of alcohol: "In small amounts it does good, in large quantities it is a poison."[430] His colleague Vasyl Rasevych (b. 1966) similarly refers to the "national memory" of the sort the UINP has propagated with a similar poison allegory, arguing "We live on a territory, cursed by history, and get drunk on historical poison, mistaking her as a universal remedy against all ills. We do not want to understand that history divides us and that the deep cleavage in societal attitudes will not go away anytime soon."[431] Whereas many professional historians are well aware of the liabilities of the instrumentalization of history, resistance to openly address the painful issues of the past remains significant. Nevertheless, as historian Grzegorz Rossoliński-Liebe (b. 1979) at Freie Universität Berlin has noted, there are few alternatives to openly and candidly addressing the difficult issues of the past: without proper *Aufarbeitung*, it will be easier for Putin

---

429 Serhy Yekelchyk, "A Long Goodbye: The Legacy of Soviet Marxism in Post-Communist Ukrainian Historiography," *Ab Imperio* 4 (2012): 401–16, here: 416.
430 "Yaroslav Hrytsak: Shchob uviintu do Evropy, treba shchos' robyty z istorieiu," *Velyka ideia*, 23 August 2015, https://bigidea.com/practices/1443/ (accessed 1 October 2015).
431 Vasyl' Rasevych, "Vyverty propahandy: Vystavka iak sproba nav'iazaty svii kanon suchasnoho istorychnoho naratyvu," *Zaxid.net*, 30 September 2015, http://zaxid.net/news/showNews.do?viverti_propagandi&objectId=13675 92 (accessed 1 October 2015).

and other actors to destabilize the country. Ukrainian history—
and society—will remain a powder keg.[432]

Paradoxically, all this is happening at a time when unprecedented access to archival materials has significantly improved our understanding of Stalinist, Nazi, and Ukrainian Nationalist atrocities. Our knowledge about the famine of 1932-33, the pogroms of 1941, the Holocaust, the OUN(b)/UPA's massacres of 1943-44, and the brutal Soviet counter-insurgency campaigns of the late 1940s has never been deeper. At the same time, the gulf between what historians know, and what the governmental memory managers *want* their citizens to believe, has been widening over the past two decades. Had the Ukrainian government relied on international expertise, rather than relying on its memory managers, some of these memory conflicts could have been avoided or defused before turning into diplomatic conflicts with very real political consequences for Ukraine.

---

432 Stefan Korinth, "'Ohne historische Aufarbetung bleibt die Ukraine ein Pulverfass," *Telepolis*, 10 February 2015, http://www.heise.de/tp/artikel/44/44107/1.html (accessed 11 February 2015).

4. "Not Quite Klaus Barbie, but in That Category" Mykola Lebed', the CIA, and the Airbrushing of the Past*

One morning in January 1986, three journalists from the left-liberal New York newspaper *The Village Voice* appeared on the doorstep of 76-year-old Mykola Lebed' in Yonkers, New York. The journalists asked specific and pointed questions regarding the old man's background as an alumnus of a German Security Police School in Zakopane, in Nazi-occupied Poland, in 1940 as Germany was preparing for war against the Soviet Union.[433] Having briefly answered the questions in the negative, Lebed' slammed the door on the journalists. As he did so, they managed to snap his picture. The photo accompanied a large article with the sensational headline, "To Catch a Nazi," which appeared a couple of weeks later.[434]

The article in *The Village Voice*, with its detailed description of war crimes, collaboration in the Holocaust, and allegations that the CIA was sheltering a terrorist and convicted assassin, trig-

---

* A previous version of this chapter appeared in *Rethinking Holocaust Justice: Essays across Disciplines*, ed. Norman J. W. Goda (New York and Oxford: Berghahn Books, 2018), 158-187, with whose kind permission it is reproduced.
433 Whereas the Zakopane school was located in the building used by the local Gestapo headquarters, it was a school run by the *Abwehr*, and the units trained by Lebed and Shukhevych were so-called *peredovye hrupy*, diversionary soldiers from among Nationalist volunteers who would go on to serve in the Nachtigall and Roland Battalions and other units in June 1941. Later, the Zakopane school moved to Rabka where Ukrainian militia were trained. According to testimonies by Jewish survivors, as many as three hundred Jews were murdered at the center, many of whom were women and children. Robin O'Neill, *The Rabka Four: A Warning from History* (London: Spiderwize, 2011), 27; Berkhoff, *Harvest of Despair*, 289; "Protokol doprosa osuzhdennogo BIZANTSA Al'freda Ioganovicha ot 23 noiabria 1949," HDA SBU, f. 65, spr. S-7448, ark. 15-22, published in Volodymyr Serhiichuk, ed., *Roman Shukhevych u dokumentakh radians'kykh orhaniv derzhavnoi bezpeky (1940-1950), Tom II* (Kyiv: PP Serhiichuk, 2007), 381-392.
434 Joe Conason, "To Catch a Nazi," *The Village Voice*, 11 February 1986, 17-21. The issue was actually published a week earlier.

gered an historiographical firestorm with a massive Ukrainian nationalist response—coordinated partially by the CIA. Only now, following the opening of the Soviet archives and the release of documents in accordance with the Nazi War Crimes Disclosure Act in 2005 and 2007 can the remarkable story of Mykola Lebed' and the CIA be told.[435] As the case of SS-*Hauptsturmführer* and Gestapo officer Klaus Barbie illustrates, Nazi war criminals in the service of Western intelligence services during the Cold War can be a politically sensitive issue.[436] By studying one—particularly prominent—case, this article aims at expanding our understanding the CIA's use of former Nazis and collaborators in the spy games of the Cold War, with a particular focus upon how the community of interest impacted the representation of a difficult past.

---

[435] Notable recent studies include Richard Breitman, Norman J.W. Goda, Timothy Naftali, and Robert Wolfe, *U.S. Intelligence and the Nazis* (New York: Cambridge University Press, 2005); Breitman and Goda, *Hitler's Shadow*; Peter Hammerschmidt, *Deckname Adler: Klaus Barbie und die westlichen Geheimdienste* (Frankfurt am Main: Fischer Verlag, 2014), and Kerstin von Lingen, *Allen Dulles, the OSS, and Nazi War Criminals: The Dynamics of Selective Prosecution* (New York: Cambridge University Press, 2013). Important studies on this topic are currently being undertaken by Jared McBride and Jeffrey Burds. Since 2009, some of the former operatives themselves have written about their experiences within AERODYNAMIC/QRPLUMB. Anatol Kamins'kyi, *Proloh u kholodnii viiny proty Moskvy: Prodovzhennia vyzvol'noi borot'bi iz-za kordonu* (Hadiach: "Hadiach," 2009); Taras Kuzio, "U.S. Support for Ukraine's Liberation during the Cold War: A Study of Prolog Research and Publishing Corporation," *Communist and Post-Communist Studies* 45, nos. 1–2 (2012): 51–64.

[436] Klaus Barbie was a former SS-*Hauptsturmführer* who commanded the Security Police in Lyon from 1942 to 1944. In 1947, he was recruited as an agent for the US Army Counter Intelligence Corps (CIC) as part of their efforts to further anti-communist efforts in Europe. The CIC helped him flee French extradition requests to Bolivia through the "rat line." In 1965 he was recruited by West German intelligence, for which he worked until 1971. In 1987, he was convicted to life imprisonment in Lyon for war crimes, dying in prison in 1991. On Barbie, see Alan A. Ryan, Jr. *Klaus Barbie and the United States Government: A Report to the Attorney General of the United States* (Washington, DC: U.S. Department of Justice 1983), retrieved March 2016 from https://www.justice.gov/sites/default/files/criminal-hrsp/legacy/2011/02/04/08-02-83 barbie-rpt.pdf.

Who was Mykola Lebed'?

The old man living on the upper floor of a two-story building, above that of the building's owner, his former driver and bodyguard "from the days of World War II clandestine operations in Western Ukraine,"[437] was not just any New York suburbanite. A former leader of the far-right Organization of Ukrainian Nationalists (OUN) and the organizer of its dreaded security service, the Sluzhba Bezpeky (SB OUN), Mykola Lebed' (1909 or 1910–1998) was a convicted murderer with a long resume of political violence, including a stint as a collaborator with Nazi Germany. In 1934, Lebed' attended a training camp near Rome, run by the Croatian Ustaša.[438] He was instrumental in the assassination of Bronisław Pieracki (1895–1934), the Polish minister of the interior, in June of that year. In January 1936, Lebed' was sentenced to death for having organized the murder, a sentence commuted to life in prison.[439] Released after the German attack on Poland in 1939, Lebed' became one of the leading figures in the more radical wing of the OUN following the 1940 split of the organization.[440]

This organization, known as the OUN-Bandera, or OUN(b) after its leader, Stepan Bandera, sought to establish a totalitarian Ukrainian state under its control.[441] In an unsuccessful attempt on 30 June 1941 to establish Ukrainian statehood, the self-proclaimed OUN(b) "Prime Minister" Yaroslav Stets'ko declared that his new state was to "cooperate closely with National Socialist Greater

---

437 "Memorandum for the Record. Subject: Meeting with QRPLUMB/2," 8 May 1990, Mykola Lebed Name File, NARA, College Park, MD, Record Group [RG] 263, Records of the Central Intelligence Agency, entry ZZ-18, box 16, folder 2 of 2.
438 "Mykola Lebed," biographical sketch, (1st draft) p. 2," undated, (February 1986), "Lebed Archives, Biographical materials about Mykola Lebed (1935–1992)," Ukrainian Research Institute Archives, Harvard Ukrainian Research Institute, Cambridge, MA, [hereafter URIA-HURI], UI0019, Mykola Lebed Papers, box 1, Biographical material: Mykola Lebed.
439 Rossoliński-Liebe, *Stepan Bandera*, 117–66.
440 Oleksandr Panchenko, *Mykola Lebed': zhyttia, diial'nist, derzhavno-pravivi poliady* (Hadiach: "Hadiach," 2001). A lawyer by training, Panchenko is a local political activist for the far-right party VO Svoboda. Highly ideological in nature, his Lebed biography needs to be treated with caution.
441 Bruder, *"Den ukrainischen Staat erkämpfen oder sterben!"*

Germany ... under the Führer Adolf Hitler."[442] Stets'ko assured Adolf Hitler, Benito Mussolini, Francisco Franco, and Ante Pavelić that the new state was a new, committed member of Hitler's New Order in Europe.[443] The state proclamation was accompanied by a wave of pogroms in over 140 localities across western Ukraine, organized by the OUN(b) in the summer of 1941, in which thousands of Jews were murdered.[444] Lebed', the number three person in the OUN(b) hierarchy, arrived in L'viv on 3 July 1941.[445]

Declarations of loyalty notwithstanding, Hitler had no interest in an OUN(b) state. His plan was to colonize Ukraine. OUN(b) activities were soon sharply curtailed. Bandera and Stets'ko were brought to Berlin where they were interrogated, but otherwise free to move around the city and to continue to pester the German authorities with pleas to cooperate with their group.[446] Following the assassination of two high-profile Ukrainian nationalists from the rival Melnyk wing of the OUN, which stood in open cooperation with the Gestapo and refused to acknowledge the 30 June declaration, Bandera and Stets'ko were detained. They spent much of the war held as *Ehrenhäftlinge* in the Zellenbau, a special annex to the Sachsenhausen camp used for particularly important political figures.[447] The Gestapo issued an arrest warrant for Lebed', and, in connection with this, issued a wanted poster for

---

442 Volodymyr Serhiichuk (ed.), *OUN-UPA v roky viiny: novi dokumenty i materialy* (Kyiv: Dnipro, 1996), 239.
443 Grzegorz Rossoliński-Liebe, "The 'Ukrainian National Revolution' of 1941: Discourse and Practice of a Fascist Movement," *Kritika: Exploration in Russian and Eurasian History* 12, no. 1 (2011): 83–114, here: 99.
444 Struve, *Deutsche Herrschaft*, 671.
445 Struve, *Deutsche Herrschaft*, 262, n64.
446 Rossoliński-Liebe, *Stepan Bandera*, 247–49; Marco Carynnyk, "'A Knife in the Back of Our Revolution': A Reply to Alexander J. Motyl's 'The Ukrainian Nationalist Movement and the Jews: Theoretical Reflections on Nationalism, Fascism, Rationality, Primordialism, and History'," *The American Association for Polish-Jewish Studies*, 2014, http://aapjstudies.org/manager/external/ckfinder/userfiles/files/Carynnyk%20Reply%20to%20Motyl%202%20.pdf (accessed 26 July 2017).
447 The two assassinated members of the more conservative OUN wing under Andrii Melnyk (1890–1964), known as OUN(m), were Omelian Senyk (1891–1941) and Mykola Sts'ibors'kyi (1898–1941), killed in Zhytomyr on 30 August 1941. Kai Struve, *Deutsche Herrschaft*, 202; Rossoliński-Liebe, *Stepan Bandera*, 249.

Lebed' on 4 October 1941. Lebed' went underground and, between September 1941 and May 1943 he served as acting leader of the OUN(b).

During this period, the OUN(b) actively infiltrated various German auxiliary police units in the occupied Soviet Union, gaining weapons training and combat experience, but also getting intimately involved in the execution of the Holocaust in Ukraine and Belorussia.[448] In February 1943, the OUN(b) and its paramilitary branch, the Ukrainian Insurgent Army (*Ukrains'ka Povstans'ka Armiia*, UPA), launched a coordinated campaign of ethnic cleansing and mass murder against the civilian Polish population in western Ukraine, claiming between 60,000 and 100,000 lives.[449] The precise date of the OUN(b) decision to remove the Poles is unclear, as is the exact role of Lebed'. Archival sources, including a postwar Polish interrogation with a local OUN(b) commander make explicit references to an SB OUN(b) "Order No. 1," for a "massive liquidation of the Polish population, starting in Polissia and then in Volhynia," issued in early 1943, at a time when Roman Shukhevych was eclipsing Lebed' as the dominant figure of the OUN(b).[450]

ZCh OUN and zpUHVR

Upon Bandera's release in August 1944, the OUN(b) again resumed its strategic collaboration with the German authorities.[451]

---

448 Gabriel N. Finder and Alexander V. Prusin, "Collaboration in Eastern Galicia: The Ukrainian Police and the Holocaust," *East European Jewish Affairs* 34, no. 2 (2004): 95–118, here: 105–6; Timothy Snyder, "The Causes of Ukrainian-Polish Ethnic Cleansing 1943," Past and Present 179 (2003): 210; Martin Dean, *Collaboration in the Holocaust: Crimes of the Local Police in Belorussia and Ukraine, 1941–44* (New York: St. Marten's Press, 2000), 106.

449 Jared McBride, "Peasants into Perpetrators: The OUN-UPA and the Ethnic Cleansing of Volynia, 1943–1944," *Slavic Review* 75, no. 3 (Fall 2016): 630–54.

450 A recent work by the author of the most detailed study of the OUN-UPA anti-Polish violence estimates the number of Polish victims at 91,200, 43,987 of which are known by name. Siemaszko, "Stan badań nad ludobójstwem," 311–36.

451 See Instytut Pamięci Narodowej, Warsaw [hereafter IPN] 0192/354, t. 1, k. 100109 and IPN 0192/354, t. 1, k. 309-312, published in Serhii Bohunov *et al.*, eds., *Pol'shcha ta Ukraina u trydtsiatykh-sorokovykh rokakh XX stolittia: Nevidomy*

The contact was established by Lebed', through his intermediary Ivan Hryn'okh (1907-1994).[452] At the same time, the OUN(b) sought to establish contact with the Western allies. Lebed' was tasked with establishing relations with US intelligence. The unreconstructed totalitarians Bandera and Stets'ko remained committed to one-party dictatorship, authoritarianism, and political terror, whereas Lebed's group, after the German defeat at Stalingrad, paid lip service to a certain degree of political pluralism. The fallout between Lebed' and Bandera was personal, political, and violent, culminating in Lebed' firing a pistol at Bandera during a dispute in mid-March 1947, upon which Bandera, in turn, ordered Lebed's assassination.[453] Bandera's group, the Foreign Section of the OUN (*Zakordonne Chastyny OUN*, ZCh OUN) parted ways with Lebed's Foreign Representation of the Ukrainian Supreme Liberation Council (*Zakordonne Predstavnytstvo Ukrains'koi Holovnoi Vyzvol'noi Rady*, zpUHVR) in 1948. In western Ukraine, the UPA continued armed resistance against the Soviets until 1949-1950. The insurgency was crushed with utmost brutality, claiming the lives of an estimated 153,000 people.[454]

Centered in Munich, Bandera's group, the largest and most militant émigré political organization, soon lost the support of the

---

dokumenty z arkhiviv spetsial'nykh sluzhb, Tom 4, Poliaky i ukraintsi mizh dvoma totalitarnymy systemamy 1942-1945: Chastyna persha (Warsaw and Kyiv: Derzhavnyi Arkhiv SBU, IPN, 2005), 186 and 194. For the background and discussion of this order, see McBride, "A Sea of Blood and Tears'," 324-25 and McBride, "Peasants into Perpetrators," 637.
452 Rossoliński-Liebe, *Stepan Bandera*, 285.
453 "O sovmestnoi deial'nosti OUN-UPA s okhrannoi politsiiei i nemetskoi 'SD'," 7 October 1944, Derzhavnyi arkhiv l'vivs'koi oblasti (DALO) f. 3, op. 1, d. 67, ll. 78-104, published in Dzheffri [Jeffrey] Burds, *Shpionazh i natsionalizm: Pervye gody "kholodnoi voiny" na Zapadnoi Ukraine (1944-1948)* (Moskva: Sovremennaia istoriia, 2010), 146-72. Ivan Hryn'okh (1907-1994), a former chaplain on the Ukrainian Nachtigall Battalion and OUN(b) liaison with the Germans in 1944 would later become vice president of the zpUVHR. A witting CIA operative, Hryn'okh was also Lebed's man in Munich.
454 Jeffrey Burds, *The Early Cold War in Soviet West Ukraine, 1944-1948*, (=*The Carl Beck Papers in Russian & East European Studies* 1505) (Pittsburgh: Center for Russian and Easy European Studies, University of Pittsburgh, 2001), 16; "Dokladnaia zapiska o sostoianii OUN za kordonom i meropriiatiiakh MVD USSR protiv zarubezhnykh natsionalisticheskikh tsentrov," 1953, HDA SBU, f. 16, op. 1, spr. 9, ark. 151.

United States due in equal measure to its reliance on political assassinations, organized crime, drug and alcohol black marketeering, and the counterfeiting of US banknotes.[455] The OUN(b) continued, however, to work with British, Italian, and West German intelligence until the end of the 1950s, at which time it came to rely increasingly on Franco's Spain and Chiang Kai-Shek's Taiwan for funding.[456] Bandera was himself assassinated by a Soviet Ukrainian agent in 1959, but his organization continued its clandestine and largely unsuccessful attempts to infiltrate the USSR throughout the Cold War.[457] In Canada, where many of its followers settled, the OUN(b) benefited from government funding under the aegis of official multiculturalism after 1971.[458] In 1992, the OUN(b) repatriated much of its organization to Ukraine.

AERODYNAMIC, QRDYNAMIC, QRPLUMB

Lebed's group was tiny by comparison. It consisted of two overlapping CIA-funded organizations, the above-mentioned ZpUHVR, and the OUN abroad (zakordonnyi), or OUN(z), established in 1954. In 1949, the CIA secretly brought Lebed' to the United States, where he came to run one of the most successful and long-lasting covert programs aimed against the Soviet Union. In the immediate postwar years Lebed' appears to have been involved in the program OHIO (later BINGO, 1949–1950), a US government program that used Ukrainian nationalist agents in the Displaced Person (DP) camps to track down and liquidate suspected Soviet moles in the US zones of occupation in Germany and Austria.[459]

---

455 In addition, 134,000 were arrested, and 203,000 people deported from Western Ukraine. Motyka, *Ukraińska partyzantka 1942–1960*, 649.
456 Breitman and Goda, *Hitler's Shadow*, 83.
457 "Zvernennia chleniv provodu ZCh OUN do vsikh chleniv OUN," p. 4. March 1960, LAC, Ottawa, MG 31, D130, vol. 6, folder 66.
458 On the Bandera assassination, see Serhii Plokhy, *The Man with the Poison Gun: A Cold War Spy Story* (New York: Basic Books, 2016).
459 On Canadian multicultural funding for Ukrainian diaspora nationalism, see Per A. Rudling, "Multiculturalism, Memory, and Ritualization: Ukrainian Nationalist Monuments in Edmonton, Alberta," *Nationalities Papers* 39, no. 5 (2011): 733–68.

From 1948 to 1952, Lebed' and his associate Evhen Stakhiv (1918–2014) played key roles in CIA covert operations in which OUN members loyal to his faction were airdropped into the Ukrainian RSR in conjunction with anti-Soviet guerilla operations.[460]

From 1952 until 1977, Lebed' led the CIA's covert action program AERODYNAMIC (later QRDYNAMIC and QRPLUMB), which operated until President George H. W. Bush discontinued its funding in September 1990. Its objective was "to exploit and increase nationalist and other dissident tendencies in the Soviet Ukraine."[461] A primary task was the smuggling of anti-Soviet materials, published in New York by a front organization titled Prolog Research Corporation, Inc., into the Ukrainian RSR. From 1961, Prolog published the journal *Suchasnist'* [*Contemporary Times*]. Different in tone and content from the militant, ideologically inflexible journals of Bandera's OUN(b), *Suchasnist'* became one of the most important journals of the Ukrainian emigration. By not admitting any new members into his inner circle of confidents until the 1970s, Lebed's zpUHVR—unlike other émigré nationalist organizations—avoided KGB penetration. The CIA described the AERODYNAMIC program as the "principal vehicle through which the Agency conducts its operations against the Ukrainian Soviet Socialist Republic. The main purpose of the project is to exploit contacts with Soviet Ukrainian citizens in order to encourage national and intellectual unrest in the Ukrainian SSR."[462]

Lebed's clandestine circle, which the CIA characterized as "more 'moderate' than most, i.e., it is not fanatically anti-Bolshevik, monarchist or neo-Fascist,"[463] was an unlikely vehicle for its aim "to encourage liberal sentiment in the USSR as a

---

460   Burds, *The Early Cold War*, 57.
461   Along with Hryn'okh, Lebed's closest collaborator was Yevhen Stakhiv, a veteran of the OUN expeditionary groups during World War II, and later a leading figure of the OUN(z) in New York.
462   "PDDYNAMIC evolution, QRPLUMB," dated "late 1974," QRPLUMB, NARA, RG 263, entry ZZ-19, box 59, vol. 1, folder 1 of 2.
463   "Secret CA/PEO PROJECT DATA SHEET," 17 May 1971, QRPLUMB, NARA, RG 263, entry ZZ-19, box 59, vol. 2, folder 2 of 2.

whole."[464] In this marriage of convenience, the CIA supported, in the name of liberal democracy, an ethnonationalist group run by a convicted assassin whereas the zpUHVR/OUN(z), in turn, worked for a government that did not support their cause of Ukrainian independence.[465]

Over the course of the 1950s and 1960s, the Holocaust spurred limited attention in North America. Whereas dissenting liberal and socialist émigré voices occasionally raised concerns about Lebed's wartime past, much of the criticism of Lebed' originated from the OUN(b), which resented the CIA funding for Lebed's group. This changed in the late 1970s, as the Holocaust entered Western historical memory, through, among other things, the broadcast in 1978 of the miniseries *Holocaust*.[466] To many postwar Ukrainian émigrés and their offspring this development was often a painful process. As a disproportionate number of the roughly 250,000 Ukrainian Displaced Persons that remained in Western Europe by 1947 had served the German occupation authorities in various capacities during the war, the émigré community was sensitive to allegations of war criminality or complicity in the Holocaust.[467] Many émigrés were stung by accounts of Ukrainian collaboration, perceiving it as besmirching their national hon-

---

464 "Memorandum for John H. Stein, Associate Deputy Director for Operations From: [redacted], Chief, Evaluations and Program Design Staff, Subject: Proposed Renewal of OPACY PDDYNAMIC," 19 May 1981," QRPLUMB, NARA, RG 263, entry ZZ-19, box 59, vol. 4.
465 "Memorandum for: The 303 Committee, Subject: Political, Propaganda ad Intelligence Activity Directed Against the Soviet Ukraine," p. 2, 4 December 1968, AERODYNAMIC, NARA, RG 263, entry ZZ-19, box 21, vol. 38, vol. 2 of 2.
466 "While Prolog reflects and encourages Ukrainian nationalism, it does not attempt in any way to provoke active separatist manifestations in the Ukrainian SSR," the CIA specified. "Memorandum for: The 303 Committee, Subject: Political, Propaganda ad Intelligence Activity Directed Against the Soviet Ukraine," p. 2, 4 December 1968, AERODYNAMIC, NARA, RG 263, entry ZZ-19, box 21, vol. 38, vol. 2 of 2.
467 Wulf Kansteiner, "Entertaining Catastrophe: The Reinvention of the Holocaust in the Television of the Federal Republic of Germany," *New German Critique* 90 (Fall 2003): 135–62, and Wulf Kansteiner, "Losing the War, Winning the Memory Battle: The Legacy of Nazism, World War II, and the Holocaust in the Federal Republic of Germany," in *The Politics of Memory in Postwar Europe*, ed. Richard Ned Lebow, Wulf Kansteiner, Claudio Fogy (Durham, NC: Duke University Press, 2006), 124–25.

or.[468] The relative ignorance of the general public further complicated matters: the average American often knew little about these Eastern Europeans, other than their reputation as antisemites and as collaborators in the Holocaust.[469]

The Office of Special Investigations

The creation of the Office of Special Investigations (OSI) within the Department of Justice in 1979 increased the unease within the Ukrainian émigré community. The OSI was charged with investigating the past of immigrants who had entered the United States after World War II who were suspected of having collaborated with the Nazi regime. Following investigations, the OSI undertook denaturalization proceedings in civil courts on the grounds that its targets had lied on their visa forms when entering the United States. Ideally, guilty subjects would be stripped of their US citizenship and then deported. Allegations of war criminality and collaboration with the Nazis served as a rallying cry for much of the Ukrainian diaspora.[470] The case of John Demjanjuk (1920–2012), a former Sobibór death camp guard who had immigrated to the United States in 1952 and settled in Ohio, became a cause célèbre for much of the Ukrainian community, which raised over $1 million for his legal defense alone.[471] And Demjanjuk was but one of several alleged war criminals facing denaturalization and de-

---

468 John-Paul Himka and Joanna Beata Michlic, "Introduction," in *Bringing the Dark Past to Light: The Reception of the Holocaust in Postcommunist Europe*, ed. John-Paul Himka and Joanna Beata Michlic (Lincoln, NE: University of Nebraska Press, 2013), 3; John-Paul Himka, "The Reception of the Holocaust in Postcommunist Ukraine," in Himka and Michlic, *Bringing the Dark Past to Light*, 648; John-Paul Himka, "Ukrainian Memories of the Holocaust: the Destruction of Jews as Reflected in Memoirs Collected in 1947," *Canadian Slavonic Papers / Revue canadienne des slavistes* 54, no. 3-4, (September–December 2012): 429.

469 Himka, "The Reception," 649. See also Dietsch, *Making Sense of* Suffering, 125.

470 John-Paul Himka, "Obstacles to the Integration of the Holocaust into Post-Communist East European Historical Narratives," *Canadian Slavonic Papers / Revue canadienne des slavistes* 50, no. 3-4 (September–December 2008): 361.

471 Per A. Rudling, *The OUN, the UPA, and the Holocaust: A Study in the Manufacturing of Historical Myths*, (=*The Carl Beck Papers in Russian & Eastern European Studies*, no. 2107) (Pittsburgh: University Center of Russian and East European Studies, University of Pittsburgh, 2011).

portation in the 1980s. Former Treblinka death camp guard Fedor Fedorenko (1907–1987) was denaturalized in 1981 and sent back to the Ukrainian SSR in December 1984 where he was found guilty of war crimes, sentenced to death, and executed by firing squad in 1986 or 1987. Estonian concentration camp guard Karl Linnas (1919–1987) was denaturalized and deported to the USSR in 1987, where he died in a prison hospital awaiting trial.[472] Other prominent cases included Andrija Artuković (1899–1988), former minister of the interior in the fascist Croatian Ustaša government, who was arrested in November 1984 and extradited to Yugoslavia in November 1986.[473] These cases stirred strong emotions with the Ukrainian community in North America.[474]

Lebed' was one of twelve individuals investigated by the US General Accounting Office (GAO) in its 1985 report.[475] Concerned about a possible exposure of Lebed' and his connection to the Agency, on 16 August 1985, the CIA approached the OSI chief Neal M. Sher (1947-2021) directly concerning its involvement with the old nationalist. Sher, according to the CIA's records, "agreed to protect the secrecy of QRPLUMB if and when the investigation of P/2 [Lebed'] resumed and promised that OSI would inform CIA of any new developments in P/2's case. This agreement was

---

472 Lawrence Douglas, *The Right Wrong Man: John Demjanjuk and the Last Great Nazi War Crimes Trial* (Princeton, NJ: Princeton University Press, 2016); Myron B. Kuropas, "OSI: Still Untouchable," *The Ukrainian Weekly* no. 37, 14 September 2003, retrieved 20 December 2013 from http://www.ukrweekly.com/old/archive/2003/370314.shtml.
473 On Linnas, see Jerome S. Legge, Jr. "The Karl Linnas Deportation Case, the Office of Special Investigations, and American Ethnic Politics," *Holocaust and Genocide Studies* 24, no. 1 (2010): 26–55.
474 On Artuković, see Tomislav Dulić, *Utopias of Nation: Local Mass Killing in Bosnia and Herzegovina, 1941–1942* (=Studia Historica Uppsalensia, 218) (Uppsala: Uppsala University Library, 2005), 81, 91, 221, n.19.
475 For reactions and commentaries from nationalist veterans linked to the OUN(m) and (b), respectively see, for instance, Zynovyi Knysh, *Vid'molovy: (Slovo v oboroni proty zhydivs'koi napasty na ukrainstiv i na narody skhidn'oi Evropy)* (Toronto: Vydavnytstvo "Novyi Shliakh," 1989), 73–80, and Petro Mirchuk, *Zustrichi i rozmovy v Izrailiu* (New York: Soiuz Ukrains'kykh Politviazniv, 1982), 121.

re-confirmed in December 1985 when OSI informed CIA that it planned to approach the Polish government on the case."[476]

The CIA followed the Lebed' case with increasing concern after October 1985 when the OSI began looking into Lebed's background "on allegations that he may have collaborated with the Germans and as a leader of the OUN during World War II [and that] he may have been responsible for the OUN's alleged war crimes" and conducted an interview with the former OUN(b) leader.[477] Roman Kupchinsky (1944–2010),[478] Lebed's successor as Prolog president, was convinced the Soviets were behind the allegations and demanded that both the CIA and GAO apologize to Lebed'.[479] The transcript of that communication remains inaccessible to researchers, but the materials available indicate that some form of agreement was reached:

> Agency representatives from the Office of the General Counsel and this office met with the Head of the Office of Special Investigation (OSI) [Neal Sher] at the Department of Justice and advised him of the case and our concern for the security of QRPLUMB operations. Chief, OSI stated that his office does not have a file on Mr. Lebed and at the moment has no basis for initiating an investigation of him; and if such investigation is warranted in the future, he will inform the Agency of his action. He advised against taking any action intended to correct the public GAO statement on Mr. Lebed lest it attract unfavorable media investigative reporting. Additionally, he recommended that we inform our Congressional oversight committees and Congressman [Peter W.] Rodino [D-NJ (1909-2005)] of the case and our security concerns, especially since he had indications that Congressman

---

476 Kevin Conley Ruffner, "Eagle and Swastika: CIA and Nazi War Criminals and Collaborators (U)," CIA Working paper (Washington, DC: Central Intelligence Agency, 2003), 26 n.58.
477 [redacted] "Memorandum for the Record. Subject: Justice Department Interest in QRPLUMB/2," 31 October 1991. Lebed Name File, NARA, RG 263, entry ZZ-18, box 16, folder 2 of 2; Ruffner, "Eagle and Swastika," 26 n.58.
478 "SUBJECT: GAO Report with Potential for Compromise of QRPLUMB Operation", p. 3, 7 October 1985, Lebed Name File, NARA, RG 263, entry ZZ-18, box 16, folder 2 of 2.
479 Roman Kupchinsky was recruited to the AERODYNAMIC program by zpUHVR activist and CIA operative Yevhen Stakhiv, a family friend, in 1964. After a year in Vietnam in 1968 he became a CIA operative, joining the zpUHVR inner circle in 1971, and Prolog as a full-time staffer in 1972, succeeding Lebed' as director in 1977. After the CIA funding ceased, he worked for RFE/RL in 1990, setting up its Ukrainian bureau in Kyiv in 1994.

Rodino was under pressure from certain quarters to hold a hearing on the GAO report.[480]

The CIA's concerns were justified. Soon thereafter, Lebed's case caught the attention of investigative journalists. The first serious journalistic inquiry into Lebed's wartime past was not initiated by one of the large New York papers, but by a relatively small, left-liberal community newspaper, *The Village Voice*. A research team of investigative journalists, led by the young journalist Joe Conason (b. 1954) spent months researching Lebed's wartime past before approaching the OUN veteran and CIA operative in his Yonkers home in January 1986.[481] Conason went through a wealth of sources, including partially redacted records from the US Army Counterintelligence Corps (CIC) obtained under the Freedom of Information Act, immigration records, interviews with Ukrainian émigrés, and eyewitness accounts, obtained via a research fellow at Yad Vashem in Jerusalem.[482] Even more alarming for the CIA was that Conason's article contained a specific, detailed timeline of Lebed's whereabouts in 1939–1941. These details posed a direct challenge to the Ukrainian diaspora's—and the CIA's—official versions of Lebed's past.[483] A key focus was on his background as a Nazi collaborator: "Only hints of what Lebed was actually doing in 1940 and 1941 appear in the CIC file . . . a card in the CIC file identifies Lebed as 'a graduate of the Zakopane, Poland criminal police school," Conason wrote.

Conason further cited the memoirs of Mykola Kosakivs'kyi (1900-1961),[484] a fellow alumnus and one of the older OUN mem-

---

480 Ruffner, "Eagle and Swastika," 26n58.
481 "SUBJECT: GAO Report with Potential for Compromise of QRPLUMB Operation," p. 3, 7 October 1985, Lebed Name File, NARA, RG 263, entry ZZ-18, box 16, folder 2 of 2.
482 Author interview with Joe Conason, New York City, 15 April 2015.
483 Conason, "To Catch a Nazi," 17. Conason's contact was a temporary research fellow at Yad Vashem who shared materials from a small Ukrainian émigré paper in Germany that was critical of Lebed'. I am thankful to Jeffrey Burds for providing this information.
484 Lebed's background in Zakopane was well-known to the US government. Lebed's CIC files refer to his collaboration with Nazi Germany. "Questionnaire submitted to Mr. Lebed in Connection with Clearing his Name with Immigration and Naturalization Service [8 April 1952]," Mykola Lebed Name

bers trained at the Zakopane police school, on how a "Ukrainian Training Unit" was established in November: "According to [Lebed's] declaration, the Ukrainian unit was organized by the OUN leadership and by permission of the German Security Service. It included 120 specially selected trainees . . . 'The Ukrainian commandant . . . was Mykola Lebid [sic].' The curriculum . . . emphasized 'exercises in the hardening of hearts.'" Conason cited Kosakivs'kyi's recollection how,

> At sundown, . . . [SS-*Hauptsturmführer* Hans] Krüger, [SS-*Untersturmführer* Wilhelm] Rosenbaum [1915-1984], Lebid [sic] and a few students would go to Zakopane, enter some Jewish home on the way, grab a Jew, and bring him to the Unit. One evening, late in November or early in December 1939, they returned with a young Jew. In the presence of Ukrainian seniors, including myself, Krüger and Rosenbaum, fortified with alcohol, [they] proceeded with their demonstration of the proper methods of interrogation.

---

file, NARA, RG 263, entry ZZ-18, box 80, folder 1 of 2. Lebed's Immigration and Naturalization Service fi le contains information from the FBI investigation on how Lebed' attended a "terroristic school in a small Polish city of Krynitza" and explicitly, how, "in Zakopane a Gestapo school for training diversionists is created." See the 5 June 1953, and 28 February 1957 investigation reports and memoranda; NARA, RG 85, Records of the Federal Bureau of Investigation, Lebed, Mykola, box 5, folder 1 of 2. Thanks to Jared McBride for copying and sharing this folder.

"NOT QUITE KLAUS BARBIE, BUT IN THAT CATEGORY" 147

Figure 4.1. First page of Joe Conason's article "To Catch a Nazi," *The Village Voice*, 11 February 1986.

Conason continued:

Seeking to induce the innocent Jew to confess that he had raped an Aryan woman, the German officers beat and tortured him, using their fists, a sword, and iron bars. When he was bloody from head to toe, they applied salt and flame to his wounds. The broken man then confessed his fictional crimes. But that was not the end . . . [According to Kosakivs'kyi,] "Rosenbaum beat the Jew again with an iron pipe and Lebed too assisted manually in that 'heroic action.' One of the senior Ukrainians and I withdrew from the spectacle to our rooms. We learned afterwards that the tortured man was stripped naked, stood-up in front of the school as 'a sentry' and doused with water in heavy frost."

The next day, Kosakivs'kyi recalled, he and a friend protested to Lebed', but the commandant told them bluntly that "it was the duty of every member of the OUN to show the Germans that his nerves are just as tough as a German's and that the heart of any nationalist is as hard as steel."

On Conason's direct question, Lebed' conceded that he had been at the Zakopane school, but said it was in the winter of 1940-1941, rather than 1939-1940, as Kosakivs'kyi had stated, adding "I left after five weeks. I have exactly the dates. I quit."[485] Conason's team not only researched Lebed's background in the Zakopane training camp, but also his postwar CIA service, for which they presented very strong indications. Even though the CIA had declined to comment on the matter, *The Village Voice* felt it had secured enough evidence to state, unambiguously, "The CIA brought Mykola Lebed to the US under an assumed name and concealed his past from the INS."[486]

A Historiographical Fire Storm

The Village Voice story generated significant interest and was soon taken up by larger outlets including the *New York Post*, *The Herald Statesman*,[487] *The New York Time*[488] as well as several Jewish

---

485 Mykyta Kozakivs'kyi (1900-1961) was an OUN(b) activist, trained in Zakopane on the eve of Operation Barbarossa in June 1941. After the war he became disenchanted with the OUN. His recollections of the Zakopane school were published in émigré publications after his death. Mykyta Kosakivs'kyi, *Z nedavn'oho mynuloho* (London: Vydavnytstvo Nashe Slovo, 1965), 2; Mykyta Kosakivs'kyi, "Z nedavn'oho mynuloho," *Nashe Slovo*, Zbirnyk 5, (1977)/ *Our Word*, Review 5 (1977): 66–80, http://diasporiana.org.ua/wp-content/uploads/books/8251/file.pdf.
486 Conason, "To Catch a Nazi," 19–20.
487 Conason, "To Catch a Nazi," 17–18, 21.
488 Marie Cortissoz, "City Man Collaborated with Nazis, Says Report," The Herald Statesman, 6 February 1986, URIA-HURI, Lebed Papers, box 1, Biographical material: Mykola Lebed, folder Lebed Archives, "Newspaper clippings about Mykola Lebed and allegations of collaboration with Nazis (1986-1992)".

community newspapers.[489] The article quickly became a liability that threatened to unravel one of the CIA's most extensive covert action programs. Unlike Demjanjuk and Fedorenko, who had not been politically active after the war, Lebed' had been a senior operative who headed a propaganda outfit and who retained important connections and support from the CIA. With decades of experience of covert action and clandestine operations, Lebed' was not one to accept quietly the exposure of his and his organizations' pasts. Utilizing his old Prolog contacts, he fought back. Roman Kupchinsky, Lebed's successor, launched a coordinated counteroffensive in the Ukrainian press in North America. Whereas the CIA was well aware of Lebed's past—and by 1986 of his training in Zakopane—in The Ukrainian Weekly, Kupchinsky denied everything, responding with a litany of direct and deliberate falsehoods. Kupchinsky charged *The Village Voice* with sloppy journalism and ignorance, dismissed the article as part of a Soviet conspiracy, and questioned Conason's mental health. "[Lebed's] friends spent [World War II] in jail," Kupchinsky said. "His wife spent the war held by Germans, his daughter was born in a concentration camp. Anyone who says [Lebed'] is a Nazi war criminal is downright loony," Kupchinsky told *The Herald Statesman*.[490]

The Ukrainian Weekly launched its own attack on Conason. The Village Voice, it asserted, had "a well-honed reputation for engaging in a type of reporting known as muckracking journalism." It also quoted a source close to Lebed', who asked not to be identified, who noted that "the story was obviously orchestrated by Moscow."[491] The following week The Ukrainian Weekly published an interview with Kupchinsky, who claimed *The Village*

---

489 Ralph Blumenthal, "CIA Said to Have Let Nazi into US," *The New York Times*, 6 February 1986. See also Ralph Blumenthal, "Nazi Hunter Says CIA Has Files on Man Accused of War Crimes," *The New York Times*, 17 September 1992, URIA-HURI, Lebed Papers, box 1.
490 Carolyn Weiner, "Innocent Until Proven Guilty," *The Jewish Chronicle*, 14 February 1986," URIA-HURI, Lebed Papers, box 1.
491 Marie Cortissoz, "City Man Collaborated with Nazis, Says Report," *The Herald Statesman*, 6 February 1986. URIA-HURI, Lebed Papers, box 1, folder Lebed Archives, "Newspapers clippings about Mykola Lebed and allegations of collaboration with Nazis (1986–1992)".

Voice article contained "nothing to show that he [Mr. Lebed'] was a collaborator," and denied Lebed' had ever commanded the SB.[492] Curiously, while denying Lebed's collaboration with the Nazis, Kupchinsky admitted Lebed's Zakopane training, but presented it as a rather unproblematic episode of the past, for which Lebed' had accounted fully.[493] "Lebed never hid the fact that he was at Zakopane . . . He was there for only five weeks and he left after he discovered it was a Gestapo police school." Kupchinsky attached a copy of the Gestapo wanted poster of 4 October 1941. The poster, which *The Ukrainian Weekly* published, Kupchinsky explained, "raises further doubt about Mr. Lebed's alleged close association with the Nazis." Conason had pointed out that Prolog, in addition to its New York office, maintained mysterious offices in Munich, London, and Cairo, and that its publication of eight to ten volumes annually, plus two or three small-circulation magazines would hardly provide a sufficient source of revenue to maintain activity on this scale.[494] Kupchinsky went on to deny both Lebed's and Prolog's connection to the CIA, insisting that Prolog's book publishing program and donations from the Ukrainian community provided the organization's funding. "Lebed," he said,

---

492 Michael B. Bociurkiw, "OUN Leaders Branded as Nazi: Sources say Allegations are Scurrilous," *The Ukrainian Weekly*, 9 February 1986, 10.

493 The Kupchinsky interview is in Michael B. Bociurkiw, "Prolog chief defends Lebed," *The Ukrainian Weekly*, February 16, 1986, 1, 4. Kupchinsky's assertion is false. Lebed' led the SB OUN(b) from its foundation, and as OUN(b) leader he personally ordered terror against communists, Soviet sympathizers, and Melnykites. Iaroslav Antoniuk, *Diial'nist' SB OUN na Volyni* (Luts'k: Volyns'ka knyha, 2007), 10; Petro J. Potichnyj, "The Struggle against the Agentura," in *Litopys Ukrains'koi Povstans'koi Armii, vol. 43, Struggle against Agentura: Protocols of Interrogation of the OUN SB in Ternopil Region 1946–1948. Book I*, ed. Petro J. Potichnyj (Toronto: Litopys UPA, 2006) http://www.litopysupa.com/main.php?pg=2&bookid=260 (Accessed 20 November 2013); see also "Protokol zaiava protokol zaiavy Pavlyshyna L. S.," L'viv, 13 May 1986, p. 2. YAV, RG 0.32, file 112. Thanks to Jeffrey Burds for bringing this document to my attention.

494 In reality, Lebed' was less than forthcoming, and the CIA less interested in the Zakopane episode than when they brought him to the United States. In April 1952, Lebed' told the CIA that he had left the Zakopane school immediately.

"NOT QUITE KLAUS BARBIE, BUT IN THAT CATEGORY" 151

has nothing to hide . . . He came to this country perfectly legally and he was never a CIA agent. The bottom line is that this article is an attack on anybody who supports Ukrainian independence . . . The Soviets have consistently tried to discredit the Ukrainian liberation movement, and the *Voice* article appears at a time when the Soviets are continuing to smear the Ukrainian underground.

Kupchinsky claimed that Prolog "for years has been trying to improve Ukrainian-Jewish relations," and he called on the Ukrainian community "not to perceive this latest attack on Ukrainian nationalists as a 'Jewish conspiracy.'"[495] Kupchinsky cast Lebed's legacy as one of reconciliation while, at the same time seeking to preempt expressions of open antisemitism from his community.

United in Denial

On its end, *The Ukrainian Weekly* urged the Ukrainian community to rally their wagons and unite around Lebed', whom they equated with Ukraine itself and to "unmask" what it described as a Muscovite conspiracy:

> The Ukrainian community should unite to unmask and fight the smear campaign which originates in Moscow. Likewise, the Ukrainian community should oppose the disinformation disseminated by Western elements, regardless of whether they are the result of ignorance or deliberate malice. It is the duty of the entire Ukrainian community to enlighten those who defame its noble struggle for freedom and denounce its inalienable right to seek justice for Ukrainians to determine their own fate in their homeland. The most recent attacks are not directed against a single person, or one political group, this is an offensive against our entire community, against the honor of Ukrainians and their good name. We can defend the truth successfully only as a single community and a united front.[496]

---

495 The affidavit, in which Lebed' was asked to account for this episode was not even translated into English until 22 January 1986, strongly suggesting that it was never even read by any of his CIA contacts. "Questionnaire submitted to Mr. Lebed in connections with clearing his name with immigration and naturalization services," 8 April 1952, p. 36, and 55, Lebed Name File, NARA RG 263, ZZ-18, box 80, folder 1 of 2.
496 Conason, "To Catch a Nazi," 21.

Lebed' summoned the aid of historian and OUN veteran Taras Hunchak,[497] who Lebed's successor Kupchinsky had recruited to serve as editor of *Suchasnist'* in 1984.[498] Hunchak admired Lebed' and shared his commitment to the pro-nationalist historical narrative.[499] In his memoirs Hunchak describes how "attacks" on alleged war criminals from Ukraine, constituted "an affront to my feelings of national dignity and therefore I reacted to them, writing replies to papers and journals."[500] Hunchak wrote to *The New York Times* as an academic and scholar. Signing as "Taras Hunczak, Professor of History," he lamented their 6 February 1986 article, titled, "C.I.A. Said to Have Let Nazi into U.S.," which he claimed to have read "with considerable dismay":

> I find it difficult to understand how Mr. Lebed can be referred to as a "Nazi collaborator" when from July 1941, he was a de facto leader of the Ukrainian Anti-Nazi underground movement known as the Organization of Ukrainian Nationalists. As all modern nationalist movements, that Ukrainian movement aimed at the establishment of an independent Ukrainian state—an objective that conflicted with the Nazi objectives in

---

497 Michael B. Bociurkiw, "Prolog chief defends Lebed," *The Ukrainian Weekly*, 16 February 1986, 1, 4. Kupchinsky's claims were, of course, completely false. In 1981, QRPLUMB received 80 percent of its funds from the CIA. "Memorandum for John H. Stein, Associate Deputy Director for Operations From: [redacted], Chief, Evaluations and Program Design Staff, Subject: Proposed Renewal of OPACY PDDYNAMIC," 19 May 1981," QRPLUMB, NARA, RG 263, entry ZZ-19, box 59, vol. 4. As the final CIA audit shows subscriptions covered less than 5 percent of the QRPLUMB revenue. [Redacted], Inspector General 2 T 21 NHB, "Audit of Operational Activity QRPLUMB Newark Office Income Statement, 1 January 1989–30 September 1990, Exhibit B," 26 April 1991, p. 8, QRPLUMB, NARA, RG 263, entry ZZ-19, box 59, vol. 5; Sign. [redacted], Chief, Central Cover Staff, "Approval of 1989 OPACT QRPLUMB," 21 December 1988.
498 "Statement: In Protest against Defamation of Ukrainian Liberation Movement," *The Ukrainian Weekly*, 2 March 1986, 7, 11.
499 Taras Hunchak (b. 1932) immigrated to the United States in 1949 and was naturalized in 1954. BS Fordham, 1955; MA Fordham, 1958; Ph.D. Vienna, 1960; US Army Military Intelligence, 1956–1958; affiliated in various CIA projects from 1959; editor, *Suchasnist'* 1984–1991. "Memorandum for the Record, Subject: Report of Contact with AECASSOWARY/2 in Washington, 3–4 November 1960," 18 November 1960, p. 7, AERODYNAMIC, NARA, RG 263, Entry ZZ-19, box 23, vol. 45, folder: 1; "HUNCHAK Taras," 15 January 1961, AERODYNAMIC, NARA, RG 263, entry ZZ-19, box 13, vol. 20.
500 Taras Hunchak, *Moi spohady-stezhky zhyttia* (Kyiv: Vydavnytstvo Dnipro, 2005), 67; Kamins'kyi, *Proloh*, 89.

Eastern Europe. The struggle of the OUN against the Nazis is a matter of record for which there is indisputable evidence.

Hunchak thereafter repeated the diaspora's canonical narration: the OUN's victimization at the hands of the Nazis, with particular emphasis on Bandera and Stet'sko's imprisonment in Sachsenhausen. Hunchak, who did not forget to submit a copy of Lebed's 1941 wanted poster, emphasized that Lebed's wife and daughter spent time in the Ravensbrück concentration camp. Hunchak concluded, "In view of the above facts it should be obvious that a charge of collaboration with the Nazis on the part of Mr. Lebed is absurd."[501] *The New York Times* did not publish his letter. It appeared, the following month, in *The Ukrainian Weekly*, the leading Ukrainian diaspora newspaper.[502]

---

501 Hunchak, *Moi spohady*, 16, 22.
502 Hunchak, *Moi spohady*, 72.

Figure 4.2 German Wanted Poster of Mykola Lebed' (October, 1941).

Evidently troubled by the renewed, massive interest in Lebed's person, the CIA responded by placing a new coat of whitewash on Lebed's past. On 18 February, the CIA's acting chief of Political and Psychological Staff spelled out the Agency's strategy: "[We] see no reason at this time not to stick by the established cover story for QRPLUMB."[503] "We are," a report from the following week said, "currently working with our Central Cover Staff and legal people to determine possible areas of vulnerability in Agency relationship with the QRPLUMB organization and ensure the cover and security of this relationship."[504]

CIA Concerns

To the dismay of the CIA, on 14 March, Lebed himself entered the discussion. In a letter to the editor of *The Jewish Chronicle*, Lebed described the *Village Voice* article as "attempts at character assassination." He argued that "contrary to the allegations made by Mr. Conason, I was never in collaboration with Germany nor with any other power. Neither was I ever involved in any anti-[S]emitic activities, directly or indirectly."[505] Like Kupchinsky and Hunchak, Lebed illustrated his story by attaching a copy of the Gestapo wanted poster. Lebed also wrote *New York Times* to offer an alternate version of the past. He approached *New York Times* journalist Ralph Blumenthal, who had covered the Lebed story.

> I was never a Nazi nor did I collaborate with the Germans. I was never trained in any German police school nor was I engaged in persecuting Jews or any other nationals. After the head of the Organization of Ukrainian Nationalists (OUN) Stepan Bandera and his deputy Yaroslav Stetsko had been placed under house arrest in July 1941, subsequently to be incarcerated at the Sachsenhausen concentration camp from September 1941 to September 1944, I headed the underground anti-Nazi resistance of the OUN (mid-July

---

503   Taras Hunczak, unpublished letter to the editor of *The New York Times*, dated 10 February 1986. URIA-HURI Lebed Papers, box 1.
504   Taras Hunczak, "Nazi Charges are Absurd," *The Ukrainian Weekly*, 30 March 1986, Lebed Papers, URIA-HURI, box 1.
505   Sign. [redacted], Acting Chief, Political and Psychological Staff, SUBJECT: Recent Press Allegations Regarding QRPLUMB," QRPLUMB (Development and Plans, 1982-88), 18 February 1986, NARA, RG 263, entry ZZ-19, box 59, vol. 4.

156   TARNISHED HEROES

1941 to May 1943) . . . Our struggle has never been directed against any other people; we opposed only those foreign powers which enslaved and aided the enslavement of Ukraine.[506]

Through his lawyer Nestor L. Olesnycky (b. 1946), Lebed' drafted an answer for *The Village Voice*, in which he questioned all the major points in Conason's article. Lebed's response systematically denied the OUN(b)'s anti-Jewish violence, instead depicting Ukrainian Nationalists as rescuers of Jews while reversing the roles of victims and perpetrators by linking Jews to Stalinist terror:

> Mr. Conason does not give any concrete proof that Lebed was a Nazi collaborator, . . . Mr. Lebed never ran the security force of the OUN, . . . As to the alleged fascism of the OUN, Mr. Conason throws this phrase out without any proof.
> How was the OUN fascistic? Did it, in its program call itself "Fascist"? No. Did it propagate the killing of Jews? No. The OUN might not have been particularly pro-Jewish, for understandable reasons . . . It is abundantly clear that the Ukrainians suffered terribly at the hands of the GPU, OGPU and NKVD. Thus it is understandable to some degree why they were not particularly pro-Jewish. It must also be kept in mind that Jews in Ukraine did not always share the concerns of their countrymen, the Ukrainians, on the vital question of Ukrainian independence . . . It was only in 1943 when the UPA was formed, that some Jews joined the UPA as doctors, printers and arms specialists.[507]

In regard to the more specific claims, Lebed, through his attorney, denied them completely:

> Mykola Lebed never attended a Gestapo training school or any other police school. He never took part in any anti-Jewish activities. From the later part of December 1939 to January 1940 Lebed was in a camp in Zakopane, Poland. During his stay there, there were two members of the German SD, an officer Kruger, and an NCO "Mutti," whose name was never given. The Germans did not interfere in the daily life of the camp. On January 22, 1940, Kruger told Lebed that the aim of Hitler's policy is to expand the German Reich on the territory of the Soviet Union and that in the near fu-

---

506   Sign. [redacted], Acting Chief, Political and Psychological Staff, "New Public Inquiries Regarding QRPLUMB" 24 February 1986, ibid.
507   Mykola Lebed, "Letter to the Editor," *The Jewish Chronicle*, 14 March 1986, URIA-HURI, Lebed Papers, box 1.

ture all participants in the camp will have to fill out personnel questionnaires and be photographed. Lebed then left the camp.[508]

Having Lebed dragged into a public discussion about his terrorist past, his relations with Nazi Germany, the role of the OUN during the Holocaust, and not least, his long-term affiliation with the CIA was a growing liability for the Agency. Officers at CIA headquarters instead suggested the following response: "Write a serious, well-documented letter to prominent newspapers with the goal of clearing Lebed" and "Have a prominent Ukrainian scholar prepare a scholarly study explaining Lebed's role in the OUN organization during World War II for . . . an appropriate publication."[509] At the same time the Agency sought to dissuade the Ukrainian community from filing a libel action: "[T]here is pressure from within the Ukrainian community," noted a CIA report, "to pursue a libel suit against the 'Village Voice' as a means of clearing [Lebed's] name and the reputation of the Ukrainian community." Having been advised that Lebed was considering taking legal action, Political and Psychological Staff representatives requested a meeting to discuss options and consequences: "Our main objective has been to avoid any legal action which could jeopardize the current Agency relationship with the organization, QRPLUMB."[510] The CIA secured Lebed's coopera-

---

508 Mykola Lebed', unpublished letter to the editor of *The New York Times*, dated 2 April 1986, URIA-HURI, Lebed Papers, box 1. Lebed' supplied the CIA with a copy of the letter as it also appears in the CIA records. See Lebed Name file, NARA, RG 263, entry ZZ-18, box 80, folder 2 of 2.
509 "(draft response to the Village Voice article) For Nestor O[lesnycky]," Lebed Papers, URIA-HURI, Lebed Papers, box 1.
510 "(draft response to the Village Voice article) For Nestor O[lesnycky],". That SS-*Hauptsturmführer* Hans Krüger (1909-1988) would have informed Lebed' about this on 22 January 1940 is highly unlikely, as the decision to attack the Soviet Union had not yet been made. See Gerd R. Ueberschär, "Hitlers Entschluß zum 'Lebensraum'-Krieg im Osten: Programmatisches Ziel oder militärstrategisches Kalkül?," in *Der deutsche Überfall auf die Sowjetunion: "Unternehmen Barbarossa" 1941*, ed. Gerd R. Ueberschär and Wolfram Wette, (Frankfurt am Main: Fischer Verlag, 1991), 25. On Hans Krüger, see Dieter Pohl, "Hans Krüger—der 'König von Stanislau,'" in *Karrieren der Gewalt: Nationalsozialistische Täterbiographien*, ed. Klaus-Michael Mallmann (Darmstadt: Primus, 2004), 134–44. That Krüger would have informed Lebed' about the upcoming invasion plans on January 22, 1941 is, however, a possibility, and

tion. He agreed "not to initiate a libel suit against the 'Village Voice' at this time since he understands that such action on his part could destroy the QRPLUMB organization."[511] The CIA also feared incidents of vigilante justice. Even though Lebed already had a bodyguard, the agency considered whether they should relocate Lebed "to some other place outside the New York metropolitan area . . . The FBI will be in contact if and when they believe Lebed was in danger. The local police force was also contacted and made aware of the situation."[512]

If Kupchinsky coordinated the media response, Professor Hunchak provided academic legitimacy to the denial and, the third leg of the effort to clear Lebed was political. *The Ukrainian Weekly* published a statement of blanket denial by the zpUVHR in English; *Suchasnist'* carried it in Ukrainian.[513] The argument was not new, but one that the émigré nationalists had mechanically repeated since the mid-1940s. Lebed', it read, "was never in collaboration with Nazi Germany or any other power;" the OUN fought Hitler from 1941, and OUN members "were incarcerated in Auschwitz, Dachau, Sachsenhausen, Bergen-Belsen and other death camps. Many perished, including the two brothers of Stepan Bandera who were murdered by the Nazis in Auschwitz." The OUN "was never fascist in any way . . . although it had elements of authoritarianism in its founding program, it never espoused racism, xenophobia or anti-Semitism." Rather, in August 1943, "it adopted a democratic program with guaranteed equal rights to all citizens of Ukraine regardless of their nationality, race or reli-

---

would — if true — support the account Lebed initially gave Conason of being in Zakopane in the winter of 1940-41, rather than 1939-40. The OUN(b) enthusiastically endorsed the German invasion, and several OUN(b) units served in German uniform at the time. It is not plausible that Lebed' would have left Zakopane out of disagreement with the Nazi invasion plans.

511 Sign. [redacted] PPS/SEO/SIB, "Update on Mykola Lebed's Situation. Memorandum for the Record" 25 March 1986, Lebed Name File, NARA, RG 263, entry ZZ-18, box 80, folder 2 of 2.
512 "Update on Mykola Lebed's Situation," Memorandum for Deputy Director for Operations from Acting Chief, Political and Psychological Staff, 10 April 1986, Lebed Name File, NARA, RG 263, entry ZZ-18, box 80, folder 2 of 2.
513 Sign. [redacted] PPS/SEO/SIB, "Update on Mykola Lebed's Situation, Memorandum for the record," 25 March 25, 1986, ibid.

gion." The OUN "was a revolutionary organization of freedom-fighters—not a terrorist organization. Only the oppressors of the Ukrainian nation refer to OUN members as terrorists." Contrary to Conason's claims, the OUN "was not counting on Nazi Germany as the liberator or ally of Ukraine. In the first weeks of the Nazi occupation of Ukraine, the OUN began an underground resistance against the occupation which continued for three years."

In September 1986, *Suchasnist'* returned to the topic, publishing a statement by the Political Council of the Organization of Ukrainian Nationalists Abroad, OUN(z).[514] The OUN(z) statement presented Conason and *The Village Voice* as tools of Moscow, dedicated to destroying the Ukrainian nation: "The groundlessness of the entire complex of 'Nazi collaborator' accusations were revealed immediately following the German occupation of the Ukrainian territory. The OUN, under the leadership of Stepan Bandera—and, in his absence from the country—Lebed, fought the National Socialist occupation authorities actively and violently."[515] In connection with the denunciation of the "dishonoring of the Ukrainian name" an open letter, signed by 110 well-known community leaders and émigré politicians was published. The signatories expressed "alarm" about how "Communist Moscow" "exterminates all expression of cultural particularities of the Ukrainian people." They lamented how "the Muscovite communists and their representatives in Ukraine falsify our history, blacken our traditions, spread lies against our fighters for the freedom of the Ukrainian people as supposed servants of foreign powers." To the OUN(z), Conason's article was part of a broader campaign by Moscow and "Mykola Lebed . . . one of the most outstanding organizers of the anti-German struggle during the time of the Nazi occupation of Ukraine."[516]

---

514 Sign. [redacted] PPS/SEO/SIB, "Update on Mykola Lebed's Situation"
515 Zakordonne predstavnytsvo Ukrains'koi Holovnoi Vyzvol'noi Rady, "Proty zneslavlennia ukrais'koho vyzvol'noho rukhy," *Suchasnist'* 4 (1986): 110–13.
516 The OUN(z), the smallest of the three OUN wings, was also the most moderate. It appeared out of a splinter group of the OUN(b), led by Zynovyi Matla (1910–1993) and Lev Rebet (1912–1957), who after 1943 rejected the Banderites' totalitarianism. From the early 1950s it was funded by the CIA.

This damage control was coordinated and professionally managed by the QRPLUMB organization. Documentary evidence, recording all the rebuttals were forwarded to Lebed, who, although retired, remained a regular visitor and grey cardinal of sorts at the Prolog office on 875 West End Avenue. The zpUHVR statement was published no less than thirteen times in Ukrainian and English in Ukrainian diaspora papers in the United States, Great Britain, Australia, and Canada.[517] By 10 June 1986, the Prolog circle could report to Lebed that no less than fifty-nine articles in rebuttal to Conason had appeared in the Ukrainian émigré press.[518] The strategy was to maintain a fixed narrative of World War II in Ukraine, with the OUN both as the Nazis' primary victim and leader of the anti-Nazi resistance in Ukraine. Lebed himself was placed at the heart of this narrative, using the October 1941 Gestapo wanted poster akin to a "get out of jail free" card, while dismissing *The Village Voice* as a tool of the KGB.

Despite the significant resources mobilized in order to clear Lebed's record, the results were mixed. The interest in Lebed' would not dissipate. In 1987 and 1988, the CIA noted with concern the continued OSI inquiries into Lebed's past, commenting that "if OSI were to bring formal charges, this could subject our relationship with the QRPLUMB organization to closer scrutiny, possible exposure."[519] The categorical denial of CIA operatives stand in contrast to the concerned tone of the CIA's internal correspondence. Well aware of the OUN's collaboration with Nazi Germany, the CIA internally acknowledged this much. It was concerned less with maintaining a sanitized and heroic account of the OUN than about the political liabilities of the Agency's long-term collaboration with Lebed should his past become publicly known.

---

517 Politychna rada Orhanizatsii ukrains'kykh natsionalistiv za kordonom, "Do kampanii zneslavliuvannia ukrains'koho imeny," *Suchasnist'* 9 (1986): 112.
518 "Zaiava ukrainskoi soloidarnosti," *America: Ukrainian Catholic Daily*, 25 April 1986, 1; "Zaiava ukrains'koi solidarnosty," *Ukrains'ki visti*, 20 April 1986, p. 1; "Zaiava ukrains'koi solidarnosty," *Ukrains'ke slovo*, 27 April 1986, URIA-HURI, Lebed Papers, box 1.
519 "Reestr stattei z presy v spravi M. Lebedia na 10 chervnia 1986," URIA-HURI, Lebed Papers, box 1.

"NOT QUITE KLAUS BARBIE, BUT IN THAT CATEGORY" 161

Although we do not believe P/2 [Lebed] ever engaged in a war crime himself, he was, during WW II, leader of the Organization of Ukrainian Nationalists (OUN) during the absence of Stepan Bandera, who spent the war in a Nazi concentration camp for having proclaimed an independent Ukrainian republic after the Nazi invasion in July 1941. For a few weeks after the German invasion, the OUN did collaborate with the Nazis. The collaboration ended quickly, however, and Bandera was incarcerated, as were P/2's wife and daughter who also spent WW II in a Nazi concentration camp. (We have given the OSI a copy of a Gestapo "wanted" poster issued in 1941 for the capture of P/2.) . . . There is a strong likelihood that the Poles and possibly the Soviets will publicize such a request and thus try to link P/2—an old nemesis—to war crimes, knowing, as they would, the significance that the request had come from OSI. This not only would damage our Ukrainian program, but would personally tarnish P/2, who is 78 and has served us for nearly 40 years. Also, if we fail to protect P/2 from inquiries [by] the Poles, there would be a strong reaction from the Ukrainian (indeed, probably the entire East European) émigré community, with whom we work closely, particularly if the Poles publicize the case. We do believe that there is some risk that our attempt to block an inquiry [by] the Poles could become public through a leak in the Justice Department. This could bring about a difficult issue for us—not quite Klaus Barbie, but in that category—but we still recommend that we request Justice refrain from contacting any bloc country with regard to its investigation of P/2.[520]

As the Cold War came to an end, the administration of George H. W. Bush ended the funding of the QRPLUMB project, which was terminated on 30 September 1990. *Suchasnist'* was transferred to Kyiv in January 1992 and lost its institutional affiliation with the zpUHVR circle.[521] The OSI continued to take an interest in Lebed' until the end of his life. On 4 October 1991, the OSI informed the CIA that they intended "to initiate inquiries with the governments of Germany, Poland and the USSR re P/2's [Lebed's] activities during World War II."[522] Yet, following the termination

---

520 "Reestr stattei z presy v spravi M. Lebedia na 3 kvitnia 1986," and "Reestr stattei z presy v spravi M. Lebedia na 10 chervnia 1986," URIA-HURI, Lebed Papers, box 1.
521 Sign. [redacted], C/PPS, "FY-88 Approval of Operational Activity—QRPLUMB," 11 December 1987, p. 6, QRPLUMB, NARA, RG 263, entry ZZ-19, box 59, vol. 4; Sign [Redacted] C/PPS, 14 November 1988, "FY-89 Approval of Operational Activity—QRPLUMB," p. 11, ibid.
522 [Redacted] "Memorandum for Deputy Director for Operations from Chief, Political and Psychological Staff. SUBJECT: Department of Justice Investiga-

of the QRPLUMB program, the CIA's internal documentation suggests that the Agency treated the allegations rather dismissively. As one report noted, "Other than a few allegations, possibly politically motivated by hostile Ukrainian émigré informants, OSI has not pursued the case since 1985 . . . [Lebed] is now 78 years old and in poor health. Aside from potential security considerations (possible exposure of CIA support of the QRPLUMB project for 43 years) there is also the human factor to be considered."[523] When Congresswoman Elizabeth Holtzman (D-NY) (b. 1941) in 1992 requested access to the CIA's files on Lebed', the CIA replied that "no records have been found on Lebed."[524] This point-blank denial continued until Lebed's death.[525]

Lebed's final years were darkened by illness. He suffered from Alzheimer's disease and died peacefully in his bed in Pittsburgh, on 18 July 1998 at the age of 89.[526] He faced no legal consequences for his wartime activities. During a tense period of the Cold War, when alleged war criminals without Lebed's connections were fully investigated and sometimes denaturalized, Lebed's case stands out. To a Ukrainian émigré community heavily vested in an airbrushed and highly ideological version of the recent past, the stakes were high; if Lebed' fell, so would their entire wartime narrative. To the CIA, it would have risked exposure of one of their most long-running covert action programs, which Lebed'—a terrorist and convicted murderer—ran for more than a quarter century. While significant CIA materials on Lebed' remain inaccessible, materials available from Polish, German,

---

tion of QRPLUMB/2," 6 January 1987, Lebed Name File, NARA, RG 263, entry ZZ-18, box 80, folder 2 of 2.
523 Kamins'kyi, *Proloh*, 149.
524 [redacted] "Memorandum for the Record. Subject: Justice Department Interest in QRPLUMB/2," 31 October 1991. Lebed Name File, NARA, RG 263, entry ZZ-18, box 80, folder 2 of 2.
525 [redacted] "Memorandum for the Record"
526 W. O. Studeman to Elizabeth Holtzman, 10 August 1992, Lebed Name File, NARA, RG 263, entry ZZ-18, box 80, folder 2 of 2. The CIA claims notwithstanding, Mykola Lebed's CIA name file, released in 2005, contains several hundred pages, the files for AERODYNAMIC and successor programs, constitute well over fifty boxes, with several hundred pages of material in each box.

Ukrainian, American, and Russian archives support historian Jeffrey Burds's (1958-2024) characterization of Lebed' as "a major war criminal, perhaps the highest ranking Nazi murderer ever to arrive in America."[527] Conason's investigative journalism in 1986 was no minor feat at a time when historians were only beginning to understand the complex and violent past of the OUN and UPA. If one objection was to be raised, it is that Conason's heavy focus on Lebed's collaboration with Nazi Germany distracted attention from the atrocities carried by the OUN(b) during Lebed's tenure as acting leader of that organization. The OUN(b) and UPA massacres of tens of thousands of Poles, and thousands of Jews, and the SB OUN(b)'s political violence against political rivals inside Ukraine and in the American and British occupation zones in the immediate postwar years greatly eclipse the atrocities committed in the Zakopane school.

CIA loyalty to a long-term employee and valuable asset resulted in Lebed receiving preferential treatment that other, less prominent alleged war criminals, did not enjoy. Lebed's central role as a CIA operative provided him a platform from which his circle launched a counter-initiative, rallying the politically active segments of his community to his defense. Having taken little, if any, interest in Lebed's past in the Zakopane training camp when he first arrived in the United States, the CIA, in 1986, accepted, at face value, Lebed's own claims of having attended the Zakopane training school for several weeks without knowledge of its sponsors.[528] Available documentation strongly suggests the CIA intervened for their long-term operative, partly as a reward for his long and faithful service to the Agency, but also because a community of interest formed over the decades: an inquiry into Lebed's criminal and terrorist past would also incriminate the

---

527 In 1996, however, both the CIC and CIA began releasing files to Jeffrey Burds, confirming that Lebed' had a CIA relationship. The same year, Harry Rositzke (1911–2002), who was in charge of running agents against the Soviet Union and Eastern Europe out of Munich between 1952–1954, confirmed to Burds that Lebed' had worked with him in the CIA. These developments took place simultaneously as the CIA continued its official denial. Burds, *The Early Cold War*, 17, 56–57.
528 Kamins'kyi, *Proloh*, 148.

CIA. Émigré nationalist politics, clandestinely funded by the CIA, not only delayed inquiry into Mykola Lebed's past until after his death; it hampered our understanding of the role of Ukrainian nationalists during World War II generally.

5. The Cult of Roman Shukhevych in Ukraine
Myth Making with Complications*

On October 12, 2007, in order to mark the 65th anniversary of the founding of the *Ukrains'ka Povstans'ka Armiia* [UPA; Ukrainian Insurgent Army] and the centennial of the birth of its commander, Roman Shukhevych, Ukrainian president Viktor Yushchenko posthumously awarded Shukhevych the highest honor of the Ukrainian state—the order of Hero of Ukraine, 'in recognition of his special contributions to the national liberation struggle for the freedom and independence of Ukraine.'[529]

Yushchenko's designation of Shukhevych as a national hero was intended as a state endorsement of the organizations he led; in addition to commanding the UPA Shukhevych was the *de facto* leader of the Bandera wing of the OUN; during most of 1943 and 1944. The president stated that his recognition of the insurgents was necessitated by the 'importance of establishing the historical truth about the activities of the UPA,'[530] identifying its two enemies as Nazism and Communist terror.

---

* A previous version of this chapter appeared in a special issue edited by Matthew Kott and Tomislav Dulić, in *Fascism: Journal of Comparative Fascist Studies* vol. 5, no. 1 (2016): 26–65. See Matthew Kott and Tomislav Dulić, "Guest Editors' Note," *Fascism: Journal of Comparative Fascist Studies*, vol. 5, no. 1 (2016): 1-2.

529 Viktor Yushchenko, "Ukaz prezydenta Ukrainy No. 965/2007 pro prysvoennia R. Shukhevvychu zvannia Heroi Ukrainy," *President of Ukraine: Official Website*, October 12, 2007, accessed February 22, 2008, http://www.president. gov.ua/documents/6808.html. In August, 2011, under Yanukovych's administration, the title was revoked by the Supreme Administrative Court of Ukraine, due to a technicality. As the title 'Hero of Ukraine' can only be bestowed to citizens of Ukraine, the conferring of these titles, posthumously, on Shukhevych and Bandera were ruled invalid. "Higher Administrative Court rules Shukhevych's Hero of Ukraine title illegal," *Kyiv Post*, August 2, 2011, accessed April 6, 2016, http://www.kyivpost.com/article/content/ukraine/higher-administrative-court-rules-shukhevychs-hero-109922.html

530 "Yushchenko doruchav Tymoshenko vyznaty UPA," *Ukrains'ka Pravda*, October 14, 2007, accessed November 18, 2007, http://www.pravda.com.ua/news/2007/10/14/65361.htm.

Roman Shukhevych remains a highly controversial and divisive person in Ukrainian history. A freedom fighter and martyr for Ukraine to some, a Nazi collaborator to others. Yushchenko's decision exposed the divided and polarized historical memory in post-Soviet Ukraine. Brought to power in a wave of popular protest against a corrupt government's falsification of elections, Yushchenko's own term in office, from 2005 to 2010, was marred by inefficiency, infighting, and an inability to address the pressing concerns about misrule, endemic corruption, and abuse of power that had fueled the wave of popular protest that brought him to power. Under Yushchenko, Ukraine remained one of the most poorly governed states in Europe.[531] Pressing concerns such as corruption, social cohesion, and economic performance largely went unaddressed. Yushchenko, however, left a more discernible legacy in regards to politics of memory, some of it highly controversial, such as the decision to rehabilitate the legacy of Ukrainian radical nationalism of the 1930s and '40s.

Shukhevych was not the first radical nationalist to be reassessed by Yushchenko; in May, 2007 he issued a presidential edict to honor the memory of Yaroslav Stets'ko, who led the OUN(b) from 1968 to 1986, and his wife Yaroslava Stets'ko (b. Hanna-Evhennia Muzyka, 1920–2003), who eventually succeeded her husband as leader of the OUN(b) in 1991–2003.[532] The couple were glorified in mass media; streets, squares, and buildings were renamed after them, a museum in their honor was to be established

---

531 Andrew Wilson, "Ukrainian Politics since Independence," in *Ukraine and Russia: People, Politics, Propaganda and Perspectives*, ed. Agnieszka Pikulicka-Wilczewski and Richard Sakwa (Bristol: E-International Relations Publishing, 2015), 103.

532 There is no academic biography on Yaroslav Stets'ko, self-proclaimed OUN(b) "Prime Minister" of Ukraine on June 30, 1941. A two-volume collection of his essays was posthumously published by the OUN(b). Yaroslav Stets'ko, *Ukrains'ka vyzvol'na kontseptsiia: Tvory, chastyna* 1 (Munich: Orhanizatsiia ukrains'kykh natsionalistv, 1987); and Yaroslav Stets'ko, *Ukrains'ka vyzvol'na kontseptsiia: Tvory, chastyna* 2 (Munich: Orhanizatsiia ukrains'kykh natsionalistv, 1991). Scholarly works on Stets'ko's politics include Karel C. Berkhoff and Marco Carynnyk, "The Organization of Ukrainian Nationalists and Its Attitude towards Germans and Jews: Iaroslav Stets'ko's 1941 Zhyttiepys," *Harvard Ukrainian Studies* 23, no. 3/4 (1999) 149–184; Carynnyk, "'A Knife in the Back of Our Revolution'."

in Kyiv.[533] After losing the first round of the 2010 presidential elections, Yushchenko in January, 2010 posthumously elevated OUN(b) leader Stepan Bandera to a national "Hero of Ukraine," triggering an intense de- bate on the legacy of the OUN.[534] The "Bandera debate" took place at a dramatic junction in Ukrainian politics, as Yushchenko did not make it to the second round of the elections, and Ukrainians elected Viktor Yanukovych and his Party of Regions to lead the country.[535] As it is the name and person of Bandera, rather than Shukhevych that has come to be most intimately linked with Ukrainian radical nationalism, the "Bandera debate" eventually came to eclipse the controversy surrounding the elevation of Shukhevych to national hero. At the time, however, this was a major symbolic event which polarized public opinion and sharply divided supporters and opponents of the decision, and, unlike previous controversial choices became a matter of international attention and protests.

The award ceremony for Shukhevych was preceded by a march of UPA veterans through Kyiv. Shukhevych's son Yurii, the leader of the far-right paramilitary organization UNA-UNSO,

---

533 Viktor Yushchenko, "Ukaz prezydenta Ukrainy No. 416/2007 Pro vshanuvannia pam'iati Yaroslava Stets'ka i Yaroslavy Stets'ko," *President of Ukraine: Official Website*, accessed April 10, 2008, http://www.president.gov.ua/documents/6145.html

534 On Stepan Bandera, see Rossoliński-Liebe, *Stepan Bandera*. On the discussion, see Tarik Syril [Cyril] Amar, Ihor Balyns'kyi, and Yaroslav Hrytsak, ed., *Strasti za Banderuiu: statti ta esei* (Kyiv: Hrani-T, 2010); Rossoliński-Liebe, *Stepan Bandera*, 459–530; Eleonora Narvselius, "The 'Bandera Debate': The Contentious Legacy of World War II and Liberalization of Collective Memory in Western Ukraine," *Canadian Slavonic Papers/Revue canadienne des slavistes* 54, no. 3–4 (2012): 61–83.

535 As one analyst has noted, the ideology of Yanukovych's now-defunct Party of Regions defied Western political science definitions: "unique in the former Soviet space in being launched by a nexus of new oligarchs, old Soviet Red Directors, Pan-Slavic and regional activists, and organized crime figures," it brought together 'oligarchs . . . former Communist Party voters, and uph[e]ld Soviet ideological tenets, such as state paternalism, anti-fascist discourse, and distrust of the West, particularly the us and NATO.' Taras Kuzio, "The Origins of Peace, Non-Violence, and Conflict *in Ukraine*," in *Ukraine and Russia: People, Politics, Propaganda and Perspectives*, ed. Agnieszka Pikulicka-Wilczewski and Richard Sakwa (Bristol: E-International Relations Publishing, 2015), 111.

accepted the medal on his father's behalf.[536] Uniformed members of this, and other radical right-wing groups, dressed in brown shirts and black ties joined the UPA veterans. Far from becoming a dignified, solemn manifestation of a nation united behind the late UPA commander, the march degenerated into street brawls between octogenarian veterans of the Red Army and UPA, as well as between radical nationalists and protesters from the communist and progressive socialist parties.[537] The small Ukrainian Jewish community was outraged.[538]

Speaking to a meeting of UPA veterans, Yushchenko stated that "The memory of each hero and every victim of the struggle for Ukraine's liberation, freedom, and independence is sacred and indivisible. Let us not avoid any difficult pages of our history and in such a way let us restore the truth which is based on the Ukrainian nation's great exploits—the exploits of the people who defeated death and established their state."[539]

Against this backdrop, the credibility of Yushchenko's words about the establishment of historical 'truth' and an indivisible

---

[536] On UNA-UNSO, see Andreas Umland and Anton Shekhovtsov, "Ultraright Party Politics in Post-Soviet Ukraine and the Puzzle of the Electoral Marginalism of Ukrainian Ultranationalists in 1994–2009," *Russian Politics and Law* 51, no.5 (2013): 33–38; on Shukhevych's role in UNA-UNSO, see Rudling, "Anti-Semitism and the Extreme Right in Contemporary Ukraine," 189–206.

[537] Pavel Korduban, "Leftist, Pro-Russian Extremists defy Yushchenko over History," *Eurasia Daily Monitor* 4, no. 197 (October 24, 2007), accessed January 17, 2008, http://www.jamestown.org/edm/article.php/?article_id=2372530. Despite its name, Natalia Vitrenko's (b. 1951) Progressive Socialist Party could rather be placed on the far right, ideologically, being affiliated with the Lyndon LaRouche movement. On the Ukrainian Communist and Progressive Socialist parties, see Volodymyr Ishchenko, "The Ukrainian Left During and After the Maidan Protests: Study requested by Die Linke delegation in the GUE/NGL," (GUE/NGL, 2015), 13–17, accessed April 5, 2016, https://www.academia.edu/20445056/The_Ukrainian_Left_during_and_after_the_Maidan_Protests.

[538] Wadim Rabinowitsch, Jan Tabatschnik and Aleksandr Feldman, "Jüdischer Protest in der Ukraine," *Kontakte-Kontakty: Verein für Kontakte zu Ländern der ehemaligen Sowjetunion*, October 15, 2007, accessed April 10, 2008, http://www.kontakte-kontakty.de/deutsch/verein/2005-2009/upa.php.

[539] "President speaks to UPA veterans," *Press Office of President Victor Yushchenko*, October 14, 2007, accessed April 10, 2008, www.president.gov.ua/done_img/b/7/7836.jpg. On the discussions surrounding the event, see Ostriitchouk, *Les Ukrainiens face à leur passé*, 343–345.

national memory was limited among many Ukrainians. Rather than promoting national reconciliation, the government's attempts to turn Shukhevych into a national hero opened up old wounds and exposed deep divisions in Ukrainian society—between the right and left, east and west, and between Ukrainian nationalists and representatives of the Jewish community.[540]

Given Yushchenko's expressed ambition of orienting Ukraine towards membership in the European Union and NATO, his designation of ultranationalist collaborators with Nazi Germany as national heroes paradoxically put some of his interpretations of history more at odds with the European mainstream than even Yanukovych and his pro-Russian electorate in the east.[541]

As Yushchenko and the western parts of Ukraine celebrated the centennial of Shukhevych's birth, the Kharkiv City Assembly, dominated by Yanukovych's Party of Regions, called on the public to stop glorifying the memories of OUN and UPA.[542] The Party of Regions described Shukhevych's award as an endorsement of integral nationalism and as an attack on the peoples of eastern Ukraine: "the population of the non-western areas of Ukraine feel an ever stronger ideological pressure from the brand of Banderite

---

[540] There is a consensus among sociologists and political scientists who study Ukraine's regions that regional differences do exist and are important. Whereas the east/west dynamic is real, these divisions are, however, complex, with sub-regions within regions. See, for instance, Yitzhak M. Brudny and Evgeny Finkel, "Why Ukraine is not Russia: Hegemonic National Identity and Democratization in Russia and Ukraine," *East European Politics and Societies* 25, no. 4 (2011): 813–833; Sebastian Klüsener, "Die Regionen der Ukraine: Abgrenzung und Charakterisierung," *Ukraine-Analysen* 23 (2007): 2–11; Katchanovski, *Cleft Countries*; Karina V. Korostelina, 'Mapping National Identity Narratives in Ukraine,' *Nationalities Papers* 41, no. 2 (2013): 293–315.
[541] Andreas Umland, "Die andere Anomalie der Ukraine: ein Parlament ohne rechtradikale Fraktionen," *Ukraine-Analysen* 41 (2008): 6–11, accessed May 1, 2009, http://www.laender-analysen.de/ukraine/pdf/UkraineAnalysen41.pdf.
[542] Wilfried Jilge, "Competing Victimhoods: Post-Soviet Ukrainian Narratives on World War II," in *Shared History – Divided Memory: Jews and Others in Soviet-Occupied Poland, 1939-1941*, ed. Elazar Barkan, Elizabeth A. Cole and Kai Struve (Leipzig: Leipziger Universitätsverlag, 2008), 125, fn. 98.

Nazism and xenophobia."[543] In the *Verkhovna Rada*, Ukrainian Communist Party leader Petro Symonenko (b. 1952), an ally of Ianukovych, protested "the raising to sainthood today of one who received two Iron Crosses from the hands of Hitler with his order to celebrate his 100th anniversary at an official level."[544] Another high-profile communist, Oleksandr Holub, condemned the move as part of "the president's attempts to impose pro-fascist, neo-Nazi policy on society."[545] After Ukrainian-Canadian political scientist Petro Potichnyj (b. 1930), a former child soldier of the UPA and a leading authority on the history of his movement, refuted Symonenko's claims,[546] the president of the Ukrainian World Congress responded by suing Symonenko for libel.[547]

OUN and UPA

Yushchenko's ambition of building national myths around the OUN was controversial. Founded in 1929, the OUN was the largest and most important Ukrainian far-right organization. Explicitly totalitarian, the movement embraced the *Führerprinzip*, a cult of political violence, racism, and an aggressive anti-Semitism.[548] It sought the establishment of Ukrainian statehood at any price, and utilized political murder as legitimate means to this end. A typical fascist movement, the OUN cultivated close relations with Fascist

---

543 Georgii Gerashchenko, "Koe-chto o 'zabyvchivosti' v panegirikakh Romanu Shukhevych," *Vremia Regionov Kharkovshchiny* 27, no. 74 (2007), accessed May 18, 2008, http://pr.kharkov.ua/full.php?g=newspaper&id=1275.
544 Zenon Zawada, "UWC president set to sue Communists over defamation of Roman Shukhevych," *The Ukrainian Weekly*, August 26, 2007, accessed November 18, 2007, http:// www.ukrweekly.com/Archive/2007/340703.shtml.
545 Korduban, "Leftist, Pro-Russian Extremists."
546 Zawada, "UWC president." While Shukhevych did not himself earn an Iron Cross, Shukhevych's comrade, *Nachtigall* soldier Yurii Lopatyns'kyi (1906-1982) received the Iron Cross of the second class. Andrii Bolianovs'kyi, *Ukrains'ki viis'kovi formuvannia v zbroinykh sylakh Nimechchyny (1939-1945)* (L'viv: L'vivs'kyi Natsional'nyi Universytet im. Ivana Franka and Canadian Institute of Ukrainian Studies, 2003), 71. Petro J. Potichnyj, personal correspondence, May 24, 2008.
547 Zawada, "UWC president"
548 Bruder, *"Den ukrainischen Staat erkämpfen oder sterben!"*; Rossoliński-Liebe, *Stepan Bandera;* and Myroslav Shkandrij, *Ukrainian Nationalism: Politics, Ideology, and Literature, 1929-1956* (New Haven, CT: Yale University Press, 2015).

Italy, Nazi Germany, the Spanish *Falange*, and the Croatian *Ustaše*.[549] Following the 1938 assassination by the Soviet NKVD of its founding leader or *vozhd'*,[550] Evhen Konovalets', the movement split in 1940, as his successor, his brother-in-law, Colonel Andrii Mel'nyk, was soon challenged by a faction of younger, more radical nationalists led by Stepan Bandera. The two wings, known as the OUN(m) and OUN(b), both courted Nazi Germany, hoping to enlist support for Ukrainian statehood in the form of a Nazi client state of the Slovak or Croatian model.[551] Certain circles in the Nazi leadership, particularly within the *Abwehr* — Germany's military intelligence agency — and Alfred Rosenberg's (1893-1946) office indicated some sympathy for the aspirations of the oun. Hitler's war aims, however, did not include vassal states in formerly Soviet territories, and Germany rejected the OUN(b)'s invitations for an alliance with the Ukrainian state, hastily declared by Bandera's deputy Stets'ko in L'viv on June 30, 1941, in the wake of Barbarossa.

---

[549] For a discussion on the OUN's ideology, see Umland, "Der ukrainische Nationalismus zwischen Stereotyp und Wirklichkeit"; Andreas Umland, "Challenges and promises of comparative research into post-Soviet fascism. Whereas the characterization of the OUN at this time as fascist is accepted by a growing number of historians in the field, Oleksandr Zaitsev has attempted to revive a historical dichotomy between 'integral nationalism' and 'fascism', introducing the term "Ustashism" to categorize OUN ideology. Oleksandr Zaitsev, "Fascism or Ustashism? Ukrainian Integral Nationalism in Comparative Perspective, 1920s-1930s," *Communist and Post-Communist Studies* 48, no. 2-3 (2015): 183-193.

[550] *Vozhd'*, Leader, was the term used to refer to Konovalets'. After the 1940 split the term was used primarily by the OUN(m) to refer to their leader, whereas the OUN(b) referred to theirs as the *Providnyk*. Rossoliński-Liebe, *Stepan Bandera*, 180, 548-549.

[551] Melnyk assured, in a May 2, 1939 letter to Joachim von Ribbentrop that his organization shared the *Weltanschaaung* of the National Socialists and Fascists, and offered to help in the 'reorganization' of Eastern Europe. Politisches Archiv des Auswärtigen Amtes, PA AA, R 104430, Po. 26, No. 1m, Pol.V. 4784, p. 2. Thanks to Ray Brandon for this reference. Stets'ko's June 30, 1941, declaration of Ukrainian statehood included a statement that the new polity would 'cooperate closely with National Socialist Greater Germany under the Führer Adolf Hitler.' Stets'ko assured Hitler, Mussolini, Franco and Pavelić the loyalty of his state to the new Europe. Serhiichuk, ed., *OUN-UPA v roky viiny*, 239; Rossoliński-Liebe, 'The "Ukrainian National Revolution" of 1941,"99.

Who was Roman Shukhevych?

Like Stepan Bandera, Roman Shukhevych's person is associated with a number of myths and legends. Shukhevych became active in nationalist radicalism as an adolescent. As a teenager he was already involved in assassination plots against Polish officials in response to the assimilatory policies of the Polish government. He committed his first political murder, that of the Lwów school curator Stanisław Sobiński (1872-1926), at the age of nineteen in 1926.[552] In 1934, Shukhevych, along with Lebed' and Bandera, was arrested for his involvement Pieracki murder, and spent two and a half years in prison, where he was allegedly tortured by the Polish authorities.[553] Throughout the 1930s, the OUN stepped up its campaign of political terrorism against the Polish state, assassinating Polish politicians and political opponents.[554] At least sixty-three persons were murdered by the OUN in interwar Poland.[555] The Polish authorities responded with a campaign of "pacification" against the OUN, including raids in 494 villages in eastern Galicia.[556]

In January, 1938, Shukhevych crossed the border from Poland to Carpathian Ukraine in Czechoslovakia, which, according to his son Yurii became his new political base. From there, he often traveled on missions to Prague, Vienna, Berlin, and illegally across the border to Lwów in Poland.[557] In the spring and summer

---

552 Rossoliński-Liebe, "Erinnerungslücke Holocaust," 421.
553 P. Sokhan and P. Potichnyi, ed., *Litopys' UPA. Nova seriia, tom 10: Zhyttia i borot'ba henerala 'Tarasa Chuprynky (1907-1950): Dokumenty i materialy* (Kyiv and Toronto: Litopys UPA, 2007), 16-17; Vasyl' Kuk, *Heneral-khorunzhyi Roman Shukhevych: Holovnyi komandyr Ukrainskoi povstans'koi armii, vydannia druhe, dopovnene* (L'viv: Tsentr dolidzhen' vyzvol'noho rukhu, 2007), 22.
554 Kulińska, *Działalność terrorystyczna i sabotażowa nacjonalistycznych organizacji ukraińskich*, 207-302; Alexander J. Motyl, "Ukrainian nationalist political violence in inter-war Poland, 1921-1939," *East European Quarterly* 19, no. 1 (1985): 50.
555 Motyka, *Ukraińska partyzantka 1942-1960*, 34-74.
556 Timothy Snyder, *Sketches from a Secret War: A Polish Artist's Mission to Liberate Soviet Ukraine* (New Haven, NJ: Yale University Press, 2005), 76.
557 Yurii Shukhevych, 'Komandyr bezimennykh,' *Ukraina moloda: shchodenna informatsiino-politychna hazeta*, June 24, 2007, accessed December 5, 2007, http://www.umoloda.kiev.ua/print/84/45/34292/.

of that year, according to some sources, he was educated as an officer at a German Military Academy in Munich.[558] From May to September, 1940, Shukhevych joined Mykola Lebed' and over 120 other Ukrainian nationalists for training at a secret Abwehr espionage school in Zakopane, which by then was German-occupied Poland.[559]

After the OUN split, Shukhevych belonged to the inner circle of its leader- ship around Stepan Bandera, and played a key role in organizing the *II Velykyi Zbir* [Second Congress] of the Bandera Wing of the OUN, held in Krakow in April, 1941.[560] He was one of the authors of the OUN(b) blueprint for action for 1941, *Borot'ba i diialnist' OUN(b) pid chas viiny* [Struggle and Activities of the OUN(b) at Times of War], outlining the establishment of a totalitarian state through the indiscriminate use of violence, urging the removal of all "non- Ukrainians" living on Ukrainian territory and the liquidation of "Polish, Muscovite, and Jewish activists."[561]

Prior to the invasion of the Soviet Union, German military intelligence set up two small Ukrainian formations: *Sonderformation Nachtigall*, and *Organisation* Roland. Formed in Krakow on March,

---

558 Alexandr Feldman, "Thirty Years After the Death of Roman Shukhevych," *Contact* 2-3 (1980): 77; Mykola Posivnych, "Roman Shukhevych (30.vi.1907–5.iii.1950)," in *Litopys Ukrains'koï Povstans'koi Armii. Tom 45: Heneral Roman Shukhevych – 'Taras Chuprynka' Holovnyi Komandyr UPA*, ed. Petro J. Potichnyj and Mykola Posivnych (Toronto and L'viv: Vydavnytstvo Litopys UPA, 2007), 28; Anatolii Kentii and Volodymyr Lozyts'kyi, "From UVO fighter to Supreme Commander of the UPA," *Litopys UPA. Nova seria, Tom 10: Zhyttia i borot'ba henerala 'Tarasa Chuprynky' (1907–1950): Dokumenty i materialy*, ed. P. Sokhan' and P. Potichnyj (Kyiv and Toronto: Litopys UPA, 2007), 86. What is probably meant is *Abwehr* training at the Munich *Kriegsschule*.

559 "Protokol doprosa osuzhdennogo bizantsa Al'freda Ioganovicha ot 23 noiabria 1949 goda," HDA SBU f. 65, spr. S-7448, ark. 15–22, published in Serhiichuk, ed., *Roman Shukhevych u dokumentakh, Tom II*, 383; Berkhoff, *Harvest of Despair*, 289, 298. On the Zakopane training camp, see Burds, *The Early Cold War*, 68.

560 Petro Duzhyi, *Roman Shukhevych – polityk, voin, hromadianyn* (L'viv: Halyts'ka vydavnycha spilka, 1998), 57–60.

561 "Borot'ba i diial'nist' OUN pid chas viiny," Tsentral'nyi Derzhavnyi Arkhiv Vyshchykh Orhaniv Vlady ta Upravlinnia Ukrainy (hereafter TsDAVOVU), f. 3833, op. 2, spr. 1, ark. 77–89; Ivan Patryliak, *Viis'kova diial'nist' OUN(b) u 1940–1942 rokakh* (Kyiv: nan Ukrainy, 2004), 128, citing TsDAVOVU, f. 3833, op. 2, spr. 1; TsDAVOVU f. 3833, op. 1, spr. 9, ark. 1.

2, 1941, the *Nachtigall* battalion consisted mostly of Ukrainian Nationalists. Established for the purpose of the immanent attack on the Soviet Union, its members received their training at Neuhammer, Silesia. Its volunteers bore German uniforms and weapons, and were attached to the 1st Battalion of the Regiment Brandenburg-800.[562] Shukhevych not only became the highest-ranking Ukrainian officer in the *Nachtigall* battalion; he also enjoyed the greatest standing among its Ukrainian members.

In the field, *Nachtigall* was a mixed unit with three companies, each made up of one German platoon and two Ukrainian platoons. A fourth company appears to have been employed in small groups elsewhere. All Ukrainian officers had German doubles, in the case of Shukhevych, it was Theodore Oberländer (1905-1998).[563] Shukhevych, as the ranking Ukrainian, probably conveyed battalion orders to the Ukrainian men of the unit. He received the orders from Hans-Albrecht Herzner (1907- 1942), *Nachtigall's* military commander. Herzner, in turn, took his orders from the leadership of the First Battalion of Regiment 800. When the unit was rounded out with Herzner and the German platoons, Oberländer served as liaison between *Nachtigall* and Regiment 800 on one hand, and between *Nachtigall* and Abwehr-II Headquarters in Kraków (before the invasion) and the military intelligence department of Army Group South (following the invasion).

Shukhevych's role was that of a courier of orders and a company commander. He was an efficient, but harsh officer, who did not hesitate to use physical violence against his own men.[564]

---

562 Bolianovs'kyi, *Ukrains'ki viis'kovi formuvannia*, 66, 571. The Ukrainian nationalist historiography usually refers to *Roland* and *Nachtigall* as the *Druzhyny Ukrains'kykh Natsionalistiv* [DUN; Units of Ukrainian Nationalists], to give the impression that they constituted autonomous units. Bruder, *"Den ukrainischen Staat erkämpfen oder sterben!"*, 130-132

563 Philipp-Christian Wachs, *Der Fall Theodor Oberländer (1909–1998): Ein Lehrstück deutscher Geschichte* (Frankfurt: Campus-Verlag, 2000), 55–71.

564 Nachtigall member Viktor Kharkiv, pseud. "Khmara" (1918-1988) described in 1948 the physical abuse at the hands of Shukhevych he was subjected to after having gone to the barber without Shukhevych's explicit permission. "He attacked me on the spot, asked me how I could have managed to get out, despite the curfew regarding leaving the sealed-off area around the casern. I began explaining that I had only been to the barber. Captain Shukhevych did

Nachtigall participated in the invasion of the Soviet Union in June, 1941, and took part in the capture of L'viv, Zolochiv, Ternopil' and Vinnytsia.[565]

Before retreating from the advancing German forces, the NKVD massacred many of the inmates it held in prisons across western Ukraine.[566] Among the thousands of people murdered was Shukhevych's brother.[567] The NKVD murders radicalized local sentiment, and was instrumentalized by the German forces and local nationalists to incite violent anti-Jewish pogroms. Roman Shukhevych personally helped set up the Ukrainian nationalist militia, which played a key role in the L'viv pogrom.[568] Soldiers of *Nachtigall* partook in the July 1, 1941 L'viv pogrom as well as massacres of Jews in the vicinity of Vinnytsia.[569] The German re-

---

not listen to that and punched me in the face." TsDAVOVU, f. 3833, op. 1, spr. 57, ark. 18.

565 According to the protocols of the 1949 interrogation of Alfred Bizanz, the marching route of the unit was L'viv–Ternopil'–Proskurov–Vinnytsia. "Protokol doprosa osuzhdennogo Bizantsa Al'freda Ioganovicha ot 23 noiabria 1949 goda," HDA SBU f. 65, spr. S-7448, ark. 15–22, published in Serhiichuk, *Roman Shukhevych u dokumentakh radians'kykh orhaniv derzhavnoi bezpeky (1940–1950). Tom II*, 385; "With the military detachment I went through an entire campaign during the first weeks of the war along the line Radyme-Yavoriv-L'viv-Proskuriv-Brailiv-Vinnytsia," wrote Ivan Hryn'okh (1907–1994), *Nachtigall's* military chaplain. Andrii Bolianovs'kyi, "Ivan Hryn'okh—providnyi diiach ukrains'koho pidpillia," in *Boh i Ukraina ponad use*: o. Ivan Hryn'okh, ed. Oleksandr Panchenko (Hadiach: Vydavnytstvo 'Hadiach', 2007), 64–65, citing Tsentral'nyi Derzhavnyi Istorychnyi Arkhiv m. L'viv (TsDIAL) f. 201, op. 46, spr. 2689, ark. 26–28. See also Petro Sodol', "U rokovyny zahybeli Romana Shukhevycha: Interv'iu z Mykoloiu Lebedem," *Suchasnsist'*, no. 3 (March 1986): 98–104.

566 Marco Carynnyk, "The Palace on the Ikva: Dubne, 18 September 1939 and 24 June 1941," in *Shared History – Divided Memory*: ed. Barkan, Cole, and Struve, 273–302. The most detailed study estimates the victims of Soviet mass shootings in the prisons of East Galicia during the first week of the war at 7,500–10,000. Struve, *Deutsche Herrschaft*, 215–216.

567 Struve, *Deutsche Herrschaft*, 281, 360; Rossoliński-Liebe, "Der Verlauf und die Täter des Lemberger Pogrom," 236; Rossoliński-Liebe, *Stepan Bandera*, 209.

568 Rossoliński-Liebe, "Der Verlauf und die Täter," 223.

569 Struve, *Deutsche Herrschaft*, 354–360, concludes that there are clear indications that members of the *Nachtigall* battalion took part in violence against Jews in all three L'viv prisons on July 1, but adds that they were but one of the perpetrators, and responsible but for a minor part of the anti-Jewish violence carried out that day. On *Nachtigall* and the L'viv pogrom, see also Rossoliński-Liebe, "Der Verlauf und die Täter," 236–237. On the L'viv pogrom, see:

fusal to accept the OUN(b)'s proclamation of Ukrainian independence led to a conflict with the leadership of the *Nachtigall* battalion. On August 13, 1941, it was disarmed and ordered to return from Vinnytsia to Neuhammer in Silesia, from which its members were transported to Frankfurt an der Oder.

Shukhevych in Belarus

On October 21, 1941, the soldiers were reorganized as the 201st Ukrainian *Schutzmannschaft* Battalion, consisting of four companies. Shukhevych's rank was that of *Hauptmann* (captain) of the first company and deputy commander of the Legion.[570] Even

---

Struve, *Deutsche Herrschaft*, 247–432; Himka, "The Lviv Pogrom of 1941"; Amar, *The Paradox of Ukrainian Lviv*, 93–101; Sergei Chuev, *Ukrainskii Legion* (Moscow: Iauza, 2006), 180; Frank Golczewski, "Die Kollaboration in der Ukraine," *Beiträge zur Geschichte des Nationalsozialismus* 19 (2003): 162; Christoph Mick, "Ethnische Gewalt und Pogrome in Lemberg 1914 und 1941," *Osteuropa* 53 (2003): 1810–1811, 1824–1829; Hannes Heer, "Einübung in den Holocaust: Lemberg Juni/Juli 1941," *Zeitschrift für Geschichtswissenschaft* 49 (2001): 409-427, here: 410, 424; Bruder, "*Den ukrainischen Staat erkämpfen oder sterben!*", 140–150; Frank Grelka, *Die ukrainische Nationalbewegung unter deutscher Besatzungsherrschaft 1918 und 1941/1942* (Wiesbaden: Harassowitz, 2005), 276–286; Dieter Pohl, *Nationalsozialistische Judenverfolgung in Ostgalizien 1941–1944: Organization und Durchführung eines staatlichen Massenverbrechens*. 2. Aufl. (München: Oldenbourg, 1997), 60–62; Wachs, *Der Fall Theodor Oberländer*, 71, 78–80; Eliyahu Yones, *Die Straße nach Lemberg: Zwangsarbeit und Widerstand in Ostgalizien 1941–1944* (Frankfurt am Main: Fischer Taschenbuch Verlag, 1999), 18. On the shooting of Jews in the Vinnytsia area, *Nachtigall* member Viktor Kharkiv, pseudo "Khmara" later wrote, "At the time of our march eastwards we saw with our own eyes the victims of the Judeo-Bolshevik terror, and the sight of it so strengthened our hatred of the Jews, that in two villages we shot all the Jews we encountered. I recall one example. At the time of our march through one village we saw many vagrant people. Asked where they were going, they answered that the Jews were threatening them and that they were afraid of spending the night in their houses. As a result of that, we shot all the Jews we encountered there." TsDAVOVU, f. 3833, op.1, spr. 57, ark. 17.

570 Yevhen Pobihushchyi-Ren, *Mozaika moikh spomyniv* (Ivano-Frankiv'sk: Lileiahb, 2002), 62. Pobihushchyi, the former commander of the *Roland* battalion, served as an officer in *Schutzmannschaft* Battalion 201, and became an officer in the *Waffen-SS* Division *Galizien* in 1943. Bolianovs'kyi, *Ukraïns'ki viis'kovi formuvannia*, 60, 143, 360; Rudling, "Szkolenie w mordowaniu." The commanders of the other three companies were Hauptmann Bryhyder, who later continued as an officer in *Waffen-SS Galizien*, Vasylyi Sydor and Volodymyr Pavliuk. Haluzevyi derzhavnyi arkhiv Sluzhba Bezpeky Ukrainy, Kyiv

though enrollment was voluntary, of the three hundred remaining members of the *Nachtigall* unit, only about fifteen declined to sign up for service in the *Schutzmannschaft*.[571] Almost all of its members belonged to the OUN.[572] To the battalion were added sixty Soviet pows from Poltava and Dnipropetrovs'k districts, selected by Shukhevych.[573] After training in Germany, *Schutzmannschaft* Battalion 201 was assigned to Belarus on February 16, 1942. The soldiers signed a one-year contract with the Germans.[574] The men of *Schutzmannschaft* Battalion 201 wore German Order Police field uniforms without national symbols. On March 16, 1942, the battalion arrived in Belarus and was spread out over twelve different points in the triangle Mahileu–Vitsebsk–Lepel', guarding a territory of 2,400 square kilometers.[575]

Soviet post-war investigations into the unit's whereabouts show that the Soviet authorities were particularly interested in any evidence of *Schutzmannschaft* Battalion 201 fighting Soviet partisans. The way the interrogators formulated their questions indicates that the Soviet state security organs were more interested in activities they regard as treason and under- mining of Soviet government, than atrocities against "peaceful Soviet citizens." "Before the battalion was reassigned to Belarus the fascists gave it the name 'Schutzmannschaft Battalion 201,' which carried out

---

(hereafter HDA SBU) f. 5, spr. 67418, t. 1, ark. 208–241, in *Roman Shukhevych u dokumentakh radians'kykh orhaniv derzhavnoi bezpeky (1940–1950). Tom I*, ed. Volodymyr Serhiichuk (Kyiv: PP Serhiichuk M.I., 2007), 529.

571 Parmen Posokhov, "Shukhevych: Beloe piatno v biografii," *Fraza*, August 15, 2007, accessed November 18, 2007, http://fraza.org.ua/zametki/15.08.07/40 788.html?c=post&i=113503. On October 15, 1941, in Neuhammer, Silesia Nachtigall had a total of 288 men. In Vienna, Roland counted 210 men at the time.

572 Chuev, *Ukrainskii legion*, 180; Volodymyr V"iatrovych, "Roman Shukhevych: soldat," *Ukrains'ka Pravda*, May 2, 2008, accessed May 6, 2008, http://www.pravda.com.ua/news/ 2008/4/25/75222.htm; Pobihushchyi-Ren, *Mozaika moikh spomyniv*, 115; Bolianovs'kyi, *Ukrains'ki viis'kovi formuvannia*, 143.

573 Bolianovs'kyi, *Ukrains'ki viis'kovi formuvannia*, 144; Myroslav Kal'ba, ed., *U lavkah druzhynnykiv: Druzhyny Ukrains'kykh Nationalistiv v 1941–1942 rokakh* (Denver: Vyd-ia Druzhyny ukrainsks'kykh nationalistiv, 1953), 91.

574 Posivnych, "Roman Shukhevych," 29.

575 Bolianovs'kyi, *Ukrains'ki viis'kovi formuvannia*, 183.

punitive action against Belarusian partisans,"[576] we read in a statement from 1986 by a former regional leader of the OUN and UPA. Soviet internal records emphasize how, in 1942, "The Konovalets' Legion [i.e., *Nachtigall*] was renamed 'Schutzmannschaft Battalion 201' by the Germans and sent to Belarus, where it partook, along with a German punitive detachment, in the struggle with Soviet partisan detachments, and the protection of German military objects."[577]

Interrogated by the Soviet authorities in November, 1949, Alfred Bisanz (1890–1951),[578] the liaison for Ukrainian matters in Hans Frank's *Generalgouvernement* who retained unofficial contacts with the Ukrainian nationalists throughout the war, recalled Shukhevych having visited his department three times in L'viv during 1942; in February, May, and November. Regarding their May, 1942 meeting, Bisanz stated that "I asked [Shukhevych] about the activities of the Ukrainian battalion at that time. He answered that the battalion takes part in the Germans' punitive operations against Soviet partisans in Belarus. In connection with this, SHUKHEVYCH told me, that his battalion several times got involved in battles against Soviet partisans and had some losses among its men."[579] As the military situation was deteriorating for the Germans over the course of 1942, *Schutzmannschaft* Battalion 201 faced problems of desertions. "In November, 1942, I received SHUKHEVYCH in L'viv in connection with the large number of deserters from the battalion. SHUKHEVYCH said that his battalion

---

576 Statement by former UPA activist and OUN military liaison Luka Pavlyshyn. "Protokol zaiava," Luka Stepanovych Pavlyshyn, (b. 1907), L'viv, Ukrainian SSR, May 13, 1986, p. 3, Yad Vashem Archives (hereafter YVA), Record Group 0.32, file number 112, inventory number 99999, number M.37/111. Thanks to Jeffrey Burds for providing a copy of this document.
577 "Spravka o prestuplennoi deiatel'nosti ukrains'koi emigratsii vo vremia voiny Germanii s SSSR," HDA SBU, f. 13, spr. 372, ch. 35, l. 32.
578 For a biography of Bisanz, see Struve, *Deutsche Herrschaft*, 97.
579 "Protokol doprosa osuzhdennogo Bizantsa Al'freda Ioganovicha ot 23 noiabria 1949 goda," HDA SBU f. 65, spr. S-7448, ark. 15–22, published in Serhiichuk, *Roman Shukhevych u dokumentakh, Tom II*, 388. Many years later Mykola Lebed' recalls having met Shukhevych in L'viv "in mid-1942," during which they discussed the situation. Sodol, "U rokovyny zahybeli Romana Shukhevycha," 99.

was conducting frequent punitive operations not only against Soviet partisans, but also against the civilian population of Belarus."[580]

Current research points to the intimate link between the "anti-partisan warfare" of the German forces and their local auxiliaries, and mass violence against the local population in occupied Belarus. Waitman Beorn's (b. 1977) study on the German military and the Holocaust in Belarus demonstrates a staggering disproportionality between German and "partisan" losses, and notes that the label 'partisan' was a very wide concept, which included various non-combatants: former Red Army soldiers separated from their units during the German advance as well as "suspicious" civilians and unarmed Jewish civilians.[581]

Beorn refers to what he calls "the Jew-Bolshevik-partisan calculus" according to which, "all Jews were Bolsheviks, all Bolsheviks were partisans, and thus, all Jews were also partisans or partisan supporters."[582] This formula, Beorn argues, "is important in explaining the murder of Jews under the guise of anti-partisan war."[583] Thus, this anti-partisan warfare needs to be understood in the context of genocide. "The Holocaust and the anti-partisan war have long remained separated in the historiography, with anti-Jewish actions inhabiting the history of Nazi genocide and the anti-partisan war the military history of the war on the eastern front. This is a false division."[584] Beorn points out that from August to December, 1941, "roughly 30 partisans [were] killed for every German," noting how this "hardly indicate[s] a vibrant and dangerous insurgency."[585]

This contextualization is helpful for assessing the activities of the *Schutzmannschaft* Battalion 201. During its ten-month deploy-

---

580 "Protokol doprosa osuzhdennogo bizantsa Al'freda Ioganovicha ot 23 noiabria 1949 goda," HDA SBU f. 65, spr. S-7448, ark. 15–22, published in Serhiichuk, *Roman Shukhevych u dokumentakh, Tom II*, 388–389.
581 Waitman Wade Beorn, *Marching into Darkness: The Wehrmacht and the Holocaust in Belarus* (Cambridge, MA: Harvard University Press, 2014), 95.
582 Beorn, *Marching into Darkness*, 95.
583 Beorn, *Marching into Darkness*, 95
584 Beorn, *Marching into Darkness*, 118.
585 Beorn, *Marching into Darkness*, 95.

ment in Belarus, the battalion lost forty-nine men, and forty of its members were wounded. At the same time, it killed over two thousand "partisans."[586] Even if all the battalion's losses were due to war deaths, this means a discrepancy in the casualty ratio between *Schutzmannschaft* Battalion 201 and enemy "bandits" of over 1:40.[587] The report of the activities of the battalion for October 30, 1942, by SS-*Obergruppenführer* Erich von dem Bach-Zelewski (1899–1972), the commander of the so-called *Bandenkämpferverbände*, or "bandit-fighting units," appears in a folder of fifteen reports on counterinsurgency activities (titled *Meldungen an den Führer über Bandenbekämpfung*), addressed to *Reichsführer*-SS Heinrich Himmler, who in turn passed them to Adolf Hitler personally.[588] Report number 51, summarized the anti-partisan activities in Russia-South, Ukraine, and the Białystok area from September to November, 1942. Passed to Hitler on December 29, 1942, this report lists a ratio of killed *Schutzmänner* and Germans to "bandits" and "bandit helpers" (excluding the category of "Executed Jews") of over 1:52. If we were to include the 363,211 executed Jews, listed as "suspected bandits," the ratio would be 1:843.[589] The reports for autumn of 1942 for *Russland- Mitte and Gebiet Weissruthenien* similarly report 28,360 enemy losses, but only 381 "own losses," a ratio 1:74.[590] The staggering disproportionality in the number of casualties provides a troubling context in which *Schutzmannschaft* Battalion 201 and other anti-partisan auxiliaries under von dem Bach's command operated in occupied Belarus in late 1942. As the parti-

---

586 I. K. Patryliak, *Viiskova diial'nist OUN(b) u 1940–1942 rokakh* (Kyiv: Kyivs'kyi natsional'nyi universytet im. Tarasa Shevchenko, Instytut istorii Ukrainy NAN Ukrainy, 2004), 386.
587 Rudling, "Szkolenie w mordowaniu," 203.
588 Meldung Nr. 36, "Ergebnisse im Gebiet Russland Mitte. Gefecht des Schutzmannschafts- Batallions 201, 20km nördlich Lepel, Feld-kommandostelle Nov. 3, 1942," Records of the Reich Leader of the ss and Chief of the German Police [Reichsführer-SS und Chef der deutschen Polizei], NARA, Washington, DC, EAP T-175, item 161-b-12/250, reel 124, frame 2599081; and Philip W. Blood, *Hitler's Bandit Hunters: The SS and the Nazi Occupation of Europe* (Washington, DC: Potomac Books, 2006), 90–91.
589 Reichsführer-SS Chef der Deutschen Polizei, Meldungen 35, 36, 37, 38, 40, 41, 42, 45, 46, 47, 48, 49, 51, 55, and 56, issued Nov. 3, 1943 to Jan. 17, 1943: NARA MF-3293, T-175, roll 124.
590 Rudling, "Szkolenie w mordowaniu," 204.

san war escalated in Belarus over the course of that year, the occupiers responded with indiscriminate use of violence against the civilian population, with Baltic and Ukrainian *Schutzmannschaften* being central to implementation of the brutal pacification. The incomplete source base for *Schutzmannschaft* Battalion 201 strongly suggests that this also unit—like other *Schutzmannschaft* battalions—was involved in brutal "anti-partisan" counterinsurgency measures that targeted civilians, equating Jews with partisans. The extreme disproportionality in terms of losses supports Bisanz's testimony that also the 201st battalion, similar to other *Schutzmannschaften* active in Belarus in 1942–43, disproportionally targeted the civilian population.

From *Schutzmannschaften* into the UPA

As the German Sixth Army was getting trapped in Stalingrad, the OUN(b) leadership was forced to reassess the situation, and was slowly abandoning its pro- German orientation, one recent study finds, "at first reluctantly and never completely."[591] "As long as the struggle against the Soviets continued," the OUN-B argued, "our political reason tells us to bide our tine," that is, to avoid confrontation with the Germans.[592] Acting OUN(b) leader Mykola Lebed' opposed taking up armed attacks on German interests, as did Shukhevych.[593] Local initiatives, such as the repeated requests from UPA-North to take up arms against the German forces, were turned down.[594] Yet, many years after the war, Lebed claimed that it was he who, at the end of 1942, suggested that Shukhevych should transfer the entire *Schutzmannschaft* Battalion 201 from Belarus to Polissia and Volhynia to "include it in the struggle

---

591 Tarik Cyril Amar, "A Disturbed Silence: Discourse on the Holocaust in the Soviet West as am Anti-Site of Memory," in *The Holocaust in the East: Local Perpetrators and Soviet Responses*, ed. Michael David-Fox, Peter Holquist and Alexander M. Martin (Pittsburgh: University of Pittsburgh Press, 2014), 169.
592 Amar, "A Disturbed Silence"
593 Interrogation of Mykailo Stepaniak, HDA SBU, f. 6, d.1510.tom 1, ll. 61 and 71–72.
594 Report from Soviet agent "Yaroslav" to the Third Department of Soviet counterintellgence directorate Smersh, Nov. 23, 1944, HDA SBU, f. 13, sbornik 372, tom 5, l. 25.

against the Germans, as well as the Red partisans," to which Shukhevych responded, according to Lebed, that he "would take this into consideration and let me know his decision."[595]

The men of *Schutzmannschaft* Battalion 201 had signed a contract of service until December 31, 1942. However, in late 1942 the German authorities unilaterally extended the term of service indefinitely.[596] When the battalion was ordered back to L'viv in January, 1943, Shukhevych left the unit.[597] In the spring of 1943, the men of the *Schutzmannschaft* Battalion 201, who had crossed over from Belarus to Volhynia came to constitute the hard core of the OUN(b) security service, the *Sluzhba Bezpeki*, or SB.[598] Others stayed and were transferred to the *Waffen-SS Galizien*.[599] The men of *Schutzmannschaft* Battalion 201 who continued their service were transferred to Battalion 57, which was returned to Belarus where it continued with anti-partisan operations and partook in

---

595 Sodol', "U rokovyny zahybeli Romana Shukhevycha," 99. Lebed's post-war accounts of the UPA are highly selective and need to be treated with great caution.
596 Martin C. Dean, "The German Gendarmerie, the Ukrainian Schutzmannschaft and the "Second Wave" of Jewish killings in Occupied Ukraine: German Policing at the Local Level in the Zhitomir Region, 1941-1944,' *German History* 14, no. 2 (1996): 179.
597 According to *Nachtigall* veteran Myrosla Kal'ba (1916-2013) and L'viv OUN(b)-affilated historian Mykola Posivnych (b. 1980), the unit was ordered to L'viv on January 6, and most of its soldiers arrived on January 8. Posivnych, 'Roman Shukhevych,' 29. According to Pobihushchyi, the officers arrived in L'viv on January 5, and the last of its soldiers left Belarus on January 14, 1943. Yevhen [Pobihushchyi]-Ren, "Spohady pro generala Romana Shukhevycha," in *U lavkah druzhynnykiv: Druzhyny Ukrains'kykh Nationalistiv v 1941-1942 rokakh*, ed. Myroslav Kal'ba (n.p: Vyd-ia Druzhyny ukrains'kykh nationalistiv, 1953), 40; Pobihushchyi-Ren, *Mozaika moikh spomyniv*, 85. The details differ in that pro-nationalist accounts often present it as Shukhevych went underground after an arrest warrant against him was issued; in reality, the sequence of events seems to be the reversed, with an arrest warrant being issued after he broke the unilaterally extended contract.
598 Ivan Katchanovski, "The Politics of World War II in Contemporary Ukraine," *The Journal of Slavic Military Studies* 27, no. 2 (2014): 220. Other officers of Schutzmannschaft Battalion 201 became officers in the *Waffen-SS Galizien*. HDA SBU, f. 5, spr. 67418, t. 1, ark. 208-241, in Serhiichuk, *Roman Shukhevych u dokumentakh, Tom II*, 529-530.
599 Andrii Bolianovs'kyi, *Dyviziia 'Halychyna': Istoriia* (L'viv: A. Bolianovs'kyi, 2000) 61, lists ten *Nachtigall* Officers and NCOs and four *Roland* officers in *Waffen-SS Galizien*.

mass killing over the course of 1943, in particular in connection with the large-scale action against the Belski partisans in the Naliboki Forest.[600]

Together with several thousand Ukrainian policemen who had deserted the Germans, the veterans of *Schutzmannschaft* Battalion 201 now came to form the backbone of the UPA. From March 15 to April 15, 1943, close to four thousand Ukrainian former *Schutzmänner* joined the ranks of the UPA.[601]

---

600 "Mit'ko i drugikh," HDA SBU f. 5, delo 65509, tom 5, l. 361. Page 331 of this file contains a list of 50 men from *Schutzmannschaft* Battalion 201 transferred to *Schutzmannschaft* Battalion 57 following the dissolution of the former. See also: HDA SBU f. 5, delo 65509, tom 3, ll. 261–262. Within the ranks of *Schutzmannschaft* Battalion 57 many former members of the 201 Battalion took part in the burning of the villages of Pochatovo and Zatareshch in the Naliboki forest to the ground; destroying thirty-four houses in the village of Goridishki; abducting civilians from the village of Zastarenia for forced labor in Germany; burning, in their entirety, the villages of Yatry and Zatop'e; as well as destroying thirty-six houses in Zazhokhe. They took part in the shooting of Jews and forced forty-six people into the *dusheguby*, "soul killers," i.e. portable gas vans. The men of *Schutzmannschaft* Battalion 57 took part in burning the entire village of Gorodishche in the Baranovichi District, where the residents were accused of aiding the partisans. Men, women, elderly, and children were chased into a house, where they were burnt alive. They grabbed children by the legs and smashed them to death against the corners of the house, throwing their little bodies into the fire, in which the adults were immolated alive. Those trying to escape were mowed down by machine gun fire. In all, 124 houses were burnt, 360 people—men, women, and children killed. In Pochaiov fifty-six houses were burnt, seventeen people killed; in the village of Yatra seventy-five houses, five people murdered; in Zapol'e thirty-six houses, seven persons killed. "Mit'ko i drugikh" HDA SBU f. 5, delo 65509, tom. 4, ll. 7, 12, 18, 19, 20, 30, 39, 43, 65, 74, 76, 78, 79–96, 105, 114, 117, 118, 121, 128, 131–131, 143, 174, 179, 184. *Schutzmänner* Derikh and Pelik were sentenced to death and executed on June 29, 1945. They were denied legal rehabilitation on December 25, 2000. HDA SBU, f. 5, delo 65509, t.5, l. 336. For the complete statement of its members: HDA SBU f. 5, delo 65509, tom 5, ll. 33–120. A summary appears in connection with the rejected rehabilitation in 2000: HDA SBU f. 5, delo 65509, tom 5, ll. 350–390. On the Belski partisans, see: Nechama Tec, *Defiance* (Oxford: Oxford University Press, 2009) and Peter Duffy, *The Bielski Brothers: The True Story of Three Men Who Defied the Nazis, Built a Village in the Forest, and Saved 1,200 Jews* (New York: Harper Collins Publishers, 2004).

601 Volodymyr Serhiichuk, ed., *Roman Shukhevych u dokumentakh radians'kykh orhaniv derzhavnoi bezpeky (1940–1950). Tom I* (Kyiv: pp Serhiichuk M.I., 2007), 11. The most detailed works to date on local perpetrators in Volhynia are: McBride, '"A Sea of Blood and Tears"; McBride, "Peasants into Perpetrators"; Jared McBride, *Contesting the Malyn Massacre: The Legacy of Inter-Ethnic Vio-*

They applied the skills acquired in 1941-1942 for carrying out systematic massacres of the civilian Polish population in the massacres against the civilian Polish population in 1943 and 1944.[602] *Schutzmannschaft* Battalion 201, in particular, became an important nursery for future UPA commanders. Other than Shukhevych himself, its alumni included Oleksandr Luts'kyi, the organizer and first Commander of the UPA-West, based mainly in Galicia, and Vasyl Sydor, Commander of UPA-West from 1944 to 1949.[603]

According to several accounts, acting OUN(b) leader Mykola Lebed' issued orders in April, 1943 to cleanse the "entire revolutionary territory" of Poles.[604] Yet, on April 13, 1943, Lebed' was replaced by a triumvirate, in which Shukhevych was "the first among equals."[605] Shukhevych consolidated his position in both the UPA and the OUN(b), which appointed him commander of the UPA in August 1943.[606] The massacres of the Volhynian Poles appear to have been initiated somewhat earlier, in February, 1943, on a local initiative by the commander of UPA-North, Dmytro Kliachkivs'kyi (1911-1945), *nom de guerre* "Klym Savur." Shukhevych endorsed Savur's methods and expanded them to other territories under UPA control. The campaign reached its climax in

---

lence and the Second World War in Eastern Europe (=The Carl Besck Papers in Russian and East European Studies no. 2405) (Pittsburgh: The Center for Russian and East European Studies, University of Pittsburgh, 2016).

602 Timothy Snyder, *The Reconstruction of Nations: Poland, Ukraine, Lithuania, Belarus, 1569-1999* (New Haven: Yale University Press, 2003), 162.

603 Petro Sodol', *Ukrains'ka povstancha armiia, 1943-1949: Dovidnyk* (New York: Proloh, 1994).

604 Timothy Snyder, "The Causes of Ukrainian-Polish Ethnic Cleansing 1943," *Past and Present*, no. 179 (2003): 202; Taras Bul'ba-Borovets', *Armiia bez derzhavy: Slava i trahediia ukrains'koho povstans'koho rukhu. Spohady* (Kyiv: Knyha Rodu, 2008), 250-266. Petro Balei, *Fronda Stepana Bandery v oun 1940 roku* (Kyiv: Tekna, 1996), 141.

605 Motyka, *Ukraińska partyzantka*, 117; Kentii and Lozyts'kyi, "From UVO Fighter to Supreme Commander of the UPA," 98-99; David R. Marples, *Heroes and Villains: Creating National History in Contemporary Ukraine* (Budapest and New York: Central European University Press, 2007), 195.

606 Kentii and Lozytskyi, "From UVO Fighter to Supreme Commander of the UPA," 99.

July, 1943.[607] The most detailed studies of the OUN-UPA mass murders of Poles estimates the OUN and UPA's Polish victims to range between 70,000 and 100,000, their Jewish victims in the thousands.[608]

In the pro-nationalist rendering of history, the OUN's collaboration with Nazi Germany, the anti-Jewish pogroms, and the massacres of the Polish minority in Volhynia and eastern Galicia are ignored, glossed over, or outright denied. The period from August, 1941, to January, 1943, is either downplayed or omitted from most Shukhevych biographies, the focus instead being heavily centered on Shukhevych's role, from 1943 until his death in 1950, as commander of the UPA, the largest armed national resistance in the Soviet Union. Shukhevych's defiant resistance to Stalinism has a powerful appeal to the patriotic imagination of many Ukrainians, particularly in the western part of the country. However, as Shukhevych was turned into an official hero of Ukraine and the organization he led presented as representing the Ukrainian people, questions also emerged in regards to the 'missing years,' omitted from the hagiographies. The assessment of Shukhevych's whereabouts in Belarus differ sharply. If University of Hamburg historian Frank Golczewski (b. 1948) describes the activities of *Schutzmannschaft* Battalion 201 as "fighting partisans and killing Jews,"[609] in *Litopys Ukrains'koi Povstans'koi Armii* [The Chronicle of the Ukrainian Insurgent Army], a massive undertaking by the UPA veterans to establish a positive history of their organization, we read: "In taking direct part in battles against the

---

607 Motyka, *Ukraińska partyzantka*, 366–367. Extract from a record of the interrogation of Mykhailo Stepaniak, regarding the third conference of the OUN held in February 1943. Note "From the reflections of an elderly OUN member," HDA SBU, f. 13, spr. 376, t. 34, p. 268, reprinted in J. Bednarek, ed., *Poland and Ukraine in the 1930s and 1940s* (Warsaw: Institute of National Remembrance, 2009), 407; "Protokol doprosa obviniaemogo Stepaniaka Mikhaila Dmitrievicha ot 25 avgusta 1944 goda," HDA SBU, f. 13, spr. 372, t. 1, k. 21–59, *Pol'shcha ta Ukraina u trydtsiatykh-sorokovykh rokakh xx stolittia*, 230.
608 Siemaszko, "Stan badań nad ludobójstwem," 341; Motyka, *Ukraińska partyzantka*, 410–412, 649–650; Grzegorz Hryciuk, *Przemiany narodowościowe i ludnościowe w Galicji Wschodniej i na Wołyniu w latach 1931–1948* (Toruń: Wydawnytswo Adam Marszałek, 2005), 281.
609 Golczewski, "Die Kollaboration," 176.

Belarusian partisans and studying the Nazis' anti-partisan operations, Shukhevych not only acquired combat experience but also absorbed the rules of partisan warfare. In our opinion, he became one of the finest adepts of this specific form of armed struggle in the ranks of the Ukrainian liberation movement."[610]

Heroic Representations of Shukhevych

Since the early 1950s the figure of Shukhevych as a hero and martyr has been central to the identity of the Ukrainian diaspora.[611] In 2007, on the centennial of Shukhevych birth, the editors of the *Litopys Ukrains'koi Povstans'koi Armii* published two massive volumes "dedicated to the glorious memory" of Shukhevych. Volume 45 of the *Litopys* remains largely silent on Shukhevych's whereabouts in 1942, deliberately avoiding the word *Schutzmannschaften* altogether. Shukhevych is presented as the man who 'in the late 1940s headed the struggle against the two largest totalitarian regimes in the world—the Soviet Union and Nazi Germany. In these memoirs this celebrated military-political figure, leading member of the OUN, and commander in chief of the UPA is portrayed as "a brilliant student, athlete, musician, military man, politician, and businessman."[612] The account of his whereabouts from fall 1941 to early 1943 is short:

> In August the Legion was removed from the front, its members interned and then transferred to Germany. Here the Ukrainian soldiers reorganized themselves into Defensive Battalion No. 201, and in keeping with a separate contract were compelled to agree to an additional year of service. On 16 March 1942 the battalion was deployed to Belarus, to the vicinity of the

---

610 Kentii and Lozytskyi, "From UVO Fighter to Supreme Commander of the UPA," 94. Litopys UPA was initiated and edited by UPA veterans and covertly funded by the CIA until 1991. On the CIA funding of *Litopys UPA*, see: '"Renewal of Operational Activity" from A iad/seg/ib,' January 24, 1983, p. 2, NARA, QRPLUMB, vol. 4, RG 263, box 59, NN3-263-02-008.

611 After the Second World War, hundreds of thousands of Ukrainians found themselves in exile. In emigration, they established their own organizations, parties, institutions, and educational networks. From around 1980, they started to refer to themselves as a diaspora, rather than as émigrés.

612 Petro J. Potichnyj and Mykola Posivnych, ed., *Litopys Ukrains'koi Povstans'koi Armii, Tom 45, Heneral Roman Shukhevych – 'Taras Chuprynka' Holovnyi Komandyr UPA* (Toronto and L'viv: Vydavnytstvo Litopys UPA, 2007), 522.

town of Borovka, to protect military installations and fight Soviet partisans. After one year of service all the soldiers, led by Shukhevych, refused to continue serving. On 6 January 1943 they were sent under guard to L'viv, where they arrived on 8 January 1943. Shukhevych, who knew that all of the officers would be arrested, slipped away from the Gestapo and disappeared.[613]

Volume 10 of the New Series of *Litopys UPA* is a little more elaborate, alluding to atrocities in Belarus, but that Shukhevych managed to maintain human decency:

> The struggle against the partisans in Belarus was difficult and exhausting, and the laurels of victory did not fall to either the Germans or their allies, including the soldiers of the Ukrainian police battalion. According to V. Yaniv, 'this was a horrible time' in Shukhevych's life, who was forced 'to play the role of the Germans' friend to the last minute' although 'his heart was breaking from pain.' Myroslav Kal'ba recalls that Shukhevych and other Ukrainian commanders sought to avoid taking part in the Nazis' punitive actions against the local population and tried to evade the food requisitions, declaring 'that we were sent here to fight, not loot.'

In taking direct part in battles against the Belarusian partisans and studying the Nazis' anti-partisan operations, Shukhevych not only acquired combat experience but also absorbed the rules of partisan warfare. In our opinion, he became one of the finest adepts of this specific form of armed struggle in the ranks of the Ukrainian liberation movement.[614] Mykola Posivnych's introduction to volume 45 concisely articulates the traditional diaspora view:

> Roman Shukhevych occupies an exceptional place in the twentieth century pantheon of Ukraine's national warriors. He was one of the organizers of the struggle against all occupiers of Ukraine. The life and deeds of the

---

613 Posivnych, "Roman Shukhevych," 29.
614 Kentii and Lozytskyi, "From UVO Fighter to Supreme Commander of the UPA," 93–94. The *Litopys* remains less than forthcoming with information which does not conform with the aim to promote the UPA commander. O. Ishhuk and S. Kokin, in *Litopys UPA. Nova seria, Tom 10: Zhyttia i borot'ba henerala 'Tarasa Chuprynky' (1907–1950): Dokumenty i materialy*, ed. P. Sokhan' and P. Potichnyj (Kyiv and Toronto: Litopys UPA, 2007), 329, omits a section in which it is noted that "Bandera has a low opinion of Shukhevych." Jeffrey Burds, "Archival Practices in the Post-Soviet Zones," paper presented at the 2008 National Convention of the American Association for the Advancement of Slavic Studies, Philadelphia, November 23, 2008.

commander in chief of the UPA, Brigadier-General Roman Shukhevych—'Taras Chuprynka'—are a shining example of the heroic struggles for Ukrainian statehood and should serve as a model to be emulated by future generations of Ukrainians.[615]

Shukhevych is referred to as "a beacon that shows the path for the young generation," and his service in Belarus as "a great example of heroic character, the highest ethical values, national honor, and Christian morality."[616]

Shukhevych as Hero on the Silver Screen

Iziaslav Kokodniak, writing in the nationalist newspaper *Za vil'nu Ukrainu* in 2000, argued that the Ukrainian people needs to be nationally conscious, and that the Ukrainian state must become national in content. He explicitly called for the dissemination of "nationalist myths" to counter Soviet myths on the crimes of UPA. Nationalist organizations, according to Kokodniak, must "impose their will" on the state and mass media. Shukhevych, Kokodniak argues, would be an ideal instrument for the construction of a new nationalist myth.[617] One example of this is Oles' Yanchuk's motion picture *Neskorenyi* [*The Undefeated*] from 2000. The movie introduces Shukhevych as:

> a genteel family man forced by brutal circumstances and his own sense of duty to lead the fight to deliver his people from the savageries of both the Nazis and Soviets Yanchuk explores the complex character of Shukhevych, his revulsion at ethnic discrimination, his love of music, his genius in combat. The film smolders with the passion of the man and ignites that viewer with the same fire that Shukhevych fueled in his countrymen—the unquenchable flame of freedom. It is a personal story of faith and commitment and ultimately, the victory over tyranny.[618]

Yanchuk portrays Shukhevych as a valiant hero, something of a combination of George Washington and James Bond: a remarkably handsome man, always surrounded by young, attrac-

---

615 Posivnych, "Roman Shukhevych," 19, 33.
616 Potichnyj and Posivnych, *Litopys Ukrains'koi Povstans'koï Armii, Tom 45*, 361.
617 Marples, *Heroes and Villains*, 261.
618 "The Undefeated (Neskorenyi)," Metro Cinema, accessed April 17, 2008, http://www.metrocinema.org/film_view?FILM_ID=1663.

tive females, yet ever faithful to his wife and family. Shukhevych's attitude to the Germans is portrayed as defiant, even domineering. His German superiors tremble in his presence, speaking in a soft and hesitant voice, avoiding eye contact as Shukhevych, in a loud voice demands the release of Bandera and declares his loyalty to Ukraine, not Hitler or Germany. This is followed by a battle scene in which the hero overpowers his German captors on a train, and discreetly departs into the majestic nature of the Carpathian Mountains just as the leaves are turning. The viewer gets the impression of a clean break with the Germans in the fall of 1941 and that Shukhevych thereafter pursued an active armed resistance against both the Nazis and the Soviets. The hero dramatically sheds his German uniform as a voice announces in first person: "I left the *Wehrmacht*, earlier than we had anticipated. The OUN went into the deep underground. The Hitlerite terror forced the leadership to establish self-defense forces. Thus, the Insurgent Army developed into a regular army."

The movie then makes a hefty jump forward in the chronology. The period between July, 1941, to August, 1943, during which the bulk of the Ukrainian Jews were murdered and the fortunes of the Germans turned, are simply omitted. Left out are also UPA's massacres of tens of thousands of Volhynian Poles during the summer of 1943, while Shukhevych headed the organization.[619] The viewer is re-introduced to the historical narrative only in autumn of 1943. The UPA is presented as an inclusive, multi-ethnic organization. The hero reminds the viewers that ethnic minorities, such as Armenians, Azerbaijanis, Jews, and Kazakhs were allowed in the UPA.[620]

---

619 Ihor Ivanovych Il'iushyn, *Volyns'ka trahediia 1943–1944 rr.* (Kyiv: Instytut istorii Ukrainy NAN Ukrainy, 2003), 198.
620 The portrayal of the UPA as a multi-ethnic organization has become a cornerstone in the pro-UPA narrative, often used in response to allegations that the organization indulged in anti-Semitic activities. Yet, even the *Schutzmannschaft* Battalions were multi-ethnic. For instance, Turkmens and Uzbeks served in Ukrainian *Schutzmannschaft* Battalion 134.

Nationalist Assessments of *Schutzmannschaft* Battalion 201

More research is needed in order to establish the exact role and whereabouts of the 201st Battalion and its activities. Older pro-OUN/pro-UPA accounts tend to overlook or ignore the period between August 1941 and January 1943 entirely.[621] Recent accounts either diminish the importance of his whereabouts in 1942, or portray Shukhevych's presence in Belarus as a benign tutorial in patriotism for the Belarusian population, an opportunity for them to advance the relatively underdeveloped Belarusian national consciousness.[622] They also deny that there were any "real" partisans in Belarus at this point, or, alternatively, that there were civilian victims of the activities of the *Schutzmannschaft* Battalion 201. "In Belarus, the members of the battalion strived to help the local population in any way they could—even though it was strictly forbidden," wrote Myroslav Kal'ba (1916–2013), the last surviving veteran of *Schutzmannschaft* Battalion 201 in 2005.[623] Nationalist historians concur:

> On February 20, 1942, the Legion was sent on military operations. It was sent to a part of Belarus, terrorized by Muscovite-MGB partisans. Much like in the adjacent Ukrainian territories, [the MGB] terrorized the population mercilessly, purposely provoking the German Army and their Polish allies into harsh punitive actions. During its nine-month protective assignment the officers and soldiers of the Legion took every chance to work to enhance the national consciousness of the local population and to implant a conviction that a free and prosperous life is possible only in a powerful, independent state. With that aim the officers and the instructors pro-

---

621 Hryhorij Waskowycz, *Roman Šuchevyč – Kommandeur des Befreiungskrieges: Aus Anlass des 30. Todestages* (Munich: Ukrainische Freie Universität, 1981); Petro Mirchuk, *Roman Shukhevych (Gen. Taras Chuprynka): Komandyr armiï bezsmertnykh* (New York, Toronto and London: Tovarystvo kolishnykh voiakiv UPA v ZSA, Kanadi i Evropi, 1970), 108; Vasyl' Kuk, *Heneral Roman Shukhevych: Holovnyi komandyr Ukrains'koi postans'koi armii* (UPA) (Kyiv: Biblioteka ukraintsia, 1997), 36–37.

622 Such was Pobihushchyi-Ren's own assessment of the battalion's role in Belarus. Ievhen Pobihushchyi-Ren, *Mozaika moikh spomyniv. Tom druhyi* (Munich and London: Ievhen Pobihushchyi-Ren and the Association of Ukrainian Former Combatants in Great Britain, 1985), 243.

623 Myroslav Kal'ba, *DUN v rozbudovi UPA* (Detroit and Ternopil': Dzhura, 2005), 103.

vided specialized education for hundreds of young Belarusians, preparing them for struggle, not only against the Russian-Bolshevik invaders. This could not be talked about openly. Yet, the Ukrainian legionnaires were able to rescue many Belarusian patriots, supporters of state independence from both the Gestapo, and the MGB, which operated under the auspices of Bolshevik partisans. There were many such cases, when such people were able to engage [the local Belarusians] in serious battles or assist them through powerful military support.[624]

Memory Management

Under President Yushchenko, most Ukrainian textbooks came to present Shukhevych in a very favorable light. "Relentlessly and almost infallibly, the OUN and the UPA are portrayed as victims and not perpetrators," writes Johan Dietsch.[625] This perspective of Ukrainian resistance is set up in deliberate contrast to the Soviet narrative of unity with Russia as the natural state of affairs for Ukraine. The post-socialist perspective is juxtaposed with the "a-historic, amoral, and a-ethical realm" of Soviet socialism. The new, "national" history is presented as "true history," in contrast to the "false Soviet history."[626]

Since 2006 decade, the perhaps most influential promoter of the Banderite heritage in Ukraine has been the young and charismatic Volodymyr V"iatrovych.[627] From 2002, he was the driving

---

[624] Duzhyi, *Roman Shukhevych*, 145–146, citing *Druzhyny Ukrains'kykh Natsionalistiv u 1941–1942 rokakh*, 65, 88. This collection of memoirs, the only published account besides Pobihushchyi, was also used as the basis for Posivnych's account of Shukhevych's whereabouts in 1941–1942 in volume 45 of *Litopys UPA*, 29.

[625] Dietsch, *Making Sense of Suffering*, 172; Marples, *Heroes and Villains*, 132–141, 277–278; and Wilfred Jilge, "The Politics of History and the Second World war in Post-Communist Ukraine (1986/1991–2004/2005)," *Jahrbücher für Geschichte Osteuropas* 54 (2006): 62.

[626] Peter Niedermüller, "Der Mythos der Gemeinschaft: Geschichte, Gedächtnis und Politik im heutigen Osteuropa," in *Umbruch im östlichen Europa: Die nationale Wende und das kollektive Gedächtnis*, ed. Andrea Corbea Hoise, Rudolf Jaworski and Monika Sommer (Innsbruck: Studien Verlag, 2004), 11–26. On the use of history in the period of the dissolution of the USSR, see also: Klas-Göran Karlsson, *Historia som vapen: Historiebruk och Sovjetunionens upplösning 1985–1995* (Stockholm: Natur och Kultur, 1999), 57–61.

[627] On V"iatrovych's Institute and his memory activism, see Rudling, *The OUN, the UPA, and the Holocaust*; Per A. Rudling "Warfare or War Criminality?" *Ab Imperio*, no. 1 (2012): 356–381; Rossoliński-Liebe, *Stepan Bandera*, 476–479;

force of the above-mentioned OUN(b) front organization The Center for the Study of the Liberation Movement, TsDVR in Ukrainian aimed at popularizing and promoting a whitewashed, heroic legacy of the OUN and UPA.[628] In addition to running the TsDVR, Yushchenko appointed him director of the HDA SBU the Special State Archives of the Ukrainian Security Services in 2008, a position he held until the election of Yanukovych.[629] From these positions, V"iatrovych invested significant efforts in elevating Shukhevych into a national hero and, in particular, absolving the organizations he led from allegations of anti-Semitism and collaboration with the Third Reich. A cornerstone of his strategy has been to seek to deflect the significant emerging scholarship of the OUN(b)'s involvement in the Holocaust and systematic massacres of Poles by an extensive focus on a handful of Jews who served in

---

Grzergorz Rossoliński-Liebe, "Debating, Obfuscating and Disciplining the Holocaust: Post-Soviet Historical Discourses on the OUN-UPA and Other Nationalist Movements," *East European Jewish Affairs* 42, no. 3 (2012): 207–208; John-Paul Himka, "The Lontsky Street Prison Memorial Museum: An Example of Post-Communist Holocaust Negationsm," in *Perspectives on the Entangled History of Communism and Nazism: A Comnaz Analysis*, ed. Klas-Göran Karlsson, Johan Stenfeldt, and Ulf Zander (Lanham, MD: Lexington Books, 2015), 137–166.

628 Lypovets'kyi, *Orhanizatsiia Ukrains'kykh Natsionalistiv (banderitvtsi)*, 84.
629 After the overthrow of Yanukovych in 2014, V"iatrovych was appointed director of the Ukrainian Institute of National Memory, with considerable influence of the government's memory policy, even of the drafting of legislation. On the Ukrainian Institute of National Memory, see Georgii Kas'ianov, "K desiatiletiia Ukrainskogo institut natsional'noi pamiati (2006–2016)," *Historians.in.ua*, January 14, 2016, accessed February 19, 2016, http://historians.in.ua/index.php/en/dyskusiya/1755-georgij-kas-yanov-k-desyatiletiyu-ukrainskogo-instituta-natsional-noj-pamyati-2006-2016. In May, 2015, V"iatrovych, together with Yurii Shukhevych (1933-2022), the son of the UPA commander, Soviet-era dissident and radical nationalist, drafted a set of laws banning Soviet symbols, outlawing the Communist Party, and prohibiting 'disrespect' for the "fighters of Ukrainian statehood in the 20th century," such as the OUN and UPA. The laws have been sharply criticized by historians, human right groups, and the Council of Europe. David R. Marples et al., "Open Letter from Scholars and Experts in Ukraine Re. the So-Called 'Anti-Communist Law'," *Krytkya*, April 2015, accessed April 6, 2016, http://krytyka.com/en/articles/open-letter-scholars-and-experts-ukraine-re-so-called-anti-communist-law; Jared McBride, "How Ukraine's New Memory Commissar Is Controlling the Nation's Past," *The Nation*, August 13, 2015, accessed March 31, 2016, http://www.thenation.com/article/how-ukraines-new-memory-commissar-is-controlling-the-nations-past/.

the UPA, mainly as physicians and nurses.[630] In an apparent attempt to reconcile the veneration of the ethno-nationalists with European expectations of recognition of the Holocaust, Yushchenko's legitimizing historians sought to establish a narrative of World War II in which Ukrainian nationalists and Jews fought together, as comrades-in-arms against a common Bolshevik-Muscovite enemy. They employed a highly selective use of documents, systematically downplaying the OUN's anti-Semitism, ignoring the nationalists' mass murder of thousands, and focusing instead on a handful of exceptions.[631] This marked a departure from a tendency in the nationalist historiography to portray Jews as enemies and tormentors of Ukrainians, and as accomplices in Communist crimes.[632] The claims by the memory management agencies run by V"iatroych notwithstanding there now exists a body of scholarly literature, which demonstrates how OUN anti-Semitism radicalized over the 1930s, reaching a high point in 1941–43.[633] There is no shortage of radical, eliminatory anti-

---

630 Rudling, *The OUN, the UPA, and the Holocaust*, 28–32.
631 "V"iatrovych," John-Paul Himka writes, "manages to exonerate the OUN of charges of antisemitism and complicity in the Holocaust only by employing a series of highly dubious procedures: rejecting sources that compromise the OUN, accepting uncritically censored sources from émigré OUN circles, failing to recognize antisemitism in OUN texts, limiting the source base to official OUN proclamations and decisions, excluding Jewish memoirs, refusing to consider contextual and comparative factors, failing to consult German document collections, and ignoring the mass of historical monographs on his subject written in the English and German languages." John-Paul Himka, "True and False Lessons from the Nachtigall Episode," *Brama*, March 19, 2008, accessed March 19, 2008, http://brama.com/news/press/2008/03/080 319himka_nachtigall.html. See also: Taras Kurylo and John-Paul Himka [Ivan Khymka], "Iak OUN stavylasia do ievreiv? Rozdumy nad knyzhkoiu Volodymyra V"iatrovycha Stavlennia OUN do ievreiv: Formuvannia pozytsii na tli katastrofy," *Ukraina Moderna* 13 (2008): 252–265.
632 See, for example, the OUN(b)-affiliated historian Petro Mirchuk, *My Meetings and Discussions in Israel (Are Ukrainians 'Traditionally anti-Semites'?)* (New York, London and Toronto: Ukrainian Survivors of the Holocaust, 1982), 66. And, on the diaspora press in North America: Himka, "A Central European Diaspora," 29.
633 Himka, "A Central European Diaspora," 22; Taras Kurylo, "The 'Jewish Question' in the Ukrainian Nationalist Discourse of the Interwar Period," in Yohanan Petrovsky-Shtern and Antony Polonsky, *Polin: Studies in Polish Jewry, Volume 26: Jews and Ukrainians*, 233-258 (Oxford and Portland OR: The

Semitism in the writings of senior OUN ideologues and intellectuals.[634] After Stalingrad, the OUN leadership systematically manipulated the organization's past. Original documents were retyped, pro-German and anti-Semitic statements omitted, sensitive documents withheld or released selectively, producing a distortingly selective view, which avoided thorny and compromising issues.[635] V"iatrovych uncritically relied on the nationalists' own doctored accounts while dismissing emerging scholarship as Soviet propaganda. Avoiding the sensitive issues in Shukhevych's biography, he instead focused on the work of the KGB of the Ukrainian SSR to discredit the OUN,[636] dismissing criticism of Shukhevych as a baseless political campaign against the UPA commander's memory.[637] The OUN's anti-Semitism is reduced to Soviet propaganda lies and the emerging body of scholarship on Ukrainian involvement in anti-Jewish violence to rehash of Soviet propaganda:

Littman Library of Jewish Civilization, 2014): 233–258; H. V. Kas'ianov, "Ideolohiyia OUN: Istoryko-retrospektyvnyi analiz," *Ukrains'kyi istorychnyi zhurnal*, no. 2 (Feb. 2004): 38–39.

[634] See, for instance Oleksandr Zaitsev, "Voenna doktryna Mykhaila Kolodzins'koho," *Ukraina Moderna* 20 (2013): 245–256; and Mykhailo Kolodzins'kyi, "Natsionalistychne povstannia: Rozdil iz pratsi 'Voenna doktryna ukrains'kykh natsionalistiv'," *Ukraina Moderna* 20 (2013): 257–295; Rossoliński-Liebe, *The Fascist Kernel of Ukrainian Genocidal Nationalism*.

[635] Himka, "A Central European Diaspora," 22; Berkhoff and Carynnyk, "The Organization of Ukrainian Nationalists," 149; Rossoliński-Liebe, "Erinnerungslücke Holocaust," 397–430, on Shukhevych, see 421–424. On Mykola Lebed's doctoring on documents on the Volhynian massacres, see Krzysztof Łada, "Creative Forgetting: Polish and Ukrainian Historiographies on the Campaign against the Poles in Volhynia during World War II," *Glaukopis*, no. 2/3 (2005), 346.

[636] "U Sluzhbi bezpeki Ukrainy…" and "Dokumenty SBU sprostovuiut' zvynuvachennia proty batal'ionu 'Nakhtihal'," Press release, Press Office of the Embassy of Ukraine in Canada, no. 20, March 22, 2008, accessed March 22, 2008, http://www.ukremb.ca/canada/ua/news/detail/11684.htm; Volodymyr V"iatrovych, "Kukhnia antysemityzmu vid KGB," in *Isotriia z hryfom "Sekretno": Taemnytsi ukrains'koho mynuloho z arkhiviv KGB*, Volodymyr V"iatrovych (L'viv: Tsentr doslidzhen' vyzvol'noho rukhu, 2011), 239–255.

[637] See, for instance, the article by his wife, TsDVR-affiliated journalist and editor Yaryna Yasynevych, "V"iatrovych: Kampania proty Shukhevycha ne maie istorychnoï osnovy," *Narodna Pravda*, March 4, 2008, accessed March 16, 2008, http://narodna.pravda.com.ua/history/47cd371e88b05/.

According to the canon of Soviet propaganda, anti-Semitism was one of the basic elements of the ideology and the practice of the Organization of Ukrainian Nationalists . . . . Unfortunately, that is the way many contemporary publicists and historians behave, who, in this old manner look at Ukrainian history through the glasses of 'Agitprop.' One of the most widespread accusations against the Ukrainian nationalists is the allegation of their participation in the anti-Jewish pogroms in L'viv in the beginning of July, 1941.[638]

Rehabilitation with Complications

Yushchenko's rehabilitation of Shukhevych did not benefit Ukrainian-Jewish reconciliation. Moshe Kantor (b. 1953), the head of the European Jewish Congress, describing Shukhevych as a "Nazi collaborator" and citing the growth in anti- Semitism and far-right activism in Ukraine, refused to accept a posthumous Order of Hero of Ukraine from Yushchenko on behalf of Major Anatolii Shapiro (1913-2005), a Soviet Jewish commander who liberated Auschwitz in 1944.[639]

During a state visit to Israel the following month, Yushchenko was sharply criticized for his decision to honor Shukhevych. At Yad Vashem, Yushchenko was confronted by the Chairman of its Council, Joseph (Tommy) Lapid (1931-2008), a Holocaust survivor and former deputy Israeli Prime Minister. A journalist and politician — not a historian — Lapid alleged that he had proof that Shukhevych participated in the July, 1941, Pogrom in L'viv.[640] To this Yushchenko responded that, "I have materials, documents, saying that in the course of grander context of Ukrainian insurgency

---

638 Volodymyr V"iatrovych, "Iak tvorylasia lehenda pro Nachtigall," *Dzerkalo Tyzhnia*, no. 6 (685), February 16–22, 2008, accessed March 16, 2008, http://www.dt.ua/3000/3150/62036/.
639 "Jewish Leaders Snub Ukraine Award Citing Rise in anti-Semitism," *Kyiv Post*, October 24, 2007, accessed April 8, 2016, https://www.kyivpost.com/article/content/ukraine-politics/jewish-leaders-snub-ukraine-award-citing-rise-in-a-27668.html.
640 "Visit of Ukrainian President Yuschenko to Yad Vashem: Yad Vashem Chairman Chalev Thanks Ukrainian President Yushchenko for Instructing the Relevant Professionals to Reach an Agreement regarding the Bruno Schultz Murals, Chairman of the Council Lapid Protest Granting Honor to man Involved in Murder of Jews During Holocaust," Yad Vashem website, accessed April 10, 2008, http://yad-vashem.org.il/about_yad/what_new/data_whats_new/Yuschenko.html.

Shukhevych signed a petition that prohibited massive persecutions (of civilians)," even adding that "there is not a single fact to confirm that any single Ukrainian national liberation organization participated in punitive actions, the deportation and murder of Jews."[641]

The Lapid-Yushchenko confrontation at Yad Vashem resembled the debate in Ukraine. Lapid's objections resembled the attitudes towards Shukhevych, common in the east and the south of the country, and within the Ukrainian left. "Sometimes you can be both a hero of Ukrainians and a murderer of Jews," Lapid summarized his position.[642] On January 6, 2008, Lapid further embellished his claims, stating that "We have an entire file that certifies that Shukhevych participated in mass murder. The Ukrainian side has not contacted us with a request to handle over those documents. If we were to receive such a request, I think we would be happy to respond to it."[643]

V"iatrovych skillfully utilized of the opportunity Lapid had provided. He lost no time organizing and heading a delegation to Yad Vashem. In Jerusalem, V"iatrovych requested to see this folder, to which the Yad Vashem archivists could only confirm what they already knew: that no such file existed.[644] V"iatrovych returned triumphantly to Ukraine, declaring the allegations baseless, proclaiming Shukhevych's innocence. Lapid's irresponsible claims served Shukhevych's hagiographers a propaganda victory at the expense of Yad Vashem's authority. More seriously, given the significant media noise surrounding this episode, it had an adverse effect on the Holocaust education and awareness Yad

---

641 "Yushchenko ne dospustyt' ksenofobii, ale i proty shtampiv," *Ukrains'ka Pravda*, November 15, 2007, accessed November 18, 2007, http://www.pravda.com.ua/news/2007/11/15/66920.htm.

642 "Ukraine President Defends National Hero," *Unian*, November 16, 2007, accessed January 17, 2008, http://www.unian.net/eng/news/news-221993.html.

643 "SBU sprostuvala Yad Vashem shchodo Shukhevycha," *BBC Ukrainian*, March 4, 2008.

644 "V arkhivi izrail'skoho memorial'noho kompleksu 'Yad Vashem' nemae dos'e na Romana Shukhevycha," *Sluzba bezpeki Ukraïny*, March 4, 2008, accessed April 23, 2008, http:// www.ssu.gov.ua/sbu/control/uk/publish/article?art_id=76079&cat_id=73817.

Vashem is dedicated to promote. The pro-Shukhevych camp used Lapid's misleading intervention as a vindication not only of Shukhevych, but also of the organizations he led, the OUN(b) and the UPA, from allegations of anti- Semitism and collaboration in the Holocaust.[645] The dynamics of the exchange between Lapid and Yushchenko—two experienced politicians—highlight the complexity of Ukrainian-Jewish relations. Ukrainian nationalists deliberately overinterpreted Lapid's attack as an expression of deep-seated Jewish stereotypes of the Ukrainian *pogromshchik*, some of the reactions emanating in Ukraine invoked the image of the Jews as the stooges of Bolshevism and Moscow. The *Kyiv Post* editorialized that

> it's time the worldwide Jewish community, known for its high standards in scholarship, quit being the pawns of the Soviet, and now Russian, propaganda machine. Instead of over-relying on Russian scholarship, distorted by Soviet nostalgia and post-Soviet nationalism, Jewish scholars should consider Ukrainian scholarship, and that of other post-Soviet satellite states, as a more reliable and objective record of events during those horrid days.[646]

In an open letter to Yushchenko, Roman Krutsyk (1945-2023), a former MP for the Congress of Ukrainian Nationalists (KUN),[647] chairman of the Kyiv *Memorial* Society and director of the Kyiv Museum of the Soviet Occupation, requested the Ukrainian president to obtain all incriminating documents for the Ukrainian SBU and the Ukrainian Institute of National Memory so that the Ukrainian researchers can ascertain their authenticity. He complained that Israel was pushed into an anti-Ukrainian stance by Russia, and expressed his concern that "Israel does not want to recognize the *Holodomor* of 1932–33 as an act of genocide against Ukrainians," since it "only recognizes the Holocaust as the sole genocide in history." Furthermore, Krutsyk requested Yushchen-

---

645 John-Paul Himka, "Debates in Ukraine over Nationalist Involvement in the Holocaust, 2004–2008," *Nationalities Papers* 39, no. 3 (2011): 363–365.
646 "Trust Ukraine scholars," *Kyiv Post*, March 13, 2008, accessed April 8, 2016, https://www.kyivpost.com/opinion/editorial/trust-ukraine-scholars-28583.html.
647 On KUN, see chapter 6.

ko to set up a "state program for patriotic training and education of the citizens of Ukraine." Krutsyk felt that such a program would "enlighten every Ukrainian citizen about the truth about the Ukrainian national liberation movement in the 20th century, especially about the fight of the Ukrainian Insurgent army and the Organization of Ukrainian Nationalists for the freedom and independence of the Ukrainian people. [This is necessary] to counteract any dirty insinuations and manipulations of the national consciousness in regards to that question."[648]

Shukhevych's admirers reject the notion that there would have been anything unethical in Shukhevych's collaboration with the Germans in 1941 and 1942, and instead compare the role of their hero in 1942 to either that of the *Judenräte*, de Gaulle, Churchill or the leaders of the struggle against British colonialism. Commenting on Shukhevych's collaboration, V"iatrovych insisted that the OUN had adopted an anti-German line from 1941: "After the Germans failed to recognize the Act of Renewal of Ukrainian Independence on June 30, 1941 and Stet'sko's government, and instead began to repress its leadership, the OUN pursued an anti-German political line." To the obvious follow-up question, as to why Shukhevych then collaborated with the *Abwehr* from 1939 and then signed up for the *Schutzmannschaften*, V"iatrovych answered:

> Shukhevych, as an individual, had the right to collaborate with the [German military] intelligence. We cannot overlook that episode, but we also need evaluate the goals he set up for himself. That goal was one—the formation of an armed formation, which could become the kernel of a Ukrainian army. Very many of the officers of the *Nachtigall* later became commanders of the UPA. And why did France and Britain have the right to collaborate with Germany during 1938–1939, why did the Soviet Union have the right to collaborate with Germany during 1939–1941? The OUN-UPA was a force that dared to challenge both totalitarianisms: the German, as

---

648 Roman Krutsyk, "Memorial: Pane Prezydente, zaberit' nareshti dokumenty Shukhevycha z iad Vashem," *Maidan*, December 20, 2007, accessed January 17, 2008, http://maidan.org.news/for-print.php3?bn=maidan_mai&key=1198164610.

well as the Soviet. Even Churchill made compromises with one evil in order to fight the other.[649]

V″iatrovych presupposes that *Schutzmannschaft* Battalion 201 targeted only the wicked, primarily NKVD agents who terrorized the Belarusians on Moscow's orders, that Shukhevych avoided shedding innocent blood, venturing to state, conclusively, that Shukhevych did not participate in the Holocaust:

> Did [Shukhevych] have the right to collaborate with evil Germany? In order to answer that question, we again need to evaluate the situation not from the perspective of 2008, or even 1945, but only 1941, when that decision was made. However, for us the German army is synonymous with millions of victims. [To us, it] represents what was put on trial at in Nuremberg in 1945. Yet, in 1941 this all laid in the future. Yes, Shukhevych fought in 1941-1942 in a German uniform, but donning it does not mean that he assumed responsibility for all crimes, committed by the soldiers of the German army. There are practically no documentary sources on Roman Shukhevych's stay in Belarus, and the [only known] recollections of the activities of that period are the memoirs of one colleague from the Battalion. Despite this, after it has been established that Shukhevych's alleged participation in anti-Jewish actions in 1941 was a hoax, [some people] have instead sought to disentangle the issue of his possible participation in the pacification against the Belarusian population in 1942. However, if there are no documents, then it will be difficult to prove that Shukhevych did not participate in such actions. Again, there is a presumption of guilt.[650]

V″iatrovych similarly denies that *Schutzmannschaft* Battalion 201 committed any crimes against civilians:

> In Belarus the 201st Ukrainian battalion was not concentrated in one place, as it was protecting bridges over the rivers Biarezina and Dzvina. The detachments in the small villages were also assigned to protect the local German administration. Towards the end of November 1942, the Ukrainian officers decided to maximally curtail the battalions' active participation in German military actions in order to avoid further losses. On December 1, 1942 the soldiers of the battalion refused to renew the contract with the Germans, which led to the arrest of many of them, particularly their leaders. Others, including Roman Shukhevych, were able to escape. Altogether, many soldiers of the battalion joined the Ukrainian Insurgent Army, where

---

649 Masha Mishchenko, "Pratsivnyk SBU: My izdyly v Izrail' pobachaty dos'e proty Shukhevycha—a ioho prosto one isnue," *UNIAN*, March 25, 2008, accessed April 8, 2008, http://unian.net/news/print.php?id=242913.
650 V″iatrovych, "Roman Shukhevych: soldat." On the discussion, see Himka, "Debates in Ukraine," 364-365.

they, as well-prepared soldiers, chose to take up commanding positions. In the functions of that army, defending the Ukrainian population, they fought honorably against their former allies, the Germans.[651]

On the question why Shukhevych did not immediately turn his weapons against the Germans after they had lied to him and arrested the leadership of the OUN, V"iatrovych responded:

> Let's be realistic. Roman Shukhevych commanded 700 soldiers. The *Wehrmacht*, at that time, close to half a million. To turn the weapons against the *Wehrmacht* in 1941 and tell them: 'now *Roland* and *Nachtigall* will fight the *Wehrmacht*' would have meant that they would have been killed on the spot. Until the end of 1942 the soldiers were bound by a contract, which tied them to the *Schutzmannschaft* battalion. When the contract ended, those people declared: we will no longer serve with you. That decision cost many of them their lives.

Q: They say that after 1942, Shukhevych fought against Belarusian partisans and Poles?
A: The *Schutzmannschaft* battalion, in which the former *Nachtigall* members, among them Shukhevych, served, ended its activities in the end of 1942. After that the majority of the boys joined the ranks of the Ukrainian Insurgent Army. And anyway, what partisans were there in 1942 in Belarus?

Q: Vasil Bykau[652] writes, that there were...
A: Vasil Bykau was a novelist. Let's look at the documents. The documents show that there were special groups, created under the leadership of the NKVD, who infiltrated and carried out acts of sabotage behind the German lines. To call them partisans is difficult, since partisans are rebels, organized by the local population.

Q: As a historian, can you say that Shukhevych did not participate in [anti-] Jewish pogroms?
A: Yes.

Q: Likewise, can you say that Shukhevych did not participate in the killing of peaceful Belarusian and Polish civilians?
A: Very interesting question regarding peaceful population during partisan warfare. In conventional warfare, one soldier differs from another by his uniform. Is it possible to consider Poles or Belarusians a peaceful population, if they at day time work as ordinary villagers, but in the evening

---

651 V"iatrovych, "Yak tvorylasia lehenda pro Nachtigall."
652 One of the most important Belarusian writers, Vasil Bykau (1924–2003) was known, in particular, for his realistic accounts of World War II. On Bykau, see Zina J. Gimpelevich, *Vasil Bykau: His Life and Works* (Montreal: McGill-Queen's University Press, 2005).

arm themselves and attack the village? How should they be regarded—as Polish or Ukrainian [soldiers]? With a machine gun—he is a soldier, with a hoe—a peaceful civilian? When such a person is killed in an armed conflict, should he be regarded as a killed civilian or as a military casualty?[653]

V"iatrovych's narration differs little from that of the *Schutzmänner* themselves, which lack any reference to abuse or atrocities committed against the local population in Belarus, whereas killings, and attacks carried out by the pro-Soviet partisans are described in great detail.[654]

An alternative explanation to the question of Shukhevych's whereabouts was offered by Parmen Posokhov, an "independent researcher," who questioned the claim that *Schutzmannschaft* Battalion 201 guarded communication infrastructure, such as bridges over the rivers Biarezina and Dzvina. Posokhov argued that the protecting the bridges of the Biarezina river was not included in the battalion's responsibilities, that the Lepel' railroad station was little more than a shack, the town connected to the outside world by just one paved road, and that its population was so small, that it would be an unlikely place to store weapons and ammunition. As an alternative explanation, Posokhov suggested that there could have been a secret *Abwehr* training camp in Lepel'. There was a sanatorium twenty-eight kilometers from Lepel', *Lesnye Ozera*, where the Germans vacationed. They had entrusted its protection to members of the OUN.[655] Posokhov refers to the memoirs of Nikolai Obryn'ba (1913-1996), a Soviet Ukrainian painter, who as a POW was interned in Lepel'. In his memoirs,

---

653 V"iatrovych, "Yak tvorylasia lehenda pro Nachtigall."
654 Pobihushchyi-Ren, *Mozaika moikh spomyniv; Myroslav Kal'ba, Druzhyny Ukrains'kykh Natsionalistiv* (Detroit: Vyd-ia Druzhyny ukrains'kykh natsionalistiv, 1994); Myroslav Kal'ba, *My prysiahaly Ukraini: DUN 1941-1942* (L'viv: Memuarna biblioteka NTSh, 1999); Myroslav Kal'ba, *U lavkah druzhynnykiv: spohady uchasnykiv. Materialy zibrav i vporiadkuvav Myroslav Kal'ba* (Denver: Vyd-ia Druzhyny ukrains'kykh natsionalistiv, 1982); Myroslav Kal'ba, ed., *Druzhyny Ukraïns'kykh Nationalistiv v 1941-1942 rokakh* (n.p: Vyd-ia Druzhyny ukrainsks'kykh nationalistiv, 1953), 63, 71, 77–78. Pobihushchyi even presents the *Schutzmänner* as victims: "The Legion did not carry out a single execution. Instead, unfortunately, a soldier from the Legion was executed [by the Germans] (I do not remember his name)." Ibid., 40.
655 Posokhov, "Shukhevych"

Obryn'ba mentions German "diversion schools in Lepel', which prepared the saboteurs for provocations, intelligence work, the mining of roads, the destruction of wells, and the murder of partisan commanders."[656]

Ukrains'ka Pravda published a similar assessment by Serhii Hrabovs'kyi (b. 1957), a former deputy editor of the above-mentioned journal *Suchasnist'*: "[T]he supreme commander of the UPA and the people he commanded were hardly any more 'collaborators' than, say, the leaders of the *Judenräte* in the Nazi-occupied territories, and no more 'fascists' than the Gaullists of the French resistance." Hrabovs'kyi claims there was an "absence of a serious popular partisan movement and battles between 'real' partisans...and the police and parts of the *Wehrmacht* until 1943. ...the 201st battalion ... did not rush into battle, but at times reached a neutrality agreement with the partisans (Shukhevych, in particular, was interested in such an agreement), though, without doubt, there were battles with victims on both sides."[657] To illustrate the situation of mutual victimhood cites atrocities committed against the local Belarusian population by Soviet partisans. Specifically citing a Jewish Soviet partisan cutting the throat of an under-aged girl:

> It was this kind of 'operations' the Kutuzov Soviet partisan division, commanded by Izrail Lapidus carried out. The people were of the same lot as Lazar Kaganovich, who pathetically stressed, 'I am not a Jew, I am a Bolshevik!' Do we need to question whether the Ukrainian nationalists had the moral right to fight *such* partisans? . . My purpose is not to 'justify' Roman Shukhevych—after all, his political principles, expressed in the program of the Third Congress of the OUN(b), have today entered the Ukrainian constitution, while the Bolshevik ideology has been thrown on the dust heap of history. I call on politicians and journalists, among them

---

656 Nikolai Ippolitovich Obryn'ba, *Sud'ba opolchentsa* (Moscow: Yauza, Eksmo, 2005), 283–284, accessed November 18, 2007, http://militera.lib.ru/memo/russian/obrynba_ni/ index.html.
657 Serhii Hrabovs'kyi, "Tak proty koho zh voiuvav Shukhevych u Bilorusi?" *Ukrains'ka Pravda*, November 13, 2007, accessed November 18, 2007, http:// www.pravda.com.ua/ news/2007/11/13/66774.htm.

Israeli: do not rush to make simple conclusions regarding 'Ukrainian fascists'.[658]

Alas, there was virtually no partisan resistance in Belarus at the time Schutzmannschaft battalion 201 was positioned there, and if the *Schutzmänner* under Shukhevych's command targeted Jews, they targeted them as communists, not as Jews—and the ethics of this needs no problematization. Soviet atrocities are linked to Jews, whereas the *Schutzmänner* are compared to the French resistance.

Shukhevych's son Yuri, who received the highest state award on behalf of his father, insisted that Shukhevych was just an independence fighter, whose alliance with Nazi Germany was strictly tactical:

> Let us look at the events of World War II in other countries. In Burma there was Aun Sang, who formed military formations on the side of the Japanese to fight the English colonizers. As a result, Burma became an independent state in 1948! The Indian legions, created by Chandra Bos—the leader of Indian National Congress—fought England as an ally not only of the Japanese, but also of the Germans. It was formed in Europe out of captive Hindus. This is not held against them. The Union of Young Officers, which under the leadership of Gamal Abdel Nasser fought for the independence of Egypt against the English, received assistance from Mussolini. That cooperation did not discredit Nasser [in the eyes of the Soviets] who, after becoming president of Egypt, received the order of Hero of the Soviet Union!
>
> **Q: *Nachtigall*, together with Roland, formed the *Schutzmannschaft* Battalion 201, which fought partisans in Belarus. Is it correct that Roman Shukhevych on October 14, 1942, did not desert from the battalion, but was assigned the task to track down Jews, hiding in Belarusian and Ukrainian forests?**
> A: Nonsense. The dissolution of the battalion began in the fall of 1942. Initially the privates were dismissed, but my father stayed there until January

---

658   Hrabovs'kyi refers to the partisan Izrail Abramovich Lapidus (1909-1986), commander of the Kutozov detachment of the second Minsk partisan brigade, and the secretary of the Minsk rural underground *raion* committee of the KP(b)B. E. G. Ioffe, G. D. Knat'ko and V. D. Selemenev, *Kholokost v Belarusi, 1941–1944* (Minsk: Natsional'nyi Arkhiv Respubliki Belarus', 2002), 219–221. Invoking Lapidus and Kaganovich as representatives of Soviet atrocities is not not a random choice; there were few Jewish commanders among Soviet partisan formations. Hrabovs'kyi does not explain how and when the OUN(b)'s 1943 political programs entered the Ukrainian constitution.

1943. And when the leader of the battalion was taken to Germany my father, at the time in Konotop or in Bakhmach, was informed that Gestapo may arrest him. Also, the leading members of the *Provid* of the OUN, led by Bandera, had been arrested, as we know, already in July of 1941. What kind of killing of Jews in Ukraine could there have been, when he was stationed around Vitsebsk?[659]

The disagreements regarding Shukhevych's whereabouts in 1942 concern not only the interpretations of the events, but also about basic facts surrounding the German occupation of Belarus. Shukhevych's critics portray him as a war criminal; his admirers either overlook this episode or regard his collaboration with Nazi Germany as unproblematic.

Conclusion

Independence called for a re-evaluation of Ukrainian history. As the polarized discussions regarding the legacy of Shukhevych and other OUN leaders show, this process is not without its difficulties. At the heart of this discussion lies the question of what sort of society Ukraine should be, its geopolitical orientation, and what sort of "national heroes" and role models this society needs. Some commentators have argued that the glorification of the leaders of the OUN and UPA does not mean rehabilitation of their ideology:

> One piece of good news, however, is that attempts to rehabilitate OUN and UPA followers as freedom fighters and glorify their leaders as national heroes, are not accompanied by attempts to revive the ideology of integral nationalism or promote any kind of militancy and intolerance. The emphasis typically is put on ethical rather than ideological values. The UPA fighters . . . are praised first of all for their patriotism and commitment to the national-liberation cause, for their idealism and dedication, for spiritual strength and self-sacrifice. We see here the makings of a heroic myth to counterbalance the long-dominant image of the impeccable Red Army. Any nation invents some historical myths of the sort, and we can only

---

[659] "Yurii Shukhevych: Ya hadaiu, Prezydent udostoidet' moho bat'ka naivyshchoi nahorody," *L'vivs'kyi portal*, July 6, 2007, accessed February 22, 2008, http://portal.lviv.ua/citizens/ 2007/07/06/174417.html.

hope that every nation will be able to keep the irrational energy of its historical myths under rational control.[660]

A historian may object that this sort of semi-mythical, moral tales of the exploits of "national liberators" belongs in the nineteenth, rather than the twenty-first century, and that the role of the professional historian is to be to facilitate the understanding of the past rather than producing edifying patriotic myths, using the organs of state security. The professional historian would also raise the question of whether it is possible to turn Shukhevych into a national hero without legitimizing the ideology of the organizations he led.

"Ukraine for Ukrainians" was implemented as brutal policy. Members of both wings of the OUN engaged in pogroms in 1941 and ethnic cleansing in 1943, in the ranks of the Wehrmacht, the Ukrainian police in occupied Ukraine, the UPA and *Waffen-SS Galizien*. The ideology of the OUN(b) was not static. Yet, at the same time as the OUN(b) officially moderated its political positions in the summer of 1943, the UPA was systematically massacring the Polish population of Volhynia, expanding the ethnic cleansing to eastern Galicia in 1944.[661] While Bandera himself remained a committed anti-democrat until his death at the hands of a Soviet assassin in 1959, the organization went through periods when its totalitarianism was toned down.[662]

The nationalistic accounts tend to focus on what has been done to Ukrainians and not by them.[663] In the quest for victim

---

660 Mykola Riabchuk, "Ukraine: Neither Heroes nor Villains: Review of Heroes and Villains: Creating National History in Contemporary Ukraine, by David Marples (Budapest: Central European Press, 2007)," *Transitions Online*, February 6, 2007.
661 Ivan Lysiak-Rudnyts'kyi, "Natsionalizm i totalitaryzm (Vidpovid' M. Prokopovi)," *Journal of Ukrainian Studies* 7, no. 2 (1982): 83–85; Per Anders Rudling, "Theory and Practice: Historical Representation of the War Time Activities of OUN-UPA (the Organization of Ukrainian Nationalists—the Ukrainian Insurgent Army)," *East European Jewish Affairs* 36, no. 2 (2006): 163–189; and Łada, "Creative Forgetting," 340–375.
662 John Armstrong, *Ukrainian Nationalism*, 3rd ed. (Englewood, CO: Ukrainian Academic Press, 1990), 117.
663 John-Paul Himka, "War Criminality: A Blank Spot in the Collective Memory of the Ukrainian Diaspora," *Spaces of Identity* 5, no. 1 (2005), 13–14.

status it is easily forgotten that Ukrainians were found not only among the victims, but also among the perpetrators of the totalitarian regimes.[664] Referring to this phenomenon as "the nationalism of the victim," Timothy Garton Ash (b. 1955) notes that the focus on the suffering of one's own group often comes at the expense of the interest taken in the suffering of others, that it is linked to "a reluctance to acknowledge in just measure the sufferings of other peoples, an inability to admit that the victim can also victimize."[665] Günther Grass (1927-2015) — of all people — referred to the uneven and selective approach of dealing with the past as "disabled memory."[666]

Much as both sides in the controversy squabbled over caricatures which are a legacy of Soviet and nationalist propaganda, the designation of Shukhevych as a national hero is best understood as continuing this tradition. Ironically, the controversy took place at a time when recent scholarship raised very serious question about the suitability of the OUN and UPA as symbols of an aspiring democracy. Rather than more myth making, Ukrainian society may arguably be better served by critical inquiry and critical engagement with the difficult episodes of it recent past.

---

[664] Andreas Kappeler, *Der schwierige Weg zur Nation: Beiträge zur neuern Geschichte der Ukraine* (Vienna: Böhlau, 2003), 19.
[665] Timothy Garton Ash, "The Life of Death," *The New York Review of Books*, December 19, 1985, 32.
[666] Richard S. Esbenshade, "Remembering to Forget: Memory, History, National Identity in Postwar East-Central Europe," *Representations*, no. 49 (1995), 84, citing Gunter Grass, "Losses," *Granta* 42 (1992): 102.

6. Yushchenko's Fascist
The Bandera Cult in Ukraine and Canada*

Introduction

Having suffered a humiliating defeat in the first round of the 2010 Ukrainian presidential elections, the outgoing president Viktor Yushchenko on 28 January 2010 took the step of posthumously designating the wartime leader of the most radical wing of the Organization of Ukrainian Nationalists—also known as the OUN(b)—Stepan Bandera, as "Hero of Ukraine," the highest honor of the Ukrainian state. This controversial decision, some observers suggested, was aimed at mobilizing pro-Yanukovych voters in the east and south of the country against the "Orange" candidate Yuliia Tymoshenko.[667] Yushchenko and Tymoshenko, former allies during the 2004–2005 popular protests against the mass electoral fraud by then-prime minister Viktor Yanukovych, soon became bitter enemies.[668] Yushchenko's lionizing of Bandera was not an isolated incident, but a culmination of a long process of rehabilitating the legacy of the OUN(b) and the Ukrainian Insurgent Army (UPA), which was escalated during his last years in office. This article seeks to contextualize the debates against the backdrop of current scholarship, which has significantly advanced our understanding of wartime Ukrainian nationalist violence. Following a section on the historical background of the OUN, it surveys various statements and actions by Ukrainian governmental organizations, politicians, memory activists, and legitimizing historians, followed by an interpretation of the historical discussions, and a concluding analysis.

---

* A previous version of this chapter was published in the *Journal of Soviet and Post-Soviet Politics and Society*, vol. 3, no. 2 (2017): 129-178.
667 Taras Kuzio, "Yushchenko Facilitates Yanukovych's Election and Buries the Orange Revolution," *Eurasia Daily Monitor* 7, no. 31 (2010).
668 On this conflict see, for instance Peter Johnsson, *Ukraina i historien: Från äldsta tid till 2015* (Stockholm: Carlssons bokförlag, 2015), 351–60.

The OUN and Fascism

Much of the controversy surrounding the legacy of the OUN(b) concerns the question of which terms should be used to characterize this organization. Especially sensitive for admirers of the OUN is the question whether the organization can be described as fascist. In order to contextualize the discussion, this essay starts by sketching out the historical background.

The OUN emerged, in 1929, out of an amalgamation between the Ukrainian Military Organization (UVO) and a number of other extreme right-wing organizations—the Union of Ukrainian Nationalist Youth (SUNM), the Group of Ukrainian Nationalist Youth (HUNM), and the League of Ukrainian Nationalists (LUN). The latter, in turn, had been formed in 1925 as a merger of the Ukrainian National Association (UNO), the Union of Ukrainian Fascists (SUF), and the Union for the Liberation of Ukraine.[669] While there were fascists among the founders of the organization, the OUN did not, as a rule, use the term itself; it would appear that the motivation here was the desire to emphasize the "originality" of Ukrainian nationalism.[670] Since 1945, of course, the use of the term fascism has been anything but neutral. Often used as a term of abuse, it is emotionally loaded, and not seldom misused for political purposes.

One of the earliest Western researchers of the OUN was John A. Armstrong (1922-2010). An active participant and product of the Cold War, Armstrong made no secret of his admiration of the OUN. His categorization of the OUN(b) was, however, ambiguous. While acknowledging that "[t]he theory and the teachings of the nationalists were very close to fascism, and in some respects, such as the insistence on 'racial purity,' even went beyond the original fascist doctrines,"[671] Armstrong contended that,

---

669 Bruder, *"Den ukrainischen Staat erkämpfen oder sterben!"*, 32; Panchenko, *Mykola Lebed'*, 15; Anatol' Kamins'kyi, *Krai, emihratsiia i mizhnarodni zakulisy: Z peredmovoiu Darii Rebet* (Manchester, Munich, New York: Vydannia Polytychnoi Rady OUNz Nakladom Kraevoi PR OUNz u Velykobrytanii, 1982), 39–42.
670 Bruder, *"Den ukrainischen Staat erkämpfen oder sterben!"* 35.
671 John A. Armstrong, *Ukrainian Nationalism, 1939-1945* (New York: Columbia University Press, 1955), 279.

[a]t least as a start, it seems preferable not to call the OUN's ideology "fascism" but to designate it "integral nationalism," in accordance with Carlton Hayes' classification of the Action Française model. In any case, it is clear that the relationship of the OUN to Nazism was in no way one of affiliation but, at the most, one of affinity.[672]

At the same time, Armstrong did not regard these categories as mutually exclusive, and he included German National Socialism in the "integral nationalist" category. By contrast, Ukrainian diaspora scholars, in particularly those of the post-war third wave of Ukrainian émigrés, tend to reject the label of fascism for the OUN.[673]

There are a number of definitions of fascism, and the OUN(b) fits rather neatly within most. Ernst Nolte's (1923-2016) characterization from 1963 is still useful for conceptualizing the OUN(b) ideology, particularly during the war years: "Fascism is anti-Marxism which seeks to destroy the enemy by the evolvement [sic] of a radically opposed and yet related ideology and by the use of almost identical and yet typologically modified methods, always, however, within the unyielding framework of national self-assertion and autonomy."[674] The OUN(b) similarly fulfills the six points of a "fascist minimum" which Nolte regarded as the criteria for categorizing an organization as fascist: anti-Communism, anti-liberalism, anti-conservatism, the leadership principle, a party-army, and the aim of totalitarianism.[675] There are, of course, other definitions of fascism. Helpful in this regard is Roger Griffin's (b. 1948) identification of an ideological nucleus of

---

672 John A. Armstrong, "Collaborationism in World War II: The Integral Nationalist Variant in Eastern Europe," *Journal of Modern History* 40, no. 3 (1968): 396-410, here: 400-01.
673 For a discussion on the ideology of the OUN in comparative perspective, see Andreas Umland, "Challenges and Promises of Comparative Research into Post-Soviet Fascism: Methodological and Conceptual Issues in the Study of the Contemporary East European Extreme Right," *Communist and Post-Communist Studies* 48, no. 2-3 (2015): 169-81.
674 Ernst Nolte, *Three Faces of Fascism: Action Française, Italian Fascism, National Socialism*, trans. Leila Vennewitz (New York: New American Library, 1969), 40.
675 Stanley G. Payne, "The Concept of Fascism," in *Who Were the Fascists?: Social Roots of European Fascism*, eds. Stein Ugelvik Larsen, Bernt Hagtvet, and Jan Petter Myklebust (Bergen: Universitetsforlaget, 1980), 17.

fascism in a synthesis of ultra-nationalism, populism, and, in particular, the myth of rebirth, or palingenesis, of the nation—characteristics that are all heavily present in the OUN(b)'s rhetoric.[676]

Academically, i.e. for the purpose of comparative historical analysis, the characterization of the OUN(b), in particular during the war years, as a fascist organization, has gained acceptance by a growing number of specialists in the field.[677] The OUN, and, in particular the Bandera wing should be understood in the larger European context, in which there were many varieties within the fascist tradition, of which "integralism" was one.[678] Historian Franziska Bruder (b. 1965), the author of the most detailed academic study of the OUN, describes the organization as "a classic representative of a nationalist movement with fascist characteristics that appeared in east-central Europe."[679] Similar characterizations are used by other scholars of Ukrainian nationalism. Timothy Snyder notes that "Bandera aimed to make of Ukraine a one-party fascist dictatorship without national minorities" and that he "remained faithful to the idea of a fascist Ukraine until assassinated by the KGB in 1959."[680] David R. Marples, of the Universi-

---

[676] Roger D. Griffin, *The Nature of Fascism* (New York: Routledge, 1991). See also "Section III: Fascist Ideology—The Quest for the 'Fascist Minimum'," in Aristotle A. Kallis (ed.), *The Fascism Reader* (New York: Routledge, 2003).

[677] Umland, "Der ukrainische Nationalismus zwischen Stereotyp und Wirklichkeit," 9. Oleksander Zaitsev of the Ukrainian Catholic University in L'viv has sought to revive a historical dichotomy between "integral nationalism" and fascism, introducing the neologism "Ustashism" to categorize the OUN's ideology. See chapter eight and Zaitsev, "Fascism or Ustashism?" 183–93; and idem., "De-Mythologizing Bandera: Towards a Scholarly History of the Ukrainian Nationalist Movement," *Journal of Soviet and Post-Soviet Politics and Society* 1, no. 2 (2015): 411–20.

[678] Juan J. Linz, "Political Space and Fascism as Late-Comer: Conditions Conducive to the Success or Failure of Fascism as a Mass Movement in Inter-War Europe," in Larsen, Hagtvet, and Myklebust (eds.), *Who Were the Fascists?*, 169, 187.

[679] Bruder, *"Den ukrainischen Staat erkämpfen oder sterben!"* 51.

[680] Timothy D. Snyder, "A Fascist Hero in Democratic Kiev," *The New York Review of Books*, 24 February 2010. http://blogs.nybooks.com/post/4094768 95/a-fascist-hero-in-democratic-kiev (accessed 7 March 2010).

ty of Alberta, describes the OUN as "a typically fascist movement of the interwar period not dissimilar to the Italian version."[681]

This author concurs with Bruder's and Marples' characterization of the OUN, in particular in regards to the crucial period between 1938 and 1943, during which that organization's most controversial policies were executed. Like similar organizations at the time, it shared common attributes such as the raised arm salute,[682] anti-Semitism, the *Führerprinzip* (leader principle), and an expansive, jingoistic nationalism. Its core "Decalogue" of principles explicitly condoned "enslaving foreigners" and called upon its members not to hesitate to "commit the greatest crime if the good of the cause requires it."[683] Its red-and-black banner, adopted in 1941, symbolized *Blut und Boden* (blood and soil) ideology, and members of its youth organization performed military drill and wore brown shirts with black ties. Akin to similar movements in eastern Europe, such as Jozef Tiso's (1887-1947) Hlinka Guard in Slovakia, Corneliu Zelea Codreanu's (1899-1938) Legionnaires in Romania, Ante Pavelić's (1889-1959) Croatian *Ustaše*, Ferenc Szálasi's (1897-1946) Arrow Cross in Hungary or Gustavs Celmiņš' (1899-1968) *Pērkonkrusts* in Latvia, the OUN(b) embraced

---

681 David Marples, "Hero of Ukraine Linked to Jewish killings: Honorary Title Sure to Provoke Divisions among Ukrainians Today," *Edmonton Journal*, 7 February 2010: A 12.
682 The fascist salute was adopted at the Second Conference of the OUN(b). This entailed raising the right arm "slightly to the right, slightly above the peak of the head," while exclaiming "Glory to Ukraine!" to which members were to respond "Glory to the Heroes!"; *Postanovy II. Velykohu Zboru Orhanizatsii Ukrains'kykh Natsionalistiv*, 37; Tsentral'nyi Derzhavnyi Arkhiv Hromads'kykh Ob'iednan' Ukrainy (hereafter: TsDAHOU), f. 1, op. 23, spr. 926, l. 199. After the war, the OUN omitted this section from their published texts from the conference in a conscious and deliberate effort to misrepresent the past of the organization in accordance with the new conditions of the post-1945 era. See, for instance *OUN v svitlu postanov Velykykh Zboriv* (n.p.: Zakordonni Chastiny Orhanizatsii Ukrains'kykh Natsionalistiv, 1955), 44-45. For a discussion on the fascist salute, see Rossoliński-Liebe, "The 'Ukrainian National Revolution'," 89; and Rossoliński-Liebe, *Stepan Bandera*, 179-80.
683 "The Decalogue of the OUN" was a set of ten commandments, written in 1929 by Stepan Lenkavs'kyi, who succeeded Bandera as OUN(b) leader, that was to guide the actions and behavior of the OUN members. The wording was later changed to "the most dangerous task"; Golczewski, *Deutsche und Ukrainer*, 598.

violence, ethnic hatred, terrorism, and an open worship of violence.[684] It was corporatist and explicitly totalitarian.

Background: Who was Stepan Bandera?

Stepan Bandera was twenty-four years old when, in 1933, he became the leader of the National Executive of the OUN in Galicia, then in interwar Poland.[685] The OUN, in particular the local Galician leadership or *Provid,* embraced terrorism and assassinations as a way to achieve its goal—a homogenized, totalitarian Ukrainian state where the OUN would hold an absolute monopoly of power. Bandera personally ordered the murder of employees at the Soviet consulate in L'viv, and of Bronisław Pieracki, the Polish minister of the interior.[686] Bandera used the Pieracki murder trial

---

684 Useful recent comparative studies include: Arnd Bauerkämper and Grzegorz Rossoliński-Liebe (eds.), *Fascism without Borders: Transnational Connections and Cooperation between Movements and Regimes in Europe from 1918 to 1945* (New York and Oxford: Berghahn Books, 2017); Aristotle A. Kallis, *Genocide and Fascism: The Eliminationist Drive in Fascist Europe* (New York: Routledge, 2009); and Rebecca Haynes and Martyn Rady (eds.), *In the Shadow of Hitler: Personalities of the Right in Central and Eastern Europe* (London and New York: I.B. Tauris, 2011)—see here on Bandera in a European context, in particular the chapter by David R. Marples, "Stepan Bandera: In Search of a Ukraine for Ukrainians," 227–44.

685 The most detailed recent studies of Stepan Bandera and his movement are Franziska Bruder, *"Den ukrainischen Staat erkämpfen oder sterben!"* and Rossoliński-Liebe, *Stepan Bandera.* Among the various review articles on the latter book are André Härtel, "Bandera's Tempting Shadow: The Problematic History of Ukrainian Radical Nationalism in the Wake of the Maidan," *Journal of Soviet and Post-Soviet Politics and Society* 1, no. 2 (2015): 421–28; and Yuri Radchenko, "From Staryi Uhryniv to Munich: The First Scholarly Biography of Stepan Bandera," *Journal of Soviet and Post-Soviet Politics and Society* 1, no. 2 (2015): 429–58.

686 Lucyna Kulińska, *Działalność terrorystyczna i sabotażowa nacjonalistycznych organizacji ukraińskich w Polsce w latach 1922–1939* (Kraków: Księgarnia Akademicka, 2009), 273–83; and Yaroslav Stets'ko, "Rozmovy dostoinoho Iaroslava Stets'ko z d-rom Anatolem Berdiem perevedeni i zapysany na lentakh dvanatsats' kasetok v chasi vid 17 do 23 chervnia 1985 v mistsi postoiu. Vidpys ruchno z lent zrobyv i opisla mahynopys vyhotovyv inzh. Dmytro Romanyshyn i tym potverdzhue virnist' zi zapysamy z lent. Vsiu pratsiu zakincheno v ponedilok, dnia 24 liutoho 1986 roku," Arkhiv OUN[b], Ukrains'ka Informatsiina Sluzhba, London (hereafter Arkhiv OUN-UIS) fond 23, l. 18, http://ounuis.info/library/handwritten-manuscripts-typed-

to make his name known and to promote the cause of the OUN brand of radical Ukrainian nationalism. He spent five years in prison for his involvement in the 1934 murder, after having his original death penalty commuted to seven consecutive life terms in prison.[687] During the trial, the young firebrand argued that no crime was too heinous that served the OUN's agenda. "The OUN values the value of the lives of its members, values it highly; but— our idea in our understanding is so great, so that when we talk about its realization, not individual, nor hundreds, but millions of lives need to be sacrificed, in order to realize it," he asserted.[688]

The NKVD's 1938 assassination of the OUN founder and original leader, Yevhen Konovalets' triggered a leadership crisis in the organization. Against the local, younger, and more radical Galician sections of the OUN stood an older, more conservative émigré wing of the OUN, under Konovalets' brother-in-law Andrii Mel'nyk. Like Konovalets', Mel'nyk was a veteran of World War I. He lacked, however, Konovalets' authority, and his cautious strategy of linking the OUN cause to the Third Reich, to which they remained loyal until the end of the war, was controversial for the more radical Galician leadership.

Anti-Semitism was integral to the ideology of both wings of the OUN, in particular after 1938. The *Literaturno-naukovyi vistnyk* (Literary-Scientific Herald), from 1933 *Vistnyk* (*The Herald*), edited by Dmytro Dontsov, perhaps the single most influential ideologue of Ukrainian "integral" nationalism, regularly contained Ukrainian translations of articles by Goebbels, Hitler, Rosenberg, Mussolini, and the leading Nazi racial theoretician Hans Günther (1891–1968).[689] In 1938, Volodymyr Martynets' (1899–1960), the editor of

---

manuscripts/567/rozmovy-yaroslava-stetska-z-anatoliiem-bedriiem.html (accessed 22 April 2017).
687 Panchenko, *Mykola Lebed'*, 23–32.
688 Petro Mirchuk, *Narys istorii Orhanizatsii Ukrains'kykh Natsionalistiv. Pershii tom 1920-1939 za redaktsiieiu Stepana Lenkavs'koho* (Munich: Ukrains'ke Vydavnytstvo, 1968 [2003]), 408.
689 See Kurylo, "The 'Jewish Question,'" 207–31. While Dontsov never joined the OUN, he not only inspired the organization intellectually, but, until his death in Montreal in 1973, cooperated closely with the organization, in particular with the OUN(b) leader Yaroslav Stets'ko, who invited him to write the ideo-

the OUN's official organ and most important ideological journal *Rozbudova Natsii* (The Building of a Nation),[690] published a pamphlet titled *The Jewish Problem in Ukraine*, in which he described Jews as "parasitical," "morally damaging," "corrupting," and a "hostile element," "racially unsuited for miscegenation and assimilation." To rid Ukraine of Jews, Martynets' called for "a total and absolute isolation of the Jews from the Ukrainian people," as the solution to the "Jewish problem":

> It is easier to liquidate 44,000 Jews using these methods, than to liquidate 3 ¼ million with more radical methods... All of the possibilities, especially if combined, will decrease the current strength of Jewry and will not only bring an end to their expansion in our country, but assure a continuous decline in the number of Jews, not only through emigration, but also through the decline of their natural growth rate. As the Jews will not be able to make a living, the Jews will take care of themselves.[691]

The Nazi aims of destroying the Second Polish Republic and the Soviet Union overlapped with that of the OUN. In a letter to Joachim von Ribbentrop on 2 May 1939, Andrii Mel'nyk assured the German Foreign Ministry that the OUN ideology was closely related to that of the Nazis and the Fascists, and offered its help in the "re-organization" of Eastern Europe.[692] OUN activists took up arms against the Second Polish Republic as Germany and the Soviet Union invaded the country. Current scholarship estimates the number of people killed, as a result of OUN violence in September 1939, at between 1,800 and 4,000.[693] Bandera was released from prison following the Nazi invasion of Poland but never again set

---

logical manifesto for the 1968 OUN(b) "IV Velykyi Zbir" (4th Grand Assembly); see W. Dankiw [Yaroslav Stets'ko] to Dmytro Dontsov, undated letter, 1967 (or late 1966), LAC, Ottawa, ON, MG 31, D130, Vol. 3, Folder 42.

690 On *Rozbudova natsii*, see Kurylo, "'Jewish Question,'" 237. After 1940, Martynets' remained loyal to the Mel'nyk wing of the OUN.

691 Volodymyr Martynets', *Zhydivs'ka problema v Ukraini* (London: Williams, Lea & Co., 1938), 10, 14–15, 22.

692 In 1939, Mel'nyk assured von Ribbentrop that the OUN was "ideologically related to similar movements in Europe, in particular National Socialism in Germany and Fascism in Italy", PA AA, Berlin, R 104430, Po. 26, No. 1m Pol. V. 4784, p. 2. Thanks to Ray Brandon for this reference.

693 Struve, *Deutsche Herrschaft*, 109–10; Ewa Siemaszko, "Bilans zbrodni," *Biuletyn Instytutu Pamięci Narodowej* 7–8 (2010): 80–81.

foot in what is today's Ukraine. After Bandera declared the establishment of a "revolutionary leadership," from Kraków in the *Generalgouvernement* on 10 February 1940, the OUN split into two wings, which have become known as OUN(m) and OUN(b), after their leaders Mel'nyk and Bandera. Nazi Germany offered the OUN prospects of collaboration, training several hundreds of their men in covert *Abwehr* schools in the *Generalgouvernement* prior to the invasion of the Soviet Union.[694] Both wings of the OUN knew the alliance between the Nazis and the Soviets was temporary, and after Operation Barbarossa was decided upon in December 1940, they were alerted and informed about the upcoming war.[695]

In April 1941, the Bandera wing of the OUN declared its intention to "combat Jews as supporters of the Muscovite-Bolshevik regime."[696] Its propaganda directives from the following month demanded the destruction of the Jews: "Ukraine for the Ukrainians! [...] Death to the Muscovite-Jewish commune! Beat the commune, save Ukraine!"[697] Referring to itself as a "natural ally" of Nazi Germany, the OUN(b) now declared its readiness to go to war against the USSR.[698] It received further encouragement on 10 April 1941, as Ante Pavelić and the *Ustaše* movement declared the establishment of the Independent State of Croatia in the wake of the German invasion of Yugoslavia. Throughout the 1930s, the OUN had collaborated closely with the *Ustaše*, trained its combatants at the same camps, and emulated its ideology and methods.[699]

---

694 McBride, "'A Sea of Blood and Tears'," 78, n. 96; Struve, *Deutsche Herrschaft*, 165–66; and "LEBED, Mykola," Ref. D 82270, Memo 22 July 1947, NARA, Washington, DC., RG 319, Entry A1 134-B, Container 457, Lebed, Mykola, Folder 1." CIC. Thanks to Jared McBride for generously sharing this document.
695 Tadeusz Piotrowski, *Genocide and Rescue in Wolyn: Recollections of the Ukrainian Nationalist Ethnic Cleansing Campaign against the Poles during World War II* (Jefferson, NC: McFarland, 2000), 231.
696 Stanislav Kul'chyts'kyi et al. (eds.), *OUN v 1941 rotsi: Dokumenty. V 2-kh ch. Ch. 1.* (Kyiv: Instytut Istorii Ukrainy NAN Ukrainy, 2006), 43.
697 Kul'chyts'kyi et al. (eds.), *OUN v 1941 rotsi*, 159, 165.
698 Kul'chyts'kyi et al. (eds.), *OUN v 1941 rotsi*, 12, 61.
699 "Akt Oskarżenia" in the Pieracki case, p. 31, in Archiwum Akt Nowych (AAN), Warsaw, MSZ 9378. Thanks to David Petruccelli for bringing this document to my attention. See also Kulińska, *Działalność terrorystyczna*, 278; and Danuta Gibas-Krzak, "Działalność terrorystyczna i dywersyjno-

On his part, Andrii Mel'nyk, leader of the rival wing, that same month proposed to Hitler the creation of a Greater Ukraine, stretching from the Danube to the Caspian Sea.[700]

With the launching of Operation Barbarossa in the summer of 1941, the OUN(b)'s anti-Semitic activities reached a crescendo. Marco Carynnyk describes the anti-Semitism of the OUN(b) in 1941 as "programmatic and pogrommatic."[701] This attitude was reflected in a 25 June 1941 letter from Bandera's deputy, the 29-year-old firebrand Yaroslav Stets'ko to Bandera, in which he, *en route* to L'viv informed his *Providnyk* (leader): "We are setting up a militia that will help remove the Jews and protect the population."[702]

OUN activists participated in the July 1941 pogroms, in which many of them displayed an above-average brutality.[703] Bernd Boll has concluded that the participation of the OUN was planned and premeditated—"the OUN leadership had certainly planned to murder their political and ethnic opponents."[704] Upon their arrival in L'viv, the commando of the Ukrainian *Wehrmacht*

---

sabotażowa nacjonalistów ukraińskich w latach 1921-1939," *Przegląd Biezpieczeństwa Wewnętrznego* 3 (2010): 174-186, here: 185.
700   Kul'chyts'kyi *et al.* (eds.), *OUN v 1941 rotsi*, 10.
701   Marco Carynnyk [Marko Tsarynnyk], "Zolochiv movchyt," *Krytyka* 14 (2005): 27-28. On the radicalization of anti-Jewish sentiment in the OUN leadership from 1938, see Carynnyk, "Foes of Our Rebirth"; Carynnyk, "'A Knife in the Back of Our Revolution'".
702   TsDAVOVU, Kyiv, f. 3833, op. 1, spr. 12, l. 10 (Telegram from Yaroslav Stets'ko no. 13, 25 June 1941).
703   The most detailed study of the OUN(b)'s role in the 1941 pogroms is Kai Struve's *Deutsche Herrschaft*. Other important works are John-Paul Himka, "The Lviv Pogrom of 1941: The Germans, Ukrainian Nationalists, and the Carnival Crowd," *Canadian Slavonic Papers / Revue canadienne des slavistes* 53, no. 2-3 (2011): 209-34; Rossoliński-Liebe, *Stepan Bandera*, especially 195-236; Grzegorz Rossoliński-Liebe, "Der Verlauf und die Täter des Lemberger Pogroms vom Sommer 1941," *Jahrbuch für Antisemitismusforschung* 22 (2015): 207-43; and Grzegorz Rossoliński-Liebe, "Erinnerungslücke Holocaust: Die ukrainische Diaspora und der Genozid an den Juden," *Vierteljahrshefte für Zeitgeschichte* 62, no. 3 (2014): 397-430.
704   Bernd Boll, "Złoczów, July 1941—The Wehrmacht and the Beginning of the Holocaust in Galicia: From a Criticism of Photographs to a Revision of the Past," in *Crimes of War: Guilt and Denial in the Twentieth Century*, eds. Omer Bartov, Atina Grossmann, and Mary Nolan (New York: The New Press, 2002), 73.

Battalion *Nachtigall* could rely on a fanatically anti-Semitic auxiliary contingent with good knowledge of the local conditions.[705] OUN(b) flyers, distributed in the first days of the German invasion, urged the population "Don't throw away your weapons yet. Take them up. Destroy the enemy...People!—Know this!— Moscow, Poland, the Hungarians, the Jews—these are your enemies. Destroy them."[706]

On 30 June 1941, the OUN(b) summarily declared Ukrainian "statehood," hoping that Ukraine would obtain a status similar to that of Tiso's Slovakia or Pavelić's Croatia.[707] Yaroslav Stets'ko presented himself as its self-proclaimed Prime Minister on behalf of the *Providnyk* Bandera.[708] The very declaration of statehood specified that the new state would "cooperate closely with National Socialist Greater Germany (...) under the Führer Adolf Hitler."[709] The OUN was committed to a "Ukraine for the Ukrainians," an ethnically cleansed totalitarian state, where all other political parties were to be banned.[710]

The main propagandist of the OUN(b)-dominated "government," Stepan Lenkavs'kyi (1904–77), advocated the physical destruction of Ukrainian Jewry, while "Prime Minister" Stets'ko expressed his support for "the destruction of the Jews and the expedience of bringing German methods of exterminating Jewry to Ukraine, barring their assimilation and the like."[711] Between 30

---

705 Hannes Heer, "Blutige Ouvertüre: Lemberg, 30. Juni 1941: Mit dem Einmarsch der Wehrmachttruppen beginnt der Judenmord," *Die Zeit* 26 (2001), http://www.zeit.de/2001/26/200126_a-lemberg.xml (accessed 23 August 2017), also published in: *Zeitschrift für Geschichtswissenschaft* 5 (2001); and Israel Gutman, "Nachtigall Battalion," *Encyclopedia of the Holocaust* (New York: Macmillan, 1995), 1029-30.
706 Pohl, *Nationalsozialistische Judenverfolgung in Ostgalizien 1941–1944*, 57.
707 Kul'chyts'kyi, *OUN v 1941 rotsi*, 11; and John-Paul Himka, "A Central European Diaspora under the Shadow of World War II: The Galician Ukrainians in North America," *Austrian History Yearbook* 37 (2006): 19.
708 Berkhoff and Carynnyk, "The Organization of Ukrainian Nationalists," 150.
709 Serhiichuk (ed.), *OUN-UPA v roky viiny: novi dokumenty i materialy*, 239.
710 Rossoliński-Liebe, "'Ukrainian National Revolution' of 1941," 87.
711 Finder and Prusin, "Collaboration in Eastern Galicia," 102; and Berkhoff and Carynnyk, "Organization of Ukrainian Nationalists," 1999: 171. Taras Hunczak has made an unconvincing attempt to show that Stets'ko's statement was a forgery. See Taras Hunczak, "Problems of Historiography: Histo-

June and 3 July 1941, when *Nachtigall* was stationed in L'viv, massive pogroms claimed the lives of 4,000 Jews.[712]

The participation of OUN militias in the murder of Jews is well documented, from OUN correspondence with the Nazis, and their own fliers and directives, down to movies and photos of Ukrainian militiamen in action. Some of the perpetrators are identifiable from the photos.[713] Violent pogroms followed the L'viv pogrom in Zolochiv, Ternopil, and other localities.[714] Recent research dispels all doubt that soldiers of the *Nachtigall* battalion, consisting almost exclusively of OUN activists serving in German uniform under Roman Shukhevych's command, took part in the anti-Jewish violence during the L'viv pogrom.[715] *Nachtigall* soldiers also carried out mass shootings of Jews in two villages in the Vinnytsia area in July 1941.[716] Throughout the German occupation, leading members of the Bandera wing wanted the Ukrainian

---

ry and Its Sources," *Harvard Ukrainian Studies* 25, no. 1–2 (2001): 129–42. For a discussion, see Taras Kurylo and Ivan Khymka [John-Paul Himka], "Iak OUN stavylasia do ievreiv? Rozdumy nad knyzhkoiu Volodymyra V"iatrovycha," *Ukraina Moderna* 13(2) (2008): 252–65, here: 253.

712 Heer, "Blutige Ouvertüre." In his book, Struve provides more specific numbers: The number of Jewish pogrom victims ranged between 7,295 and 11,309, of which between 3,015 and 4,359 fell victim to anti-Jewish violence inflicted by local perpetrators; Struve, *Deutsche Herrschaft*, 671.

713 On eyewitness testimonies and photographs from the L'viv pogrom see Ivan Khymka [John-Paul Himka], "Dostovirnist' svidchennia: reliatsiia Ruzi Vagner pro l'vivs'kyi pohrom vlitku 1941 r," *Holokost i suchasnist': studii v Ukraini i sviti* 4, no. 2 (2008): 43–79. Himka's work on militiamen in photographs comes from the research of Jeffrey Burds.

714 Marco Carynnyk, *Furious Angels: Ukrainians, Jews, and Poles in the Summer of 1941*, forthcoming; Marco Carynnyk, "The Palace on the Ikva – Dubne, September 18th, 1939 and June 24th, 1941," in Elazar Barkan, Elizabeth A. Cole, Kai Struve (eds.), *Shared History – Divided Memory: Jews and Others in Soviet-Occupied Poland, 1939–1941* (Leipzig: Leipziger Universitätsverlag, 2007), 273–302; and Carynnyk [Tsarynnyk] "Zolochiv movchyt."

715 Struve, *Deutsche Herrschaft*, 354–60; and Rossoliński-Liebe, "Der Verlauf und die Täter des Lemberger Pogroms," 236–37; Rudling, "Dispersing the Fog," 237.

716 See the 1944 testimony of Viktor Khar'kiv "Khmara," a member of both *Nachtigall* and *Schutzmannschaft* battalion 201; TsDAVOVU, f. 3833, op. 1, spr. 57, ark. 17–18.

Jews killed or removed, and offered to participate in the process.[717]

Bandera's relationship with the Nazis was complex. He had been liberated from prison as a consequence of the 1939 invasion, but in 1941 the German authorities demanded that Bandera retract the "Act of June 30th" and that he stop the OUN(b)'s armed attacks on the OUN(m), something he refused to do. Bandera was therefore taken to Berlin, where he was held in "*Ehrenhaft*," a form of honorary house arrest. Bandera and Stets'ko continued their political activities for some time. During the first week of July 1941, Stets'ko sent letters to the fascist leaders of Europe, Hitler, Mussolini, Franco, and Pavelić, seeking to assure them of his fascist credentials and hoping to enlist their support for his newly declared state.[718] After two leading members of the OUN(m) were assassinated, the German authorities correctly suspected the hand of the OUN(b) behind the murders, and had Bandera and Stets'ko incarcerated in the Berlin Spandau prison.[719]

The OUN continued to infiltrate German auxiliary police formations, obtaining weapons and training, but also getting deeply involved in the process of exterminating the Jewish population in Ukraine and Belarus. Many ranking OUN(b) leaders, among them Roman Shukhevych, interrupted their collaboration with Nazi Germany only in January 1943, during the time of the Stalingrad battle, after it became obvious that the Axis powers would lose the war.[720] By August 1943, the OUN(b) — from May

---

717 Berkhoff, *Harvest of Despair*, 83.
718 Rossoliński-Liebe, "'Ukrainian National Revolution' of 1941," 99, citing TsDAVOVU, f. 3833, op. 1, spr. 22, ll. 1–3.
719 David R. Marples, "Stepan Bandera: The Resurrection of a Ukrainian National Hero" *Europe-Asia Studies* 58, no. 4 (2006): 562; Philip Friedman, "Ukrainian-Jewish Relations during the Nazi Occupation," in *idem, Roads to Extinction: Essays on the Holocaust* (New York and Philadelphia: The Jewish Publication Society of America, 1980), 176-208, here: 195; Berkhoff and Carynnyk, "Organization of Ukrainian Nationalists," 149–52; and Bruder, "*Den ukrainischen Staat erkämpfen oder sterben!*" 57.
720 Per A. Rudling, "Szkolenie w mordowaniu: Schutzmannschaft battalion 201 i Hauptmann Roman Szuchewycz na Białorusi w 1942 r.," in Bogosław Paź (ed.), *Prawda historyczna a prawda polityczna w badaniach naukowych: Ludobójst-*

1943 under Shukhevych's leadership—began paying lip service to political pluralism, while continuing its massacres of Volhynian Poles and Jews. From early 1944, the OUN(b) and UPA expanded the anti-Polish massacres into East Galicia.[721] The exact number of victims is impossible to ascertain, but the author of the most extensive study on the topic lists the documented number of Poles, killed by the OUN(b) and UPA, as 91,200. Of these, 43,987 are identified by name.[722] To that should be added several thousands of Western Ukrainian Jews, killed by the OUN and UPA.

During the period of his detention, Bandera's direct contacts with the UPA insurgents were limited, but not non-existent. In March 1943, Bandera was moved to the Sachsenhausen camp, north of Berlin, where he and Stets'ko were placed in the *Zellenbau*, a special residential for high profile political prisoners. He had privileges other Sachsenhausen inmates did not. He received parcels from his wife who lived nearby, in Berlin-Charlottenburg. On 16 May 1944, his son Andrii was born, which means that in August 1943, he was either allowed to leave the *Zellenbau*, or allowed conjugal visits by his wife.[723] Upon his release in late 1944

---

wo na Kresach południowo-wschodniej Polski w latach 1939–1946 (Wrocław: Wydawnictwo uniwersytetu Wrołavskiego, 2011), 191–212.

721   On the UPA massacres in Eastern Galicia, in March to April 1944, see, for instance "ZVIT z protypol's'kykh aktsii," 1 June 1944, TsDAVOVU, f. 4620, op. 3, spr. 378, ark. 43–44, and Alexander Statiev, *The Soviet Counterinsurgency in the Western Borderlands* (Cambridge and New York: Cambridge University Press, 2013, 86–87, citing "Protokol v spravi vidplatnykh aktsii na poliakakh v pov. Peremyshliany [Retaliatory actions against Poles in the Peremyshliany District]" (12 May 1944), TsDAHOU, f. 57, op.4, d. 339, l. 422.

722   Siemaszko, "Stan badań nad ludobójstwem," 341. In regards to Ukrainians were killed by Polish forces during this period, Grzegorz Motyka estimates the number of Ukrainians killed by Poles at between 10,000 and 15,000, of which 8,000-10,000 perished west of the Curzon line. See Grzegorz Motyka, *Od rzezi wołyńskiej do akcji "Wisła:" Konflikt polsko-ukraiński 1943–1947* (Kraków: Wydawnictwo Literackie, 2011), 448. See also Ryszard Torzecki, *Polacy i Ukraińcy: Sprawa ukraińska w czasie II wojny światowej na terenie II Rzeczpospolitej* (Warsaw: PWN, 1993), 267. On the historiography of the conflict, see Grzegorz Rossoliński-Liebe, "Der polnisch-ukrainische Historikerdiskurs über den polnisch-ukrainischen Konflikt 1943-1947," *Jahrbücher für Geschichte Osteuropas* 57 (2009): 54–85.

723   D.V. Vedeneev and O.E. Lysenko, "Orhanizatsiia ukrains'kykh natsionalistiv i zarubizhni spetssluzhby (1920-1950-ti rr.)," *Ukrains'kyi istorichnyi zhurnal* 3 (2009): 132–46, here: 137; and Rossoliński-Liebe, *Stepan Bandera*, 285–86.

he resumed his cooperation with Nazi Germany, which continued until the collapse of the Third Reich in May 1945.[724]

Bandera was instrumental for the radicalization of the OUN(b) in 1939–41, where he helped drafting the blueprint for the violent uprising of June–July 1941, but was not—unlike Shukhevych and Stets'ko—physically present in L'viv during the pogroms in June–July 1941. During the OUN(b)'s and UPA's ethnic cleansing of the Poles and Jews of Western Ukraine, he was in prison; during the brutal post-war Soviet pacification of Western Ukraine, he was in hiding in Austria and Germany. During their tenacious insurgency, the OUN(b) and UPA killed at least 18,000, but perhaps as many as 30,000 people in a campaign of underground warfare which the Soviet authorities quashed with utter brutality, killing over 107,166 people, and capturing and arresting 230,217.[725] The OUN(b)'s postwar attempts to infiltrate Soviet Ukraine failed disastrously, and by 1949 the CIA was distancing itself from Bandera's increasingly sidelined group. His cooperation with British, Italian, and West German intelligence services continued for much of the 1950s, as a rule with similarly tragic results, penetrated as his organization was by Soviet agents.[726] In October 1959 Stepan Bandera, that uncompromising revolutionary and assassin, was himself murdered by the KGB outside his Munich apartment.[727] In the eyes of his followers this turned him into a martyr and consolidated the Bandera myth.

Despite the Ukrainian government's identification of Ukraine with the OUN and UPA, it is important to keep in mind that, official policy notwithstanding, these extremist organizations were

---

724 Rossoliński-Liebe, *Stepan Bandera*, 285; and "O sovmestnoi deial'nosti OUN-UPA s okhrannoi politsiiei i nemetskoi 'SD'," 7 October 1944, State Archives of L'viv Region, Derzhavnyi arkhiv l'vivs'koi oblasti (DALO) f. 3, op. 1, d. 67, ll. 78–104, published in: Burds, *Shpionazh i natsionalizm*, 146–72.
725 Jeffrey Burds, "AGENTURA: Soviet Informants' Networks & the Ukrainian Underground in Galicia, 1944–1948," *East European Politics and Societies* 11, no. 1 (1997): 97, 108–9. See also Burds, *The Early Cold War*.
726 The CIA used several of Bandera's cronies to run agents into Ukraine. Bandera himself did not work for the CIA, but the BND established contact with Bandera in 1956. Until his death Bandera helped to bring Ukrainian agents into the USSR. See Breitman and Goda, *Hitler's Shadow*, 73–97.
727 Plokhy, *The Man with the Poison Gun*.

not synonymous with the Ukrainian people. Even at the height of their activities, the Banderites were largely a regional force which never counted more than some tens of thousands of people and never commanded the support of more than a small minority of Ukrainians. Timothy Snyder reminds us that "it is necessary to remember, that there were many other Ukrainian activists in that time, who were not glorifying violence. The majority of Ukrainian politicians at that time were not fascists and were not terrorists. They embraced entirely different political ideals."[728] Few of the democratic alternatives to the OUN, however, survived the destruction of Poland in 1939, and many of those who were not targeted by the unprecedented Soviet repressions that befell Western Ukraine in 1939–41 were intimidated, attacked, or even murdered by the OUN(b).[729]

Nationalist Myth Making in the Diaspora

The Ukrainian diaspora has played a key role in preserving, defending, and legitimizing the legacy of the OUN. The Ukrainian community in Canada got a very significant boost in the late 1940s and early 1950s, as many refugees, so-called Displaced Persons, arrived in that country after the war. These immigrants brought with them their nationalist politics, and became, with the onset of the Cold War useful allies against the Soviet Union.[730] In North America, they set up institutions, schools, papers and fraternal organizations dedicated to the preservation of the nationalist heritage.[731] In the diaspora, they developed their own historical and

---

[728] "Profesor Snaider: proholoshennia heroiamy—radians'ka ideia," *BBC Ukrains'ka Sluzhba*, 3 March 2010, http://www.bbc.co.uk/ukrainian/Ukraine/2010/03/100303_snyder_ie_it.shtml (accessed 3 March 2010).

[729] Marples, *Heroes and Villains*, 311. On OUN(b) and UPA violence against Ukrainians, see also Kudelia, "Choosing Violence in Irregular Wars," 149–81; Burds, "AGENTURA," 97, 108–109; and Burds, "Early Cold War."

[730] See, for instance, Anna Holian, "Anticommunism in the Streets: Refugee Politics in Cold War Germany," *Journal of Contemporary History* 45, no. 1 (2010): 134–61.

[731] See, for instance, Boshyk, Isajiw, and Senkus (eds.), *The Refugee Experience*; Grzegorz Rossoliński-Liebe, "Celebrating Fascism and War Criminality in Multicultural Canada: The Political Myth and Cult of Stepan Bandera in Mul-

political culture, preserving organizational structures and maintaining their nationalist ideology. Presenting the OUN as "a national liberation movement," the nationalist rendition of the past was organized around a number of central claims:

1. there never existed a Ukrainian anti-Semitic movement or party;[732]
2. the OUN could not have been a fascist organization, as it did not have its own state or government;[733]
3. Ukrainian war-time Nationalists cannot be considered collaborators, since they had no state;
4. integral nationalists are not fascists;
5. the detention of Bandera, Stets'ko, and other OUN leaders in German concentration camps in 1943–44 qualifies them as prime victims of the Nazis;
6. the OUN(b) and UPA took up arms against Hitler and Stalin.[734]

Instead, this tradition presents both the OUN(b) and the UPA as democratic movements, and Bandera, Shukhevych, and Stets'ko as anti-Nazi resistance fighters. Admirers and adherents of these organizations tend to rely on an uncritical reading of the declarations of the OUN(b) August 1943 III *Velykyi Zbir* (Grand Assembly), taking its official statements about moderating its ide-

---

ticultural Canada," *Kakanien Revisited*, December 29 (2010): 1–16, and Rudling, "Multiculturalism, Memory, and Ritualization."

732 For this claim, see, for instance, Bohdan Wytwytsky, "Anti-Semitism," in Volodymyr Kubijovyč (ed.), *Encyclopedia of Ukraine*, Vol. 1 (Toronto: CIUS Press, 1984), 82.

733 For this argument, see, for instance, Motyl, *The Turn to The Right*, 166. In 2010, Motyl repeats this argument in: Alexander Motyl, "Ukraine, Europe, and Bandera," *Cicero Foundation Great Debate Paper* 5 (2010): 12, http://www.cicerofoundation.org/lectures/Alexander_J_Motyl_UKRAINE_EUROPE_AND_BANDERA.pdf (accessed 2 April 2010); and Alexander J. Motyl, "Difficult Task Defining Bandera's Historic Role," *The Moscow Times*, 11 March 2010, available at http://historynewsnetwork.org/article/124267 (accessed 23 August 2017).

734 For this claim, see, for instance, Petro R. Sodol, *UPA: They Fought Hitler and Stalin: A Brief Overview of Military Aspects from the History of the Ukrainian Insurgent Army, 1942-1949* (New York: Committee of the World Convention and Reunion of Soldiers in the Ukrainian Insurgent Army, 1987).

ology at face value, overlooking the Nationalists' continued, systematic anti-Polish and anti-Jewish violence, ignoring or dismissing survivors' accounts.

The OUN(b) went to great lengths to cover up their atrocities. As early as October 1943, the organization ordered the production of documents "that would confirm that the Germans carried out anti-Jewish pogroms and liquidations by themselves, without the participation or help of the Ukrainian police" but which would instead "clearly confirm that Poles had initiated and taken part in anti-Jewish pogroms and at the same time that they had served as the hirelings and agents of the Germans in their struggle with Ukrainians."[735]

From the earliest years of the Cold War, nationalist Ukrainian émigrés worked closely with Ukrainian scholars sympathetic to their cause, promoting their agenda through academic, or quasi-academic venues. During the Cold War, pro-nationalist Ukrainian émigré academics in the US were underwritten by the CIA and other Western intelligence services as part of the efforts to counteract and weaken the Soviet Union.[736] In Canada, where the Ukrainian presence is considerably stronger, University of Alberta historian Frances Swyripa (b. 1950) notes, Ukrainian nationalists successfully lobbied "for a multiculturalism policy to serve what they saw as their special needs as a fully functioning microsociety aided by public funds and access to government institutions and programs."[737] Indeed, as another Alberta historian, Aya Fujiwara has argued, "the multicultural movement...began under the initiative of Ukrainian nationalists,"[738] who she describes as "by far the

---

735 Carynnyk, "Foes of our Rebirth," 345, citing TsDAVOVU f. 3833, op.1, spr.43,ark.9, facsimile on page 346.
736 On the Prolog Research and Publication Corporation, see chapter three, Breitman and Goda, *Hitler's Shadow*, 73–97; Kuzio, "U.S. Support for Ukraine's Liberation," 51–64; John-Paul Himka, "Assessing the Prolog Legacy," *Current Politics in Ukraine*, 31 May 2013, https://ukraineanalysis.wordpress.com/2013/05/31/assessing-the-prolog-legacy/ (accessed 7 July 2017).
737 Frances Swyripa, *Storied Landscapes: Ethno-Relious Identity and the Canadian Prairies* (Winnipeg, MB: University of Manitoba Press, 2010), 140.
738 Aya Fujiwara, "From Anglo-Conformity to Multiculturalism: The Role of the Scottish, Ukrainian, and Japanese Ethnicity in the Transformation of Canadian Identity, 1919–1971" (PhD dissertation, University of Alberta, 2007), 210.

most active group in the pursuit of multiculturalism and collective ethnic rights."[739] In the chronically underfunded humanities, this political symbiosis has developed into economic interdependence. Ukrainian studies centers in North America are dependent on the generosity of community donors who, in turn, expect a certain representation of history.[740]

During the Cold War, émigré nationalist historians released documents selectively, re-typing original documents, whereby wording and phrasing that would have contradicted the sanitized historiography were omitted.[741] For instance, when Paris-based historian and ranking OUN(b) activist Volodymyr Kosyk (1924–2017) republished Stets'ko's 1941 declaration of statehood, he omitted the pledge that this state would exist "in close cooperation with the Greater German Reich under the *Führer* Adolf Hitler." Other pro-OUN historians took this one step further. Émigré Ukrainian historian and OUN veteran Taras Hunchak maintains that with the declaration of Ukrainian statehood the OUN had "crossed its Rubicon in the very first days of the German-Soviet war, placing it in an adversarial position vis-à-vis the

---

739 Fujiwara, "From Anglo-Conformity to Multiculturalism," 223.
740 The Canadian Institute of Ukrainian Studies (CIUS), perhaps the most prominent center for Ukrainian studies in Canada, is largely funded by donations from the diaspora community, and the researchers, with few exceptions, reflect the dominant view. University of Alberta professor David Marples, whose collaboration with the CIUS dates back to the 1970s, notes that "[M]y colleagues at the Canadian Institute of Ukrainian Studies hold views that vary only in the smallest degree from those of the community at large. In only one case there is an exception: John-Paul Himka, whose investigations into the Holocaust in Ukraine has led him to the conclusion that his compatriots have never admitted responsibility for their complicity at various times during the war"; David R. Marples, "Studying Ukraine," Modern European History Seminar, University of Cambridge, http://www.hist.cam.ac.uk/seminars_events/seminars/modern-european/marples-writing-history-of-ukraine.pdf (date of last access 27 January 2010, link no longer active as at 23 August 2017), 5. On the complications of émigré donors, Canadian official multiculturalism, and its influence on historiography, see Rossoliński-Liebe, "Celebrating Fascism"; Dietsch, *Making Sense of Suffering*, 120–21; Karyn Ball and Per Anders Rudling, "The Underbelly of Canadian Multiculturalism: Holocaust Obfuscation and Envy in the Debate about the Canadian Museum for Human Rights," *Holocaust Studies: A Journal of Culture and History* 20, no. 3 (2014): 33–80.
741 Rudling, *The OUN, the UPA, and the Holocaust*, 20.

Germans."⁷⁴² Diaspora political activists, in turn, rehashed academic discourses, often in an exaggerated and reductive manner. Only the opening of the archives after 1991 has allowed historians to reconstruct the events more closely and to expose the ideologically motivated distortions.

After Ukraine became independent in 1991, several influential émigré nationalists returned to Ukraine, seeking to repatriate their ideology. Whereas this group was limited in numerical terms, the émigré impact on Ukrainian political life, public intellectuals, and opinion making was significant. The returning émigrés included such figures as the first lady of Ukraine, Kateryna (Chumachenko) Yushchenko (b. 1961), and OUN(b) activist Roman Zvarych (b. 1953), who briefly served as Justice Minister under Yushchenko. A significant role in the repatriation of the Banderite heritage to Ukraine was played by the widow of OUN(b) leader Yaroslav Stets'ko, Yaroslava, or Slava. Under her leadership the OUN(b) reconstituted itself in Ukraine as the *Konhres Ukrains'kykh Natsionalistiv* (KUN—Congress of Ukrainian Nationalists). Slava Stets'ko who was, for some time, an MP and seniority speaker or Mother of the House, i.e. the Oldest Member of the Ukrainian parliament, the *Verkhovna Rada*.⁷⁴³

---

742 Berkhoff and Carynnyk, "Iaroslav Stets'ko," 151; and Taras Hunczak, "Between Two Leviathans: Ukraine during the Second World War," in *Ukrainian Past, Ukrainian Present: Selected Papers from the Fourth Congress for Soviet and East European Studies, Harrogate, 1990*, ed. Bohdan Krawchenko (New York and London: Macmillan, 1993), 99. On Hunczak's background in the OUN and his work for US intelligence, see "Memorandum for the record, Subject: Report of Contact with AECASSOWARY/2 in Washington, 3-4 November 1960," 18 November 1960, p. 7. AERODYNAMIC, vol. 45, NARA, College Park, MD, Record Group [RG] 263, NN3-263-02-008, Box: 23, Folder: 1, Document: 2; "HUNCHAK Taras," 15 January 1961, Aerodyniamic, vol. 20, *NARA*, RG 263, Box 13, NN3-263-02-008; and Taras Hunchak, *Moi spohady-stezhky zhyttia* (Kyiv: Dnipro, 2005), 16, 22, 30, 39-40, 66-67.

743 Born in Yonkers in 1953, Zvarych, aide and personal secretary to Yaroslav Stets'ko, moved to Ukraine in 1992 to set up the Congress of Ukrainian Nationalists (KUN) together with Yaroslava Stets'ko. Following the Orange Revolution, Zvarych became Minister of Justice, but was forced to resign after having lied about holding MA and PhD degrees from Columbia University; Andrew Wilson, *Ukraine's Orange Revolution* (New Haven and London: Yale University Press, 2005), 161.

Following the collapse of the USSR, diaspora histories of Ukraine replaced the Soviet textbooks. The most widely used was Canadian Ukrainian historian Orest Subtelny's above-mentioned *Ukraine: A History*, the English original version of which was initially published by the University of Toronto Press in 1988. Even though Subtelny had not worked in Ukrainian archives, in the immediate post-Soviet period the book was regarded as indispensable. By 1998, its Ukrainian and Russian translations alone had sold over 800,000 copies.[744] "No Ukrainian article between 1991 and 1995 was considered complete without a reference to Subtelny in the footnotes. Subtelny, if you like, became the new Lenin," University of Alberta historian David Marples observed, tongue in cheek.[745] An ethnocentric history of Ukrainians, rather than a history of Ukraine, only five of its nearly 700 pages are devoted to non-Ukrainians.[746]

Under Yushchenko, a slightly modified version of the diaspora narrative of history was adopted as government policy. Whereas the archives had been largely opened already in the 1990s and the situation regarding their access was relatively good, Yushchenko placed them in the hands of ideological activists, whom he tasked with the production of an edifying national mythology. One of the cornerstones of Yushchenko's memory politics was the Ukrainian Institute of National Memory (UINP), established in 2006.[747] One of the main tasks of his institute its founding director Yukhnovs'kyi stated, was to "return Stepan Bandera's good

---

744 Johan Öhman [Dietsch], "*Holodomor* and the Ukrainian Identity of Suffering: The 1932-1933 Ukrainian Famine in Historical Culture," *Canadian-American Slavic Studies* 37, no. 3 (Fall 2003): 27-44; here: 37.
745 Marples, "Studying Ukraine," 2.
746 Kuzio, *Theoretical and Comparative Perspectives on Nationalism*, 331.
747 On the UINP and memory policy in Ukraine, see, in particular, Georgiy Kasianov, "History, Politics, and Memory (Ukraine 1990s–2000s)," in *Memory and Change in Europe: Eastern Perspectives*, eds. Małgorzata Pakier and Joanna Wawrzyniak (New York and Oxford: Berghahn Books, 2015), 193–211; Georgii Kas'ianov, "K desiatiletiiu Ukrainskogo instituta natsional'noi pamiati (2006-2016)," *Historians.in.ua*, 14 January 2016, http://www.historians.in.ua/index.php/en/dyskusiya/1755-georgij-kas-yanov-k-desyatiletiyu-ukrainskogo-instituta-natsional-noj-pamyati-2006-2016 (accessed 7 July 2016); and Heorhii Kas'ianov, *Past Continuous: Istorychna polityka 1980-kh – 2000-kh rr. Ukraina ta susidy*, Kyiv: Antopos-Logos-Film, 2018.

name to the whole territory of Ukraine."⁷⁴⁸ The promotion of Bandera started, however, almost immediately after Yushchenko took office. Initially the instrumentalization took place within the auspices of the Archives of the Ukrainian Security Services (HDA SBU), in 2008-2010 under V"iatrovych's directorship. V"iatrovych simultaneously led the above-mentioned OUN(b) "façade structure" the Center for the Study of the Liberation Movement (TsDVR).⁷⁴⁹ On of the first tasks of their new center, OUN(b) leader Haidamacha stated, was a "broad civic activity campaign," entitled "The Truth about the UPA."⁷⁵⁰ One of the first joint projects was a portable exhibit glorifying the UPA, accompanied by a book with the same purpose, *The Ukrainian army – The History of the Undefeated*.⁷⁵¹ V"iatrovych and his institutes have been subject to sharp criticism by historians for employing dubious methods, which can be characterized as selective at best, but often directly misleading.⁷⁵²

---

748 *Stepan Bandera: Zbirnyk materialiv i dokumentiv* (Kyiv: Ukrains'kyi Instytut National'noi Pamiati, 2009), 10.
749 In the words of one of its central operatives: "The Organization [of Ukrainian Nationalists] is today a global (world-wide) closed structure, and much of the [work] done remains unannounced [...]. At the same time, a large segment of [its] activity is known thanks to various façade structures *[zavdiaki riznym fasadnym strukturam]* founded by the OUN: from political [...] to academic [ones, like] the 'Center for the Study of the Liberation Movement' (TsDVR) [...]"; Lypovets'kyi, *Orhanizatsiia ukrainskikh natsionalistiv (banderivtsi)*, 84.
750 "No. 77. Lyst holovy provodu OUN Andriia Haidamakhy do holovnoi upravy TV UPA v ZSA 20 travnia 2006 r." In Homziak and Kovalyk, eds., *Al'manakh Tovarystva voiavakiv UPA,. Knyha 3, 2001-2015*, 175-176, here: 176.
751 Volodymyr V"iatrovych, Roman Hrytsiv, Ihor Derevianyi, Ruslan Zabilyi, Andrii Sova, Petro Sodol', *Ukrains'ka Povstans'ka Armiia: Istoriia neskorennykh* (L'viv: Center for the Study of the Liberation Movement, 2007. In the TsDVR 2014 became a member of the reputed Ukrainian NGO umbrella organization "Reanimation Package of Reforms." Andreas Umland, "The Ukrainian Government's Memory Institute against the West," *New Eastern Europe*, 7 March 2017, http://neweasterneurope.eu/articles-and-commentary/2284-the-ukrainian-government-s-memory-institute-against-the-west (accessed 7 July 2017).
752 On the official, legitimizing historians' lionizing of the OUN, UPA, and their selective representation of the past, see Khymka and Kurylo, "Yak OUN stavylasia do ievreiv?" 252-65. See also the 2012 review forum in *Ab Imperio* on V"iatrovych's book *Druha pol's'ko-ukrains'ka viina*, in which he presents the UPA's ethnic cleansing in Volhynia and east Galicia as mutual warfare; Per Anders Rudling, "Warfare or War Criminality?" *Ab Imperio* 2 (2012): 356-81; Igor' Iliushin, "Plokho zabytoe staroe: o novoi knige Vladimira Viatrovycha,"

Bandera as Hero of Ukraine

Bandera was not the first OUN(b) leader to be posthumously granted the highest Ukrainian state honor. As we have seen in chapter five, the designation of Shukhevych as a Hero of Ukraine in 2007, proved highly controversial, not only in Ukraine itself, where Kyiv saw street brawls between octogenarian UPA and Red Army veterans. The rehabilitation of Shukhevych triggered angry protests, not only in Russia, but also in Israel, Poland, and Belarus, and deepened the polarization within Ukraine itself.[753] In Ukraine, the protests came mostly from the Ukrainian left, and the southern and eastern parts of the country, whereas in Poland, the strongest reactions came from the community of expellees from the former borderlands of the Second Polish Republic and their families, and from nationalist groups—many of them on the political right. Shukhevych is a much more problematic figure than Bandera, since he was directly involved in mass murders of Poles, Belarusians, and Jews—as a commanding officer in the *Nachtigall* battalion in 1941, as a commanding officer in *Schutzmannschaft* Battalion 201 in 1942, and as supreme commander of the UPA from 1943.[754]

Nevertheless, the rehabilitation of Bandera generated far more international attention than that of Shukhevych. There are a number of reasons for this. Internationally, Bandera's name is much better known than that of Shukhevych, and the term "Banderites" has become a kind of shorthand for the atrocities committed by his followers. Domestically, no less controversial was Yushchenko's exploitation of a highly divisive symbolic issue after

---

Ab Imperio 2 (2012): 382–86; Gzhegozh [Grzegorz] Motyka, "Neudachnaia kniga," *Ab Imperio* 2 (2012): 387–402; Andzhei Zemba [Andrzej Zięba], "Mifologizirovannaia 'voina'," *Ab Imperio* 2 (2012): 403–21. See also: Jared McBride, "How Ukraine's New Memory Commissar is Controlling the Nation's Past," *The Nation*, 13 August 2015, https://www.thenation.com/article/how-ukraines-new-memory-commissar-is-controlling-the-nations-past/ (accessed 7 July 2017); and Rudling, *The OUN, the UPA, and the Holocaust*, 28–32.
753 See chapter five.
754 On Shukhevych's men taking part in mass shootings of Jews in the vicinity of Vinnytsia and mass violence in occupied Belarus in 1942, see Rudling, "Szkolenie w mordowaniu," 191–212.

having been crushingly rejected in the first round of the 2010 presidential elections. Many people, including those sympathetic to the Bandera cult itself, regarded this a cynical move.[755]

The order "Hero of the Ukraine" is a modified version of the highest Soviet civilian award, "Hero of the Soviet Union." The decoration ceremony, broadcast live on TV, echoed the Byzantine pageantry of the Brezhnev era. On a stage in front of heavy curtains, accompanied by orchestra and to resounding cheers and applause Yushchenko handled over the medal to Stepan Bandera's Canadian grandson, Stephen, or Stefko, Bandera (b. 1970), referring to the OUN leader in a most un-Galician fashion, with patronymic name, as "Bandera, Stepan Andriiovych."[756] A week later, on 29 January 2010, Yushchenko issued another edict officially recognizing the entire Ukrainian Insurgent Army, and both wings of the OUN.[757]

---

[755] "I approve of this decision, but Yushchenko should have taken it back in 2005, or at least in 2009, when he marked Bandera's birth centenary," Ihor Losiev argues. See Ihor Siundiukov, "Time to Gather Stones," *Den'*, 4 February 2010, https://day.kyiv.ua/en/article/close/time-gather-stones (accessed 23 August 2017). Similar opinions were expressed by activists in the Ukrainian Canadian community. "Many Ukrainians here would even argue that such recognition is long overdue and should have been granted in the first year of Ukraine's independence and not in the last weeks of Yushchenko's presidency"; Lubomyr Markevych, "Coming to Grips with the Past," *Edmonton Journal*, 14 February 2010: A15.

[756] "Stepan Bandera—Heroi Ukrainy," *TCH.ua*, 22 January 2010, https://tsn.ua/video/video-novini/stepan-bandera-geroy-ukrayini.html (accessed 15 September 2017).

[757] This implicitly included the 14. Grenadier-Divison SS *Galizien*, or the 1st Ukrainian Division, as the SS veterans prefer to call themselves; Ukaz Prezydenta Ukrainy No. 75/2010 "Pro vshanuvannia uchasnykiv borot'by za nezalezhnist' Ukrainy u XX stolitti," available at official website of Ukrainian parliament: http://zakon3.rada.gov.ua/laws/show/75/2010 (accessed 23 August 2017).

Figure 6.1 Philatelic "all-inclusive" memory. Multi-totalitarian cover, on which postal stamps with red star, red banner and the ribbon of St. George on the occasion of the 60th anniversary in the Great Patriotic War (2005) share space with stamps with the emblem and red-and-black banner of the OUN(b) paying tribute to Shukhevych (2007) and Bandera (2009) on the centennials of their births. In the author's private collection.

The Diaspora as Echo-Chamber

In Canada, Yushchenko's move was greeted with enthusiasm by the Ukrainian Canadian Congress, an umbrella organization of Ukrainian nationalist groups: "We commend President Victor Yushchenko for recognizing those who struggled and perished for Ukraine's independence," stated Paul Grod (b. 1970), National President of the Ukrainian Canadian Congress:

> "President Yushchenko has made incredible progress in elevating the national consciousness of Ukrainians. It is critical now that Ukraine's Cabinet of Ministers and the Parliament of Ukraine bring forth the appropriate legislation, regulations and educational programs to implement this decree... The UCC calls upon the Government of Canada to make changes to Canada's War Veterans Allowance Act by expanding eligibility to include designated resistance groups such as OUN-UPA and to limit eligibility of Soviet War Veterans to those who served after 1941 when the Soviet Union

switched from being allies of Nazi-Germany to become allies of Canada."[758]

The UCC's attempts to transplant the OUN cult to Canada and the history writing of the outgoing president attracted the attention of scholars and Western journalists. In an op-ed in *The Edmonton Journal*, David R. Marples expressed his concern about the rehabilitation of this "typical fascist movement of the interwar period," recalling the OUN(b)'s totalitarian ideology, political violence, and its involvement in the 1941 pogroms. "Yushchenko surely erred" when conferring the posthumous order to Bandera, Marples concluded.[759] The op-ed was circulated in pro-nationalist Ukrainian diaspora circles far beyond Alberta, who flooded the *Edmonton Journal* with letters of complaint. These in turn triggered emotional, agitated discussions in a number of internet fora. The discussion laid bare stark differences in interpretation between diaspora admirers of the OUN(b), not least of the so-called "third wave," i.e. postwar immigrants from Western Ukraine, diaspora political activists and lobbyists on the one hand, and professional historians, who treat Bandera, OUN, and the UPA as objects of inquiry, on the other.[760]

---

758 Ukrainian Canadian Congress, "Ukraine's President Recognizes Ukraine's Freedom Fighters," Press release, 1 February 2010.
759 David Marples, "Hero of Ukraine linked to the Murder of 4000 Jews," *Edmonton Journal*, 7 February 2010.
760 Historian and UCC activist Roman Serbyn (b. 1939) has long lobbied for a unifying nationalist mythology, based upon a heroization of the UPA, arguing that "if Ukrainian today honors the veterans of the Red Army, then it is unworthy to relate to the veterans of the Ukrainian [*Waffen-SS*] Division 'Galicia' with any less respect," and has taken Yushchenko to task for failing to include the Ukrainian Waffen-SS veterans "and other units of the armed forces of the Axis powers" in his myth making; Roman Serbyn, "Erroneous Methods in J.-P. Himka's Challenge to 'Ukrainian Myths,'" *Current Politics in Ukraine*, 7 August 2011, http://ukraineanalysis.wordpress.com/2011/08/07/erroneous-methods-in-j-p-himka's-challenge-to-"ukrainian-myths"/ (accessed 18 January 2012); Roman Serbyn, "Fotohrafii dyvizii 'Halychyna'," in Bohdan Matsiv (ed.), *Ukrains'ka dyviziia "Halychyna:" Istoriia u svitlynakh vid zasnuvannia u 1943 r. do zvil'nennia z polony 1949 r.* (L' viv: ZUKTs, 2009), 223. Conversely, Ukrainians opposing the recognition of the UPA and *Waffen-SS* veterans, Serbyn insisted, must bear a burden of responsibility "before their own conscience and before history"; cited in Marples, *Heroes and Villains*, 262, 299.

Marples' op-ed compelled Grod, who, in addition to heading the Ukrainian Canadian Congress was a ranking member of the OUN(b)-affiliated *Spilka Ukrains'koi Molodi* (SUM—Ukrainian Youth Association) to organize a "task force" to counteract the scholarly criticism. In a series of Canada-wide telephone conferences, Grod called for the development of a "Community Strategy regarding recent attacks on Ukraine's Liberation Movement," coordinating the efforts of the OUN admirers in the Ukrainian-Canadian community against what he described as OUN "detractors," primarily scholars at the Department of History at the University of Alberta.761 The "task force" discussed a number of measures aimed at regaining the initiative and disciplining critical scholars:

> Organize pressure on EU representatives who voted in support of the resolution to rescind the honour of Hero of Ukraine to Bandera ...organize a meeting with the Editorial Board of the Edmonton Journal, [and] [p]ut pressure on North American academic institutions which are funded by community money (Harvard, CIUS, Chair of Ukr Studies, etc., [and] ... consider legal action (libel, hate propaganda).762

"Task force" letters sent to the *Edmonton Journal* combined disavowal, denial, and allegations of stereotyping. Its coordinated responses illuminate how the diaspora elite affirms and sustains its mythology, and warrant analysis.

---

761 Grod's "task force" included, among others, Daria Luciw, the President of the Albertan Provincial Council of the UCC; Stephen Bandera, the grandson of the late OUN(b) leader; Taras Podilsky of the OUN(b) front organization The League of Ukrainian Canadians (LUC); Roman Serbyn; Lubomyr Luciuk, a geography professor at the Royal Military College of Canada; Marco Levytsky, the editor of the *Ukrainian News*; and Jaroslaw Balan of the CIUS. However, the community elite does not appear to have been united behind these "measures" against critical scholars. Of the community leaders invited to take part, Roman Petryshyn, then the director of the Ukrainian Resource and Development Centre at Grant MacEwan University in Edmonton, and Petro Savaryn (1926–2017), a veteran of the *Waffen-SS Galizien*, former Chancellor of the University of Alberta and former President of the World Congress of Free Ukrainians, declined to participate.

762 Paul Grod, "Task Force Meeting—Developing Community Strategy regarding recent attacks on Ukraine's Liberation Movement," E-mail to community leaders, 14 March 2010. Thanks to John-Paul Himka for sharing this material with the author. On the UCC "task force," see also Himka, "Interventions."

The Nationalists as Victims

From Toronto, Stephen Bandera, a former editor of the *Kyiv Post*, alleged that Marples had "smeared" the Bandera family name:

> David Marples' column is a rehash of misinformation he's been passing off as academic research for more than a decade... It is a shame The [Edmonton] Journal is providing a forum for people to smear our family name. If Stepan Bandera was even guilty of half the crimes of which Marples and his ilk accuse him, then he would have been swinging from the gallows at Nuremberg 65 years ago.[763]

Daria Luciw, the President of the Alberta Provincial Committee of the Ukrainian Canadian Congress (UCC-APC), arguably the best organized and most influential ethnic lobby group in Western Canada, claimed her community was victimized by Marples' article:

> The Ukrainian Canadian Congress-Alberta Provincial Council (UCC-APC) is stunned by the inaccurate headline and content of David Marples' ... column. The headline is inflammatory and reminiscent of articles written in Alberta papers a century ago, which discriminated against various ethnic groups. Today, some 110 years later, our office is receiving calls from respected individuals in Alberta who are being harassed at work as a result of this headline and column.[764]

No less remarkable was the intervention by academic researchers to Marples' article. Zenon Kohut (b. 1944), who at the time was Director of the Canadian Institute of Ukrainian Studies, also invoked the danger of stereotyping Ukrainians. Kohut, a scholar of 17th century Cossackry who has not published on the OUN or the Holocaust in Ukraine, took it upon himself to correct Marples' claims:

> The pogrom of Jews in the summer of 1941 occurred under Nazi German occupation and was encouraged and initiated by German authorities. Ukrainians were involved in the pogrom, but ultimate responsibility lies with German authorities.... Marples's characterization of the Organization

---

763 Stephen Bandera, "Family Name Cleared," *Edmonton Journal*, 9 February 2010: A 13. Of course, the Nuremberg tribunal was set up to try the leaders of the Third Reich, not local Nazi supporters, allies, or collaborators. Tiso, Antonescu, Szalasi, Quisling, and Laval were all tried locally.

764 Daria Luciw, "Congress Offended," *Edmonton Journal*, 14 February 2010: A 15.

of Ukrainian Nationalists (OUN) as a typically fascist movement is also not correct. It was a national liberation movement whose ideology may have been influenced by fascism, but it was characterized as "integral nationalist" by John A. Armstrong.[765]

While denying the fascist nature of the OUN and deflecting responsibility for the pogroms to German authorities, Kohut expressed concerns that a focus on anti-Jewish violence, committed by the OUN(b) would contribute to stereotyping of Ukrainians: "we must be careful about our allegations or inferences, especially as they may encourage the stereotyping of entire ethnic groups."[766]

The perhaps most heavy-handed reaction to Marples' article came from Marco Levytsky, the editor of *The Ukrainian News*, an Edmonton-based Ukrainian paper, who linked Marples to the Kremlin: "This headline is a Vladimir Putin-style ex-KGB falsification, topping an article by David Marples which is misleading," Levytsky wrote.[767] In his attempt to exonerate the OUN from its well-documented role in the pogroms, Levytsky dwelled on the role of Jews in the NKVD. "The Soviet NKVD, in which Jews had disproportionate membership, was involved in the killing of 4,000 to 8,000 civilian prisoners—a fact the Nazis hoped would provoke Ukrainian retaliation,"[768] Levytsky claimed, with no mention of the fact that any Jew who joined the rank of the Soviet security organs had to leave his or her Jewish background behind, and acted as a representative of the Soviet government, rather in the capacity of representing a particular religious, or ethnic community.[769] Whereas Jews—like Poles and Latvians—were disproportionately represented in the Soviet security organs during the first decades after

---

765 Zenon E. Kohut, "Ukrainian Nationalism," *Edmonton Journal*, 10 February 2010: A 16.
766 Kohut, "Ukrainian Nationalism"
767 Marco Levytsky, "Ukrainian Nationalists Played No Part in Massacre of 4,000 Jews," *Edmonton Journal*, 9 February 2010: A13.
768 Levytsky, "Ukrainian Nationalists Played No Part in Massacre of 4,000 Jews"
769 Dieter Pohl, "Bohdan Musial: 'Konterrevolutionäre Elemente sind zu Erschiessen.' Die Brutalisierung des deutsch-sowjetisches Krieges im Sommer 1941," *H-Soz-u-Kult Online*, 30 April 2001, http://www.hsozkult.de/publicationreview/id/rezbuecher-546 (accessed 23 August 2017).

the October Revolution, most had been removed during the purges. Therefore, at the time of the Soviet invasion of Eastern Poland, Jews constituted less than four per cent of the leading NKVD cadres.[770] Thus, at the time of Galicia's first encounters with the NKVD during the brutal Soviet occupation of 1939-41, the number of Jews in leading positions of the NKVD did not stand out in a region where the percentage of Jews were in the double digits.[771]

The rationalization and justification of anti-Semitism as national self-defense has a long tradition and deep roots in Eastern Europe, pre-dating the 1917 revolution by several decades, and the concept of the *zhydokomuna* is a staple in the ideology of many Eastern and Central European far right groups.[772] For the OUN, the concept is central to understanding the reason for its participa-

---

[770] By 1 July 1939, Jews constituted 3.92 per cent, on 1 January 1940 3.49 per cent, and on 26 February 1941, 5.49 per cent of the leading cadres (*rukovodiashchie*) of the NKVD; Petrov and Sorokin, *Kto Rukovodil NKVD 1934-1941*.

[771] At the beginning of the German occupation of Western Ukraine—Eastern Galicia and Volhynia, the Jewish population numbered 870,000 people, around 540,000 of whom lived in East Galicia; Ahron Weiss, "Jewish-Ukrainian Relations in Western Ukraine During the Holocaust," in *Ukrainian-Jewish Relations in Historical Perspective*, eds. Peter J. Potichnyj and Howard Aster (Edmonton: CIUS Press, 1990), 409. In the cities where some of the bloodiest pogroms took place, Jews constituted large minorities, or pluralities. According to the 1931 Polish census, Jews constituted 31.9% of the population in Lwów, 41.1% in Stanisławów, 39.3% in Tarnopol, 42.4% in Kolomyja, 40.1% in Drohobycz, and 35.7% in Stryj. Maciej Siekierski, "The Jews in Soviet-Occupied Eastern Poland at the End of 1939: Numbers and Distribution," in *Jews in Eastern Poland and the USSR, 1939-46*, eds. Norman Davies and Antony Polonsky (New York: St. Martin's Press, 1991), 111. Jews constituted 1,600,000 people, or roughly one-tenth of the former *Kresy* population of a little over 13 million; Jan T. Gross, *Revolution from Abroad: The Soviet Conquest of Poland's Western Ukraine and Western Belorussia*, expanded ed. (Princeton and Oxford: Princeton University Press, 2002), 3-4. As for the number of Jews in the Ukrainian Communist Party, a frequently cited estimate is 13.4% in 1940; Mordechai Altschuler, *Soviet Jewry since the Second World War: Population and Social Structure* (Studies in Population and Urban Demography 5) (Westport, CT: Greenwood Press, 1987), 208-9.

[772] In Poland, the image of the Jew as the harmful other emerged in the post-1864 period, and crystallized from 1880 to 1918. Anti-Semitic views and the tendency to single out the Jews as the chief enemy were not unique to the Polish integral nationalists. Similar attitudes were found among contemporary French, German, Hungarian, and Romanian groups; Joanna Beata Michlic, *Poland's Threatening Other: The Image of the Jew from 1880 to the Present* (Lincoln and London: University of Nebraska Press, 2006), 24-25, 55.

tion in the 1941 pogroms. Levytsky's argument is that Jews were targeted for the pogroms due to their association with Bolshevism echoes the very allegation that the OUN(b) used to fuel the anti-Semitic violence in the first place.[773] Paradoxically, in a follow-up editorial in the *Ukrainian News*, Levytskyi identified the OUN's critics as those who "fan ethnic discord."[774]

The assertion of Jewish overrepresentation in the NKVD became something of a *Leitmotif* to Bandera's diaspora admirers. In the *Kyiv Post*, Askold Lozynskyj (b. 1952), a senior OUN(b) activist in New York and a former chair of the World Congress of Ukrainians took up a similar line of argumentation. Lozynskyj had, for years, actively promoted the legacy of the OUN(b) to large audiences in Ukraine and in diaspora through meetings, commemorations, mass media, motion pictures, education, and the internet.[775] While it was a commentary by David Marples that triggered the discussion, Lozynskyj sought to shift focus on John-Paul Himka (b. 1949), Marples' colleague at the University of Alberta, whose research into OUN(b) and UPA involvement in mass murder of Jews has been a particular irritant for adherents and admirers of the OUN. "Marples relies on Himka for his assertions" Lozynskyj alleged, denouncing the latter as "a notorious Soviet apologist and ... a Ukraine detractor." Lozynskyj offers an alternative explanation as to Himka's research into the Holocaust in Ukraine:

---

773 Scholars of this phenomenon have chosen to look for different explanations to the pogroms. Ahron Weiss argues that "the cause for taking revenge on the Jews on account of the NKVD murders was secondary.... The main reason for these pogroms and the further consistent hostile measures against the Jews was rooted in two sources: the traditional anti-Semitism among various layers of the Ukrainian population and the fostering of Nazi ideology by the Ukrainian extremists, especially by the OUN"; Weiss, "Ukrainian-Jewish Relations During the Holocaust," 413.
774 Marko Levytsky, "UPA Detractors Fan the Flames of Ethnic Discord," *Ukrainian News*, 16 February 2010: 2.
775 Askold Lozynskyj, in his position as president of the OUN(b)-dominated Ukrainian Congress Committee of America and the World Congress of Ukrainians, served as the main consultant for Oles' Yanchuk's 2000 movie *Neskorennyi* (The Undefeated) (dir. Oles' Yanchuk, Ukraine/USA), an heroic account of UPA commander Roman Shukhvych, with an English translation by Stefko Bandera. On *Neskorennyi*, see chapter five, pages 176-177.

To his credit Prof. Himka did acknowledge that his paper was paid for with a fellowship from the Holocaust Memorial Museum. This goes to motive. Simply put, Himka for his remuneration had to produce one or more demons. [...] What is also indisputable is that many Jews served in the Soviet secret police during that period of Soviet rule in Western Ukraine. Naturally, Himka fails to mention the Jewish complicity which may have pointed to the motive of any number of oppressors.... While being Jewish in and of itself, certainly, was not a reason to be killed, being Jewish was not immunity from being attacked when you sided and fought with the enemy.[776]

A couple of days later, Lozynskyj repeated, and expanded his allegations:

> [Bandera] even issued directives to his members to fight the Germans and the Soviets, but not to participate in the German plans against the Jews. He did this in spite of the fact that Jews in disproportion to the population served as the bloody murdering agents of the Soviets in the two years of Soviet rule in Western Ukraine between 1939 and 1941...It was Moscow that issued the orders that starved to death 7–10 million Ukrainians during the Great Famine of 1932–33. Here once again disproportionately Jews acted as agents of that murderous plan. They sided with the enemy in Moscow against their neighbors in Ukraine.[777]

Lozynskyj's depiction of Jews as perpetrators, servants of Moscow, NKVD murderers, falsifiers of history and "producers of demons," contrasts sharply to his account of Ukrainians, who figure exclusively in the role of victims, and illustrates the émigré OUN(b)'s rather crude Manichean perception of Ukrainian history.

Other pro-nationalist writers in *Kyiv Post* expanded on Lozynskyj's comments. The lawyer and diaspora Ukrainian activist Andriy J. Semotiuk argued that "the current backlash against ... Bandera diverts attention from both Soviet and Nazi crimes

---

[776] Askold S. Lozynskyj, "Rewriting History: An Evidentiary Evidence," *Kyiv Post*, 16 February 2010, https://www.kyivpost.com/article/opinion/op-ed/rewriting-history-an-evidentiary-perspective-59650.html (accessed 23 August 2017).

[777] Askold Lozynskyj, "Inna Rogatchi, Shame on You!" *League of Ukrainian Canadians*, 23 February 2010, http://www.lucorg.com/news.php/news/4151 (accessed 2 May 2010).

YUSHCHENKO'S FASCIST 239

against humanity."[778] In a statement, rather representative of the dominant view within the Ukrainian diaspora, Semotiuk alleged that:

> [The OUN] never advocated a dictatorship for Ukraine. On the contrary, it sought to overthrow one. It never maintained that the Ukrainian people or race was superior to others. On the contrary, it sought to unite with other oppressed nations in its struggle for justice and freedom. It never sought to conquer foreign territories, but only to liberate its own. And, at the end of the day, it had no fascist political program to implement. But instead, it was prepared to advance that mix of social-democratic policies, principles and programs as would meet the needs and desires of the western and eastern halves of the country, including the national minorities that constituted an essential part of both.[779]

Semotiuk argues that the victims of the UPA were targeted, not primarily due to their ethnicity, but rather for siding with the enemies of Ukraine:

> As for the actions of the Organization of Ukrainian Nationalists and the Ukrainian Insurgent Army in Volhynia, as Professor Peter Potichnyj of Canada, editor of the book *Poland and Ukraine: Past and Present*, points out, if minorities fought in support of the NKVD secret police or other oppressors, they ran the risk of falling victims in the war. Those who opposed the Organization of Ukrainian Nationalists and the Ukrainian Insurgent Army, including Poles who sought to restore the 600-year oppression of Ukrainians under Poland, chose to do so at their own peril. There is no denying, however, that thousands of innocent Poles were slaughtered in Volhynia.[780]

Other diaspora commentators, such as Stephen Velychenko (b. 1950), a research fellow associated with the Chair of Ukrainian Studies at the University of Toronto, argued that the debate on Bandera required "a balanced approach. Ideally, they should also be competitive and collaborative in approach. In the case of Jews and Ukrainians the recent discussions concerning OUN and Bandera seem rather one-sided." One way to achieve such a balance, according to Velychenko, would be to relate wartime OUN mur-

---

778 Andriy J. Semotiuk, "The Stepan Bandera Quandary," *Kyiv Post*, 19 April 2010, https://www.kyivpost.com/article/opinion/op-ed/the-stepan-bandera-quandary-64386.html (accessed 23 August 2017).
779 Semotiuk, "The Stepan Bandera Quandary"
780 Semotiuk, "The Stepan Bandera Quandary"

der of Jews to post–1948 Israeli policy towards the Palestinians. "If some Ukrainians wanted a Ukraine without Jews, how different were they from those Jews who wanted an Israel without Arabs? And if there was a difference, what was it?" Stephen Velychenko asked rhetorically, citing David Ben Gurion, "We must expel Arabs and take their places... We must use terror, assassination, intimidation, land confiscation, and the cutting of all social services to rid the Galilee of its Arab population... We must do everything to ensure that [the Palestinian refugees] do not return."[781]

The logic that "a balanced approach" would be achieved by comparing OUN pogroms to post-war Israeli transgressions vis-à-vis Palestinians, or the suggestion that critical attention to the crimes of the OUN would somehow hamper the study of Nazi and Stalinist crimes is not entirely clear. On the contrary, as UCLA Holocaust scholar Michael Rothberg notes, focusing on one atrocity does not have to divert from other atrocities, but could also help animate mindfulness of other atrocities through what he refers to as "multidirectional memory."[782]

New research on OUN and UPA political violence has made nationalist myth-making more difficult. Since the focus of the crimes challenges some core myths held by the diaspora, the unwelcome focus on the atrocities of their heroes challenges their own representation of history in which they figure solely in the role of victims. Attitudes, such as those illustrated above, are recurrent in the largest and most representative English language Ukrainian publications—not only in the *Kyiv Post* and Levytskyj's *Ukrainian News*, but also on a regular basis in the *Ukrainian Weekly*.[783] John A. Armstrong, himself an admirer of Bandera, in 1990 referred to this as "hypersensitivity" which "tended, in turn, to

---

781 Stephen Velychenko, "Ukrainians, Jews, and Double Standards," *The Ukraine List*, no. 442 (2010).
782 Michael Rothberg, *Multidirectional Memory: Remembering the Holocaust in the Age of Decolonization* (Stanford, CA: Stanford University Press, 2009).
783 On Myron Kuropas' representation of Jews in his regular column in *The Ukrainian Weekly*, see Per Anders Rudling, "Organized Anti-Semitism in Contemporary Ukraine: Structure, Influence and Ideology," *Canadian Slavonic Papers/Revue canadienne des slavistes*, vol. XLVIII, nos. 1-2 (March-June 2006), 81-118, here: 96.

exacerbate the problem of influencing agencies and opinion outside the Ukrainian communities."[784]

International Responses

Yushchenko's designation of Stepan Bandera as a national hero prompted condemnation from Jewish groups, including the Wiesenthal Center, which expressed its "deepest revulsion at the recent honor awarded to Stepan Bandera, who collaborated with the Nazis in the early stages of World War II, and whose followers were linked to the murders of thousands of Jews and others."[785] Mark Weitzman, Director of Government Affairs for the Simon Wiesenthal Center, expressed his concern about the development in Ukraine, something he saw as part of a trend of "relativizing the Holocaust." "They [US officials] didn't even know this was happening until recently," but expressed his belief that the US silence on the matter was about to change, given the seriousness of the situation.[786]

The Anti-Defamation League (ADL), in a statement, similarly called on Viktor Yanukovych, the recently elected president of Ukraine, to withdraw the "Hero of Ukraine" title awarded to two partisans who fought alongside the Nazis against the Soviets in World War II and who had direct involvement in atrocities against Jews and Poles. "The Ukrainian state does a grave disservice to its own history and its reputation by lionizing those complicit in the mass murder of Jews," said Abraham H. Foxman, ADL National Director and a Holocaust survivor.[787]

---

784 John A. Armstrong, *Ukrainian Nationalism*, 3rd ed. (Englewood, CO: Ukrainian Academic Press, 1990), 237.
785 "Wiesenthal Center Blasts Ukrainian Honor for Nazi Collaborator," *Simon Wiesenthal Center*, 28 January 2010, http://www.wiesenthal.com/site/apps/nlnet/content2.aspx?c=lsKWLbPJLnF&b=5711859&ct=7922775 (accessed 26 April 2010).
786 Mark Ames, "The Hero of the Orange Revolution Poisons Ukraine," *The Nation*, 12 February 2010, https://www.thenation.com/article/hero-orange-revolution-poisons-ukraine/ (accessed 23 August 2017).
787 "ADL Calls on New Ukrainian President to Withdraw 'Hero' Title Bestowed by Predecessor on Nazi Collaborators," *Anti-Defamation League*, 11 March 2010, https://www.adl.org/news/press-releases/adl-calls-on-new-ukrainian-president-to-withdraw-hero-title-bestowed-by (accessed 26 July 2017).

The Chief Rabbi of Chabad in Ukraine, Moshe Reuven Asman announced he would, in protest, relinquish his Order of Merit honor, bestowed upon him by the Ukrainian government, describing the Bandera award as "a hideous blow to Ukraine's international image." Frank Dimant, CEO of B'nai Brith Canada, expressed his concerns about the UCC proposal to use Canadian tax payers' money to fund OUN or UPA veterans, opining that: "Any consideration of a proposal involving Canadian taxpayer-funded pensions must be scrutinized by the government of Canada to ensure that the individuals who are seeking these pensions did not in any way collaborate with the Nazi regime during the World War II era."[788]

Polish Reactions

During the so-called Orange Revolution the Polish government had been one of Yushchenko's staunchest supporters. The national conservative government of Jarosław Kaczyński, Prime Minster in 2006–2007, continued the policy of supporting Ukrainian integration with European institutions, envisioning a key role for Poland in this process. Poland's association with, and open support for Yushchenko now increasingly appeared, however, as a political liability. The Polish government, which had kept a relatively low profile following Yushchenko's rehabilitation of Shukhevych in 2007, faced increasing pressure from parts of their constituencies as the Ukrainian government intensified their cult of the OUN and UPA.

In 2009, two years after the designation of Roman Shukhevych an official hero of Ukraine, the Polish Sejm officially characterized the UPA's anti-Polish massacres in genocidal terms, describing them as "mass murders characterized by ethnic cleansing with features of genocide" ("masowych mordów o charak-

---

The "two partisans who fought alongside the Nazis" Foxman referred to are, of course, Shukhevych and Bandera. At least for Bandera, who was not present in today's Ukraine after 1934, this characterization is debatable.

788 "Ukraine Chief Rabbi to Give Up Honour in Protest of 'Hero' Recognition," *Jewish Tribune* (Canada), 10 February 2010.

terze czystki etnicznej i znamionach ludobójczych").[789] A sociological survey conducted by the Polish Museum of World War II in August 2009 showed that 1,200 people surveyed remembered Polish wartime relations with Ukrainians as more negative than those with Germans and Russians.[790]

Commemorative practices by far-right Ukrainian groups, not least those taking place on Polish territory, were increasingly perceived as provocations. In the summer of 2009, Bandera admirers, organizing a pilgrimage in the form of a bicycle rally to Bandera's grave in Munich to commemorate the fiftieth anniversary of the *Providnyk*'s death, were met with angry protests on the Ukrainian–Polish border, where many were denied Polish entry visas.[791]

By 2010, Yushchenko's memory policies had become a very real political issue, with direct political implications for Ukrainian–Polish relations. Voices within the Roman Catholic Church in Poland were increasingly expressing criticism and concern about the Bandera cult in their neighboring country. *Niedziela: Tygodnik katolicki*, a leading Roman Catholic daily, emphasized the need to openly address the OUN and UPA atrocities, and that any sensible reconciliation also required willingness on the part of the Ukrainian authorities to address the past honestly. Honoring Bandera, it argued, meant:

> honoring not only the legitimate fight of Ukrainian nationalists against the Soviet Union, but also mass killings that have been neither condemned nor morally accounted for. Only by condemning those crimes can we reach a

---

789 Bronisław Komorowski, "Uchwała Sejmu Rzeczypospolitej Polskiej z dnia 15 lipca 2009 r. w sprawie tragicznego losu Polaków na Kresach Wschodnich," http://orka.sejm.gov.pl/opinie6.nsf/nazwa/2183_u/$file/2183_u.pdf (accessed 18 October 2009).
790 Asked "How would you define your country's relation to the following groups during World War II?" in August 2009, 64 per cent of respondents answered that relations with Ukrainians were bad, a higher number even than Germans (63%) and Russians (57%); Wojciech Szacki and Marcin Wojciechowski, "Sondaż 3: Źli Niemcy, źli Ukraińcy," *Gazeta Wyborcza*, 24 August 2009, http://wyborcza.pl/1,75398,6956564,Sondaz_3__Zli_Niemcy__zli_Ukraincy.html (accessed 16 July 2017).
791 Marcin Wojciechowski, "Gdy Lach z Kozakiem się kłócą, Moskal zaciera ręce," *Gazeta Wyborcza*, 8–9 August 2009, 2; and Marcin Kobiałka, "Szlaban na rajd Bandery," *Gazeta Wyborcza*, 8–9 August 2009, 3.

genuine mutual understanding. Future relationships cannot be built on silence concerning crimes that have not been condemned and on deformations of the memory of the victims. In a long perspective, such false "reconciliation" will always create aversion, misunderstanding of one's reasons, injustice and consequently, hostility. Truth is the only way out of the blind alleys of this kind of "dialogue."[792]

The criticism was not limited to the political right. The left-wing weekly *Przegląd tygodniowy* argued that Yushchenko's designation of Bandera a national hero represented a failure of Kaczyński's eastern policy:

> Yushchenko, at the very end of his term in office gave his Polish promoters and enthusiasts the finger... by awarding Stepan Bandera the title of Hero of Ukraine. The very same Bandera, who had on his conscience acts of terror in the 1930s, the murder of Poles, Ukrainians, and Jews in the summer of 1941, when the soldiers of the *Nachtigall* battalion entered L'viv along with the Wehrmacht under the slogan: *"Liachiv vyrezmo, zhydiv vydushym, a Ukrainu stvoryty musymo"* [We will kill the Poles and strangle the Jews but we must create Ukraine] carried out bestial blood baths against the local population. This was, however, only a foretaste of the mass genocide of Poles in Volhyn and East Galicia, which took place in the beginning of 1943... The Volhynian crimes had their ideologists and perpetrators: Bandera, Dontsov, Shukhevych, and Savur.[793] President Yushchenko's Ukraine has erected monuments and renamed squares and streets in their honor.[794]

Polish president Lech Kaczyński (1949-2010) now openly condemned Yushchenko's move.[795] While the Ukrainian president

---

[792] Marek Jurek, "Stepan Bandera—nowy symbol Ukrainy?" *Niedziela: Tygodnik katolicki*, no. 6 (2010), http://niedziela.pl/artykul/90908/nd/Stepan-Bandera---nowy-symbol-Ukrainy (accessed 14 September 2017).

[793] Dmytro Kliachkivs'kyi, pseud. "Klym Savur" (1911–45), commander of the UPA-North in Volhynia and Polissia, was one of the key initiators of the mass murder of the Volhynian Poles in early 1943. He was killed in battle against Soviet forces in February 1945. See, on Kliachkivs'kyi, see Grzegorz Motyka, *Cień Kłyma Sawura: Polsko-ukraiński konflikt pamięci* (Gdańsk: Wydawnictwo Oskar oraz Muzeum II Wojny Światowej, 2013); and Yuliia Yurchuk, "Proshloe pod pritselom amnezii: pamiat' ob OUN i UPA v Volynskom regione na primere pamiatnika Klimu Savuru," *Forum noveishei vostochnoevropeiskoi istorii i kul'tury* 14, no. 2 (2016): 87–101.

[794] Jerzy Domański, "Bandera—bohater Juszczenki," *Przegląd tygodniowy*, no. 5(527) (2010): 3.

[795] "Kancelaria Prezydenta: sprzeciw L. Kaczyńskiego wobec decyzji Juszczenki," *Gazeta Wyborcza*, 4 February 2010, http://wiadomosci.gazeta.pl/Wiadomosci/1,81048,7530132,Kancelaria_Prezydenta__sprzeciw_L_Kaczynskiego_w

had previously been very popular in Poland, one reporter noted, "many Poles greeted Yushchenko's ouster from the presidency with unrestrained joy."[796]

The critical reactions were not limited to Poland. On 22 February 2010, the European Parliament condemned Yushchenko's recognition of Bandera, passing a resolution stating that it "[d]eeply deplores the decision by the outgoing President of Ukraine, Viktor Yushchenko, posthumously to award Stepan Bandera, a leader of the Organization of Ukrainian Nationalists (OUN) which collaborated with Nazi Germany, the title of 'National Hero of Ukraine'; hopes, in this regard, that the new Ukrainian leadership will reconsider such decisions and will maintain its commitment to European values."[797]

In public discussions, Marples' assessment of the OUN(b) was seconded by others. In a blog post for the *New York Review of Books*, Timothy Snyder left no uncertainty as to how to characterize the OUN(b)'s political belonging, referring to Bandera as a fascist half a dozen times, arguing that Yushchenko's celebration of Bandera had "cast a shadow over his own political legacy."[798]

Reactions within Ukraine and by the Diaspora

As the designation of Bandera as a Ukrainian state hero developed into an international controversy, the *Providnyk*'s admirers urged Ukrainians to rally around Bandera's legacy. Associate Professor Ihor Losiev at the Kyiv-Mohyla Academy equated support for Ukrainian independence with support for Bandera: "It is necessary to pass a law on the status of veterans of national liberation movements, rather than award selected individuals.... Everyone

---

obec.html (accessed 5 February 2010; URL no longer active as at 28 September 2017).
796 Jan Cienski, "Why Poles Cheered Yushchenko's Ouster: 20th century Ukrainian Nationalist Stepan Bandera still Divides Poland and Ukraine," *Global Post*, 2 March 2010.
797 Joint motion for a resolution RC-B7-0116/2010. http://www.europarl.europa .eu/sides/getDoc.do?type=MOTION&reference=P7-RC-2010-0116&languag e=EN (accessed 26 April 2010).
798 Snyder, "Fascist Hero."

who values the independence of Ukraine will clearly approve of the step taken by President Yushchenko."[799]

The most enthusiastic admirers of the OUN(b), among them far-right groups such as Oleh Tiahnibok's *Svoboda* (Freedom) party and Yurii Shukhevych's Ukrainian National Assembly-Ukrainian National Self-Defense (UNA-UNSO), and the leadership of the Ukrainian Canadian Congress, responded angrily to the international reactions.[800] Tiahnybok and the émigré OUN(b) started to collect signatures against the European Union's condemnation of Bandera. Tiahnybok argued that:

> The European Parliament is not going to tell Ukraine who their heroes are… It is not up to the pseudo-European liberal and left-wing Europarliamentarians to tell the Ukrainians who to designate Heroes and how to honor them. Our Heroes were shaped in bloody battle with the occupants when the so-called "civilized Europe" ran away. Therefore, to judge Bandera is to spit in the face of the Ukrainian national-liberation movement, which was anti-colonial in its nature, first and foremost anti-communist and anti-Nazi. It means spitting on the right of Ukrainians to have their own state… It is typical that this defamatory and humiliating paragraph about Bandera was introduced by deputies from Germany and Poland. The anti-Ukrainian position of Germany is explained by the complexes of the German leadership and their failure to take responsibility for crimes committed during the Second World War and to blame them on others, Ukrainians in particular.[801]

Other pro-OUN voices leveled similar criticism at the European Union. In the diaspora forum *ePOSHTA*, Boris Danyk, a prominent diaspora activist from New Jersey, argued that:

---

[799] Siundiukov, "Time to Gather Stones."
[800] On the All-Ukrainian Union "Svoboda," see Anton Shekhovtsov, "The Creeping Resurgence of the Ukrainian Radical Right? The Case of the Freedom Party," *Europe-Asia Studies* 63, no. 2 (2011): 203–28. Yurii Shukhevych was the son of the UPA commander and former dissident. On the UNA-UNSO, see Per Anders Rudling, "Anti-Semitism and the Extreme Right in Contemporary Ukraine," in *Mapping the Extreme Right in Contemporary Europe: From Local to Transnational*, eds. Andrea Mammone, Emmanuel Godin, and Brian Jenkins (London and New York: Routledge, 2012), 189–206.
[801] Oleh Tiahnybok, "Evroparlament ne vkazuvatyme Ukraini, koho vyznavaty Heroiamy," *Ukrains'ka Pravda Blohy*, 26 February 2010, http://blogs.pravda.com.ua/authors/tiahnybok/4b88066cc9c5f/ (accessed 26 April 2010).

Stepan Bandera was and is the symbol of Ukrainian national anti-Nazi and anti-Soviet resistance. The European Union alleges that he collaborated with the Nazi occupation regime. The *Kyiv Post*, Ukraine's leading English-language newspaper, responded with an editorial (March 4): "The continent that spawned Hitler has no business telling Ukraine who should and shouldn't be its heroes." The *Kyiv Post* is right on target. It tells it like it was, and still is, about Stepan Bandera, with the Poles, Moscow, and now the European Union smearing his legacy.[802]

The petition to censure the European Union for its criticism of the state cult of Bandera was based upon the claim that Bandera's critics had the basic facts wrong:

> this official document of the highest legislative body of the European Union implies, without grounds, that Stepan Bandera was a Nazi collaborator during the Second World War. We believe that the European Parliament's decision is historically groundless and is based on disinformation about the so-called "collaboration" between the OUN and the Third Reich that was spread by Soviet propaganda. On 30 June 1941, Stepan Bandera and his colleagues announced the renewal of independent Ukrainian statehood in L'viv against the will of Hitler's Germany. For this they were killed or incarcerated in Nazi concentration camps.[803]

The success of the petition was, however, modest. By spring 2010, it had gathered just over five thousand signatures, with diaspora and western Ukrainians heavily overrepresented. Its concerns about double standards in Germany, France, and Poland with regard to communist crimes were, moreover, not entirely convincing. The year 2009 saw the passing of resolutions by pan-European institutions on the 70th anniversary of the Molotov-Ribbentrop treaty in 2009, denouncing both fascism and Stalinism in no uncertain terms.[804]

---

802 Boris Danik, "Disrobing the European Union," *ePOSHTA*, 10 March 2010, http://www.eposhta.com/newsmagazine/ePOSHTA_100316_CanadaUS.html#ed2 (accessed 27 April 2010).
803 "Petytsiia: vidkryte zvernennia do deputativ evropeis'koho parlamentu z pryvodu naklepu proty S. Bandery v teksti rezoliutsii evropeis'koho parlamentu shchodo Ukrainy vid 25 liutoho 2010 r.," *Onlain Petytsii*, 4 February 2010, http://www.petition.org.ua/petition/detail.php?ELEMENT_ID=617 (last accessed 26 April 2010, link no longer active as at 14 September 2017).
804 On 3 July 2009, the parliamentary assembly of the OSCE condemned Stalinism and fascism as genocidal ideologies, jointly responsible for the outbreak of World War II, condemning the two ideologies for crimes against humani-

If the cases above represent the diaspora and the stauncher of the nationalists, the reaction of West Ukrainian public intellectuals self-identifying as liberals is more complex. One such example is the writer Mykola Riabchuk, a frequent commentator on Ukrainian politics and memory. Riabchuk does not object to the promotion of Shukhevych and Bandera, whom he regards as indispensable and necessary for national mobilization in Ukraine, but he divorces them and the OUN from the political and ideological context of the 1930s and 1940s. Riabchuk instead points to their "ethical rather than ideological values. The UPA fighters... are praised first of all for their patriotism and commitment to the national-liberation cause, for their idealism and dedication, for spiritual strength and self-sacrifice."[805] Utilizing post-colonial references, Riabchuk argued that Ukraine should not be measured by the same standards as those applied for its western neighbors:

> Ukraine is not just a postcommunist but also a postcolonial country shared nearly equally by the "aboriginal" and "settler" communities, with their own myths, symbols, historical narratives, heroes, cultures, and languages. The numerical preponderance of aborigines is counter-balanced by a socially higher status of settlers... There is also a huge swing group of aborigines assimilated historically, to different degrees, into the dominant Creole-type culture, and a much smaller but still important group of settlers who opted for a "dancing-with-wolves" identification with aborigines... Ukraine is not just a "normal" nation, with [a] firm identity and secure statehood, that chooses presumably between authoritarianism and democracy, i.e. in this case, between [the] crypto-fascist legacy exemplified by Bandera and [the] OUN and [the] liberal-democratic values promoted by the EU... [F]or Ukrainians, the real choice is not between OUN-style nationalistic dictatorship and EU-style liberal democracy. Most of them made this choice long ago, and virtually nobody but a few marginals praise the former today, and deny the latter. The real choice is to either defend the national sovereignty, dignity, and identity, or give them away to Russia and/or its "Creole" subsidiaries. Under these circumstances, the second part of Bandera's legacy remains relevant—that of patriotism, national sol-

---

ty, and designated 23 August, the day the Molotov-Ribbentrop Treaty was signed in 1939, as a day of memory of the victims of Nazism and Stalinism. The OSCE explicitly called upon Russia to refrain from glorifying its Stalinist past; Nastassia Shamrei, "ABSE asudila Stalinism. Shto z Liniiai Stalina?" *Nasha Niva*, 8 July 2009, 6; and "OBSE priravnila SSSR k natsistskoi Germanii," *Narodnaia Volia* 103–104(3029–3030) (2009): 1.

805 Riabchuk, "Ukraine: Neither Heroes nor Villains"

idarity, self-sacrifice, idealistic commitment to common goals and values.[806]

Europe needs to have more tolerance for the Ukrainian aborigines' reverence for idols—irrespective of their ideological underpinnings and their actual historical record, the argument goes. Another self-identifying liberal, L'viv historian Yaroslav Hrytsak makes a similar distinction. To him the question is less whether Bandera was a fascist than whether he is lionized as one. He warns that "the European Parliament call for stripping Bandera of the title of Hero of Ukraine today aids Russia's monopolizing of the memory of the peoples of eastern Europe," and that "Brussels and Moscow will appear like potential allies." This, Hrytsak argues, is why "small" peoples, like the Ukrainians, have the "right" to have "inconvenient" heroes:

> [T]he "small"peoples have the right to have them, as long as they celebrate those heroes not as symbols of violence against other people, but as symbols of resistance and struggle for their own survival and their own dignity. In the case of Bandera, the issue is not whether he was a fascist—the question is whether the majority of people who celebrate him, celebrate him *as* a fascist.[807]

If some commentators called for measuring Ukraine by a double standard, others accused the European Parliament of just that. Rutgers University's Alexander J. Motyl, a diaspora Ukrainian political scientist and blogger, warned about European double standards, and that the European Parliament's denunciation of the Bandera cult meant that the European Parliament had objectively joined forces with the anti-democrats:

> Does conferral of Hero of Ukraine status represent a disregard for European values? The answer to this question partly depends on what one means by European values. Viewed historically, European values include above all militarism, racism, anti-Semitism, imperialism, and chauvinism. [...] In

---

806 Mykola Riabchuk, "Bandera's Controversy and Ukraine's Future," *Russkii vopros* 1 (2010), http://www.russkiivopros.com/?pag=one&id=315&kat=9&cs l=46#_edn13 (accessed 28 April 2010).
807 Yaroslav Hrytsak, "Klopoty z pam'iattiu," *Zaxid.net*, 8 March 2010, http://www.zaxid.net/article/60958/ (accessed 12 April 2010), republished in Amar, Balyns'kyi, and Hrytsak, eds., *Strasti za Banderuiu*, 346-57, here: 354.

condemning Bandera's hero of Ukraine status, the European Parliament injected itself into contemporary Ukrainian politics in a way that has thus far had primarily unfortunate consequences. Many nationally conscious Ukrainians—who represent the core of Ukraine's civil society and democratic movement—resent being singled out for their views of their heroes and point to double standards and European hypocrisy. In turn, the anti-democratic forces—who generally support sanitized Soviet versions of the past and tend to align with the Kremlin's authoritarian project—have used the resolution to promote their anti-democratic and anti-Ukrainian agendas. Ironically, if unintentionally, the European Parliament has effectively joined forced with the anti-democrats and chauvinists and served to undermine Ukrainian democracy.[808]

Post-colonial references and imagery were invoked to advance the post-structural argument that Ukrainians have a "right" to lionize native fascists, and that no one—neither scholars, nor governments, nor the parliamentary assembly of the European Union—has the right to impinge on this subjective truth. Higher aims of national consolidation, and—paradoxically—democratization, this argument goes, may require a rehabilitation of totalitarian figures. From this perspective, the fascistoid icons of the subaltern are not only admissible, but indeed desirable, and, conversely, the European Union's objections to the Bandera cult hurt the prospect of democracy in Ukraine.

Conclusion

There is no obvious reason why democratic Ukrainians, supportive of Ukrainian independence, should embrace the legacy of the OUN(b). In fact, a June 2009 poll showed that less than one in eight Ukrainians had positive views of the OUN and UPA. In 2010, Yushchenko received 5.4% of the popular vote, whereas 53% of Ukrainians polled wanted Bandera's posthumous award revoked.[809] In 2010, the pro-OUN voices were limited largely to the

---

808 Motyl, "Ukraine, Europe, and Bandera."
809 "Ukrainians in other regions have much more negative attitudes, compared to the respondents in Galicia, towards the OUN-B and the UPA. Only 6 per cent of the respondents in Ukraine as [a] whole express very positive, and 8 per cent mostly positive, attitudes towards the Bandera faction of the Organization of Ukrainian Nationalists. Forty percent of the respondents believe that the OUN-B and the UPA were involved in mass murder of Ukrainians,

western oblasts and its overseas diaspora.[810] Bandera's posthumous tenure as Hero of Ukraine was brief. Shortly after coming to power, Yushchenko's successor, Viktor Yanukovych announced his intention to strip Bandera of his official status as Hero of Ukraine.[811] The repeal of the status was not, however, carried out by presidential degree, but through a judicial decision. In April 2010, a Donetsk court revoked Yushchenko's decree as unconstitutional, ruling that the order can only be bestowed upon citizens of Ukraine—which Bandera never was.[812]

* * *

The collapse of the Soviet Union and the partial opening of Ukrainian archives has brought a surge of interest in the topic of wartime Ukrainian Nationalism. The wave of new scholarship that has appeared since the turn of the century constitutes a challenge to nationalist mythmakers. All the key historical issues which make Bandera a highly controversial official hero for an

---

Jews, and Poles in the 1940s, while only 14 per cent, mostly in Galicia, deny such an involvement"; Ivan Katchanovski [Kachanovskii], "Ukraintsy ne veriat v mify ob OUN i UPA," *Fraza*, 14 October 2010, https://fraza.ua/analyti cs/76064-ukraincy-ne-veryat-v-mify-ob-oun-i-upa (accessed 14 September 2017). An opinion poll of 2,000 Ukrainians, carried out during the first week of February 2010, found that 53% of Ukrainians were in favor of revoking Yushchenko's decree of turning Bandera into a hero of Ukraine; "53% ukraintsiv za skasuvannia ukazu po Banderi—sotsopytuvannia," *Zaxid.net*, 29 March 2010, http://www.zaxid.net/newsua/2010/3/29/120623/ (last accessed 29 March 2010, link no longer active as at 14 September 2017).

810 However, in recent years, in particular following the military conflict and the Russian annexation of Crimea 2015–2017, the approval of Bandera and his legacy is increasing. If, according to polls by the Rating Group, 22 per cent of Ukrainians were positively disposed towards Bandera in 2010, in 2014, that number had increased to 31, and, in November 2016 to 35 per cent; "Lukash Adamskii: v Pol'she boiatsia ne kul'ta Bandery, a lozhnogo predstavleniia istorii," *Levyi Bereg*, 9 February 2017, http://lb.ua/news/2017/02/09/358189_lukash_adamskiy_polshe_boyatsya.html (accessed 12 February 2017).

811 "Ukraine's Yanukovych to Repeal Bandera Hero Decree," *Reuters*, 19 March 2010, http://www.reuters.com/article/idUSTRE62I32J20100319 (accessed 19 March 2010).

812 "Donets'kyi sud skasuvav ukaz Yushchenka pro prysvoennia Banderi zvannia Heroia," *Novyny UNIAN*, 2 April 2010, http://unian.net/ukr/news/news-370692.html (accessed 2 April 2010).

aspiring democracy—the OUN(b)'s political violence, its role in the 1941 pogroms, the UPA's ethnic cleansing of Poles, Jews, and other minorities in 1943-44, and the OUN's totalitarian, anti-Semitic ideology—were already well-documented at the time Yushchenko designated Shukhevych and Bandera official, national heroes of Ukraine. Since 2010, this knowledge has been outlined in more detail in a number of peer-reviewed scholarly studies published, under the auspices of reputed academic presses, by researchers at respected universities.[813] Others are bound to appear in the near future, and are likely to generate further interest, as this subject matter slowly enters historical consciousness. For the nationalist faithful, raised on stories about the heroism and martyrdom of Bandera and Shukhevych, this is and will be, no doubt, a painful process.

As to the political utility of these myths, it is hard to regard Yushchenko's attempt to mobilize the perceived moral capital of Bandera's legacy as anything but unsuccessful. Not only to a majority of Ukrainians, but perhaps even more so to Poles and Jews, the OUN and UPA are unacceptable as Ukrainian national heroes. In 2010, the strongest reactions to Yushchenko's 2010 rehabilitation of Bandera came from Jewish groups in Europe and North America whereas Yushchenko's memory policies began to seriously alienate public opinion in Poland—perhaps Ukraine's strongest advocate in the EU. Rather than uniting the country, Bandera's legacy divides Ukraine, between east and west, left and right. It antagonized—and continues to antagonize—Ukraine's neighbors and partners in the European Union. Politically counterproductive, the Bandera cult has been inefficient as an instrument of nation-building.

When it comes to scholarship, the sharp polarization around these matters has crystallized and clarified positions. Yushchenko's and the UCC's veneration of Bandera and the OUN(b)

---

[813] Recent important monographs include Burds, *Holocaust in Rovno*; Golczewski, *Deutsche und Ukrainer*; Motyka, *Od rzezi wołyńskiej do akcji "Wisła;"* Motyka, *Cień Kłyma Sawura*; Ostriitchouk, *Les Ukrainiens face à leur passé*; Rossoliński-Liebe, *Stepan Bandera*; Shkandrij, *Ukrainian Nationalism*; Statiev, *The Soviet Counterinsurgency*; and Struve, *Deutsche Herrschaft*; Zaitsev, *Ukrains'kyi intehral'nyi natsionalizm*.

brought an important debate to the fore. The increased interest in the topic has not only generated renewed efforts at cementing the nationalist mythology, but has also forced Bandera's promoters to respond to the challenges of a new wave of research. Despite the noise and the shrill tone of the debate, the involvement of critical scholars in the controversy also raised awareness of Bandera, the OUN, and their ideology. This discussion lays bare what one analyst refers to as "the rawest of nerves in Ukrainian Studies and in the Ukrainian community": the legacy of the OUN and Ukrainian memories of World War II.[814] For all its shortcomings, misrepresentations, and misunderstandings, the debate has trained a new spotlight on the OUN's ideology and wartime activities, forcing a necessary discussion upon the Ukrainian and Canadian public sphere. From the perspective of historians who treat Bandera and the OUN as objects of inquiry, this is a welcome development.

---

814 Dominique Arel, "On Context, Comparison, and Dialogue," *Current Politics in Ukraine*, 21 June 2013, https://ukraineanalysis.wordpress.com/2013/06/21/on-context-comparison-and-dialogue/ (accessed 6 July 2017).

7. Eugenics and Racial Anthropology in the Ukrainian Radical Nationalist Tradition[*]

Introduction

Only in recent years has the intellectual history of eugenics in Eastern Europe become the subject of a more systematic academic inquiry. A number of important studies have significantly expanded our understanding of eugenic thought in the European states that emerged following the collapse of the multiethnic empires at the end of World War I.[815] Eugenic thought in nationalist movements of the stateless groups remains understudied. This is not, in itself, surprising, as eugenics was closely connected to modernizing policies of emerging nation states, and the study of eugenics to a considerable extent becomes the study of institutions and agencies.

However, eugenic thought in the interwar radical Ukrainian nationalist tradition remains a historiographic *terra incognito*.[816] This chapter constitutes a first attempt at a more systematic study of eugenics and racial anthropology in Ukrainian nationalist thought from the 1930s to the 1960s.

---

[*] A previous version of this chapter appeared in a special issue of *Science in Context*, vol. 32, no. 1 (March 2019): 67-91.9o See Nadav Davidovitch and Rakefet Zalashik, "Scientific Medicine and the Politics of Public Health: Minorities in Interwar Eastern Europe," *Science in Context*, vol. 32, no.1 (2019): 1-4.

[815] Marius Turda and Paul J. Weindling, *Blood and Homeland: Eugenics and Racial Nationalism in Central and Southeast Europe, 1900-1940* (Budapest: CEU Press, 2007); Marius Turda, ed. *The History of East-Central European Eugenics, 1900-1945: Sources and Commentaries.* (Houndsmills, Basingstone: Macmillan, 2015); Aleksandar Boskovic and Chris Hann, eds. *The Anthropological Field on the Margins of Europe, 1945-1991* (=Halle Studies in the Anthropology of Eurasia) (Berlin: LIT, 2013); Björn M. Felder and Paul J. Weindling, eds. *Baltic Eugenics: Bio-Politics, Race and Nation in Interwar Estonia, Latvia and Lithuania 1918-1940.* (Amsterdam: Brill, 2013).

[816] Partial exceptions include Rossoliński-Liebe, *The Fascist Kernel of Ukrainian Genocidal Nationalism* and Aleksei Bakanov, "*Ni katsapa, ni zhida, ni liakha*" *Natsional'nyi vopros v ideologii Organizatsii ukrainskikh natsionalistov, 1929-1945 gg.* (Moscow: Algoritm, 2014), the primary focus of which are, however, more on race and racial violence in the Ukrainian ultranationalist tradition.

What role did eugenics play in Ukrainian radical nationalist thought in the 1930s and 40s, and what role did these radicals envision for eugenic engineering in their intended state? How did eugenic thought manifest itself in Ukrainian nationalist ideology after 1945, as many of the nationalist activists were dispersed across the Western world?

Eugenics and Modernity

Current scholarship increasingly approaches eugenics from the perspective of regional and transnational comparative analysis. Historian Marius Turda places eugenics at the center of the modern project, as an attempt to bring about the nation's redemption and rejuvenation.[817] Eugenicists were particularly concerned about perceived social and biological degeneration, which they sought to counteract by state intervention to reverse negative demographic trends, replacing it with biological rejuvenation. According to Turda and his colleague Paul Weindling, "The 'blood and soil' mythology, in addition to a whole range of modern techniques aimed at improving the health of the nation, helped to create a new political biology, whose purpose it was to prepare the 'chosen' race at the expense of others, for the onset of racial utopia: the ethnic state."[818]

A transnational approach is particularly helpful to understand the role of racial anthropology and eugenics in the case of the radical Ukrainian nationalist tradition. The Ukrainians were interwar Europe's largest stateless group, whose area of settlement spanned several European states. According to the 1926 Soviet census, 31.2 million ethnic Ukrainians lived in the USSR, 23.2 million of them in the Ukrainian RSR. In addition, an estimated 5.87 million Ukrainians lived in Poland, and 1.1 million in Romania, and nearly half a million in interwar Czechoslovakia.[819] In

---

[817] Marius Turda, *Modernism and Eugenics*. (New York: Palgrave MacMillan, 2010), 15, 124.
[818] Turda and Weindling, *Blood and Homeland*, 12-13.
[819] Rostislav Yendyk, *Vstup do rasovoi budovoi Ukrainy: osnov. pytania z zah. i susp. antropolohii ta evheniky Ukrainy* (=*Naukove Tovarystvo im. Shevchenka, Biblioteka Ukrainoznavstva*, 1) (Munich: Naukove Tovarystvo im. Shevchenka., 1949),

EUGENICS AND RACIAL ANTHROPOLOGY 257

all these states—Poland, Czechoslovakia, and, not least, Romania—eugenic societies were established.[820] The direction of eugenic research and its role in the respective societies varied greatly among the states where the Ukrainians lived.

The role of eugenicists in the new nation-states of Eastern Europe was also dependent on international political relations; not least of their respective states' relation to Germany. Czechoslovak and Polish eugenicists tended to reject German racial hygiene. The Polish eugenic movement was dominated by left-wing and liberal advocates of state welfare; it tended to be class- rather than race-oriented, and generally abstained from anti-Semitic and racist phraseology.[821] The attitude of the Polish authorities in the 1930s towards eugenics, cultural anthropologist Olga Linkiewicz (b. 1977) argues, was "ambivalent if not reluctant": not only did the Roman Catholic Church resist state-based eugenics; important state actors sought to limit the proliferation of eugenics, consciously seeking to prevent or block sterilization laws.[822] Eugenics did not become part of Polish state ideology, and proposals for compulsory sterilization and prenuptial certificates were firmly rejected by the regime.[823]

German models of racial hygiene did, however, have a significant impact in countries such as Hungary, Romania, Bulgaria, and Greece, and the Nordic states.[824] In Romania and other states on the Balkan peninsula, eugenics was pursued as part of a larger,

---

366; Paul Robert Magocsi, *A History of Ukraine: The Land and Its Peoples*, 2nd ed. (Toronto: University of Toronto Press, 2012), 611, 646.
820 Maria Bucur, *Eugenics and Modernization in Interwar Romania* (Pittsburgh: University of Pittsburgh Press, 2002), 49.
821 Magdalena Gawin, "Progressivism and Eugenic Thinking in Poland, 1905-1939," in Turda and Weindling eds., *Blood and Homeland*, 167-183, here: 167, 176-177.
822 Olga Linkiewicz, "Applied Modern Science and the Self-Politicization of Racial Anthropology in Interwar Poland," *Ab Imperio* no. 2 (2016): 154, 179-180.
823 Gawin, "Progressivism and Eugenic Thinking in Poland," 178.
824 Turda and Weindling, *Blood and Homeland*, 9.

modernist project intended to propel these states from an underdeveloped periphery and to become part of modern Europe.[825]

Today, as eugenics and racial anthropology tend to be popularly associated with National Socialism and the far right, it may be helpful to keep in mind that the early eugenic movement included political positions from across the political spectrum. In Sweden, for instance, the eugenic project included representatives from the authoritarian right to liberals, progressives, and radical socialists, whereas Soviet racial anthropologists in the 1920s sought to reconcile eugenics with official Marxist ideology.

In Sweden, a pioneer in state eugenics, which had set up a State Institute for Racial Biology (*Statens Institut för Rasbiologi*, SIFR) in 1921. Operating within a conceptual framework of *völkisch* nationalism, during the first decade of its existence, the institute was preoccupied with the aim of preserving the quality of the nation's racial stock. Under its first director, Herman Lundborg (1868-1943), a primary focus was to document and categorize population sub-groups according to phenotypes within a conceptual framework of racial purity. Racial anthropology, or "Racial biology" was closely associated with "racial hygiene," or "racial culture" and in some European languages the terms were used interchangeably.[826] Lundborg, for instance, used the terms eugenics and racial biology, respectively, for the theoretical and practical aspects of the same discipline: "racial hygiene (eugenics) con-

---

825 Interwar Romanian eugenics belongs to the best researched in Eastern Europe (regarding Romania, see, for instance, Bucur, *Eugenics and Modernization in Interwar Romania*; Solonari, *Purifying the Nation*, 62-94; and Maria Bucur, "Remapping the Historiography of Modernization and State-Building in Southeastern Europe through Health, Hygiene, and Eugenics," in Christian Promitzer, Sevasti Trubeta, and Marius Turda (eds.), *Health, Hygiene, and Eugenics in Southeastern Europe to 1945*, (Budapest: CEU Press, 2011), 429-445, here: 433.

826 See, for instance the journal *Födelsekontroll: Organ för nymalthusianism och raskultur*, no. 1-2, (Jan-Feb 1925). Värmlandsarkiv, (VA), Karlstad, Sweden, Karlstads stifts- och läroverksbiblioteks handskriftssamling, Per Clarholms Samling IV, folder diverse 29d, Tidningsklipp.

stitutes, so to say, the practical implementation of racial biology".[827]

The rise of National Socialism and, in particular, Adolf Hitler's *Machtübernahme* in 1933 became a watershed to eugenicists. The Social Democratic government that took office in 1932 replaced the leadership of SIFR in 1936. The new leadership explicitly rejected the racial mysticism of its founding director. Swedish eugenic legislation, in effect 1934-1975, was largely aimed at reversing a falling nativity. There was no state policy for sterilization in Sweden, and most of the 62,888 documented cases of sterilizations were, in principle voluntary.[828]

The close connection between eugenics, modern nationalizing states, and national projects, delineating ideology and scholarship is not always easy. This article seeks to distinguish between academic inquiry and its political instrumentalization. Let us look at these two categories in order.

Eugenics and Raciology as Academic Disciplines

In academia, two Ukrainian émigrés gained some international prominence in eugenic circles in the interwar era: Borys Matiushenko (1883-1944) and Aleksandr Makletsov (1884-1948). Both belonged to a wave of émigrés who had been actively engaged during the turbulent years of civil war in Ukraine during the years around the end of World War I. After the Bolsheviks prevailed in the civil war, both eugenicists emigrated, initially to Czechoslovakia. Matiushenko found employment with the Czechoslovak Institute for National Eugenics in Prague from 1923, whereas Makletsov later moved to Ljubljana where, in 1937, he became one of the founders of the Section for Anthropology, Genealogy, and

---

827 Herman Lundborg, *Rasbiologi och rashygien: Nutida kultur- och rasfrågor i etisk belysning*, 2nd ed. (Stockholm: Norstedts, 1922), 2.
828 Mattias Tydén, *Från politik till praktik: de svenska steriliseringslagarna 1935–1975. Rapport till 1997 års steriliseringsutredning*. (=SOU 2000:22), (Stockholm: Socialdepartementet, 2000), 41, 59, 529–30.

Eugenics.[829] Ethnicity and identity during the late imperial period were rather fluid concepts, and the identities and political choices of these two Ukrainian eugenicists testify to this.

Makletsov was born in Kharkiv, where he became a *privat-dozent* at Kharkiv University in 1912. He came to chair the Kharkiv city duma in 1919, representing the Constitutional Democratic Party (*Konstitutsionno-demokraticheskaia partiia*, popularly known as the *Kadet* Party, from the abbreviation KD). In 1918-1919 he was editor of the Russian-language paper *Novaia Rossiia*, the leading paper of Anton Denikin's White forces, with whose slogan "For one Great, United, Indivisible Russia" (*Za velikuiu, Edinuiu i Nedelimuiu Rossiu*), he identified. Makletsov left Kharkiv shortly before the Bolsheviks, in December 1919, designated the city as the capital of the newly proclaimed Ukrainian RSR. Upon emigration, Makletsov's scholarship centered on criminal law, and he wrote articles with titles like "Biological Directions in Contemporary Criminology" and "The Struggle to Improve the Race".[830]

Borys Matiushenko, one the other hand, identified as Ukrainian, even though he was born in St Petersburg. He engaged in Ukrainian nationalist politics, and came to serve briefly as Minister of Public Health in the Council of People's Ministers (*Rada Narodnykh Ministriv*), the executive branch of the Ukrainian People's Republic in 1917-1918.[831] Matiushenko was affiliated first with the Revolutionary Ukrainian Party (*Revoliutsiina Partiia Ukrainy*, RUP), later with the Ukrainian Social Democratic Workers' Party (*Ukrains'ka sotsiial-demokratychna robotnycha partiia*,

---

829 Turda, *The History of East-Central European Eugenics*, xviii; Danylo Husar Struk, ed. *Encyclopedia of Ukraine*, vol. 3 (Toronto: University of Toronto Press, 1993a), 346–347.
830 G. Meshko, "Vklad professor Makletsova, A. V. v stanovleniie i razvitie slovenskoi kriminologii," *Iuridicheskaia nauka i provookhranitel'naia praktika* vol. 4(34), (2015): 16-21; Janko Polec, "Maklecov, Aleksander (1884-1948)," in *Slovenska biografija*. (Ljubljana: Slovenska akademija znanosti in umetnosti, Znanstvenoraziskovalni center SAZU, 2013), http://www.slovenska-biogra fija.si/oseba/sbi343178/ (last accessed 2 April, 2017).
831 Ivan Katchanovski, Zenon E. Kohut, Bohdan Y. Nebesio, and Myroslav Yurkevich, eds. *Historical Dictionary of Ukraine*, 2nd edition. (Lanham MD: Scarecrow Press, 2013), 105.

USDRP), and, in the 1920s remained loyal to the émigré group led by Symon Petliura.[832]

For eugenicists who stayed in Soviet Ukraine, the new regime appeared to offer considerable promise; eugenic research was underwritten by the young Soviet state, which set up a number of eugenic societies, the most important of which was the Bureau of Eugenics at the Russian Academy of Sciences in Petrograd. Established in 1921, in 1925 it was reorganized as the Bureau of Genetics and Eugenics. Soviet eugenic research was largely concentrated in the leading academic centers in Leningrad and Moscow, even though it was also conducted at institutes in Kyiv and Minsk. In the Ukrainian RSR, from 1918 the geneticist and selection scientist Andrii O. Sapiehin (1883-1946) led an experimental farm in Odesa, which in 1928 became the All-Union Selection and Genetics Institute. Soviet Ukrainian eugenics and racial anthropological thought was heavily influenced by the geneticist Yurii Filipchenko (1882-1930), the father of Soviet eugenics, who came to train and influence a generation of Soviet racial anthropologists.[833] Trained in the late imperial era, Filipchenko taught the first university course in genetics in Russia in 1913, and remained, in the eyes of his radical critics, a middle-class intellectual.[834] Filipchenko academic work not only bridged the late imperial and early Soviet eras, but also, as we shall see, had an impact on international scholarship in genetics and racial anthropology. He was the mentor of Viktor V. Bunak (1891-1979), for over half a century was a key figure in Soviet racial science, with broad interests in topic

---

832 Christopher Gilley, *The "Change of Signposts" in the Ukrainian Emigration: A Contribution to the History of Sovietophilism in the 1920s*. With a foreword by Frank Golczewski (Stuttgart: ibidem-Verlag, 2014), 104, 168, 247.
833 His Ukrainian-sounding name notwithstanding, Filipchenko was from the Orel *guberniia*, today a border region between the Russian Federation and Ukraine, and most of his academic work was concentrated to Petrograd/Leningrad.
834 See Daniel A. Alexandrov, "Filipchenko and Dobzhansky: Issues in Evolutionary Genetics in the 1920s," in *The Evolution of Theodosius Dobzhansky: Essays on His Life and Thought in Russia and America*, edited by Mark B. Adams, 49-62. Princeton NJ: Princeton Legacy Library, 1994, 49.

varying from blood groups, craniology, into racial history and phenotypes.[835]

Soviet eugenicists regarded the existence of human races as a biological fact. Understanding human races from the perspective of historical materialism, they argued that the 'present racial face' of the earth should be understood as a 'phase,' and rejected assertions that human races did not exist as a "subjective-idealistic" position.[836] Eugenics, as a separate discipline, had a rather short history in the USSR, limited largely to the period 1918-1930. The Russian Eugenics Society was disbanded and, from 1930, eugenics was denounced as "fascist," or a "bourgeois doctrine."[837] The Soviets juxtaposed eugenics with racial research, "raciology," (*rasovedenie*) which they perceived as an apolitical science that could be utilized in the "struggle against anti-scientific racist ideas of some reactionary scholars and political and societal figures of the capitalist countries."[838]

Filipchenko was also the mentor of the Ukrainian racial anthropologist, Theodosius [Teodosii] Dobzhansky (1900-1975). Born in Nemyriv in the Podols'k *guberniia*, (today in the Vinnytsia oblast in Ukraine), Dobzhansky emigrated to the United States in 1927, and is often described as "Ukrainian-American." Yet, like so many others in the borderlands of the Russian Empire at the time, Dobzhansky's ethnic identity was fluid. He spoke Russian, identified as a Russian, and belonged to a Russian Orthodox Church in

---

835 Per Anders Rudling, "Eugenics and Racial Biology in Sweden and the USSR: Contacts across the Baltic Sea." *Canadian Bulletin of Medical History/Bulletin canadien d'historie de la medicine* vol. 31, no,1 (2014): 42, 48, 66, 68.
836 Francine Hirsch, "Race without the Practice of Racial Politics," *Slavic Review* vol. 61, no. 1 (2002): 34-36.
837 Mark B. Adams, "The Soviet Nature-Nurture Debate," in Loren R. Graham (ed.), *Science and the Soviet Social Order*, (Cambridge: Harvard University Press, 1990), 94-138, here: 103; Loren R. Graham, "Science and Values: The Eugenics Movement in Germany and Russia in the 1920s," *American Historical Review* vol. 82, no. 5 (1977): 1156, 1158.
838 Mikhail F. Nesturkh, *et al.* (eds.), *Sovremennia antropologiia* (=*Trudy Moskovskogo obshchestva ispytatelei prirody*, vol. 14), (Moscow: Izdatel'stvo Moskovskogo Universiteta, 1964), 13.

emigration. A humanist and critic of racism, Dobzhanskyi was quite skeptical of nationalist doctrines.[839]

Whereas Filipchenko and Bunak were forced to conform and adjust to the political dictates of the Soviet state, their work—like that of Dobzhanskyi—was academic, and within the mainstream of the day. Despite the very different political conditions under which the three had to operate, all were in agreement that variations in the human population are properly identified in racial terms. Human races were a reality, Dobzhanskyi argued, and race the appropriate conceptual tool to use in order to talk about and understand evolution at a subspecies level[840] "[M]ost biological species are composed of races, and *Homo Sapiens* is no exception," he asserted.[841] Despite resembling the attitudes of the early Soviet era, described by Francine Hirsch as "Race without the Practice of Racial Politics,"[842] Dobzhanski's theory on race rather reflected a continuity from late imperial Russian anthropological scholarship. Dobzhanskyi, sociologist Jenny Reardon writes, offered a concept of race "grounded in the genetics of natural populations, which treated race as an open genetic system in which races overlapped and changed over time."[843] "Races," Dobzhanskyi argued, "are genetically open systems while species are closed ones."[844]

To the extent that it is at all possible to disentangle the question about the existence of human races from political and ideological preferences, Dobzhanskyi's argument that variations of human population are properly characterized in term of races was

---

839 Dobzhanskyi was not only a Russophone. According to his daughter, Dobzhanskyi "always regarded himself a Russian," even though "The only country, of which my father always regarded himself a citizen, was a country that would not know any borders—that is, the land of science." Mikhail D. Golubovskii, "Dobzhanskii v dvukh mirakh," *Vestnik* no. 24(231), (November 23, 1999), http://www.vestnik.com/issues/1999/1123/koi/golubov.htm (last accessed May 4, 2018).
840 Jenny Reardon, *Race to the Finish: Identity and Governance in an Age of Genomics* (Princeton: Princeton University Press, 2005), 37.
841 Theodius Dobzhansky, "A Debatable Account of the Origin of Races." *Scientific American* no. 208, (1963), 169-70, cited in Reardon, *Race to the Finish*, 35.
842 Hirsch, "Race without the Practice of Racial Politics.", 33.
843 Reardon, *Race to the Finish*, 34.
844 Theodius Dobzhansky, "Comment," *Current Anthropology* vol. 3, no. 3 (1962): 279, cited in Reardon, *Race to the Finish*, 34.

a scholarly argument by a geneticist, rather than a political statement by an ideologue. As we will see, Dobzhansky would have a significant impact on discussions of race in the postwar era.

Racial Thought in the Ukrainian Nationalist Tradition

Racial anthropology, or racial hygiene also had direct applications in political platforms of various nationalist ideologues and organizations across Europe. The Ukrainian nationalist movement was no exception in this regard. Racial and eugenic thought started to enter Ukrainian nationalist thought at the turn of the twentieth century, as Ukrainian national and ethnic consciousness was taking hold. In the interwar period, the radical strand in Ukrainian nationalism, to which Matiushenko belonged, would be challenged by more radical currents. One of the portal figures of this radicalism was Mykola Mikhnovs'kyi, a native of the village of Turivka of the Poltava *guberniia*. Mikhnovs'kyi endorsed revolutionary violence as a means to establish an ethnically defined Greater Ukraine "from the river Sian to the Caucasus."[845] The problem was, of course, that this enormous landmass—from the Lublin area in what today is Poland to what today is Dagestan on the shores of the Caspian Sea—was inhabited by highly diverse populations, most of whom had a weak sense of ethnic, or national, identity. Many of the residents—as the examples of Makletsov and Dobzhanskyi illustrate—did *not* choose to self-identify as Ukrainians but instead identified with rivaling identity projects: Russian, Polish, Rusyn, and others.

In 1903, Mikhnovs'kyi published the so-called "Decalogue of the Ukrainian National Party." This "Decalogue" was intended to guide the ideological and private ethics of Ukrainian nationalists. Its third commandment demanded a "Ukraine for the Ukrainians," the sixth "commandment" designated Muscovites (*moskale*), Poles (*liakhy*) and Jews (*zhydy*) as enemies and ethnic others, whereas the tenth and final policed the sexual life of its adherents: "Do not marry a foreign woman because your children will be

---

845 Mykola Mikhnovs'kyi, *Samostiina Ukraina*. (Kyiv: Diokor, 2002), 6, 9-10.

EUGENICS AND RACIAL ANTHROPOLOGY 265

your enemies."[846] Mikhnovs'kyi's use of racial characteristics to delineate Ukrainians from ethnic others, in particular Jews, Poles, and Russians, would become canonical to the Ukrainian radical nationalist tradition.

Another pioneer of this radical ethno-nationalism thought was Dmytro Dontsov. Born in Melitopol in the Tauria *guberniia*, into a primarily Russian-speaking family, he studied in Vienna and Lemberg at the turn of the century.[847] During the Great War, Dontsov metamorphosed from an orthodox Marxist into a radical nationalist. His thought was not particularly original; his amoral nationalism, historian Frank Golczewski argues, was merely a vulgarization of Friedrich Nietzsche's concept of the "will to power."[848] Dontsov emphasized genetic continuity as a supreme value at the center of Ukrainian nationalist ideology.[849] Denouncing humanism and democracy as leading to mediocrity and degeneration and associating it with Jews and freemasonry, Dontsov instead conceptualized history in social Darwinist terms as a struggle between "master races" and "plebeian races," "nation-carrying" and "provincial peoples." Dontsov called for a new concept of heroism, a "new man" of "burning faith and a heart of stone" who would mercilessly destroy Ukraine's ethnic enemies. "Only philistines can absolutely condemn and moralize over war, murder, and violence—philistines and people with atrophied life instincts, thickened 'eunuchs'." Rather, only great spirits and "poets of the

---

846   Rossoliński-Liebe, *The Fascist Kernel of Ukrainian Genocidal Nationalism*, 22; Ostriitchouk, *Les Ukrainiens face à leur passé*, 77-78.
847   Dontsov studied at the University of Vienna from 1909 to 1914 and received his Ph.D. from the University of Lemberg (now L'viv) in 1917. Certificate issued Vienna, January 8, 1915; Demetri Donzow, Ph. D. Diploma, Univerisitatis Leopolensis, July 4, 1917, LAC, Dmytro Dontsov Collection, MG 31, D130, Vol. 1, Folder 2.
848   Frank Golczewski, "Politische Konzepte des ukrainischen nichtsozialistischen Exils (Petliura-Lypynskyj-Donzow)" in Guido Hausmann and Andreas Kappeler, eds. *Ukraine: Gegenwart und Geschichte eines neuen Staates* (Baden-Baden: Nomos, 1993), 110-118.
849   On the intellectual history of Dontsov, see Erlacher, "The Furies of Nationalism"; Oleksandr Zaitsev, *Natsionalist u dobi fashyzmu: L'vivs'kyi period Dmytra Dontsova 1922-1939 roky* (Kyiv: Krytyka, 2019), 157-236; Shkandrij, *Ukrainian Nationalism*, 79-100.

deed," not eunuchs, are builders of empires, Dontsov asserted.[850] From 1923 Dontsov was an enthusiastic admirer of fascism; he extolled Benito Mussolini's "creative leadership" and praised Adolf Hitler in quasi-religious terms, as "the real Messiah."[851]

Dontsov became an important transmitter of *völkisch* and radical nationalist thought into Ukraine, not least as a translator and publisher of the works of Alfred Rosenberg, Joseph Goebbels, Adolf Hitler, and Hans F. K. Günther (1891-1968), the leading ideologue of National Socialist racial theory.[852] Conversant in French and Italian, Dontsov also translated Mussolini and Georges Sorel (1847-1922), and called for the creation of a literature infused with irrational yearnings and what he referred to as a 'barbaric' philosophy of myth and legend.[853] Dontsov rejected the more tolerant stance of earlier Ukrainian activists, viewing Jews and Poles as parasitical communities to be suppressed or eradicated, while regarding Russians as the major oppressor. His statist and xenophobia worldview, Dontsov's biographer Trevor Erlacher notes, was really "closer to protofascist Russian nationalist movements (such as the Black Hundred and the Union of Russians) than to anything from contemporary Ukrainian intellectual circles."[854] Borrowing heavily from Günther, by the late 1930s Dontsov had developed a full-fledged racialist discourse. To the racial ideologues of Ukrainian nationalism, the application of *völkisch* nationalism to the racially fractious lands "from the Danube to the Caspian Sea" constituted particular difficulties. If *völkisch* racial theoreticians like Lundborg in North-western Europe regarded themselves and their ethnic communities as representa-

---

850 Dmytro Dontsov, *Natsionalizm*, (Kyiv: FOP Stebeliak, 2015), 191, 206.
851 Shkandrij, *Ukrainian Nationalism*, 86-97; Zaitsev, *Ukrains'kyi integral'nyi natsionalizm*, 179.
852 On Günther, see Kramár, *Rasismens Ideolog*, 207-231; Terje Emberland and Matthew Kott. *Himmlers Norge: Nordmenn i det storgermanske prosjekt* (Oslo: H. Aschehoug & Co., 2013), 56–65.
853 Kurylo, "The 'Jewish Question'", 233-258 (Oxford and Portland OR: The Littman Library of Jewish Civilization, 2014), 249; Shkandrij, *Ukrainian Nationalism*, 11, 96; Rossoliński-Liebe, *The Fascist Kernel of Ukrainian Genocidal Nationalism*, 10; Ostriitchouk, *Les Ukrainiens face à leur passé*, 102-103.
854 Erlacher, "The Furies of Nationalism," 35.

tives of a racially superior group, their Ukrainian counterparts wrestled with significant variations in phenotype in the enormous geographic area the Ukrainian nationalists claimed for a future Ukrainian state.[855]

Following Günther, Dontsov argued that there were five original racial groups in Europe: the Nordic, Mediterranean, Alpine (*Ostisch*, in German, translated into Ukrainian by Dontsov as *ostiitsa*),[856] East Baltic, and Dinaric racial groups, with the Nordics at the top of this evolutionary hierarchy. Günther theorized that the respective subgroup also possessed a "racial soul," reflected in their emotional traits and religious beliefs, characterizing the Nordic types as cold and clear-thinking, self-controlled, domineering, and lacking in empathy and human feelings, whereas he portrayed the Alpine racial type as sneaky, perverted petty criminals.[857] In Dontsov's work, these ideas were articulated most clearly in his book *The Spirit of Our Antiquity* [*Dukh nashoi davnyny*], the first edition of which was published in German-occupied Prague 1944, and which has since been reprinted in many editions. Dontsov was enchanted with the "Nordic race," which he believed had the best possibility to realize its full "biological potential"[858]:

---

855 One expression of this is Yendyk's anthropological map of Ukraine, which outlines, in exact detail The distribution of "Nordic," "Subnordic," "Dinaric," "Armenoid," "Mediterranean," "Sub-Laponoid," "Laponoid" and "Central Asians" on the map of Ukraine." Dr. Rostyslav Yendyk, Antropolohichna karta Ukrainy," in idem. *Vstup do rasovoi budovoi Ukrainy*, 440. Similar difficulties faced contemporary Romanian eugenicists. See, for instance Solonari, *Purifying the Nation*, 62-74.

856 Soviet raciologist Bunak translated *Ostisch*, as *karpatidy*, or "Carpathoids." T. I. Alekseeva, *Etnogenez vostochnykh slavian*, (Moscow: MGU, 1973), 232.

857 Anne Maxwell, *Picture Imperfect: Photography and Eugenics, 1870-1940* (Sussex: Sussex Academic Press, 2010), 150-152.

858 In *Dukh*, Dontsov adds a section on "The Most Important Literature," which, on racial matters, lists, among others, Lothar Stenzel von Rutkowski, *Was ist ein Volk?*, Kretschmer, *Körperbau und Charakter*; P. Lester and J. Millot, *Les races humaines*; Louis Figur, *Les races humaines*; E. Pittard, *Les races et l'histoire*; H. Günther, *Rassen und Stil*; H. Günther, *Rassenkunde des deutschen Volkes*; L.F. Claus, *Die nordische Seele*; *Rasse und Seele*. Dmytro Dontsov, *Dukh nashoi davnyny*. Druhe vydannia. (Drohobych: Vydavnytstvo "Vidrodzhennia", 1991), 337.

The least represented in the contemporary Ukrainianhood is the Nordic race. Its characteristics of personality and physical of that race are: tall stature, blond hair, blue eyes, elongated faces, straight nose, tall and thin, a sharply marked, outstanding chin, reddish skin color of their faces. That race is most spread in Scandinavia, England, Northern Germany, Belgium, Northern France. The characteristics of success and intelligence of that race are the *characteristics of a state-building race*."[859]

To Dontsov's regret, the "Pontic, Mediterranean type" (*pontiitsa, medyterantisa, seredezamortsia*) were more prevalent among Ukrainians. Even more alarmingly, from Dontsov's perspective, "The most common type among us is the *Dinaric* type and, unfortunately, the *Ostische (ostiitsa)*."[860]

Dontsov explained the misfortunes of the Ukrainians by its substandard racial qualities of its people, and, in particular, of its political elite. The *Ostisch*, or Alpine race, he lamented, constituted "the *dominant type of our democratic leadership*, which played a decisive role in Ukraine in 1917. "According to Günther," Dontsov lamented, "the *Ostisch* type lacks 'the Nordics' ruling spirit' — his is of the 'calmly subjugated' type. [Hector] MacLean,[861] presents the Ostische as brachycephalic, broad-faced, of short stature, referring to him as a Sancho Pancha of sorts."[862] "No heroism is to be found in the works of the *Ostisch*," Dontsov continued,

> In the civic and political life the sole dream of the [representatives of the] *Ostisch* [racial group] is state welfare, hence his love for government positions, pensions, for socialism and bureaucracy, [societies] where everybody works for the government. ... He hates all expressions of greatness — talent, geniality, extraordinary individuality. ... The *Ostische* thinks within the parochial framework of his family, community, parish, village or province — the 'limits of his fatherland is too far from his own limited vision.' ... [The *Ostische*] are characterized by 'resentment,' complex of inferiority, *hinaufgassen*" — that is, hatred of everything greater than themselves, everything heroic and noble.[863]

---

859 Dontsov, *Dukh nashoi davnyny*. Druhe vydannia, 232; emphasis in original.
860 Dontsov, *Dukh nashoi davnyny*, 232, 221; emphasis in original.
861 On the romantic linguist and Celtic nationalist Hector MacLean (1818-1893), see Richard McMahon, *The Races of Europe: Construction of National Identities in the Social Sciences, 1839-1939* (London: Palgrave MacMillan, 2016), 265-266.
862 McMahon, *The Races of Europe*, 221-222.
863 McMahon, *The Races of Europe*, 225-226.

Perceiving his imagined community as occupying an intermediary position between the racially most valuable Nordic and Sub-Nordic groups, and less desirable Dinaric, Pontic, Mediterranean, and Alpine/*Ostisch* racial groups, Dontsov rejected miscegenation with racial types regarded as less valuable, while encouraging miscegenation with racial types he regarded as more valuable.

The Anthropological Features of the Ukrainian People

For his popularization of this heavily politicized *völkisch* raciology Dontsov was aided by Rostislav Yendyk (1906-1974), one of his most faithful followers. Like Dontsov, Yendyk had been a communist as a young man, before trading his far-left views for far-right ones. Yendyk developed his theories on race and purity of blood in his 1934 *The Anthropological Features of the Ukrainian People* (*Antropolohichni prekmety ukrains'koho narodu*) where he argued that psychological and cultural features are racially determined, and that a merciless struggle rages between superior and inferior races. Lesser races, Yendyk asserted, "lack the physiological antibodies that would defend them from new diseases, the mental energy to find work and bread in the conditions imposed on them. The cold embrace of death is their only end."[864] Following Dontsov, Yendyk argued for the need of Ukrainian Nationalists to adopt Nazi practices and experiences of racial hygiene, and promote the strengthening Nordic element within the Ukrainian people.[865] Dontsov and Yendyk's investment in *völkisch* raciology was part of a larger ideological project. Yendyk's popular 1934 biography *Adolf Hitler*, published and prefaced by Dontsov, interpreted the role of the Jews essentially as determined by their racial character.

> "Schopenhauer said, that 'the fatherland of the Jews are other Jews,' therefore Germany cannot be the fatherland of German Jews. That is why they have never had a common interest with the German fatherland... There are

---

[864] Shkandrij, *Ukrainian Nationalism*, 97, citing Rostislav Yendyk, *Adol'f Hitler*. (L'viv: Knyhozbirnia Vistnyka, 1934), 37.
[865] Zaitsev, *Ukrains'kyi integral'nyi nationalism*, 342-343.

about 600,000 Jews in Germany. But they play a disproportional role in German life—as lawyers, judges, administrators, editors (almost the entire press was in their hands), politicians, at the universities, in the literature and so on, in finance and trade—and, from 1918—leading politicians and statemen. Depriving that small minority and its disproportionate role in the liberal arts, the press, and politics—generally in the life of the German nation, Hitler only deprived the German people influence and leadership of an alien, non-German race, to whom Germany was never its fatherland, who did not think the way the nation did, and did not want what she wanted."[866]

If Polish nationalism tended to be anti-German, the Ukrainian nationalist movement in the former Habsburgs lands was, as historian John-Paul Himka has noted, pro-German; in the late 1930s, National Socialism generated considerable interest and sympathy among the western Ukrainian nationalists, as their plans to restructure eastern Europe became increasingly obvious.[867] In the second half of the 1930s, there was a tangible radicalization, and the nationalists' anti-Semitic attitudes rhetoric became markedly more radical, in particular from 1938. In September, 1939 Dontsov's journal *Vistnyk* published sections of *Mein Kampf*, emphasizing the Jewish danger to the Aryan race.[868]

---

[866] Rostislav Yendyk, *Adol'f Hitler* (L'viv: Knyhozbirnia Vistnyka, 1934), 58-59. Iendyk also translated Hans F. K. Günther's *Ritter, Tod und Teufel: Der heldische Gedanke* and wrote an introduction to the Ukrainian edition. Hans F. K. Ginter [Günther]. *Lytsar, Smert' i chort: Herois'ka mysl'. Vstup ta pereklad iz IV. nimets'koho vydannia Rostyslava Yendyka.* (L'viv: Vydavnytstvo "Prometei.", 1937). Dontsov never joined the OUN, whereas Yendyk was affiliated with Dmytro Paliiv's Front of National Unity (FNE), a far-right rival to the OUN. Ihor Mel'nyk, "Rostyslav Iendyk—pys'mennyk i antropoloh." *Zbruch*, 2016, May 28. http://zbruc.eu/node/52015 (last accessed March 20, 2017). On Paliiv, see Volodymyr Kubiiovych "Propamiatna knyha Dmytra Palieva" LAC, MG 31, D203, Vol.17.
[867] John-Paul Himka, "Ukrainian Collaboration in the Extermination of the Jews during the Second World War: Sorting Out the Long-Term and Conjunctural Factors," in Jonathan Frankel (ed.), *Studies in Contemporary Jewry: Vol. XIII: The Fate of the European Jews, 1939-1945: Continuity of Contingency?* (Oxford: Oxford University Press, 1997), 170-189, here: 174.
[868] Kurylo, "The 'Jewish Question'", 249; Shkandrij, *Ukrainian Nationalism*, 87, 284, n.5.

Eugenics, Biopolitics, and Ukrainian Nationalism

Nationalism, in the common understanding of the word—the desire to build a nation-state for a particular group, appears in a variety of forms and manifestations. Many of the expressions of Ukrainian nationalism in the 1910s and 1920s, as in the example illustrated by Matiushenko above, were liberal, socialist, and, for the most part, democratic. From 1919, the racial-eugenic current in Ukrainian nationalist thought was increasingly dominated by Galician Ukrainians, who up until 1918 had been Austrian citizens. The attempts to establish a Ukrainian nation state ended in bitter frustration in the 1921 Riga Peace Treaty, which divided the Ukrainian lands and reduced Ukrainians to national minorities in intensely nationalistic—and nationalizing—states like Poland and Romania, where they were submitted to attempts at political assimilation.[869] Under the leadership of colonel Yevhen Konovalets', the Ukrainian Military Organization (*Ukrains'ka Viis'kova Orhanizatsiia*, UVO) was established in 1921 by Ukrainian war veterans who, disillusioned with democracy, sought to set up a Ukrainian state through armed struggle. Increasingly under the influence of Dontsovian nationalism, in 1929, the UVO united much of the Ukrainian far right into the Organization of Ukrainian Nationalists (*Orhanizatsiia Ukrains'kykh Natsionalistiv*, OUN).[870]

The OUN policed the sexual and reproductive life of its imagined community, which it understood in biological and spiritual terms. Organized, in accordance with Dontsovian ideology like an order, the organization condensed its biopolitical postulates in terms of violent, mystical, quasi-religious doctrines articulated in terms of "44 Rules of Life of a Ukrainian Nationalist," a new "Decalogue," introduced in 1929, and "12 Characteristics of a Ukrainian Nationalist." The latter stipulated that the Nationalist was to constitute the physical and psychological flower of the nation: "Ukraine needs strong, healthy sons, strong to spirit and body. ... The Ukrainian Nationalist harbors the Great Idea in his heart, the fire of the revolutionary Spirit in his heart, powerful and

---

869 Bruski, *Between Prometheism and Realpolitik*, 29-59
870 Ostriichouk, *Les Ukrainiens face à leur passé*, 67.

flexible muscles, nerves of steel, a quick eagle vision and hearing, and a hard fist." The "44 Rules of Life of a Ukrainian Nationalist," a supplement to the Decalogue was intended to guide the lives and daily activities of its members. It characterized intermarriage with other races "a crime of national treason," which would lead to "degeneration" and therefore needed to be banned. Its 40th rule read: "Cherish motherhood as the source of re-generation of life. Make your family a ciborium for the purity of Your Race and Nation."[871]

These biopolitical postulates were not mainly theoretical concepts, but a categorical imperative to guide the Nationalists in the most intimate aspects of their lives. In his memoirs the leading OUN activist Mykola Sukhovers'kyi (1913-2008) recalled how, in the 1930s his *Burschenschaft* in Cernauti/Chernivtsi, then in Romania, forbade its members to marry non-Ukrainians, citing Mikhnovs'kyi's "Do not marry an alien, because your children will become your enemies," a postulate, taken quite literally by the Nationalist faithful.[872]

Practical guidelines to direct the Nationalist vanguard in the most intimate aspects on life was one thing; bringing about their revolutionary, Ukrainian ethno-state would require state planning and eugenic engineering on a grand scale. How did the Nationalist ideologues envision the implementation of their doctrines? From about 1936, the theoretical basis for this project started to crystallize.

Yurii Lypa: *The Ukrainian Race*

Yurii Lypa, one of the ideologues of the biopolitical thought of Ukrainian Nationalism, rose to prominence in the late 1930s. Lypa admired Dontsov's style and "implacable militancy" and was a contributor to Dontsov's journal *Vistnyk* over the 1930s.[873] After the 1940/41 split, Lypa came to side with the more radical Ban-

---

871 Lypovets'kyi, *Orhanizatsiia Ukrainkykh Natsionalistiv (banderivtsy)*, 92-94.
872 Mykola Sukhovers'kyi, *Moi spohady*. (Kyiv: Vydavnytstsvo "Smoloskyp," 1997), 50.
873 Shkandrij, *Ukrainian Nationalism*, 90, 136.

dera wing of the OUN. A poet and physician, Lypa worked as a military doctor in the UPA, and was killed by the Soviets at the end of the war. Radical nationalists today refer to him as a "classic of Ukrainian geopolitics and raciology."[874] Like Dontsov and Yendyk, Lypa sought to reconcile radical ethnonationalism with the significant genetic variation among the Ukrainian-speaking community. While emphasizing that "biological anthropology indicates that Muscovite (*moskvyns'koi*) blood is related to the blood of Finno-Mongolian and not to the Western and Southern neighbors," his conceptualization of the Ukrainian race resembled that of Dontsov and Yendyk, as consisting of that of plural racial groups which needed to be amalgamated. "The term 'race' meant for him a nation with roots in an *ethnie*—more correctly, several *ethnies*," literary scholar Myroslav Shkandrij (b. 1950) notes.[875]

Trained as a physician, Lypa was preoccupied with practical eugenics, and paid particular attention to the role of women. A OUN publication of the time states that the main task of women was "the upbringing of the new generation, a physically, spiritually and morally healthy generation."[876] Lypa argued that "the physical love to one's own and the physical hatred towards foreigners" was a duty of the Ukrainian woman. To Lypa, gender become the criteria for establishing boundaries, and as historian Olena Petrenko has observed, he perceived the Ukrainian woman as different from other women.[877]

Lypa called for a more systematic eugenic managing of his ethnocommunity. In his 1936 essay "The Ukrainian Race," Lypa argued

---

874 Yurii Lypa, "Ukrains'ka rasa," *Vatra: national'-revoliutsiinyi chasopys*, (July 21, 2009) http://www.vatra.cc/rasa/yuriy-lypa-ukrayinska-rasa.html (last accessed 7 January, 2012).
875 Shkandrij, *Ukrainian Nationalism*, 210.
876 Olesia Khromeychuk, "What Place for Women in Ukraine's Memory Politics?" *Open Democracy*, (October 10, 2016), https://www.opendemocracy.net/od-russia/olesya-khromeychuk/what-place-for-women-in-ukraine-s-memory-politics (last accessed October 13, 2016).
877 Olena Petrenko, "Geschlecht, Gewalt, Nation: Die Organisation Ukrainischer Nationalisten und die Frau." *Osteuropa* vol. 66, no. 4 (2016): 89.

every woman has to get married. Marriage is the duty of women to their own kin (*rid*). To aid her in that task is the duty of the state. Sexual prodigality (*statevoho marnotratsva*) is not acceptable, neither among women, nor among men. We need to realize that the 300 ovulations of every Ukrainian woman, as well as 1,500 ejaculations of every Ukrainian man are the same sort of national resources, as, say, its energy supplies and iron, coal, or oil deposits. The state has to relate to the sexual lives [of its citizens] in the same way it does to other matters—in accordance with the traditions and culture.[878]

In order to achieve these aims, Lypa called for extensive authority of a future Ukrainian state to intervene into the most intimate aspects of its citizens' lives. "In order to maintain that order of life there will be sexual and eugenic advisors, sexual courts and tribunals"[879]

Volodymyr Martynets: *The Jewish Problem in Ukraine*

Volodymyr Martynets' was one of the more prominent OUN ideologues to seek a practical solution to what he called the "Jewish problem" in Ukraine.[880] In 1938, from his Paris exile Martynets' published a booklet entitled *The Jewish Problem in Ukraine*, where he argued "Our Jews are, from a political perspective a hostile element, from a socio-economic perspective parasitic, from a cultural and national perspective harmful, from a moral and ideological perspective corruptive ... and from a racial perspective unsuitable for mixing and assimilation." Martynets' pondered five methods to solve the "Jewish problem": assimilation, 'racial-national isolation,' agrarianization or settling on the land, expulsion, and 'complete isolation'".[881] In order to prevent miscegenation with Jews, which, he argued, would lead to the "Judaization" (*ozhydovlennia*) of Ukrainians, Martynets' argued that a whole range of methods be introduced—not only a ban on mixed mar-

---

878 Lypa, "Ukrains'ka rasa"
879 Lypa, "Ukrains'ka rasa"
880 Martynets remained loyal to Mel'nyk's wing after the 1940-41 split. After the war, Martynets' immigrated to Winnipeg, Manitoba, Canada where he became an influential publicist and active participant in émigré politics.
881 Volodymyr Martynets', *Zhydivs'ka problema v Ukraini*, (London: Williams, Lea & Co, 1938), 10.

riages, but the total isolation of Jews from any economic, political, and cultural contacts with Ukrainians, something he hoped would force the Jews to a mass exodus.

> All of the options, especially if combined, will decrease the current strength of Jewry, stop their expansion in our country, and assure their continuous decline in numbers, not only through emigration, but also through the decline of their natural growth rate. As the Jews will not be able to make a living, they will take care of this themselves.[882]

Exactly what "complete isolation" was supposed to mean, and how it was to be implemented, remained, however, unclear.[883]

Mykhailo Kolodzins'kyi: *The Military Doctrine of Ukrainian Nationalists*

On March 10, 1938, Konovalets' tasked the young firebrand Yaroslav Stets'ko to draft a military doctrine for the OUN. Stets'ko, who was also arranging the ideological preparations for a second Grand Assembly of the OUN, scheduled to be held in Rome in August 1939, in turn delegated this to Mykhailo Kolodzins'kyi. A veteran of the UVO since 1922, and the military *referent* of the Galizian OUN since 1929, Kolodzins'kyi had considerable military experience. In the early 1930s, Kolodzins'kyi had been trained at a joint OUN and Ustasha military camp in Mussolini's Italy, where he had befriended the future Croatian dictator Ante Pavelić (1889-1959). Stets'ko requested Kolodzins'kyi to have the policy document, entitled "The Military Doctrine of Ukrainian Nationalists," completed by June 1, in order to have it published that summer. Kolodzins'kyi wrote the document in April-May 1938.[884]

Some of its eugenic components we recognize from works by other OUN ideologues at the time. The "Military doctrine" characterizes Polish rule not only as socioeconomically oppressive, but also as sexually demoralizing and exploitative: "In the Polish settlements all poor Ukrainian girls lose their innocence, when they

---

882 Martynets', *Zhydivs'ka problema v Ukraini*, 14-15.
883 Carynnyk, "'Foes of Our Rebirth,'" 323.
884 Oleksandr Zaitsev "Voenna doktryna Mykhaila Kolodzins'koho." *Ukraina Moderna*, vol. 20 (2013b): 246-248.

go there for work."⁸⁸⁵ The "Military doctrine" reflects a further radicalization. Kolodzins'kyi openly called for the removal, "literally, to the last man of the Polish element from the Western Ukrainian Lands, thereby end the Polish pretentions about the Polish character of those lands."⁸⁸⁶

If Martynets' one year earlier, had proposed "total isolation" of its Jews, Kolodzins'kyi now called for a partial extermination of minorities "who are hostile to Ukr[ainian] independence. The fury of the Ukrainian people towards the Jews will be particularly horrific," he continued. "We have no need to hamper this rage; on the contrary, we need to increase it, since the more Jews killed during the uprising, the better for the Ukrainian state, because the Jews will be the only minority, which we will not be able to envelop through our denationalizing policies. All other minorities, who will remain alive after the uprising, we will denationalize."⁸⁸⁷

On May 23, 1938, Konovalets' was assassinated by an NKVD agent in Rotterdam. This, notes historian Taras Kurylo, "paved the way to the adoption of Nazi anti-Jewish discourse and the further radicalization of anti-Jewish motifs in the Ukrainian nationalist movement."⁸⁸⁸ Konovalets' successor, his brother-in-law Andrii Mel'nyk lacked his predecessor's authority, leading to a growing rift in the organization, between the émigré leadership and a younger generation of radicals in the Galician "homeland" leadership.⁸⁸⁹ Following the German occupation of Czechoslovakia, on March 15, 1939, Transcarpathia declared independence, only to promptly be invaded and absorbed by Hungary. Kolodzins'kyi went to fight in Transcarapthia and was killed on March 18 or 19. A first section of Kolodzins'kyi's doctrine was published in 1940,

---

885 Mykhailo Kolodzins'kyi, "Natsionalistychne povstannia (rozdil iz pratsi 'Voenna doktryna ukrains'kykh nationalistiv'). Publikatsiia ta komentari O. Zaitseva." *Ukraina moderna* vol. 20, (2013): 264.
886 Kolodzins'kyi, "Natsionalistychne povstannia, 266.
887 Kolodzins'kyi, "Natsionalistychne povstannia, 290.
888 Kurylo, "The 'Jewish Question'", 257.
889 See, for instance Stets'ko's unpublished 1986 memoirs, Yaroslav Stets'ko, "Rozmovy dostoinoho Yaroslava Stets'ko" Osobovyi fond Ya. Stets'ka, Archive OUN-UIA, Fond 23, p. 41.

whereas a second part did not appear in print until 1957, and then not in its entirety.[890]

Yaroslav Stets'ko

Possibly the most intelligent of the OUN leaders, Stets'ko was certainly one of the most radical, and his role in the radicalization of the Galician OUN cannot be overstated. In his unpublished memoirs, Stets'ko recalls how "We were happy to read Dontsov ... we were captivated by his faith, fanaticism, his unabashed affirmation of the national idea and the apotheosis of the Fatherland."[891]

Stets'ko claimed not only to have given Kolodzins'kyi the idea to write the Military Doctrine, but also that "it contains many of my suggestions."[892] While Stets'ko did not specify exactly which the suggestions were, he would, over the next three years, develop his racial and eugenic ideas in some detail.

In 1938 Stets'ko denounced democracy "as a corruption of morality... . The rule of money is absolute, and the financial bourgeoisie, Masonry, and a clique of international criminals led by Jews control governments."[893] In May 1939, *Novyi Shliakh*, the leading OUN paper in Canada, published Stets'ko's article "We and Jewry" (*"Zhydivstva i my"*), penned under his pseudonym Zynovyi Karbovych, in which he characterized Jews as "nomads and parasites," a nation of "swindlers, materialists, and egoists," interested only in "personal profit," who found "pleasure in the satisfaction of the basest instincts," and determined "to corrupt the heroic culture of warrior nations." Stets'ko further elaborated on the issue of separation of Jews from Ukrainians. He argued that Ukrainians constituted "the first people in Europe to understand

---

890 Zaitsev. "Voenna doktryna Mykhaila Kolodzins'koho," 248.
891 Iaroslav Stets'ko, "Spohady/Vidredagovanyi tekst rozmov dostoinoho Yaroslava 'Stets'ka z d-Rom Anatoliem Bedriem, perevedenykh i zapysanykh na 12 kasetkakh vid 17 do 23 chervnia 1985 roku," p. 5, Arkhiv TsDVR, L'viv, fond 639, electronic document spohady_fond639Arkhiv.
892 Stets'ko. "Spohady," (1985) p. 8 Arkhiv TsDVR, L'viv, fond 639, electronic document spohady_fond639Arkhiv.
893 Carynnyk, "'A Knife in the Back of Our Revolution'," 6.

the corrupting work of Jewry," which, according to Stets'ko, was the reason why they had separated themselves from the Jews for centuries, something which, in turn, had enabled them to retain "the purity of their spirituality and culture."[894] The material from the preparation of the Rome Grand Assembly—of which Stets'ko was a key organizer—unsurprisingly differed little from those of Kolodzins'kyi. Stets'ko was of the opinion that the "minority question" in Ukraine would be solved by means of the minorities ceasing to exist. He envisioned three paths to achieve that goal: assimilation, deportation or "physical measures," proposing the setup of ghettos, even though he felt that the ideal solution to the Jewish question would be the deportation of all Jews from Ukraine to the far east.[895] The preference for exclusion and isolation is reflected also in Mykola Stsibors'kyi's (1898-1941) OUN draft constitution of September 1939, which stipulated that "Ukraine is a sovereign, authoritarian, totalitarian" state under the OUN's exclusive control, in which Jews are excluded from citizenship.[896]

Ukrainian Nationalism in the *Generalgouvernement*

The German and Soviet partition and occupation of Poland in September 1939 radically altered the preconditions for Western Ukrainian Nationalist activism. The top leadership of the Galician OUN, among them Stepan Bandera and Mykola Lebed—who both served lifetime sentences for terrorism and murder—were released from prison. Under Bandera's leadership, the radicals soon broke with Mel'nyk's leadership and set up their own organization, taking the bulk of the Galician "homeland" organization

---

894 Carynnyk, "'A Knife in the Back of Our Revolution'," 13.
895 Marek Wojnar, "Wizije przemocy." *Nowa Europa Wschodnia*, July 6, 2016 online edition, http://new.org.pl/2643,post.html (last accessed 20 February, 2017).
896 Mykola Stsibors'kyi, "Narys proektu osnovnykh zakoniv (konstytutsii) Ukrains'koi Derzhavy," reprinted in O. Kucheruk and Iu. Cherchenko (eds.), *Dokumenty i materialy z istorii Orhanizatsii Ukrains'kykh Natsionalistiv, Tom 7, Dokumenty komisii derhzvnoho planuvannia OUN (KDP OUN)*, 8-23, here; 8, 20; Carynnyk, "Foes of Our Rebirth", 324.

with them. Stets'ko sided with Bandera and became his first deputy.

Kraków quickly became the most important center for Ukrainian Nationalist activism in 1939-41. In the *Generalgouvernement*, the OUN was not only tolerated, but actively supported by the German authorities. The OUN set up military units in German uniform in preparation for Operation Barbarossa and their activities were conducted openly and with *Abwehr* support.[897] From their base in Kraków the radicals could witness, first-hand the German authorities' implementation of racial policies, intended to alter the ethnic makeup of the lands. As the German population constituted less than 10 per cent of the population in the *Generalgouvernement* the German leadership sought to increase and strengthen the German presence in this territory. *Lebensborn* homes were set up in Kraków and Warsaw, and, from 1941, also in L'viv.[898] Similar notions of ethnic restructuring of Ukrainian ethnic lands are echoed in the rhetoric of the so-called Ukrainian Central Committee, the officially sanctioned Ukrainian political and community organization in the *Generalgouvernment*, led by Volodymyr Kubiiovych.[899]

The establishment of the OUN(b) was formalized by its own, rivalling Grand Assembly in Kraków in April, 1941, in which the followers of Stepan Bandera broke with Mel'nyk's leadership. The radical splinter group, which in size and influence would soon greatly eclipse Mel'nyk's group, referred to itself as the Revolutionary Leadership of the OUN, but is better known as the OUN-

---

897 Struve, *Deutsche Herrschaft*, 162-185.
898 The total number of children "Germanized" through the Lebensborn project was limited, around 350 children in East- and Southeast Europe, and hardly any in the occupied Soviet Union Georg Lilienthal, *Der 'Lebensborn e.V.': Ein Instrument nationalsozialistischer Rassenpolitik* (Frankfurt a M: Fischer, 1993), 219, 222, 223.
899 Kubiiovych, who was close to the OUN(m), repeatedly requested Hans Frank "to cleanse [the Kholm and eastern Lublin] area from Polish and Jewish elements through re-settlement," thereby establishing "in the east, a purely Ukrainian border region...a protective eastern wall for Greater Germany" and "a territorial basis for the German-Ukrainian community of interest." Volodymyr Kubiiovych to Hans Frank, February 1943, pp. 1 and 8, LAC MG 31, D 203, Vol. 27, Folder 1.

Bandera, or OUN(b). In April 1941 the Banderites adopted a banner with the colors red and black, symbolizing *Blut und Boden*, and adopted the fascist, raised arm salute.[900]

The April 1941 OUN(b) program called for "a state-organized plan for the for national health, expansion, and unity of the Ukrainian race by the means of a) universal, mandatory, complimentary medial services and the use of all achievements of medical science and treatments for the entire community b) assistance to large families c) guardianship and protection of mothers and children, d) elevating the level of national resuscitation, through improved housing, and standard of living , e) the nourishing of the physical health of the people."[901]

The OUN(b) regarded Ukrainians as the sole autochthonous people of the land, and thereby exclusive proprietors to the multiethnic borderlands of Eastern Galicia, Volhynia, and Podlachia. The 1941 program stipulated that the "Jews in the USSR are the most dedicated supporters of the ruling Bolshevik regime and the vanguard of Muscovite imperialism in Ukraine" and that "the Organization of Ukrainian Nationalists fight the Jews as supporters of Muscovite-Bolshevism, at the same time enlightening the popular masses the Moscow is the main enemy."[902] It also pledged that it would fight Masonry and "unmask their organizations wherever they appear."[903] The resolutions of the April, 1941 Kraków Second Grand Assembly also referred explicitly to the "military doctrine," which suggests that the Organization's leadership—and not only Stets'ko—has read and approved it.[904]

Immediately following the Kraków Grand Assembly, Bandera summoned his closest associates; in addition to Stets'ko, also Lenkavs'kyi and Shukhevych. The four drafted a master plan to be activated in connection with Operation Barbarossa.[905] The re-

---

[900] Volodymyr Serhiichuk, ed. *Ukrains'kyi zdvih: Zakerzonnia. 1939-1947. Vydannia druhe, dopovnene.* (Kyiv: PP Serhiichuk, M.I, 2011), 106; Rossoliński-Liebe, *Stepan Bandera*, 179-180.
[901] Serhiichuk (ed.), *Ukrains'kyi zdvih*, 95.
[902] Serhiichuk (ed.), *Ukrains'kyi zdvih*, 100.
[903] Serhiichuk (ed.), *Ukrains'kyi zdvih*, 105.
[904] Serhiichuk (ed.), *Ukrains'kyi zdvih*, 101-102.
[905] Carynnyk, "Foes of Our Rebirth," 329.

sult was the 71-page blueprint for action, entitled "Struggle and Activities of the OUN(b) in Wartime" ("Borot'ba i diial'nist' OUN(b) pid chas viiny"). The language of this document echoed that of Kolodzins'kyi: "Jews are to be isolated, eliminated from official positions in order to avoid sabotage, Russian and Poles all the more so," Stets'ko, Bandera, Lenkavs'kyi and Shukhevych wrote. "If there should be an insurmountable need to leave a Jews in the economic administration, place one of our militiamen over him and liquidate him for the slightest offense. Administrators of various branches can only be Ukrainians, never hostile aliens"[906]

We also encounter this language in the anonymous OUN pamphlet "Nation as a Species" (*"Natsiia iak spetsies"*), which appeared in 1941 and which stipulates the OUN(b)'s absolute rejection of miscegenation with other peoples living together with Ukrainians: "we fight against mixed marriages (Ukrainian-Polish, Ukrainian-Muscovite, Ukrainian-Hungarian, Ukrainian-Jewish [*(ukr.-pol'., ukr.-mosk., ukr.,-madiar., ukr.-zhyd.)*] and need to eliminate the possibility of them taking place. The very fact of their existence or establishment we regard as a crime and national treason."[907] The only author given is "Organization of Ukrainian Nationalists," yet from the language, style, and content it would not be unreasonable to assume Stets'ko's authorship of this programmatic document:

> The Ukrainian Nation is against mixed marriages—we regard them a crime. The Stalinist-Leninist concept of unity of the peoples we regard as hostile. We do not recognize them, since it is aimed at out extermination, by means of [creating a] (Muscovite or, nowadays, Soviet) people. The content of our family has to be a Ukrainian (father, mother, and children). The family is the highest organic unit of the national collective, whose Ukrainian purity we are obliged to defend.[908]

---

906 Carynnyk, "Foes of Our Rebirth," 330.
907 Orhanizatsiia Ukrains'kykh Natsionalistiv, 1941, HDA SBU, f. 13, spr. 376, t. 1 ark. 7.
908 Orhanizatsiia Ukrains'kykh Natsionalistiv, 1941, HDA SBU, f. 13, spr. 376, t. 1, ark. 7-8.

"On the Content of State Life"

Stets'ko was in many ways the ideological mastermind of the new group that immediately started to draft policy documents on strategies to accomplish the state, but also on how it was be run. In his memoirs Stets'ko referred to this group as a "Commission for State Planning," and stated that it consisted of four departments.[909] In all likelihood, it was during this period, between April and June 1941, on the eve of Operation Barbarossa, that Stets'ko authored the "working paper" entitled "On the Content of State Life" ("*Za zmist derzhavnoho zhyttia*"), outlining the OUN(b)'s eugenic agenda.[910] In section 11 of the document, entitled "Eugenics, protection of people's health and physical education," Stets'ko spells out the need for a national, governmental eugenic policy: "Set up a State Agency of People's Eugenics with branches all over the entire territory of the state."[911] This state agency, Stets'ko wrote, "should not only treat diseases, but also prevent diseases from gaining a foothold. Therefore, it will obligate not only state doctors from the people's institute of eugenics, but also private ones" to carry out its activities.[912] Throughout, the document refers to society as "organic life," and life of the nation as a unified organism.[913] A key task of this agency would be to ban marriages with physically unhealthy people.[914] "[N]ationalism," Stets'ko

---

909 Stets'ko, "Spohady," (1985) pp. 34-35 Arkhiv TsDVR, L'viv, fond 639, electronic document spohady_fond639Arkhiv.
910 Yaroslav Stets'ko, "Za zmist derzhavnoho zhyttia," unpublished document, 1941. HDA SBU, f. 13, spr. 372, t. 12, ark. 215-271 Also available as facsimile on *Elektronnyi arkhiv Ukrains'koho vyzvol'noho rukhu*, http://avr.org.ua/index.php/viewDoc/11291/ (last accessed 16 April, 2018).
911 Stets'ko, "Za zmist derzhavnoho zhyttia", 39. HDA SBU, f. 13, spr. 372, t. 12, ark. 260.
912 Stets'ko, "Za zmist derzhavnoho zhyttia", 41. HDA SBU, f. 13, spr. 372, t. 12, ark. 262.
913 See, in particular, Stets'ko, "Za zmist derzhavnoho zhyttia", 49. HDA SBU, f. 13, spr. 372, t. 12, ark. 270. By contrast, in the contemporary OUN(m) materials, references to eugenics are absent. The Minister of Health in the intended OUN(m) state "Will be tasked with the issue of the spiritual hygiene of the people" Kucheruk, and Cherchenko, *Dokumenty i materialy z istorii Orhanizatsii Ukrains'kykh Natsionalistiv, Tom 7*, 28-31.
914 Stets'ko, "Za zmist derzhavnoho zhyttia," 40-41, HDA SBU, f. 13, spr. 372, t. 12, ark. 261-262.

wrote, "can permit the assimilation only of those elements, the content of their lives were and are heroic, whose culture is similar to the Ukrainian. Only those can be assimilated who are on the same level of development as the spiritual-cultural type of the Ukrainian."[915]

The interrelated aims of national palingenesis through segregation and assimilation was now coordinated into a coherent set of governmental policies for the intended state. "The purpose of OUN education is to create a new, heroic type of Ukrainian," Stets'ko wrote.[916] "Therefore Nationalism will allow for the assimilation only of those elements, the content of their lives was and is heroic, the culture of whom is similar to the Ukrainian. The assimilation aims at creating a spiritual-cultural type of Ukrainian."[917]

The Ukrainian National Revolution

Operation Barbarossa, the German invasion of the Soviet Union on June 22, 1941, marked the beginning, as Hitler put it, not only of a world crusade against Bolshevism, but also of a national uprising, a Ukrainian national revolution, as envisioned by the OUN(b). Not Bandera, but his deputy, the 29-year-old Stets'ko was the dominant figure in the crucial final week of June 1941, which the OUN(b) referred to as the "Ukrainian national revolution."[918] Having crossed the Soviet border in the first days of the German-Soviet war, Stets'ko wrote to Bandera on June 25, 1941, "We are establishing a militia that will help eliminate Jews and protect the population."[919] In L'viv, on June 30, 1941, Stets'ko declared himself head of a government of a "renewed" Ukrainian state which, he emphasized, would "work closely together with

---

915 Stets'ko, "Za zmist derzhavnoho zhyttia," 42, HDA SBU, f. 13, spr. 372, t. 12, ark. 263.
916 Stets'ko, "Za zmist derzhavnoho zhyttia," 47. HDA SBU, f. 13, spr. 372, t. 12, ark. 268.
917 Stets'ko, "Za zmist derzhavnoho zhyttia," 42. HDA SBU, f. 13, spr. 372, t. 12, ark. 263.
918 Armstrong, John A. "Heroes and Human: Reminiscences Concerning Ukrainian National Leaders During 1941-1944." *The Ukrainian Quarterly*, Vol. 51 (nos. 2-3 Summer-Fall, 1995): 219.
919 Struve, *Deutsche Herrschaft*, 263, 267.

National Socialist Greater Germany which under the leadership of its Führer Adolf HITLER creates a new order in Europe."[920] The renewal of Ukrainian statehood was followed by a wave of anti-Jewish mass violence in the entire area of OUN(b) operation. The discovery of thousands of bodies of inmates, murdered in Soviet prisons by the retreating NKVD, appears to have stoked local resentment further, as OUN(b) militia launched a wave of pogroms in which thousands of Jews were murdered, many in locations without a local prison where there had been no NKVD massacres.[921]

In letters to Hitler, Mussolini, Franco, and Pavelić, Stets'ko reassured them that his newly declared state belonged to Adolf Hitler's New Order in Europe.[922] The German authorities refused to recognize this state, and both Stets'ko and Bandera were detained and brought to Berlin, where they were questioned by the Gestapo but were otherwise free to move around in the city, meet other OUNites, and petition the German government to cooperate with him.[923] At this point, Stets'ko's attitude to Jews has been further radicalized. In May 1939, Stets'ko advocated the expulsion and ghettoizing of Jews. The OUN September, 1939, draft of the Ukrainian constitution excluded Jews from citizenship. In May 1941, the OUN(b) issued a blueprint for a national uprising which spelled out the need for mass violence against Jews and its intended head of government drew up the lines for a eugenic agency to specify the requirements for who would be allowed to assimilate into the Ukrainian national organism. However, Stets'ko had not

---

920 TsDAVOVU f. 3833, op.1, spr. 5, ark. 3.
921 Kai Struve, author of the most detailed study of the anti-Jewish violence in Western Ukraine in 1941, estimates the victims of the Soviet prison massacres to be in the range of 7,500-10,000 and the victims of the anti-Jewish violence to between 7,295 and 11,309 victims, 4,280-6,950 of which he attributes to the Waffen-SS Division *Wiking*, and 3,015-4,359 to local Ukrainian perpetrators. Struve, *Deutsche Herrschaft*, 216 and 671. For a different, higher estimate, see Dieter Pohl, "Anti-Jewish Pogroms in Western Ukraine: A Research Agenda," in Barkan, Cole, and Struve (eds.), *Shared History – Divided Memory*, 305-314, here: 306.
922 Rossoliński-Liebe, "The 'Ukrainian National Revolution' of 1941"
923 Rossoliński-Liebe, *Stepan Bandera*, 247-249; Carynnyk, "'A Knife in the Back of Our Revolution'," 3.

yet openly addressed the issue of what to do with to those excluded who had survived the violence of the initial uprising. In Berlin, in July 1941 the self-proclaimed Prime Minister of Ukraine now explicitly spelled out what to do with those inassimilable: "I therefore support the destruction of the Jews and the expedience of bringing German methods of exterminating Jewry to Ukraine, barring their assimilation and the like."[924]

Stets'ko spent the time from September 15, 1941, to September 30, 1944, in German captivity, albeit in relative comfort in an annex to the KZ Sachsenhausen. During this period his, and Bandera's influence on their movement was marginal. The OUN(b), struggling with how to relate to its former sponsor, initially urged its activists to volunteer for, and infiltrate the auxiliary police formations. After Stalingrad, as it became clear that Nazi Germany would lose the war, thousands of policemen defected the police, and went underground, where they formed the backbone of the Ukrainian Insurgent Army (UPA), under OUN(b)'s command. In 1943, the rivalry over the claims to the ethnically mixed Polish-Ukrainian borderland escalated into a brutal violent conflict as the UPA launched a campaign of mass ethnic cleansing of the Polish minority in Volhynia and East Galicia, in which at least 70,000 people, perhaps as many as 100,000 were killed.[925] Following the return of the Soviets, the OUN(b) launched a tenacious insurgency against the Soviet authorities, which was crushed with utter brutality, claiming the lives of 110,825 people.[926]

After their release, Stets'ko and Bandera resumed strategic cooperation with Nazi Germany for the remainder of the war. After a meeting with Dontsov in Prague during the final days of the war, Stets'ko was seriously wounded as the German caravan in which he travelled was attacked in the vicinity of Prague by the US Air Force on May 10, 1945. A bullet fired from the air tore off

---

[924] Berkhoff and Carynnyk, "The Organization of Ukrainian Nationalists," 152, 171.
[925] Jared McBride, "Peasants into Perpetrators: The OUN-UPA and the Ethnic Cleansing of Volhynia, 1943-1944," *Slavic Review* vol. 75, no. 3, (Fall 2016): 639; Siemaszko, "Stan badań nad ludobójstwem," 341.
[926] Burds, "AGENTURA," 97.

his arm at the elbow before ricocheting into his lower abdomen, causing irreversible injury of his genitalia and permanently paralyzing his left arm. Stets'ko received seven serious wounds, was hospitalized for five months, and underwent surgery eight times. He would suffer from poor health and spend the remainder of his life in physical pain.[927]

Phenotype and Genotype

The collapse of Nazi Germany and the Axis powers in 1945, de-colonization, and the civil rights movement forced a discussion on race, and racism. Much like the political situation of the 1930s and 40s had a direct impact on scholarly discussions on race and eugenics, so did de-colonization and the civil rights movement in the 1960s. Until about 1950, almost all geneticists believed that visible, physical traits corresponded to underlying genetic characteristics, and regarded phenotype to be a realization of the genotype. Discussions on race was intimately linked to politics and was often intensely politicized. The very question of whether human races exist has been subject to intense debates also among self-identified anti-racists—between those who emphasize the role of race, and those who argue that the eradication of racism depended on the deliberate non-recognition of race.[928]

During the 1950s, the concept of human races was redefined and re-conceptualized. From his position as a professor at Rockefeller University in New York and president of the Behavior Genetics Association Dobzhansky would find himself at the center of this discussion on human race. His *Genetics and the Origins of Spe-*

---

[927] On the attack and Stets'ko's health situation, see "SUBJECT: Yaroslav STETSKO aka Wasyl DANKIW," July 1957, NARA, RG 263, E ZZ-18, Box 126, Jaroslav Stetsko name file, v. -02-008, Box 126; Roman Petrenko, "Poranennia Iaroslava Stets'ka," *Homin Ukrainy*, (October 9, 2012): 5, https://issuu.com/31054/docs/jaroslav_stecko_new/2 (last accessed 9 December, 2016); Iaroslav Stets'ko to Dontsov February 2, 1950., LAC, MG 31, D130, Vol. 5, Folder 21; Wasyl DANKIW Application for Assistance, July 7, 1949, MUZYKA, Anna CM Files 1, Germany, 79019639_0_1.jpg, ITS Collections, Archive of the United States Holocaust Memorial Museum, Washington, DC.
[928] Reardon, *Race to the Finish*, 55.

cies appeared in in three editions and was recognized as one of the most important books ever written in his field of research. With a reputation as "a founder of the field of population genetics and a noted anti-racist," Dobzhansky perhaps became the most authoritative proponent of the concept of race and would play a prominent role in the scholarly debates on race of the 1950s and 1960s.[929] Arguing that "to claim that there are no objective criteria for classifying human races is not necessarily to argue that races do not exist, or that concepts of race are meaningless," Dobzhansky saw no contradiction between recognizing the existence of human races, which he regarded as a biological reality, and opposition to political racism.[930] "The relevant question for Dobzhansky was not whether race was a valid scientific concept, but rather which concept of race was valid. He advocated for a populationist concept in which race did not refer to a discrete type, but rather to a natural phenomenon," Reardon noted.[931]

Believing that population genetics would provide a new, sounder basis for systems of classification, in Dobzhansky's view, the classification systems based upon ideal racial types "did not correspond to nature and obscured biological processes." Instead, he suggested that "the naming of races should follow the discovery of a barrier that limited gene exchange between populations — whether they be national, ethnic, religious, linguistic, or class boundaries. ... Nature would determine categories rather than human-constructed categories being imposed on nature."[932]

Dobzhansky not only belonged to the academic mainstream; he himself regarded his scholarship on race as apolitical.

Rostislav Yendyk: *Introduction to the Racial Structure of Ukraine*

The politicized application of race for the national cause was not, however, exhausted. As the Ukrainian émigrés spread over the

---

929 Reardon, *Race to the Finish*, 34, 54, 56.
930 Reardon, *Race to the Finish*, 53.
931 Reardon, *Race to the Finish*, 35.
932 Reardon, *Race to the Finish*, 39.

world from the DP camps where they spent the immediate postwar years, not only to Canada, Britain, Australia, the United States, but also to destinations like Brazil, Venezuela, Paraguay, Peru, and Tunisia, the Ukrainian émigrés encountered new, unfamiliar ethnic groups. Under the specific conditions of forced emigration, racial science gained a renewed, but somewhat different urgency. A 1954 volume published by the Ukrainian Youth Association (*Spilka ukrains'koi molodi*, SUM), the OUN(b)'s paramilitary youth organization, described the situation of the Ukrainian émigrés as "now living in small communities which are grouped like tiny islands of an extensive archipelago in the midst of an ocean of different cultural and racial elements."[933]

In June 1947, the Shevchenko Scientific Society (*Naukove tovarystvo imeni Shevchenka*, NTSh), the oldest and most prominent Ukrainian scholarly association was reactivated in Munich, in the US Zone of occupied Germany. Volodymyr Kubiiovych was elected its General Secretary. Under his leadership, the NTSh resumed the interwar tradition of *völkisch* racial biology. In fact, the first volume of the flagship publication series of the reconstituted society, *The Library of Ukrainian Studies* (*Biblioteka ukrainoznavstva*), published in 1949, was dedicated to the topic of raciology and eugenics. Authored by Rostislav Yendyk, it was entitled *Introduction to the Racial Structure of Ukraine: Basic Questions on the General and Societal Anthropology and Eugenics of Ukraine* (*Vstup do rasovoi budovoi Ukrainy: osnov. Pytania z zah. i susp. antropolohii ta evheniky Ukrainy*).[934] In content, style, focus, and language Yendyk's study offered a continuity from the his interwar racial inquires.[935] It

---

933 I. Fedchynia and Ia. Deremenda, eds. *Spil'ka Ukrains'koi Molodi: S.U.M. na chuzhyny*. (London: Mercurius Press, 1954), 170, 234.
934 Yendyk, *Vstup do rasovoi budovoi Ukrainy*; Shkandrij, *Ukrainian Nationalism*, 97-98; Yendyk spent most of his postwar years in Munich writing as a journalist mainly in the OUN(b) press. Yendyk retained a good reputation in the émigré community until his death. Ihor Mel'nyk, "Rostyslav Yendyk." In the 1960s, Volodymyr Kubiiovych tasked Yendyk with the writing of all the entries on physical anthropology for the *Entsyklopediia ukrainoznavstava*, of which he was the editor. In the 1980s, John-Paul Himka argued with Kubiiovych against including them in the English version, published by the University of Toronto Press (John-Paul Himka, email to author, January 31, 2017).
935 Yendyk, *Vstup do rasovoi budovoi Ukrainy*, 171, 173, 235. Yendyk's views on the racial characteristics of Ukrainians were also summarized in "Rasovi prob-

EUGENICS AND RACIAL ANTHROPOLOGY 289

praised racial theorists, in particular Gobineau and Günther, advocated for a racial worldview, racial purity and racial determinism.[936]

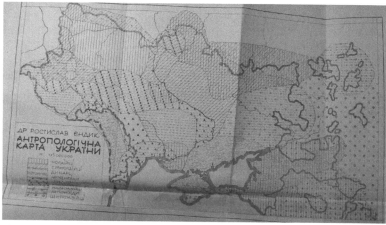

Figure 7.1 Dr. Rostislav Yendyk, Anthropological Map of Ukraine, delineating the various Ukrainian racial groups: Nordic, Sub-Nordic, Dinaric, Armenoid, Mediterranean, Sub-Laponoid, Paleo-Asiatic, Laponoid, and Central Asiatic. Yendyk, *Vstup do rasovoi budovy* (1949), 440.

Interspersed between illustrations of the various racial phenotypes, Yendyk reminded his readers about the duty and imperative of a bio-politically conscious Ukrainian living under Muscovite occupation to maintain his community's racial hygiene and shelter it from degenerative influence from the east:

> The essential differences, which we can ascertain between Muscovites (*moskali*) and Ukrainians are very important for us, not only from the perspective of racial science (*rasoznavstvo*) and racial hygiene (*rasova higiena*), but also for the national instinct, so that our people does not degenerate, regardless of Bolshevism, and continue to exist, and a factor of delineation, to prevent us to flourish and lose our specific characteristics.[937]

---

liemy," *Krakivs'ki visti*, no. 120(275), June 6, 1941. Gyidel, "The Ukrainian Legal Press," 33, n77.
936 Gyidel, "The Ukrainian Legal Press," 34.
937 Gyidel, "The Ukrainian Legal Press," 378.

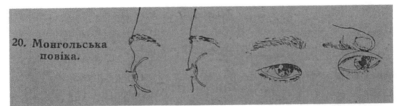

Figure 7.2. "Epicanthic fold." Yendyk, *Vstup do rasovoi budovy Ukrainy* (1949), 59.

Yendyk's book not only categorized the various racial phenotypical into neat groups and sub-groups, but also offered practical, eugenic advice to the ethnically conscious émigré youth, urging them to "Be clean in body and spirit," to "Piously cherish the racial type of your kin and the nature of your stock," called upon them to "Marry timely, if you want your kin to inherit health," and to "Aim at having at least four children."[938]

Figure 7.3. "Nordic Race," from Yendyk, *Vstup do rasovoi budovy Ukrainy* (1949), 57.

---

938 Gyidel, "The Ukrainian Legal Press,"', 329. Kubiiovych, who after the war headed the Scientific Shevchenko Society in Europe liked Yendyk's book. However, as it contained comments on Jews, Kubiiovych lamented, which "now offend oversensitive Jews," he felt compelled to withdraw it from circulation. To Kubiiovych, this illustrated the absurdity of the US press, where one "is not free to touch Jews-Masonry [zhydiv-masonerii]." Gyidel, "The Ukrainian Legal Press," 34.

"National and National Jewry"

After the war, Dontsov immigrated to Canada where he found employment as an adjunct professor at the Université de Montréal. After having his immigration application to the US rejected, the disabled Stets'ko spent the rest of his life in Munich. Citing his incarceration in Sachsenhausen, Stets'ko after 1945 presented himself as a victim of Nazism.[939] Like Yendyk, Dontsov's and Stets'ko's outlooks remained essentially unchanged after 1945. In 1951, Dontsov's *The Spirit of Our Antiquity* appeared in a second edition by the OUN(b) publishing house in Munich. Like Dontsov, Stets'ko was ill at ease with the post-1945 era, which he saw as denationalized, degenerate, and unprincipled. Presenting himself as the "Former Prime Minister of Ukraine" in 1946 Stets'ko set up the Anti-Bolshevik Bloc of Nations (ABN), an OUN(b) front organization which brought together veterans the now-defunct "New Order." Funded and underwritten by Chiang Kai-Shek's Nationalist China and Franscisco Franco's Spain from the mid-1950s, the ABN connected the émigré Ustasha, Romanian Iron Guardists, and former members of Tiso's Slovak government.

Stets'ko remained preoccupied with Jewry and Freemasonry for the rest of his life. In May 1957, in the OUN(b)'s most important ideological journal Stets'ko — again under a pseudonym — published a long article entitled "National and International Jewry" revisiting the Jewish question: "Some Jews, particularly their elites, have an internationalist attitude. They long for a world empire under the aegis of international capital and a world government, which Masonry also supports."[940] If the rootless, cosmopolitan Jewry repulsed the former OUN prime minister, Stets'ko felt more sympathy for "national Jewry," who, like Zionists, sought to

---

939 "Bestätigung zur Vorlage bei P.C. IRO Control Center" for Wasyl DANKIW, nr. 753/48 of August 11, 1948, CM 1 Files, Germany for MUZYKA, Anna. Central Name Index, USHMM, ITS Collection, 0.1, document no. 79019642.
940 Yaroslav Stets'ko, "Natsional'ne i international'ne zhydivstvo." In Yaroslav Stets'ko, *Tvory: Ukrains'ka vyzvol'na kontseptsiia, Tom druhyi*, edited by Volodymyr Kosyk, (Munich: Vydannia Orhanizatsii ukrains'kykh natsionalistyv, 1991), 350-354, here: 351.

give up their nomadic lifestyle and root themselves in a national homeland of their own.

> The organized national idea of a Christian Ukraine with its longing for liberty, truth, and justice is opposite the idea of international Jewry. ... The Ukrainian people has never opposed the Jewish minority in Ukraine and has always been ready to ensure it equal rights ... but it cannot agree to become a minority in its lands. ... Jews will enjoy all the liberties in the Ukrainian state ... if they do not try to overturn it. We have no basis or intention to limit the civic rights of Jews, but they cannot give them special privileges. Equality for all.[941]

In his correspondence with Donstov, Stets'ko complained in less than egalitarian language about what he perceived as the decline of the West. Stets'ko perceived this decline not only in spiritual and metaphysical forms—something that found racial expression. After having been denied a visa to the US, Stets'ko explained this by the power of "Muscovites, Jews, Freemasons and fifth columns" in the United States: "Eisenhower is a puppet in the hands of the mafia. I do not understand how they can force people to school together with negroes—Is that democratic? ... Why do white people have to sit together with blacks?"[942]

---

941 Stets'ko, "Natsional'ne i international'ne zhydivstvo", 351–352.
942 Yaroslav Stets'ko to Dmytro Dontsov, September 12, 1957, LAC, MG 31, D 130, Vol. 6, file 1.

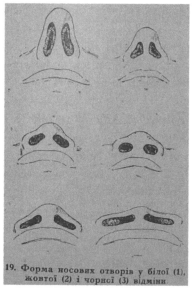

Figure 7.4. "Nasal forms of whites (1), yellows (2), and blacks (3)"Yendyk, *Vstup do rasovoi budovy Ukrainy*, 59.

Following the assassination of Bandera by a Soviet agent in October 1959, Stets'ko further strengthened his position in the OUN(b), becoming the leader of that organization in 1968.

Following the Eichmann trials of 1961-62, and the Frankfurt Auschwitz trials of 1963-65, the Holocaust was slowly entering public consciousness in Bavaria, and Munich, a process that would continue over the following decades.

Stets'ko was increasingly frustrated with how his own anti-Semitic publication record—even though much had been published under pseudonym—hampered the effectiveness of his anti-communist activism. Also this, he charged on the Jews. To Dontsov he lamented how "They send me my anti-Jewish articles, because I signed them, and thus the entire odium of world Jewry attack me (*otzhe uves' odium svitovoho zhydivstvo pide na mene*)."[943] Bitterly disillusioned with the United States and increasingly disenchanted also with Franz-Josef Strauss Bavaria, Stets'ko increas-

---

943 Yaroslav Stets'ko to Dmytro Dontsov, November 22, 1967, LAC, MG 31, D130, Vol. 5, Folder 21.

ingly saw Franco as Europe's—and indeed Christian civilization's last hope.[944]

To the Nationalist faithful, the biological language was integral to their conceptualization of their nation, their community, and the Organization itself. If, to its members and followers, "the OUN was like a mother for the nation," they regarded Stets'ko as the "father of the nation."[945] Among his followers in the diaspora, a curious cult of personality developed around Stets'ko's persona, exalted as a "man of iron determination, although weak in health, a man of principle, a man dedicated to a great idea—the idea of nationalism which will overcome all opposition."[946] With his paralyzed arm, somewhat high-pitched voice, the sickly Stets'ko was a rather paradoxical incarnation of the Dontsovian amoral, heroic beast of "burning faith and with a heart of stone." Exalted in the OUN(b) press as a "man of iron determination," a "father of the Ukrainian nation," this man infatuated with notions of heroic nationalism, racial hierarchies, and uncompromising disdain for weakness—was a eunuch.[947] Soviet propagandists did not hesitate to exploit his personal tragedy against Stets'ko, enforcing rumors,

---

944 "Spain already stands on the verge of evil democratization," Stets'ko lamented to Dontsov, "When Franco dies, there will be a liberal democracy. ... They are still holding the banner high, but for how long?" Sign. "Orach" [Yaroslav Stets'ko] to Dmytro Dontsov, undated letter, 1967, LAC, MG 31, D130, Vol. 5, Folder 21.

945 Lubomyr Y. Luciuk, *Searching for Place: Ukrainian Displaced Persons, Canada, and the Mingration of Memory* (Toronto: University of Toronto Press, 2000), 5; "Funeral of Former Prime Minister of Ukraine," 1986, 2.

946 Volodymyr Masur, "Yaroslav Stetsko: Prominent Statesman of the 20th Century," *ABN Correspondence*, 1-2, 47(Spring/Summer 1996): 3.

947 On Stets'ko's medical condition, see "Jaroslav STECKO (STETSKO) or KARBOVSKI" Undated, but marked with a handwritten note: "date of info: 1950" Iaroslav Stetsko name file, http://iwpchi.files.wordpress.com/2014/03/cia_wwii_nazi_war_criminals_files_stetsko_yaroslav.pdf (accessed 30 June 30, 2014); "Jaroslaw Stetzko, Prime Minster of Ukraina" to "his Excellence General Mr. Eisenhower," May 10, 1945, Mykola Lebed Papers, 1930-1995; Political material; Other political material; Proclamation of Ukrainian statehood (1941) [Box 23, folder 03] Ukrainian Research Institute, Harvard University, Cambridge, Mass., Sequence 37, http://pds.lib.harvard.edu/pds/view/47119890?n=37&imagesize=1200&jp2Res=.25&printThumbnails=no (Accessed 8 August 8, 2013); "DANKIW, Wasyl and Anna, geb. Muzyka, Application for Assistance, CM/1, 7.7. 1949, 79019639_0_1.jpg, ITS collection, USHMM, Washington, DC.)

circulating in the Ukrainian émigré community about his assertive, power-hungry and frivolous wife's supposed infidelities.[948]

Sectarian and increasingly anachronistic, at the time of his death, Stets'ko's organization was largely irrelevant and detached from the motherland. When the Soviet Union collapsed, five years after his death in 1986, it did so, not as a result of thermonuclear confrontation, nor an apocalyptic World War III. The Soviet system collapsed under its own weight, as a consequence of the inability of the political elites to reform and restructure an inflexible and inefficient economic model.

Conclusion

As the writings of ideologues like Dontsov, Yendyk, Kolodzins'kyi, Lypa, and Stets'ko show, interwar Ukrainian Nationalism had strong undercurrents of racial anthropology and eugenics. Racial thought played an important role in the project to chart and categorize the diverse populations in the vast territories claimed by Ukrainian Nationalists for their intended state "from the Danube to the Caspian Sea." Ukraine was no anomaly; rather, these currents reflected larger European trends. The centrality of notions of race, miscegenation, and eugenics to the OUN(b) is underscored by the fact that their rather extensive agendas were drafted by the intended Prime Minster himself.

Since Stets'ko's state failed to obtain recognition by his intended Axis partners the eugenic programs spelled out in *For the Content of State Life* never materialized as Ukrainian state policy. We will never know how they would have played out if materialized. The implementation of similar eugenic programs in the Independent State of Croatia (NDH) between 1941 and 1945, a source of inspiration for the OUN(b) could indicate a possible path of development.[949]

---

948 Taras Mihal, *ABN – assembly of buffoonish nationalists* (Kyiv: The Association for Cultural Relations with Ukrainians Abroad, 1968), Copy in Arkhiv New_Yorku_03004.pdf, Arkhiv TsDVR, L'viv, Ukraine, 17-18, 21.
949 On Ustasha racial laws and eugenics, see Rory Yeomans, "Fighting the White Plague: Demography and Abortion in the Independent State of Croatia," in Christian Promitzer, Sevasti Trubeta, and Marius Turda, eds., *Health, Hygiene*

Notions of race clearly informed OUN(b) ethno-political violence during the war, the anti-Jewish pogroms of 1941 as well as and the massacres of the Polish minority in Volhynia and Eastern Galicia in 1943-44. Some of these notions survived the collapse of the Axis powers, and retained a role not only in the sectarian and fractious Galician Ukrainian émigré politics; eugenics, as a discipline was revived by its postwar émigré scholarly association.

---

and *Eugenics in Southeastern Europe to 1945*, 385-426 (Budapest: CEU Press, 2011) and Rory Yeomans, "'If Our Race Did Not Exist, It Would Have to be Created': Racial Science in Hungary, 1940-1944," in Anton Weiss-Wendt and Rory Yeomans, eds. *Racial Science in Hitler's New Europe 1938-1945*, (Lincoln and London: University of Nebraska Press, 2013), 237-258; Dulić, *Utopias of Nation*, 89-93.

8. "Saving the OUN from a Collaborationist and Possibly Fascist Fate" On the Genealogy of the Discourse on the OUN's "Non-Fascism"*

Beyond the Ukrainian community, the classification of the OUN as a fascist organization is both common and unproblematic. In the Ukrainian historiography, however, the term remains hotly contested. Once a topic which generated little interest outside the Ukrainian community, over the past decades, the OUN has been increasingly integrated into comparative studies of European fascism.[950] This growing interest is indicative of a field coming of age and entering the academic mainstream. Yet recent years have seen attempts at introducting alternative classifications of the OUN. One of the more sophisticated belong to historian Oleksandr Zaitsev (b. 1964) of the Ukrainian Catholic University of L'viv,[951] who suggested the introduction of a new term, "ustashism" to the followers of Stepan Bandera.[952]

This chapter seeks to addres a set of interrelated issues in regards to the OUN(b) and its legacy. Was it fascist? How did it, and

---

* A previous version of this chapter appeared in the *Journal of Soviet and Post-Soviet Politics and Society*, vol. 7, no. 1 (2021): 179-214.
950 See, for instance the thematic issue "Fashyzm i pravyi radykalizm na skhodi Evropy," *Ukraina Moderna* 20 (2013): 35-122; Bauerkämper and Rossoliński-Liebe (eds.), *Fascism without Borders:*, eds. Roland Clark and Tim Grady (eds.), *European Fascist Movements: A Sourcebook* (New York: Routledge, 2023); Rebecca Haynes and Martyn Rady (eds.), *In the Shadow of Hitler: Personalities of the Right in Central and Eastern Europe* (New York: I.B. Tauris, 2011); and Grzegorz Rossoliński-Liebe, "Der europäische Faschismus und der ukrainische Nationalismus: Verflechtungen, Annäherungen und Wechselbeziehungen," *Zeitschrift für Geschichtswissenschaft* 65, no. 2 (2017): 153–69.
951 On the discussion, see Zaitsev, "Fascism or Ustashism?" and Tomislav Dulić and Goran Miljan, "The Ustašas and Fascism: 'Abolitionism,' Revolution, and Ideology (1929–42)," *Journal of Soviet and Post-Soviet Politics and Society* 6, no. 1 (2020): 277–306.
952 See also, more recently: Oleksandr Zaitsev, "Integral Nationalism in the Absence of a Nation-State: The Case of Ukraine," in *Conservatives and Right Radicals in Interwar Europe,* ed. Marco Bresciani (New York: Routledge, 202o): 118–42.

its successor organizations, shape the memory and narration of its legacy, and how does this play out in Ukraine today? What are the political and diplomatic implications of its rehabilitation and glorification?

Was the OUN Fascist?

As noted above, the OUN(b) fits rather neatly most of the more common scholarly definitions of fascism; it meets Ernst Nolte's requirements for "fascist minima," and suits Stanley Payne (b. 1934) and Roger Griffin's revolutionary ultranationalism and palingenetics.[953] Listing the fascist attributes of the OUN—its leader principle, its red-and-black flag, its raised-arm salute, its aspiration to ban all other parties, its fascist-style slogan, its xenophobia and anti-Semitism, its cult of violence, and its identification with Hitler, Mussolini, and the new fascist Europe—historian John-Paul Himka asks, rhetorically: "What's not fascist here?"[954] Indeed, for many historians who work on the OUN's ethnic violence and local collaboration in the Holocaust, its fascism is all but self-evident.[955]

In Ukraine, the situation is different. Under the official nomenclature "national liberation movement," the Organization of

---

953 Ernst Nolte, *Three Faces of Fascism: Action Française Italian Fascism, National Socialism*, trans. Leila Vennewitz (New York: New American Library, 1969), 40; Roger Griffin, *The Nature of Fascism* (New York: St. Martin's Press, 1991), 1-19; and Stanley G. Payne, *A History of Fascism, 1914-1945* (Madison: The University of Wisconsin Press, 1995), 3–52.

954 John-Paul Himka, "The Organization of Ukrainian Nationalists and the Ukrainian Insurgent Army: Unwelcome Elements of an Identity Project," *Ab Imperio* 4 (2010): 83–101, here: 87.

955 Umland, "Der ukrainische Nationalismus zwischen Stereotyp und Wirklichkeit," 9; Ihor Iljuszyn, "[Review of:] Grzegorz Rossoliński-Liebe, *Bandera. Życie i mit ukraińskiego nacjonalisty: faszyzm, ludobójstwo, kult*, Wydawnictwo Pruszyński i S-ka, Warszawa 2018, ss. 904," *Europa Orientalis: Studia z Dziejów Europy Wschodniej i Państw Bałtyckich* 10 (2019): 255–63, here: 257; Rossoliński-Liebe, *The Fascist Kernel of Ukrainian Genocidal Nationalism*; Thomas Sandkühler, *Das Fußvolk der "Endlösung": Nichtdeutsche Täter und die europäische Dimension des Völkermords* (Darmstadt: Wissenschaftliche Buchgesellschaft Academic, 2020), 370; and Alexander Statiev, "The Strategy of the Organization of Ukrainian Nationalists in its Quest for a Sovereign State, 1939-1950," *Journal of Strategic Studies* 43, no. 3 (2020): 443–71, here: 444–46.

Ukrainian Nationalists (OUN) and its armed forces, the Ukrainian Insurgent Army (UPA) have received official recognition; its leaders have been designated national heroes glorified by postage stamps, monuments, and street names. In 2015, Petro Poroshenko signed into law the criminalization of "disrespect" for these groups.[956] Rather than reiterating these discussions, this article seeks to put the disavowal of the OUN's fascism in its historical, genealogical context.

The historiographical situations in Ukraine and Croatia resemble one another. Historians of Ukraine will have no difficulty relating to Tomislav Dulić's and Goran Miljan's observation: "Dominating much of Croatian scholarship are voluminous but descriptive accounts of military and political history, where the role of fascism is given scant attention at best." They will also find familiar how this stand in sharp contrast to international scholarship which tends to focus on the Ustaša "genocide and other forms of mass violence," accompanied by more detailed studies of anti-Semitism.[957]

Scholars of the OUN and UPA recognize only too well the phenomenon of massive, multi-volume collections of documents on the "Ukrainian national liberation movement" with titles like *Ukrains'kyi zdvyh* (*The Ukrainian Feat*), or hagiographies with edifyingly patriotic titles such as *Victory or Death, Stand Up and Fight,* and *The Power of Freedom,* which overlook, marginalize, or outright deny their massacres of Jews, Poles, and political opponents.

To a significant degree, this narrative follows a narration developed by pro-nationalist émigré scholars. The *Encyclopedia of Ukraine*, edited by no less than the war-time head of the Ukrainian Central Committee at Kraków Volodymyr Kubiiovych himself, lacked entries for the Holocaust as well as the Volhynian Massacres.[958] Instead, it informed its readers that "there has never been

---

956 Amar, "Ukraine's Nationalist 'Decommunization' Laws" and David R. Marples, "Decommunization, Memory Laws, and 'Builders of Ukraine in the 20th Century'," *Acta Slavica Iaponica* 39 (2018): 1–22.
957 Dulić and Miljan, "The Ustašas and Fascism," 278–79.
958 The entry under "Jews," written by Volodymyr Kubiiovych and Vasyl Markus, contains eight(!) sentences on the murder of the Jews, including the

... a Ukrainian anti-Semitic organization or political party."[959] Taras Hunczak, an emeritus Professor of History at Rutgers University-Newark, insisted that "In Ukraine there were no collaborationists seduced by Nazi ideology ... Unlike the French, Belgians, Dutch and Russians, Ukrainians did not establish fascist organizations."[960]

As many Ukrainian scholars have limited knowledge of foreign languages other than Russian or Polish, their exposure to scholarship in German, French, and English is often restricted; sometimes this literature is accessed in Russian translation. Consequently, what in Ukraine is referred to as *"vitchynznanyi"* ("fatherland") historiography is often disconnected from international scholarship. The Holocaust is only partially integrated into Ukrainian historiography; the most authoritative studies on the pogroms and Holocaust in Galicia, the OUN(b) and UPA's massacres of the Volhynian Poles, even the first scholarly biography of Stepan Bandera, were all written by non-Ukrainians.[961]

Official Rehabilitation

Rather than underwriting original research or critical inquiry, from its establishment in 2006 until the election of Viktor Yanukovych in 2010 — and again after his overthrow in 2014 — the Ukrainian Institute of National Memory (UINP) has sought to affix the OUN at the center of national mythology, through the renaming of streets and squares, the drafting of history laws and

---

following: "Apart from the involvement of individuals and some organized auxiliary units, the Ukrainian population did not take part in these genocidal actions. Despite the penalty of death for aiding Jews, a number of Ukrainians, among them Metropolitan A. Sheptytsky, tried to save Jews"; V. Kubijovyč and V. Markus, "Jews," in *Encyclopedia of Ukraine: Vol. II G-K*, ed. Volodymyr Kubijovyč, (Toronto: University of Toronto Press, 1988), 385–93, here: 389. On Kubiiovych, see Markiewicz, *Unlikely Allies*.

959 Wytwycky, "Anti-Semitism," in *Encyclopedia of Ukraine*, 1, ed. Kubijovyč, 82.
960 Taras Hunczak, "Ukrainian-Jewish Relations during the Soviet and Nazi Occupations," in *Ukraine during World War II: History and Its Aftermath*, ed. Yuri Boshyk (Edmonton: CIUS Press, 1986), 39–57, here: 42, 45.
961 Motyka, *Ukraińska partyzantka*; Pohl, *Nationalsozialistische Judenverfolgung in Ostgalizien 1941-1944*; Rossoliński-Liebe, *Stepan Bandera* and Struve, *Deutsche Herrschaft*.

propaganda initiatives, and by seeking to set up a national pantheon of Ukrainian heroes in Kyiv.[962]

The OUN(b) greeting *"Slava Ukraini! – Heroiam Slava!"* – the equivalent of the Ustašas' *"Za dom! Spremni!"* – has been introduced as official salutation in the Ukrainian Army.[963] Ukrainian military uniforms have been redesigned after those of the UPA.[964] As of 2015, Ukraine had no less than 100 streets, 46 statues or busts, 14 memorial plaques, and five museums dedicated to Bandera alone.[965] A gulf has opened between international scholarship on the Holocaust in Ukraine and the state-sanctioned Ukrainian narration of the OUN's history.

Ustashism

Unlike many of his Ukrainian colleagues, multilingual and prolific Oleksandr Zaitsev is well integrated into the international scholarly community and has made valuable contributions to the field.[966] In the discussion about how to classify the OUN he has advanced the neologism "ustashism" to describe that organization. Previously, Zaitsev has used other alternatives to the term fascism.[967]

---

[962] Deputy Director Alina Shpak of the UINP, to Ukrainian Cabinet of Ministers, Appendix "Dodatok, Propozytsii Ukrains'koho instytutu natsional'noi pam''iaty shchodo zasnuvannia Ukrains'koho natsional'noho panteonu," 13 November 2014, 3; and Per Anders Rudling, "Warfare or War Criminality?" *Ab Imperio* 1 (2012): 356–81, here: 357.

[963] Tea Sindbæk Andersen, "Šimunić and the 'Za dom spremni' Chant," in *Disputed Memory: Emotions and Memory Politics in Central, Eastern and South-Eastern Europe*, eds. Tea Sindbæk Andersen and Barbara Törnquist-Plewa (Berlin: De Gruyter, 2016), 297–318.

[964] "V armii deokomunizuvaly pohony i uniformu," *Gazeta.ua*, 5 July 2016, https://gazeta.ua/articles/regions/_v-armiyi-dekomunizuvali-pogoni-i-uniformu/708787?mobile=true (accessed 1 March 2021).

[965] Kuzio, *Ukraine: Democratization, Corruption, and the New Russian Imperialism*, 180.

[966] Other noteworthy works include: Oleksandr Zaitsev, "Ukrains'kyi natsionalizm ta italiis'kyi fashyzm (1922-1939)," *Ukraina Moderna*, 3 January 2012, uamoderna.com/md/98-zaitsev; idem., "Ukrainian Integral Nationalism in Quest of a 'Special Path' (1920s–1930s)," *Russian Politics & Law* 51, no. 5 (2013): 11–32; idem, "De-Mythologizing Bandera," 411–20; and idem., *Natsionalist u dobi fashyzmu*.

[967] Zaitsev, *Ukraiins'kyi intehral'nyi natsionalizm*, 426.

Zaitsev's attempts at contextualizing OUN(b) mass violence using the Ustaša as a point of reference highlight a number of similarities.[968] The organizations appeared at the same time, and were both totalitarian and anti-Semitic. Operating mainly in exile, both were sponsored by Mussolini's Italy and Nazi Germany. Both relied on assassinations and political violence; both carried out their most spectacular acts of terrorism in 1934—the OUN assassinated the Polish Minister of the Interior Bronisław Pieracki in June,[969] and the Ustaša murdered King Alexander I of Yugoslavia and the French Foreign Minister Louis Bartou in October of that year.[970]

The Radicalization of the OUN, 1935–43

There is no space here for anything other than the most cursory account of the OUN's political history. By way of background as to why many scholars conclude that the OUN is most properly classified as fascist, let us revisit some key documents from the period between 1935 and 1943, the period when the movement reached the height of its power, and its politics was the most radical.

In 1938, Volodymyr Martynets' member of the OUN *provid* (leadership) and one of its main ideologists, penned the booklet *The Jewish Problem in Ukraine*, in which he characterized Jews as a "parasitical," "morally damaging," "corrupting" and "hostile element," "racially unsuitable for miscegenation and assimilation." Martynets' solution to the "Jewish problem" was the "*total and absolute isolation* of the Jews from the Ukrainian people" (em-

---

968 Dulić, *Utopias of Nation*; and Rory Yeomans, *Visions of Annihilation: The Ustasha Regime and the Cultural Politics of Fascism 1941–1945* (Pittsburgh: University of Pittsburgh Press, 2013).
969 The Polish authorities cracked down on the assassins, sentencing the top Galician leadership to lengthy prison sentences.
970 Zaitsev, *Ukrains'kyi intehral'nyi natsionalizm*, 324, citing Alexander J. Motyl, *Dilemmas of Independence: Ukraine after Totalitarianism* (Council on Foreign Relations Press, 1993), 95. Motyl, though, also declines to use the term "terrorist" to describe the OUN's political violence; see *idem*, "Ukrainian Nationalist Political Violence in Inter-War Poland, 1921-1939," *East European Quarterly* 19, no. 1 (1985): 45–55, here: 54.

phasis in original). His "solution" was, moreover, "to assure a continued decline in the number of Jews not only through emigration, but also through decline of their natural growth rate."[971]

Mykhailo Kolodzins'kyi's *Military Doctrine of the Ukrainian Nationalists* was written in late 1935 or early 1936, edited and reworked before the final version was completed in spring 1938.[972] The doctrine, with its open calls for an OUN insurgency that would exterminate "the entire hostile population and all those minorities, hostile to Ukr[ainian] independence," reflects a further radicalization.[973] According to the *Military Doctrine of Ukrainian Nationalists*, "[t]he more Jews that are killed during the time of the uprising, the better for the Ukrainian state."[974] The OUN struggle against communists, Polish police, settlers, "Muscovite" workers, Ukrainian "sellouts and traitors," it stipulated, would

> be merciless, harsh and zoological. Thus, our insurgency does not only aim at changing the political system. It has to cleanse Ukraine from alien, hostile elements and those malignantly disposed to our own culture. Only during the time of the insurgency will there be an opportunity to uproot, literally to the last person the Polish element from the W[estern] U[krainian] L[ands] and thereby end Polish pretentions about the Polish character of these lands.[975]

No less brutal treatment awaited the Jews:

> Without doubt, the fury of the Ukrainian people towards the Jews will be particularly horrific. There is no reason to diminish that fury — on the contrary [it is necessary to] strengthen it further, because the more Jews that die during the uprising, the better it will be for the Ukrainian state, since

---

971 Volodymyr Martynets', *Zhydvis'ka problema v Ukraini* (London: Williams, Lea & Co., 1938), 10, 14–15, 22.
972 Oleksandr Zaitsev, "Voenna doktryna Mykhaila Kolodzins'koho," *Ukraina Moderna* 20 (2013): 245–56, here: 247–48.
973 Mykhailo Kolodzins'kyi, "Natsionalistychne povstannia: Rozdil iz pratsi 'Voenna doktryna ukrains'kykh natsionalistiv'," *Arkhiv OUN u Kyive*, f. 1, op. 2, spr. 466, ark. 91–139; published in: *Ukraina Moderna* 20 (2013): 257–95, here: 289.
974 Kolodzins'kyi, "Natsionalistychne povstannia, 290.
975 Kolodzins'kyi, "Natsionalistychne povstannia, 266–67.

Jews will be the sole minority, which will not be able to be included in our denationalizing policy.[976]

Mykola Stsibors'kyi's (1897-1941) 1939 draft constitution outlined the government of the future OUN "authoritarian, totalitarian state,"[977] in which "[t]he entire Ukrainian Nation acts through the Head of State-Leader of the Nation [*Holova Derzhavy-Vozhdia Natsii*]." Jews were to be ineligible for citizenship, the OUN the only political movement allowed.[978] The OUN Second Grand Assembly (*II Velykyi Zbir OUN*), held in Rome in August 1939 affirmed the foundations of Stsisbors'ky's concept of "*natsiokratiia*" (natiocracy), as well as "anti-partisanship [*proty-partiinist'*] and the replacement of old parliamentary forms by new forms of *syndicalist-solidarist organization of the state.*"[979]

The radicalization was reflected not only in doctrine and policy documents produced by the organization's top leadership but also in its increasingly radical anti-Semitic propaganda from 1937.[980] The radicalization escalated following the collapse of Poland and the release from prison of Stepan Bandera, Mykola Lebed', and other radical leaders of the Galician OUN. The OUN split as Galician radicals, known as OUN-Bandera or OUN(b), held a founding Grand Assembly in Krakow in April 1941 (*II*

---

976 Kolodzins'kyi, "Natsionalistychne povstannia, 290.
977 "Narys proektu osnovnykh zakoniv (konstitutsii) Ukrains'koi Derzhavy. Opratsiuvav inzh. M. Stsibors'kyi," in *Dokumenty i materialy z istorii Orhanizatsii Ukrains'kykh Natsionalistiv. Tom 7: Dokumenty komisii derzhavnoho planuvannia OUN (KDP OUN)*, eds. O. Kucheruk, Iu. Cherchenko, and N. Myronets' (Kyiv: Vydavnytstvo imeni Oleny Telihy, 2002), 8–23, here: 8.
978 "Narys proektu osnovnykh zakoniv (konstitutsii)," 8, 20.
979 "Predmova do poltychnoi prohramy i ustroiu OUN," in *Politychna prohrama i ustrii Orhanizatsii Ukrains'kykh Natsionalistiv* (n. p., 1941), 1–20, here: 15, Arkhiv Tsentru Doslidzheni Vyzvol'noho Rukhu (hereafter Arkhiv TsDVR), L'viv, f. 17, t. 1, rozdil 4.3.4, Vyshkil'ni materialy OUN(m). Emphasis in the original.
980 Myroslav Shkandrij, "Radio Vienna: Broadcasts by the Organization of Ukrainian Nationalists, 1938-1939," *Kyiv-Mohyla Humanities Journal* 2 (2015): 121–36. Shkandrij, however, characterizes this as "a symptom ... of its hope for German support," suggesting that "the strong anti-Jewish line taken by the OUN in the first months of broadcasting was likely the required payment for being allowed to broadcast." Shkandrij, "Radio Vienna," here: 133 and 121.

Velykyi Zbir OUN(b)), breaking off from the more conservative, mostly émigré *provid* (leadership) of Andrii Mel'nyk. The declaration of the Independent State of Croatia (NDH) on 10 April 1941 was greeted with unrestrained joy by the OUN(b) leadership in Krakow.[981] In May 1941, on the eve of Operation Barbarossa, its leadership released the policy document *Struggle and Activities of the OUN(b) in Times of War*, the OUN(b)'s blueprint for violent action. The document explicitly called for the extermination of Jews and Poles. Merging the tactics of Kolodzins'kyi's *Military Doctrine* with the totalitarianism of Stsibors'kyi's *natiocracy*[982] it stipulated that "The system of state government will be a *political-military dictatorship of the OUN*,"[983] and that its "[n]ational minorities are divided into a) those friendly towards us, that is, members of the hitherto subjugated peoples; b) people hostile to us: Muscovites, Poles, Jews."[984] Those falling into the second category were to be dealt with harshly: "[a]t a time of chaos and confusion one can allow oneself the liquidation of undesirable Polish, Muscovite, and Jewish activists, especially adherents of the Bolshevik-Muscovite imperialism."[985] Jews, in particular, were to be subjected to particularly violent treatment: "Jews are to be isolated, elim-

---

[981] [Borys Lewytzkyj], "Natsional'nyi rukh pid chas Druhoi svitovoi viiny: Interv"iu z B. Levyts'kym," *Diialoh: Za demokratiiu i sotsiializm v samostiinii Ukraini* 2 (1979): 4–31, here: 15.

[982] Stsibors'kyi himself remained loyal to Mel'nyk, and was murdered, in all likelihood by the OUN(b), in August 1941 after refusing to acknowledge its government. "Provid Ukrains'kykh Natsionalistiv usim Ukrainstsam i chlenam Orhanizatsii Ukrains'kikh Natsionalistiv podae do vidoma," TsDAVOVU, f. 3833, op. 1, spr. 42, l. 33; and "Dvi klepsydry," TsDAVOVU, f. 3833, op. 1, spr. 42, l. 49.

[983] "Vkazivky na pershi dni orhanizatsii derzhavnoho zhyttia z Instruktsii Revoliutsiinoho Provodu OUN (S. Bandery) dlia orhanizatsiinoho aktyvu v Ukraini na period viiny 'Borot'ba i diial'nist' OUN pid chas viiny'," May 1941, TsDAVOVU, f. 3833, op. 2, spr. 1, ark. 33–57, reprinted in *OUN v 1941 rotsi: Dokumenty. Chastyna 1*, eds. S. Kul'chyts'kyi et al. (Kyiv: Instytut istorii Ukrainy NAN Ukrainy, 2006), 94–126, here: 95 (emphasis in the original).

[984] "'Borot'ba i diial'nist' OUN pid chas viiny'," TsDAVOVU, f. 3833, op. 2, spr. 1, ark. 33–57, in Kul'chyts'kyi et al. (eds.), *OUN v 1941 rotsi*, 103–104.

[985] "Viis'kovi instruktsii z Instruktsii Revoliutsiinoho Provodu OUN (S. Bandery) dlia orhanizatsiinoho aktyvu v Ukraini na period viiny 'Borot'ba i diial'nist' OUN pid chas viiny'," May 1941, TsDAVOVU, f. 3833, op. 2, spr.1, ark. 25–33, in Kul'chyts'kyi et al. (eds.), *OUN v 1941 rotsi*, 93.

inated from official positions" and the militiamen were to liquidate Jews "for the slightest transgression."[986] Slogans like "Ukraine for the Ukrainians! Ukrainian power on Ukrainian lands! ... Death to the Muscovite-Judeo commune! Beat the *komuna*, save Ukraine!"[987] were advanced for the forthcoming national revolution.

Zaitsev is not only well acquainted with these documents. In 2013, he published a critical, complete annotated version of *Military Doctrine* in the journal *Ukraina Moderna*, doing the field a major service by bringing it to wider attention beyond a narrow circle of specialists. In his comments, however, Zaitsev appears to question whether the policy articulated in the doctrine was but a marginal phenomenon in the OUN(b) by the late 1930s:

> How widely disseminated were the ideas that Kolodzins'kyi represented in the OUN circles? There is no reason to assume that his work obtained the status of an official OUN doctrine. There is no information that the OUN *Provid* [leadership] somehow officially endorsed the *Military Doctrine of Ukrainian Nationalists*. We can only conclude that, among the OUN activists there was a group which supported radical views with regard to the future uprising, the solution to the "Polish" and "Jewish" questions and that of a future "Ukrainian empire." More research is needed. Exactly how numerous and influential was the circle of people sharing Kolodzins'kyi's views? How well known was his work among the members of the organization? Finally: was there a connection between the theoretical concept of the OUN activists in 1938–1939 and the practical deeds of the OUN(b) and UPA during World War II?[988]

Still reluctant to draw conclusions similar to those of many Western colleagues in assessing the ideology of the OUN, Zaitsev limits himself to the quite narrow source base of the OUN programs. He stresses that "Programs of the OUN of 1929 and 1939

---

986 "'Borot'ba i diial'nist' OUN pid chas viiny'," TsDAVOVU, f. 3833, op. 2, spr. 1, ark. 33–57, in Kul'chyts'kyi *et al.* (eds.), *OUN v 1941 rotsi*, 104.

987 "Propagandyvni vkazivky na peredvoennyi chas, na chas viiny i revoliutsi ta pochatkovi dni derzhavnoho budivnytstva z Instruktsii Revoliutsiinoho Provodu OUN (S. Bandery) dlia orhanizatsiinoho aktyvu v Ukraini na period viiny 'Borot'ba i diial'nist' OUN pid chas viiny," TsDAVOVU, f. 3833, op. 2, spr. 1, ark. 77–87, in Kul'chyts'kyi *et al.* (eds.), *OUN v 1941 rotsi*, 154–76, here: 159.

988 Zaitsev, "Voenna doktryna Mykhaila Kolodzyns'koho," 25.

contained no racist or anti-Semitic statements."[989] When anti-Semitic wording in 1941 actually *did* enter the program it did not contain, Zaitsev emphasizes, "*Nazi* racial theory and anti-Semitism." According to him, "[t]he OUN never adopted Nazi racist theory and racial anti-Semitism as part of its political program," though "[a]dmittedly, *some* OUN members shared the anti-Semitic ideology of the Nazis."[990]

Zaitsev raises pertinent questions: How are we to understand these sources? Should they be regarded as statements by "some individuals" who happened to be OUN members? Or do they reflect actual policies pursued by the OUN(b) at the time?

Political Programs and Their Limitations

Political programs are typically concise. The programs of the 1929, 1939, 1941, 1943, and 1968 OUN/OUN(b) Grand Assemblies are 8,[991] 10,[992] 10,[993] 6,[994] and 6[995] pages in length, respectively. While

---

989 Zaistev, "Fascism or Ustashism?" 7, n. 8.
990 Zaistev, "Fascism or Ustashism?" 7. Emphasis added.
991 "Resolutions of the First Congress of the Organization of Ukrainian Nationalists 28 January-2 February 1929," transl. by Taras F. Pidzamecky, Roman Waschuk, and Andriy Wynnyckyj, in *Ukraine during World War II: History and its Aftermath*, ed. Yury Boshyk (CIUS Press, 1986), 165–72. See Arkhiv TsDVR, f. 9, t. 14, retyped version from *Arkhiv Zakordonnoho predstavnytsva Ukrains'koi holovnoi vyzvol'noi rady*, "Zbrika dokumentiv Mykoly Lebedia (Arkhiv Prolohy, N'iu-Iork)" of the resolutions of the I Vienna Grand Assembly 1929, II Kraków Grand Assembly of 1941, and the III Extraordinary Grand Assembly of August 1943. In total, it consists of 33 type-written pages, but omits the August 1939 Rome II Grand Assembly; http://avr.org.ua/viewDoc/9066 (accessed 31 December 2020).
992 "Politychna prohrama i ustrii orhanizatsii Ukrains'kykh natsionalistiv: Ukhvaleno II Velykym Zborom Ukrains'kykh Natsionalistiv u serpni 1939 r.," in *Politychna prohrama i ustrii Orhanizatsii Ukrains'kykh Natsionalistiv* (n.p., 1941), 21–41, Arkhiv TsDVR, f. 17, t. 1, rozdil 4.3.4, Vyshkil'ni materialy OUN(m); and "Ustrii orhanizatsii ukrains'kykh natsionalistiv. Ukhvaleno II Velykym Zborom Ukrains'kykh Natsionalistiv u serpni 1939 r.," HDA SBU, f. 13, spr. 376, t. 4, http://avr.org.ua/viewDoc/1376 (accessed 31 December 2020).
993 "Postanovy II. Velykoho Zboru Orhanizatsii Ukrains'kykh Natsionalistiv [April 1941]," in *Ukrains'kyi zdvyh: Zakerzonnia. 1939-1947*, ed. Volodymyr Serhiichuk, 2nd ed. (Kyiv: PP Serhiichuk M.I., 2011), 93–102.
994 "Programmatic and Political Resolution of the Organization of Ukrainian Nationalists' Third Congress 21-5 August 1943," in Boshyk (ed.), *Ukraine dur-*

not unimportant, these summary documents provide but a limited picture of the movement.

Similarly, the political program of the NSDAP is so short and concise that its 25 points fit on one page.[996] From the eighth party congress of 1919 until the 22nd in 1961, the Soviet Communist Party retained one party program. Considerably longer than those of the NSDAP and the OUN, the Bolsheviks' 1919 party program was a document of 31 pages.[997] While not unimportant, these programs tell us preciously little on the nature on the Nazi and Soviet rule. Just as few scholars of the Holocaust turn to the NSDAP's 25 point-program to understand Nazi political violence, the utility of the 1919 party program, or the 1936 are of limited use to scholars of Stalinism.

Sven Reichardt argues that it is "more helpful to think of fascism as a genre — an ensemble of overlapping and intersecting practices and attitudes — than it is to regard it as a strictly logical ideology."[998] It is difficult to separate the study of fascism from that of violence. Reichardt uses the concept of "fascist warfare," "to describe ultranationalist wars with eliminatory and genocidal tendencies marked by an especially rapid, brutal form of war conduct." According to Reichardt, "Ruthlessness and extreme violence merged with ethnic cleansing. The convergence of armed

---

ing World War II, 186–91; or, in a different edition, "Resolutions of the Third Extraordinary Grand Assembly of the Organization of Ukrainian Nationalists 21-5 August 1943," in *Political Thought of the Ukrainian Underground, 1943-1951*, eds. Peter J. Potichnyj and Yevhen Shtendera (Edmonton: CIUS Press, 1986) (the programmatic resolutions are ten pages in English translation, 342–51).

995 "Holovni ideolohichni i politychni pryntsypy OUN," *Vyzvol'nyi shliakh*, kn. 11-12 (248-9) (November–December 1968): 1268–1273.

996 "Das 25-Punkte-Programm der NSDAP vom 24. Februar 1920," Universität Wien, Institut für Zeitgeschichte, http://www.kurt-bauer-geschichte.at/PDF_Lehrveranstaltung%202008_2009/04_25-Punkte-Programm.pdf (accessed 31 December 2020).

997 *Programma Rossiiskoi kommunisticheskoi partii (bolshevikov): priniata VIII s"ezdom partii 18-23 marta 1919 goda* (=Rabochaia biblioteka Pravdy, no. 4), (Moscow: Izd. Gazety "Pravdy," 1920).

998 Sven Reichardt, "Fascism's Stages: Imperial Violence, Entanglement, and Processualization," *Journal of History of Ideas* 82, no. 1 (January 2021): 85–107; here: 88.

encounters and ideological exaggeration led in turn to intensified fascistization of the regimes themselves."[999] A focus on the role of violence and warfare is helpful in providing a deeper understanding of fascist movements. Taking the cue from Holocaust studies, cutting edge research into OUN(b) and UPA has focused on its political violence, combining survivor testimonies with newly available materials such as interrogation protocols, legal proceedings, immigration records, and intelligence reports.[1000]

Cherchez le Premier ministre!

Another way to approach a totalitarian, hyper-centralized sectarian group organized according to the *Führerprinzip* (leader principle) is to study the actions and positions of its top leadership. In this regard, the person of Yaroslav Stets'ko is of particular interest. A man of considerable intellectual and organizational ability, Stets'ko became a key figure in the Galician *provid* (leadership), later the OUN(b). The self-proclaimed Prime Minister and future OUN(b) leader not only commissioned the *Military Doctrine*. In his taped memoirs of 1985, Stets'ko proudly stressed that Kolodzins'kyi's doctrine "contains many of my suggestions."[1001]

---

999 Reichardt, "Fascism's Stages"
1000 Marta Havryshko, "Illegitimate Sexual Practices in the OUN Underground and UPA in Western Ukraine in the 1940s and 1950s," *Journal of Power Institutions in Post-Soviet Societies* 17 (2016); Himka, "The Lviv Pogrom of 1941"; Kudelia, "Choosing Violence in Irregular Wars," 149–81; McBride, "'A Sea of Blood and Tears'"; Olena Petrenko, *Unter Männern: Frauen im ukrainischen nationalistischen Untergrund 1944-1954* (Paderborn: Ferdinand Schöningh, 2018), 189–96; Władysław Siemaszko and Ewa Siemaszko, *Ludobójstwo dokonane przez nacjonalistów ukraińskich na ludności polskiej Wołynia 1939-1945*, 2 vols, 3rd ed. (Warsaw: Wydawnictwo von Borowiecky, 2008); Statiev, "Strategy of the Organization of Ukrainian Nationalists;" and Struve, *Deutsche Herrschaft*. The IPN is currently building an interactive database where survivors and family members are able to submit their family stories; "Konferencja prasowa IPN dotycząca Bazy Ofiar Zbrodni Wołyńskiej," *IPN TV*, https://przystanekhistoria.pl/pa2/tematy/oun-upa (accessed 2 January 2021).
1001 Yaroslav Stets'ko, "Spohady/Vidredagovanyi tekst rozmov dostoinoho Yaroslava Stets'ka z d-rom Anatoliem Bedriem, perevedenykh i zapysanykh na 12 kasetkakh vid 17 do 23 chervnia 1985 roku," Arkhiv TsDVR, fond 639, electronic document, 8; and "Rozmovy dostoinoho Yaroslava Stets'ko, Arkhiv OUN-UIS, fond 23, l. 15.

In practice, I added a great deal to that work, since I had [myself already] developed a concept of a military doctrine, a theme on which I spoke with him at great length. Therefore, significant parts of [Kolodzins'kyi's doctrine] consist of my ideas, among others.[1002]

Yaroslav Stets'ko's role in the development of OUN ideology between 1935 and 1941 can hardly be overstated.[1003] Stets'ko drafted the ideological declarations of the OUN's Second Grand Assembly at Rome in August 1939,[1004] and played a similar role in the preparation of the OUN(b)'s II Grand Assembly at Kraków in April 1941. The following month, he authored *The Struggle and Activity of the OUN in Times of War* together with Bandera, Lenkavs'kyi, and Shukhevych. Following the German invasion of the Soviet Union, Stets'ko went eastwards to L'viv with a special marching group tasked with declaring statehood.[1005] On 25 June 1941 Stets'ko, en route to L'viv, reported back to Bandera in Krakow: "We are establishing a militia that will help eliminate the Jews and protect the population."[1006]

Stets'ko was the dominant figure in L'viv during the fateful final week of June when OUN(b) statehood was declared.[1007] In the evening of 30 June 1941 he announced the "renewal" of Ukrainian Statehood and the forming of a government with himself as Prime Minister. On 1 July, his OUN(b) circulated leaflets

---

1002 "Rozmovy dostoinoho Yaroslava Stets'ko," Arkhiv OUN-UIA, fond 23, l. 36.
1003 See chapter seven.
1004 Yaroslav Stets'ko, "Mii zhyttiepys," TsDAVOVU, f. 3833, op. 3, spr. 7, ark. 1–3, facsimile available at https://training.ehri-project.eu/sites/training.ehri-project.eu/files/A7%20Stetsko.pdf (accessed 4 May 2019); Yurii Cherchenko, "Dzherela do istorii vyzvol'noho rukhu," *Ukrains'kyi vyzvol'nyi rukh: Naukovyi zbirnyk* 18 (2013), 6–24, here: 9; and Zaitsev, *Ukrains'kyi intehral'nyi natsionalizm*, 280, citing Arkhiv OUN[m] u Kyivi (hereafter AOUN u Kyivi), f. 1, op. 1, spr. 108, 118 ("Ukrains'ka national'na revoliutsiia abo Ukraina na shlikahu vidnovy i tvorennia novykh vnutrishnikh vartostei i vstanovliuvannia svoei velykoderzhavnoi ratsii v Evropi i sviti").
1005 Vasyl' Kuk, "Derzhavotvorcha diial'nist' OUN Akt Vidnovlennia Ukrains'koi Derzhavy 30 chervnia 1941 r.," in *Ukrains'ke derzhavotvorennia: Akt 30 chervnia 1941. Zbirnyk dokumentiv i materialiv*, eds. Yaroslav Dashkevych and Vasyl' Kuk (L'viv and Kyiv: Piramida, 2001), v–xxiii, here: xi.
1006 Struve, *Deutsche Herrschaft*, 263, 267.
1007 John A. Armstrong, "Heroes and Human: Reminiscences Concerning Ukrainian National Leaders During 1941-1944," *The Ukrainian Quarterly* 51, nos. 2–3 (1995): 213–27, here: 219.

calling the Ukrainian population to violent action: "Ukrainians! ... Don't throw away your weapons yet. Take them up. Destroy the enemy ... People!—Know this: Moscow, the Hungarians, the Jews—these are your enemies. Destroy them!"[1008] During the following days, a wave of anti-Jewish violence swept through at least 143 localities of Western Ukraine, claiming the lives of between 7,295 and 11,309 Jews.[1009]

On 3 July, presenting himself as Prime Minister of Ukraine, Stet'sko assured Hitler, Mussolini, Franco, and Pavelić that the new state was a part of "the new Europe."[1010] To Ante Pavelić he wrote that "both revolutionary nations [i.e., the Croatians and Ukrainians], hardened in battle, will guarantee the establishment of healthy circumstances in the Europe of the new order."[1011] Under house arrest in Berlin after his attempted state failed to get German support, he authored a biographical statement for the German authorities, in which he endorsed "the destruction of the Jews and the expedience of bringing German methods of exterminating Jewry to Ukraine."[1012]

Though the OUN(b) failed to obtain recognition for its statehood, it carried out political violence on a substantial scale. From the fall of 1941 it encouraged its men to join various auxiliary police formations set up by the German authorities. This brought combat experience, but also deep involvement in the Holocaust.[1013]

1008 "Ukrains'kyi narode!" TsDAVOVU, f. 3833, op. 1, spr. 42, l. 33.
1009 Struve, *Deutsche Herrschaft*, 671. Dieter Pohl provides a higher estimate of 13,000–35,000; Pohl, "Anti-Jewish Pogroms in Western Ukraine" in *Shared History–Divided Memory*, eds. Barkan, Cole, and Struve, 305–13, here: 306.
1010 Rossoliński-Liebe, "The 'Ukrainian National Revolution' of 1941."
1011 TsDAVOVU, f. 3833, op. 1, spr. 22, ll. 1–27. See also Rossoliński-Liebe, "The 'Ukrainian National Revolution' of 1941," 99.
1012 Stets'ko, "Mii zhyttiepys," ark. 3; Berkhoff and Carynnyk, "The Organization of Ukrainian Nationalists," 171.
1013 Gregorz Rossoliński-Liebe, "Ukraińska policja, nacjonalizm i zagłada Żydów w Galicji Wschodniej i na Wołyniu," *Zagłada Żydów: Studia i Materiały* 13 (2017): 57–79, here: 74, 79; and Per Anders Rudling, "Rehearsal for Volhynia: Schutzmannschaft Battalion 201 and Hauptmann Roman Shukhevvych in Occupied Belorussia, 1942," *East European Politics and Societies and Cultures* 34, no. 1 (2020): 158–93.

The ideological underpinnings of the OUN did inform its actions in the summer of 1941, and also in 1943, when it violently took over and reorganized the Ukrainian Insurgent Army (UPA).[1014] Less than 7,000 men under the command of Dmytro Kliachkivs'kyi (1911–45), the commander of UPA-North, were able to kill around 60,000 mostly civilian Poles in Volhynia, within a matter of months.[1015] The most detailed studies suggest that taken together, the UPA's systematically organized massacres in Volhynia and Galicia in 1943–44 claimed the lives of 91,200 Poles.[1016] Such levels of political violence required planning, preparation, and premeditation.

This radicalization, not only in words but in deeds, strongly suggests that Zaitsev's question: "Was there a connection between the theoretical concept of the OUN activists in 1938–1939 and the practical deeds of the OUN(b) and UPA during World War II?"[1017] must be answered in the affirmative. This, to be sure, is not to argue a strictly intentionalist line. The trajectory from the formulation of the ideological-doctrinal underpinnings for mass violence, through practical preparations for the "removal" and killing of Poles and Jews, to the actual massacres was influenced by a variety of short-term and conjunctural factors, which need to be taken into consideration.[1018] What cannot be dismissed, however, is that the change in rhetoric reflected a radicalization of the ideological

---

[1014] On the OUN(b)'s hijacking of Bul'ba Borovets'' original organization, see "Holovna komanda Ukrains'koi Narodn'oi Revoliutsiinoi Armii no. 501, dnia, 24.9.1943 do Provodu OUN-UPA i holovnoi komandy UPA," HDA SBU, f. 65, spr. S-9133, t. 2. Ch. III, ark. 25–27, in *Taras Bul'ba-Borovets': Dokumenty. Statti. Lysty*, ed. Volodymyr Serhiichuk (Kyiv: PP Serhiichuk M. I., 2011), 212–215; Taras Bul'ba-Borovets', *Armiia bez derzhavy: Slava i trahediia ukrains'koho povstans'koho rukhu. Spohady* (Kyiv: Knyha rodu, 2008), 250–67; and McBride, "'A Sea of Blood and Tears'," 265.
[1015] Volodymyr Koval'chuk, "Skil'ky zh soldativ bulo v UPA? Sekrety rozkryvae Klym Savur," *Ukrains'ka pravda*, 12 March 2010, http://www.istpravda.com.ua/articles/2010/12/3/7410/ (accessed 6 February 2012).
[1016] Siemaszko, "Stan badań nad ludobójstwem," 333.
[1017] Zaitsev, "Voenna doktryna Mykhaila Kolodzyns'koho," 253.
[1018] Himka, "Ukrainian Collaboration." On the genealogy of the anti-Polish sentiments in the radical Ukrainian nationalist tradition, see Krzysztof Łada, "The Ukrainian Topos of Oppression and the Volhynian Slaughter of Poles, 1841-1943/44" (Ph.D. thesis, Flinders University, 2012), in particular 229–344.

"SAVING THE OUN" 313

positions of the OUN, in particular its Galician *provid*, and that these must be integral to any analysis of this political violence.[1019] The OUN(b)'s August 1943 strategic change of rhetoric—at the peak of the Volhynian massacres—and the abandonment of fascist symbolism such as the raised arm salute took place when Stets'ko and Bandera were in German detention.[1020] As to the OUN(b), the years 1944 to 1948 were defined by its leadership's reconsolidation of the authoritarian order and the violent purge of those more pragmatic and strategically minded figures who, jockeying for support from Western intelligence agencies, adopted a more acceptable language. The result was a second split of the organization as Bandera and Stets'ko restored control over the OUN(b) in emigration.[1021]

Stets'ko would play a dominant role in that organization, serving as its leader from 1968 until his death in 1986.[1022] In emigration, the OUN(b) aligned itself with other authoritarian, anti-Semitic ultra-nationalist east European groups neatly qualifying in the fold of "generic fascism." These included remnants of the Tiso regime, organized around its former Foreign Minister Ferdinand

---

1019 See Bruder, "*Den ukrainischen Staat erkämpfen oder Sterben!*" and Rossoliński-Liebe, *Stepan Bandera*.
1020 The raised arm salute as OUN(b) salutation was introduced in April 1941, and dropped, discreetly, in August 1943; Archiwum Wiktora Poliszczuka (AWP), Derzhavnyi Arkhiv Rivnens'koi oblasti (hereafter DARO), Rolka 15, number klatki 00059—rozkaz komendanta Rejonu Wojskowego "Kostomarowa" z 1.09.44 o podziale ziemi po wymordowanych Polakach. Rękopis w języku ukraińskim" and "Nakaz komendanta raionu ['Iskra' Kostopil'skho rajonu VO "Zahrava"] "Kostomarova" (vid 1 veresnia 1943 r.)," DARO, f. R.-30, op.2, spr. 64, ark. 38–40. The author wishes to thank Wiesław Tokarczuk for bringing these documents to his attention.
1021 See, for instance Stepan Bandera, "A Letter to the Members of the OUN," February 1953, NARA, College Park, MD, AERODYNAMIC, Record Group [RG] 263, Records of the Central Intelligence Agency, entry ZZ-19, box 10, vol. 12, document 57, Location (RC), 230-86-25-02. Available online, https://www.cia.gov/readingroom/document/519a2b74993294098d50f0be (accessed 24 February 2021).
1022 On the IV Grand Assembly of the OUN(b), see *Vyzvol'nyi shliakh*, kn. 10 (247), (October 1968): 1139–1217; and *Vyzvol'nyi shliakh*, kn. 11–12 (248-9) (November–December 1968): 1267–1314.

Ďurčanský (1906-1974),[1023] Romanian Iron Guard leader Horia Sima (1907-1993) and Ante Pavelić's (1889-1959) Ustaša, reorganized in Argentinian exile as the Croatian Liberation Movement (HOP).[1024]

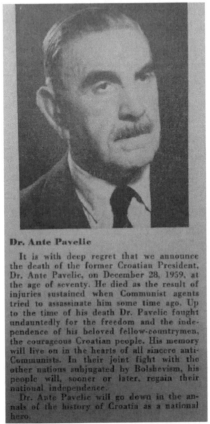

Figure 8.1. Obituary to Ante Pavelić in the OUN(b)'s *ABN Correspondence* XI, no. 2 (March-April 1960): 13.

1023 On the Tiso regime, see James Mace Ward, *Priest, Politician, Collaborator: Jozef Tiso and the Making of Fascist Slovakia* (Ithaca: Cornell University Press, 2013); and Jerome S. Legge, Jr., "Collaboration, Intelligence, and the Holocaust: Ferdinand Ďurčanský, Slovak Nationalism, and the Gehlen Organization," *Holocaust and Genocide Studies* 32, no. 2 (2018): 224–48.

1024 On the Ustaša after 1945, see Mate Nikola Tokić, *Croatian Radical Separatism and Diaspora Terrorism During the Cold War* (West Lafayette: Purdue University Press, 2020).

An unreconstructed authoritarian organization, the émigré OUN(b) continued to rely on political violence. It the U.S. and British Zones of occupied Germany it was linked to organized crime and engaged in substantial, systematic violence against political opponents in the DP camps. Moreover, it was penetrated by Soviet intelligence agents. The CIA instead collaborated with a splinter group which violently split off from the OUN(b) in 1948: the Foreign Representation of the Ukrainian Supreme Liberation Council (zpUHVR) and the interlinked Organization of Ukrainian Nationalists Abroad (*Orhanizatsiia Ukrain'skykh Natsionalistiv za kordonom*, OUN[z]), established formally in 1954.[1025] The central figure in this project was Mykola Lebed', the former acting leader of the OUN(b) (1941–43), who after the war ran the Prolog Research and Publishing Corporation (1952-92) in New York, a façade for a CIA operation under the cryptonyms AERODYNAMIC, QRDYNAMIC, PDDYNAMIC and QRPLUMB.[1026]

A Matter of Sources

Taras Kuzio has aptly observed how "Glasnost is alien to OUNb, and the only information we have access to is largely from the OUNb failures that were brought into the public domain by the Soviet authorities with the purpose of boasting at their successful efforts at 'liquidating' émigré nationalist activity."[1027] While glasnost was not exactly a characterizing feature of Lebed's conspiratorial zpUHVR either, from the late 1980s, the opening of Polish and Soviet archives made a wealth of new materials available to researchers shedding new light on these groups. In the US, the 1998 Nazi War Crimes Disclosure Act made numerous CIA materials available, enabling the reconstruction of the activities of these

---

[1025] Oleksandr Panchenko, *Orhanizatsiia Ukrains'kykh Natsionalistiv za kordonom (Naukovo-populiarnyi narys)* (Hadiach: Vydavnytstvo "Hadiach," 2003).
[1026] Breitman and Goda, *Hitler's Shadow*, 90; and Kuzio, "U.S. Support for Ukraine's Liberation," here: 51.
[1027] Kuzio, *Ukraine: Democratization, Corruption, and the New Russian Imperialism*, 140.

groups during the Cold War, not least their attempts at shaping and policing their own legacies.[1028]

It is thus unsurprising that the publication of an annotated version of Stets'ko's autobiography by Karel Berkhoff and Marco Carynnyk in 2002 created consternation among pro-nationalist diaspora scholars.[1029] For instance, Taras Hunczak, long-term Prolog affiliate and editor of its journal *Suchasnist'*, dismissed the text as a forgery "written in the offices of KGB functionaries."[1030] Hunczak's former associate at Prolog, Alexander J. Motyl,[1031] argued that "even if authentic, Yaroslav Stetsko's autobiographical sketch is not, I suggest, of much use here, primarily because a document produced in Nazi Germany after interrogation and before arrest may not be assumed to represent the truthful views of the author."[1032] Alas, the argument of the former Prolog col-

---

1028 See chapter four.
1029 Berkhoff and Carynnyk, "The Organization of Ukrainian Nationalists." The issue of *Harvard Ukrainian Studies* in which this article appeared was published in 2002 but dated 1999.
1030 Taras Hunczak, "Problems of Historiography: History and Its Sources," *Harvard Ukrainian Studies* 25, nos. 1–2 (2001): 129–42, here: 138. According to his memoirs, Hunczak's association with the CIA started in 1959; Taras Hunchak, *Moi spohady – stezhky zhyttia* (Dnipro, 2005), 39–40; "HUNCHAK, Taras," 15 January 1961, AERODYNAMIC, NARA, RG 263, entry ZZ/19, box 13, vol. 20; "Dossier opening request, from G-2 to "Chief, Central Registry Division, Dossier Franch, 66th CIC Group, Thru [redacted], November 21, 1956," "Nr. 332, HUNCZAK, Taras, FE017222," declassified NWCDA11/3/2014, NARA RG 319, IRR Hunczak, Taras, FE017222. Thanks to Jared McBride for sharing this material with the author.
1031 On Motyl's association with Prolog, see "[redacted], QRDYNAMIC – New York, N.Y. and Munich, Germany – Support of ZP/UHVR (Zakordonne Predstavnytstvo Ukrains'koi Holovnyi Vyzvol'noi Rady – Foreign Representation of the Ukrainian Supreme Liberation Council) FY 1974 Cost $ [redacted] ($[redacted] in the Congressional Budget plus $ [redacted] to cover effects of devaluation)," ANNEX 1 CONTINUED, PAYROLL, New York Office" QRPLUMB, NARA, RG 263, entry ZZ-19, box 59, vol. 2, RC NN3-263-02-008, (Development and Plans, 1970-1978). On Motyl's work on *Litopys UPA*, see *Litopys Ukrains'koi Povstans'koi Armii, Tom 6. UPA v svitli nimets'kykh dokumentiv. Knyha persha: 1942-cherven' 1944*, ed. Taras Hunchak (Toronto: Vydavnytstvo Litopys UPA, 1983), 5, 6.
1032 Alexander J. Motyl, "The Ukrainian Nationalist Movement and the Jews: Theoretical Reflections on Nationalism, Fascism, Rationality, Primordialism, and History," *Polin: Studies in Polish Jewry* 26 (2014): 275–95, here: 287, n. 14.

leagues goes, Stets'ko probably did not author that autobiography, and even if he did these were not his true views.

The OUN(b)'s own Volodymyr Kosyk rejected Hunczak's suggestion that the document was a forgery. Instead, Kosyk argued that Stets'ko's "'*zhyttiepys*' can under no circumstances be regarded as an official document of the *Provid* [leadership] of the OUN(b). It is a personal biography of a person, who speaks for himself."[1033] To suggest that the "Prime Minister" and long-term OUN(b) leader Stets'ko, Kosyk argued, was representative of anything other than himself would be "to cast an unjustified shadow over all further activities of the OUN(b) and its struggle for Ukrainian independence."[1034]

Zaitsev does not avoid the difficult questions this material raises. He cites Kolodzins'kyi's words: "The more Jews will die during the uprising, the better for the Ukrainian state." He cites Stets'ko's endorsement of "German methods of exterminating Jewry,"[1035] questioning neither the authenticity of the document, nor that it would reflect the head of government's actual views.

The plights of the Ustaša and OUN states differed. In September 1941, as Stets'ko and Bandera were incarcerated in an annexe to Sachsenhausen, the concentration camp was visited by Vjekoslav Luburić (1914–69), the head of the Ustaša camp system. Much impressed by the camp, the NDH built the Jasenovać camp as a copy of Sachsenhausen-Oranienbaum. It would become but one of about forty concentration camps operated by the Ustaša.[1036] There was no OUN equivalent of the Jasenovać concentration camp. Similarly, absence of a state precluded the establishment of a "Ukrainian State Agency of National Eugenics with branches all

---

[1033] Volodymyr Kosyk, "Harvard patronue nenaukove metody istorychnoho doslidzhennia," *Ukrains'kyi vyzvol'nyi rukh* 1 (2003): 176–89, here: 186.
[1034] Kosyk, "Harvard patronue nenaukove metody," 187. Neither did Volodymyr V"iatrovych of the OUN(b)'s Center for the Study of the Liberation Movement (TsDVR) deny the authenticity of Stets'ko's autobiography, instead taking the study to task for "using the same documents as did Soviet propagandists"; Volodymyr V"iatrovych, *Stavlennia OUN do evreiv: Formuvannia pozytsii na tli katastrofy* (L'viv: Vydavnytstvo "Ms," 2006), 9.
[1035] Zaitsev, "Fascism or Ustashism?" 7.
[1036] Reichardt, "Fascism's Stages," 93.

over the entire territory of the state," as envisioned by Stets'ko.[1037] Controlling the mechanisms of a state machinery makes a significant difference in the ability to implement policies. Luburić and Stets'ko got to see Sachsenhausen from different angles.

According to Zaitsev's argument, without statehood, the OUN(b) remained "proto-fascist," whereas the Ustaša entered the world of fascism on 10 April 1941. From Zaitsev's taxonomy is not entirely clear whether after the Ustaša became fully fascist, it ceased to be ustashist. Further, for a taxonomy structured around the issue of statehood, puppet states ought to constitute particular problems. How sovereign the NDH really was, under the conditions of German and Italian occupations, with large territories controlled by partisan insurgents, is debatable. Conversely, what do we make of the claims by the OUN(b), that the polity declared on 30 June 1941 was legitimate, and the UPA its legal armed forces? Stets'ko insisted that "in the forties, Ukrainian statehood, and the Ukrainian government continued as long as even the tiniest strip of land remained defended by the Ukrainian weapons of the OUN-UPA."[1038] For the rest of his life, Stets'ko regarded himself Head of the Ukrainian State Administration (*Holova Ukrains'koho Derzhavnoho Pravlinnia*), and introduced himself as the "former Prime Minster of Ukraine."[1039] Viktor Yushchenko's posthumous

---

[1037] Ustaša's attitude to eugenics was complex and contradictory; see Rory Yeomans, "Fighting the White Plague: Demography and Abortion in the Independent State of Croatia," in *Health, Hygiene and Eugenics in Southeastern Europe to 1945*, eds. Christian Promitzer, Sevasti Trubeta, and Marius Turda (Budapest: CEU Press, 2011), 385–426; and Rory Yeomans, "Eradicating 'Undesired Elements': National Regeneration and the Ustasha Regime's Program to Purify the Nation, 1941-1945," in *Racial Science in Hitler's New Europe, 1938-1945*, eds. Anton Weiss-Wendt and Rory Yeomans (Lincoln: University of Nebraska Press, 2013), 200–36.

[1038] Yaroslav Stets'ko, "Zaiava Holovy UDP Ya. Stets'ka shchodo roli UDP v derzhavotvorenni ta terminu 'vidnovelnnia derzhavnosti'," 11–12 May 1986, document AOUN_001_001_000092.pdf, *Arkhiv OUN-UIS*, Provid OUN, f.1, op. 1, ad. zb. 92, ark. 10, http://ounuis.info/fonds/executive-oun-f-1/1449/pravni-rishennia-yastetska-shchodo-oun-ta-udp-zrobleni-nym-v-ostanni-dni-zhyttia-piznishi-dokumenty.html (accessed 22 February 2021).

[1039] Stets'ko, "Zaiava Holovy UDP," f.1, op. 1, ad. zb. 92, ark. 10; Yaroslav Stets'ko business card, LAC, Ottawa, The Dontsov Collection, MG 31, D130, Vol. 5, folder 21, "Yaroslav Stetsko 1953-1968"; and Yaroslav Stets'ko to Jan Tokarzewski-Karaszewicz, 10 January 1950, Jan Tokarzewski-Karasewicz Pa-

rehabilitation of Stets'ko in 2007 sanctioned the "Prime Minister"'s activities by mandating the renaming of streets, boulevards, squares, and a museum in his honor.[1040] Volodymyr V"iatrovych, the former head of the Ukrainian Institute of National Memory, claimed the entire Soviet period in Ukraine constituted an illegal occupation, whereas he presented the UPA as a regular, national army of a recognized state, down to fulfilling the requirements of the Hague Convention.[1041] The same memory activists who are intensely preoccupied with the issue of statehood, paradoxically need the absence of statehood in order to legitimate the OUN(b) as "non-fascist". It remains on open question how the retroactive, official recognition of the OUN(b) and its leaders impact their categorization.

Saving Us from Fascism

To a historian, the sustained efforts to refute categorizations of the OUN as fascist are no less interesting than the taxonomy as such. This concerns not least the institutional networks that facilitated and underwrote the glorification of these organizations.[1042] Over the course of the 1960s and '70s, Ukrainian émigré nationalists came to appropriate an anti-colonial rhetoric, applying it to Ukraine. It served, directly or indirectly, their purpose to salvage

---

pers, Ukrainian Research Institute, Harvard University, Box 3, Folder 27, "Stetsko, Yaroslav," https://iiif.lib.harvard.edu/manifests/view/drs:51452 950$100i (accessed 17 March 2017).

1040 Viktor Yushchenko, "Ukaz prezidenta Ukrainy Pro vshanuvannia pam"iaty Iaroslava Stets'ka i Iaroslavy Stets'ko," *Verkhovna rada Ukrainy*, doc. 419/2007, 16 May 2007, https://zakon.rada.gov.ua/laws/show/419/2007#Text (accessed 6 February 2021).

1041 Volodymyr V"iatrovych, "Perebuvannia Ukrainy u skladi SRSR — tse okupatsiia, — V"iatrovych," *Tsenzor.net*, 7 January 2018, https://censor.net/ua/news/3043120/perebuvannya_ukrayiny_u_skladi_srsr_tse_okupatsiya_vyatrovych (accessed 24 February 2021); and idem., *Druha pol's'ko-ukrains'ka viina, 1942-1947* (Kyiv: Vydavnychyi dim "Kyevo-Mohylians'ka akademiia," 2011), 27.

1042 Per Anders Rudling, "Terror Remembered, Terror Forgotten: Stalinist, Nazi, and Nationalist Atrocities in Ukrainian 'National Memory'," in *World War II Re-explored: Some New Millenium Studies in the History of the Global Conflict*, eds. Jarosław Suchoples, Stephanie James, and Barbara Törnquist-Plewa (Berlin: Peter Lang, 2019), 401–28.

and rehabilitate the legacy of the OUN(b) and UPA, in part or in full, divorcing it from a legacy of collaboration, fascism, and ideologically motivated ethnic cleansing of ethnic minorities.[1043] The perhaps most eloquent promoter of this narrative, Alexander J. Motyl, summarized the narration thus:

> The OUN began as a radical youth movement, then morphed into a quasi-authoritarian movement, adopted fascist elements by the late 1930s and early 1940s, abandoned them by 1943-4, and began acquiring progressively more democratic and social-democratic characteristics by the mid to late 1940s and 1950s.[1044]

From around 1980, the pretense that that the OUN(b) had undergone a democratic conversion in August 1943 became a leitmotif of the discourse from the Prolog circle.[1045]

Motyl's conceptualization of generic fascism differs in some key regards from the more common definitions, not least by separating it from nationalism, instead making it dependent on statehood.

> Must fascism have nationalist components? The answer is no. Fascism, whether ideology, movement, or system of rule, presupposed an independent state and then proposes to reorganize it along specifically fascist lines. Statehood is thus a necessary condition of fascism: genuinely fascist ideologies, movements, and systems of rule can exist if and only if an independent state is already in existence.[1046]

1043 For this argument see, for instance, V. Z. Ukhach, I. I. Martsias', and O. V. Koval's'kyi, "Akt proholoshennia vidnovlennia Ukrains'koi derzhavy 30 chervnia 1941 roku: Istoriko-pravovyi analiz (Suchasna vitchyzna istoriohrafiia)," *Iurydychnyi naukovyi elektronnyi zhurnal* 6 (2015): 34–37. For a critical discussion on this disavowal, see Gyidel, "The Ukrainian Legal Press," 11–12.
1044 Motyl, "Ukrainian Nationalist Movement and the Jews," 279–80.
1045 See, for instance, Potichnyj and Shtendera (eds.), *Political Thought of the Ukrainian Underground*; Petro R. Sodol, *UPA: They Fought Hitler and Stalin: A Brief Overview of Military Aspects from the History of the Ukrainian Insurgent Army, 1942-1949* (New York: Committee for the World Convention and Reunion of Soldiers in the Ukrainian Insurgent Army, 1987); and the CIA-funded *Litopys UPA*. On the CIA funding of *Litopys UPA*, see "Renewal of Operational Activity," IAD/SEG/IB, 24 January 1983, 2, QRPLUMB, NARA, RG 263, entry ZZ-19, box 59, vol. 4, RC NN3-263-02-008.
1046 Motyl, "The Ukrainian Nationalist Movement and the Jews," 278.

"SAVING THE OUN" 321

From this, it follows that

> neither Bandera nor the Organization of Ukrainian Nationalists was fascist, although both had fascist inclinations—particularly in 1940 and 1941. Fascists run or aspire to run existing states. Nationalists in contrast, aspire to create nations.[1047]

In accordance with such a definition, as the OUN(b) failed to set up a state, it was "saved" from fascism:

> Bandera hoped for an alliance with Nazi Germany against the Soviet Union. But the Nazis failed to oblige, cracking down on the nationalists in mid-1941, imprisoning Bandera in Sachsenhausen and inadvertently saving him and his supporters from a collaborationist and possibly fascist fate.[1048]

This argument is quite popular among Ukrainian researchers. Zaitsev follows Motyl's argument closely, yet differs in his assessment in regard to what a OUN(b) state may have looked like.

> The Independent State of Croatia of 1941-1945 is a good model of what a Ukrainian state under the aegis of the Third Reich might have looked like had the Nazis agreed to its creation. The Croatian experience shows that, under such conditions, Ustashism soon turns into full-fledged fascism. Thus, by breaking up the Ukrainian government that Yaroslav Stetsko had created in L'viv, the Nazis saved Ukrainian nationalism from such a fate. "Paradoxically, —wrote Alexander J. Motyl—repression proved to be the best thing that could have happened to the OUN, saving it from the collaborationist fate of the Croatian Ustasha and the Slovak People's Party."[1049]

Motyl, on the other hand, suggests the possibility that Stets'ko's state, had it been accepted as a member of the Axis camp, would have rejected fascism:

> It is, of course, perfectly possible that the Ukrainian nationalist movement would have moved toward full fascism had it been permitted to establish

---

1047 Alexander Motyl, "Stepan Bandera: Hero of Ukraine?" *New Atlanticist*, 15 March 2010, https://www.atlanticcouncil.org/blogs/new-atlanticist/stepan-bandera-hero-of-ukraine/ (accessed 28 December 2020).
1048 Motyl, "Stepan Bandera: Hero of Ukraine?"
1049 Zaitsev, "Fascism or Ustashism?" 9; and idem., *Ukrains'kyi intehral'nyi natsionalizm*, 324, citing Motyl, *Dilemmas of Independence*, 95.

an independent state in 1941. It is also perfectly conceivable that the seemingly inexorable upward trajectory ... would have stopped well short of fascism. There is no way of knowing empirically... Only a counterfactual experiment resting on already implicit theoretical views could suggest such an outcome. Thus, if one already believes that the nationalists were fascists to the core, then fascism is the only imaginable outcome.[1050]

As now readily accessible archival material clearly demonstrates, many claims of the Prolog circle do not hold up to scrutiny. Not only did the OUN and UPA's anti-Polish massacres continue unabatedly in the days and weeks following the OUN(b)'s supposed democratic change of heart at the III Grand Assembly 1943,[1051] but these massacres included some of the largest and brutal atrocities of the anti-Polish campaign, such as the massacres at Wola Ostrowiecka and Ostrowski on 30 August 1943.[1052] Subsequently, the violence was expanded into East Galicia. The OUN and UPA's anti-Jewish violence follows a similar pattern.[1053] The opening of the archives conclusively shows how the pretense of a democratic change of heart in August 1943 does not hold up for scrutiny. Rather, this was a façade which the OUN(b) sought to project to the Western allies, as it sought new allies among the Western allies. In order to back up this new, "democratic" image,

---

1050 Motyl, "The Ukrainian Nationalist Movement and the Jews," 280.
1051 On the massacres on 29–30 August 1943, see, for instance, "Protokol doprosa obviniaemogo STEL'MASHCHUK Yuriia Aleksandovicha ot 20-go fevralia 1945 goda," HDA SBU, f. 5, spr. 67424, ark. 41–49, reproduced in Litopys UPA, Nova seriia, tom 9. Borot'ba proty povstans'koho rukhu i natsionalistychnoho pidpillia: protokoly dopytiv zaareshtovanykh radians'kymy orhanamy derzhavnoi bezpeky kerivnykiv OUN i UPA, 1944-1945, eds. P. Sokhan, P. Potichnyj et al. (Toronto and L'viv: Litopys UPA, 2007), 442.
1052 Tadeusz Piotrowski, Poland's Holocaust: Ethnic Strife, Collaboration with Occupying Forces and Genocide in the Second Republic, 1918-1947 (Jefferson, NC: McFarland, 1998), 246–47; idem., Genocide and Rescue in Wołyń, 81; Berkhoff, Harvest of Despair, 285–86; and Leon Popek, "Wołyńskie ekshumacje w latach 1992-2015," Instytut Pamięci Narodowej, https://ipn.gov.pl/pl/aktualnosci/37305,Leon-Popek-Wolynskie-ekshumacje-w-latach-19922015.html?search=1915 0659558585 (accessed 10 February 2021).
1053 Bruder, "Den ukrainischen Staat erkämpfen oder sterben," 217-223; John-Paul Himka, "Former Ukrainian Policemen in the Ukrainian National Insurgency: Continuing the Holocaust outside German Service," Lessons and Legacies XII: New Directions in Holocaust Research and Education, eds. Wendy Lower and Laureen Faulkner Rossi (Evanston, IL: Northwestern University Press, 2017), 139–63.

the OUN(b), immediately after the III Grand Assembly issued orders to falsify the organization's immediate history, denying collaboration with the Germans and blaming the anti-Jewish pogroms of the Poles.[1054]

The obvious incongruency between the claim that the OUN(b)/UPA underwent a supposed democratic transformation amidst a brutal guerrilla war and the ethnic cleansing of western Ukraine of Poles and Jews may account for its limited effectiveness outside the Ukrainian community. The historian is interested in the methodological problem: if we cannot pin fascism on the OUN in the pre-1943 documents, then how can we pin democracy on them post-1943? The OUN(b) and UPA did not use the term democracy in 1943; the term rather starts to appear in emigration around 1948.[1055]

The memory production, to be sure, differed between the three rival groups who claimed to represent the legacy of the OUN. Whereas Bandera and Stets'ko's OUN(b) kept promoting, for instance, the legacy of the Ustaša, the US government-funded zpUHVR/Prolog did not. Political scientist John Armstrong, an admirer of the OUN(b), made a distinction between Stets'ko, a "heroic type" who "radiated unflinching determination,"[1056] while criticizing him for collaborating with "some questionable groups" — among which he presumably counted the Ustaša.[1057] If

---

1054 Carynnyk, "Foes of Our Rebirth," 345–46. Jeffrey Kopstein and Jason Wittenberg refer to this as "an important piece of evidence for the historians' equivalent of mens rea — evidence of a guilty mind in criminal law"; Jeffrey S. Kopstein and Jason Wittenberg, *Intimate Violence: Anti-Jewish Pogroms on the Eve of the Holocaust* (Ithaca: Cornell University Press, 2018), 92.
1055 The claim appears to have entered the discourse through Motyl in 1980; Oleksander Motyl', "Orhanizatsiia ukrains'kykh natsionalistiv i robitnytstbo (kil'ka zavvah)," *Suchasnist* 2 (1980): 51–63, here: 61. For others repeating the claim, see Myroslav Shkandrij, "Breaking Taboos: The Holodomor and the Holocaust in Ukrainian-Jewish Relations," *Polin: Studies in Polish Jewry* 26 (2014): 259–73, here: 268; Taras Kuzio, "European Identity, Euromaidan, and Ukrainian Nationalism," *Nationalism and Ethnic Politics* 22, no. 4 (2016): 497–508, here: 504; and Volodymyr V"iatrovych, *Stavlennia OUN do evreiiv: Formuvannia pozytsii na tli katastrofy* (L'viv: Vydavytsvo "Ms," 2006), 73.
1056 Armstrong, "Heroes and Human," 219.
1057 Armstrong, "Heroes and Human," 213.

Stets'ko regarded the Ustaša as a kindred liberation movement, his admirer Armstrong did not.

Zaitsev's conceptualization is indebted to Motyl: fascism, Zaitsev argues, "arises in state nations bent on national rebirth" while "Ustašism" develops "under conditions of perceived foreign occupation."[1058] At the same time Zaitsev stresses the similarities between the OUN and the Ustaša which the Prolog circle sought to downplay, placing the two in the same category.

Problems of Methodology

The thesis that the lack of statehood precluded fascism "popular among a considerable part of Ukrainian historians," historian Taras Kurylo (b. 1974) argues, "treats fascism somewhat mechanically."[1059] Indeed, there are a number of objections that could be made. Since only a few fascist groups in Eastern Europe managed to come to power and operate machineries of state, what do we do with those who failed to come to power?[1060] An analytical model which makes the distinction between fascism and ustashism on the basis of "conditions of perceived foreign occupation" becomes particularly complicated in regard to an organization such as the OUN, active as an underground organization in four multi-ethnic states; Poland, Romania, Czechoslovakia, and the USSR. Applied to the Galicia at the time Kolodzins'kyi authored the military doctrine of the Ukrainian Nationalists, a taxonomy making fascism dependent on statehood would place a Polish ethnonationalist far-right group such as the OZN-Falanga squarely in the fascist category, whereas it would not pertain to the OUN. Applied to Czechoslovakia, the OUN would be accompanied in the "non-fascist" fold not only by the Hlinka Guard, but also the Sudeten

---

1058 Zaitsev, "Fascism or Ustashism?" 9.
1059 Taras Kurylo, "Shche raz pro OUN ta fashyzm," *Zakhid*, 15 March 2012, https://zaxid.net/shhe_raz_pro_oun_ta_fashizm_n1250264 (accessed 28 December 2020).
1060 Daniel Ursprung, "Faschismus in Ostmittel- und Südosteuropa: Theorien, Ansätze, Fragestellungen," in *Der Einfluss von Faschismus und Nationalismus auf Minderheiten in Ostmittel- und Südosteuropa*, eds. Marianna Hausleitner and Harald Roth (Munich: IKGS-Verlag, 2006), 22.

German German National Socialist Workers' Party (*Deutsche Nationalsozialistische Arbeiterpartei*, DNSAP), and Konrad Henlein's (1898-1945) *Sudetendeutsche Partei*.[1061] Applied to other parts of interwar Europe, this analytical model would lead to similar confusion; it would similarly leave the NSDAP in the Free City of Danzig, Saargebiet, and Memel[1062] — or, for that matter, Gabriele D'Annunzio's (1863-1938) Regency of Carnaro in Fiume in 1919-20 in the non-fascist category.[1063] Taken to its logical conclusion, Alfred Rosenberg(1893-1946) would cease to be fascist during the final year of his life, since Germany had ceased to exist as a state. This "mechanical" interpretation would, ipso facto, "save" a group such as DSU (*Vseukrains'ke politychne ob"iednannia "Derzhavna samostiinist' Ukraini"* – the All-Ukrainian Political Union "State Independence of Ukraine"), a far-right party open only to ethnic Ukrainians which "openly propagated the idea of establishing a national dictatorship and adhered to the fascist legacy of the OUN's ideologists Dontsov, Stsibors'kyi and Bandera," at least for the period from its establishment in May 1990 until 24 August 1991.[1064] Conversely, Kurylo notes, Stets'ko *would* have been a fascist until his arrest on 11 July 1941, as long as his *Derzhavne Upravlinnia* (State Administration) actually operated and controlled OUN militias and other armed formations under its control.[1065]

1061 Mark Cornwall, "The Czechoslovak Sphinx: 'Moderate and Reasonable' Konrad Henlein," in *In the Shadow of Hitler: Personalities of the Right in Central and Eastern Europe*, eds. Rebecca Haynes and Martyn Rady (London: I. B. Tauris, 2011), 206–26. See also Nancy M. Wingfield, "Czechoslovakia's Germans," in Roland Clark and Tim Grady (eds.), *European Fascist Movements: A Sourcebook* (London and New York: Routledge, 2023), 327-347.
1062 Mads Ole Balling, *Von Reval bis Bukarest: Statistisch-Biographisches Handbuch der Parlamentarier der deutschen Minderheiten in Ostmittel- und Südosteuropa 1919-1945*, 2 vols. (Copenhagen: Dokumentation Verlag, 1991).
1063 Göran Hägg, *D'Annunzio: Dekandent, diktare, krigare och diktator* (Stockholm: Norstedts, 2015), 203–36.
1064 Anton Shekhovtsov, "The Creeping Resurgence of the Ukrainian Radical Right? The Case of the Freedom Party," *Europe-Asia Studies* 63, no. 2 (2011): 203–28, here: 210.
1065 "If we are to follow the thesis that a fascist movement can exist only in a nation state, then we need to consider Yaroslav Stets'ko a 'fascist' as soon as he declared the renewal of the Ukrainian State in L'viv on 30 June 1941, and,

Zaitsev's taxonomy excludes even Ukrainian groups who self-identified as fascist, such the Union of Ukrainian Fascists (*Soiuz ukrains'kykh fashystiv*, SUF), established in emigration in 1924.[1066] According to Zaitsev, "that they called themselves fascists does not constitute a fact that they truly were."[1067] As a tool to understand historical phenomena better, the taxonomy raises serious questions.

The insistence on a Ukrainian *Sonderweg*, that Western Ukraine, unique in the post-Habsburg realm, somehow "escaped" or was "saved" from fascism, sets it apart from a European memory culture, which takes a point of departure, as Claus Leggewie argues, in a realization that "anti-Semitism and fascism were all-European phenomena, and the murder of the Jews would not be possible without extensive collaboration."[1068] For students of fascism it is not self-evident why, specifically, Western Ukraine should be treated differently and Ukrainian fascists be regarded as an anomaly and exception.

Right into Left

Having divorced the OUN(b) from its ideology Motyl asserts: "I argue that the Ukrainian nationalist movement was a typical national liberation movement whose primary goal was political—to

---

accordingly, cease to regard him as such, as soon as it was understood, that the Germans would not agree to it. We acknowledge that this does not look particularly serious"; Kurylo, "Shche raz pro OUN ta fashyzm."

1066 The following year SUF merged with the League of Ukrainian Nationalists, which in 1929 became a founding member of the OUN. Its leader, Petro Kozhevnikiv (1896–1980), was a delegate at the OUN's *I Velykyi Zbir* (First Grand Assembly) in 1929. H. V. Kas'ianov, "Ideolohiia orhanizatsii ukrans'kykh natsionalistiv," in *Orhanizatsiia ukrains'kykh natsionalistiv i Ukrains'ka povstans'ka armiia: Istorychni narysy*, ed. S. V. Kul'chyts'kyi (Kyiv: Naukova dumka, 2005), 445–78, here: 457.

1067 "'Soiuz ukrains'kykh fashystiv ne buv fashysts'koiu orhanizatsiieiu'— istoryk," *Gazeta.ua*, 15 July 2013, https://gazeta.ua/articles/history/_soyuz-ukrayinskih-fashistiv-ne-buv-fashistskoyu-organizaciyeyu-istorik/507018 (accessed 2 January 2021).

1068 Claus Leggewie and Anne Lang, "Sieben Kreise europäischer Erinnerung: 1. Der Holocaust als negativer Gründungsmythos Europas," in *idem*, *Der Kampf um die europäische Erinnerung: Ein Schlachtfeld wird besichtigt* (Munich: C. H. Beck, 2011), 15-48.

achieve independent statehood for the Ukrainian nation—and not ideological."[1069] This, he contends, is something adherents of liberal democracy ought to support: "It makes perfect sense for liberals and democrats always to oppose fascism. When it comes to nationalism, their attitude should be welcoming but cautious. Welcoming, because liberals and democrats should welcome every form of liberation."[1070]

A similar logic has informed the rehabilitation of the OUN(b) in Ukraine, where positive aspects of its legacy are stressed. Writer Mykola Riabchuk highlights Bandera's "patriotism, national solidarity, self-sacrifice, idealistic commitment to common goals and values,"[1071] whereas Viktor Yushchenko cited Bandera's "unbreakable spirit in defending the national idea, expressions of heroism and self-sacrifice" in posthumously awarding the OUN leader the highest recognition of the Ukrainian state.[1072]

Motyl places the OUN(b) into an ulterior context of anti-colonial, mostly left-leaning nationalist groups active outside Europe:

> the ethnic violence in Volhynia bears comparison not with the state-directed destruction of ethnic groups by Nazi Germany, Ustaša Croatia, or Vichy France, but with the ethnic violence of Algerians against pied-noirs French, of Irish nationalists against the British, of Palestinian nationalists against Israelis, and of Jewish nationalists against Palestinians.

According to Motyl, while the OUN's methods "may be despicable," they "are not necessarily more despicable than the horrors of state-generated wars."[1073] Therefore, he explains, "Roman

---

1069 Motyl, "The Ukrainian Nationalist Movement and the Jews," 275.
1070 Alexander J. Motyl, "On Nationalism and Fascism, Part 3," *World Affairs Blog*, 25 June 2013, http://www.worldaffairsjournal.org/blog/alexander-j-motyl/nationalism-and-fascism-part-3 (accessed 12 February 2019).
1071 Mykola Riabchuk, "Bandera's Controversy and Ukraine's Future," *Russkii vopros* 1 (2010), http://www.russkiivopros.com/ruskii_vopros.php?pag=on e&id=315&kat=9&csl=46 (accessed 2 January 2021).
1072 Viktor Yushchenko, "Ukaz prezydenta Ukrainy Pro prysvoennia S. Banderi zvannia Heroi Ukrainy," *Verkhovna Rada Ukrainy*, doc. 46/2010, 20 January 2010 (redaction of 2 April 2010), https://zakon.rada.gov.ua/cgi-bin/laws/m ain.cgi?nreg=46/2010#Text (accessed 6 February 2020).
1073 Motyl, "The Ukrainian Nationalist Movement and the Jews," 288.

Shukhevych and Stepan Bandera are rather more like Ahmed Ben Bella, Yasser Arafat, Menachem Begin, Avraham Stern, and Billy McKee, than like Benito Mussolini, Francisco Franco, and Adolf Hitler."[1074] His former colleague at Prolog/QRPLUMB, Taras Kuzio, expands the list of alternative references further, adding Malcolm X and Nelson Mandela.[1075] In a recent article, *Litopys UPA* editor Oleksandr Pahiria (b. 1987) added a few additional names for context: Charles de Gaulle, Draža Mihailović, and Aung San—and a long line of other leaders of "anticolonial national liberation" movements.[1076]

Ivan Patryliak,[1077] places the OUN in the context of the Viet Cong, Mau Mau, Serbian, Croatian, Macedonian, and Irish revolutionary movements of the late 19th and early 20th centuries: "The guilt of the OUN was only that this anti-colonial and national liberation organization existed and was active at the same time as the expansion of the fascist movement in Europe and in the period of its colossal popularity."[1078] Stets'ko's nephew Oleh Romanyshyn (b. 1941), editor of the OUN(b) journal *Homin Ukrainy*, explained that that the organization was akin to the "Irish Republican Army, the Jewish Haganah and Irgun, South African African National Congress and all other liberation movements of the peoples of the world."[1079] In this narration, OUN(b) was a national liberation movement which merely happened to have had the misfortune to exist in a region and in an era in which fascist movements were in vogue—elsewhere.

1074 Motyl, "The Ukrainian Nationalist Movement and the Jews," 282.
1075 Taras Kuzio, "How Not to Debate Ukrainian History (at Columbia University or Elsewhere)," *The Ukrainian Weekly*, no. 20, 19 May 2013, 6, 13.
1076 Oleksandr Pahiria, "OUN ta UPA v konteksti vyzvol'nykh rukhiv: sproba komparativnoho analizu," *Novitnia doba* 7 (2019): 150–77, here: 164–65.
1077 Ivan Patryliak, *"Peremoha abo smert": ukrains'kyi vyzvol'nyi rukh u 1939-1960 rr.* (L'viv: Tsentr doslidzhen' vyzvol'noho rukhu, 2012), back cover.
1078 Ivan Patryliak, "Zapytannia do Forumu 'Fashyzm na skhodi Evropy'," *Ukraina Moderna* 20 (2013): 30–31, here: 30.
1079 [Oleh Romanyshyn] "Nasha porada deiakim istorikam," *Homin Ukrainy*, March 27, 2012, p. 8.

The Fascism of Others

The stringency of Motyl's criteria for fascism in regard to the OUN(b) contrasts sharply with the generosity of the definitions he applies in his analysis of the Russian Federation. Already before the 2008 Russian–Georgian war, Motyl referred to Russia in terms of fascism.[1080] If in 2012 he conceptualized the Russian Federation as a "fascistoid" "hybrid authoritarian-fascist system,"[1081] by 2015, he insisted, it had developed into a full-fledged "fascist state."[1082] Motyl argues that "[c]alling Putin's system fascist will mark a conceptual breakthrough in Western attitudes—and perhaps policies—toward Russia."[1083] Not all scholars of fascism concur.[1084] Andreas Umland has taken Motyl to task for an unconventional use of terminology which "deprives researchers of Russian nationalism of an important analytical tool."[1085] "Motyl," Umland contends,

> misses *all* of the dozens of previous scholarly and publicist discussions on [the Weimar/Russia comparison, meaning of fascism in Russia, rise of fascist movements in post-Soviet Russia, etc.]. Motyl's terminological-conceptual obfuscation around the attributes "fascist" and "fascistoid" makes both verification and falsification of his argument difficult.[1086]

1080 Alexander J. Motyl, "Is Putin's Russia Fascist?" *The National Interest*, 3 December 2007, https://nationalinterest.org/commentary/inside-track-is-putin s russia fascist-1888 (accessed 6 February 2020).
1081 Alexander J. Motyl, "Fascistoid Russia: Whither Putin's Brittle Realm?" *World Affairs* (March–April 2012), http://www.worldaffairsjournal.org/article/fascistoid-russia-whither-putin's-brittle-realm (accessed 15 May 2015).
1082 Alexander Motyl, "Is Ukraine Fascist?" *The World Post*, 2 March 2015, http://www.huffingtonpost.com/alexander-motyl/putin-calls-ukraine-fasci_b_6600292.html (accessed 15 May 2015).
1083 Alexander J. Motyl, "Is Putin's Russia Fascist?" *Atlantic Council*, 23 April 2015, http://www.atlanticcouncil.org/blogs/new-atlanticist/is-putin-s-russia-fascist (accessed 15 May 2015).
1084 Marlene Laruelle, *Is Russia Fascist?: Unraveling Propaganda East and West* (Ithaca: Cornell University Press, 2021).
1085 Andreas Umland, "Is Putin's Russia Really Fascist? A Response to Alexander Motyl," *Katholische Universität Eichstätt-Ingolstadt*, 17 January 2008, https://www.ku.de/news/is-putins-russia-really-fascist-a-response-to-alexander-motyl (accessed 15 March 2021).
1086 Andreas Umland, "Challenges and Promises of Comparative Research into Post-Soviet Fascism: Methodological and Conceptual Issues in the Study of

A definition of fascism which qualifies Putin's Russia but disqualifies the polity declared by Stets'ko in 1941 constitutes a discrepancy in terminology which cannot be explained by terminological conservatism, but rather by an ideological use of history.

Taxonomy, Terminology, and Genealogy

The heroization of the OUN and UPA may have been a central feature of the memory culture of the Ukrainian diaspora. Yet even here there were important voices of dissent. Among the scholars who characterize the OUN as fascist, Ukrainian émigré historian Ivan Lysiak-Rudnyts'kyi (1919–84) may be counted among the more authoritative. In 1973, the politically conservative and strongly anti-Soviet Lysiak-Rudnyts'kyi described the *"banderivshchyna"* as "our home-grown fascism" and "Ukrainian Black Hundreds."[1087] In a letter to his uncle Ivan Kedryn Rudnyts'kyi (1895–1991), he wrote that

> the Banderites continue the traditional line of the old OUN. They still remain a totalitarian group today. The examples of this are many: the strivings for monopolizing control over all Ukrainian societal-political life; the organic incapacity for honest cooperation with other groups on an equal footing; the infiltration of non-political communal and cultural organizations and their subordination under the orders of party *politruks*, its mafiosi-conspiratorial modus operandi in regards to its own community members, an extreme obscurantism, hatred of independent artistic creation, systematic suppression of free thought, criticism and discussion, distorting public opinion by means of shouting it down with shrill, hysterical propaganda and hurrah-patriotic demagoguery; and, finally, the *vozhdyzm* in the form of Stets'ko, never mind the grotesqueness of that candidate for dictator.[1088]

---

the Contemporary East European Extreme Right," *Communist and Post-Communist Studies* (2015), 6–7, http://dx.doi.org/10.1016/j.postcomstud.2015.07.002 (accessed 28 July 2015).

1087 Ivan Lysiak Rudnyts'kyi to Ivan Kedryn Rudnytsky, 23 December 1973, p. 1, 84–155, item 804, University of Alberta Archives (hereafter UAA) Ivan L. Rudnytsky Collection, 84–155, item 804. Thanks to John-Paul Himka for sharing this document with the author.

1088 Ivan Lysiak Rudnyts'kyi to Ivan Kedryn Rudnyts'kyi, 26 April 1974, pp. 3-4, UAA, Ivan L. Rudnytsky Collection, 84–155, item 808.

Lysiak-Rudnyts'kyi based his assessment on empirical experience from his own community. We may never be able to reach a consensus on how to classify the OUN. To the empirical historian, taxonomy and terminology may ultimately be of secondary importance to the reconstruction and understanding of the dynamics and actions of the movement. Here, Sven Reichardt's concept of "fascist warfare" could be helpful for our understanding of the OUN(b). The opening of the archives has allowed us to get a good understanding of the anti-Jewish violence in the summer of 1941. While the larger picture on OUN penetration of the auxiliary police in 1941-42 is clear, further microstudies of individual perpetrators remains to be carried out to ascertain the dynamics of the Holocaust on the local level. The same pertains to the OUN(b)/UPA's systematic massacres of the Polish population in Volhynia and East Galicia. On 10-11 July 1943 alone, no less than 99 Polish villages in Volhynia were assaulted, many mass graves and massacre sites of which remain unexamined and undocumented. In 2017 the Ukrainian authorities banned Polish archeologists from conducting excavations of OUN(b)-UPA massacre sites. Following the election of Zelens'kyi, the ban was lifted. Much work in archives and massacre sites remains to be conducted in order to get the full picture of the dynamics and scope of the OUN(b)-UPA massacres. Similarly, research into SB OUN(b) terror, kidnappings, and murder of political opponents in the Displaced Persons' camps in post-war Germany is still in its infancy. Similarly to how scholars of Stalinism have benefited more from studying the practices of the terror, camps, and violence than exegesis of the 1936 Stalin Constitution, inquiry into OUN(b) would learn more from its deeds, rather than its programs or declarations.

In order to separate facts from fiction, no less important is the genealogy, institutional networks, overt and covert government interventions during and after the Cold War, all of which have been factors in an intense politicization of the legacy of the OUN. One explanation for the reluctance to accept the identification of the OUN(b) with fascism has to be sought in identity politics. The more the source base continues to expand, the stronger the arguments for classifying the OUN as fascist appear.

9. "Benderites," UkroNazis and *Rashizm* Studying the Historical Ukrainian Far Right in Times of Disinformation and Hybrid Warfare*

Russia's full-scale war of aggression launched against Ukraine on 24 February 2022 conclusively ended the post-Cold War era. At the time of writing, 14 million people have been displaced, and torture chambers and mass graves of civilians have been uncovered; the UN "has found an array of war crimes, violations of human rights and international humanitarian law" committed in Ukraine.[1089] At a time when Russia is flooding the media with systematic disinformation about "Ukrainian neo-Nazis," is this the right time to problematize the red-and-black tradition of 1941, which the Russian Federation has chosen as the basis for its propaganda to justify its own war crimes? This author contends that it is; the Russian propaganda campaign, which serves as an underpinning to its war of aggression is a reminder of the political liabilities of leaving the difficult past to propagandists and memory managers. Dispassionate inquiry based upon scholarly method is a powerful remedy to disinformation. This article argues against putting critical inquiry on hold at times of war while seeking to problematize the Russian Federation's egregious abuse of history. It also seeks to contextualize the promiscuous use of the terms "fascism," "Nazism," and "genocide" that has accompanied the greatest military conflict in Europe since 1945.

---

* A previous version of this chapter was published in *The Journal of Soviet and Post-Soviet Politics and History*, vol. 9, no. 2 (2023): 11-63.
1089 "Independent International Commission of Inquiry on Ukraine," A77/533, Agenda item 69(c), 18 October 2022, *Office of the United Nations High Commissioner for Human Rights* official website, https://www.ohchr.org/sites/defau lt/files/2022-10/A-77-533-AUV-EN.pdf (accessed 20 October 2022); "Kriget i Ukraina," *Sverige för UNHCR: FN:s flyktingorgan*, https://www.sverigeforunh cr.se/ukraina (accessed 22 October 2022).

Enter Zelens'kyi

On 21 April 2019 incumbent president Petro Poroshenko, running on the slogan "Army, Language, Faith" (*Armiia, Mova, Vira*), was resoundingly defeated as Volodymyr Zelens'kyi (b. 1978) won a landslide 73 per cent of the votes in the second round of the presidential elections. In the parliamentary elections in July that year his party Servant of the People, *Sluha narodu*, won an absolute majority in the *Verkhovna Rada*.[1090] The election of a politically inexperienced, Russophone popular actor of Jewish descent caused alarm and consternation in diaspora circles. Diaspora Ukrainian veteran political analyst Adrian Karatnycky (b. 1954) dismissed Zelens'kyi as "probably the least prepared individual to head a democracy in world history."[1091] The Ukrainians, Karatnycky lamented, "rejected an experienced incumbent— President Petro Poroshenko, who had rebuilt Ukraine's military and competently marshalled international aid and diplomatic support—and took a chance on a political novice."[1092] Karatnycky vented a dismay, he claimed was shared with "much of Ukraine's civil society and intellectual class" about the election of a sitcom actor, the Ukrainian voice of Paddington the Bear.[1093] Karatnycki's is a close associate of Motyl, a cooperation that goes back to the QRDYNAMIC project of the 1970s. Their work straddles the worlds of opinion making, political activism,[1094] and academic

---

1090 Roman Dubasevych and Matthias Schwartz, "Einleitung," in idem., (eds.) *Sirenen des Krieges: Diskursive und affektive Dimensionen des Ukraine-Konflikts* (=*LiteraturForschung*, vol. 38) (Berlin: Kulturverlag Kadmos, 2020), 7-46; and Matthias Schwartz, "Servants of the People: Populism, Nationalism, State-Building, and Virtual Reality in Contemporary Ukraine," *Telos: Critical Theory and the Contemporary*, Heft 195 (2021): 65–81.
1091 Adrian Karatnycky, "The World Just Witnessed the First Entirely Virtual Presidential Campaign," *Politico Magazine*, 24 April 2019, https://www.politico.com/magazine/story/2019/04/24/ukraine-president-virtual-campaign-226711/ (accessed 14 November 2022).
1092 Karatnycki, "The World Just Witnessed."
1093 Mattias Schwartz, "'Diener des Volkes': Eine TV-Serie zwischen satirischer Fiktion und politischer Realität," *INDES: Zeitschrift für Politik und Gesellschaft* 10: no. 1–2 (November 2022): 70–75.
1094 On Karatnycky and Motyl's work with the zpUHVR and Prolog as part of the QRDYNAMIC project in the 1970s, see [redacted], "QRDYNAMIC—New York, N.Y. and Munich, Germany—Support of ZP/UHVR," ANNEX 1

inquiry, and their prominent voices to a significant degree representative of the diaspora elite.[1095] In regards to Zelens'kyi, "Critics [...] see him as insufficiently committed to Ukraine's national and cultural identity," Karatnycky and Motyl opined.[1096] Motyl expressed a frustration felt in many Ukrainian diaspora quarters with the Ukrainians who would not re-elect the incumbent billionaire oligarch Poroshenko: "Poroshenko transformed the broken Ukraine he inherited after the 2014 Maidan Revolution: He made it more independent, more pro-Western, more pro-Ukrainian, more efficient, more secure, more market-oriented, and more democratic."[1097] Motyl denounced the "pretend president" as "disastrous for the country,"[1098] demanding that "the forces that made a Zelensky presidency inevitable should acknowledge re-

---

CONTINUED, PAYROLL, New York Office" National Archives Records Administration, College Park, MD, QRPLUMB Vol. 2, RG 263, NN3-263-02-008. Also available in the CIA's digital reading room at https://www.cia.gov /library/readingroom/docs/QRPLUMB%20%20%20VOL.%202%20%20%28 DEVELOPMENT%20AND%20PLANS%2C%201970-78%29_0018.pdf (accessed 21 December 2020).

1095 A senior member of the executives of the Ukrainian Free Academy of Science (UVAN) and Shevchenko Scientific Society in America (NTShA) characterized Motyl as "one of the best;" his positions are rather representative of the Ukrainian diaspora elite. Anna Procyk, "Challenges and Achievements of Ukrainian Scholarly Institutions in the United States during the Cold War, the Period of Co-existence and the Three Decades of Ukraine's Independence," presentation at the conference "Ukraine in North America: Diaspora Activism, Academic Institutions," The Harriman Institute at Columbia University, 5 November 2022, available online: "Academic Institutions, Libraries, and Archives (11/5/22)," *The Harriman Institute's Youtube channel*, https://www.youtube.com/watch?v=-X0ccs5cSVI&t=3557s (accessed 7 November 2022), 33:00–33:07.

1096 Adrian Karatnycky and Alexander J. Motyl, "The End of Volodymyr Zelensky's Honeymoon," *Foreign Policy*, 26 February 2020, https://foreignpolicy. com/2020/02/26/zelensky-ukraine-russia-corruption/ (accessed 14 November 2022).

1097 Alexander J. Motyl, "Ukraine's Pretend President Now Faces a Real Test," *Foreign Policy*, 22 April 2019, https://foreignpolicy.com/2019/04/22/Ukrain es-pretend-president-now-faces-a-real-test/ (accessed 14 November 2022).

1098 Alexander J. Motyl, "Is Zelensky Ukraine's George Washington?," *Los Angeles Times*, 27 February 2022, available at: https://news.yahoo.com/op-ed-zelens ky-ukraines-george-234659357.html (accessed 14 November 2022).

sponsibility and attempt to contain the damage he may well do to Ukraine's sovereignty."[1099]

Also campaigning against Zelens'kyi was Volodymyr V"iatrovych, who as head of the Ukrainian Institute of National Memory (2014–2019) pursued an ambitious policy of "decommunization," aggressively renaming cities, banning political parties, and drafting laws policing the writing of history.[1100] Through his Center for the Study of the Liberation Movement, TsDVR, V"iatrovych's campaign against Zelens'kyi was coordinated with the network of other OUN(b) front organizations. The émigré OUN(b) were alarmed by Zelens'kyi's victory in the 2019 presidential elections, regarding him as ideologically void and oblivious in regards to "national memory." As Zelens'kyi's Jewish grandfather lost all three of his brothers and his parents in the Holocaust,[1101] the cult of the OUN(b) and UPA, historians Grzegorz Rossoliński-Liebe (b. 1979) and Bastiaan Willems (b. 1985) note, runs contrary to "his self-understanding as a Ukrainian of Jewish descent and a president of a democratic country."[1102] Acidulously, they added: "Although he has worked as a comedian and did not study the Ukrainian past, his family's wartime ordeal makes him adhere to a more accurate historical narrative than many 'professional' historians in Ukraine."[1103]

Homin Ukrainy, the main political organ of the OUN(b) in Canada, took Zelens'kyi to task for erroneously referring to the OUN(b) leader as "Bendera," a mispronunciation many nationalists regard as evidence historical illiteracy and of being under the

---

1099 Motyl, "Ukraine's Pretend President."
1100 Georgiy Kasianov, *Memory Crash: The Politics of History in and around Ukraine, 1980s-2010s* (Budapest: Central University Press, 2022), 255.
1101 Gillian Brockell, "Putin Says He'll 'Denazify' Ukraine: Its Jewish President Lost Family in the Holocaust," *Washington Post*, 25 February 2022, https://www.washingtonpost.com/history/2022/02/25/zelensky-family-jewish-holocaust/ (accessed 28 October 2022).
1102 Grzegorz Rossoliński-Liebe and Bastiaan Willems, "Putin's Abuse of History: Ukrainian 'Nazis', 'Genocide', and a Fake Threat Scenario," *Journal of Slavic Military Studies* 35, no. 1 (2022): 1–10, here: 7.
1103 Rossoliński-Liebe and Willems, "Putin's Abuse of History," 7.

sway of Soviet myths.[1104] The Canadian Banderites were concerned by Zelens'kyi's vague responses to inquiries about the new government's priorities in the field of ideology, during his July 2019 visit to Ottawa—in particular, his noncommittal answers to the hard right's inquiries about the future of the Ukrainian Institute of National Memory (UINP). Zelens'kyi dodged their inquiries about ideology and memory with a deflective laughter:

> Well, this is something they are asking about here. My ideology is very simple: to end the war and restore the economy, and to have people return. Right now I am not even speaking about the Institute of National Memory. I have one ideology: all people, all efforts, all draft laws— all that transpires in our country that has the potential to divide the country is something we have to react to and change.[1105]

Zelens'kyi cautiously characterized the UINP's work under V"iatrovych as "too radical."[1106] "Stepan Bandera is a hero for a certain percentage of Ukrainians, and this is normal and cool," the newly elected president said in a 2019 interview. "He is one person who defended the freedom of Ukraine. But I think that when we call so many streets and bridges by the same name, this is not entirely correct."[1107] Under the new president the Ukrainian authorities quietly abandoned the state policies of glorifying the OUN(b) and UPA. V"iatrovych was dismissed as head of the UINP to the "reticence" of voices in the diaspora who found this "disturbing."[1108]

On 4 December 2019, V"iatrovych was replaced by a low-key cultural studies scholar, Anton Drobovych (b. 1986) of the Drahomanov National Pedagogical University, in what the old director

---

1104 "Zelens'kyi zaproponuvav nazvaty vulytsi na chest' boksera Usyka, a ne 'Bendery'," *Homin Ukrainy*, 15 October 2019, 2.
1105 "Zelens'kyi zaproponuvav nazvaty vulytsi na chest' boksera Usyka"
1106 Roman Medyk and Orest Steciw, "President Zelenskyy's visit to Canada: League of Ukrainian Canadians' view," *The Ukrainian Weekly*, 1 August 2019, https://www.ukrweekly.com/uwwp/president-zelenskyys-visit-to-canada-league-of-ukrainian-canadians-view/ (accessed 5 July 2022).
1107 David Klion, "At the Limits of Nationalism: Confronting Ukraine's Past to Imagine its Future," *Stranger's Guide*, undated (16 November 2022), https://strangersguide.com/articles/at-the-limits-nationalism-klion/ (accessed 23 November 2022).
1108 Medyk and Steciw, "President Zelenskyy's Visit to Canada."

decried as a "U-turn" in the direction of the Institute's Activities.[1109] Under Drobovych's tenure, the UINP's parochialism continued; like his predecessor, he did not master any foreign languages (other than Russian), and the institute remains largely detached from the international scholarly community.[1110] Ending the TsDVR's dominance over the UINP, Drobovych switched the focus of the memorial activism away from the 1930s and 1940s — that is, from World War II, the OUN(b), UPA — to the period of World War I, the UNR, ZUNR, Petliura, Skoropads'kyi, and the Directory — and the 2013–2014 Euromaidan protests.[1111] To the TsDVR's overseas sponsors, this was a red herring; depicting Zelens'kyi as a defeatist, in October 2019 the OUN(b) and other nationalist right-wing groups co-organized a front organization entitled the Capitulation Resistance Movement (*Rukh oporu kapituliatsii*).[1112] The 2022 Russian full-scale assault on Ukraine would, almost overnight, reconfigure much of this political landscape.

Terminological Inflation: "Fascist Russia"

The Ukrainian–Russian conflict has been accompanied by an intensive instrumentalization of the term "fascism." The trivialization is not new; since the 1920s the Soviet Union applied the term "fascism" to its critics with little discernment.[1113] During the Cold

---

1109 Kateryna Iakovenko, "Meet the Man in Charge of Ukraine's National Memory," *openDemocracy*, 11 June 2020, https://www.opendemocracy.net/en/odr/anton-drobovich-natsionalnaya-pamyat-en/ (accessed 14 November 2022).

1110 Volodymyr Pyrih, "Novym dyrektorom Ukrains'koho instytutu natsional'noi pam'iati stav Anton Drobovych," *Zaxid.net*, 4 December 2019, https://zaxid.net/anton_drobovich_biografiya_golovi_institutu_natsionalnoyi_pamyati_n1494067 (accessed 5 December 2019).

1111 Iakovenko, "Meet the Man."

1112 Roman Medyk, "Vizyt Prezydenta Zelens'koho do Kanady: pohliad Ligi Ukraintsiv Kanady," *Homin Ukrainy*, 9 July 2019, 6; and Medyk and Steciw, "President Zelenskyy's visit to Canada."

1113 Manfred Agethen, Eckhard Jesse, and Ehrhart Neubert, *Der missbrauchte Antifaschismus: DDR-Staatsdoktrin und Lebenslüge der deutschen Linken* (Freiburg: Verlag Herder, 2002); Neuber Lea Haro, "Entering a Theoretical Void: The Theory of Social Fascism and Stalinism in the German Communist Party," *Critique: Journal of Socialist Theory* 39, no. 4 (2011): 563–82; and Andreas

War, both sides used the fascist epithet against one another; communism was often referred to as "Red Fascism."[1114] The characterization of the Russian Federation as a fascist system dates back to 1995, when, during the first Chechen War (1994–96), Chechen president Dzhokhdar Dudaev (1944–96), argued that the Russian Federation was a fascist system, coining the term *Rusizm*, which he described as "a particular form of humanity-hating ideology, based on great power chauvinism, total lack of spiritual values and immorality. It differs from the familiar forms of fascism, racism, nationalism by a particular cruelty, to man as well to nature."[1115]

In 2007 Motyl suggested that the Russian Federation was a fascist state,[1116] arguing the advantage of employing the fascist label was that it would enhance analytical clarity: "Calling Putin's system fascist will mark a conceptual breakthrough."[1117] Outside the diaspora echo chamber, Motyl's proposition had limited trac-

---

Umland, "Concepts of Fascism in Contemporary Russia and the West," *Political Studies Review* 3 (2005): 34–49.

1114 Thomas R. Maddux, "Red Fascism, Brown Bolshevism: The American Image of Totalitarianism in the 1930s," *The Historian* 40, no. 1 (November 1977): 85–103.

1115 Dzhokhar Dudaev, "Rusizm—shizofrenicheskaia forma manii mirovogo gospodarstva," *Argument*, 19 March 2014, https://argumentua.com/tsitaty/rusizm-shizofrenicheskaya-forma-manii-mirovogo-gospodstva (accessed 25 October 2022). Dudaev was supported by the ABN and his views echoed in the radical segments of the Ukrainian diaspora. See, for instance "Chechen Republic—Ichkeriya," *ABN Correspondence* XLV, no. 4 (Winter 1994): 15–18; and Oleksander Skypalsky, "Russia Should Not Undermine the Chechens," *ABN Correspondence* LI, no. 3 (Autumn 2000): 1–5.

1116 In 2007 Motyl used the term "an unconsolidated fascist state;" Alexander J. Motyl, "Is Putin's Russia Fascist?," *National Interest Online*, 3 December 2007, http://www.nationalinterest.org/Article.aspx?id=16258; idem., "Surviving Russia's Drift to Fascism," *Kyiv Post*, 17 January 2008 http://www.kyivpost.com/opinion/oped/28182/ (accessed 23 October 2022).

1117 Alexander J. Motyl, "Is Putin's Russia Fascist?," *Atlantic Council*, 23 April 2015, http://www.atlanticcouncil.org/blogs/new-atlanticist/is-putin-s-russia-fascist (accessed 4 October 2022). If Motyl in 2007 was rather alone among political scientists regarding the concept of fascist Russia, following the 2014 Russian invasion of Ukraine the notion of fascist Russia started to gain traction beyond the Ukrainian diaspora, and was embraced by, among others, Yale historian Timothy Snyder; Marlene Laruelle, *Is Russia Fascist?: Unravelling Propaganda East and West* (Ithaca, NY: Cornell University Press, 2021), 16–19.

tion; political scientist Andreas Umland (b. 1967) took Motyl's interpretation to task as "unhelpful, if not misleading." In Umland's view, Motyl obfuscated the issue of Russian fascism by introducing a conceptualization of fascism so wide that "we might find so many 'fascisms' that the term would lose much of its heuristic and communicative value." Therefore, Umland argued, "Motyl's comment is so far unconstructive as he deprives researchers ... of an important analytic tool."[1118]

In Ukraine, Motyl's school prevailed: since 2022, Ukrainian law stipulates that Russian Federation is a Nazi, terrorist state, and totalitarian state engaged in genocide. Law 2265-IX, signed into effect on 22 May 2022, formally designates Russia a "Nazi totalitarian regime" and "state terrorist state," outlawing its propaganda on Ukrainian territory.[1119]

"Nazi Ukraine"

The instrumental use of the fascist label by Ukrainian circles pale in comparison to the use of the term by its north-eastern neighbor. By 2022, Russian propaganda had employed *reductio ad Hitlerum* for nearly two decades; claims of fascism, Nazism, and genocide appeared as *Leitmotifs* in Russian disinformation from 2003 — that is, since before the Orange Revolution.[1120] From their introduction on a rather modest scale, the use was amplified over the next nineteen years, reaching a shrill crescendo in 2022. As Yushchenko's

---

[1118] Andreas Umland, "Is Putin's Russia Really 'fascist'?: A Response to Alexander Motyl," *History News Network*, 26 March 2008.

[1119] Zakon Ukrainy 2265-IX, "Pro zaboronu propahandy rosiis'koho natsysts'koho totalitarnoho rezhymu, zbroinoi ahresii Rosiis'koi Federatsii iak derzhava-terorysta proty Ukrainy, symboliky voennoho vtorhnennia rossiis'koho natsists'koho totalitarnoho rezhymu v Ukrainy," passed by Verkhovna Rada 22 May 2022, https://zakon.rada.gov.ua/laws/show/2265-IX, registered with the Presidium of the Verkhovna Rada under the number 7214, 26 March 2022.

[1120] In response to this misrepresentation, Yushchenko himself invoked the rhetorical figure of genocide, referring to the campaign against him as "political genocide;" Egbert Fortuin, "Ukraine Commits Genocide on Russians: The Term 'Genocide' in Russian Propaganda," *Russian Linguistics* (in advance of publication, 7 September 2022), 12, https://link.springer.com/article/10.1007/s11185-022-09258-5 (accessed 9 September 2022).

Nasha Ukraina electoral bloc—which at that point included Slava Stets'ko's Congress of Ukrainian Nationalists—held a conference in Donetsk in 2003, billboards appeared with Yushchenko in SS uniform performing a raised arm salute. Media clandestinely funded by circles close to the Yanukovych government demonized *Nasha Ukraina* as *nashisty* – that is, *Nasha Ukraina* merged with *fashisty*.[1121] At this time, the "Nazi-genocide" rhetorical figure was not yet used by the Russian government and state media. The more systematic Russian misuse of the term "fascist" began in earnest with the Orange Revolution. From 2006, Russian media applied it systematically to a number of democratic Ukrainian politicians. The misrepresentations were greatly aided by Yushchenko's historical revisionism and his projects of rehabilitating the OUN(b) and UPA. Russian claims of a "cultural genocide" of the Russian-speaking majority population in the Donbas can be dated to 2008.[1122]

Though Russia has taken this terminological misuse further than any other memory actor in the region, mutual allegations of fascism, Nazism, and genocide played central roles in the political culture and rhetoric across the post-Soviet space, where arguments *reductio ad Hitlerum* are staples of the political rhetoric.[1123]

1121 Andrew Wilson, *Ukraine's Orange Revolution* (New Haven, CT: Yale University Press, 2005), 91; Kuzio, *Ukraine: Democratization, Corruption, and the New Russian Imperialism*, 231, 258; and Fortuin, "Ukraine Commits Genocide on Russians," 13.

1122 Fortuin, "Ukraine Commits Genocide on Russians," 14, 17; and "Yushchenko will Push the Verkhovna Rada to Recognize Soldiers of the OUN-UPA," *Kharkiv Human Rights Protection Group*, 16 October 2006, https://khpg.org/en /1160949835 (accessed 12 December 2022). A brainchild of Raphael Lemkin, "cultural genocide," is not included in the United Nations Genocide Convention of 1948. Rossoliński-Liebe and Willems, "Putin's Abuse of History," 7.

1123 Dovile Budrytė, "'We Call It Genocide': Soviet Deportations and Repression in the Memory of Lithuanians," in R. S. Frey (ed.), *The Genocidal Temptation: Auschwitz, Hiroshima, Rwanda, and Beyond* (Lanham, MD: University Press of America, 2004): 79–101; Alexandra Goujon, "'Genozid': A Rallying Cry in Belarus: A Rhetoric Analysis of Some Belarusian Nationalist Texts," *Journal of Genocide Research* 1, no. 3 (1999): 353–66; Rebekah Moore, "'A Crime Against Humanity Arguably Without Parallel in European History': Genocide and the 'Politics' of Victimhood in Western Narratives of the Ukrainian Holodomor," *Australian Journal of Politics and History* 58, no. 3 (September 2012): 367–79; and Anton Weiss-Wendt, *A Rhetorical Crime: Genocide in the Geopolitical*

Activists gathering in Kyiv in November 2008 for the 75th anniversary of the famine rallied around a poster with the text "Holodomors—bloody crimes of communo-fascism."[1124] In 2013 Yanukovych's Party of Regions organized "anti-fascist rallies" in Odesa in May 2013 under the slogan "Fascism will not pass,"[1125] whereas pro-Orange, pro-Euromaidan media regularly referred to the Russian president as "Putler."[1126] The systematic misuse of the term genocide, the promiscuous and mutual accusations of fascism dulled sensibilities; in the Ukrainian case this obfuscated the Holocaust. The historical revisionism, the state cult of the OUN(b) and UPA played into the hands of the Kremlin, aiding their quest to produce the strawman of a "Nazi" Ukraine.[1127] Whereas the Ukrainian revisionism remained, for the most part a rhetorical devise, aimed at rallying political support, in Russia the misrepresentations was constructed as a *casus belli*. When the Russian Federation called upon its soldiers to repeat the exploits of their grandfathers, to take up arms and destroy the "Ukronazis," it was an actual call to arms. A call for an actual military aggression. As Oksana Dudko has shown, "Russia's war against Ukraine has

---

    Discourse of the Cold War (New Brunswick, NJ: Rutgers University Press, 2018).
1124 "Holodomory—kryvavy zlochyny komunofashyzmu." The reference is to Holodomors, in plural, as a strategy of genocidal annihilation of the Ukrainian nation, reading not only the 1932–33 famine but the famines of 1921 and 1947 as acts of genocide aimed at the Ukrainian ethnic group; Kuzio, *Ukraine: Democratization, Corruption, and the New Russian Imperialism*, 258.
1125 Kuzio, *Ukraine: Democratization, Corruption, and the New Russian Imperialism*, 262.
1126 Marlene Laruelle traces the terms Putler—that is, Putin plus Hitler—and Rashizm, i.e. Russia and fascism—to the Ukrainian press; Marlene Laruelle, *Is Russia Fascist?*, 3.
1127 On the instrumental and systematic falsification of history in the Russian Federation, see Anton Weiss-Wendt, *Putin's Russia and the Falsification of History: Reasserting Control of the Past* (London: Bloomsbury Academic Press, 2020); and Anton Weiss-Wendt and Nanci Adler (eds.), *The Future of the Soviet Past: The Politics of History in Putin's Russia* (Bloomington, IN: Indiana University Press, 2021).

become one of the most exemplary cases of how the term 'genocide' can be misused to justify and fuel civilian destruction."[1128]

2014: From Hybrid to Physical Warfare

In the spring of 2014, the Russian Federation went from rhetorical to physical aggression against Ukraine; the popular uprising against Yanukovych triggered contingency plans of hybrid warfare and outright military invasion. In a 19 October 2014 interview Russian Foreign Minister Sergei Lavrov stated, "We cannot lose Ukraine [...] Ukraine is for us a brotherly people, with whom we share historical, cultural, philosophical and civilizational roots, to say nothing about language and literature."[1129] The Kremlin reserved for itself the agency to make the key decisions on the geopolitics of Ukraine, over the heads of the citizens of Ukraine and in blatant violation of international law. In order to deny Ukrainian sovereignty Russian hybrid warfare included measures to systematically misrepresent its democratically elected government as a "junta," reminiscent of dictatorial regimes in South America.[1130] This systematic misrepresentation may have been accepted by significant sections of the increasingly isolated Russian society. Beyond Russia its effectiveness was limited. In Ukraine, the 2014 invasion discredited Russia in the eyes of the bulk of the people; the Putin regime's criminal assault served as midwife for the Ukrainian nation. Its attempts to stir up a separatist "uprising" in Kharkiv and Odesa backfired, and Russian proxies failed to control even the full Donetsk and Luhansk *oblasti*. From the mid-2010s, the Russian rhetoric radicalized. Its officials now openly called into question the very existence of the Ukrainian nation.[1131]

1128 Oksana Dudko, "A Conceptual Limbo of Genocide: Russian Rhetoric, Mass Atrocities in Ukraine, and the Current Definition's Limits," *Canadian Slavonic Papers/Revue Canadienne des Slavistes* 64, nos. 2–3 (2022): 133–45, here: 140.
1129 Winfried Schneider-Deters, *Ukrainische Schicksaalsjahre 2013-2019: Band 1. Der Volksaufstand auf dem Majdan im Winter 2013/2014* (Berlin: Berliner Wissenschafts-Verlag, 2021), 465.
1130 Fortuin, "Ukraine Commits Genocide on Russians," 15.
1131 Schneider-Deters, *Ukrainische Schicksaalsjahre, Band 1*, 463–65, 466.

"On the historical unity of Russians and Ukrainians"

In his July 2021 essay "On the historical unity of Russians and Ukrainians," Putin articulated the ideological underpinnings of the forthcoming assault. The edge was aimed at Lenin and the Bolsheviks, who Putin described as having robbed Russia and chopped up the country:

> modern Ukraine is entirely the product of the Soviet era ... it was shaped — for a significant part — on the lands of historical Russia ... The Bolsheviks treated the Russian people as inexhaustible material for their social experiments ... It is no longer important what exactly the idea of the Bolsheviks leaders who were chopping the country in to pieces was ... One fact is crystal clear: Russia was robbed, indeed.[1132]

The Russian autocrat insisted that Russians and Ukrainians constituted one people, one unity, ruined by malicious foreign interests. Putin reneged on a century of Soviet and Russian policy, presenting Ukraine as a renegade province which he reserved himself the right to control and subjugate: "The owners of this project took as a basis the old groundwork of the Polish-Austrian ideologists to create an 'anti-Moscow Russia.' And there is no need to deceive anyone that this is being done in the interest of the people of Ukraine."[1133] The Russian president claimed "that Russians and Ukrainians were one people—a single whole. These words were not driven by some short-term considerations or prompted by the current political context. It is what I have said on numerous occasions and what I firmly believe."[1134]

Putin's 2021 essay provided the ideological foundation to revert Russia not to the pre-1991, but pre-1918 geopolitical situation:

> the situation in Ukraine...involved a forced change of identity ... It would not be an exaggeration to say that the path of forced assimilation, the formation of an ethnically pure Ukrainian state, aggressive towards Russia, is comparable in its consequences to the use of weapons of mass destruction against us. As a result of such a harsh and artificial division of Russians

---

[1132] Vladimir Putin, "On the Historical Unity of Russians and Ukrainians," *President of Russia official website*, 12 July 2021, http://en.kremlin.ru/events/president/news/66181 (accessed 27 October 2022).
[1133] Putin, "On the Historical Unity of Russians and Ukrainians"
[1134] Putin, "On the Historical Unity of Russians and Ukrainians"

and Ukrainians, the Russian people in all may decrease by hundreds of thousands or even millions.[1135]

As his military planners prepared the full-scale assault on Ukraine, the Russian autocrat insisted that it was not the Russian aggressor, but Ukraine's Western partners that denied Ukraine its sovereignty: "In the anti-Russia project, there is no place for a sovereign Ukraine or for the political forces that are trying to defend its real independence."[1136] In an Orwellian fashion Putin invoked the language of popular sovereignty and democracy: "Russia has never been and will never be 'anti-Ukraine'. And what Ukraine will be — it is up to its citizens to decide."[1137]

A Botched *Blitzkrieg*

Until the archives become available to researchers the full picture behind the disastrous decision to launch the war cannot be reconstructed. Investigative journalists have, however, been able to reconstruct some of the key events of the botched Russian assault in some detail.[1138] The plan was to seize Kyiv in three to four days while Spetsnaz special forces would track down and kill Zelens'kyi if necessary, installing a puppet regime in his place. Having captured Kyiv, Kharkiv, and Chernihiv, the strategy of the Russian invaders was to push westward, occupying the territory

---

1135 Putin, "On the Historical Unity of Russians and Ukrainians"
1136 Putin, "On the Historical Unity of Russians and Ukrainians"
1137 Putin, "On the Historical Unity of Russians and Ukrainians"
1138 Caroline Anders, "The Lead-Up to the War in Ukraine Revisited," *Washington Post*, 19 August 2022, https://www.washingtonpost.com/politics/2022/08/19/lead-up-war-ukraine-revisited/; Greg Miller and Catherine Bolton, "Russia's Spies Misread Ukraine and Misled Kremlin as War Loomed," *Washington Post*, 19 August 2022, https://www.washingtonpost.com/world/interactive/2022/russia-fsb-intelligence-ukraine-war/; Shane Harris, Karen DeYoung, Isabelle Khurdursyan, "Road to War: U.S. Struggled to Convince Allies, and Zelensky, of Risk of Invasion," *Washington Post*, 16 August 2022, https://www.washingtonpost.com/national-security/interactive/2022/ukraine-road-to-war/; Paul Sonne, Isabelle Khurdursyan, and Sergey Morgurov, "Battle for Kyiv: Ukrainian Valor, Russian Blunders Combined to Save the Capital," *Washington Post*, 24 August 2022, https://www.washingtonpost.com/national-security/interactive/2022/kyiv-battle-ukraine-survival/ (all accessed 5 December 2022).

up to a north-south line between Moldova and western Belarus, leaving a rump Ukrainian state to the west of that line.[1139]

The Russian military, however, demonstrated a remarkable lack of prowess. Failing to capture Kyiv, they chaotically retreated from the Kyiv and Chernihiv oblasts, and were routed out of Kharkiv oblast. The confused and poorly led troops were disorganized and militarily ineffective.

US intelligence agencies appears to have ascertained Russia's contingency plans with some precision, but appear to have underestimated the level of corruption and incompetence in the Russian forces. The CIA, according to leaked intelligence reports, predicted Kyiv would fall quickly, in a week, or two at the most.[1140] Zelens'kyi's calm, his composed and defiant demeanor helped uphold morale and likely contributed to taking the edge off the "shock and awe effect" of the Russian *Blitzkrieg*.[1141] At a crucial moment, when the future of Ukraine appeared to be in the balance, Zelens'kyi did not flinch: "When it became clear that the agency's predictions of a rapid Russian victory had been wrong, the Biden administration sent the clandestine assets that had been pulled out of Ukraine back into the country, the military and intelligence officials said."[1142] The FSB, for whom Ukraine was the most important intelligence mission outside Russia, "either did not fathom how forcefully Ukraine would respond, Ukrainian and Western officials said, or did understand but couldn't or wouldn't convey such sober assessment to Russian President Vladimir Putin."[1143]

1139 Harris, DeYoung, and Khurdursyan, "Road to War."
1140 James Risen and Ken Klippenstein, "The CIA thought Putin would Quickly Conquer Ukraine: Why Did They Get it So Wrong?," *The Intercept*, 5 October 2022, https://theintercept.com/2022/10/05/russia-ukraine-putin-cia/ (accessed 27 October 2022).
1141 Shane Harris, Karen DeYoung, and Isabelle Khurdursyan, "Road to War: U.S. Struggled to Convince Allies, and Zelensky, of Risk of Invasion," *Washington Post*, 16 August 2022, https://www.washingtonpost.com/national-security/interactive/2022/ukraine-road-to-war/ (accessed 27 October 2022).
1142 Risen and Klippenstein, "The CIA thought Putin would Quickly Conquer Ukraine."
1143 Greg Miller and Catherine Bolton, "Russia's Spies Misread Ukraine and Misled Kremlin as War Loomed," *Washington Post*, 19 August 2022,

In a pre-recorded televised appeal to the Ukrainian people released as he launched his war of aggression, Putin openly called for Ukraine's armed forces to commit treason:

> Do not allow neo-Nazis and Benderites [sic!] to use your children, your wives and the elderly as a human shield. Take power into your own hands. It seems that it will be easier for us to come to an agreement than with this gang of drug addicts and neo-Nazis who settled in Kyiv and took all Ukrainian people hostage.[1144]

Apparently, the leadership of the Russian Federation had expected its aggression would be welcomed by the Ukrainians; it is otherwise hard to make sense of the astonishing attempt to subjugate 45 million Ukrainians and a European country of 600,000 square kilometres with 190,000 soldiers; Ludendorff budgeted 53 divisions in March 1918, Hitler deployed 797,000 men for Ukraine in 1941, whereas the Warsaw Pact deployed a quarter million to subjugate ten million Czechoslovaks. The Russian leaders apparently envisioned a short, swift war. On 26 February, at 8 AM sharp, seemingly by mistake, *RIA Novosti* released an article declaring victory, praising the Russian success in having solved the Ukrainian "problem," claiming that "Ukraine has returned to Russia" through the military action, rectifying that "terrible catastrophe" of the collapse of the Soviet Union in 1991. The result of the successful military action supposedly heralded "Russia's return of its historical space and its place in the world," which, according to the officious article, puts the Anglo-Saxons of Europe and the US in their place since "Western global domination can be considered completely and finally over."[1145] According to *RIA Novosti*, the swift Russian victory established a new geopolitical world order: "Ukraine, as an anti-Russia, will no longer exist. Rus-

---

https://www.washingtonpost.com/world/interactive/2022/russia-fsb-intelligence-ukraine-war/ (accessed 5 December 2022).
1144 "Putin References Neo-Nazis and Drug Addicts in Bizarre Speech to Russian Security Council—Video," *The Guardian*, 25 February 2022, https://www.theguardian.com/world/video/2022/feb/25/putin-references-neo-nazis-and-drug-addicts-in-bizarre-speech-to-russian-security-council-video (accessed 5 July 2022).
1145 Alistair Coleman, "Ukraine Crisis: Russian News Agency Deleted Victory Editorial," *BBC News*, 28 February 2022.

sia restores its historical completeness [*polnota*], gathering the Russian world, the Russian people together—through uniting the Great Russians, Belarusians, and Little Russians."[1146]

With the assault on Ukraine and the international security order, Russia exited the community of civilized states, becoming an outlaw, rogue state.

The Russian Federation's blunt rejection of international norms reverberated not only among former Soviet republics of the "near abroad" and former satellites of the Warsaw Pact; Russia reserved itself a veto right over the foreign policy decisions of sovereign states further afield. Already during his first visit to Helsinki as head of state in September 2001 Putin bluntly told his Finnish hosts that he wished Finland to remain neutral and stay out of NATO.[1147] In December 2021, as the Russian Federation mobilized for its full-scale assault on Ukraine it demanded that NATO be reduced in size to the states which were members of that organization in May 1997, presenting Washington with a draft treaty, in which the US "shall undertake to prevent further eastward expansion of the North Atlantic Treaty Organization and deny accession to the Alliance to the states of the former Union of Soviet Socialist Republics."[1148] This open disdain for its neighbors to chose their own foreign and security arrangements backfired. The lack of a reaction from some European partners to

---

[1146] Petr Akopov, "Nastuplenie Rossii i novogo mira," *RIA Novosti*, 26 February 2022, https://web.archive.org/web/20220226051154/https://ria.ru/20220226/rossiya-1775162336.html (accessed 5 July 2022).

[1147] Stefan Lundberg, "Putin önskar ett neutralt Finland," *Dagens Nyheter*, 2 September 2001.

[1148] Henry Meyer and Ilya Arkhipov, "Russia Demands NATO Pullback in Security Talks With U.S." *Bloomberg*, 17 December 2021, https://www.bloomberg.com/news/articles/2021-12-17/russia-demands-nato-return-to-1997-in-security-treaty-proposals (accessed 4 October 2022); "Treaty between The United States of America and the Russian Federation on Security Guarantees," 17 December 2021, *Ministerstvo inostrannykh del Rossiiskoi Federatsii*, 17 December 2021, https://mid.ru/ru/foreign_policy/rso/nato/1790818/?lang=en (accessed 4 October 2022).

the Russian declaration convinced Finnish president Sauli Niinistö (b. 1948) about the need to join NATO.[1149]

In Sweden, the ruling Social Democrats remained opposed to join NATO. Still one week prior to the Russian assault on Ukraine, Swedish foreign Minster Ann Linde (b. 1961) had declared that her country's non-allied status "served Sweden well."[1150] The naked Russian aggression and Niinistö's decision would soon force their hand. On 25 February 2022, one day after the assault on Ukraine, Kremlin spokesperson Mariia Zakharova (b. 1975) stated that "accession of Finland and Sweden to NATO ... would have serious military and political consequences, which would require our country to take response steps."[1151] After some initial hesitation, on 30 March 2022, Swedish Prime Minister Magdalena Andersson (b. 1967) opened up the path to a Swedish membership in NATO on the grounds that the Russian aggression had fundamentally changed the security situation in Europe.[1152] According to Lena Hallin (b. 1961), the head of Swedish Military Intelligence and Security Service, the Swedish and Finnish NATO applications had not been part of the Russian calculations.[1153] In April, ex-

---

1149 Karin Thurfjell, "Ninistö: Kärnvapen kommer inte på fråga," *Svenska Dagbladet*, 13 May 2022, https://www.svd.se/a/y4B1g2/niinisto-jag-komm er-att-ringa-putin-om-nato (accessed 2 October 2022); Kristian Klarskov, "Finlands præsident er ekspert i Putin: Når han bruger humor, skal man for alvor være vågen," *Politiken*, 1 January 2023, https://politiken.dk/udland/art9121 144/Når-han-bruger-humor-skal-man-for-alvor-være-vågen (acccessed 3 January 2023)
1150 Peter Wallberg and Maria Davidsson, "Så gick det till när Sverige sade ja till Nato," *Svenska Dagbladet*, 16 May 2022, https://www.svd.se/a/V97Pd4/sa-gick-det-till-nar-sverige-sa-ja-till-nato (accessed 2 October 2022).
1151 Nitin J. Ticku, "Russia Sends Bone-Chilling Message to Sweden & Finland; Threatens 'Military Implications' If They Go The Ukraine Way," *The Eurasian Times*, 25 February 2022, https://eurasiantimes.com/russia-sends-bone-chilli ng-message-to-sweden-threatens-with-military-implications-if-they-go-the-u kraine-way/ (accessed 4 October 2022).
1152 Wallberg, Davidsson, "Så gick det till när Sverige sade ja till Nato"; and Maggie Strömberg and Torbjörn Nilsson, "Så gick det till när Sverige svängde om Nato," *Svenska Dagbladet*, 2 July 2022 https://www.svd.se/a/Qy1gXx /sa-gick-det-till-nar-magdalena-andersson-kovande-om-nato (accessed 2 October 2022).
1153 "Mustchefen Lena Hallin: Sveriges och Finlands Natoansökan fanns inte med i Rysslands kalkyl," *Dagens Nyheter*, 10 June 2022, https://www.dn.se/sveri

president Dmitrii Medvedev (b. 1965) added that Russia would have to "strengthen its land, naval and air forces in the Baltic Sea to restore military balance" if the two countries were to join NATO: "There can be no more talk of any nuclear-free status for the Baltic—the balance must be restored."[1154] The bluster again backfired—in another sharp reversal of decades-long policies, the Finnish and Swedish governments now opened for the possibility of stationing NATO nuclear weapons on their territories.[1155]

Germany, long reluctant to meet the NATO guidelines for defense spending, and which had further increased its dependency on Russian energy following the 2014 invasion of Ukraine, now reconsidered decades of eastern policies. Its new chancellor Olaf Scholz (b. 1958) heralded a *Zeitenwende*; a doubling of Germany's defense expenditures, and an indication that the federal republic would now be willing to shoulder its share of the European defense. Poland, Lithuania, and Latvia, who held the border when Lukashenka in July 2021 sought to weaponize asylum seekers and threatened to "flood" the EU with migrants, opened their borders to Ukrainian refugees. Across the board, Putin's policies backfired disastrously.

From Pretend President into George Washington and Moses

Zelens'kyi, who may not have distinguished himself during his initial term in office, now quickly took the lead, courageously

---

ge/mustchefen-lena-hallin-sveriges-och-finlands-natoansokan-fanns-inte-med-i-rysslands-kalkyl/ (accessed 27 October 2022).

1154 "Russia's Medvedev Issues Warning about Finland, Sweden NATO Membership," YLE, 14 April 2022, https://yle.fi/news/3-12405420 (accessed 4 October 2022).

1155 "Överbefälhavare Micael Bydén om kärnvapen på svensk mark: 'Inga förbehåll'," *Sveriges Television*, 1 November 2022, https://www.svt.se/nyheter/inrikes/forsvarsmakten-haller-presstraff-1; and Tea Oscarsson, "Försvarsministern stänger inte dörren för kärnvapen i Sverige," *Svenska Dagbladet*, 4 November 2022, https://www.svd.se/a/nQyrro/forsvarsministern-oppnar-for-karnvapen-i-sverige (both accessed 16 November 2022).

defying the Russian assault.[1156] His background as a "pretend president" now unexpectedly turned out to be an asset; the actor skilfully shouldered the role of a wartime leader, rejecting Western offers of help to leave Kyiv. The war's most famous—though unsubstantiated—quote is attributed to Zelens'kyi. Turning down a U.S. offer of evacuation, the president was supposed to have said: "The fight is here; I need ammunition, not a ride."[1157] Through his personal bravery Zelens'kyi became a unifying symbol of resistance, and one of the most admired politicians worldwide.[1158] In his trademark green military T-shirt, Zelens'kyi emerged as something akin to a modern Winston Churchill, a unifying, defiant symbol of resistance in the face of naked aggression. A *New York Times* op-ed summed up the reason for the veneration:

> We admire Zelensky because of who and what he faces. Vladimir Putin represents neither a nation nor a cause, only a totalitarian ethos. The Russian dictator stands for the idea that truth exists to serve power, not the other way around, and that politics is in the business of manufacturing propaganda for those who will swallow it and impose terror on those who

---

1156 Confidence in Zelens'kyi's prowess as commander in chief had been weak. In a November 2021 poll by the Kyiv International Institute of Sociological Studies the question "In the event of a full-scale Russian invasion, which is now being warned about by Ukrainian and foreign intelligence services, will Volodymyr Zelens'kyi be able to effectively function as Supreme Commander and organize the defense of the country?" 51.6 per cent answered "no," and only 35.9 per cent in the affirmative; "Suspil'no-politychni nastroi naselennia Ukrainy: Aktual'ni politychni podii za rezul'tatamy telefonnoho opytuvannia, provedenoho 26-29 lystopada 2021 roku," *Kyivs'kyi mizhnarodnyi instytut sotsiolohii*, https://www.kiis.com.ua/?lang=ukr&cat=reports&id=1074&page=1 (accessed 27 October 2022); and Mats Larsson, "Kriget har inte gått som någon tänkt sig," *Expressen*, 24 August 2022, https://www.expressen.se/kronikorer/mats-larsson/kriget-har-inte-gatt-som-nagon-tankt-sig/ (accessed 24 August 2022).

1157 Glenn Kessler, "Zelensky's Famous Quote of 'Need Ammo, Not a Ride' Not Easily Confirmed," *Washington Post*, 6 March 2022, https://www.washingtonpost.com/politics/2022/03/06/zelenskys-famous-quote-need-ammo-not-ride-not-easily-confirmed/ (accessed 28 October 2022).

1158 In the U.S. Zelens'kyi became the most admired world leader with a popularity eclipsing President Biden; Sarah Mucha, "Zelensky is America's Most Popular World Leader," *Axios*, 6 April 2022, https://www.axios.com/2022/04/06/zelensky-is-americas-most-popular-world-leader (accessed 28 October 2022).

will not. Ultimately, the aim of this idea isn't the mere acquisition of power of territory. It's the eradication of conscience.[1159]

Russia's grotesque propaganda offensive was even more disastrous. Its clumsy attempts to instrumentalize genocide backfired. Even Zelens'kyi's harshest critics now realized the political potential a Jewish president offered. "The fact that Zelensky is a Russian-speaking Ukrainian Jew is of immense symbolic as well as political importance.... His comedy poked fun at patriotic Ukrainians, and he did not appear to pay attention to the way he personifies three identities. But all that has changed in the last few days and weeks," Motyl opined. The "pretend president," recently denounced as "disastrous for the country," the political scientist now surmised, "will go down in history as a new type of Ukrainian patriot who fought for his homeland's freedom. And in the end, he may deserve to be considered Ukraine's George Washington."[1160] Even the Banderites were enchanted. In a November 2022 lecture for the League of Ukrainian Canadians (LUC) in Toronto, Canadian geographer Lubomyr Luciuk (b. 1953) noted "thankfully, we have a president, in the person of Volodymyr Zelenskyi, who is Ukraine's Moses … a man that has risen to heights no one of us who've met him had expected."[1161]

Whither Genocide?

Since the years of *hlasnist*, the term "genocide" has occupied a central role in the political rhetoric in Ukraine. The 1986 Chernobyl nuclear catastrophe was characterized as genocide in both

---

1159 Bret Stephens, "Why We Admire Zelensky," *New York Times*, 19 April 2022, https://www.nytimes.com/2022/04/19/opinion/why-we-admire-zelensky.html (accessed 28 October 2022).
1160 Alexander J. Motyl, "Op-Ed: Is Zelensky Ukraine's George Washington?," *Los Angeles Times*, 27 February 2022, https://news.yahoo.com/op-ed-zelensky-ukraines-george-234659357.html (accessed 14 November 2022).
1161 "Forum TV: Dr. Lubomyr Luciuk, Book Presentation," LUC event "Operation Payback," organized by Orest Steciw, The Old Mill Inn, Toronto, *Youtube* channel, Forum TV Canada, 28 November 2022, https://www.youtube.com/watch?v=q8shFxO85oY (accessed 30 November 2022), quote at 46:48-47:07. The LUC, founded in 1948 as the League for the Liberation of Ukraine, is the front organization of the OUN(b) in Canada.

Ukraine and Belarus.[1162] For the construction of a new, nationalizing historical narrative post-Soviet memory activists have centered their explanatory and illustrative schemes around the word "genocide."[1163] As historian Nicolas Dreyer of the Otto-Friedrich Universität in Bamberg demonstrates, "it has been greatly banalized, being used hyperbolically in all sorts of contexts of every-day and social life."[1164] It is of little consequence that "genocide" is a legal term, codified and regulated in binding international treaties, the most important being the 1948 UN Convention on the Prevention of the Crime of Genocide.[1165]

Regional memory actors have been less than consistent in their utilizing the term. While Ukraine lobbied governments around the world to recognize the 1932–33 famine as genocide, it opposed, and opposes recognition of the massacres of Armenians in 1915 as genocide; the Ukrainian foreign ministry is instructed always to place the term "Armenian genocide" within quotation marks.[1166] Poland's 2016 recognition of the 1943 Volhynian massa-

---

[1162] Adriana Petryna, "A Technical Error: Measures of Life after Chernobyl," *Social Identities: Journal for the Study of Race, Nation, and Culture* 4, no. 1 (1998): 72–92.

[1163] Kasianov, *Memory Crash*, 178, 184. The over-utilization of the term "genocide" rivals that of "fascism," and often they are used in tandem. For one recent example, see Taras Kuzio in collaboration with Stefan Jajecznyk-Kelman, *Fascism and Genocide: Russia's War Against Ukraine* (Stuttgart: ibidem-Verlag, 2023).

[1164] Nicolas Dreyer, "Genocide, *Holodomor* and Holocaust Discourse as Echo of Historical Injury and as Rhetorical Radicalization in the Russian–Ukrainian Conflict of 2013–2018," *Journal of Genocide Research* 20, no. 4 (2018): 545–64, here: 555–56.

[1165] On the 1948 genocide convention, see Malin Isaksson, *The Holocaust and Genocide in History and Politics: A Study of the Discrepancy between Human Rights' Law and International Politics* (Gothenburg: University of Gothenburg School of Global Studies, 2010); Michelle Jean Penn, "The Extermination of Peaceful Soviet Citizens: Aron Trenin and International Law" (Ph.D. Dissertation, University of Colorado, 2017); Philippe Sands, *East West Street: On the Origins of Genocide and Crimes Against Humanity* (London: Weidenfeld & Nicholson, 2017); and Anton Weiss-Wendt, *The Soviet Union and the Gutting of the UN Genocide Convention* (Madison, WI: The University of Wisconsin Press, 2017).

[1166] Per Anders Rudling, "Institutes of Trauma Re-Production in a Borderland: Poland, Ukraine, and Lithuania," in Ninna Mörner (ed.), *Constructions and Instrumentalization of the Past: A Comparative Study on Memory Management in the*

cres as genocide was angrily rejected by Kyiv. Various atrocities have been upgraded to genocide rather selectively, in accordance with shifting geopolitical interests. Nicolas Dreyer notes how, "Following the Russian annexation of the Crimea, after two decades of neglecting the Crimean Tatars, and of much indifference towards their interests and history, Ukraine under President Petro Poroshenko's leadership placed emphasis on framing the Tatar deportation of 1944 as 'genocide'."[1167]

Dreyer shows how the instrumental use of the term "genocide" casts Russia and the Russian-speaking population in Ukraine as victim of Ukrainian and Western policies: "It also creates the sense of an extraordinary threat being built up to which Russia must react with extraordinary measures ... and it serves to externalize the culpability for Russia's resulting international isolation and worsening of her social and economic situation. It therefore fulfils a classic propaganda function of radicalizing public opinion."[1168]

Given the political use of the term "genocide," the employment of explicit references to the Shoah are unsurprising. "Just as the Nazis exterminated Jewish people during World War II, Russians are exterminating people in Ukraine today," one Ukrainian academic argued.[1169] Less than a week after Putin's launch of his full-scale assault on Ukraine, Alexander Motyl ascertained genocide as a fait accompli, already in the past tense:

> Will Russian President Vladimir Putin commit genocide in Ukraine? The short answer is that he already has, at least according to the definition provided by the Convention on the Prevention and Punishment of the Crime of Genocide ... Ukrainians are to Putin as Jews were to Hitler: a menace that must be exterminated. Unsurprisingly, one of Putin's leading propa-

---

Region (=*CBEES State of the Region Report 2020*) (Huddinge: Centre for Baltic and East European Studies, 2020), 55–68, here: 63.
1167 Dreyer, "Genocide, *Holodomor* and Holocaust Discourse," 553.
1168 Dreyer, "Genocide, *Holodomor* and Holocaust Discourse," 552-553.
1169 Viacheslav Kudlai, "A Brief Diary of a Witness," *Baltic Worlds* XV, nos. 1–2 (June 2022): 4–7, here: 7.

gandists has even suggested that Ukrainians be subjected to a "final solution."[1170]

Motyl's former Prolog/QRPLUMB associate Taras Kuzio, operating within the same analytical paradigm, characterized Putin's July, 2021 essay as "the Kremlin's equivalent of Adolf Hitler's treatise *Mein Kampf* justifying the needs for a final solution to the Ukraininian and Jewish 'questions' respectively." According to Kuzio, "the goal of denazification was the Kremlin's equivalent of the Nazi's final solution, the former of Ukrainians and the latter of Jews. Russia's FSB would act in the same manner as the Nazi's Einsatzgruppen paramilitary death squads in searching out ene-

---

[1170] Alexander Motyl, "Vladimir Putin Is Committing Genocide in Ukraine," *1945*, 2 March 2022, https://www.19fortyfive.com/2022/03/vladimir-putin-is-co
mmitting-genocide-in-ukraine/ (accessed 20 July 2022). Motyl's criteria for what constitutes genocide are rather inconsistent. In 2016 when Poland recognized the OUN(b)/UPA's massacres of Poles in Volhynia as genocide, Motyl sounded alarm about "trivializing genocide," dismissing this as a "dangerous distraction" since "the concept of genocide will be trivialized and lost in demagoguery." He went on to argue, "Unfortunately, the Genocide Convention does not reasonably distinguish between genocide and lesser atrocities. Its definition of genocide is so broad as to include everything from a hate crime to the Holocaust." The scope of the OUN-UPA murders, he asserted, was insufficient to qualify as them genocide. Moreover, Motyl contended, "the killings took place in the midst of armed conflict between Poles and Ukrainians ... neither side was helpless .... if thousands or hundreds of deaths constitute a genocide, then the history of Ukrainians and Poles, like the history of all nations everywhere, becomes transformed into an endless series of 'genocides';" Alexander J. Motyl, "Trivializing Genocide: A Dangerous Distraction," *World Affairs Blog*, 18 August 2016, https://web.archive.org/web/20160825042823/http://www.worldaffairsjournal.org/blog/alexander-j-motyl/trivializing-genocide-dangerous-distraction (accessed 19 August 2016). If the numbers were a crucial factor as to why Volhynia could *not* constitute genocide, in regards to the *Holodomor* the opposite was the case: "the question of numbers ... is irrelevant to and a distraction from the far more important issues ..., namely, the existential reality of the Holodomor, the enormous suffering that its victims experienced, and the genocidal nature of Stalin's assault on Ukrainian peasants;" Bohdan Klid and Alexander J. Motyl, "Introduction," in Bohdan Klid and Alexander J. Motyl (eds.), *The Holodomor Reader: A Sourcebook on the Famine of 1932-1933 in Ukraine* (Edmonton: CIUS Press, 2012), xxxii.

mies and denationalizing, torturing, deporting, and liquidating them."[1171]

Yet, Putin's rhetoric suggests something else; if Hitler regarded Jews an anti-race, to be subjected to isolation, expulsion, and annihilation, Putin insisted on a shared origin, identity, and nationality with Ukrainians: "We are not just close neighbors; we are actually, as I've repeatedly said, the same nation. Kiev is the mother of Russian cities. Ancient Rus is our common origin; we cannot live without each other."[1172]

Ukrainian philosopher Volodymyr Yermolenko (b. 1980) offers an interpretation that seeks to reconcile Putin's claims with the Hitler/genocidal interpretive frame—he characterizes Putin's attitudes to Ukrainians as follows: "Jews were for the Nazis 'the Other' which wanted to 'be like you.' Ukrainians are for Russians 'like us' which now want to be 'the Other.' And therefore have to be exterminated as major enemy par excellence ('anti-Russia')."[1173]

To Putin and his ideologues of revenge, Ukraine had become an "anti-Russia"—an unnatural, artificial and illegitimate polity, a satanical neo-Nazi polity Frankenstein's monster of sorts, subjecting its own, triune Russian people to autogenocide. Putin's analysis is not entirely consistent: as "Neanderthals" he places Ukraini-

---

1171 Kuzio with Jajecznyk-Kelman, *Fascism and Genocide: Russia's War Against Ukraine*, 79; Taras Kuzio, "The Russian Imperialist War Against Ukraine," 2 December 2022, event organized by Orest Steciw and the LUC under the auspices of the OUN(b)'s Ucrainica Research Institute, Toronto, "Forum TV: Taras Kuzio," posted 11 December 2022, https://www.youtube.com/watch?v=_Ciy0TZN51o, quote at 7:59–8:03 (accessed 12 December 2022). Curiously, Kuzio made this analysis without having read *Mein Kampf*. Taras Kuzio, "Chy mav Bandera ratsiio shchodo Rosii ta rosiian? Chomu Rosiia rozpochala henotsyd ukraintsiv," lecture at the Ukrainian Catholic University, L'viv, June 15, 2023
1172 Denys Kiryukhin, "Russia and Ukraine: The Clash of Conservative Projects," *European Politics and Society* 17, no. 4 (2016): 438–52, 449, citing Vladimir Putin, "Obrashchenie Prezidenta Rossiiskoi Federatsii," *RF President official website*, 18 March 2014, http://kremlin.ru/events/president/news/20603.
1173 Yermolenko, cited in Mikhail Fishman, "Putin's Dehumanized Russia," *The Russia File: A Blog of the Kennan Institute*, 7 June 2022, https://www.wilsoncenter.org/blog-post/putins-dehumanized-russia (accessed 14 December 2022).

ans beyond the pale of humanity—while at the same time insisting on sharing blood, lineage, and community with them.[1174]

The attempts to equate Putin with Hitler and *Mein Kampf* resulted in confused and muddled analyses, of limited help as a tool to understand the actions of the Russian regime.

The full Russian assault re-energized Ukrainian genocide claims which had been heard from the start of the Russian proxy war in Donbas from 2014.[1175] Zelens'kyi regularly invoked the term genocide to describe what is taking place in Ukraine, and opinion polls suggest the vast majority of Ukrainians share that assessment.[1176] On 14 April 2022 the Rada passed declaration 2188-IX which established that the Russian Federation was "committing genocide in Ukraine."[1177] Other legislatures have followed suit: Canada, Poland, Lithuania, Latvia, the Czech Republic, and Ireland have declared the abuses committed by the Russian army constitute genocide.[1178]

Leading authorities on international law such as Amherst Law Professor Douglas R. Lawrence (b. 1959) question whether

---

1174 Testimonies by Ukrainian refugees in the Western democracies are currently being documented to be used for post-war trials. See, for instance, "Ukraine: Apparent War Crimes in Russia-Controlled Areas. Summary Executions, Other Grave Abuses by Russian Forces," *Human Rights Watch*, 3 April 2022, https://www.hrw.org/news/2022/04/03/ukraine-apparent-war-crimes-russia-controlled-areas (accessed 28 October 2022).
1175 Matthew Kupfer and Thomas De Waal, "Crying Genocide: Use and Abuse of Political Rhetoric in Russia and Ukraine," *Carnegie Endowment for International Peace*, 28 July 2014, https://carnegieendowment.org/2014/07/28/crying-genocide-use-and-abuse-of-political-rhetoric-in-russia-and-ukraine-pub-56265 (accessed 20 July 2022).
1176 89 per cent of the respondents to a 27 April 2022 poll supported the recognition of the actions of the Russian troops in Ukraine as "genocide of the Ukrainian people;" "The Tenth National Survey: Ideological Markers of the War (April 27, 2022)," *Sotsiolohichna hrupa Reitinh*, 5 May 2022, https://ratinggroup.ua/en/research/ukraine/desyatyy_obschenacionalnyy_opros_ideologicheskie_markery_voyny_27_aprelya_2022.html (accessed 20 July 2022).
1177 "Postnova Verkhovnoi Rady Ukrainy 'Pro vchynennia Rosis'koiu Federatsieiu henotsydu v Ukraini," passed by the Verkhovna Rada April 14, 2022, has number 2188-IX and does not use terms "(neo-) nazism" or "fascism" in regards to Russia; http://zakon.rada.gov.ua/laws/shows/2188-20#Text (accessed 20 July 2022).
1178 Dudko, "A Conceptual Limbo of Genocide," 134.

the Russian aggression qualifies as genocide.[1179] Similarly, Philippe Sands (b. 1960) has cautioned against overusing the term; the Director of the Centre on International Courts and Tribunals at University College London emphasized that "from a legal point of view, it is very difficult to prove genocide. Given the assessments of the courts and tribunals, it is not yet clear to me whether this is genocide from a legal point of view."[1180] While not disputing Russian atrocities on a mass scale, Sands argued: "On the basis of what I've seen there is no genocide of the Ukrainian population in its legal parlance, going on. I do not see an intention to destroy a group in whole or in part, within the meaning of the 1948 convention."[1181]

Legislating genocidal narrations of history further widens the gulf between politics and scholarship. There are reasons to be conservative in regard to terminology; random and selective definitions of genocide and fascism for transparent political reasons deprives us of critically needed analytical tools. Anton Weiss-Wendt (b. 1973) at the Oslo Center for Studies of the Holocaust and Religious Minorities pointed at dangers of its over-utilization: "When everything is genocide, nothing is genocide."[1182] A similar note of caution could be used for the term "fascism."

"Nazi" Spamming

As already noted, Russian state-controlled media systematically maligned Poroshenko's democratically elected government as

---

1179 Lawrence Douglas, hosted by Denise Gamon, "Is Russia a Verbrecherstaat? – A Perspective from International Law," *The American Academy in Berlin*, 29 April 2022. https://www.americanacademy.de/videoaudio/is-russia-a-verbrecherstaat-a-perspective-from-international-law/ (accessed 3 October 2022), quote at 17:00-17:15.
1180 Philippe Sands, "Prosecuting Putin's Aggression," *The Nation*, 14 April 2022, https://www.thenation.com/article/world/ukraine-putin-aggression-crime/ (accessed 20 July 2022).
1181 Sam Wolfson, "'It's a Slam Dunk': Philippe Sands on the Case against Putin for the Crime of Aggression," *The Guardian*, 31 March 2022, https://www.theguardian.com/law/2022/mar/30/vladimir-putin-ukraine-crime-aggression-philippe-sands (accessed 20 July 2022).
1182 Anton Weiss-Wendt, "Hostage of Politics: Raphael Lemkin on 'Soviet Genocide,'" *Journal of Genocide Research* 7, no. 4 (2005): 551–59, here: 556.

fascists and death squads (Ru: *karateli*), invoking the imagery of *Einsatzgruppen* in the process of committing genocide against ethnic Russians in eastern Ukraine. Until 2022, Putin himself, and the members of his government had refrained from using the term "fascist junta," leaving this epithet to be articulated by members of the Duma, where Vladimir Zhirinovskii (1946–2022) and Gennadii Ziuganov (b. 1944) denounced the "Banderite-fascist junta."[1183]

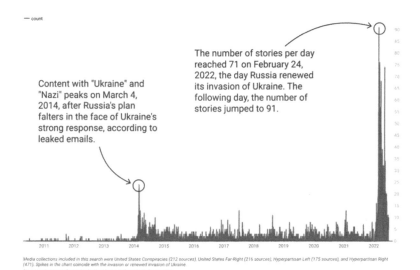

Figure 9.1. Courtesy of website *Hoaxlines*. "Stories about 'Ukrainian Nazis' were rare before 2014 when they surged at the moment when Russia's plans faltered," *Hoaxlines*, 3 August 2022, https://hackmd.io/@Hoaxlines/aug-3-2022 (accessed 7 August 2022).

With the launching of his war of aggression against Ukraine, Putin abandoned all restraint. Denouncing not only the Ukrainian government as fascist and neo-Nazi, he dehumanized the victims of his assault by literally placing them beyond the confines of the human species. He inflated the tally of supposed genocide victims, claiming that no less than four million people in Ukraine faced "genocide," as he put it, "only because these people did not agree with the West-supported coup in Ukraine in 2014 and op-

---

1183 Laruelle, *Is Russia Fascist?*, 79.

posed the transition towards the Neanderthal and aggressive nationalism and neo-Nazism which have been elevated in Ukraine to the rank of national policy."[1184] Stories with the words "Ukraine" and "Nazi" now flooded the Russian media.[1185]

Beyond Russia, the blunt misrepresentations convinced few people. Indeed, Putin's hyperbolic claims diverged so evidently from an easily verifiable reality that many observers called the mental health of the Kremlin strongman into question. The blunt misuse of Holocaust terminology was sharply condemned by authoritative academic institutions such as the United States Holocaust Memorial Museum and the Wiener Holocaust Library.[1186] In an uncharacteristically blunt statement, the USHMM sharply condemned Russia's "outrageous attack," stressing that "Putin has misrepresented and misappropriated Holocaust history by claiming falsely that democratic Ukraine needs to be 'denazified'. Equally groundless and egregious are his claims that Ukrainian authorities are committing 'genocide' as a justification for the invasion of Ukraine."[1187] The UN General Assembly condemned the Russian aggression as unlawful by 141 to 5 votes.[1188]

Whereas some pundits identify Russia's actions in the light of Nazism, *Mein Kampf* and the Holocaust, cooler heads identity

---

[1184] Vladimir Putin, "Address by the President of the Russian Federation," *President of Russia official website*, 21 February 2022, http://en.kremlin.ru/events/president/news/67828 (accessed 5 July 2022).

[1185] "Stories about 'Ukrainian Nazis' were rare before 2014 when they surged at the moment when Russia's plans faltered," Hoaxlines, 3 August 2022, https://hackmd.io/@Hoaxlines/aug-3-2022 (accessed 7 August 2022). On the term "fashizm" on Google Russia, see Laruelle, *Is Russia Fascist?*, 38.

[1186] "Museum Condemns Russia's Invasion of Ukraine," *The United States Holocaust Memorial Museum*, 24 February 2022, https://www.ushmm.org/information/press/press-releases/museum-condemns-russias-invasion-of-ukraine (accessed 28 October 2022); and Rossoliński-Liebe and Willems, "Putin's Abuse of History," 3.

[1187] "Museum Condemns Russia's Invasion of Ukraine"

[1188] 141 countries voted in favor, with 35 abstentions. Other than the belligerents, Russia and Belarus, themselves, only three other countries voted against the resolution: Syria, North Korea, and Eritrea. "UN Resolution ES-11/1. Aggression against Ukraine, March 18, 2022," *Official Documents Systems of the United Nations*, https://documents-dds-ny.un.org/doc/UNDOC/GEN/N22/293/36/PDF/N2229336.pdf?OpenElement (accessed 28 October 2022).

precedence, sources inspiration and patterns in other parts of historical experience.

A Clash of Conservative Projects

The Russian-Ukrainian conflict arose, political philosopher Denys Kiryukhin (b. 1977) argues, as the liberal tendencies of the immediate post-Soviet years yielded to conservatism.[1189] In Russia and Ukraine, Kiryukhin argues, "many former supporters of the Communists re-oriented themselves towards the political forces whose agenda combined 'left' and conservative 'right' rhetoric — the promise of social security and appellation to the national cultural and historic tradition."[1190] Russia's increasingly aggressive insistence that the Ukrainian and Russian peoples constituted one social and cultural unity gradually evolved into an ideological underpinning a Russian aggression. In the eyes of Ukrainians, Russia developed into an aggressive Other, an existential threat to the maintenance of Ukrainian statehood.[1191]

Federation Without Borders

In his study of Finland's "Imperial decades" of 1830-1890, historian Max Engman (1945-2020) noted how:

> An empire lacks sharp outward boundaries. At the borders of an empire, one finds various sorts of buffer zones and spheres of influence; there are border zones, vassal states and client states. To these unclear outward borders belongs what in Soviet context have been referred to as satellites or outer empires."[1192]

Putin's neo-imperial project entails continuities with, but also significant discontinuities from, the Soviet tradition. In the decade following his ascent to power, Putin concentrated power in the center by targeting, weakening, and depleting the already weak tradition of federalism in Russia, facilitating a highly re-

---

1189 Kiryukhin, "Russia and Ukraine," 439.
1190 Kiryukhin, "Russia and Ukraine," 440.
1191 Kiryukhin, "Russia and Ukraine," 438.
1192 Max Engman, *Lejonet och dubbelörnen: Finlands imperiella decennier 1830-1890* (Stockholm: Atlantis, 2000), 22.

centralizing dynamic.[1193] Having dislodged the mechanisms of modern federalism domestically, Russia, from 2007-8 embarked on an externally expansive policy. From the perspective of 2022, Putin's speech at the Munich Security Conference in February 2007, Russia's invasion of Georgia in August 2008 and the assault on Ukraine in March 2014 now all appear like ominous forebodings of what was to come. One quote, from a speech Putin gave to the Russian Geographical Society in November 2016, now appear as particularly ominous: "The borders of Russia are endless."[1194] In 2020 was turned into a slogan around which a propaganda campaign was centered.[1195] From our latter-day vantage point, also the name of the ruling party, *Edinaia Rossiia*, United Russia can be given a similarly ambiguous reading. Leonid Nikitinskii (b. 1953), founder of the oppositional *Novaia gazeta*, describes the 2001 launching of that party as the beginning of a "civil war" in that the authorities only regarded those who supported Putin as "united," whereas those who did not were treated as schismatics and deviants.[1196] *United Russia* could be understood in terms of uniting, consolidating the country—that is, the Russian Federation. After 2014, and even more so after 24 February 2022, the party's title could also be understood in the tradition of "gatherer of Russian lands," ("*sobiratel' russkoi zemli*") of tsar Ivan III (r. 1462–1505). Given the Russian Federation's disdain for international law and de-facto rejection of modern understandings of statehood, how to understand the regime's actions becomes informed by what is understood by "Rus'ian" lands? Is that Rus', Musovy, the Russian empire, the USSR, the RSFSR, or Russian Federation? With a regime that systematically violate international treaties with refer-

---

1193 Jörg Broschek, "Federalism in Europe, America and Africa: A Comparative Analysis," in Wilhelm Hofmeister (ed.), *Federalism and Democratization: Perceptions for Political and Institutional Reforms* (Singapore: Konrad Adenauer Stiftung Singapore, 2016), 23–52, here: 37, 40–41.
1194 "Putin: 'Granitsy Rossii nigde na zakanchivaiutsia," *BBC News Russkaia sluzhba*, 24 November 2016, https://web.archive.org/web/20210410182349/https://www.bbc.com/russian/news-38093222 (accessed 25 October 2022).
1195 https://uk.wikipedia.org/wiki/Рашизм#/media/Файл:Границі_Росії_нід е_не_закінчуються.jpg (accessed 25 October 2022).
1196 Kristian Gerner, *Rysslands historia* (Lund: Historiska Media, 2022), 354.

ences to disinformation and misrepresentation, then fall back upon random, mystical concepts based on uncertain boundaries of language, culture, and history.

Figure 9.2. Russian propaganda poster, "Russia's Borders are Endless" 2020. https://uk.wikipedia.org/wiki/Рашизм#/media/Файл:Границі_Росії_ніде_не_закінчуються.jpg (accessed 25 October 2022).

Munich, Georgia, Crimea and Donbass all marked various stages of the Russian neo-imperial revenge. Yet with the botched 2022 assault on Ukraine Russia's use of systematic destabilization of the post-Soviet republics of the "near abroad" would take another turn; if Moscow's proxy wars in Moldova, Georgia, and Ukraine had destabilized and slowed down these states integration with European integration, the destabilization and legal grey zones it had created for many of its neighbors now became a problem for Russia itself. In October 2022 the Russian Federation unilaterally declared four conquered *oblasti* of Ukraine part of the Russian Federation. This, seemingly ad hoc decision effectively made the term "federation" discordant. At the time of writing, the Russian Federation is not even able to delineate its legal borders, or even to provide information about the size of the country. As the State Duma on 3 October 2022 voted 409 to 0 to annex the Kherson *oblast'*, the Russian Ministry of Defense was forced to admit that the Russian military supply lines had been severed. Putin's spokesperson said it was unclear where the border ran, and that this was something for the residents themselves to determine.[1197] The neo-imperial slogan "Russia's Borders are Endless" in a literal sense became state policy in the fall of 2022.

The reneging upon seventy years of Soviet nation-building sent a chilling message to other former Soviet republics, none of which could now expect their sovereignty to be respected. When Kazakhstani president Kasym-Zhomart Tokaev (b. 1953) declared at a June 2022 meeting of the Organization for Collective Security (ODKB) in St Petersburg that he would not recognize the Donetsk and Luhansk People's Republics as independent states Putin ominously reminded him that the Soviet Union covered the same territory as "the historical Russia," the same rhetoric he had employed with regard to Ukrainian territories prior to invading them.[1198]

While the propaganda campaign is no doubt aimed as a display of strength, Russia's military incompetence and erratic leadership signal the opposite. The anarchy reflected in the Russian Federation's blurred boundaries in the Kherson, Zaporizhzhia, and Luhansk *oblasti* exposes the profound dysfunctionality of the Russian Federation and its erratic regime. The Russian Federation has reverted to a modus operandi reminiscent of 19th-century imperial practices, with their uncertain military frontiers — curiously anachronistically for an industrialized, supposedly federal state in the 21st century.

Imperial Nationalism

Does Putin's project constitute nationalism or imperialism? As we have seen, the two concepts do not have to be mutually exclusive.[1199] Its name notwithstanding, the Russian Federation current-

---

1197 Maria Persson Löfgren, "P1-Morgon," *Sveriges Radio*, 4 October 2022, https://sverigesradio.se/tabla.aspx?programid=132 (accessed 4 October 2022), quote at 1:09:30–1:10:05.
1198 Jan Majlard and Jesper Sundén, "Putin 'glömde' namnet på allierad president," *Svenska Dagbladet*, 19 June 2022, 27.
1199 See the section on OUN ideologues Mykhailo Kolodzins'kyi and Yurii Lypa above, and Wojnar, *Imperium ukraińskie*. For some of the key texts of Ukrainian imperialism, see Per A. Rudling, "Ukrainians," in Roland Clark and Tim

ly de facto comports itself as an empire. The definition that comes closest to capture this phenomenon is the concept of "imperial nationalism." This seemingly contradictory concept was given a more systematic theoretical underpinning in the writings of émigré Eurasianist ideologue Peter Savitskii (1895–1968), a contemporary of Lypa and Kolodzins'kyi. The three ideologues of empire were all born in Ukraine. They grew up in a borderland at a time of uncertainty and transformation, something reflected in divergent geopolitical orientations. If the Odesa native Lypa and the Galician Koldzins'kyi came to argue for Ukrainian empire, the Chernihiv native Savits'kyi maintained that there is no distinct, clear-cut border between nation and empire, and that Ukrainians and Belarusians, along with the Russians, were part of the same center, or ethnic core, of the all-Russian nation.[1200] Savitskyi developed a "dialectical concept of 'protonation'," according to which "the Ukrainian people are simultaneously an independent nation and a part of a larger national whole."[1201]

As Putin discarded Lenin's and Stalin's understanding of Ukrainians as a distinct nationality, the Russian autocrat returned to the pre-revolutionary imperial understanding of Ukrainians constituting a branch of the triune, or pan-Russian nation. Putin, and other adherents of this narration sought ideological legitimization the works of Ivan Il'in (1883–1954), published in 28 volumes between 1993 and 2008. In his addresses to the Federal Assembly Putin repeatedly quoted the émigré ideologue. In October

---

Grady (eds.), *European Fascist Movements* (London and New York: Routledge, 2023), 366-385, here: 368-370.
1200 Andrzej Nowak, "Russia, Empire, and Evil: Dilemmas and Temptations in Contemporary Russian Political Imagination," in Zdzisław Krasnodębski, Stefan Garsytecki, and Rüdiger Ritter (eds.), *Politics, History and Collective Memory in East Central Europe* (Hamburg: Krämer, 2012), 163-93, here: 170. On Savitskii, see Sergey Glebov, *From Empire to Eurasia: Politics, Scholarship, and Ideology in Russian Eurasianism, 1920s-1930s* (DeKalb, IL: NIU Press, 2017), 26-32. On Eurasianism, see Marlene Laruelle and Mischa Gabowitsch, *Russian Eurasianism: An Ideology for Empire* (Baltimore, NJ: Johns Hopkins University Press, 2008); and Mark Bassin, *The Gumilev Mystique: Biopolitics, Eurasianism, and the Construction of Community in Modern Russia* (Ithaca, NY: Cornell University Press, 2016).
1201 Glebov, *From Empire to Eurasia*, 28.

2005 Il'in's mortal remains, along with those of the Supreme Commander of the White Forces, Anton Denikin and conservative émigré writer Ivan Shemelev (1873–1950) were returned to Russia and interned at the necropolis of the Donskoi Monastery in Moscow. The reburial was funded by president Putin personally.[1202] The Russian strongman's highly publicized 24 May 2009 pilgrimage to the gravesite was reported broadly in Russian mass media. Putin, citing Denikin's diary on the relation between "Great and little Russia, Ukraine," stressed that the late White Commander had said that "nobody should be allowed to intervene between us. This is only Russia's right."[1203]

Trading Lenin for Denikin and Savitskii

For Putin—as it did for Denikin, Savitskii, and Il'in—Ukraine constitutes an artificial state, a fiction, a figment of the Bolsheviks' imagination, illegitimately detached from Russia. After 1991 Lenin vanished from official iconography and memory culture. The authorities' went to great lengths seeking to ignore and downplay the centennial of his 1917 coup d'état—an event which for over seven decades had been massively heralded as the most important event in human history.[1204] The official Lenin cult had ended in 1991, the Bolshevik leader disappeared from the fond of the plenary hall of the Russian parliament in 1991 and from its bank notes in 1993. In October that year Yeltsin removed the honor guards from the Lenin mausoleum. Whereas Lenin's economic, social, and political legacy was discarded, in the public sphere, the ghost

---

[1202] Larysa Yakubova, "Ivan Il'in: Patriarkh rosiis'koho fashyzmu," *Ukrains'kyi Tyzhden*, 19 July 2022, https://tyzhden.ua/History/255363 (accessed 14 November 2022). Denys Kiryukhin is currently working on a larger study of Putin's ideology; Pavel Tereshkovich is editing an encyclopedia of the "Russkii mir."

[1203] "Putin: 'You Certainly Should Read' Anton Denikin's Diary; Specifically, the Part about 'Great and Little Russia, Ukraine. He Says Nobody Should Be Allowed to Interfere between Us. This is Only Russia's," *Kyiv Post*, 24 May 2009, https://www.kyivpost.com/article/content/ukraine-politics/putin-you-cert ainly-should-read-anton-denikins-dia-42032.html (accessed 14 November 2022).

[1204] Christopher Read, "Centennial Thoughts of an Exhausted (?) Revolution," *Revolutionary Russia* 31, no. 2 (2018): 194–207.

of the old Bolshevik, lingered in in the form of street names and old Soviet monuments. Yet the process of demoting Lenin's legacy continued under Putin.[1205] On 27 December 2004 the State Duma replaced 7 November, the day of the 1917 Bolshevik takeover of power as a national holiday with 4 November as the "Day of Reconciliation and Agreement." The Interregional Council of Russia, which formally recommended the change of symbolic dates cast the October Revolution as an event that led to a "tragic division of Russia." November 4, the new national holiday commemorated the liberation of Moscow in 1612 from from Polish-Lithuanian "foreign invaders," and was entitled the Day of National Unity.[1206] A day commemorating the communist takeover of power in 1917 was replaced in the calendar with a day marking the end of the "Time of Troubles" and Muscovy's return to a policy of imperial expansion. Historian John-Paul Himka notes how "Russia has a history of imperialism, and Lenin was correct to think of it as an imperialist country."[1207] There could be no place for Lenin's 1917 coup d'etat in the Russian official memory; it was discarded in favor of symbols of revenge.

The Big Lie as Raison d'être

Echoing Stalin's words that what matters in history is not sources, rather a "correct attitude,"[1208] Russian Minister of Culture Vladimir Medinskii (b. 1970) stated: "You are naïve to think that facts are the main thing in history. Open your eyes: nobody pays atten-

---

[1205] Though, paradoxically, the restoration of monuments to Lenin, removed during the "*Leninopad*," and "decommunization" of 2014 and 2016 have been a prioritized issue by the Russian occupation authorities in eastern Ukraine, for instance in razed Mariupol; "Russia Plans to Restore Statues of Lenin in Occupied Mariupol," *The New Voice of Ukraine*, 18 November 2022, https://english.nv.ua/nation/russia-plans-to-restore-statues-of-lenin-in-occupied-mariupol-news-50285188.html (accessed 18 November 2022).
[1206] Evgenii Pchelov, "Khronologicheskii kommentarii k 'Dniu narodnogo edinstva'," *Gerboved* 85 (2005): 138–41.
[1207] John-Paul Himka, "Ukraine's Geopolitical Precarity: A Historian's Perspective," *The Spectre Magazine*, 6 July 2022, https://spectrejournal.com/ukraines-geopolitical-precarity/ (accessed 7 August 2022).
[1208] Andrei Zubov, *Istoriia Rossii: XX vek, 1894–1939* (Moscow: Astrel, 2009), 933.

tion to them! What matters is its interpretation, point of view, and mass propaganda."[1209]

Alternative reality has been a *Leitmotif* in Russian propaganda since the initial military intervention into Ukraine in 2014. Conspiracy theories have come to play an increasingly central role, in military institutions and official think tanks, possibly making inroads into the top leadership of the Russian state.[1210]

Outside of the Russian Federation, the increasingly hysterical disinformation was ineffective. The International Court in the Hague ruled that the court had not obtained any evidence that supports the Russian allegations of an ongoing genocide in Ukraine and ruled on 16 March that the Russian Federation "shall immediately suspend the military operations that it commenced on February 24, 2022."[1211]

There are apparent drawbacks to taking the state down into a conspiratorial alternative reality. The Russian Federation's systematic use of disinformation and falsehood in foreign and domestic communication risks inform analysis and decision making, with detrimental effects on its operations and actions. In an authoritarian system with weak feedback mechanisms, such as the Russian Federation, unwarranted beliefs about the outside world are less likely to be challenged, not least in situations when such beliefs exist within the military and security establishment.[1212]

Russian academia failed to challenge the regime's obvious falsehoods and conspiratorial misrepresentation. On the contrary,

---

1209 David Gaunt, "Targeting Ukrainians that Praise the Armed Resistance to USSR: Putin's Authoritarian Turn Justified by the Past," *Baltic Worlds* XV: 1–2 (June 2022): 165–67, here: 165. On Medinskii, see Robert F. Baumann, "Russia's Latest Historical Revisionism and Reinventing the Future," *Military Review Online Exclusive* (November 2022): 1–15, here: 5–7, 11–12.

1210 Martin Kragh, Erik Andermo, and Liliia Makashova, "Conspiracy Theories in Russian Security Thinking," *Journal of Strategic Studies* 45, no. 3 (2020): 334–68, here: 339.

1211 Joan E. Donoghue *et al.*, The International Court of Justice, "Allegations of Genocide Under the Convention on the Prevention and Punishment of the Crime of Genocide (Ukraine v. Russian Federation): Order," General List No. 182, 16 March 2022, 17, https://www.icj-cij.org/public/files/case-related/182/182-20220316-ORD-01-00-EN.pdf (accessed 11 July 2022).

1212 Kragh, Andermo, and Makashova, "Conspiracy Theories in Russian Security Thinking," 361, 362.

it partook in mobilizing society for the war of aggression, sanctioning the officious falsehoods. On 4 March 2022, over 260 members of the Russian Union of Rectors signed a declaration in support of the Russian assault, to "achieve demilitarization and de-Nazification of Ukraine and thus protect itself from growing military threats," stressing the need, "in the face of economic and information attacks, to rally firmly around our President."[1213]

As the war did not develop according to plan, official rhetoric was further radicalized. On 3 April 2022, the journalist and political consultant Timofei Sergeitsev (b. 1963) wrote a long article, published by the Russian government agency *RIA Novosti*, in which called for Ukraine to be "de-Nazified" and for the Ukrainian language and culture to be annihilated.[1214] Upholding the official lies required further repression still. Even referring to this war of aggression as "war" was made a punishable offense in the Russian Federation. The failure to meet his objectives increasingly apparent, in his Victory Day speech on 9 May 2022 Putin now blamed NATO for his invasion of Ukraine, insisting that "Russia has pre-emptively repulsed an aggression."[1215]

Zelens'kyi's very persona complicated Russian propaganda. In an interview with the Italian television channel *Rete 4*, when asked why a Jewish president would be committed to neo-Nazism, Lavrov got himself entangled in anti-Semitically tainted

---

1213 "Obrashchenie rossiiskogo soiuza rektorov," *Rossiiskii soiuz rektorov*, 4 March 2022, https://rsr-online.ru/news/2022-god/obrashchenie-rossiyskogo-soyuza-rektorov1/ (accessed 1 November 2022); Scott Jaschik, "Russian Rectors' Union Defends War," *Inside Higher Education*, 7 March 2022, https://www.insidehighered.com/quicktakes/2022/03/07/russian-rectors'-union-defends-war (accessed 4 November 2022).
1214 Anna-Lena Laurén, "Hur kan någon vilja dränka ukrainska barn?" *Dagens Nyheter*, 31 October 2022, https://www.dn.se/varlden/anna-lena-lauren-hur-kan-nagon-vilja-dranka-ukrainska-barn/ (accessed 1 November 2022). This was received with dismay in Ukraine as a "blueprint for genocide." Yanina Sorokina, "Who Is the Author of Russia's 'Blueprint for Genocide' Essay?," *The Moscow Times*, 7 April 2022 https://www.themoscowtimes.com/2022/04/06/who-is-the-author-of-russias-blueprint-for-genocide-essay-a77223 (accessed 4 November 2022).
1215 "Putin Scolds West and Blames NATO for Ukraine Invasion during Victory Day Speech," *CBC*, 9 May 2022, https://www.cbc.ca/news/world/russia-ukraine-war-1.6446322 (accessed 4 July 2022).

conspiracy theories: "well, I think that Hitler also had Jewish origins, so it does not mean anything," the Russian foreign minister claimed. "For a long time now, we've been hearing the wise Jewish people say that the biggest anti-Semites are the Jews themselves," Lavrov asserted.[1216]

The war of aggression turned the Russian Federation into a pariah state and escalated the totalitarian transformation of that country. On 7 July, Aleksei Gorinov (b. 1961), a municipal councilor from Moscow, was sentenced to seven years in jail for calling what the Russian authorities insist is a "special military operation" a war.[1217] At the time of writing, the Russian Federation has imprisoned more than 16,000 people for having criticized the war or calling for peace.[1218]

Studies conducted using open sources strongly indicate that the Russian soldiers deployed in operations in Ukraine were disproportionally from peripheral areas in the North Caucasus, Siberia, and the Russian Far East, many from socially disadvantaged groups.[1219] A wealth of testimonies and evidence of massive sexual violence, atrocities, and indiscriminate violence against the civilian population have been gathered by human rights organizations. In places like Bucha and Izium torture chambers have been discovered; bodies with traces of torture found, with ears and other body parts severed. "Russia's dehumanizing rhetoric in the war has over time become demonizing. In the so-called de-Nazification the victims are not regarded as human beings," Da-

---

1216 "Israel Summons Russian Envoy Over Lavrov's Hitler Comment," *RFE/RL*, 2 May 2022, https://www.rferl.org/a/lavrov-israel-hitler-jewish-zelenskiy-ukraine-denazification/31830525.html (accessed 6 July 2022).

1217 "Russia: Municipal Councilor Sentenced to Seven Years in Jail for Opposing the Ukraine War," *Amnesty international*, 8 July 2022, https://www.amnesty.org/en/latest/news/2022/07/russia-municipal-councillor-sentenced-to-seven-years-in-jail-for-opposing-the-ukraine-war/ (accessed 11 July 2022).

1218 Jesper Sundén, "Rysk lokalpolitiker till SvD: Slutet närmar sig för Putin," *Svenska Dagbladet*, 12 September 2022, 14.

1219 Niklas Bernsand, "Minoritetssoldater i det ryska kriget i Ukraina: Hur framställs 'specialoperationen' i burjatiska, ossetiska och dagestanska sociala medier?" *Östbulletinen: Temanummer om Ukraina och Rysslands anfallskrig* 2 (2022): 8–17, http://www.sallskapet.org/download/ostbulletinen/Ostbulletinen_20 22_nr2.pdf (accessed 10 July 2022).

vid Bergman (b. 1979), military psychologist at the Swedish Defense University stated, stressing how this is a result of the relentless dehumanizationof the enemy: "We have seen similar atrocities in Georgia and Chechnya, this is nothing new. I am surprised that we have not seen more of this."[1220] Indeed, during 2022 Russian media was saturated with calls for even more severe violence against Ukrainians. Analyst Hugo von Essen (b. 1994) of the Stockholm Centre for East European Studies (SCEEES) at the Swedish Institute of International Affairs similarly noted that:

> The growing criticism against the war emanating from Russia is not focused on Russian war crimes but rather on the contrary; that war is going so poorly and that Russia has not crushed the Ukrainian resistance and the people harshly enough; this may sound horrible, but many Russians do not see Ukrainians as human beings and many Russians, unfortunately want to see *more* of these kinds of pictures.[1221]

Surveying attitudes in an authoritarian society is notoriously difficult. Yet discussions in Russian social media networks also among national minorities overrepresented among the occupying forces in Ukraine reflect the official narration. Many have internalized the official narrative about "Ukrainian Nazis," and, as one analyst noted, "express the same lack of empathy and inability to self-reflection as large parts of Russian majority society."[1222]

As the Russian fiasco on the battlefield became apparent, Russian rhetoric brutalized further. The chief editor of *RT*, Margarita Simon'ian (b. 1980) tweeted on 30 September 2022, that the war had two possible outcomes: the victory of Russia or nuclear war.[1223] Later that day, TV journalist Anton Krasovskii (b. 1975) argued on *RT* that Ukrainian children ought to be drowned in the river Tisza in the Carpathians. "Let them claim that they are occu-

---

[1220] Jan Majlard, "Kroppar visar tecken på tortyr: 'Offren ses inte som människor'," *Svenska Dagbladet*, 17 September 2022, 22; and David Bergman, *Stridens psykologi: Konsten att döda och överleva* (Lund: Studentlitteratur, 2022).
[1221] Hélène Benno, "Ryssland retirerar från delar av Ukraina," *Sveriges Radio* P1, 18 September 2022, https://sverigesradio.se/avsnitt/ryssland-retirerar-fran-delar-av-ukraina (accessed 19 September 2022).
[1222] Bernsand, "Minoritetssoldater i det ryska kriget i Ukraina," 17.
[1223] Margarita Simon'ian, 11:19, *Twitter*, 20 September 2022.

pied, we'll throw them in the river with its strong undercurrent. We lock them up in their ugly *khata* and burn them down."[1224]

Political scientist and former United Russia Duma deputy Sergei Markov (b. 1958), head of the Institute of Political Research in Moscow argued that the population in Kyiv, which had turned against Russia, deserved to be punished by having an "angel bomb" dropped over the city, while consistently referring to Ukraine as a "terror state." The use of a rhetoric so unhinged that it becomes difficult to be taken seriously is not clear; one analyst suggests that is serves to the adversary off balance by shocking and frightening them.[1225]

The Russian propaganda stepped up its rhetoric from "denazification" to "desatanization" of Ukraine: "As the special operation continues it has become obvious that Ukraine has desatanized," Aleksei Pavlov (b. 1971), a deputy secretary on the Security Council of Russia told TASS.[1226] In a choreographed ceremony marking the illegal annexation of the four Ukrainian regions, president Putin invoked Satan and Goebbels, hurling furious allegations against the West: "They drowned the truth in an ocean of myths, illusions and fakes, using extremely aggressive propaganda, lying recklessly, like [Nazi propaganda chief] Goebbels," denouncing "satanic" gender policies in the Western world, and lamented that "the Russophobia articulated across the entire world is nothing but racism." The president dressed his neo-imperial conquest in anti-colonial language: announcing the illegal annexation of Ukrainian territory, Putin reiterated the claims

---

[1224] This led to Krasovskii's dismissal, following reactions from the Kremlin-loyal Human Rights Council–a paradox, as Russian state media was a main outlet for the regime's hate propaganda; Laurén, "Hur kan någon vilja dränka ukrainska barn?"
[1225] Laurén, "Hur kan någon vilja dränka ukrainska barn?"
[1226] "V RF zagovorili o 'desatanizatsii' Ukrainy: v ISW ob'iasnili, pochemu rossiiane pridumali novye tseli v voine," *RIA Novosti*, 26 October 2022, https://ria-m.tv/news/302122/v_rf_zagovorili_o_desatanizatsii_ukrainyi_v _isw_obyyasnili_pochemu_rossiyane_pridumali_novyie_tseli_v_voyne.html.

of the leaked February 26 RIA news dispatch; that "It's obvious that the current [Western] neo-colonial model is doomed."[1227]

Western observers have keenly been looking for cracks in the propaganda front. In March 2022 Odesa-born news anchor Marina Ovsiannikova (b. 1978), for many ordinary Russians the face of the state-controlled *First Channel*, gained much goodwill in the democratic West when disrupting a news broadcast, protesting the war and the lies of her own agency—lies which she had herself conveyed since 2003. Ovsiannikova noted, following her spectacular protest, that Russians had been "zombified by propaganda." Her self-reflection upon nearly 20 years of voluntarily disseminating disinformation at a key propaganda venue did not involve much introspection or soul-searching. "I was an ordinary cog in the propaganda machine. Until the very last moment I didn't think about it too much," the long-term propaganda indifferently noted.[1228] She evidenced more passion on social media, where she insisted that "Russian people should not carry collective responsibility for what transpired in Ukraine. The blame for that rests only on Vladimir Putin." She denounced the notion that Russian society also carries responsibility for Putin's war as "unacceptable Russophobia."[1229] Her disavowal is all too familiar to many Ukrainians.

There are countless reports of Ukrainians reaching out friends and family in the Russian Federation, telling them about the atrocities and consequences of the war affecting them on their bare skin—only to have their stories of sexual violence and murder dismissed.[1230] Reports of war crimes, massacres, and sexual

---

1227 Vladimir Isachenkov, "Putin Invokes Satan, Slavery, Goebbels, Nukes to Denounce West in Annexation Speech," *The Times of Israel*, 1 October 2022, https://www.timesofisrael.com/with-pomp-and-bluster-putin-bucks-west-in-speech-before-signing-annexation-treaties/ (accessed 4 October 2022).
1228 "Marina Ovsyannikova: Protesting Journalist says Russians Zombified by Propaganda," *BBC News*, 17 March 2022, https://www.bbc.com/news/world-europe-60778554 (accessed 4 November 2022).
1229 Marina Ovsiannikova, sign. "Ovsiannikova6219," *Instagram*, 27 March 2022.
1230 Ryan Lucas, "Ukrainian-Russian Families are being Torn Apart by Russia's Invasion," *NPR Weekend Edition*, 7 March 2022, https://wamu.org/story/22/03/07/relationships-across-the-ukraine-russia-border-feel-the-strain-of-war/ (accessed 4 November 2022); Ilia Hercules, "Putin's War in Ukraine has

violence were met with indifference, disavowal or dismissed as fake news or "Nazi lies." The "silent majority's" complacent indifference to the actions of their elites facilitated the aggression.[1231]

The Land of Lost Empathy

How should this be understood? In the book *The Land of Lost Empathy* (2019) Russian sociologist Aleksei Roshchin (b. 1967), argues that Soviet society instilled among its citizens the notion that they cannot influence anything—and did it so thoroughly that it undermined the very ability to empathize.[1232]

Indeed, societal support for the aggression has been massive, as has that of Putin himself; moreover, his approval ratings soared after the invasion of Ukraine in 2014.[1233] This support reached deep into the circles of people which in the West tend to regard as "decent" Russians. Nobel Peace Prize winner Mikhail Gorbachev (1931-2022) endorsed the annexation of Crimea.[1234] Opposition leader Aleksei Naval'nyi (1976-2024) took a similar position.[1235] As of June 2022, according to the Levada Center, the only remaining independent pollster in Russia, 77% of its people supported the

---

Torn my Family Apart," *New Statesman*, 27 February 2022, https://www.ne wstatesman.com/world/europe/ukraine/2022/02/putins-war-in-ukraine-has-torn-my-family-apart (accessed 4 November 2022).

1231 Marc Bennetts, "On Putin's 'Zombie Box': Tune into 16 Hours a Day of Invasion Propaganda," *Sunday Times*, 1 May 2022, https://www.thetimes.co.uk/article/on-putins-zombie-box-tune-into-16-hours-a-day-of-invasion-propaga nda-zgds7zzw0 (accessed 21 August 2022).

1232 Aleksei Roshchin, *Strana utrachenoi empatii: Kak sovetskoe proshloe vliiaet na rossiiskoe nastoiashchee* (Moscow: Eksmo, 2019); Laurén, "Hur kan någon vilja dränka ukrainska barn?"

1233 Bo Petersson, The *Putin Predicament: Problems of Legitimacy and Succession in Russia*. With a foreword by J. Paul Goode (Stuttgart: ibidem-Verlag, 2021); Derek S. Hutcheson and Bo Petersson. "Shortcut to Legitimacy: popularity in Putin's Russia," *Europe-Asia Studies*, vol. 68, no. 7, (2016): 1107-1126.

1234 "Ukraine bans Gorbachev over support for Crimea annexation," *Reuters*, May 16, 2015, https://www.reuters.com/article/us-ukraine-crimea-gorbachev-id USKCN0YH1UD (accessed 4 October 2022).

1235 Casey Michel, "Alexei Navalny Has a Crimea Problem," *New Republic*, 4 October 2022, https://newrepublic.com/article/167944/alexei-navalny-crim ea-problem-putin (accessed 29 October 2022). He has later changed his position.

war.[1236] Putin's approval ratings remained around 80% throughout 2022, and roughly three quarters of the Russians supported the war.[1237]

The evidence runs contrary to Ovsiannikova's spurious claim that this is but Putin's war. This is Russia's war, if not of active preference, then of acceptance or passive support of the vast majority of the Russian population. It raises fundamental questions about the social, political, and intellectual culture which made this possible—and about the agency and responsibility of ordinary Russians.

Verbrecherstaat

In 1945 German sociologist Karl Jaspers (1883–1969) sought to clarify the meaning of guilt. He cautioned his countrymen against escaping their responsibility by looking only at their immediate, disastrous situation and focusing on transgressions committed by the Allies. Jaspers rejected the idea that all Germans were tainted with guilt just by being German, arguing that such a line of argumentation resembled that of the Nazis, who claimed all Jews were tainted just by being Jews.[1238] His indictment was rather that it was German society, legal authorities, and political culture had brought Germany to the abyss. In a famous 1965 interview in *Der Spiegel*, Jaspers referred to Nazi Germany as a *Verbrecherstaat*, a

---

1236 "Konflikt s Ukrainoi," Press-vyspusk, *Levada-tsentr: Analiticheskii tsentr Iuriia Levady*, 6 June 2022, https://www.levada.ru/2022/06/02/konflikt-s-ukrain oj-2/ (accessed 10 June 2022).
1237 The support for "the actions of Russian military forces in Ukraine," went from 80 per cent in March, to 72 in September 2022, "Conflict with Ukraine: September 2022," *Levada-Center: Yuri Levada Analytical Center*, 7 October 2022, https://www.levada.ru/en/2022/10/07/conflict-with-ukraine-september-2 022/ (accessed 17 November 2022). According to a November 2022 poll by the Levada Center, 42% of Russians "unequivocally support" the "actions of the Russian armed forced in Ukraine," whereas 32% "rather support." "74% of Russians support actions of their military in Ukraine, while 53% are in favor of peace negotiations; 'Levada Center' survey. INFOGRAPHICS," *Censor.net*, 4 December 2022, https://m.censor.net/en/news/3384796/74_of_ru ssians_support_actions_of_their_military_in_ukraine_while_53_are_in_favor _of_peace_negotiations (accessed 5 December 2022).
1238 Dennis L. Bark and David R. Gress, *A History of West Germany. Second edition. Vol. 1. From Shadow to Substance, 1945-1963* (Oxford: Blackwell, 1993), 162.

criminal state. That is, he identified the novel achievement of Nazism as turning the state—which, in the Western legal tradition is supposed to be the source of ordered legality—into an agent of criminality.[1239] "What basically had happened to us and by us, the Germans did not register. One did not distance oneself from the totally criminal state which we had become."[1240] Jaspers' observations resonate with us today, as the Russian war of aggression invites us to revisit his concept of *Verbrecherstaat* and the issue of collective civic responsibility.

University of Jena historian Norbert Frei (b. 1955) contends that "in states with rule of law one cannot talk about collective punishment, and [there cannot be] any accusations of collective guilt; rather, what distinguishes rule of law is that guilt always has to be concrete, individual and personal."[1241] Like Jaspers, he makes a distinction between guilt and responsibility. At the same time, Frei stresses how "Putin enjoys a large support. The Russians have elected Putin, and re-elected him again and again. He has, so to say, come to power through elections, and has been sustained [in power], and for that those who elected him, of course, bear responsibility."[1242]

University of Alberta historian Volodymyr Kravchenko (b. 1957) sought to address this question of agency:

> "Do the Russians want war?" Sixty years ago, it was a rhetorical question posed in the title of a popular song written by the Soviet poet Yevgenii Yevtushenko (1932-2017). Today, it became obvious they do. In today's

---

1239 Karl Jaspers, "Für Völkermord gibt es keine Verjährung," *Der Spiegel*, October 3, 1965; Lawrence Douglas, "From the Sentimental Story of the State to the Verbrecherstaat, Or, the Rise of the Atrocity Paradigm," in Immi Tallgren and Thomas Skouteris (eds.), *The New Histories of International Criminal Law: Retrains* (Oxford: Oxford University Press, 2019), 54–71, here: 55.
1240 Bark and Gress, *A History of West Germany*, 163, citing Karl Jaspers, *Der Spiegel*, no. 41, 1967.
1241 Nina Benner and Luise Steinberger, "Bär alla ryssar på en kollektiv skuld?" *Sveriges Radio P1*, 21 August 2022, quote at 16:36–16:59, https://Sverigesradio.se/avsnitt/1943499 (accessed 21 August 2022).
1242 Benner and Luise Steinberger, "Bär alla ryssar på en kollektiv skuld?," quote at 17:17–17:39.

Russia, more than seventy percent of citizens approve of the war started by their possessed dictator and feel proud of him.[1243]

The question "where were *you* on 24 February?" will face not only its news anchors, parliamentarians, clergy, intellectuals, and university rectors, but Russian society as a whole. The problem, as identified by Jaspers, pertains to the social, political, and civic culture that enabled the regime and facilitated its criminal war of aggression. Ovsiannikova's disavowal notwithstanding, these discussions are likely to revolve around the issue of Russian agency; of intellectual and civic responsibility.

This is not to say critical voices are missing. There are also Russian voices of introspection. On 9 May 2022, Leonid Nikitinskii noted in the online, international version of *Novaia gazeta* that it was the questions Theodore Adorno asked himself about responsibility that was important, not the answer as such. What was it in Russian society that had made the horrors possible? "These were no aliens, no homunculi produced in testing tubes, but 'our boys,' with whom we've been neighbors for years and who appeared to speak the same language. ...Where did this tribe originate and who had raised them? What is our responsibility for what they have done?"[1244]

Opinion polls conducted in an authoritarian state are problematic. The dissent of a relative small minority suggest cracks in the monolith. As the Kharkiv and Kherson fronts crumbled in August 2022 Putin declared a "partial mobilization." This triggered an exodus of men in the age of service. A week after the mobilization was announced, an estimated 300,000 Russians had left the country; as Poland, the Baltic States, and Finland closed their borders, they headed towards Kazakhstan, Georgia, and Turkey. Whereas Germany and some other European countries opened their doors for these men, the very issue of agency and responsibility were again rainsed. Michał Dworczyk (b. 1975),

---

1243 Volodymyr Kravchenko, "The Russian War against Ukraine: Cyclic History vs Fatal Geography," *East/West: Journal of Ukrainian Studies*, vol. IX, no. 1 (2022): 201–208, here: 202.
1244 Gerner, *Rysslands historia*, 352.

head of Polish Prime Minister Mateusz Morawiecki's (b. 1968), office argued "We are not going to let in Russian citizens who have backed up Vladimir Putin's regime and then suddenly become convinced democrats who want to leave the country once they realized that they would be sent to the front."[1245]

Mördersprache

Inevitably, the war has changed the world's attitudes not only to Russia, but to the political and social culture that, whether by active support or complacency, enabled the regime and facilitated its war crimes. To many, the very Russian language itself became tainted by its association with the systematic state-disseminated hate speech and war crimes — not unlike how the German language in the wake of World War II was seen as a *Mördersprache*, a language of murderers.[1246] As University of St Andrews sociologist Tomasz Kamusella (b. 1967) has noted, "Employing a language as the media for spreading genocidal propaganda, making a language into a weapon of war and a 'justification' of genocide does not leave this language unscathed. ... The Russians are now busy fashioning their language into a *iazyk ubiits*, a murderers' language." Kamusella suggests that "Until a Ukrainian Celan or Ausländer, or Ukrainian survivors ... come forward and devote their lives to exorcise Russian from its newly gained notoriety as a murderers' language, writing poetry in Russian after Bucha will be barbaric."[1247]

In Ukraine, the war radicalized attitudes. In an April 2022 essay, writer Oksana Zabuzhko (b. 1960) argued that "In many ways, it was Russian literature that wove the camouflage net for Russia's tanks."[1248] In August 2022, the Ukrainian ministry of edu-

---

1245 Tomas Lundin, "Flyende ryssar splittrar Europa: 'Är desertörer'," *Svenska Dagbladet*, 4 October 2022, https://www.svd.se/a/MoLjQJ/tyskland-gor-tva rtemot-finland-oppnar-for-flyende-ryssar (accessed 4 October 2022).
1246 Tomasz Kamusella, "Russian: A Murderer's Language," October 2022, https://www.academia.edu/89459162/Russian_A_Murderers_Language (accessed 29 October 2022).
1247 Kamusella, "Russian: A Murderer's Language"
1248 Oksana Zabuzhko, "No guilty people in the world?: Reading Russian literature after the Bucha massacre," *Times Literary Supplement*, 22 April 2022,

cation took the radical step of banning Russian—and Belarusian—authors from the curriculum "in response to the challenges that appeared in wake of the full-scale Russian invasion of Ukraine." Moves were made to rename a Kyiv subway station named after Lev Tolstoi and to close the museum to the Kyiv native Mikhail Bulgakov.[1249] Ukraine motioned to remove itself from the Russian cultural orbit, from a civic culture that enabled the atrocious war.

Lund University professor emeritus Kristian Gerner (b. 1942) argued that "Russia in 2022, is a country which similarly to Germany in 1945, morally, legally and politically found itself at point zero" and that "Russia has existed the European civilization in the positive sense of that term."[1250] The consequences of this can hardly be overstated: "Regardless of how the war ends, Russia will, for many years ahead be excluded from economic, technological, scientific and cultural relations with Europe and the USA."[1251] Gerner takes the analogy of Germany and *Stunde Null* to its logical conclusion: "Prussia was the incarnation of German militarism. Prussia was outlawed by the victorious powers in 1945. In a similar fashion in our days, a militarized Russia must be outlawed."[1252]

Whereas such a scenario currently may appear distant, there are steps the international community could take. Removing the Russian Federation as a permanent member of the UN Security Council could be one. Not only does Article 18, no. 2 of the UN charter make this legally possible; the 25 October 1971 expulsion of the Republic of China (Taiwan) offers a precedent.[1253]

---

https://www.the-tls.co.uk/articles/russian-literature-bucha-massacre-essay-oksana-zabuzhko/ (accessed 25 April 2022).
1249 Gunilla von Hall, "Ryska klassiker förbjuds i Ukraina: 'Det är tragiskt'," *Svenska Dagbladet*, 20 August 2022, 19.
1250 Gerner, *Rysslands historia*, 340.
1251 Gerner, *Rysslands historia*, 357.
1252 Gerner, *Rysslands historia*, 340.
1253 Thomas Grant, "Removing Russia from the Security Council: Part One," *Opinio Juris*, 18 October 2022, http://opiniojuris.org/2022/10/18/removing-russia-from-the-security-council-part-one/ and idem., "Removing Russia from the Security Council: Part Two" *Opinio Juris*, 19 October 2022 http://opiniojuris.org/2022/10/19/removing-russia-from-the-security-council-part-two/. Ariel Cohen and Vladislav Inozemtsev, "How to Expel Russia from the UN," *The Hill*, 3 November 2022, https://thehill.com/opinion/international/3717566-how-to-expel-russia-from-the-un/ (all accessed 22 November 2022).

The Disruptive Potential of an Undigested Past

The onslaught also changed the dynamics of Polish–Ukrainian relations. In a speech to the *Verkhovna Rada* on 23 May 2022 Polish President Andrzej Duda (b. 1972) — though from the same national conservative party, PiS — delivered a different message than had Waszczykowycz in 2017. Duda stated "I personally will not rest until Ukraine becomes a member of the European Union in the full sense of the word," and that "Poland will actively support Ukraine on its way to membership of the European Union."[1254]

At the acute stage of war, Polish–Ukrainian disputes over divisive historical topics were marginalized.[1255] Yet even in this acute phase of the war, when world opinion stood united with Ukraine the undigested past continued to mar Ukrainian diplomacy. We were reminded of its divisive potential in connection with Zelens'kyi's 20 March 2022 speech to the Knesset, in which he equated the Russian assault in 2022 to the Shoah: "listen to what is being said in Moscow. Hear how these words are said again: 'Final solution.' But already in relation, so to speak, to us, to the Ukrainian issue'." Even more sensitive was his assertion, that "The Ukrainians made their choice. Eighty years ago. They rescued Jews." Against the background of the rehabilitation of Shukhevych and Bandera many Israelis perceived this as deeply offensive. Israeli Finance Minister Bezalel Smotrich (b. 1980), leader of the Religious Zionist Party, objected to Zelens'kyi's comparison to the Holocaust as "infuriating and ridiculous" and an "attempt

---

[1254] "Speech by the President of Poland, Andrzej Duda at the Verkhovna Rada, May 22, 2022 (VIDEO)," *Kyiv Post*, 23 May 2022, https://www.kyivpost.com/ukraine-politics/speech-by-the-president-of-poland-andrzej-duda-at-the-verkhovna-rada-may-22-2022-video.html (accessed 4 July 2022); Lukash Adamski, "Chomu visit Andzheia Dudy do Kyive stav znakovym dlia vidnosyn Ukrainy ta Pol'shchi," *Evropeiska pravda*, 23 May 2022, https://www.eurointegration.com.ua/experts/2022/05/23/7139906/ (accessed 4 July 2022).
[1255] Maciej Makulski, "Poland's Ukraine Refugee Assistance as a Transformative Experience," *New Eastern Europe* LIV, no. 6 (November–December 2022): 60–65, here: 63.

to rewrite history and to erase the role of the Ukrainian people in the attempts to exterminate the Jewish people."[1256]

On 29 June 2022, Andrii Mel'nyk (b. 1975), the Ukrainian ambassador to Germany, generated headlines in Germany at a time where key decisions on arms exports to Ukraine were being discussed. A native of L'viv, Mel'nyk became known as a combative "cultural warrior," whose statements on matters of historical controversy repeatedly generated headlines in German media.[1257] The Ukrainian ambassador, whose pilgrimages to the OUN(b) leader's grave at the Munich Waldfriedhof had already raised eyebrows, now went on record denying the OUN(b)'s antisemitism and its involvement in the Holocaust as well as in the pogroms. Mel'nyk insisted that "Bandera was no mass murderer of Jews and Poles," stressed that "I am against that all sort of crimes are blamed on Bandera," reducing it to a Soviet campaign to demonize Bandera, in which German, Polish, and Israeli historians have played along.[1258] "I doubt that there were orders to kill Jews. There is no evidence."[1259]

When the interviewer read Mel'nyk, in verbatim the OUN(b) statements from the April 1941 Krakow Grand Assembly, the May 1941 policy document "The Struggle and Activities of the OUN(b) at times of War" and the OUN(b) June 1941 appeals to Ukrainians to exterminate Jews, the Ukrainian ambassador called the historical authenticity of these documents into question.[1260]

1256 Félix Krawatzek and George Soroka, "The Best Story: The Ukrainian Past in Zelenskyy's Words and the Eyes of the Public," *New Eastern Europe* LIV, no. 6 (November–December 2022): 143–52, here: 148.
1257 Tomas Lundin, "Rysslandsexpert: Länderna i väst skulle slitas sönder av frågan," *Svenska Dagbladet*, 10 July 2022: 8–9, here: 9.
1258 "'Verharmlosung des Holocausts': Israelisch Botschaft kritisiert ukrainischen Pöbel-Botschafter," *Blick*, 1 July 2022, https://www.blick.ch/ausland/umstr ittene-aussagen-zu-bandera-melnyk-schweigt-zu-kiew-distanzierung-id17624 428.html (accessed 4 July 2022).
1259 "Meron Mendel über Botschaftler Melnyk: 'Er hat der ukrainischen Sache einen Bärendienst erwiesen'," *Deutschlandsradio Kultur*, 2 July 2022, https:// www.deutschlandfunkkultur.de/ukrainischer-botschafter-verteidigt-nazi-kol laborateur-stepan-bandera-100.html (accessed 4 July 2022).
1260 "Andrij Melnyk, Botschaftler der Ukraine — Jung & Naiv: Folge 580," *Youtube.com*, July 29 2022 https://www.youtube.com/watch?v=JVEGR7apz

The Ukrainian ambassador's words caused consternation in Israel and Poland. "The statement made by the Ukrainian ambassador is a distortion of the historical facts, belittles the Holocaust and is an insult to those who were murdered by Bandera and his people," the Israeli embassy said, whereas Polish deputy Foreign Minister Marcin Przydacz (b. 1985) commented that "such an opinion and such words are absolutely unacceptable."[1261] Antisemitism scholar Meron Mendel (b. 1976) at the University of Frankfurt am Main argued that "Surely Mr. Mel'nyk has done the Ukrainian cause a disservice. This is particularly tragic at a time, when Ukraine needs all support."[1262]

Yet, under Zelens'kyi things were changing. Mel'nyk was a former advisor to Yushchenko who had been appointed ambassador to Germany by Poroshenko. In a departure from practices under their presidencies, the Ukrainian Foreign Ministry moved swiftly to distance itself from Mel'nyk's claims, stressing that "relations between Ukraine and Poland are at their peak now…. Kyiv and Warsaw share a complete understanding of the need to preserve unity in the face of shared challenges. The opinion of the Ambassador of Ukraine to Germany Andriy Mel'nyk… is his own and does not express the position of the Ministry of Foreign Affairs of Ukraine."[1263] Ten days later, Mel'nyk was dismissed, prematurely, from his position as ambassador to Germany.[1264]

---

ol (accessed 4 July 2022), quote at 1:49:07–1:49:54. English translations of the documents are available in Rudling, "Ukrainians," 374-376, 382.

1261 "Ukraine's Envoy to Germany Irks Israeli, Polish Government with WWII Comments," *Deutsche Welle*, 1 July 2022, https://www.dw.com/en/ukraines-envoy-to-germany-irks-israeli-polish-governments-with-wwii-comments/a-62335288 (accessed 4 July 2022).

1262 "Meron Mendel über Botschaftler Melnyk."

1263 "Comment of the Spokesperson of the Ministry of Foreign Affairs of Ukraine Oleg Nikolenko on the Ukrainian-Polish Relations," *Ministry of Foreign Affairs of Ukraine*, 30 June 2022, https://mfa.gov.ua/en/news/komentar-rechnika-mzs-ukrayini-olega-nikolenka-shchodo-ukrayinsko-polskih-vidnosin; "Polen rügt Melnyks Äußerungen," *Frankfurter Allgemeine Zeitung*, 1 July 2022, https://www.faz.net/aktuell/politik/ausland/polen-ruegt-andrij-melnyks-aeusserungen-ueber-stepan-bandera-18142310.html (accessed 4 July 2022).

1264 In November 2022 Melnyk made a comeback, promoted to Deputy Foreign Minister; "Kyiv's Ex-Envoy to Berlin takes Deputy Foreign Minister Post," *Deutsche Welle*, 19 November 2022, https://www.dw.com/en/kyivs-ex-

Post-Bandera?

Despite Zelens'kyi's attempts to move beyond Bandera, a decade of memory management under Yushchenko and Poroshenko, and almost as many years of Russian military aggression has left traces; growing numbers of Ukrainians identify with the legacy of the OUN(b) and UPA.[1265] A generation of young Ukrainians have grown up with the state veneration of these groups. Hundreds of streets, buildings, squares, monuments, and museums have been established to Bandera alone. Since the Russian Federation has opted to invoke the poorly conceptualized cult of the OUN(b) and UPA to caricature Ukraine as "neo-Nazi" state to justify its illegal war of imperial conquest, dispassionate inquiry into this sensitive topic, unpopular in peacetime, becomes all but impossible at a time when the Ukrainian state fights for its survival.

Yet, as the Mel'nyk episode reminds us, without *Aufarbeitung* and critical engagement, the past is bound to fester. It feeds revisionism and stokes conflict domestically. It complicates Ukraine's European integration while providing ammunition to the country's adversaries. It is imperative that Ukraine prevails in this war. In the short term, it needs heavy weapons and unwavering support of the entire democratic world.[1266] In the longer term, as Ukraine advances further on the path towards rule of law, democracy, pluralism, and integration into the Euro-Atlantic community, the Banderite heritage, the willful amnesia, the revisionist myths will need to be addressed. More than a mere image prob-

---

envoy-to-berlin-takes-deputy-foreign-minister-post/a-63816305 (accessed 20 November 2022).

1265 According to a 7–13 September 2022 opinion poll, the support for "OUN-UPA" increased from 22 per cent in 2013 to 43 per cent in 2022; Anton Hrushets'kym, "Dynamika otsinka diial'nosti OUN-UPA u chasi Druhoi Svitovoi Viiny: Rezul'taty telefonnoho opytuvannia, provedenoho 7-13 veresnia 2022 roku," *Kyivs'kyii mizhnarodnyi instytut sotsiolohii*, 12 October 2022, https://kiis.com.ua/?lang=ukr&cat=reports&id=1146&page=1&fbclid=IwA R2RbaTdO8z-ckSAHzJj_vAS9hNX3q_kOHNv8UWT-6MjnekN9SisI1f7SNQ (accessed 4 November 2022).

1266 Andreas Umland *et al.*, "Schwere Waffen jetzt! Replik auf 'Waffenstillstand jetzt'," *Focus.de*, 19 July 2022, https://www.focus.de/politik/ausland/ukrain e-krise/96-osteuropa-experten-weltweit-fordern-schwere-waffen-jetzt_id_119 428660.html (accessed 3 November 2022).

lem, Yushchenko and Porosheko's decision to identify democratic Ukraine with the totalitarian *Blut-und-Boden* tradition has come to constitute a real political liability and obstacle to its democratic transformation. Zelens'kyi's defiance not only built confidence which had immediate military implications; it offered building blocks for a new national mythology. February 2022 may have been that "violent teacher" the importance of which Langewische emphasizes for processes of national consolidation. Those fateful days in late February 2022 may have produced that Ukrainian "founding father," a role which neither the totalitarian Bandera, nor the former communist ideologue Kravchuk could ever fill.[1267] The role Yushchenko and his legitimizing historians had intended for Bandera may come to be occupied by a Russophone Jewish comedian-turn-president and war hero. This could offer an opportunity to press the "reset" button; undoing the Bandera episode of the Yushchenko and Poroshenko presidencies in favor of historical references in line with the democratic ideals for which hundreds of thousands of Ukrainians are fighting as these lines are written.

Under Zelens'kyi, much of the cult of the OUN has already been scaled down and dismantled. A victorious Ukraine will be integrated into the larger international academic community, engage the difficult past together with its Euroatlantic partners, not least those with positive experiences of overcoming difficult historical legacies. Democratic Ukraine would neither be the first, nor the last, to embark on this path.

1267 Langewiesche, *Der Gewaltsame Lehrer*, 261–63.

Archival References

AAN	Archiwum Akt Nowych, Warsaw.
AWP	Archiwum Wiktora Poliszczuka
AtsDVR	Arkhiv Tsentru Doslidzheni Vyzvol'noho Rukhu (The Archive of the Center for Research of the Liberation Movement), L'viv, Ukraine.
AOUN-UIS.	Arkhiv OUN, Ukrains'ka Informatsiina Sluzhba—London. (The Archive of the OUN, the Ukrainian Information Agency in London, UK).
AOUN v Kyive	Arkhiv Orhanizatsii Ukrains'kykh Natsionalistiv v Kyive (The Archive of the OUN[M] in Kyiv, Ukraine.)
DALO	Derzhavnyi arkhiv l'vivs'koi oblasti (State Archives of L'viv Region, Ukraine)
DARO	Derzhavnyi Arkhiv Rivnens'koi oblasti
HDA SBU	Haluzevyi Derzhavnyi Arkhiv Sluzhby Bezpeky Ukrainy (The Special State Archive of the Security Services of Ukraine, Kyiv, Ukraine).
IPN	Instytut Pamięci Narodowej, Warsaw
LAC	Libraries and Archives Canada, Ottawa, ON, Canada.
NARA	The National Archives Records Administration College Park, MD, USA.
PA AA	Politisches Archiv des Auswärtigen Amtes (The Political Archive of the Foreign Ministry), Berlin, Germany.
RA-MA	Riksarkivet Marieberg, The National Archives of Sweden, Stockholm, depot Marieberg.
TsDAHOU	Tsentral'nyi Derzhavnyi Arkhiv Hromads'kykh Ob'iednan' Ukrainy (The Central State Archive of the Civic Organizations of Ukraine), Kyiv, Ukraine.
TsDAVOVU	Tsentral'nyi Derzhavnyi Arkhiv Vyshyi Orhaniv Vlady Ukrainy (The Central State Archive of the

	Higher Organs of Government of Ukraine), Kyiv, Ukraine.
ITS Collection	The Collection of the International Tracing Service, Unites Stated Holocaust Memorial Museum (USHMM), Washington, DC, USA.
UAA	The University of Alberta Archives, Edmonton, AB, Canada (UAA)
URIA-HURI.	Ukrainian Research Institute Archives, Harvard Ukrainian Research Institute, Cambridge, MA, USA.
VA	Värmlandsarkiv, Karlstads stifts- och läroverksbiblioteks handskriftssamling, Karlstad (The Provincial Archives of Värmland, The Collection of handwritten documents of the library o the diocese and college), Karlstad, Sweden.
YVA	Yad Vashem Archives, Jerusalem, Israel

Bibliography

Adams, Arthur E. *Bolsheviks in the Ukraine: The Second Campaign, 1918–1919*. New Haven: Yale University Press, 1963.

Adams, Mark B., ed. *The Evolution of Theodosius Dobzhansky: Essays on His Life and Thought in Russia and America*. Princeton: Princeton University Press, 1994.

Adams, Mark B. "The Soviet Nature-Nurture Debate." In *Science and the Soviet Social Order*, edited by Loren R. Graham, Cambridge: Harvard University Press, 1990, 94-138.

Adamski, Lukash [Łukasz]. "Chomu visit Andzheia Dudy do Kyive stav znakovym dlia vidnosyn Ukrainy ta Pol'shchi." *Evropeiska pravda*, 23 May 2022. https://www.eurointegration.com.ua/experts/2022/05/23/7139906/ (accessed August 17, 2023).

Adamski, Łukasz. *Nacjonalista postępowy: Mychajło Hruszewski i jego poglądy na Polskę i Polaków*. Warsaw: Wydawnictwo Naukowe PWN, 2011.

Adler, Max and Rudolf Hilferding, eds. *Marx-Studien: Blätter für Theorie und Politik des wissenschaftlichen Sozialismus*, Vol. 2. Vienna: Ignaz Brand, 1907.

Agethen, Manfred, Eckhard Jesse, and Ehrhart Neubert. *Der missbrauchte Antifaschismus: DDR-Staatsdoktrin und Lebenslüge der deutschen Linken*. Freiburg: Verlag Herder, 2002.

Alekseeva, T. I. *Etnogenez vostochnykh slavian*. Moscow: MGU, 1973.

Alexandrov, Daniel A. "Filipchenko and Dobzhansky: Issues in Evolutionary Genetics in the 1920s," in *The Evolution of Theodosius Dobzhansky: Essays on His Life and Thought in Russia and America*, edited by Mark B. Adams. Princeton: Princeton University Press, 1994, 49-62.

Altschuler, Mordechai. *Soviet Jewry since the Second World War: Population and Social Structure*. Westport, CT: Greenwood Press, 1987.

Amar, Tarik Cyril. "A Disturbed Silence: Discourse on the Holocaust in the Soviet West as an Anti-Site of Memory." In *The Holocaust in the East: Local Perpetrators and Soviet Responses*, edited by Michael David-Fox, Peter Holquist and Alexander M. Martin, 158–184. Pittsburgh: University of Pittsburgh Press, 2014.

Amar, Tarik Cyril. *The Paradox of Ukrainian Lviv: A Borderland City between Stalinists, Nazis, and Nationalists*. Ithaca: Cornell University Press, 2015.

Amar, Tarik Cyril. "Ukraine's Nationalist 'Decommunization' Laws of Spring 2015: Shielding Perpetrators and Excluding Victims." *Memories at Stake* 9 (Summer–Fall 2019): 99–103.

Amar Tarik Cyril [Tarik Syril Amar], Ihor Balyns'kyi, and Yaroslav Hrytsak, ed., *Strasti za Banderuiu: statti ta esei*. Kyiv: Hrani-T, 2010.

Ames, Mark. "The Hero of the Orange Revolution Poisons Ukraine." *The Nation*, 12 February, 2010.https://www.thenation.com/article/hero-orange-revolution-poisons-ukraine/.

Anders, Caroline. "The Lead-Up to the War in Ukraine Revisited." *Washington Post*, 19 August, 2022.https://www.washingtonpost.com/politics/2022/08/19/lead-up-war-ukraine-revisited/ (accessed August 17, 2023).

Anderson, Benedict. "Introduction." In *Mapping the Nation*, edited by Gopal Balakrishnan, 1–16. London: Verso, 1996.

Andriewsky, Olga. "Towards a Decentered History: The Study of the Holodomor and Ukrainian Historiography." *East/West: Journal of Ukrainian Studies* 2, no. 1 (2015): 18–52.

Antoniuk, Iaroslav. *Diial'nist' SB OUN na Volyni*. Luts'k: Volyns'ka knyha, 2007.

Antons, Jan-Hinnerk. *Ukrainische Displaced Persons in der Britischen Zone: Lagerleben zwischen nationaler Fixierung und pragmatischen Zukunftsentwürfen*. Essen: Klartext Verlag, 2014.

Applebaum, Anne. "Nationalism Is Exactly What Ukraine Needs." May 12, 2014. https://www.anneapplebaum.com/2014/05/12/nationalism-is-exactly-what-ukraine-needs/ (accessed August 17, 2023).

Arel, Dominique. "On Context, Comparison, and Dialogue." *Current Politics in Ukraine*, 21 June 2013.https://ukraineanalysis.wordpress.com/2013/06/21/on-context-comparison-and-dialogue/ (accessed August 17, 2023).

Armstrong, John A. "Collaborationism in World War II: The Integral Nationalist Variant in Eastern Europe." *Journal of Modern History* 40, no. 3 (1968): 396–410.

Armstrong, John A. "Heroes and Human: Reminiscences Concerning Ukrainian National Leaders During 1941–1944." *The Ukrainian Quarterly* 51, nos. 2–3 (Summer-Fall, 1995): 213–227.

Armstrong, John A. *Ukrainian Nationalism, 1939–1945*. New York: Columbia University Press, 1955.

Armstrong, John A. *Ukrainian Nationalism*. 2nd edition. New York: Columbia University Press, 1963.

Armstrong, John A. *Ukrainian Nationalism*. 3rd edition. Englewood, CO: Ukrainian Academic Press, 1990.

Artizov, A. N., N. G. Tomilinaia (eds.), *Brezhnev k 109-letiiu so dnia rozhdeniia: Katalog istoriko-dokumental'noi vystavki*. Moscow: Kuchkovo pole, 2016.

Ash, Timothy Garton. "The Life of Death." *The New York Review of Books*, December 19, (1985): 26–39.

Avrutin, Eugene M. and Elisssa Bemporad, eds. *Pogroms: A Documentary History*. Oxford: Oxford University Press, 2021.

Babiracki, Patryk. "Interfacing the Soviet Bloc: Recent Literature and New Paradigms." *Ab Imperio* 4 (2011): 376–407.

Bachyns'kyi, Yuliian. *Ukraina irredenta*. Trete vydanie. Berlin: Vydavnytstvo ukrains'koi molodi, 1924. https://zbruc.eu/node/54638 (accessed August 17, 2023).

Bacon, Edwin and Mark Sandle (eds.), *Brezhnev Reconsidered*. Houndmills: Palgrave Macmillan, 2002.

Bakanov, Aleksei *"Ni katsapa, ni zhida, ni liakha": Natsional'nyi vopros v ideologii Organizatsii ukrainskikh natsionalistov, 1929–1945 gg*. Moscow: Algoritm, 2014.

Balakrishnan, Gopal, ed. *Mapping the Nation*. London: Verso, 1996.

Balei, Petro. *Fronda Stepana Bandery v OUN 1940 roku*. Kyiv: Tekna, 1996.

Ball, Karyn and Per Anders Rudling. "The Underbelly of Canadian Multiculturalism: Holocaust Obfuscation and Envy in the Debate about the Canadian Museum for Human Rights," *Holocaust Studies: A Journal of Culture and History* 20, no. 3 (2014): 33–80.

Balling, Mads Ole. *Von Reval bis Bukarest: Statistisch-Biographisches Handbuch der Parlamentarier der deutschen Minderheiten in Ostmittel- und Südosteuropa 1919–1945*, 2 vols. Bad Saulgau: Dokumentation Verlag, 1991.

Bandera, Stephen. "Family Name Cleared." *Edmonton Journal*, 9 February 2010: A 13.

Barets'kyi Osyp *et al*. (eds.). *Bila knyha: OUN na zlami II i XXI stolit'*. Kyiv: Vydavnytstvo "Kyii," 2006.

Bark, Dennis L. and David R. Gress. *A History of West Germany*. Second edition. Vol. 1. *From Shadow to Substance, 1945-1963*. Oxford: Blackwell, 1993.

Barkan, Elazar, Elizabeth A. Cole, and Kai Struve, eds. *Shared History – Divided Memory: Jews and Others in Soviet-Occupied Poland, 1939–1941*. Leipzig: Leipziger Universitätsverlag, 2007.

Barkey, Karen and Mark von Hagen, eds. *After Empire: Multiethnic Societies and Nation-Building. The Soviet Union and the Russian, Ottoman, and Habsburg Empires*. Boulder, CO: Westview Press, 1997.

Baron, Nick. "Remaking Soviet Society: The Filtration of Returnees from Nazi Germany, 1944–49." In *Warlands: Population Resettlement and State Reconstruction in the Soviet–East European Borderlands, 1945–50*, edited by Peter Gatrell and Nick Baron, 89–116. Basingstoke: Palgrave Macmillan, 2009.

Bartov, Omer. "Fascism in Practice and Contemporary Politics." *Journal of Soviet and Post-Soviet Politics and Society*, Vol. 7, No. 2 (2021): 176–184.

Bartov, Omer, Atina Grossmann, and Mary Nolan, eds. *Crimes of War: Guilt and Denial in the Twentieth Century*. New York: The New Press, 2002

Basarab, John. *Pereiaslav 1654: A Historiographical Study*. Edmonton: Canadian Institute of Ukrainian Studies, University of Alberta, 1982.

Bassin Mark, *The Gumilev Mystique: Biopolitics, Eurasianism, and the Construction of Community in Modern Russia*, Ithaca, NY: Cornell University Press, 2016.

Bauer, Otto. "Die Nationalitätenfrage und die Sozialdemokratie." In *Marx-Studien: Blätter für Theorie und Politik des wissenschaftlichen Sozialismus*, Vol. 2, edited by Max Adler and Rudolf Hilferding. Vienna: Ignaz Brand, 1907.

Bauerkämper, Arnd and Grzegorz Rossoliński-Liebe (eds.). *Fascism without Borders: Transnational Connections and Cooperation between Movements and Regimes in Europe from 1918 to 1945* (New York and Oxford: Berghahn Books, 2017.

Baumann, Robert F. "Russia's Latest Historical Revisionism and Reinventing the Future," *Military Review Online Exclusive* (November 2022): 1–15.

Bayly, Christopher A. *The Birth of the Modern World 1780–1914: Global Connections and Comparisons*. Oxford: Blackwell, 2004.

Bazhan, O. and O. Loshyts'kyi (eds.). "Stanovlennia Narodnoho rukhu Ukrainy (za dokumentamy Haluzevoho derzhavnoho arkhivu Sluzhby bezpeky Ukrainy)." *Z arkhiviv VUChK, GPU, NKVD, KGB: Naukovyi i dokumental'nyi zhurnal*, no. 2 (33) (2009): 206–326.

Bednarek, J., ed. *Poland and Ukraine in the 1930s and 1940s*. Warsaw: Institute of National Remembrance, 2009.

Beichelt, Timm and Susann Worschech, eds. *Transnational Ukraine? Networks and Ties that Influence Contemporary Ukraine*. Stuttgart: ibidem-Verlag, 2017.

Beissinger, Mark. "Ethnicity, the Personnel Weapon, and Neo-Imperial Integration: Ukraine and RSFSR Provincial Party Officials Compared." *Studies in Comparative Communism*, XXI, no. 1 (Spring, 1988): 71-85.

Bellezza, Simone Attilio. "Making Soviet Ukraine Ukrainian: The Debate on Ukrainian Statehood in the Journal Suchasnist' (1961-1971)." *Nationalities Papers* 47 no. 3 (2019): 379-393.

Bemporad, Elissa. *Legacy of Blood: Jews, Pogroms, and Ritual Murder in the Lands of the Soviets*. New York: Oxford University Press, 2019.

Beniuk, Andrew G. "The Referendum: On the Road to Ukraine's Independence." MA Thesis, University of Alberta, 1993.

Beorn, Waitman Wade. *Marching into Darkness: The Wehrmacht and the Holocaust in Belarus*. Cambridge, MA: Harvard University Press, 2014.

Berdykhovs'ka, Bogumila [Bogumiła Berdychowska] (ed.). *Ezhy Gedroits' ta ukrains'ka emigratsiia: Lystovannia 1950-1982 rokiv*. Kyiv: Krytyka, 2008.

Berglund, Christofer, Katrine Gotfredsen, Jean Hudson and Bo Petersson, eds. *Language and Society in the Caucasus: Understanding the Past, Navigating the Present*. Lund: Universus Academic Press, 2021.

Bergman, David. *Stridens psykologi: Konsten att döda och överleva*. Lund: Studentlitteratur, 2022.

Berkhoff, Karel C. and Marco Carynnyk. "The Organization of Ukrainian Nationalists and Its Attitude towards Germans and Jews: Iaroslav Stets'ko's 1941 Zhyttiepys." *Harvard Ukrainian Studies* 23, no. 3/4 (December 1999): 149-184.

Berkhoff, Karel C. *Harvest of Despair: Life and Death in Ukraine under Nazi Rule*. Cambridge, MA: The Belknap Press of Harvard University Press, 2004.

Bernsand, Niklas. "Minoritetssoldater i det ryska kriget i Ukraina: Hur framställs 'specialoperationen' i burjatiska, ossetiska och dagestanska sociala medier?" *Östbulletinen: Temanummer om Ukraina och Rysslands anfallskrig* 2 (2022): 8-17.

Bilas, Ivan. *Represyvno-karal'na systema v Ukraini, 1917-1953: suspil'no-politychnyi ta istoriko-pravovyi analiz*. Tom I. Kyiv: Lybid, 1994.

Bennich-Björkman Li, Andriy Kashyn, and Sergiy Kurbatov, "The Election of a Kleptocrat: Viktor Ianukovych and the Ukrainian Presidential Elections in 2010," *East/West: Journal of Ukrainian Studies* VI, no. 1 (2019): 91-124.

Blacker, Uilleam, Alexander Etkind, and Julie Fedor, eds. *Memory and Theory in Eastern Europe*, New York: Palgrave Macmillan, 2013.

Blood, Philip W. *Hitler's Bandit Hunters: The SS and the Nazi Occupation of Europe*. Washington, DC: Potomac Books, 2006.

Bohunov, Serhii et al., ed. *Pol'shcha ta Ukraina u trydtsiatykh-sorokovykh rokakh XX stolittia: Nevidomy dokumenty z arkhiviv spetsial'nykh sluzhb, Tom 4, Poliaky i ukraintsi mizh dvoma totalitarnymy systemamy 1942–1945: Chastyna persha*, Warsaw: IPN, NAN Ukrainy, 2005.

Bolianovs'kyi, Andrii. "Ivan Hryn'okh—providnyi diiach ukrains'koho pidpillia." In *Boh i Ukraina ponad use: o. Ivan Hryn'okh*, edited by Oleksandr Panchenko, 60–76. Hadiach: Vydavnytstvo 'Hadiach', 2007.

Bolianovs'kyi, Andrii. *Dyviziia 'Halychyna': Istoriia*. L'viv: A. Bolianovs'kyi, 2000.

Bolianovs'kyi, Andrii. *Ukrains'ki viis'kovi formuvannia v zbroinykh sylakh Nimechchyny (1939–1945)*. L'viv: L'vivs'kyi Natsional'nyi Universytet im. Ivana Franka and Canadian Institute of Ukrainian Studies, 2003.

Boll, Bernd. "Złoczów, July 1941—The Wehrmacht and the Beginning of the Holocaust in Galicia: From a Criticism of Photographs to a Revision of the Past." In *Crimes of War: Guilt and Denial in the Twentieth Century*, edited by Omer Bartov, Atina Grossmann, and Mary Nolan, 61–99. New York: The New Press, 2002.

Borowsky, Peter. "Germany's Ukrainian Policy during World War I and the Revolution of 1918-1919." In *German-Ukrainian Relations in Historical Perspective*, edited by Hans-Joachim Torke and John-Paul Himka, 84–94. Edmonton: Canadian Institute of Ukrainian Studies Press, 1994.

Borys, Jurij. *The Russian Communist Party and the Sovietization of Ukraine: A Study in the Communist Doctrine of the Self-Determination of Nations*. Stockholm: Norstedts, 1960.

Borzęcki, Jerzy. *The Soviet-Polish Peace of 1921 and the Creation of Interwar Europe*. New Haven: Yale University Press, 2008.

Boshyk, Yury (eds.), *Ukraine during World War II: History and its Aftermath*. Edmonton: CIUS Press, 1986.

Aleksandar Boskovic and Chris Hann, eds. *The Anthropological Field on the Margins of Europe, 1945-1991* (=Halle Studies in the Anthropology of Eurasia) (Berlin: LIT, 2013).

Breitman, Richard and Norman J.W. Goda. *Hitler's Shadow: Nazi War Criminals, U.S. Intelligence, and the Cold War*. Washington, DC: The National Archives, 2010.

Breitman, Richard, Norman J.W. Goda, Timothy Naftali, and Robert Wolfe. *US Intelligence and the Nazis*. New York: Cambridge University Press, 2005.

Brezhnev, Leonid Ilich. *Rabochie i dnevnikovye zapisi: V 3-kh tomakh*. Moscow: Istoricheskaia literatura, 2016.

Broschek, Jörg. "Federalism in Europe, America and Africa: A Comparative Analysis." In *Federalism and Democratization: Perceptions for Political and Institutional Reforms*, edited by Wilhelm Hofmeister, 23–52. Singapore: Konrad Adenauer Stiftung Singapore, 2016.

Brown, Kate. *A Biography of No Place: From Ethnic Borderland to Soviet Heartland*. Cambridge, MA: Harvard University Press, 2003.

Bruder, Franziska. *"Den ukrainischen Staat erkämpfen oder sterben!" Die Organisation Ukrainischer Nationalisten (OUN) 1928–1948*. Berlin: Metropol Verlag, 2007.

Brudny Yitzhak M. and Evgeny Finkel, 'Why Ukraine is not Russia: Hegemonic National Identity and Democratization in Russia and Ukraine,' *East European Politics and Societies* 25, no. 4 (2011): 813–833

Bruski, Jan Jacek. *Between Prometheism and Realpolitik: Poland and Soviet Ukraine, 1921–1926*. Krakow: Jagiellonian University Press, 2017.

Brzezinski, Zbigniew. "The Premature Partnership." *Foreign Affairs* 73, no. 2 (1994): 67–82.

Bucur, Maria. *Eugenics and Modernization in Interwar Romania*. Pittsburgh: University of Pittsburgh Press, 2002.

Budrytė, Dovilė. "'We Call It Genocide': Soviet Deportations and Repression in the Memory of Lithuanians." In *The Genocidal Temptation: Auschwitz, Hiroshima, Rwanda, and Beyond*, edited by R. S. Frey, 79–101. Lanham, MD: University Press of America, 2004.

Bul'ba-Borovets', Taras. *Armiia bez derzhavy: Slava i trehediia ukrains'koho povstans'koho rukhu. Spohady*. Kyiv: Knyha Rodu, 2008.

Burakovskiy, Alexander. "In Search of a Liberal Polity: The Rukh Council of Nationalities, the Jewish question, and Ukrainian Independence." *East European Jewish Affairs*, 45, no. 1 (2015): 109–131.

Burds, Jeffrey. "AGENTURA: Soviet Informants' Networks & the Ukrainian Underground in Galicia, 1944–1948." *East European Politics and Societies* 11, no. 1 (Winter 1997): 89–130.

Burds, Jeffrey. "Archival Practices in the Post-Soviet Zones." Paper presented at the 2008 National Convention of the American Association for the Advancement of Slavic Studies, Philadelphia, November 23, 2008.

Burds, Dzheffri [Jeffrey]. *Shpionazh i natsionalizm: Pervyi gody 'kholodnoi voiny' na Zapadnoi Ukraine (1944-1948)*. Moscow: Sovremennaia Istoriia, 2010.

Burds, Jeffrey. *The Early Cold War in Soviet West Ukraine, 1944-1948* (=The Carl Beck Papers in Russian and East European Studies. No. 1505). Pittsburgh: Center for Russian and East European Studies, University of Pittsburgh, 2001.

Burds, Jeffrey. *The Holocaust in Rovno: the massacre at Sosenki Forest, November 1941*. Basingstoke: Palgrave Macmillan, 2014.

But'ko, Serhii, ed. *Stepan Bandera: Zbirnyk materialiv i dokumentiv*. Kyiv: Ukrains'kyi Instytut Natsional'noi Pamiati, 2009.

Cameron, Sarah. *The Hungry Steppe: Famine, Violence, and the Making of Soviet Kazakhstan*. Ithaca, NY: Cornell University Press, 2018.

Canovan, Margaret. *Nation and Political Theory*. Cheltenham: Edward Elgar, 1996.

Carynnyk, Marco. "A Bit of Blood-stained Batting. Kharkiv, Saturday, 13 May 1933." *Krytyka*, XIX, issue 1-2, (May 2015): 35-39.

Carynnyk, Marco. "'A Knife in the Back of Our Revolution': A Reply to Alexander J. Motyl's 'The Ukrainian Nationalist Movement and the Jews: Theoretical Reflections on Nationalism, Fascism, Rationality, Primordialism, and History.'" *The American Association for Polish-Jewish Studies*, 2014. Retrieved on 31 January 2017. http://aapjstudies.org/manager/external/ckfinder/userfiles/files/Carynnyk%20Reply%20to%20Motyl%202%20.pdf (accessed August 17, 2023).

Carynnyk, Marco. "'Foes of Our Rebirth': Ukrainian Nationalist Discussions about Jews, 1929-1947." *Nationalities Papers* 39, no, 3 (2011): 315-352.

Carynnyk, Marco. *Furious Angels: Ukrainians, Jews, and Poles in the Summer of 1941*, forthcoming.

Carynnyk, Marco. "The Palace on the Ikva: Dubne, 18 September 1939 and 24 June 1941." In *Shared History – Divided Memory: Jews and Others in Soviet-Occupied Poland, 1939-1941*, edited by Elazar Barkan, Elizabeth A. Cole, and Kai Struve, 273-302. Leipzig: Leipziger Universitätsverlag, 2007.

Carynnyk, Marco. [Marko Tsarynnyk] "Zolochiv movchyt." *Krytyka* 14 (2005): 27-28.

Cherchenko, Yurii. "Dzherela do istorii vyzvol'noho rukhu." *Ukrains'kyi vyzvol'nyi rukh: Naukovyi zbirnyk* 18 (2013): 6-24.

Chernev, Boris. *Twilight of Empire: The Brest-Litovsk Conference and the Remaking of East-Central Europe, 1917-1918*. Toronto: University of Toronto Press, 2017.

Chernev, Borislav. "Ukrainization and Its Contradictions in the Context of the Brest-Litovsk System." In *The Empire and Nationalism at War*, edited by Eric Lohr, Vera Tolz, Alexander Semyonov, and Mark von Hagen. Bloomington, IN: Slavica Publishers, 2014, 163-188.

Chuev, Sergei. *Ukrainskii Legion* (Moscow: Iauza, 2006)

Cienciala, Anna M. and Titus Komarnicki. *From Versailles to Locarno: Keys to Polish Foreign Policy, 1919-1925*. Lawrence: University Press of Kansas, 1984.

Ciesielski, Stanisław, Wojchiech Materski and Andrzej Paczkowski. *Represje sowieckie wobec Polaków i obywateli polskich*. Wyd. II. Warsaw: Ośrodek Karta, 2002.

Cisesielski, Stanisław, Grzegorz Hryciuk and Aleksander Srebakowski. *Masowe deportacje ludności w Związku Radzieckim*. Toruń: Wyd. Adam Marszałek, 2003.

Clark, Roland and Tim Grady, eds. *European Fascist Movements: A Sourcebook*. New York: Routledge, 2023.

Conason, Joe "To Catch a Nazi," *The Village Voice*, 11 February 1986, 17-21.

Connor, Walker. "Nation-Building or Nation-Destroying?" *World Politics* 24, no. 3 (April 1972): 332-336.

Connor, Walker. *The National Question in Marxist-Leninist Theory and Strategy*. Princeton: Princeton University Press, 1984.

Conquest, Robert. *The Nation Killers: The Soviet Deportation of Nationalities*. London: Macmillan, 1970.

Conquest, Robert. *Stalin: Breaker of Nations*. New York: Penguin Random House, 1991

Corbea Hoise, Andrea, Rudolf Jaworski and Monika Sommer, eds. In *Umbruch im östlichen Europa: Die nationale Wende und das kollektive Gedächtnis*. Innsbruck: Studien Verlag, 2004.

Cornwall, Mark. "The Czechoslovak Sphinx: 'Moderate and Reasonable' Konrad Henlein." In *In the Shadow of Hitler: Personalities of the Right in Central and Eastern Europe*, edited by Rebecca Haynes and Martyn Rady, 206-226. London: I. B. Tauris, 2011.

Dahlstedt, Sten and Sven-Erik Liedman. *Nationalismens logik: Nationella identiteter i England, Frankrike och Tyskland decennierna kring sekelskiftet 1900*. Stockholm: Natur och kultur, 1996.

Dalberg-Acton, John Emerich Edward. *The History of Freedom and Other Essays*. London: Macmillan, 1907.

Dashkevych, Yaroslav and Vasyl' Kuk, eds. *Ukrains'k derzhavotvorennia: Akt 30 chervnia 1941. Zbirnyk dokumentiv i materialiv*. L'viv: Piramida, 2001.

David-Fox, Michael, Peter Holquist and Alexander M. Martin, eds. *The Holocaust in the East: Local Perpetrators and Soviet Responses*. Pittsburgh: University of Pittsburgh Press, 2014.

Davidovitch, Nadav and Rakefet Zalashik "Scientific Medicine and the Politics of Public Health: Minorities in Interwar Eastern Europe," *Science in Context*, vol. 32, no.1 (2019): 1-4.

Davies, Norman and Antony Polonsky, eds. *Jews in Eastern Poland and the USSR, 1939-46*. New York: St. Martin's Press, 1991.

Davies, R.W. and Stephen G. Wheatcroft. *The Years of Hunger: Soviet Agriculture, 1931–1933*. New York: Palgrave Macmillan, 2004.

Dean, Martin. "The German *Gendarmerie*, the Ukrainian *Schutzmannschaft* and the "Second Wave" of Jewish killings in Occupied Ukraine: German Policing at the Local Level in the Zhitomir Region, 1941-1944." *German History* 14, no. 2 (1996): 168-192.

Dean, Martin. *Collaboration in the Holocaust: Crimes of the Local Police in Belorussia and Ukraine, 1941–44*. New York: St. Martin's Press in association with the United States Holocaust Memorial Museum, 2000.

Dietsch, Johan. *Making Sense of Suffering: Holocaust and Holodomor in Ukrainian Historical Culture*. Lund: Department of History, Lund University, 2006.

Dmitrijew, S. S. "Die russische Kultur und die Kultur der Völker des Russischen Reiches in der ersten Hälfte des 19. Jh." In Netschkina *et al*. (eds.), *Geschichte der UdSSR, Band I: Von den ältesten Zeiten bis zum Jahre 1861. Urgesellschaft, Sklavenhalterordnung und Feudalismus*. Zweiter Halbband. Translated by Arno Specht. 825–866. Berlin: VEB Deutscher Verlag der Wissenschaften, 1962.

Dobzhansky, Theodius. "A Debatable Account of the Origin of Races." *Scientific American* vol. 208, (1963): 169–172.

Dobzhansky, Theodius. "Comment." *Current Anthropology* 3, no. 3 (1962): 279–280.

Domański, Jerzy. "Bandera—bohater Juszczenki." *Przegląd tygodniowy*, no. 5(527) (2010): 3.

Dontsov, Dmytro. *Dukh nashoi davnyny*. Druhe vydannia. Drohobych: Vydavnytstvo "Vidrodzhennia", 1991.

Dontsov, Dmytro. *Natsionalizm*. Kyiv: FOP Stebeliak, 2015.

Dornik, Wolfram, Georgiy Kasianov [Heorhii Kas'ianov], Hannes Leidinger, Peter Lieb, Alexei Miller, Bogdan Musial, and Vasyl Rasevych (eds). *The Emergence of Ukraine: Self-Determination, Occupation, and War in Ukraine, 1917–1922*, edited by translated by Gus Fagan. Edmonton: Canadian Institute of Ukrainian Studies Press, 2015.

Douglas, Lawrence. "From the Sentimental Story of the State to the Verbrecherstaat, Or, the Rise of the Atrocity Paradigm." In *The New Histories of International Criminal Law: Retrains*, edited by Immi Tallgren and Thomas Skouteris, 54–71. Oxford: Oxford University Press, 2019.

Douglas, Lawrence. "Is Russia a Verbrecherstaat?—A Perspective from International Law." *The American Academy in Berlin*, 29 April 2022. https://www.americanacademy.de/videoaudio/is-russia-a-verbrecherstaat-a-perspective-from-international-law/ (accessed 17 August 2023).

Douglas, Lawrence. *The Right Wrong Man: John Demjanjuk and the Last Great Nazi War Crimes Trial*. Princeton, NJ: Princeton University Press, 2016.

Dreyer, Nicolas. "Genocide, *Holodomor* and Holocaust Discourse as Echo of Historical Injury and as Rhetorical Radicalization in the Russian-Ukrainian Conflict of 2013–2018." *Journal of Genocide Research* 20, no. 4 (2018): 545–564.

Dubasevych, Roman. "Die Erinnerung an die Habsburgmonarchie in der ukrainischen Kultur der Gegenwart," (Ph.D. Dissertation, University of Vienna, 2013).

Dubasevych, Roman. "Majdan-Lyrik: Gibt es eine Poetik der Revolution?" In *Ukraine: Literatur und Kritik*, edited by Martin Pollak and Stefaniya Ptashnyk, 50–71. Salzburg: Otto Müller Verlag, 2016.

Dubasevych, Roman. "Pryvydy imperii ta demony peryferii." *Zaxid.net*, 23 May 2011. https://zaxid.net/prividi_imperiyi_ta_demoni_periferiyi_n1129717.

Dubasevych, Roman. *Zwischen kulturellem Gedächtnis, Mythos und Nostalgie: Die Erinnerung an die Habsburgermonarchie in der ukrainischen Kultur der Gegenwart*. Vienna: Böhlau, 2017.

Dubasevych, Roman and Matthias Schwartz. "Einleitung." In *Sirenen des Krieges: Diskursive und affektive Dimensionen des Ukraine-Konflikts* (=*LiteraturForschung* 38), edited by Roman Dubasevych and Matthias Schwartz. Berlin: Kulturverlag Kadmos, 2020: 7–46.

Dubasevych, Roman and Matthias Schwartz, eds. *Sirenen des Krieges: Diskursive und affektive Dimensionen des Ukraine-Konflikts* (=*LiteraturForschung* 38), Berlin: Kulturverlag Kadmos, 2020.

Dudaev, Dzhokhar. "Rusizm—shizofrenicheskaia forma manii mirovogo gospodarstva." *Argument*, 19 March 2014. https://argumentua.com/tsitaty/rusizm-shizofrenicheskaya-forma-manii-mirovogo-gospodstva (accessed 17 August 2023).

Dudko, Oksana. "A Conceptual Limbo of Genocide: Russian Rhetoric, Mass Atrocities in Ukraine, and the Current Definition's Limits." *Canadian Slavonic Papers/Revue Canadienne des Slavistes* 64, nos. 2-3 (2022): 133-145.

Peter Duffy, *The Bielski Brothers: The True Story of Three Men Who Defied the Nazis, Built a Village in the Forest, and Saved 1,200 Jews*. New York: Harper Collins Publishers, 2004.

Dulić, Tomislav. *Utopias of Nation: Local Mass Killing in Bosnia and Herzegovina, 1941-42*. Uppsala: Department of History, Uppsala University, 2005.

Dulić, Tomislav and Goran Miljan. "The Ustašas and Fascism: 'Abolitionism,' Revolution, and Ideology (1929-42)." *Journal of Soviet and Post-Soviet Politics and Society* 6, no. 1 (2020): 277-306.

Duzhyi, Petro. *Roman Shukhevych – polityk, voin, hromadianyn*. L'viv: Halyts'ka vydavnycha spilka, 1998.

Esbenshade, Richard S. "Remembering to Forget: Memory, History, National Identity in Postwar East-Central Europe," *Representations*, no. 49 (1995): 72-96.

Emberland, Terje and Matthew Kott. *Himmlers Norge: Nordmenn i det storgermanske prosjekt*. Oslo: H. Aschehoug & Co., 2013.

Emeran, Christine. *New Generation Political Activism in Ukraine, 2000-2014*. New York: Routledge, 2017.

Engman, Max. *Lejonet och dubbelörnen: Finlands imperiella decennier 1830-1890*. Stockholm: Atlantis, 2000.

Engman, Max, ed. *När imperier faller: Studier kring riksupplösningar och nya stater*. Stockholm: Atlantis, 1994.

Engman, Max. "Tillbaka till framtiden eller framåt till det förflutna? Imperieupplösningar förr och nu." In *När imperier faller: Studier kring riksuppläsningar och nya stater*, edited by Max Engman, 7-22. Stockholm: Atlantis, 1994.

Erhart, Walter and Arne Koch, eds. *Ernst Moritz Arndt (1769-1860): Deutscher Nationalismus – Europa-Transatlantische Perspektiven*. Berlin: De Gruyter, 2007.

Erklikhman, Vadim. "Poteri narodonaselenia v XX veke: spravochnik," *Radio Free Europe/Radio Liberty*. http://www.rferl.mobi/a/soviet-war-dead/26999777.html (accessed 17 August 2023)

Erlacher, Trevor. "The Furies of Nationalism: Dmytro Dontsov, the Ukrainian Idea, and Europe's Twentieth Century." PhD Diss., University of North Carolina at Chapel Hill, 2017.

Esbenshade, Richard S. "Remembering to Forget: Memory, History, National Identity in Postwar East-Central Europe." *Representations*, no. 49 (1995): 72–96.

Fairey, Jack and Brian P. Farrell. "Series Introduction: Reordering an Imperial Modern Asia." In *Empire in Asia: A New Global History. Volume 1. From Chinggisid to Qing*, 1–8. London: Bloomsbury Academic, 2018.

Farmer, Kenneth C. *Ukrainian Nationalism in the Post-Stalin Era: Myth, Symbols and Ideology in Soviet Nationalities Policy*. The Hague: Martinus Nijhoff Publishers, 1980.

Fedchynia I. and Ia. Deremenda, (eds). *Spil'ka Ukrains'koi Molodi: S.U.M. na chuzhyny*. London: Mercurius Press, 1954.

Fedevich, Klimentii. *Za Viru, Tsaria i kobziaria: Malorosiis'ki monarkisti i ukrains'kyi natsional'nyi rukh (1905–1917 roki)*, per. z. ros. Katerina Demchuk. Kyiv: Krityka, 2017.

Feldman, Alexandr. "Thirty Years After the Death of Roman Shukhevych." *Contact* 2-3 (1980): 77.

Felder, Björn M. and Paul J. Weindling, eds. *Baltic Eugenics: Bio-Politics, Race and Nation in Interwar Estonia, Latvia and Lithuania 1918-1940*. Amsterdam: Brill, 2013.

Finder, Gabriel N., and Alexander V. Prusin. "Collaboration in Eastern Galicia: The Ukrainian Police and the Holocaust." *East European Jewish Affairs* 34, no. 2 (2004): 95–118.

Finlay, Richard J. "The Rise and Fall of Popular Imperialism in Scotland, 1850-1950." *Scottish Geographical Society*, 113, no. 1 (1997): 13–21.

Fisch, Jörg. *A History of the Self-Determination of Peoples: The Domestication of an Illusion*. Cambridge: Cambridge University Press, 2015.

Fischer, Fritz. *Germany's Aims in the First World War*. New York: W.W. Norton & Company, 1967.

Fishman, Mikhail. "Putin's Dehumanized Russia." *The Russia File: A Blog of the Kennan Institute*, 7 June 2022. https://www.wilsoncenter.org/blog-post/putins-dehumanized-russia (accessed 17 August 2023).

Fortuin, Egbert. "Ukraine Commits Genocide on Russians: The Term 'Genocide' in Russian Propaganda." *Russian Linguistics*, 7 September 2022. https://link.springer.com/article/10.1007/s11185-022-09258-5 (accessed 17 August, 2023).

Fowkes, Ben. "The National Question in the Soviet Union under Leonid Brezhnev: Policy and Response." In *Brezhnev Reconsidered*, edited by Edwin Bacon and Mark Sandle, 68–89. Houndmills: Palgrave Macmillan, 2002.

Fowler, Mayhill C. *Beau Monde on Empire's Edge: State and Stage in Soviet Ukraine.* Toronto: University of Toronto Press, 2017.

Frankel, Jonathan, ed. *Studies in Contemporary Jewry: Vol. XIII: The Fate of the European Jews, 1939–1945: Continuity of Contingency?* Oxford: Oxford University Press, 1997.

Fredborg, Arvid. *Storbritannien och den ryska frågan 1918–1920: Studier i de anglo-ryska relationerna från vapenstilleståndet den 11 november 1918 till den begynnande avspänningen i januari och februari 1920 mellan Storbritannien och Sovjetryssland.* Stockholm: Norstedt & Söner, 1951.

Frey, R. S., ed. *The Genocidal Temptation: Auschwitz, Hiroshima, Rwanda, and Beyond.* Lanham, MD: University Press of America, 2004.

Friedman, Philip. "Ukrainian-Jewish Relations during the Nazi Occupation." In *Roads to Extinction: Essays on the Holocaust*, ed. Philip Friedman, 176–208. New York and Philadelphia: The Jewish Publication Society of America, 1980.

Fritz, Stephen G. *Ostkrieg: Hitler's War of Extermination in the East.* Lexington, KY: University Press of Kentucky, 2011.

Fröhlich, Florence. "Victimhood and Building Identities on Past Suffering," in Ninna Mörner, ed. *Constructions and Instrumentalization of the Past: A Comparative Study on Memory Management in the Region (=CBEES State of the Region Report, 2020)* (Huddinge: Center for Baltic and East European Studies, 2020), 23-36.

Fujiwara, Aya. "From Anglo-Conformity to Multiculturalism: The Role of the Scottish, Ukrainian, and Japanese Ethnicity in the Transformation of Canadian Identity, 1919–1971." PhD Diss., University of Alberta, 2007. Furuhagen, Birgitta, ed. *Ryssland: ett annat Europa: Historia och samhälle under 1000 år.* Stockholm: Utbildningsradion, 1995.

Gatrell, Peter and Nick Baron, eds. *Warlands: Population Resettlement and State Reconstruction in the Soviet–East European Borderlands, 1945–50.* Houndmills, Basingstoke: Palgrave Macmillan, 2009.

Gaunt, David. "Targeting Ukrainians that Praise the Armed Resistance to USSR: Putin's Authoritarian Turn Justified by the Past." *Baltic Worlds* XV: 1–2 (June 2022): 165–167.

Gawin, Magdalena. "Progressivism and Eugenic Thinking in Poland, 1905–1939." In *Blood and Homeland: Eugenics and Racial Nationalism in Central and Southeast Europe, 1900-1940*, edited by Marius Turda and Paul J. Weindling. Budapest: CEU Press, 2007, 167–183.

Gerashchenko, Georgii. "Koe-chto o "zabyvchivosti" v panegirikakh Romanu Shukhevych." *Vremia Regionov Kharkovshchiny* 27, no. 74 (2007). http://pr.kharkov.ua/full.php?g=newspaper&id=1275 (accessed 17 august 2008. Link no longer valid).

Gerner, Kristian. "Ryssland: Statsbildning som historiskt problem." In *Ryssland: ett annat Europa: Historia och samhälle under 1000 år*, edited by Birgitta Furuhagen, 265–291. Stockholm: Utbildningsradion, 1995.

Gerner, Kristian. *Rysslands historia*. Lund: Historiska Media, 2022.

Getty, J. Arch, Gábor Rittersporn and Viktor Zemskov. "Victims of the Soviet Penal System in the Pre-War Years: A First Approach on the Basis of Archival Evidence." *American Historical Review*, 98, no. 4 (1993): 1017–1049.

Gibas-Krzak, Danuta. "Działalność terrorystyczna i dywersyjno-sabotażowa nacjonalistów ukraińskich w latach 1921-1939," *Przegląd Bezpieczeństwa Wewnętrznego* 3 (2010): 174-186.

Gilley, Christopher. "Beyond Petliura: The Ukrainian national movement and the 1919 pogroms." *East European Jewish Affairs*, 47, no. 1 (2017): 45–61.

Gilley, Christopher. "Reconciling the Irreconcilable? Left-Wing Ukrainian Nationalism and the Soviet Regime." *Nationalities Papers* 47, no. 3, (2019): 341–354.

Gilley, Christopher. "Was Symon Petliura 'an anti-Semite who massacred Jews during a time of war'?" *Open Democracy* (February 2019). https://www.opendemocracy.net/en/odr/the-centenary-of-the-proskuriv-pogrom/ (accessed 17 August 2023)

Gilley, Christopher. *The "Change of Signposts" in the Ukrainian Emigration: A Contribution to the History of Sovietophilism in the 1920s*. Stuttgart: ibidem-Verlag, 2014.

Gimpelevich, Zina J. *Vasil Bykau: His Life and Works*. Montreal: McGill-Queen's University Press, 2005.

Ginter, [Günther]. Hans F. K. *Lytsar, Smert' i chort: Herois'ka mysl'. Vstup ta pereklad iz IV. nimets'koho vydannia Rostyslava Yendyka*. L'viv: Vydavnytstvo "Prometei," 1937.

Glebov, Sergey. *From Empire to Eurasia: Politics, Scholarship, and Ideology in Russian Eurasianism, 1920s-1930s*. DeKalb, IL: NIU Press, 2017.

Głowacka-Grajper, Małgorzata and Anna Wylegała (eds.) *The Burden of Memory: History, Memory and Identity in Contemporary Ukraine*. Bloomington, IN: Indiana University Press, 2020.

Goda, Norman J. W., ed. *Rethinking Holocaust Justice: Essays across Disciplines*. New York and Oxford: Berghahn Books, 2018.

Golczewski, Frank. "Die Kollaboration in der Ukraine," *Beiträge zur Geschichte des Nationalsozialismus*, vol. 19: Kooperation und Verbrechen: Formen der "Kollaboration" im östlichen Europa 1939-1945, edited by. Christoph Dieckmann, Babette Quinkert, and Tatjana Tönsmeyer (Göttingen: Wallenstein Verlag, 2003): 151-182.

Golczewski, Frank. "Politische Konzepte des ukrainischen nichtsozialistischen Exils (Petliura-Lypynskyj-Donzow)," In *Ukraine: Gegenwart und Geschichte eines neuen Staates*, edited by Guido Hausmann and Andreas Kappeler, 110–118. Baden-Baden: Nomos, 1993.

Golczewski, Frank. *Deutsche und Ukrainer 1914–1939*.Paderborn: Ferdinand Schöningh, 2010.

Golubovskii, Mikhail D. "Dobzhanskii v dvukh mirakh." *Vestnik* no. 24(231), November 23, 1999. http://www.vestnik.com/issues/1999/1123/koi/golubov.htm (accessed June 12, 2013, link no longer valid).

Gorina, Ivanna. "Ianukovychu vozvrashchaiut sudimosti." *Rossiiskaia gazeta*, no. 3819, 13 July 2005. https://rg.ru/2005/07/13/yanukovich.html (accessed 17 August, 2023).

Goujon, Alexandra. "'Genozid': A Rallying Cry in Belarus: A Rhetoric Analysis of Some Belarusian Nationalist Texts." *Journal of Genocide Research* 1, no. 3 (1999): 353–366.

Grabowski, Jan. "The Polish Holocaust Law," *Intersections* vol. 4, no. 1 (2021), 22–25.

Graham, Loren R. "Science and Values: The Eugenics Movement in Germany and Russia in the 1920s." *American Historical Review* 82, no. 5 (1977): 1133–1164.

Graham, Loren R. (ed.) *Science and the Soviet Social Order*, Cambridge: Harvard University Press, 1990.

Gramsci, Antonio. *En kollektiv intellektuell: Urval och inledning av René Coeckelberghs*. Translated by Stig Herlitz. Lund: Cavefors, 1967.

Grant, Thomas. "Removing Russia from the Security Council: Part One." *Opinio Juris*, 18 October 2022. http://opiniojuris.org/2022/10/18/removing-russia-from-the-security-council-part-one/ (accessed August 17, 2023).

Grant, Thomas. "Removing Russia from the Security Council: Part Two." *Opinio Juris*, 19 October 2022. http://opiniojuris.org/2022/10/19/removing-russia-from-the-security-council-part-two/ (accessed August 17, 2023).

Grelka, Frank. *Die ukrainische Nationalbewegung unter deutscher Besatzungsherrschaft 1918 und 1941/1942*. Wiesbaden: Harassowitz, 2005.

Griffin, Roger. *The Nature of Fascism*. New York, NY: St. Martin's Press, 1991.

Gross, Jan T. *Revolution from Abroad: The Soviet Conquest of Poland's Western Ukraine and Western Belorussia*. Princeton, NJ: Princeton University Press, 2002.

Guthier, Stephen L. "The Popular Basis of Ukrainian Nationalism in 1917." *Slavic Review*, 38, no. 1 (March 1979): 30-47.

Gyidel, Ernest. "The Ukrainian Legal Press of the General Government: The Case of *Krakivski Visti*, 1940-1944" (Ph.D. dissertation, University of Alberta, 2019).

Hai-Nyzhnyk, Pavlo. "Derzhavnyi perevorot 29 kvitnia 1918 r: prychyny ta perebi zakhoplennia vlady P. Skorodads'kym." *Ukrains'kyi istrychnyi zhurnal*, 4 (2011): 132-164.

Hai-Nyzhnyk, Pavlo. "Vizyt Het'mana Pavla Skoropads'koho do Nimechchyny u konteksti politychnoho zhyttia Ukrainy 1918 roku." *Ukraina dyplomatychna: Naukovyi shchorichnyk*, XV (2014): 605-615.

Hammerschmidt, Peter. *Deckname Adler: Klaus Barbie und die westlichen Geheimdienste*. Frankfurt am Main: Fischer Verlag, 2014.

Harasymiw, Bohdan. "Kravchuk, Leonid." *Internet Encyclopedia of Ukraine / Enstyklopediia Ukrainy v Internet*. Last modified 2020. http://www.encyclopediaofukraine.com/display.asp?linkpath=pages%5CK%5CR%5CKravchukLeonid.htm (accessed 17 August 2023)

Haro, Neuber Lea. "Entering a Theoretical Void: The Theory of Social Fascism and Stalinism in the German Communist Party." *Critique: Journal of Socialist Theory* 39, no. 4 (2011): 563-582.

Harris, Shane, Karen DeYoung, and Isabelle Khurdursyan. "Road to War: U.S. Struggled to Convince Allies, and Zelensky, of Risk of Invasion." *Washington Post*, 16 August 2022. https://www.washingtonpost.com/national-security/interactive/2022/ukraine-road-to-war/ (accessed 17 August 2023).

Härtel, André. "Bandera's Tempting Shadow: The Problematic History of Ukrainian Radical Nationalism in the Wake of the Maidan," *Journal of Soviet and Post-Soviet Politics and Society* 1, no. 2 (2015): 421-428.

Hausleitner, Marianna and Harald Roth. *Der Einfluss von Faschismus und Nationalismus auf Minderheiten in Ostmittel-und Südosteuropa*, Munich: IKGS-Verlag, 2006.

Hausmann, Guido and Andreas Kappeler, eds. *Ukraine: Gegenwart und Geschichte eines neuen Staates*. Baden-Baden: Nomos, 1993.

Havryshko, Marta. "Illegitimate Sexual Practices in the OUN Underground and UPA in Western Ukraine in the 1940s and 1950s." *Journal of Power Institutions in Post-Soviet Societies* 17 (2016). https://journals.openedition.org/pipss/4214 (accessed 17 August 2023).

Haynes, Rebecca and Martyn Rady, eds. *In the Shadow of Hitler: Personalities of the Right in Central and Eastern Europe*. London: I. B. Tauris, 2011.

Hazony, Yoram. *The Virtue of Nationalism*. New York: Basic Books, 2018.

Heer, Hannes. "Blutige Ouvertüre: Lemberg, 30. Juni 1941: Mit dem Einmarsch der Wehrmachttruppen beginnt der Judenmord." *Die Zeit* no. 26 (2001). http://www.zeit.de/2001/26/200126_a-lemberg.xml (accessed 17 August 2023).

Heer, Hannes. "Einübung in den Holocaust: Lemberg Juni/Juli 1941," *Zeitschrift für Geschichtswissenschaft* 49 (2001): 409-427.

Heimann, Mary. *Czechoslovakia: The State that Failed*. New Haven: Yale University Press, 2009.

Hercules, Ilia. "Putin's War in Ukraine has Torn my Family Apart." *New Statesman*, 27 February 2022. https://www.newstatesman.com/world/europe/ukraine/2022/02/putins-war-in-ukraine-has-torn-my-family-apart (accessed 17 August 2023).

Herder, Emil Gottfried von, (ed.) *Johann Gottfried von Herder's Lebensbild. Sein chronologisch-geordneter Briefwechsel, verbunden mit den hierhergehörigen Mittheilungen aus seinem ungedruckten Nachlasse, und mit den nöthigen Belegen aus seinen und seiner Zeitgenossen Schriften herausgeben von seinem Sohne Dr. Emil Gottfried von Herder, königl. Bayer. Regierungsrath*. Zweiter Band, in Erlangen: Verlag von Theodor Bläsing, 1846), 155-334

Herder, Johann Gottfried. *Ideen zur Philosophie der Geschichte der Menschheit*. Zweiter Teil. Neuntes Buch. Band I. Berlin and Weimar: Aufbau-Verlag, 1965.

Johann Gottfried Herder, "Journal meiner Reise im Jahr 1769," in *Johann Gottfried von Herder's Lebensbild. Sein chronologisch-geordneter Briefwechsel, verbunden mit den hierhergehörigen Mittheilungen aus seinem ungedruckten Nachlasse, und mit den nöthigen Belegen aus seinen und seiner Zeitgenossen Schriften herausgeben von seinem Sohne Dr. Emil Gottfried von Herder, königl. Bayer. Regierungsrath*. Zweiter Band, edited by Emil Gottfrid von Herder (Erlangen: Verlag von Theodor Bläsing, 1846), 155-334

Hillis, Faith. *Children of Rus': Right-Bank Ukraine and the Invention of a Russian Nation*. Ithaca: Cornell University Press, 2013.

Himka, John-Paul. "A Central European Diaspora under the Shadow of World War II: The Galician Ukrainians in North America." *Austrian History Yearbook* 37 (2006): 17-31.

Himka, John-Paul. "Assessing the Prolog Legacy," *Current Politics in Ukraine*, 31 May 2013, https://ukraineanalysis.wordpress.com/2013/05/31/assessing-the-prolog-legacy/ (accessed 7 July 2017)

Himka, John-Paul. "Debates in Ukraine over Nationalist Involvement in the Holocaust, 2004-2008." *Nationalities Papers* 39, no. 3 (2011): 353-370.

Khymka, Ivan. [John-Paul Himka], "Dostovirnist' svidchennia: reliatsiia Ruzi Vagner pro l'vivs'kyi pohrom vlitku 1941 r," *Holokost i suchasnist': studii v Ukraini i sviti* 4, no. 2 (2008): 43-79.

Himka, John-Paul. "Encumbered Memory: The Ukrainian Famine of 1932-33." *Kritika: Explorations in Russian and Eurasian History* 14, no. 2 (Spring 2013): 411-436.

Himka, John-Paul. "Former Ukrainian Policemen in the Ukrainian National Insurgency: Continuing the Holocaust outside German Service." In *Lessons and Legacies XII: New Directions in Holocaust Research and Education*, edited by Wendy Lower and Laureen Faulkner Rossi, 139-163. Evanston, IL: Northwestern University Press, 2017.

Himka, John-Paul. *Galician Villagers and the Ukrainian National Movement in the Nineteenth Century*. Edmonton: Canadian Institute of Ukrainian Studies, 1988

Himka, John-Paul. "Interventions: Challenging the Myths of Twentieth-Century Ukrainian History." In *The Convolutions of Historical Politics*, edited by Alexei Miller and Maria Lipman, 211-238. Budapest: Central European University Press, 2012.

Himka, John-Paul. "Obstacles to the Integration of the Holocaust into Post-Communist East European Historical Narratives." *Canadian Slavonic Papers/Revue canadienne des slavistes* 50, no. 3-4 (2008): 359-72.

Himka, John-Paul. *Religion and Nationality in Western Ukraine: The Greek Catholic Church and the Ruthenian National Movement in Galicia, 1870-1900*. Montreal: McGill-Queen's University Press, 1998.

Himka, John-Paul. "The Lviv Pogrom of 1941: The Germans, Ukrainian Nationalists, and the Carnival Crowd." *Canadian Slavonic Papers/Revue canadienne des slavistes* 53, no. 2 (2011): 209-243.

Himka, John-Paul. "The Lontsky Street Prison Memorial Museum: An Example of Post-Communist Holocaust Negationsm," in *Perspectives on the Entangled History of Communism ad Nazism: A Comnaz Analysis*, ed. Klas-Göran Karlsson, Johan Stenfeldt, and Ulf Zander (Lanham, MD: Lexington Books, 2015), 137-166.

Himka, John-Paul. "The Organization of Ukrainian Nationalists and the Ukrainian Insurgent Army: Unwelcome Elements of an Identity Project." *Ab Imperio* 4 (2010): 83–101.

Himka, John-Paul. "The Reception of the Holocaust in Postcommunist Ukraine," in John-Paul Himka and Joanna Beata Michlic *Bringing the Dark Past to Light: The Reception of the Holocaust in Postcommunist Europe*. Lincoln, NE: University of Nebraska Press, 2013, 626-661.

Himka, John-Paul. "True and False Lessons from the Nachtigall Episode." *Brama*, March 19, 2008. http://brama.com/news/press/2008/03/08 0319himka_nachtigall.html (accessed 17 August, 2023).

Himka, John-Paul. "Ukraine's Geopolitical Precarity: A Historian's Perspective." *The Spectre Magazine*, 6 July 2022. https://spectrejournal.com/ukraines-geopolitical-precarity/ (accessed 17 August 2023).

Himka, John-Paul. "Ukrainian Collaboration in the Extermination of the Jews during the Second World War: Sorting Out the Long-Term and Conjunctural Factors." In *Studies in Contemporary Jewry: Vol. XIII: The Fate of the European Jews, 1939-1945: Continuity of Contingency?* Edited by Jonathan Frankel, 170–189. Oxford: Oxford University Press, 1997.

Himka, John-Paul. "Ukrainian Memories of the Holocaust: the Destruction of Jews as Reflected in Memoirs Collected 1947." *Canadian Slavonic Papers/ Revue canadienne des slavistes* 44, no. 3-4 (2012): 427–442.

Himka, John-Paul. *Ukrainian Nationalists and the Holocaust: OUN and UPA's Participation in the Destruction of Ukrainian Jewry, 1941-1944*. Stuttgart: ibidem Press, 2021.

Himka, John-Paul. "War Criminality: A Blank Spot in the Collective Memory of the Ukrainian Diaspora." *Spaces of Identity* 5, no. 1 (2005): 9–24.

Himka, John-Paul, and Joanna Beata Michlic, eds. *Bringing the Dark Past to Light: The Reception of the Holocaust in Postcommunist Europe*. Lincoln, NE: University of Nebraska Press, 2013.

Himka, John-Paul and Joanna Beata Michlic. "Introduction," in *Bringing the Dark Past to Light: The Reception of the Holocaust in Postcommunist Europe*, edited by John-Paul Himka and Joanna Beata Michlic. Lincoln, NE: University of Nebraska Press, 2013, 1-24.

Hirsch, Francine. *Empire of Nations: Ethnographic knowledge and the Making of the Soviet Union*. Ithaca: Cornell University Press, 2005.

Hirsch, Francine. "Race without the Practice of Racial Politics." *Slavic Review* 61, no. 1 (2002): 30–43.

Hirsch, Francine. "Toward an Empire of Nations: Border-Making in the Formation of Soviet National Identities." *The Russian Review* 59 (April 2000): 201-226.

Hobsbawm, Eric J. *The Age of Empire, 1875-1914.* London: Cardinal, 1989.

Hofman, Tatjana. "Cultural Cringe?: Narrative Instrumentalisierungen lokaler Kulturen bei M. Rjabchuk, Ju. Andruchovych und S. Zadan." In *Alles neu macht der Majdan?: Interdiziplinäre Perspektiven auf eine Ukraine im Umbruch*, edited by Galyna Spodarets and Sabine Stöhr, 71-93. Berlin: Wissenschaftlicher Verlag Berlin, 2015.

Hofmeister, Wilhelm, ed. *Federalism and Democratization: Perceptions for Political and Institutional Reforms*, Singapore: Konrad Adenauer Stiftung Singapore, 2016.

Holian, Anna. "Anticommunism in the Streets: Refugee Politics in Cold War Germany," *Journal of Contemporary History* 45, no. 1 (2010): 134-61.

Holovakha, Yevhen. "Sub"iektyvnyi pohliad na ukrains'ku filosofiiu (Rozmova iz Kseniieiu Zborovs'koiu, Aminoiu Kkhelufi ta Vsevolodom Khomoiu)," *Sententiae*, vol. 36, no. 1 (2017): 173-214.

Homziak Ihor and Bohdan Kovalyk, eds., *Al'manakh Tovarystva voivakiv UPA im. hen-khor. Romana Shukheyvcha-'Taras Chuprynynky" v ZSA. Knyha 3, 2001-2015.* New York and L'viv: TV UPA v ZSA, 2018.

Hrabovs'kyi, Serhii. "Tak proty koho zh voiuvav Shukhevych u Bilorusi?" *Ukraïns'ka Pravda*, November 13, 2007. http://www.pravda.com.ua/news/2007/11/13/66774.htm (accessed 4 January 2009, link no longer valid).

Hrushets'kym, Anton. "Dynamika otsinka diial'nosti OUN-UPA u chasi Druhoi Svitovoi Viiny: Rezul'taty telefonnoho opytuvannia, provedenoho 7-13 veresina 2022 roku." *Kyivs'kyi mizhnarodnyi instytut sotsiolohii*, 12 October 2022-https://kiis.com.ua/?lang=ukr&cat=reports&id=1146&page=1 (accessed 17 August 2023)

Hryciuk, Grzegorz. *Przemiany narodowościowe i ludnościowe w Galicji Wschodniej i na Wołyniu w latach 1931-1948.* Toruń: Wydawnytswo Adam Marszałek, 2005.

Hrytsak, Yaroslav. "Klopoty z pam'iattiu." *Zaxid.net*, 8 March 2010. http://www.zaxid.net/article/60958/ (accessed 11 April 2010, link no longer active).

Hunczak [Hunchak], Taras. "Between Two Leviathans: Ukraine during the Second World War." In *Ukrainian Past, Ukrainian Present: Selected Papers from the Fourth Congress for Soviet and East European Studies, Harrogate, 1990*, edited by Bohdan Krawchenko, 97-106. New York and London: Macmillan, 1993.

Hunchak, Taras. *Moi spohady-stezhky zhyttia.* Kyiv: Vydavnytstvo Dnipro, 2005.

Hunczak [Hunchak], Taras. "Problems of Historiography: History and Its Sources." *Harvard Ukrainian Studies* 25, nos. 1–2 (2001): 129–142.

Hunczak [Hunchak], Taras. "Ukrainian-Jewish Relations during the Soviet and Nazi Occupations." In *Ukraine during World War II: History and Its Aftermath,* edited by Yuri Boshyk, 39–57. Toronto: CIUS Press, 1986.

Hutcheson, Derek S. and Bo Petersson. "Shortcut to Legitimacy: popularity in Putin's Russia." *Europe-Asia Studies* 68, no. 7, (2016): 1107-1126.

Hägg, Göran. *D'Annunzio: Dekandent, diktare, krigare och diktator.* Stockholm: Norstedts, 2015.

Iljuszyn, [Il'iushyn] Ihor. "[Review of:] Grzegorz Rossoliński-Liebe, Bandera. Życie i mit ukraińskiego nacjonalisty: faszyzm, ludobójstwo, kult, Wydawnictwo Pruszyński i S-ka, Warszawa 2018, ss. 904." *Europa Orientalis: Studia z Dziejów Europy Wschodniej i Państw Bałtyckich* 10 (2019): 255–263.

Iliushin Igor' [Iliiushyn, Ihor']. "Plokho zabytoe staroe: o novoi knige Vladimira Viatrovycha," *Ab Imperio* 2 (2012): 382–386.

Il'iushyn, Ihor. *Volyns'ka trahediia 1943–1944 rr.* Kyiv: Instytut istoriï Ukraïny NAN Ukraïny, 2003.

Ilchuk, Yuliya. *Nikolai Gogol: Performing Hybrid Identity.* Toronto: University of Toronto Press, 2021.

Ilnytzkyj, Oleh S. *Ukrainian Futurism, 1914–1930.* Cambridge, MA: Harvard Ukrainian Research Institute, 1998.

Ioffe, E. G., G. D. Knat'ko and V. D. Selemenev. *Kholokost v Belarusi, 1941–1944.* Minsk: Natsional'nyi Arkhiv Respubliki Belarus', 2002.

Ioffe, Grigory. *Reassessing Lukashenka: Belarus in Cultural and Geopolitical Context.* Houndmills, Basingstoke: Palgrave Macmillan, 2014.

Isajiw, Wsevolod W., Yury Boshyk, and Roman Senkus, eds. *The Refugee Experience: Ukrainian Displaced Persons after World War II.* Edmonton: The Canadian Institute of Ukrainian Studies, University of Alberta, 1992.

Ishchenko Volodymyr, 'The Ukrainian Left During and After the Maidan Protests: Study requested by Die Linke delegation in the GUE/NGL,' (GUE/NGL, 2015), 13–17, accessed April 5, 2016, https://www.academia.edu/20445056/The_Ukrainian_Left_during_and_after_the_Maidan_Protests

Jacobmeyer, Wolfgang. "The 'Displaced Persons' in West Germany, 1945-1951." In *The Uprooted: Forced Migration as an International Problem in the Post-War Era*, edited by Göran Rystad, 271-288. Lund: Lund University Press, 1990.

Jaschik, Scott. "Russian Rectors' Union Defends War." *Inside Higher Education*, 7 March 2022. https://www.insidehighered.com/quicktakes/2022/03/07/russian-rectors'-union-defends-war (accessed 17 August 2023).

Jaspers, Karl. "Für Völkermord gibt es keine Verjährung." *Der Spiegel*, October 3, 1965.

Jilge, Wilfred. "The Politics of History and the Second World war in Post-Communist Ukraine (1986/1991-2004/2005)." *Jahrbücher für Geschichte Osteuropas* 54 (2006): 50-81.

Jilge, Wilfried. "Competing Victimhoods: Post-Soviet Ukrainian Narratives on World War II." In *Shared History – Divided Memory: Jews and Others in Soviet-Occupied Poland, 1939-1941*, edited by Elazar Barkan, Elizabeth A. Cole and Kai Struve, 103-131. Leipzig: Leipziger Universitätsverlag, 2008.

Jobst, Kerstin S. *Geschichte der Ukraine*. Stuttgart: Reclam, 2015.

Johansson, Rune. "Ideér om Europa – Europa som idé: Europeiskt enhets- och samarbetstänkande." In *Europa – historiens återkomst*, edited by Sven Tägil, 48-110. Hedemora: Gidlunds bokförlag, 1993.

Johnsson, Peter. *Ukraina i historien: Från äldsta tid till 2015*. Stockholm: Carlssons bokförlag, 2015.

Jurek, Marek. "Stepan Bandera – nowy symbol Ukrainy?" *Niedziela: Tygodnik katolicki*, no. 6 (2010). http://niedziela.pl/artykul/90908/nd/Stepan-Bandera---nowy-symbol-Ukrainy (accessed 17 August, 2023).

K sobytiiam v Chekhoslovakii: Fakty, dokumenty, svidetel'stva pressy i ochevidtsev. Moscow: Press-gruppa sovetskikh zhurnalistov, 1968.

Kal'ba, Myroslav, (ed). *U lavkah druzhynnykiv: Druzhyny Ukrains'kykh Nationalistiv v 1941-1942 rokakh*. Detroit: Vyd. Druzhyny ukrainsks'kykh nationalistiv, 1953.

Kal'ba, Myroslav. *Druzhyny Ukrains'kykh Natsionalistiv*. Detroit: Vyd. Druzhyny ukrains'kykh natsionalistiv, 1994.

Kal'ba, Myroslav. *DUN v rozbudovi UPA*. Detroit and Ternopil': Dzhura, 2005.

Kal'ba, Myroslav. *My prysiahaly Ukraini: DUN 1941-1942*. L'viv: Memuarna biblioteka NTSh, 1999.

Kal'ba, Myroslav. *U lavkah druzhynnykiv: spohady uchasnykiv. Materialy zibrav i vporiadkuvav Myroslav Kal'ba.* Denver: Vyd. Druzhyny ukrains'kykh natsionalistiv, 1982.

Kallis, Aristotle A. *Genocide and Fascism: The Eliminationist Drive in Fascist Europe.* New York: Routledge, 2009.

Kallis, Aristotle A. (ed.). *The Fascism Reader.* New York: Routledge, 2003.

Kaltenbrunner, Matthias. *Das global vernetzte Dorf: Eine Migrationsgeschichte.* Frankfurt am M: Campus Verlag, 2017.

Kamins'kyi, Anatol'. *Krai, emihratsiia i mizhnarodni zasy: Z peredmovoiu Darii Rebet.* Manchester, Munich, New York: Vyd. Politychnoi Rady OUNz, 1982.

Kamins'kyi, Anatol'. *Proloh u kholodnii viiny proty Moskvy: Prodovzhennia vyzvol'noi borot'bi iz-za kordonu.* Hadiach: Vydanytstvo "Hadiach," 2009.

Kamusella, Tomasz. "Russian: A Murderer's Language." October 2022. https://www.academia.edu/89459162/Russian_A_Murderers_Language (accessed 17 August 2023).

Kansteiner, Wulf. "Entertaining Catastrophe: The Reinvention of the Holocaust in the Television of the Federal Republic of Germany," *New German Critique* 90 (Fall 2003): 135–162.

Kansteiner, Wulf. "Losing the War, Winning the Memory Battle: The Legacy of Nazism, World War II, and the Holocaust in the Federal Republic of Germany." In *The Politics of Memory in Postwar Europe,* edited by Richard Ned Lebow, Wulf Kansteiner, and Claudio Fogy, 102–146. Durham, NC: Duke University Press, 2006.

Kappeler, Andreas. *Der schwierige Weg zur Nation: Beiträge zur neuern Geschichte der Ukraine.* Vienna: Böhlau, 2003.

Kappeler, Andreas. *Kleine Geschichte der Ukraine.* Munich: Verlag C. H. Beck, 2000.

Karatnycky, Adrian and Alexander J. Motyl. "The End of Volodymyr Zelensky's Honeymoon." *Foreign Policy,* 26 February 2020. https://foreignpolicy.com/2020/02/26/zelensky-ukraine-russia-corruption/ (accessed 17 August 2023).

Karatnycky, Adrian. "The World Just Witnessed the First Entirely Virtual Presidential Campaign." *Politico Magazine.* 24 April 2019.

Karlsson, Klas-Göran. *Europeiska möten med historien: Historiekulturella perspektiv på andra världskriget, förintelsen och den kommunistiska terrorn.* Stockholm: Atlantis, 2010.

Karlsson, Klas-Göran. *Folkmord: Historien om ett brott mot mänskligheten.* Lund: Historiska Media, 2021.

Karlsson, Klas-Göran. *Historia som vapen: Historiebruk och Sovjetunionens upplösning 1985–1995.* Stockholm: Bokförlaget Natur och Kultur, 1999.

Karlsson, Klas-Göran, Johan Stenfeldt, and Ulf Zander, eds. *Perspectives on the Entangled History of Communism and Nazism: A Comnaz Analysis.* Lanham, MD: Lexington Books, 2015.

Karlsson, Ingmar. *Det omaka paret: Tjeckernas och slovakernas historia.* Lund: Historiska media, 2019.

Karmeliuk, Andronik. "Istoriia mizh politykoiu i naukoiu." *Ukrains'kyi pohliad*, 21 June 2019. http://ukrpohliad.org/national-memory/istoriya-mizh-politykoyu-i-naukoyu.html (accessed 17 August 2023).

Karpus, Zbigniew, Waldemar Rezmer, and Emilian Wiszka, eds., *Polska i Ukraina: Sojusz 1920 roku i jego następstwa.* Toruń: Wydawnictwo Uniwersytetu Mikołaja Kopernika, 1997.

Kas'ianov, Heorhii. *Danse macabre: Holod 1932-1933 rokiv u polititsi, masovii svidomosti ta istoriohrafii (1980-ti – pochatok 2000-kh)* (Kyiv: Nash chas, 2010).

Kas'ianov, H. V. "Ideolohiia orhanizatsii ukrans'kykh natsionalistiv." In *Orhanizatsiia ukrains'kykh natsionalistiv i Ukrains'ka povstans'ka armiia: Istorychni narysy*, edited by S. V. Kul'chyts'kyi, 445–478. Kyiv: Naukova dumka, 2005.

Kas'ianov, H. V. "Ideolohiya OUN: Istoryko-retrospektyvnyi analiz." *Ukrains'kyi istorychnyi zhurnal*, no. 2 (Feb. 2004): 29–42.

Kas'ianov, Georgii "K desiatiletiia Ukrainskogo institut natsional'noi pamiati (2006–2016)," *Historians.in.ua*, January 14, 2016, accessed February 19, 2016, http://historians.in.ua/index.php/en/dyskusiya/1755-georgij-kas-yanov-k-desyatiletiyu-ukrainskogo-instituta-natsional-noj-pamyati-2006-2016.

Kas'ianov Heorhii. *Past Continuous: Istorychna polityka 1980-kh – 2000-kh rr. Ukraina ta susidy.* Kyiv: Antropos-Logos-Fil'm, 2018.

Kas'ianov, Heorhii. *Rozryta mohyla: Holod 1932–1933 rokiv u polityts, pam'iati ta istorii (1980-ti–2000-ni).* Kharkiv: "Folio," 2018.

Kas'ianov, Georgii [Heorhii]. *Ukraina i sosedi: Istoricheskaia politika. 1987–2018.* n.p: NLO, 2019.

Kasianov, Georgiy [Kas'ianov, Heorhii]. "What's Past is Prologue: Politics and Historical Memory in Ukraine." Lecture at the Wilson Center, the Kennan Institute, January 26, 2018. https://soundcloud.com/the-wilson-center/01262018-whats-past-is-prologue-politics-and-historical-memory-in-ukraine (accessed 17 August 2023).

Kasianov, Georgiy. [Kas'ianov, Heorhii] "Ukraine between Revolution, Independence, and Foreign Dominance." *The Emergence of Ukraine. Self-Determination, Occupation, and War in Ukraine, 1917–1922* (2015): 76–131.

Kasianov, Georgiy. [Kas'ianov, Heorhii] *Memory Crash: The Politics of History in and around Ukraine, 1980s-2010s*. Budapest: Central University Press, 2022.

Katchanovski, Ivan, Zenon E. Kohut, Bohdan Y. Nebesio, and Myroslav Yurkevich, (eds). *Historical Dictionary of Ukraine*. Second edition. Lanham MD: Scarecrow Press, 2013.

Katchanovski, Ivan. *Cleft Countries: Regional Political Divisions and Cultures in Post-Soviet Ukraine and Moldova*. Stuttgart: ibidem-Verlag, 2006.

Katchanovski, Ivan. "The Politics of World War II in Contemporary Ukraine." *The Journal of Slavic Military Studies* 27, no. 2 (2014): 210–233.

Kachanovskii [Katchanovski] Ivan. "Ukraintsy ne veriat v mify ob OUN i UPA." *Fraza*, 14 October 2010. https://fraza.ua/analytics/76064-ukraincy-ne-veryat-v-mify-ob-oun-i-upa (accessed 26 September 2011, link no longer valid).

Kay, Alex J. *Exploitation, Resettlement, Mass Murder: Political and Economic Planning for German Occupation Police in the Soviet Union, 1940–1942*. New York: Berghahn Books, 2006.

Kharkun, Valentyna. "Reconstructing the past: narratives of Soviet occupation in Ukrainian museums," *Canadian Slavonic Papers / Revue canadienne des slavistes*, vol. 63, no. 1-2 (2021): 148-167.

Kedourie, Elie. *Nationalism*. 4th, expanded Edition. Cambridge, MA: Blackwell, 1993.

Kentii, Anatolii and Volodymyr Lozyts'kyi. "From UVO fighter to supreme commander of the UPA." *Litopys UPA. Nova seria, Tom 10: Zhyttia i borot'ba henerala 'Tarasa Chuprynky' (1907–1950): Dokumenty i materialy*, edited by P. Sokhan' and P. Potichnyj, 78–150. Kyiv and Toronto: Litopys UPA, 2007.

Kessler, Glenn. "Zelensky's Famous Quote of 'Need Ammo, Not a Ride' Not Easily Confirmed." *Washington Post*, 6 March 2022. https://www.washingtonpost.com/politics/2022/03/06/zelenskys-famous-quote-need-ammo-not-ride-not-easily-confirmed/(accessed 13 August 2023).

Khiterer, Victoria. *Jewish Pogroms in Kiev during the Russian Civil War, 1918-1920*. Lewiston: The Edwin Mellen Press, 2015.

Khromeychuk, Olesia. "What Place for Women in Ukraine's Memory Politics?" *Open Democracy*. October 10, 2016. https://www.opende mocracy.net/od-russia/olesya-khromeychuk/what-place-for-wom en-in-ukraine-s-memory-politics (accessed 17 August 2023).

Khvylovyi, Mykola, Myroslav Shkandrij, and George S.N. Luckyj. *The Cultural Renaissance in Ukraine: Polemical Pamphlets 1925-26*. Edmonton: The Canadian Institute of Ukrainian Studies Press, 1986.

Kiebuzinski, Ksenya and Alexander Motyl. "Introduction." In *The Great Ukrainian Prison Massacre of 1941: A Sourcebook*, edited by Kiebuzinski, Ksenya and Alexander Motyl, 27-67. Amsterdam: Amsterdam University Press, 2017.

Kiebuzinski, Ksenya and Alexander Motyl, eds. *The Great Ukrainian Prison Massacre of 1941: A Sourcebook*. Amsterdam: Amsterdam University Press, 2017.

Kiryukhin, Denys. "Russia and Ukraine: The Clash of Conservative Projects." *European Politics and Society* 17, no. 4 (2016): 438-452.

Kiryukhin, Denys. "The Philosophical Process in Post-Soviet Ukraine," in Mikhail Minakov, ed., *Philosophy Unchained: Development of Philosophy After the Fall of the Soviet Union* Stuttgart: ibidem-Verlag, 2023, 283-323.

Klarskov, Kristian. "Finlands præsident er ekspert i Putin: Når han bruger humor, skal man for alvor være vågen." *Politiken*, 1 January 2023. https://politiken.dk/udland/art9121144/Når-han-bruger-hu mor-skal-man-for-alvor-være-vågen (accessed 17 August 2023).

Klid, Bohdan and Alexander J. Motyl. "Introduction." In *The Holodomor Reader: A Sourcebook on the Famine of 1932-1933 in Ukraine*, edited by Bohdan Klid and Alexander J. Motyl, xixx-xvii. Edmonton: CIUS Press, 2012.

Klid, Bohdan and Alexander J. Motyl, eds. *The Holodomor Reader: A Sourcebook on the Famine of 1932-1933 in Ukraine*, edited by Bohdan Klid and Alexander J. Motyl, Edmonton: CIUS Press, 2012.

Klion, David. "At the Limits of Nationalism: Confronting Ukraine's Past to Imagine its Future." *Stranger's Guide*, 16 November 2022. https:// strangersguide.com/articles/at-the-limits-nationalism-klion/ (accessed 17 August 2023).

Klüsener Sebastian, 'Die Regionen der Ukraine: Abgrenzung und Charakterisierung,' *Ukraine-Analysen* 23 (2007): 2-11.

Knysh, Zynovyi. *Vid'molovy: (Slovo v oboroni proty zhydivs'koi napasty na ukrainstiv i na narody skhidn'oi Evropy)*. Toronto: Vydavnytsvo "Novyi Shliakh," 1989.

Kobiałka, Marcin. "Szlaban na rajd Bandery." *Gazeta Wyborcza*, 8–9 August 2009, 3.

Kohut, Zenon E. "Ukrainian Nationalism," *Edmonton Journal*, 10 February 2010: A 16.

Kolarz, Walter. *Russia and her Colonies*. Hamden, CT: Archon Books, 1967.

Kolesnikov, Andrei. *Pervyi ukrainskii: Zapisi s perevodoi*. Kyiv: Vagrius, 2005.

Kolesnychenko, Vadim, ed. Anatolii Chaikovskii, Per Anders Rudling, and Dzhon-Pol Khimka [John-Paul Himka], *"Voina ili voennaia prestupnost'?"*: *Sbornik Publikatsii*. (= *Istorychna pravda*, Tom III) Kyiv: Zolotye vorota, 2013.

Kolesnychenko, Vadim, ed. Per Anders Rudling, Timoti Shnaider [Timothy Snyder], and Gzhegozh Rossolinski-Libe [Grzegorz Rossoliński-Liebe]. *"OUN i UPA: Issledovaniia o sozdanii 'Istoricheskikh' mifiv"*: *Sbornik statei*. (=*Istorychna pravda*, Tom II) Kyiv: Zolotye vorota, 2012.

Kolodzins'kyi, Mykhailo. *Voenna doktryna ukrains'kykh natsionalistiv*. Kyiv: Tsentr Natsional'noho Vidrodzhennia, 2019.

Konieczna-Sałamatin, Joanna, Natalia Otrishchenko, and Tomasz Stryjek. *History. People. Events: Research Report on the Memory of Contemporary Poles and Ukrainians*. Warsaw: Instytut Studiów politycznych Polskiej Akademii Nauk, 2018.

Konończuk, Wojciech. "Why Poland Needs a Post-Giedroyc Doctrine towards Ukraine." *New Eastern Europe*, 22 March 2017. http://new easterneurope.eu/2018/03/22/poland-needs-post-giedroyc-doctrin e-towards-ukraine/ (accessed 17 August 2023).

Koposov, Nikolay. *Memory Laws, Memory Wars: The Politics of the Past in Europe and Russia*. Cambridge: Cambridge University Press, 2018.

Kopstein, Jeffrey S. and Jason Wittenberg. *Intimate Violence: Anti-Jewish Pogroms on the Eve of the Holocaust*. Ithaca and London: Cornell University Press, 2018.

Kordayn, Bohdan S. *Strategic Friends: Canada–Ukraine Relations from Independence to the Euromaidan*. Montreal: McGill-Queen's University Press, 2018.

Korduban, Pavel. "Leftist, Pro-Russian Extremists defy Yushchenko over History." *Eurasia Daily Monitor* 4, no. 197 (October 24, 2007). http://www.jamestown.org/edm/article.php/?article_id=2372530 (accessed October 28, 2007, link no longer valid).

Korinth, Stefan. "'Ohne historische Aufarbeitung bleibt die Ukraine ein Pulverfass." *Telepolis*, 10 February 2015. http://www.heise.de/tp/a rtikel/44/44107/1.html (accessed 17 August 2023).

Korostelina, Karina V. 'Mapping National Identity Narratives in Ukraine,' *Nationalities Papers* 41, no. 2 (2013): 293-315.

Kosakivs'kyi, Mykyta. *Z nedavn'oho mynuloho.* London: Vydavnytstvo Nashe Slovo, 1965.

Kosakivs'kyi, Mykyta. "Z nedavn'oho mynuloho," *Nashe Slovo,* Zbirnyk 5, (1977)/ *Our Word,* 5 (1977): 66-80

Koshkyna, Sonia. "Volodymyr V"iatrovych: 'Niurnberh' nad komunizmom mozhlyvyi i potribnyi." *Levyi bereg,* 20 May 2016. http://lb.ua/news/2016/05/20/335648_volodimir_vyatrovich_ny urnberg_nad.html (accessed 17 August 2023).

Kosyk, Volodymyr. "Harvard patronue nenaukove metody istorychnoho doslidzhennia." *Ukrains'kyi vyzvol'nyi rukh* 1 (2003): 176-189.

Kosyk, Volodymyr ed. *Yaroslav Stets'ko. Tvory: Ukrains'ka vyzvol'na kontseptsiia, Tom druhyi,* Munich: Vydannia Orhanizatsii ukrains'kykh natsionalistiv, 1991.

Kosyk, Volodymyr. ed. *Ukraina v Druhii svitovii viini u dokumentakh: Zbirnyk nimets'kykh arkhivnykh materiali, T. 1.* L'viv: Instytut ukrainoznavstva im. I. Krypiakievycha NAN Ukrainy.

Kott, Matthew and Tomislav Dulić. "Guest Editors' Note," *Fascism: Journal of Comparative Fascist Studies,* vol. 5, no. 1 (2016): 1-2.

Koval'chuk, Volodymyr. "Skil'ky zh soldativ bulo v UPA? Sekrety rozkryvae Klym Savur." *Ukrains'ka pravda,* 12 March 2010. http://www.istpravda.com.ua/articles/2010/12/3/7410/ (accessed 17 August 2023).

Kragh, Martin, Erik Andermo, and Liliia Makashova. "Conspiracy Theories in Russian Security Thinking." *Journal of Strategic Studies* 45, no. 3 (2020): 334-368.

Kramár, Leo. *Rasismens ideologer: Från Gobineau till Hitler.* Stockholm: Norstedts, 2000.

Kramer, Mark. "Ukraine and the Soviet-Czechoslovak Crisis of 1968 (part 2): New Evidence from the Ukrainian Archives." *Cold War International History Project Bulletin,* Issue 14/15 (2004): 273-276.

Krasnodębski, Zdzisław, Stefan Garsytecki, and Rüdiger Ritter, eds. *Politics, History and Collective Memory in East Central Europe.* Hamburg: Krämer, 2012.

Kratochvil, Alexander. "Mykola Chvyl'ovyj. Eine Studie zu Leben und Werk." *Slavistische Beiträge,* 379. Munich: Verlag Otta Sagner, 1999.

Kravchenko, Volodymyr. "The Russian War against Ukraine: Cyclic History vs Fatal Geography." *East/West: Journal of Ukrainian Studies,* vol. IX, no. 1 (2022): 201-208.

Krawchenko, Bohdan, ed. *Ukrainian Past, Ukrainian Present: Selected Papers from the Fourth Congress for Soviet and East European Studies*, Harrogate, 1990. New York and London: Macmillan, 1993.

Krawatzek, Félix and George Soroka. "The Best Story: The Ukrainian Past in Zelenskyy's Words and the Eyes of the Public." *New Eastern Europe* LIV, no. 6 (November–December 2022): 143–152.

Kruglov, Alexander. "Jewish Losses in Ukraine, 1941–1944." In *The Shoah in Ukraine: History, Testimony, Memorialization*, edited by Ray Brandon and Wendy Lower, 272–290. Bloomington: Indiana University Press, 2008.

Krutsyk, Roman. "Memorial: Pane Prezydente, zaberit' nareshti dokumenty Shukhevycha z Yad Vashem." *Maidan*, December 20, 2007. http://maidan.org.news/for-print.php3?bn=maidan_mai&key=11 98164610 (accessed Dec 30, 2007, link no longer valid).

Kuberska, D. and S. Figiel, "The Competitiveness of Ukraine and Poland," *Socioeconomic Research Bulletin* 3 (50) (2013): 72–78.

Kubijovyč, V. and V. Markus. "Jews." In *Encyclopedia of Ukraine: Vol. II G-K*, edited by Volodymyr Kubijovyč, 385–393. Toronto: University of Toronto Press, 1988.

Kubijovyč, Volodymyr ed. *Encyclopedia of Ukraine: Vol. I, A-F*. Toronto: University of Toronto Press, 1984.

Kubijovyč, Volodymyr, ed. *Encyclopedia of Ukraine: Vol. II G-K*. Toronto: University of Toronto Press, 1988.

Kucheruk, O. and Yu. Cherchenko. *Dokumenty i materialy z istorii Orhanizatsii Ukrains'kykh Natsionalistiv, Tom 7, Dokumenty komisii derhazvnoho planuvannia OUN (KDP OUN)*. Kyiv: Vyd-vo im. Oleny Telihy, 2002.

Kudelia, Serhiy. "Choosing Violence in Irregular Wars: The Case of Anti-Soviet Insurgency in Western Ukraine." *East European Politics and Societies*, vol. 27, no. 1 (February 2013): 149–181.

Kudlai, Viacheslav. "A Brief Diary of a Witness." *Baltic Worlds* XV, nos. 1–2 (June 2022): 4–7.

Kuk, Vasyl'. "Derzhavotvorcha diial'nist' OUN Akt Vidnovlennia Ukrains'koi Derzhavy 30 chervnia 1941 r." In *Ukrains'ke derzhavotvorennia: Akt 30 chervnia 1941. Zbirnyk dokumentiv i materialiv*, edited by Iaroslav Dashkevych and Vasyl' Kuk, v–xxiii. L'viv: Piramida, 2001.

Kuk, Vasyl'. *Heneral Roman Shukhevych: Holovnyi komandyr Ukrains'koi postans'koi armii (UPA)*. Kyiv: Biblioteka ukraintsia, 1997.

Kuk, Vasyl'. *Heneral-khorunzhyi Roman Shukhevych: Holovnyi komandyr Ukrainskoi povstans'koi armii, vydannia druhe, dopovnene*. L'viv: Tsentr dolidzhen' vyzvol'noho rukhu, 2007.

Kul'chyts'kyi, S. V., ed. *Orhanizatsiia ukrains'kykh natsionalistiv i Ukrains'ka povstans'ka armiia: Istorychni narysy*, 445–478. Kyiv: Naukova dumka, 2005.

Kul'chyts'kyi, Stanislav et al. (eds.). *OUN v 1941 rotsi: Dokumenty. V 2-kh ch.* Ch. 1. Kyiv: Instytut Istorii Ukrainy NAN Ukrainy, 2006.

Kulińska, Lucyna. *Działalność terrorystyczna i sabotażowa nacjonalistycznych organizacji ukraińskich w Polsce w latach 1922–1939*. Kraków: Księgarnia Akademicka, 2009.

Kupfer, Matthew and Thomas De Waal. "Crying Genocide: Use and Abuse of Political Rhetoric in Russia and Ukraine." *Carnegie Endowment for International Peace*, 28 July 2014. https://carnegieendow ment.org/2014/07/28/crying-genocide-use-and-abuse-of-political-rhetoric-in-russia-and-ukraine-pub-56265 (accessed 17 August 2023).

Kuromia, Hiroaki. *Freedom and Terror in the Donbas: A Ukrainian-Russian Borderland, 1870s-1990s*. Cambridge: Cambridge University Press, 2002.

Kurylo, Taras. "'The Biggest Calamity that Overshadowed All Other Calamities': Recruitment of Ukrainian 'Eastern Workers' for the War Economy of the Third Reich, 1941–1945." PhD Diss., University of Alberta, 2009.

Kurylo, Taras. "Shche raz pro OUN ta fashyzm." *Zakhid.net*, 15 March 2012. https://zaxid.net/shhe_raz_pro_oun_ta_fashizm_n1250264 (accessed 17 August 2023).

Kurylo, Taras. "The "Jewish Question" in Ukrainian Nationalist Thought of the Interwar Period." *Polin: Studies in Polish Jewry* 26 (2014): 233–258.

Kurylo Taras and John-Paul Himka [Ivan Khymka], "Yak OUN stavylasia do ievreiv? Rozdumy nad knyzhkoiu Volodymyra V"iatrovycha Stavlennia OUN do ievreiv: Formuvannia pozytsii na tli katastrofy," *Ukraina Moderna* 13 (2008): 252–265.

Kutkina, Anna. *Between Lenin and Bandera: Decommunization and Multivocality in (post)Euromaidan Ukraine*. Helsinki: Unigrafia, 2020.

Kuzik, Lilia. "Ihor Yukhnovs'kyi: 'Ta derzhava zh mala utvorytysia. I ya vse robyv, shchob vona utvorylas'." *Zaxid.net*, 11 August 2011. https://zaxid.net/igor_yuhnovskiyta_derzhava_zh_mala_utvoritis ya_i_ya_vse_robiv_shhob_vona_utvorilas_n1233429 (accessed 17 August 2023).

Kuzio, Taras. "Chy mav Bandera ratsiio shchodo Rosii ta rosiian? Chomu Rosiia rozpochala henotsyd ukraintsiv." Lecture at the Ukrainian Catholic University, L'viv, June 15, 2023.

Kuzio, Taras. "How America Played a Central Role in Ukraine Becoming Independent," *Kyiv Post*, 11 September 2011. http://www.kyivpost.com/opinion/op-ed/how-america-played-a-central-role-in-ukraine-becom-112603.html (accessed 11 September 2011, link no longer valid).

Kuzio, Taras. "How Not to Debate Ukrainian History (at Columbia University or Elsewhere)." *The Ukrainian Weekly*, no. 20, (19 May 2013): 6, 13.

Kuzio, Taras. "Rise and Fall of the Party of Regions Political Machine," *Problems of Post-Communism* 62, no. 3 (2015): 174–186.

Kuzio, Taras. "State and Institutions in Ukraine: A Theoretical and Comparative Introduction." In *State and Institution Building in Ukraine*, edited by Taras Kuzio, Robert S. Kravchuk, and Paul D'Anieri, 1-23. New York: St. Martin's Press, 1999.

Kuzio, Taras. *Theoretical and Comparative Perspectives on Nationalism: New Directions in Cross-Cultural and Post-Communist Studies*. Stuttgart: ibidem-Verlag, 2007.

Kuzio, Taras. "The Origins of Peace, Non-Violence, and Conflict in Ukraine." In *Ukraine and Russia: People, Politics, Propaganda and Perspectives*, edited by Agnieszka Pikulicka-Wilczewski and Richard Sakwa, 103–116. Bristol: E-International Relations Publishing, 2015.

Kuzio, Taras. "The Russian Imperialist War Against Ukraine." Ucrainica Research Institute, Toronto, 2 December 2022, "Forum TV: Taras Kuzio. https://www.youtube.com/watch?v=_Ciy0TZN51o (accessed 17 August 2023).

Kuzio, Taras. *Ukraine: Democratization, Corruption, and the New Russian Imperialism*. Santa Barbara, CA: Praeger Security International 2015.

Kuzio, Taras. *Ukraine: Perestroika to Independence*. Second edition. Houndmills, Basingstoke: Palgrave MacMillan, 2000.

Kuzio, Taras. "U.S. Support for Ukraine's Liberation during the Cold War: A Study of Prolog Research and Publishing Corporation." *Communist and Post-Communist Studies*, vol. 45, no. 1–2 (March–June 2012): 51–64.

Kuzio, Taras. "Yushchenko Facilitates Yanukovych's Election and Buries the Orange Revolution." *Eurasia Daily Monitor* 7, no. 31(2010). https://jamestown.org/program/yushchenko-facilitates-yanukovychs-election-and-buries-the-orange-revolution/ (accsessed 17 August 2023).

Kuzio, Taras, Stefan Jajecznyk-Kelman, *Fascism and Genocide: Russia's War Against Ukraine*. Stuttgart: ibidem-Verlag, 2023.

Kuzio, Taras, Robert S. Kravchuk, and Paul D'Anieri, eds. *State and Institution Building in Ukraine*, New York: St. Martin's Press, 1999.

Kyrychuk, Serhii. "Ia znaiu, chto takoe ukrainskaia revoluiutsiia." *Liva.com.ua*, Summer 2012. http://liva.com.ua/valery-soldatenko.html (accessed 17 August 2023)

Łada, Krzysztof. "Creative Forgetting: Polish and Ukrainian Historiographies on the Campaign against the Poles in Volhynia during World War II." *Glaukopis*, no. 2/3 (2005): 340–375.

Łada, Krzysztof. "The Ukrainian Topos of Oppression and the Volhynian Slaughter of Poles, 1841-1943/44" (Ph.D. thesis, Flinders University, 2012).

Lagzi, Gábor. "The Ukrainian National Movement in Inter-War Poland—the Case of the Organization of Ukrainian Nationalists (OUN)," *Regio—Minorities, Politics, Society*, No. 1 (2004): 194–206.

Langewiesche, Dieter. *Der Gewaltsame Lehrer: Europas Kriege in der Moderne*. Munich: C.H. Beck, 2019.

Larsson, Mats. "Kriget har inte gått som någon tänkt sig." *Expressen*, 24 August 2022. https://www.expressen.se/kronikorer/mats-larsson/kriget-har-inte-gatt-som-nagon-tankt-sig/ (accessed 17 August 2023).

Laruelle, Marlene. *Is Russia Fascist?: Unravelling Propaganda East and West*. Ithaca, NY: Cornell University Press, 2021.

Laruelle, Marlene and Mischa Gabowitsch, eds. *Russian Eurasianism: An Ideology for Empire*. Baltimore, NJ: Johns Hopkins University Press, 2008.

Latysh, Yurii (ed.). *Shcherbyts'kyi: Zhyttia prysviachene Ukraini*. Kyiv: Vydavnychyi Dim ADEF-Ukraina, 2018.

Latysh, Yurii. "Volodymyr Shcherbyts'kyi: liudyna ta ii epokha." *Spil'ne: zhurnal sotsial'noi krytyky*, August 10, 2017. https://commons.com.ua/en/volodimir-sherbickij/ (accessed 17 July 2023).

Lebow, Richard Ned, Wulf Kansteiner, and Claudio Fogy, eds. *The Politics of Memory in Postwar Europe*, Durham, NC: Duke University Press, 2006.

Legge, Jr., Jerome S. "Collaboration, Intelligence, and the Holocaust: Ferdinand Ďurčanský, Slovak Nationalism, and the Gehlen Organization," *Holocaust and Genocide Studies* 32, no. 2 (2018): 224–48.

Legge, Jr., Jerome S. "The Karl Linnas Deportation Case, the Office of Special Investigations, and American Ethnic Politics." *Holocaust and Genocide Studies* 24, no. 1 (2010): 26–55.

Leggewie Claus, and Anne Lang. *Der Kampf um die europäische Erinnerung: Ein Schlachtfeld wird besichtigt*, Munich: C. H. Beck, 2011.

Lenin, V. I. *Polnoe sobranie sochinenii, Tom 41. Mai-noiabr 1920*. Moscow: Gosizpolit, 1981.

Levytsky, Marko. "Ukrainian Nationalists Played No Part in Massacre of 4,000 Jews." *Edmonton Journal*, 9 February 2010: A13.

Levytsky, Marko. "UPA Detractors Fan the Flames of Ethnic Discord." *Ukrainian News*, 16 February 2010: 2.

Lewytzkyj, Borys. *Die Sowjetukraine 1944–1963*. Cologne: Kiepenhauer & Witsch, 1964.

Lewytzkyj [Levyts'kyi], Borys. "Natsional'nyi rukh pid chas Druhoi svitovoi viiny: Interv"iu z B. Levyts'kym." *Diialoh: Za demokratiiu i sotsiializm v samostiinii Ukraini* 2 (1979): 4–31.

Lewytzkyj, Borys. *Politische Opposition in der Sowjetunion 1960–1972: Analyse und Dokumentation*. Munich: Deutsche Taschenbuch Verlag, 1972.

Liber, George O. *Alexander Dovzhenko: A Life in Soviet Film*. London: British Film Institute, 2000.

Liber, George O. *Total Wars and the Making of Modern Ukraine, 1914–1954*. Toronto: University of Toronto Press, 2016.

Lieb, Peter and Wolfram Dornik. "The Ukrainian Policy of the Central Powers during the First World War." In *The Emergence of Ukraine: Self-Determination, Occupation, and War in Ukraine, 1917–1922*, edited by Wolfram Dornik, Georgiy Kasianov, Hannes Leidinger, Peter Lieb, Alexei Miller, Bogdan Musial, Vasyl Rasevych, translated by Gus Fagan, 37–75. Edmonton: Canadian Institute of Ukrainian Studies Press, 2015.

Lilienthal, Georg. *'Der Lebensborn e.V.': Ein Instrument nationalsozialistischer Rassenpolitik*. Frankfurt a M: Fischer, 1993.

Lingen, Kerstin von. *Allen Dulles, the OSS, and Nazi War Criminals: The Dynamics of Selective Prosecution*. New York: Cambridge University Press, 2013.

Linkiewicz, Olga. "Applied Modern Science and the Self-Politicization of Racial Anthropology in Interwar Poland." *Ab Imperio* no. 2 (2016): 153–181.

Linz, Juan J. "Political Space and Fascism as Late-Comer: Conditions Conductive to the Success or Failure of Fascism as a Mass Movement in Inter-War Europe." In *Who Were the Fascists?: Social Roots of European Fascism*, edited by Stein Ugelvik Larsen, Bernt Hagtvet, and Jan Petter Myklebust, 153–189. Bergen: Universitetsforlaget, 1980.

Lisevych, Ivan. "Politychni aspekty ukrains'ko-pol's'koho soiuzu 1920 r." In *Polska i Ukraina: Sojusz 1920 roku i jego następstwa*, edited by Zbigniew Karpus, Waldemar Rezmer, and Emilian Wiszka, 81–99. Toruń: Wydawnictwo Uniwersytetu Mikołaja Kopernika, 1997.

Lohr, Eric, Vera Tolz, Alexander Semyonov, and Mark von Hagen, eds. *The Empire and Nationalism at War*. Bloomington, IN: Slavica Publishers, 2014.

Loftus, John. *America's Nazi Secret*. Waterville, OR: Trine Day, 2010.

Lower, Wendy and Laureen Faulkner Rossi, eds. *Lessons and Legacies XII: New Directions in Holocaust Research and Education*. Evanston, IL: Northwestern University Press, 2017.

Lower, Wendy. *Nazi Empire-Building and the Holocaust in Ukraine*. Chapel Hill: University of North Carolina Press, 2005.

Lozynskyj, Askold S. "Rewriting History: An Evidentiary Evidence." *Kyiv Post*, 16 February 2010. https://www.kyivpost.com/article/opinion/op-ed/rewriting-history-an-evidentiary-perspective-59650.html (accessed 16 February 16, 2010, link no longer valid).

Lozynskyj, Askold. "Inna Rogatchi, Shame on You!" *League of Ukrainian Canadians*, 23 February 2010. http://www.lucorg.com/news.php/news/4151 (Accessed 24 February 2010, link no longer valid).

Lucas, Ryan. "Ukrainian-Russian Families are being Torn Apart by Russia's Invasion." *NPR Weekend Edition*, 7 March 2022. https://wamu.org/story/22/03/07/relationships-across-the-ukraine-russia-border-feel-the-strain-of-war/ (accessed 17 August 2023).

Luciuk, Lubomyr Y. *Searching for Place: Ukrainian Displaced Persons, Canada, and the Migration of Memory*. Toronto: University of Toronto Press, 2000.

Luciw, Daria. "Congress Offended." *Edmonton Journal*, 14 February 2010: A 15.

Luk"ianenko, Levko. *Zlochynna sut' KPRS-KPU: Niurnberh – 2*. Kyiv: MAUP, 2005.

Lundborg, Herman. *Rasbiologi och rashygien: Nutida kultur- och rasfrågor i etisk belysning*. Second edition. Stockholm: Norstedts, 1922.

Lypa, Yurii. *Pryznachennia Ukrainy*. L'viv: Khortitsia, 1938.

Lypa, Yurii. "Ukrains'ka rasa." *Vatra: national'-revoliutsiinyi chasopys*. July 21, 2009. http://www.vatra.cc/rasa/yuriy-lypa-ukrayinska-rasa.html (accessed 17 August 2023).

Lypovets'kyi, Sviatoslav. *Orhanizatsiia Ukrainkykh Natsionalistiv' (banderivtsy): frahmenty diial'nosti ta borot'by*. Kyiv: Ukrains'ka Vydavnycha Spilka, 2010.

Lysiak-Rudnyts'kyi, Ivan. "Natsionalizm i totalitaryzm (Vidpovid' M. Prokopovi)." *Journal of Ukrainian Studies* 7, no. 2 (1982): 80–86.

Löwenhardt, John. *The Soviet Politburo*, translated by Dymphna Clark. Edinburgh: Canongate, 1982.

Mace, James. *Communism and the Dilemmas of National Liberation: National Communism in Soviet Ukraine, 1918–1933*. Cambridge, MA: HURI Harvard, 1983.

Madajczyk, Czesław. "Vom 'Generalplan Ost' zum Generalsiedlungsplan." In *Der 'Generalplan Ost': Hauptlinien der nationalsozialistischen Planungs- und Vernichtungspolitik*, edited by Mechthild Rössler and Sabine Schleiermacher, 96–117. Berlin: Akademie-Verlag, 1993.

Maddux, Thomas R. "Red Fascism, Brown Bolshevism: The American Image of Totalitarianism in the 1930s." *The Historian* 40, no. 1 (November 1977): 85–103.

Magocsi, Paul Robert. *A History of Ukraine: The Land and Its Peoples*. Second, Revised and Expanded Edition. Toronto: University of Toronto Press, 2012.

Magocsi, Paul Robert. *The Roots of Ukrainian Nationalism: Galicia as Ukraine's Piedmont*. Toronto: University of Toronto Press, 2002.

Makulski, Maciej. "Poland's Ukraine Refugee Assistance as a Transformative Experience." *New Eastern Europe* LIV, no. 6 (November-December 2022): 60–65.

Mark, Rudolf A. "Symon Petliura und die UNR: Vom Sturz des Hetmans Skoropadskyj bis zum Exil in Polen." *Forschungen zur osteuropäischen Geschichte* 40 (1988): 7–228.

Markevych, Lubomyr. "Coming to Grips with the Past." *Edmonton Journal*, 14 February 2010: A 16.

Markiewicz, Pawieł. *Unlikely Allies: Nazi German and Ukrainian Nationalist Collaboration in the General Government During World War II*. West Lafayette: Purdue University Press, 2021.

Marková, Alena. *The Path to a Soviet Nation: The Policy of Belarusization*. Paderbron: Schönigh, 2022.

Markus, Vasyl. "Political Parties in the DP Camps." In *The Refugee Experience: Ukrainian Displaced Persons after World War II*, edited by Wsevolod W. Isajiw, Yury Boshyk, and Roman Senkus, 111-143. Edmonton: The Canadian Institute of Ukrainian Studies, University of Alberta, 1992.

Marples, David R. "Decommunization, Memory Laws, and 'Builders of Ukraine in the 20th Century." *Acta Slavica Iaponica* 39 (2018): 1–22.

Marples, David. "Hero of Ukraine Linked to Jewish killings: Honorary Title Sure to Provoke Divisions among Ukrainians Today." *Edmonton Journal*, 7 February 2010, A 13.

Marples, David R. *Heroes and Villains: Creating National History in Contemporary Ukraine*. Budapest and New York: Central European University Press, 2007.

Marples, David R. et al., 'Open Letter from Scholars and Experts in Ukraine Re. the So-Called "Anti-Communist Law",' *Krytkya*, April 2015, accessed April 6, 2016, http://krytyka.com/en/articles/open-letter-scholars-and-experts-ukraine-re-so-called-anti-communist-law

Marples, David R. "Stepan Bandera: In Search of a Ukraine for Ukrainians," in Rebecca Haynes and Martyn Rady, eds. *In the Shadow of Hitler: Personalities of the Right in Central and Eastern Europe*. London and New York: I.B. Tauris, 2011, 227–244.

Marples, David R. "Stepan Bandera: The Resurrection of a Ukrainian National Hero." *Europe-Asia Studies* 58, no. 4 (2006): 555–566.

Marples, David R. "Studying Ukraine." Lecture delivered at the Modern European History Seminar, University of Cambridge, 27 January 2010. http://www.hist.cam.ac.uk/seminars_events/seminars/modern-european/marples-writing-history-of-ukraine.pdf (Accessed 4 February 2010, link no longer valid).

Marples, David R. *The Social Impact of the Chernobyl Disaster*. Edmonton: The University of Alberta Press, 1988.

Marples, David R. "The Yanukovych Election Campaigns in Ukraine, 2004 and 2006: An Analysis," *Journal of Ukrainian Studies*, vol. 35–36 (2010–2011): 265–80.

Marples, David R. *Ukraine under Perestroika: Ecology, Economics and the Workers' Revolt*. Edmonton: The University of Alberta Press, 1991.

Marplz, Davyd [David R. Marples]. "'Zabutyi' voennyi zlochynets'," *Diialoh: Za demokratiiu i sotsiializm v samostiinii Ukraini* vol. 10 (1984): 44-50.

Martin, Terry. *The Affirmative Action Empire: Nations and Nationalism in the Soviet Union, 1923–1939*. Ithaca, NY: Cornell University Press, 2001.

Martynets', Volodymyr. *Zhydivs'ka problema v Ukraini*. London: Williams, Lea & Co., 1938.

Martyniuk, Jaroslaw. "Public Opinion in Ukraine: Attitudes Towards the 1932-33 Holodomor. The Level of Support for the Genocide Thesis among Ukrainians." *Holodomor Studies* 2, no. 1 (Winter-Spring 2010): 53–61.

Marx, Karl. "A Contribution to the Critique of Political Economy—Preface." In *Collected Works*, vol. 29, by Karl Marx and Friedrich Engels, 261–266. Moscow: Progress Publishers, 1987.

Marx, Karl and Friedrich Engels. *Collected Works*, vol. 29. Moscow: Progress Publishers, 1987.

Masur, Volodymyr. "Yaroslav Stetsko: Prominent Statesman of the 20th Century." *ABN Correspondence*, 1-2, 47 (Spring/Summer 1996): 47.

Matsiv, Bohdan, ed. *Ukrains'ka dyviziia "Halychyna:" Istoriia u svitlynakh vid zasnuvannia u 1943 r. do zvil'nennia z polony 1949 r.* L'viv: ZUKTs, 2009.

Mattingly, Daria. "'Idle, Drunk, and Good-for-Nothing': The Cultural Memory of Holodomor Rank-and-File Perpetrators," in Małgorzata Głowacka-Grajper and Anna Wylegała (eds.) *The Burden of Memory: History, Memory and Identity in Contemporary Ukraine*. Bloomington, IN: Indiana University Press, 2020, 19-54.

Maxwell, Anne. *Picture Imperfect: Photography and Eugenics, 1870–1940*. Sussex: Sussex Academic Press, 2010.

Mayer, Arno J. *Wilson vs Lenin: Political Origins of the New Diplomacy, 1917–1918*. New York: Meridan Books, 1964.

McBride, Jared Graham. "'A Sea of Blood and Tears': Ethnic Diversity and Mass Violence in Nazi-Occupied Volhynia, Ukraine, 1941–1944." PhD Diss., University of California, Los Angeles, 2014.

McBride, Jared. *Contesting the Malyn Massacre: The Legcy of Inter-Ethnic Violence and the Second World War in Eastern Europe* Pittsburgh: The Center for Russian and East European Studies, University of Pittsburgh, 2016.

McBride, Jared. "How Ukraine's New Memory Commissar Is Controlling the Nation's Past." *The Nation*, August 13, 2015. http://www.thenation.com/article/how-ukraines-new-memory-commissar-is-controlling-the-nations-past/ (accessed 17 August 2023).

McBride, Jared. "Peasants into Perpetrators: The OUN-UPA and the Ethnic Cleansing of Volhynia, 1943–1944." *Slavic Review* vol. 75, no. 3, (Fall 2016): 630–654.

McBride, Jared. "The Many Lives and Afterlives of Khaim Sygal: Borderland Identities and Violence in Wartime Ukraine," *Journal of Genocide Research*, vol. 23, no. 4 (2021): 547-567.

Medvedev, Roi. *Neizvestnyi Andropov*. Rostov-na-Donu: Feniks, 1999.

Medvedev, Zhores A. *Andropov: An Insider's Account of Power and Politics Within the Kremlin*. New York: Penguin Books, 1984.

Medyk, Roman. "Vizyt Prezydenta Zelens'koho do Kanady: pohliad Ligi Ukraintsiv Kanady." *Homin Ukrainy*, 9 July 2019.

Medyk, Roman and Orest Steciw. "President Zelenskyy's visit to Canada: League of Ukrainian Canadians' view." *The Ukrainian Weekly*, 1 August 2019. https://www.ukrweekly.com/uwwp/president-zelensk yys-visit-to-canada-league-of-ukrainian-canadians-view/ (accessed 17 August 2023).

Mel'nyk, Ihor. "Rostyslav Yendyk—pys'mennyk i antropoloh." *Zbruch*, 2016, May 28. http://zbruc.eu/node/52015 (accessed 17 August 2023).

Meshko, G. "Vklad professor Makletsova, A. V. v stanovleniie i razvitie slovenskoi kriminologii." *Yuridicheskaia nauka i provookhranitel'naia praktika* vol. 4(34), (2015): 16–21.

Meyer, Henry and Ilya Arkhipov. "Russia Demands NATO Pullback in Security Talks with U.S." *Bloomberg*, 17 December 2021. https://www.bloomberg.com/news/articles/2021-12-17/russia-demands-nato-return-to-1997-in-security-treaty-proposals (accessed 17 August 2023).

Michaluk, Dorota and Per Anders Rudling. "From the Grand Duchy of Lithuania to the Belarusian Democratic Republic: The Idea of Belarusian Statehood during the German Occupation of Belarusian Lands, 1915–1919." *The Journal of Belarusian Studies*, 7, no. 2 (2014): 3–36.

Michel, Casey. "Alexei Navalny Has a Crimea Problem." *New Republic*, 4 October 2022. https://newrepublic.com/article/167944/alexei-navalny-crimea-problem-putin (accessed 17 August 2023).

Michlic, Joanna Beata. "History 'Wars' and the Battle for Truth and National Memory," in Ninna Mörner, ed. *Constructions and Instrumentalization of the Past: A Comparative Study on Memory Management in the Region (=CBEES State of the Region Report 2020)*, Huddinge: Centre for Baltic and East European Studies, 2020, 115–38.

Michlic, Joanna Beata. *Poland's Threatening Other: The Image of the Jew from 1880 to the Present*. Lincoln and London: University of Nebraska Press, 2006.

Michnik, Adam. "Forum for the Future of Democracy 2010 Keynote speech," *Council of Europe*, https://www.coe.int/t/dgap/forum-democracy/Activities/Forum%20sessions/2010/Speeches/Text%20Michnik%20for%20proceedings_EN_061210%20fin.asp (accessed January 17, 2024).

Christoph Mick, "Ethnische Gewalt und Pogrome in Lemberg 1914 und 1941," *Osteuropa* 53 (2003): 1810–1829.

Mihal, Taras. *ABN – assembly of buffoonish nationalists*. Kyiv: The Association for Cultural Relations with Ukrainians Abroad, 1968.

Mikhnovs'kyi, Mykola. *Samostiina Ukraina*. Kyiv: Diokor, 2002.

Miliakova, Lidia B. ed. *Kniga pogromov: Pogromy na Ukraine, v Belorussii i evropeiskoi chasti Rossii v period grazhdanskoi voiny, 1918-1922 gg. Sbornik dokumentov.* Moscow: ROSSPEN, 2007.

Mill, John Stuart. "Considerations on Representative Government." In *On Liberty and Other Essays*, edited by John Gray. Oxford: Oxford University Press, 1991.

Mill, John Stuart. *On Liberty and Other Essays*, edited by John Gray. Oxford: Oxford University Press, 1991.

Miller, Alexei I. "The Role of the First World War in the Competition between Ukrainian and All-Russian Nationalism." In *The Empire and Nationalism at War*, edited by Erik Lohr, Vera Tolz, Alexander Semyonov and Mark von Hagen. Bloomington, IN: Slavica Publishers, 2014, 73–89.

Miller, Alexei and Maria Lipman, eds. *The Convolutions of Historical Politics*. Budapest: Central European University Press, 2012.

Miller, Greg and Catherine Bolton. "Russia's Spies Misread Ukraine and Misled Kremlin as War Loomed." *Washington Post*, 19 August 2022. https://www.washingtonpost.com/world/interactive/2022/Russia-fsb-intelligence-ukraine-war/ (accessed August 17, 2023).

Minakov, Mikhail, ed. *Philosophy Unchained: Development of Philosophy After the Fall of the Soviet Union*. Stuttgart: ibidem-Verlag, 2023.

Mirchuk, Petro. *Narys istorii Orhanizatsii Ukains'kykh Natsionalistiv. Pershii tom 1920-1939 za redaktsiieiu Stepana Lenkavs'koho*. Munich: Ukrains'ke Vydavnytstvo, 1968 [2003].

Mirchuk, Petro. *Roman Shukhevych (Gen. Taras Chuprynka): Komandyr armii bezsmertnykh*. New York, Toronto and London: Tovarystvo kolyshnikh voiakiv UPA v ZShA, Kanadi i Evropi, 1970.

Mirchuk, Petro. *Zustrichi i rozmovy v Izrailiu*. New York: Soiuz ukrains'kykh politviazniv, 1982.

Mishchenko, Masha. "Pratsivnyk SBU: My izdyly v Izrail' pobachaty dos'e proty Shukhevycha—a ioho prosto one isnue." *Unian*, March 25, 2008. http://unian.net/news/print.php?id=242913 (accessed 17 August, 2023).

Moore, Rebekah. "'A Crime Against Humanity Arguably Without Parallel in European History': Genocide and the 'Politics' of Victimhood in Western Narratives of the Ukrainian Holodomor." *Australian Journal of Politics and History* 58, no. 3 (September 2012): 367–379.

Mörner, Ninna, ed. *Constructions and Instrumentalization of the Past: A Comparative Study on Memory Management in the Region (=CBEES State of the Region Report 2020)*, Huddinge: Centre for Baltic and East European Studies, 2020.

Motyka, Grzegorz. *Cień Kłyma Sawura: Polsko-ukraiński konflikt pamięci.* Gdańsk: Wydawnictwo Oskar oraz Muzeum II Wojny Światowej, 2013.

Motyka, Gzhegozh [Grzegorz]. "Neudachnaia kniga," *Ab Imperio* 2 (2012): 387–402

Motyka, Grzegorz. *Od rzezi wołyńskiej do akcji "Wisła:" Konflikt polsko-ukraiński 1943–1947.* Krakow: Wydawnictwo Literackie, 2011.

Motyka, Grzegorz. *Ukraińska partyzantka 1942–1960: Działalność Organizacji Ukraińskich Nacjonalistów i Ukraińskiej Powstańczej Armii.* Warsaw: Instytut Studiów Politycznych PAN, Oficyna Wydawnicza Rytm, 2006.

Motyl, Alexander J. "A House United: Why Analysts Touting Ukraine's East-West Division are Just Plain Wrong." *Foreign Policy*, 22 February 2014. http://foreignpolicy.com/2014/02/22/a-house-united/ (accessed 17 August, 2023).

Motyl, Alexander J., "Difficult Task Defining Bandera's Historic Role," *The Moscow Times*, 11 March 2010, available at http://historynewsnetwork.org/article/124267 (accessed 23 August 2017).

Motyl, Alexander J. "Fascistoid Russia: Whither Putin's Brittle Realm?" *World Affairs* (March–April 2012). http://www.worldaffairsjournal.org/article/fascistoid-russia-whither-putin's-brittle-realm (accessed 12 June, 2012, link no longer active).

Motyl, Alexander J. "Is Putin's Russia Fascist?" *Atlantic Council*, 23 April 2015. http://www.atlanticcouncil.org/blogs/new-atlanticist/is-putin-s-russia-fascist (accessed 17 August, 2023).

Motyl, Alexander J. "Is Putin's Russia Fascist?" *The National Interest*, 3 December, 2007. https://nationalinterest.org/commentary/inside-track-is-putins-russia-fascist-1888 (accessed 4 December, 2007, link no longer active).

Motyl, Alexander. "Is Ukraine Fascist?" *The World Post*, 2 March 2015. http://www.huffingtonpost.com/alexander-motyl/putin-calls-ukraine-fasci_b_6600292.html (accessed 5 March, 2015, link no longer active).

Motyl, Alexander J. "Is Zelensky Ukraine's George Washington?" *Los Angeles Times*, 27 February 2022. https://news.yahoo.com/op-ed-zelensky-ukraines-george-234659357.html (accessed 17 August, 2023).

Motyl, Alexander J. "Let It Go: Ukraine's Occupied Donbass Region is a Pointless Burden. It's Time for Kiev to Accept that It's Better Off Without It." *Foreign Policy*, 12 August 2016. http://foreignpolicy.com/2016/08/12/let-it-go-ukraine-russia-donbass/ (accessed 17 August, 2023).

Motyl, Alexander J. "On Nationalism and Fascism, Part 3." *World Affairs Blog*, 25 June 2013. http://www.worldaffairsjournal.org/blog/alexander-j-motyl/nationalism-and-fascism-part-3 (accessed July 1, 2013, link no longer active).

Motyl, Alexander J. "Should There Be One Ukraine?" *World Affairs Journal*, 14 February 2014. http://www.worldaffairsjournal.org/blog/alexander-j-motyl/should-there-be-one-ukraine (accessed 21 February, 2014, link no longer active).

Motyl, Alexander J. "Surviving Russia's Drift to Fascism." *Kyiv Post*, 17 January 2008. http://www.kyivpost.com/opinion/oped/28182/ (accessed 23 January, 2008, link no longer active).

Motyl, Alexander J. *The Turn to the Right: The Ideological Origins and Development of Ukrainian Nationalism, 1919–1929*. Boulder, CO: East European Monographs, 1980.

Motyl, Alexander J. "The Ukrainian Nationalist Movement and the Jews: Theoretical Reflections on Nationalism, Fascism, Rationality, Primordialism, and History." *Polin: Studies in Polish Jewry* 26 (2014): 275–295.

Motyl, Alexander J. "Thinking About Empire." In *After Empire: Multiethnic Societies and Nation-Building. The Soviet Union and the Russian, Ottoman, and Habsburg Empires*, edited by Karen Barkey and Mark von Hagen, 19–29. Boulder, CO: Westview Press, 1997.

Motyl, Alexander J. "Trivializing Genocide: A Dangerous Distraction." *World Affairs Blog*, 18 August 2016, https://web.archive.org/web/20160825042823/http://www.worldaffairsjournal.org/blog/alexander-j-motyl/trivializing-genocide-dangerous-distraction (accessed 17 August 17, 2023).

Motyl, Alexander J. "Ukrainian Nationalist Political Violence in Inter-War Poland, 1921–1939." *East European Quarterly* 19, no. 1 (1985): 45–55.

Motyl, Alexander J. "Ukraine's Pretend President Now Faces a Real Test." *Foreign Policy*, 22 April 2019. https://foreignpolicy.com/2019/04/22/ukraines-pretend-president-now-faces-a-real-test/ (accessed August 17, 2023).

Motyl', Oleksander. [Motyl, Alexander] "Orhanizatsiia ukrains'kykh natsionalistiv i robitnytstbo (kil'ka zavvah)." *Suchasnist* no. 2 (1980): 51–63.

Motyl, Alexander. "Stepan Bandera: Hero of Ukraine?" *New Atlanticist*, 15 March 2010. https://www.atlanticcouncil.org/blogs/new-atlanticist/stepan-bandera-hero-of-ukraine/ (accessed 17 August, 2023).

Motyl, Alexander. "Ukraine, Europe, and Bandera." *Cicero Foundation Great Debate Paper* 5 (2010): 12. http://www.cicerofoundation.org/lectures/Alexander_J_Motyl_UKRAINE_EUROPE_AND_BANDERA.pdf (accessed August 17, 2023).

Motyl, Alexander. "Vladimir Putin Is Committing Genocide in Ukraine." *1945*, 2 March 2022. https://www.19fortyfive.com/2022/03/vladimir-putin-is-committing-genocide-in-ukraine/ (accessed August 17, 2023).

Mucha, Sarah. "Zelensky is America's Most Popular World Leader." *Axios*, 6 April 2022. https://www.axios.com/2022/04/06/zelensky-is-americas-most-popular-world-leader (accessed 17 August 2023).

Mędykowski, Witold. *W cieniu gigantów: pogromy 1941 r. W byłej sowieckiej strefie okupacyjnej: kontekst historyczny, społeczny i kulturowy*. Warsaw: Instytut Studiów Politycznych PAN, 2012.

Nakai, Kazuo. "Soviet Agricultural Policies in the Ukraine and the 1921-1922 Famine." *Harvard Ukrainian Studies*, vol. 6, no. 1 (March 1982): 43-61.

Narvselius, Eleonora. "The 'Bandera Debate': The Contentious Legacy of World War II and Liberalization of Collective Memory in Western Ukraine,' *Canadian Slavonic Papers / Revue canadienne des slavistes* 54, no. 3-4 (2012): 61-83.

Nesturkh, Mikhail F. *et al.* (eds.). *Sovremennia antropologiia (=Trudy Moskovskogo obshchestva ispytatelei prirody, vol. 14)*. Moscow: Izdatel'stvo Moskovskogo Universiteta, 1964.

Netschkina, M. W. *et al. Geschichte der UdSSR, Band I: Von den ältesten Zeiten bis zum Jahre 1861. Urgesellschaft, Sklavenhalterordnung und Feudalismus*. Erster Halbband. Translated by Arno Specht. Berlin: VEB Deutscher Verlag der Wissenschaften, 1961.

Nieberle, Sigrid. "'Und Gott im Himmel Lieder singt': Zur prekären Rezeption von Ernst Moritz Arndt Des Deutschen Vaterland." In *Ernst Moritz Arndt (1769-1860): Deutscher Nationalismus – Europa – Transatlantische Perspektiven*, edited by Walter Erhart, Arne Koch, 121-136. Berlin: De Gruyter, 2007.

Niedermüller, Peter. "Der Mythos der Gemeinschaft: Geschichte, Gedächtnis und Politik im heutigen Osteuropa." In *Umbruch im östlichen Europa: Die nationale Wende und das kollektive Gedächtnis*, edited by Andrea Corbea Hoise, Rudolf Jaworski and Monika Sommer, 11-26. Innsbruck: Studien Verlag, 2004.

Nilsson, Göran B. *Den lycklige humanisten: tio offensiva essäer*. Stockholm: Carlssons, 1990.

Nolte, Ernst. *Three Faces of Fascism: Action Française Italian Fascism, National Socialism*. Translated by Leila Vennewitz. New York, NY: New American Library, 1969.

Norman, Filip, "Svagt fredshopp i krigstrött Ukraina." *Svenska Dagbladet*, 20 April 2020.

Nove, Alec. *An Economic History of the USSR*. London: Penguin Books, 1989.

Nowak, Andrzej. "Russia, Empire, and Evil: Dilemmas and Temptations in Contemporary Russian Political Imagination." In *Politics, History and Collective Memory in East Central Europe*, edited by Zdzisław Krasnodębski, Stefan Garsytecki, and Rüdiger Ritter, 163–193. Hamburg: Krämer, 2012.

Nowosselski, A. A. "Die Ukraine und Belorussland im 17. Jh." In *Geschichte der UdSSR, Band I: Von den ältesten Zeiten bis zum Jahre 1861. Urgesellschaft, Sklavenhalterordnung und Feudalismus*. Zweiter Halbband. Translated by Arno Specht. By Netschkina *et al.*, 389–403. Berlin: VEB Deutscher Verlag der Wissenschaften, 1962.

Oberländer, Erwin. *Sowjetpatriotismus und Geschichte: Dokumentation*. Cologne: Verlag Wissenschaft und Politik, 1967.

O'Neill, Robin. *The Rabka Four: A Warning from History*. London: Spiderwise, 2011.

Obryn'ba, Nikolai Ippolitovich. *Sud'ba opolchentsa*. Moscow: Yauza, Eksmo, 2005.

Öhman [Dietsch], Johan. "Holodomor and the Ukrainian Identity of Suffering: The 1932-1933 Ukrainian Famine in Historical Culture." *Canadian-American Slavic Studies* 37, no. 3 (Fall 2003): 27-44.

Olszański, Tadeusz A. *The Great Decommunization: Ukraine's Wartime Historical Policy*. Warsaw: Centre for Eastern Studies, 2017.

Oscarsson, Tea. "Försvarsministern stänger inte dörren för kärnvapen i Sverige." *Svenska Dagbladet*, 4 November 2022. https://www.svd.se/a/nQyrro/forsvarsministern-oppnar-for-karnvapen-i-sverige (accessed 17 August 2023).

Osiecki, Grzegorz and Zbigniew Parafianowicz. "Czarna lista Waszczykowskiego. Szef ukraińskiego IPN nie wjedyie do Polski." *Dziennik.pl*, 9 November 2017. http://wiadomosci.dziennik.pl/polityka/artykuly/562162,czarna-lista-waszczykowskiego-kto-na-niej-jest-w jazd-do-polski.html (accessed 17 August 2023)

Ostriitchouk, Olha. *Les Ukrainiens face à leur passé: Vers une meilleure compréhension du clivage Est/Ouest*. Brussels: Peter Lang, 2013.

Paasivirta, Juhani. *Finland år 1918 och relationerna till utlandet*, translated by Henrik von Bonsdorff. Helsinki: Tiden, 1962.

Pahiria, Oleksandr. "OUN ta UPA v konteksti vyzvol'nykh rukhiv: sproba komparativnoho analizu." *Novitnia doba* 7 (2019): 150–177.

Pakier, Małgorzata and Joanna Wawrzyniak, eds. *Memory and Change in Europe: Eastern Perspectives*. New York and Oxford: Berghahn Books, 2015.

Palij, Michael. *The Ukrainian-Polish Defensive Alliance, 1919–1921: An Aspect of the Ukrainian Revolution*. Edmonton: Canadian Institute of Ukrainian Studies Press, 1995.

Palko, Olena. *Making Ukraine Soviet: Literature and Cultural Politics under Lenin and Stalin*. London: Bloomsbury Academic Press, 2022.

Pal'ko, Olena P. *Natsional'ne pytannia v teoriiakh lo avstromarksyzmu*. Kyiv: NAN Ukrainy, 2022.

Panchenko, Oleksandr, ed. *Boh i Ukraina ponad use: o. Ivan Hryn'okh*, edited by Oleksandr Panchenko, Hadiach: Vydavnytstvo 'Hadiach', 2007, 60–76.

Panchenko, Oleksandr. *Mykola Lebed': zhyttia, diial'nist, derzhavno-pravivi pohliady*. Hadiach: Vydavnytstvo "Hadiach," 2001.

Panchenko, Oleksandr. *Orhanizatsiia Ukrains'kykh Natsionalistiv za kordonom (Naukovo-populiarnyi narys)*. Hadiach: Vydavnytstvo "Hadiach," 2003.

Patryliak, Ivan K. *Viiskova diial'nist OUN(b) u 1940–1942 rokakh*. Kyiv: Kyivs'kyi natsional'nyi universytet im. Tarasa Shevchenko, Instytut istorii Ukrainy nan Ukrainy, 2004.

Patryliak, Ivan. *"Peremoha abo smert": ukrains'kyi vyzvol'nyi rukh u 1939–1960 rr*. L'viv: Tsentr doslidzhen' vyzvol'noho rukhu, 2012.

Patryliak, Ivan. "Zapytannia do Forumu 'Fashyzm na skhodi Evropy'." *Ukraina Moderna* 20, (2013): 30–31.

Pauly, Matthew. *Breaking the Tongue: Language, Education, and Power in Soviet Ukraine, 1923-1934*. Toronto: University of Toronto Press, 2014.

Pavlovs'kyi, Al. *Grammatika malorossiiskago narechia, ili Grammaticheskoe pokazanie sushchesvenneishikh otlichii, otdalivshikh Malorossiiskoe narechie ot chistago Rossiiskago iazyka, soprovozhdaemoe raznyi po semu predmetu zamechaniiami i sochineniiami*. St. Petersburg: Tipografiia V. Plavil'shchikova, 1818.

Payne, Stanley G. "The Concept of Fascism." In *Who Were the Fascists?: Social Roots of European Fascism*, edited by Stein Ugelvik Larsen, Bernt Hagtvet, and Jan Petter Myklebust, 14-25. Bergen: Universitetsforlaget, 1980.

Payne, Stanley G. *A History of Fascism, 1914–1945*. Madison: The University of Wisconsin Press, 1995.

Paź, Bogusław, ed. *Prawda historyczna a prawda polityczna w badaniach naukowych: Ludobójstwo na Kresach południowo-wschodniej Polski w latach 1939-1946*. Wrocław: Wydawnictwo uniwersytetu Wrocławskiego, 2011.

Pchelov, Evgenii. "Khronologicheskii kommentarii k 'Dniu narodnogo edinstva'." *Gerboved* 85 (2005): 138-141.

Petersson, Bo. *The Putin Predicament: Problems of Legitimacy and Succession in Russia*. Stuttgart: ibidem-Verlag, 2021.

Petrenko, Olena. "Geschlecht, Gewalt, Nation: Die Organisation Ukrainischer Nationalisten und die Frau." *Osteuropa* 66, no. 4 (2016): 83-93.

Petrenko, Olena. *Unter Männern: Frauen im ukrainschen nationalistischen Untergrund 1944-1954*. Paderborn: Ferdinand Schöningh, 2018.

Petrenko, Roman. "Poranennia Iaroslava Stets'ka," *Homin Ukrainy*, October 9, (2012): 5

Petrov, N. V. and K. V. Sorokin. *Kto rukovodil NKVD 1934-1941: Spravochnik*. Moscow: Zveniia, 1999.

Petrovsky-Shtern, Yohanan. *The Anti-Imperial Choice: The Making of the Ukrainian Jew*. New Haven: Yale University Press, 2009.

Petrovsky-Shtern, Yohanan and Antony Polonsky, eds. *Polin: Studies in Polish Jewry, Volume 26: Jews and Ukrainians*. Oxford and Portland OR: The Littman Library of Jewish Civilization, 2014.

Petryna, Adriana. "A Technical Error: Measures of Life after Chernobyl." *Social Identities: Journal for the Study of Race, Nation, and Culture* 4, no. 1 (1998): 72-92.

Pikulicka-Wilczewski, Agnieszka and Richard Sakwa (eds.), *Ukraine and Russia: People, Politics, Propaganda and Perspectives*. E-International Relations Publishing, 2015.

Piotrowski, Tadeusz. *Genocide and Rescue in Wołyń: Recollections of the Ukrainian Nationalist Ethnic Cleansing Campaign against the Poles During World War II*. Jefferson, NC: McFarland, 2008.

Piotrowski, Tadeusz. *Poland's Holocaust: Ethnic Strife, Collaboration with Occupying Forces and Genocide in the Second Republic, 1918-1947*. Jefferson, NC: McFarland, 1998.

Pipes, Richard. *The Russian Revolution*. New York: Vintage Books, 1990.

Pittock, Murray. *Scotland: The Global History, 1603 to the Present*. New Haven: Yale University Press, 2022.

Plokhy, Serhii. *The Man with the Poison Gun: A Cold War Spy Story*. New York: Basic Books, 2016.

Plokhy, Serhii. *Ukraine & Russia: Representations of the Past.* Toronto: University of Toronto Press, 2008.

Pobihushchyi-Ren, Yevhen. "Spohady pro generala Romana Shukhevycha." In *U lavkah druzhynnykiv: Druzhyny Ukrains'kykh Nationalistiv v 1941–1942 rokakh,* edited by Myroslav Kal'ba. n.p: Vyd-ia Druzhyny ukrainsks'kykh nationalistiv, 1953.

Pobihushchyi-Ren, Yevhen. *Mozaika moikh spomyniv.* Ivano-Frankiv'sk: Lileia-hb, 2002.

Pobihushchyi-Ren, Yevhen. *Mozaika moikh spomyniv.* Tom druhyi. Munich and London: Yevhen Pobihushchyi-Ren and the Association of Ukrainian Former Combatants in Great Britain, 1985.

Podrabinek, Alexaner. *Punitive Medicine.* Ann Arbor: Karoma Publishers, 1980.

Pohl, Dieter. "Anti-Jewish Pogroms in Western Ukraine—A Research Agenda." In *Shared History–Divided Memory: Jews and Others in Soviet-Occupied Poland, 1939–1941,* edited by Elazar Barkan, Elizabeth A. Cole, and Kai Struve, 305–313. Leipzig: Leipziger Universitätsverlag, 2007.

Pohl, Dieter. "[Review of] Bohdan Musial: 'Konterrevolutionäre Elemente sind zu Erschiessen' Die Brutalisierung des deutsch-sowjetisches Krieges im Sommer 1941." *H-Soz-u-Kult Online,* 30 April 2001. http://www.hsozkult.de/publicationreview/id/rezbuecher-546 (accessed 17 August 2023).

Pohl, Dieter. "Hans Krüger—der 'König von Stanislau.'" In *Karrieren der Gewalt: Nationalsozialistische Täterbiographien,* edited by Klaus-Michael Mallmann, 134–144. Darmstadt: Primus, 2004.

Pohl, Dieter. *Nationalsozialistische Judenverfolgung in Ostgalizien 1941–1944: Organization und Durchführung eines sluutlichen Massenverbrechens.* 2. Auflage. München: Oldenbourg, 1997.

Polec, Janko. "Maklecov, Aleksander (1884–1948)." In *Slovenska biografija.* Lubljana: Slovenska akademija znanosti in umetnosti, Znanstvenoraziskovalni center SAZU, 2013 http://www.slovenska-biografija.si/oseba/sbi343178/ (accessed 17 August, 2023).

Politychna prohrama i ustrii Orhanizatsii Ukrains'kykh Natsionalistiv. N.p., 1941.

Pollak, Martin and Stefaniya Ptashnyk, eds. *Ukraine: Literatur und Kritik.* Salzburg: Otto Müller Verlag, 2016.

Popek, Leon. "Wołyńskie ekshumacje w latach 1992–2015." *Instytut Pamięci Narodowej.* https://ipn.gov.pl/pl/aktualnosci/37305,Leon-Popek-Wolynskie-ekshumacje-w-latach-19922015.html (accessed 17 August, 2023).

Portnov, Andrii. "Memory Wars in Post-Soviet Ukraine (1991–2010)." In *Memory and Theory in Eastern Europe*, edited by Uilleam Blacker, Alexander Etkind, and Julie Fedor, 233–245. New York: Palgrave Macmillan, 2013.

Portnov, Andrii. *Istorii dlia domashn'oho vzhytku: Esei pro pol's'ko-rosiis'ko-ukrains'kyi trykutnyk pam''iati* (Kyiv: Krytyka, 2013).

Portnov, Andriy, and Andrew Wilson. "The Heart of Ukraine"? Dnipropetrovsk and the Ukrainian Revolution." *What does Ukraine think*, 62–70. Berlin: The European Council on Foreign Relations, 2015.

Posivnych, Mykola. "Roman Shukhevych (30.VI.1907–5.III.1950)." In *Litopys Ukrains'koï Povstans'koi Armii. Tom 45: Heneral Roman Shukhevych – 'Taras Chuprynka' Holovnyi Komandyr UPA*, edited by Petro J. Potichnyj and Mykola Posivnych, 7–20. Toronto and L'viv: Vydavnytstvo Litopys UPA, 2007.

Posokhov, Parmen. "Shukhevych: Beloe piatno v biografii." *fraza*, August 15, 2007. http://fraza.org.ua/zametki/15.08.07/40788.html?c=post&i=113503.

Potichnyj, Petro J. ed. *Litopys Ukrains'koi Povstans'koi Armii, Tom 43: Struggle against Agentura: Protocols of Interrogation of the OUN SB in Ternopil Region 1946–1948. Book I*. Toronto: Litopys UPA, 2006.

Potichnyj, Petro J. and Mykola Posivnych, eds. *Litopys Ukrains'koi Povstans'koi Armii, Tom 45, Heneral Roman Shukhevych – 'Taras Chuprynka' Holovnyi Komandyr UPA*. Toronto and L'viv: Vydavnytstvo Litopys UPA, 2007.

Potichnyj, Peter J. and Howard Aster, *Ukrainian-Jewish Relations in Historical Perspective*. Edmonton: CIUS Press, 1990.

Potichnyj, Peter J. and Yevhen Shtendera, eds. *Political Thought of the Ukrainian Underground, 1943–1951*. Edmonton: CIUS Press, 1986.

Procyk, Anna. "Challenges and Achievements of Ukrainian Scholarly Institutions in the United States during the Cold War, the Period of Co-existence and the Three Decades of Ukraine's Independence." Presentation at the conference "Ukraine in North America: Diaspora Activism, Academic Institutions," The Harriman Institute at Columbia University, 5 November 2022. https://harriman.columbia.edu/event/ukraine-in-north-america-diaspora-activism-academic-initiatives/ (accessed 17 August 2023)

Promitzer, Christian, Sevasti Trubeta, and Marius Turda, eds., *Health, Hygiene and Eugenics in Southeastern Europe to 1945*. Budapest: CEU Press, 2011.

Prusin, Alexander Victor, *Nationalizing a Borderland: War, Ethnicity, and Anti-Jewish Violence in East Galicia, 1914-1920*. Tuscaloosa: University of Alabama Press, 2005.

Prusin, Alexander V. *The Lands Between: Conflict in the East European Borderlands, 1870-1992*. Oxford: Oxford University Press, 2010.

Prymak, Thomas M. "Dmytro Doroshenko: A Ukrainian Émigré Historian of the Interwar Period," *Harvard Ukrainian Studies*, vol. 25, no. 1-2 (2001): 31-56.

Prymak, Thomas M. *Mykhailo Hrushevsky: The Politics of National Culture*. Toronto: University of Toronto Press, 1987.

Prymak, Thomas M. *Mykola Kostomarov: A Biography*. Toronto: University of Toronto Press, 1995.

Prymachenko, Iana. "Antykolonial'nyi dyskurs OUN/UPA v suchasnomu ukrains'komu kontektsi borot'by za evropeis'ku identychnist'," *Ukrains'kyi istorychnyi zbirnyk*, vyp. 17 (2014): 328-338.

Putin, Vladimir. "Address by the President of the Russian Federation." *President of Russia official website*, 21 February 2022. http://en.kremli n.ru/events/president/news/67828 (accessed 17 August 2023).

Putin, Vladimir. "On the Historical Unity of Russians and Ukrainians." *President of Russia official website*, 12 July 2021. http://en.kremlin.ru/ events/president/news/66181 (accessed 17 August 2023).

Pyrih, Volodymyr. "Novym dyrektorom Ukrains'koho instytutu natsional'noi pam'iati stav Anton Drobovych." *Zaxid.net*, 4 December 2019. https://zaxid.net/anton_drobovich_biografiya_golovi_instit utu_natsionalnoyi_pamyati_n1494067 (accessed 5 December 2019, link no longer active).

Rabinowitsch, Wadim, Jan Tabatschnik and Aleksandr Feldman. "Jüdischer Protest in der Ukraine." *Kontakte-Kontakty: Verein für Kontakte zu Ländern der ehemaligen Sowjetunion*, October 15, 2007. http://www.kontakte-kontakty.de/deutsch/verein/2005-2009/up a.php (accessed October 23, 2007, link no longer valid).

Programma Rossiiskoi Kommunisticheskoi Partii (bolshevikov): priniato VIII s"ezdom partii 18-23 marta 1919 goda. Rabochaia biblioteka Pravdy, Tom 4. Prague: Izd. Gazety "Pravdy," 1920.

Radchenko Yuri. "From Staryi Uhryniv to Munich: The First Scholarly Biography of Stepan Bandera," *Journal of Soviet and Post-Soviet Politics and Society* 1, no. 2 (2015): 429-58.

Rasevych, Vasyl. "The Western Ukrainian People's Republic of 1918-1919." In *The Emergence of Ukraine*, edited by Dornik et al., 132-154.

Rasevych, Vasyl'. "Vyverty propahandy: Vystavka iak sproba nav'iazaty svii kanon suchasnoho istoriychoho naratyvu." *Zaxid.net*, 30 September 2015. http://zaxid.net/news/showNews.do?viverti_prop agandi&objectId=1367592 (accessed 17 August 2023)

Read, Christopher. "Centennial Thoughts of an Exhausted (?) Revolution." *Revolutionary Russia* 31, no. 2 (2018): 194-207.

Reardon, Jenny. *Race to the Finish: Identity and Governance in an Age of Genomics*. Princeton: Princeton University Press, 2005.

Reich, Rebecca. *State of Madness: Psychiatry, Literature, and Dissent After Stalin*. DeKalb: Northern Illinois University Press, 2018.

Reichardt, Sven. "Fascism's Stages: Imperial Violence, Entanglement, and Processualization." *Journal of History of Ideas* 82, no. 1 (January 2021): 85-107.

Reiman, Michal. *The Birth of Stalinism: The USSR on the Eve of the 'Second Revolution'*. Bloomington and Indianapolis: Indiana University Press, 1987.

Reisch, Alfred A. *Hot Books in the Cold War: The CIA-funded Secret Western Book Distribution Program Behind the Iron Curtain*. Budapest: Central European University Press, 2013.

Riabchuk, Mykola. "Bandera's Controversy and Ukraine's Future." *Russkii vopros* 1 (2010). http://www.russkiivopros.com/?pag=one&id=315&kat=9&csl=46#_edn13 (accessed 17 August 2023).

Riabchuk, Mykola. "Emancipation from the East Slavonic Ummah." *New Eastern Europe* 2 (16) (2015): 14-20.

Ryabchuk, [Riabchuk] Mykola. "The Ukrainian 'Friday' and the Russian 'Robinson': the Uneasy Advent of Postcoloniality." *Canadian-American Slavic Studies* 44 (2010): 7-25.

Riabchuk, Mykola. "Ukraine: Neither Heroes nor Villains: [Review of] Heroes and Villains: Creating National History in Contemporary Ukraine, by David Marples," *Transitions Online*, February 6, 2007.

Ryabchuk [Riabchuk], Mykola. "Ukraine's Turbulent Past between Hagiography and Demonization." *Raam op Rusland: Podium voor kennis, analyse en debat*, 2 November 2016. http://www.raamoprusland.nl/dossiers/oekraine/311-ukraine-s-turbulent-past-between-hagiography-and-demonization (accessed 17 August 2023).

Risch, William Jay. *The Ukrainian West: Culture and the Fate of Empire in Soviet Lviv*. Cambridge, MA: Harvard University Press, 2011.

Risen, James and Ken Klippenstein. "The CIA thought Putin would Quickly Conquer Ukraine: Why Did They Get it So Wrong?" *The Intercept*, 5 October 2022. https://theintercept.com/2022/10/05/russia-ukraine-putin-cia/ (Accessed 17 August 2023).

[Romanyshyn, Oleh]. "Nasha porada deiakim istorikam," *Homin Ukrainy*, March 27, 2012, 8.

Roshchin, Aleksei. *Strana utrachenoi empatii: Kak sovetskoe proshloe vliiaet na rossiiskoe nastoiashchee*. Moscow: Eksmo, 2019.

Rössler, Mechthild and Sabine Schleiermacher, eds. *Der "Generalplan Ost": Hauptlinien der nationalsozialistischen Planungs- und Vernichtungspolitik*. Berlin: Akademie-Verlag, 1993.

Rossoliński-Liebe, Grzegorz. "Celebrating Fascism and War Criminality in Multicultural Canada: The Political Myth and Cult of Stepan Bandera in Multicultural Canada," *Kakanien Revisited*, December 29 (2010): 1–16.

Rossoliński-Liebe, Grzegorz. "Der polnisch-ukrainische Historikerdiskurs über den polnisch-ukrainischen Konflikt 1943-1947," *Jahrbücher für Geschichte Osteuropas* 57 (2009): 54–85.

Rossoliński-Liebe, Grzegorz. "Der Verlauf und die Täter des Lemberger Pogrom vom Sommer 1941: Zum aktuellen Stand der Forschung." *Jahrbuch für Antisemitismusforschung* 22 (2014): 207–243.

Rossoliński-Liebe, Grzegorz. "Erinnerungslücke Holocaust: Die ukrainische Diaspora und der Genozid an den Juden." *Vierteljahrhefte für Zeitgeschichte* 62, no. 3 (2014): 397–430.

Rossoliński-Liebe, Grzegorz. *Stepan Bandera: The Life and Afterlife of a Ukrainian Nationalist. Fascism, Genocide, and Cult*. Stuttgart: ibidem-Verlag, 2014.

Rossoliński-Liebe, Grzegorz. *The Fascist Kernel of Ukrainian Genocidal Nationalism*. (= *The Carl Beck Papers in Russian and East European Studies* 2402) Pittsburgh: The Center for Russian and East European Studies, University of Pittsburgh, 2015.

Rossoliński Liebe, Grzegorz. "The 'Ukrainian National Revolution' of 1941: Discourse and Practice of a Fascist Movement." *Kritika: Explorations in Russian and Eurasian History* 12, no. 1 (Winter 2011): 83–114.

Rossoliński-Liebe, Gregorz. "Ukraińska policja, nacjonalizm i zagłada Żydów w Galicji Wschodniej i na Wołyniu." *Zagłada Żydów: Studia i Materiały* 13 (2017): 57–79.

Rossoliński-Liebe, Grzegorz and Bastiaan Willems. "Putin's Abuse of History: Ukrainian 'Nazis', 'Genocide', and a Fake Threat Scenario." *Journal of Slavic Military Studies* 35, no. 1 (2022): 1–10.

Rothberg, Michael. *Multidirectional Memory: Remembering the Holocaust in the Age of Decolonization*. Stanford, CA: Stanford University Press, 2009.

Rudé, George. *Debate on Europe, 1815-1850*. New York: Harper & Row, 1972.

Rubl'ov, Oleksandr and Larysa Iakubova in their review "Pro 'imperiio pozytyvnoi dii' Teri Martyna," *Historians.in.ua*, August 1, 2013.

Rudling, Per Anders. "Dispersing the Fog: The OUN and Anti-Jewish Violence in 1941." *Yad Vashem Studies* 44, no. 2 (2016): 227-45.

Rudling, Per Anders. "Eugenics and Racial Biology in Sweden and the USSR: Contacts across the Baltic Sea." *Canadian Bulletin of Medical History/Bulletin canadien d'historie de la medicine* 31, no. 1 (2014): 41-75.

Rudling, Per Anders. "Institutes of Trauma Re-Production in a Borderland: Poland, Ukraine, and Lithuania." In *Constructions and Instrumentalization of the Past: A Comparative Study on Memory Management in the Region (=CBEES State of the Region Report 2020)*, edited by Ninna Mörner, 55-68. Huddinge: Centre for Baltic and East European Studies, 2020.

Rudling, Per A. "Multiculturalism, Memory, and Ritualization: Ukrainian Nationalist Monuments in Edmonton, Alberta." *Nationalities Papers* 39, no. 55 (2011): 733-768.

Rudling, Per Anders. "Organized Anti-Semitism in Contemporary Ukraine: Structure, Influence and Ideology," *Canadian Slavonic Papers/Revue canadienne des slavistes*, vol. XLVIII, nos. 1-2 (March-June 2006), 81-118.

Rudling, Per Anders. "Rehearsal for Volhynia: Schutzmannschaft Battalion 201 and Hauptmann Roman Shukhevvych in Occupied Belorussia, 1942." *East European Politics and Societies and Cultures* 34, no. 1 (2020): 158-193.

Rudling, Per Anders. "Szkolenie w mordowaniu: Schutzmannschaft Battalion 201 i Hauptmann Roman Szuchewycz na Białorusi 1942 roku." In *Prawda Historyczna a Prawda Polityczna w badaniach naukowych: Przykład ludobójstwa na Kresach południowo-wschodniej Polski w latach 1939-1946*, edited by Bogusław Paź, 183-204. Wrocław: Wydawnictwo uniwersytetu Wrocławskiego, 2011.

Rudling, Per Anders. "Terror Remembered, Terror Forgotten: Stalinist, Nazi, and Nationalist Atrocities in Ukrainian 'National Memory'." In *World War II Re-explored: Some New Millenium Studies in the History of the Global Conflict*, edited by Jarosław Suchoples, Stephanie James, and Barbara Törnquist-Plewa, 401-428. Brussels: Peter Lang, 2019.

Rudling, Per Anders. "Theory and Practice: Historical Representation of the War Time Activities of OUN-UPA (the Organization of Ukrainian Nationalists—the Ukrainian Insurgent Army)." *East European Jewish Affairs* 36, no. 2 (2006): 163-189.

Rudling, Per A. *The OUN, the UPA and the Holocaust: A Study in the Manufacturing of Historical Myths (=The Carl Beck Papers in Russian and East European Studies. No. 2107).* Pittsburgh: Center for Russian and East European Studies, University of Pittsburgh, 2011.

Rudling, Per A. "Ukrainians," in Roland Clark and Tim Grady (eds.), *European Fascist Movements* London and New York: Routledge, 2023, 366-385.

Rudling, Per Anders. "Warfare or War Criminality?: Volodymyr V"iatrovych, Druha pol's'ko-ukrains'ka viina, 1942-1947 (Kyiv: Vydavnychyi Dim 'Kyevo-Mohylians'ka Akademiia, 2011)," *Ab Imperio* 1 (2012): 356-381.

Ruffner, Kevin Conley. "Eagle and Swastika: CIA and Nazi War Criminals and Collaborators." Draft Working Paper. History Staff, History Staff, Central Intelligence Agency, Washington, DC, 2003) https://www.cia.gov/readingroom/docs/CIA%20AND%20NAZI %20WAR%20CRIM.%20AND%20COL.%20CHAP.%201-10%2C%20 DRAFT%20WORKING%20PAPER_0001.pdf (accessed 17 August 2023)

Ryan, Jr., Alan A. *Klaus Barbie and the United States Government: A Report to the Attorney General of the United States.* Washington, DC: US Department of Justice, 1983.

Rystad, Göran, ed. *The Uprooted: Forced Migration as an International Problem in the Post-War Era,* Lund: Lund University Press, 1990.

Sakwa, Richard. *Frontline Ukraine: Crisis in the Borderlands.* London: I.B. Tauris, 2014.

Salomon, Kim. *Refugees in the Cold War: Toward a New International Refugee Regime in the Early Postwar Era.* Lund: Lund University Press, 1991.

Sanborn, Joshua A. *Imperial Apocalypse: The Great War & the Destruction of the Russian Empire.* Oxford: Oxford University Press, 2014.

Sanborn, Joshua. "War of Decolonization: The Russian Empire in the Great War." In *The Empire and Nationalism at War,* edited by Eric Lohr, Vera Tolz, Alexander Semyonov, and Mark von Hagen, 49-71. Bloomington, IN: Slavica Publishers, 2014.

Sandkühler, Thomas. *Das Fußvolk der "Endlösung": Nichtdeutsche Täter und die europäische Dimension des Völkermords.* Darmstadt: Wissenschaftliche Buchgesellschaft Academic, 2020.

Sands, Philippe. "Prosecuting Putin's Aggression." *The Nation*, 14 April 2022. https://www.thenation.com/article/world/ukraine-putin-aggression-crime/ (accessed 17 August 2023).

Sands, Philippe. *East West Street: On the Origins of Genocide and Crimes Against Humanity*. London: Weidenfeld & Nicholson, 2017.

Savaryn, Petro. *Z soboiu vzialy Ukrainu: Vid Ternopillia do Al'berty*. Kyiv: KVITs, 2007.

Schattenberg, Susanne. *Leonid Breschnew: Staatsmann und Schauspieler im Schatten Stalins. Eine Biographie*. Cologne: Böhlau, 2017.

Schenk, Gibfried. *Zwischen Sowjetnostalgie und "Entkommunisierung": Postsowjetische Geschichtspolitik und Erinnerungskultur in der Ukraine*. Erlangen: FAU-University Press, 2020.

Schneider-Deters, Winfried. *Ukrainische Schicksaalsjahre 2013–2019: Band 1. Der Volksaufstand auf dem Majdan im Winter 2013/2014*. Berlin: Berliner Wissenschafts-Verlag, 2021.

Schneider-Deters, Winfried. *Ukrainische Schicksalsjahre 2013–2019. Band 2: Die Annexion der Krim und der Krieg im Donbass*. Berlin: Berliner Wissenschafts-Verlag, 2021.

Schwartz, Matthias. "Servants of the People: Populism, Nationalism, State-Building, and Virtual Reality in Contemporary Ukraine." *Telos: Critical Theory and the Contemporary*, Heft 195. (2021): 65–81.

Schwartz, Matthias. "'Diener des Volkes': Eine TV-Serie zwischen satirischer Fiktion und politischer Realität." *INDES: Zeitschrift für Politik und Gesellschaft* 10: no. 1–2 (November 2022): 70–75.

Sehn, Arthur. "Etniska minoriteter i Polen i svenska diplomatrapporter 1918–1939: Del 1," *Acta Sueco-Polonica* Nr. 2, (1994): 23–51. Uppsala: Seminariet i Polens kultur och historia vid Uppsala universitet.

Semczyszyn, Magdalena and Mariusz Zyalączkowski. *Giedroyc a Ukraina: Ukraińska perspektywa Jerzego Giedroycia i środowiska paryskiej "Kultury"*. Warsaw: IPN, 2014.

Semotiuk, Andriy J. "The Stepan Bandera Quandary." *Kyiv Post*, 19 April 2010. https://www.kyivpost.com/article/opinion/op-ed/the-stepan-bandera-quandary-64386.html (accessed 20 April 2010, link no longer valid)

Serbyn, Roman. "Erroneous Methods in J.-P. Himka's Challenge to 'Ukrainian Myths.'" *Current Politics in Ukraine*, 7 August 2011. http://ukraineanalysis.wordpress.com/2011/08/07/erroneous-methods-in-j-p-himka's-challenge-to-"ukrainian-myths"/ (accessed August 17, 2023)

Serbyn, Roman. "Fotohrafii dyvizii 'Halychyna'." In *Ukrains'ka dyviziia "Halychyna:" Istoriia u svitlynakh vid zasnuvannia u 1943 r. do zvil'nennia z polony 1949 r*, edited by Bohdan Matsiv, 223-234. L'viv: ZUKTs, 2009.

Serhiichuk, Volodymyr, ed. *OUN-UPA v roky viiny: novi dokumenty i materialy*. Kyiv: Vydavnytstvo khudozhnoi literatury 'Dnipro', 1996.

Serhiichuk, Volodymyr, ed. *Roman Shukhevych u dokumentakh radians'kykh orhaniv derzhavnoi bezpeky (1940-1950)*. Tom I. Kyiv: PP Serhiichuk M.I., 2007.

Serhiichuk, Volodymyr, ed. *Roman Shukhevych u dokumentakh radians'kykh organiv derzhavnoi bezpeky (1940-1950)*. Tom II. Kyiv: PP Serhiichuk, M.I., 2007.

Serhiichuk, Volodymyr, ed. *Taras Bul'ba-Borovets': Dokumenty. Statti. Lysty*. Kyiv: PP Serhiichuk M. I., 2011.

Serhiichuk, Volodymyr, ed. *Ukrains'kyi zdvih: Zakerzonnia. 1939-1947. Vydannia druhe, dopovnene*. Kyiv: PP Serhiichuk, M.I, 2011.

Shamrei, Nastassia. "ABSE asudila Stalinism. Shto z Liniiai Stalina?" *Nasha Niva*, 8 July 2009, 6.

Shapoval, Yurii and Oleksandr Yabubets'. *Sluzhytel' zalezhnosty: Volodomyr Shcherbyts'kyi za obstavyn chasu*. Kyiv: Krytyka, 2021.

Shekhovtsov, Anton. "The Creeping Resurgence of the Ukrainian Radical Right? The Case of the Freedom Party." *Europe-Asia Studies* 63, no. 2 (2011): 203-228.

Shekhovtsov, Anton. "The Ukrainian Far Right and the Ukrainian Revolution." *New Europe College Black Sea Link Program Yearbook 2014-2015*. (2014): 215-237.

Shkandrij Myroslav. "Breaking Taboos: The Holodomor and the Holocaust in Ukrainian-Jewish Relations," *Polin: Studies in Polish Jewry* 26 (2014): 259-73.

Shkandrij, Myroslav. "Radio Vienna: Broadcasts by the Organization of Ukrainian Nationalists, 1938-1939." *Kyiv-Mohyla Humanities Journal* 2 (2015): 121-136.

Shkandrij, Myroslav. *Ukrainian Nationalism: Politics, Ideology, and Literature, 1929-1956*. New Haven, CT: Yale University Press, 2015.

Shtendera, Ye. and Petro P. I. Potichnyi (eds.). *Litopys Ukrains'koi Povstans'koi Armii, Tom 25, Pisni UPA: Zibrav i zredaktovav Zenovii Lavryshyn. Peredmova anhliis'koiu movoiu*. Toronto and L'viv: Vydavnytstvo Litopys UPA, 1996.

Shurkhalo, Dmytro. "Paryz'ka myrna konferentsiia 1919 roku: na mapi Ukrainy buly Krym i Kuban," *Radio Svoboda*, April 30, 2017, https://www.radiosvoboda.org/a/28457626.html (Accessed December 22, 2019).

Shukhevych, Yurii. "Komandyr bezimennykh." *Ukraina moloda: shchodenna informatsiino-politychna hazeta*, June 24, 2007. http://www.umolo da.kiev.ua/print/84/45/34292/ (accessed June 30, 2007, link no longer valid).

Siekierski, Maciej, "The Jews in Soviet-Occupied Eastern Poland at the End of 1939: Numbers and Distribution," in *Jews in Eastern Poland and the USSR, 1939-46*, eds. Norman Davies and Antony Polonsky (New York: St. Martin's Press, 1991), 110-115.

Siemaszko, Ewa. "Bilans zbrodni," *Biuletyn Instutytu Pamieci Narodowej* 7-8 (2010): 80-81.

Siemaszko, Ewa. "Stan badań nad ludobójstwem dokonanym na ludności polskiej przez Organizację Nacjonalistów Ukraińskich i Ukraińską Powstańczą Armię." In *Prawda historyczna a prawda polityczna w badaniach naukowych: Ludobójstwo na Kresach południowo-wschodniej Polski w latach 1939-1946*, edited by Bogusław Paź, 319-344. Wrocław: Wydawnictwo uniwersytetu Wrołwskiego, 2011.

Siemaszko, Władysław and Ewa Siemaszko. *Ludobójstwo dokonane przez nacjonalistów ukraińskich na ludności polskiej Wołynia 1939-1945*, 2 vols. Third edition. Warsaw: Wydawnictwo von Borowiecky, 2008.

Sindbæk Andersen, Tea and Barbara Törnquist-Plewa, eds. *Disputed Memory: Emotions and Memory Politics in Central, Eastern and South-Eastern Europe*. Berlin: De Gruyter, 2016.

Sindbæk Andersen, Tea. "Šimunić and the 'Za dom spremni' Chant." In *Disputed Memory: Emotions and Memory Politics in Central, Eastern and South-Eastern Europe*, edited by Tea Sindbæk Andersen and Barbara Törnquist-Plewa, 297-318. Berlin: De Gruyter, 2016.

Siundiukov, Ihor. "Time to Gather Stones." *Den'*, 4 February 2010. https://day.kyiv.ua/en/article/close/time-gather-stones (accessed February 4, 2010, link no longer valid).

Sjöberg, Tommie. *The Powers and the Persecuted: The Refugee Problem and the Intergovernmental Committee on Refugees*. Lund: Lund University Press, 1991.

Skypalsky, Oleksander "Russia Should Not Undermine the Chechens," *ABN Correspondence* LI, no. 3 (Autumn 2000): 1-5.

Slezkine, Yuri. "The USSR as a Communal Apartment: or How a Socialist State Promoted Ethnic Particularlism." *Slavic Review*, vol. 53, no. 2 (1994): 414-452.

Smirnov, Egor. "Glava Gosudarstvennoi arkhivoi sluzhby Ukrainy Ol'ga Ginzburg: 'Oshchushchaiu sebia khranitelem istorii'." Versii.com, 18 January 2012. https://versii.com/news/247764/ (accessed 17 August 2023)

Snyder, Timothy D. "A Fascist Hero in Democratic Kiev." *The New York Review of Books*, 24 February 2010. https://www.nybooks.com/only ne/2010/02/24/a-fascist-hero-in-democratic-kiev/ (Accessed 17 August 2023).

Snyder, Timothy. *Black Earth: The Holocaust as History and Warning*. New York: Tim Duggan Books, 2015.

Snyder, Timothy. *Sketches from a Secret War: A Polish Artist's Mission to Liberate Soviet Ukraine*. New Haven: Yale University Press, 2005.

Snyder, Timothy. "The Causes of Ukrainian-Polish Ethnic Cleansing 1943." *Past and Present*, no. 179 (2003): 197–234.

Snyder, Timothy. *The Reconstruction of Nations: Poland, Ukraine, Lithuania, Belarus, 1569–1999*. New Haven: Yale University Press, 2003.

Sodol', Petro. *Ukrains'ka povstancha armiia, 1943–1949: Dovidnyk*. New York: Proloh, 1994.

Sodol, Petro R. *UPA: They Fought Hitler and Stalin: A Brief Overview of Military Aspects from the History of the Ukrainian Insurgent Army, 1942-1949*. New York: Committee for the World Convention and Reunion of Soldiers in the Ukrainian Insurgent Army, 1987.

Sodol', Petro. 'U rokovyny zahybeli Romana Shukhevycha: Interv'iu z Mykoloiu Lebedem,' *Suchasnsist'*, no. 3 (March 1986): 98–104.

Sokhan, P. and P. Potichnyi (ed.). *Litopys' UPA. Nova seriia, tom 10: Zhyttia i borot'ba henerala 'Tarasa Chuprynky (1907–1950): Dokumenty i materialy*. Kyiv and Toronto: Litopys UPA, 2007.

Sokhan, P. and P. Potichnyj et al., eds. *Litopys UPA, Nova seriia, tom 9. Borot'ba proty povstans'koho rukhu i natsionalistychnoho pidpillia: protokoly dopytiv zaareshtovanykh radians'kymy orhanamy derzhavnoi bezpeky kerivnykiv OUN i UPA, 1944-1945*. Toronto and L'viv: Litopys UPA, 2007.

Sokol, Sam. "Babi Yar as a Symbol of Holocaust Distortion in Post-Maidan Ukraine." *Israel Journal of Foreign Affairs* 11, no. 1 (2017): 35–46.

Sokol, Sam. "The Tension between Historical Memory and Realpolitik in Israel's Foreign Policy." *Israel Journal of Foreign Affairs* 12, no. 3 (2019): 311–324.

Solonari, Vladimir. *Purifying the Nation: Population Exchange in Nazi-Allied Romania*. Baltimore, MD: The Johns Hopkins University Press, 2010.

"'Soiuz ukrains'kykh fashystiv ne buv fashysts'koiu orhanizatsiieiu' — istoryk." *Gazeta.ua*, 15 July 2013. https://gazeta.ua/articles/history/_soyuz-ukrayinskih-fashistiv-ne-buv-fashistskoyu-organizaciyeyu-istorik/507018. (accessed 17 August 2023)

Sonne, Paul, Isabelle Khurdursyan, and Sergey Morgurov. "Battle for Kyiv: Ukrainian Valor, Russian Blunders Combined to Save the Capital." *Washington Post*, 24 August 2022. https://www.washingtonpost.com/national-security/interactive/2022/kyiv-battle-ukraine-survival/. (accessed 17 August 2023)

Soroka, Mykola. *Faces of Displacement: The Writings of Volodymyr Vynnychenko*. Montreal and Kingston: McGill-Queen's University Press, 2012.

Sorokina, Yanina. "Who Is the Author of Russia's 'Blueprint for Genocide' Essay?" *The Moscow Times*, 7 April 2022. https://www.themoscowtimes.com/2022/04/06/who-is-the-author-of-russias-blueprint-for-genocide-essay-a77223 (accessed 17 August 2023)

Spodarets, Galyna and Sabine Stöhr, eds. *Alles neu macht der Majdan?: Interdiziplinäre Perspektiven auf eine Ukraine im Umbruch*. Berlin: Wissenschaftlicher Verlag Berlin, 2015.

Stalin, J.V. "The Political Tasks of the University of the Peoples of the East," in Stalin, J.V., *Works*, Volume 7, 135–154. Moscow: Foreign Languages Publishing House, 1954.

Stalin, J.V., *Works*, Volume 7, Moscow: Foreign Languages Publishing House, 1954.

Statiev, Alexander. *The Soviet Counterinsurgency in the Western Borderlands*. Cambridge and New York: Cambridge University Press, 2013.

Statiev, Alexander. "The Strategy of the Organization of Ukrainian Nationalists in its Quest for a Sovereign State, 1939-1950." *Journal of Strategic Studies* 43, no. 3 (2020): 443–471.

Stephens, Bret. "Why We Admire Zelensky." *New York Times*, 19 April 2022. https://www.nytimes.com/2022/04/19/opinion/why-we-admire-zelensky.html (accessed 17 August 2023).

Stets'ko, Yaroslav. "Natsional'ne i international'ne zhydivstvo." In Yaroslav Stets'ko, *Tvory: Ukrains'ka vyzvol'na kontseptsiia, chastyna druha*, edited by Volodymyr Kosyk, 350–354. Munich: Vydannia Orhanizatsii ukrains'kykh natsionalistiv, 1991.

Stets'ko, Yaroslav. *Ukrains'ka vyzvol'na kontseptsiia: Tvory, chastyna* 1, edited by Volodymyr Kosyk. Munich: Orhanizatsiia ukrains'kykh natsionalistiv, 1987.

Stets'ko, Yaroslav. *Tvory: Ukrains'ka vyzvol'na kontseptsiia, Tvory, chastyna druha*, edited by Volodymyr Kosyk. Munich: Vydannia Orhanizatsii ukrains'kykh natsionalistiv, 1991.

Struk, Danylo Husar, (ed.). *Encyclopedia of Ukraine*. Volume 3. Toronto: University of Toronto Press, 1993.

Struve, Kai. *Bauern und Nation in Galizien: Über Zuhörigkeit und soziale Emanzipation im 19. Jahrhundert*, Göttingen: Vandenhoeck & Ruprecht, 2005.

Struve, Kai. *Deutsche Herrschaft, ukrainischer Nationalismus, antijüdische Gewalt: Der Sommer 1941 in der Westukraine*. Berlin and Boston: De Gruyter Oldenbourg, 2015.

Strömberg, Maggie and Torbjörn Nilsson. "Så gick det till när Sverige svängde om Nato." *Svenska Dagbladet*, 2 July 2022. https://www.sv d.se/a/Qy1gXx/sa-gick-det-till-nar-magdalena-andersson-kovande -om-nato (accessed 17 August 2023).

Ståhlberg, Per and Göran Bolin, "Having a Soul or Choosing a Face? Nation Branding, Identity and Cosmopolitan Imagination." *Social Identities* 22, no. 2 (2016): 274–290.

Stsibors'kyi, Mykola. "Narys proektu osnovnykh zakoniv (konstytutsii) Ukrains'koi Derzhavy." In *Dokumenty i materialy z istorii Orhanizatsii Ukrains'kykh Natsionalistiv, Tom 7, Dokumenty komisii derzhavnoho planuvannia OUN (KDP OUN)*, edited by O. Kucheruk and Yu. Cherchenko, 8–23.

Subtelny, Orest. *Ukraine: A History*. Fourth edition. Toronto: University of Toronto Press, 2009.

Suchoples, Jarosław, Stephanie James, and Barbara Törnquist-Plewa, eds. *World War II Re-explored: Some New Millenium Studies in the History of the Global Conflict*. Brussels: Peter Lang, 2019.

Sukhovers'kyi, Mykola. *Moi spohady*. Kyiv: Vydavnytstsvo Smoloskyp, 1997.

Sundén, Jesper. "Rysk lokalpolitiker till SvD: Slutet närmar sig för Putin." *Svenska Dagbladet*, 12 September 2022, 14.

Suny, Ronald Grigor. *The Revenge of the Past: Nationalism, Revolution and the Collapse of the Soviet Union*. Stanford, CA: Stanford University Press, 1993.

Suny, Ronald Grigor and Terry Martin, "Introduction." In idem., eds., *A State of Nations: Empire and Nation-Making in the Age of Lenin and Stalin*, 3–20. Oxford: Oxford University Press, 2001.

Suny, Ronald Grigor and Terry Martin, eds. *A State of Nations: Empire and Nation-Making in the Age of Lenin and Stalin*, Oxford: Oxford University Press, 2001.

Swyripa, Frances. *Storied Landscapes: Ethno-Religious Identity and the Canadian Prairies*. Winnipeg: University of Manitoba Press, 2010.

Szacki, Wojciech and Marcin Wojciechowski. "Sondaż 3: Źli Niemcy, źli Ukraińcy." *Gazeta Wyborcza*, 24 August 2009. http://wyborcza.pl/1,75398,6956564,Sondaz_3__Zli_Niemcy__zli_Ukraincy.html (accessed August 24, 2009, link no longer valid).

Szporluk, Roman. "West Ukraine and West Belorussia." *Soviet Studies*, vol. 31, no. 1 (1979): 76–98.

Szycht, Aleksander. "Co dalej z polsko-ukraińskim Dialogiem historycznym?" *Polska Zbrojna*, 22 November 2017. https://www.polska-zbrojna.pl/Mobile/ArticleShow/24148 (accessed 17 August 2023).

Tägil, Sven, ed. *Europa – historiens återkomst*. Hedemora: Gidlunds bokförlag, 1993.

Tatu, Michael. *Power in the Kremlin: From Khrushchev to Kosygin*. New York: The Viking Press, 1974.

Tauger, Mark. "Soviet Peasants and Collectivization, 1930–1939: Resistance and Adaptation." *The Journal of Peasant Studies*, vol. 31, nos. 3-4 (2004): 427–456.

Tec, Nechama. *Defiance*. Oxford: Oxford University Press, 2009.

Ther, Philipp. *Die neue Ordnung auf dem alten Kontinent: Eine Geschichte des neoliberalen Europas*. Berlin: Suhrkamp Verlag, 2014.

Thurfjell, Karin. "Ninistö: Kärnvapen kommer inte på fråga." *Svenska Dagbladet*, 13 May 2022. https://www.svd.se/a/y4B1g2/niinisto-jag-kommer-att-ringa-putin-om-nato (accessed 17 August 2023).

Tiahnybok, Oleh. "Evroparlament ne vkazuvatyme Ukraini, koho vyznavaty Heroiamy." *Ukrains'ka Pravda Blohy*, 26 February 2010. http://blogs.pravda.com.ua/authors/tiahnybok/4b88066cc9c5f/ (accessed 17 August 2023).

Ticku, Nitin J. "Russia Sends Bone-Chilling Message to Sweden & Finland; Threatens 'Military Implications' If They Go The Ukraine Way." *The Eurasian Times*, 25 February 2022. https://Eurasiantimes.com/russia-sends-bone-chilling-message-to-sweden-threatens-with-military-implications-if-they-go-the-ukraine-way/ (accessed 17 August 2023).

Tillett, Lowell. *The Great Friendship: Soviet Historians on the Non-Russian Nationalities*. Chapel Hill: University of North Carolina Press, 1969.

Tokić, Mate Nikola. *Croatian Radical Separatism and Diaspora Terrorism During the Cold War*. West Lafayette: Purdue University Press, 2020.

Torzecki, Ryszard. *Polacy i Ukraińcy: Sprawa ukraińska w czasie II wojny światowej na terenie II Rzeczpospolitej*. Warsaw: PWN, 1993.

Trehubova, Iaroslava. "Cherez 82 roky doslidnyky nazvaly kilkist' zhertv Holodomoru." *Radio Svoboda*, 26 November 2015. http://www.rad iosvoboda.mobi/a/27390191.html (accessed 17 August 2023).

Tscherepnin, L. W. and B. A. Rybakow. "Einleitung." In *Geschichte der UdSSR, Band I: Von den ältesten Zeiten bis zum Jahre 1861. Urgesellschaft, Sklavenhalterordnung und Feudalismus*. Erster Halbband. Translated by Arno Specht. Edited by Netschkina *et al.*, 1–7. Berlin: VEB Deutscher Verlag der Wissenschaften, 1961.

Tucker, Robert C. *Political Culture and Leadership in Soviet Russia: From Lenin to Gorbachev*. New York: W.W. Norton, 1987.

Turda, Marius and Paul J. Weindling. *Blood and Homeland: Eugenics and Racial Nationalism in Central and Southeast Europe, 1900–1940*. Budapest: CEU Press, 2007.

Turda, Marius, ed. *The History of East-Central European Eugenics, 1900–1945: Sources and Commentaries*. Houndsmills Basingstone: Palgrave Macmillan, 2015.

Turda, Marius. *Modernism and Eugenics*. New York: Palgrave MacMillan, 2010.

Tydén, Mattias. *Från politik till praktik: de svenska steriliseringslagarna 1935–1975. Rapport till 1997 års steriliseringsutredning*. Stockholm: Socialdepartementet, 2000.

Törnquist-Plewa, Barbara. "Ukraina — en territoriell och politik eller en språklig och etnisk gemenskap?" *Historisk Tidsskrift*, no. 4 (1996): 494–547.

Ueberschär, Gerd R. "Hitlers Entschluß zum 'Lebensraum'-Krieg im Osten: Programmatisches Ziel oder militärstrategisches Kalkül?" In *Der deutsche Überfall auf die Sowjetunion: "Unternehmen Barbarossa" 1941*, edited by Gerd R. Ueberschär and Wolfram Wette, 13–43. Frankfurt am Main: Fischer Verlag, 1991.

Ueberschär, Gerd R. and Wolfram Wette, eds. *Der deutsche Überfall auf die Sowjetunion: "Unternehmen Barbarossa" 1941*, Frankfurt am Main: Fischer Verlag, 1991.

Ugelvik Larsen, Stein, Bernt Hagtvet, and Jan Petter Myklebust, eds. *Who Were the Fascists?: Social Roots of European Fascism*. Bergen: Universitetsforlaget, 1980.

Ukhach, V. Z., I. I. Martsias', and O. V. Koval's'kyi, "Akt proholoshennia vidnovlennia Ukrains'koi derzhavy 30 chervnia 1941 roku: Istoriko-pravovyi analiz (Suchasna vitchyzna istoriohrafiia)," *Yurydychnyi naukovyi elektronnyi zhurnal* 6 (2015): 34–37.

Umland, Andreas. "Challenges and Promises of Comparative Research into Post-Soviet Fascism: Methodological and Conceptual Issues in the Study of the Contemporary East European Extreme Right." *Communist and Post-Communist Studies* (2015): 169–181.

Umland, Andreas. "Concepts of Fascism in Contemporary Russia and the West." *Political Studies Review* 3 (2005): 34–49.

Umland, Andreas. "Der ukrainische Nationalismus zwischen Stereotyp und Wirklichkeit: Zu einigen Komplikationen bei der Interpretation von befreiungs- vs. ultranationalistischen Tendenzen in der modernen Ukraine." *Ukraine-Analysen* 107 (2012): 7–10.

Umland, Andreas. "Die andere Anomalie der Ukraine: ein Parlament ohne rechtradikale Fraktionen." *Ukraine-Analysen* 41 (2008): 6–11. http://www.laender-analysen.de/ukraine/pdf/UkraineAnalysen41.pdf (accessed 17 August 2023).

Umland, Andreas. "Is Putin's Russia Really Fascist? A Response to Alexander Motyl." Katholische Universität Eichstätt-Ingolstadt, 17 January 2008. https://www.ku.de/news/is-putins-russia-really-fascist-a-response-to-alexander-motyl (accessed 17 August 2023).

Umland, Andreas. "The Ukrainian Government's Memory Institute against the West." *New Eastern Europe*, 7 March 2017. http://neweasterneurope.eu/articles-and-commentary/2284-the-ukrainian-government-s-memory-institute-against-the-west (accessed 17 August 2023).

Umland, Andreas et al., "Schwere Waffen jetzt! Replik auf 'Waffenstillstand jetzt'," *Focus.de*, 19 July 2022, https://www.focus.de/politik/ausland/ukraine-krise/96-osteuropa-experten-weltweit-fordern-schwere-waffen-jetzt_id_119428660.html

Umland, Andreas and Anton Shekhovtsov, "Ultraright Party Politics in Post-Soviet Ukraine and the Puzzle of the Electoral Marginalism of Ukrainian Ultranationalists in 1994–2009," *Russian Politics and Law* 51, no.5 (2013): 33–38.

Umland, Andreas and Yuliya Yurchuk, "Introduction: Diverging Evaluations of the OUN(b)'s Ideology and Activities during World War II," *Journal of Soviet and Post-Soviet Politics and Society*, Vol. 7, No. 2 (2021): 137-145.

Ursprung, Daniel. "Faschismus in Ostmittel- und Südosteuropa: Theorien, Ansätze, Fragestellungen." In *Der Einfluss von Faschismus und Nationalismus auf Minderheiten in Ostmittel- und Südosteuropa*, edited by Marianna Hausleitner and Harald Roth, 9–52. Munich: IKGS-Verlag, 2006.

Usach, Andriy. "The 'Eastern Action' of the OUN(b) and the Anti-Jewish Violence in the Summer of 1941: The Cases of Smotrych and Kupryn," *Euxeinos*, vol. 9, no. 27 (2019): 63-84.

V"iatrovych, Volodymyr. *Druha pol's'ko-ukrains'ka viina, 1942-1947.* Kyiv: Vydavnychyi Dim 'Kyevo-Mohylians'ka Akademiia, 2011.

V"iatrovych, Volodymyr. "Heroichnyi reid soten' UPA," *Natsiia i derzhava*, no. 4 (1998).

V"iatrovych, Volodymyr. "Iak Holodomor zrobyv nas natsieiu." Holodomor33.org.ua http://holodomor33.org.ua/volodymyr-vyatrovych-yak-holodomor-zrobyv-nas-natsijeyu/ (accessed 17 August 2023).

V"iatrovych, Volodymyr. "Iak tvorylasia lehenda pro Nachtigall." *Dzerkalo Tyzhnia*, no. 6 (685), February 16-22, 2008. http://www.dt.ua/3000/3150/62036/ (accessed March 2, 2008, link no longer valid).

V"iatrovych, Volodymyr, ed. *Isotriia z hryfom "Sekretno": Taemnytsi ukrains'koho mynuloho z arkiviv KGB.* L'viv: Tsentr doslidzhen' vyzvol'noho rukhu, 2011.

V"iatrovych, Volodymyr. "Kukhnia antysemityzmu vid KGB," *Isotriia z hryfom "Sekretno": Taemnytsi ukrains'koho mynuloho z arkiviv KGB*, L'viv: Tsentr doslidzhen' vyzvol'noho rukhu, 2011, 239-255.

V"iatrovych, Volodymyr. "Perebuvannia Ukrainy u skladi SRSR—tse okupatsiia,—V'iatrovych." *Tsenzor.net*, 7 January 2018. https://censor.net/ua/news/3043120/perebuvannya_ukrayiny_u_skladi_srsr_tse_okupatsiya_vyatrovych (accessed 17 August 2023).

V"iatrovych, Volodymyr. "Roman Shukhevych: soldat." *Ukraïns'ka Pravda*, May 2, 2008. http://www.pravda.com.ua/news/2008/4/25/75222.htm (accessed May 4, 2008, link no longer valid)

V"iatrovych, Volodymyr. *Stavlennia OUN do evreiv: Formuvannia pozytsii na tli katastrofy.* L'viv: Vydavnytstvo "Ms," 2006.

V"iatrovych, Volodymyr. "Taktyka povstan's'kykh reidiv," *Vyzvol'nyi shliakh*, 6 (1999).

Viatrovich, Vladimir [V"iatrovych, Volodymyr]. "Vtoraia pol'sko-ukrainskaia voina i diskussii vokrug nee." *Ab Imperio*, no. 2 (2012): 422-433.

V"iatrovych, Volodymyr Roman Hrytsiv, Ihor Derevianyi, Ruslan Zabilyi, Andrii Sova, Petro Sodol', *Ukrains'ka Povstans'ka Armiia: Istoriia neskorennykh.* L'viv: Center for the Study of the Liberation Movement, 2007.

Vallin, Jacques, France Meslé, Serguei Adamets, and Serhii Pyrozhkov. "A New Estimate of Ukrainian Population Losses during the Crises of the 1930s and 1940s." *Population Studies* 56, no. 3 (2002): 249-264.

van den Bergh, Godfried van Benthem. "Herder and the Idea of a Nation," *Human Figurations: Long-term perspectives on the human condition*, Vol. 7, issue 1 (May 2018), https://quod.lib.umich.edu/h/hu mfig/11217607.0007.103?view=text;rgn=main (accessed 17 August 2023).

Vedeneev, D.V. and O.E. Lysenko. "Orhanizatsiia ukrains'kykh natsionalistiv i zarubizhni spetssluzhby (1920–1950-ti rr.)." *Ukrains'kyi istrorichnyi zhurnal* 3 (2009): 132–146.

Veidlinger, Jeffrey. *In the Midst of Civilized Europe: The Pogroms of 1918-1921 and the Onset of the Holocaust*. New York: Metropolitan Books, 2021.

Velikanova, Olga. *Popular Perceptions of Soviet Politics in the 1920s: Disenchantment of the Dreamers*. London: Palgrave Macmillan, 2013.

Velychenko, Stephen. "Ukrainians, Jews, and Double Standards." *The Ukraine List*, no. 442 (15 March 2010)

Vil'chyns'kyi, Oleksandr. "Mykola Ribachuk: Iashchirky, iakym shkoda pozbutys' khvosta, pozbuvaiut'sia holovy—Interv'iu." *Zaxid.net*, 9 August 2010. http://zaxid.net/home/showSingleNews.do?mikola_ ryabchuk_yashhirki_yakim_shkhoda_pozbutis_hvosta_pozbuvayut sya_golovi&objectId=1110717 (accessed 17 August 2023).

Viola, Lynne. *Contending with Stalinism*. Ithaca: Cornell University Press, 2002.

Viola, Lynne. *Stalinist Perpetrators on Trial: Scenes From the Great Terror in Soviet Ukraine*. Oxford: Oxford University Press, 2017.

von Hagen, Mark. *War in a European Borderland: Occupations and Occupation Plans in Galicia and Ukraine 1914-1918*. Seattle: University of Washington Press, 2007.

von Hall, Gunilla. "Ryska klassiker förbjuds i Ukraina: 'Det är tragiskt'." *Svenska Dagbladet*, 20 August 2022.

von Lingen, Kerstin. *Allen Dulles, the OSS, and Nazi War Criminals: The Dynamics of Selective Prosecution*. New York: Cambridge University Press, 2013.

Vushko, Iryna. "Historians at War: History, Politics and Memory in Ukraine." *Contemporary European History* 27, no. 1 (2018): 112–24.

Wachs, Philipp-Christian. *Der Fall Theodor Oberländer (1909–1998): Ein Lehrstück deutscher Geschichte*. Frankfurt: Campus-Verlag, 2000.

Wallberg, Peter and Maria Davidsson. "Så gick det till när Sverige sade ja till Nato." *Svenska Dagbladet*, 16 May 2022. https://www.svd.se/a/ V97Pd4/sa-gick-det-till-nar-sverige-sa-ja-till-nato (accessed 17 August 2023).

Ward, James Mace. *Priest, Politician, Collaborator: Jozef Tiso and the Making of Fascist Slovakia*. Ithaca: Cornell University Press, 2013.

Waskowycz, Hryhorij. *Roman Šuchevyč – Kommandeur des Befreiungskrieges: Aus Anlass des 30. Todestages*. München: Ukrainische Freie Universität, 1981.

Way, Lucan. *Pluralism by Default: Weak Autocrats and the Rise of Competitive Politics*. Baltimore, MD: Johns Hopkins University Press, 2015.

Weeks, Theodore R. "The 'End' of the Uniate Church in Russia: The 'Vozsoedinenie' of 1875." *Jahrbücher für Geschichte Osteuropas*, 44, no. 1 (1996): 28–40.

Weiner, Amir. *Making Sense of War: The Second World War and the Fate of the Bolshevik Revolution*. Princeton: Princeton University Press, 2001.

Weiss, Ahron. "Jewish-Ukrainian Relations in Western Ukraine During the Holocaust." In *Ukrainian-Jewish Relations in Historical Perspective*, edited by Peter J. Potichnyj and Howard Aster, 409–420. Edmonton: CIUS Press, 1990.

Weiss-Wendt, Anton. *A Rhetorical Crime: Genocide in the Geopolitical Discourse of the Cold War*. New Brunswick, NJ: Rutgers University Press, 2018.

Weiss-Wendt, Anton. "Hostage of Politics: Raphael Lemkin on 'Soviet Genocide.'" *Journal of Genocide Research* 7, no. 4 (2005): 551–559.

Weiss-Wendt, Anton, *Putin's Russia and the Falsification of History: Reasserting Control of the Past*. London: Bloomsbury Academic Press, 2020.

Weiss-Wendt, Anton. *The Soviet Union and the Gutting of the UN Genocide Convention*. Madison, WI: The University of Wisconsin Press, 2017.

Weiss-Wendt, Anton and Rory Yeomans, eds. *Racial Science in Hitler's New Europe 1938–1945*. Lincoln and London: University of Nebraska Press, 2013.

Weiss-Wendt, Anton and Nanci Adler (eds.), *The Future of the Soviet Past: The Politics of History in Putin's Russia* Bloomington, IN: Indiana University Press, 2021.

Wilson, Andrew. *The Ukrainians: Unexpected Nation*. Fourth edition. New Haven: Yale University Press, 2015.

Wilson, Andrew. *Ukraine Crisis: What it Means for the West*. New Haven: Yale University Press, 2014.

Wilson, Andrew. *Ukraine's Orange Revolution*. New Haven: Yale University Press, 2005.

Wilson, Andrew. "Ukrainian Nationalism: A Minority Faith." *Slavonic and East European Review*, 73, no. 2 (April 1995): 282–288.

Wilson, Andrew. *Ukrainian Nationalism in the 1990s: A Minority Faith.* Cambridge: Cambridge University Press, 1997.

Wilson, Andrew. "Ukrainian Politics since Independence." In *Ukraine and Russia: People, Politics, Propaganda and Perspectives,* edited by Agnieszka Pikulicka-Wilczewski and Richard Sakwa, 101–108. Bristol: E-International Relations Publishing, 2015.

Wingfield, Nancy M., "Czechoslavakia's Germans," in Roland Clark and Tim Grady (eds.), *European Fascist Movements: A Sourcebook.* London and New York: Routledge, 2023, 327-347.

Wojciechowski, Marcin. "Gdy Lach z Kozakiem się kłócą, Moskal zaciera ręce." *Gazeta Wyborcza,* 8–9 August 2009, 2.

Wojnar, Marek. *Imperium ukraińskie: Źrodla idei i jej miejsce w myśli politycznej ukraińskiego pierwszej połowy XX wieku.* Warsaw: Arcana, 2023.

Wojnar, Marek. "Wizije przemocy." *Nowa Europa Wschodnia.* July 6, 2016, online edition. http://new.org.pl/2643,post.html (accessed July 7, 2016, link no longer valid).

Wojnowski, Zbigniew. *The Near Abroad: Socialist Eastern Europe and Soviet Patriotism in Ukraine, 1956–1985.* Toronto: University of Toronto Press, 2017.

Wolff, Larry. *The Idea of Galicia: History and Fantasy in Habsburg Political Culture.* Stanford: Stanford University Press, 2010.

Wolowyna, Oleh. "The Famine-Genocide of 1932–1933: Estimation of Losses and Demographic Impact." In *The Holodomor Reader: a Sourcebook on the Famine of 1932–1933 in Ukraine,* edited by Bohdan Klid and Alexander Motyl, 59–64. Edmonton: Canadian Institute of Ukrainian Studies, 2012.

Wytwycky, Bohdan. "Anti-Semitism." In *Encyclopedia of Ukraine: Vol. I,* edited by Volodymyr Kubijovyč, 81–83. Toronto: CIUS Press, 1984.

Yakovenko, Kateryna. "Meet the Man in Charge of Ukraine's National Memory," *Open Democracy,* 11 June 2020. https://www.opendemocracy.net/en/odr/anton-drobovich-natsionalnaya-pamyat-en/ (accessed 17 August 2023).

Yakubova, Larysa. "Ivan Il'in: Patriarkh rosiis'koho fashyzmu." *Ukrains'kyi Tyzhden,* 19 July 2022. https://tyzhden.ua/History/2553 63 (accessed 17 August 2023).

Yekelchyk, Serhy. "A Long Goodbye: The Legacy of Soviet Marxism in Post-Communist Ukrainian Historiography." *Ab Imperio* 4 (2012): 401–416.

Yekelchyk Serhy. *Stalin's Empire of Memory: Russian-Ukrainian Relations in the Soviet Historical Imagination.* Toronto: University of Toronto Press, 2014.

Yekelchyk, Serhy. *Ukraine: Birth of a Modern Nation.* Oxford: Oxford University Press, 2007.

Yendyk, Rostislav. *Adol'f Hitler.* L'viv: Knyhozbirnia Vistnyka, 1934.

Yendyk, Rostislav. *Vstup do rasovoi budovoi Ukrainy: osnov. pytania z zah. i susp. antropolohii ta evheniky Ukrainy. (=Biblioteka Ukrainonazstva, vol. 1)* Munich: Naukove Tovarystvo im. Shevchenka, 1949.

Yeomans, Rory. "Eradicating 'Undesired Elements': National Regeneration and the Ustasha Regime's Program to Purify the Nation, 1941-1945," in *Racial Science in Hitler's New Europe, 1938-1945,* eds. Anton Weiss-Wendt and Rory Yeomans. Lincoln: University of Nebraska Press, 2013, 200-236.

Yeomans, Rory. "Fighting the White Plague: Demography and Abortion in the Independent State of Croatia," in Christian Promitzer, Sevasti Trubeta, and Marius Turda, eds., *Health, Hygiene and Eugenics in Southeastern Europe to 1945,* 385-426. Budapest: CEU Press, 2011.

Yeomans, Rory. "'If Our Race Did Not Exist, It Would Have to be Created': Racial Science in Hungary, 1940-1944," in Anton Weiss-Wendt and Rory Yeomans, eds. *Racial Science in Hitler's New Europe 1938-1945.* Lincoln and London: University of Nebraska Press, 2013.

Yeomans, Rory. *Visions of Annihilation: The Ustasha Regime and the Cultural Politics of Fascism 1941-1945.* Pittsburgh: University of Pittsburgh Press, 2013.

Yones, Eliyahu. *Die Straße nach Lemberg: Zwangsarbeit und Widerstand in Ostgalizien 1941-1944.* Frankfurt am Main: Fischer Taschenbuch Verlag, 1999.

Yurchuk, Yuliya. "Global Symbols Local Meanings: The 'Day of Victory' after Euromaidan." In *Transnational Ukraine? Networks and Ties that Influence contemporary Ukraine,* edited by Timm Beichelt and Susann Worschech, 89-110. Stuttgart: ibidem-Verlag, 2017.

Yurchuk, Yuliya. "Historians as Activists: History Writing in Times of War: The Case of Ukraine in 2014-2018," *Nationalities Papers,* vol. 49, no. 4 (2021): 691-709.

Yurchuk, Yuliia. "Proshloe pod pritselom amnezii: pamiat' ob OUN i UPA v Volynskom regione na primere pamiatnika Klimu Savuru," *Forum noveishei vostochnoevropeiskoi istorii i kul'tury 14, no. 2 (2016): 87-101.*

Yurchuk, Yuliya. *Reordering of Meaningful Worlds: Memory of the Organization of Ukrainian Nationalists and the Ukrainian Insurgent Army in Post-Soviet Ukraine* (=Stockholm Studies in History 103). Stockholm: Stockholm University, 2014.

Yushchenko, Viktor. "President speaks to UPA veterans." *Press Office of President Victor Yushchenko*, October 14, 2007. www.president.gov.ua/done_img/b/7/7836.jpg (accessed October 14, 2007, link no longer valid).

Zabuzhko, Oksana. "No guilty people in the world?: Reading Russian literature after the Bucha massacre." *Times Literary Supplement*, 22 April 2022. https://www.the-tls.co.uk/articles/russian-literature-bucha-massacre-essay-oksana-zabuzhko/.

Zaitsev, Oleksandr. "De-Mythologizing Bandera: Towards a Scholarly History of the Ukrainian Nationalist Movement," *Journal of Soviet and Post-Soviet Politics and Society* 1, no. 2 (2015): 411–20.

Zaitsev, Oleksandr. "Fascism or Ustashism? Ukrainian Integral Nationalism of the 1920s–1930s in Comparative Perspective." *Communist and Post-Communist Studies* 48, nos. 2–3 (2015): 183–193.

Zaitsev, Oleksandr. *Natsionalist u dobi fashyzmu: L'vivs'kyi period Dmytra Dontsova 1922–1939 roky*. Kyiv: Krytyka, 2019.

Zaitsev, Oleksandr. *Ukrains'kyi intehral'nyi natsionalizm (1920–1930-ti roky): Narysy intelektual'noi istorii*. Kyiv: Krytyka, 2013.

Zaitsev, Oleksandr. "Voenna doktryna Mykhaila Kolodzins'koho." *Ukraina Moderna* 20 (2013): 245–256.

Zamoyski, Adam. *Warszawa 1920: Lenins misslyckade erövring av Europa*. Translated by Andreas Wadensjö. Stockholm: Dialogos förlag, 2008.

Zawada, Zenon. "UWC president set to sue Communists over defamation of Roman Shukhevych," *The Ukrainian Weekly*, August 26, 2007.

Zayarnyuk, Andriy, *Framing the Ukrainian Peasantry in Habsburg Galicia, 1846-1914*. Edmonton: Canadian Institute of Ukrainian Studies Press, 2013.

Zhigunova, Lidia S. and Raymond C. Taras. "Under the Holy Tree: Circassian activism, indigenous cosmologies and decolonizing practices." In *Language and Society in the Caucasus: Understanding the Past, Navigating the Present*, edited by Christofer Berglund, Katrine Gotfredsen, Jean Hudson and Bo Petersson, 190–213. Lund: Universus Academic Press, 2021.

Zięba Andrzej [Zemba, Andzhei]. "Mifologizirovannaia 'voina'," *Ab Imperio* 2 (2012): 403–421.

Zięba, Andrzej A., ed. *OUN, UPA i zagłada żydów*. Krakow: Księgarnia akademicka, 2016.

Zubov, Andrei. *Istoriia Rossii: XX vek, 1894–1939*. Moscow: Astrel, 2009.

Index

People

Acton, Lord John Emerich Edward Dalberg 27
Adorno, Theodore 377
Alexander I 302
Amelina, Victoria 120
Andersson, Magdalena 349
Andrukhovych, Yurii 120-122
Antonescu, Ion 234
Antoniuk, Dmytro 122
Antonov, Oleg 116
Applebaum, Anne 17
Arafat, Yasser 328
Armstrong, John A. 208-209, 235, 240, 323-324
Arndt, Ernst Moritz 32
Artuković, Andrija 143
Ash, Timothy Garton 206
Asman, Moshe Reuven 242
Babiracki, Patryk 74
Bachyns'kyi, Yuliian 36, 42
Bach-Zelewski, Erich von dem 180
Balan, Jaroslaw 233
Balfour, Arthur 78
Bandera, Andrii 220
Bandera, Stefko (Stephen) 230, 237
Bandera, Stepan 19-20, 29, 59, 67, 89-90, 106, 109, 116, 124-125, 127, 135-140, 153, 155, 158-159, 161, 165, 167, 171-173, 187, 189, 204-205, 207, 210, 212, 215-221, 223, 227-234, 237-253, 272-273, 278-281, 283-285, 293, 297, 300-301, 304, 310, 313, 317, 321, 323, 325, 327-328, 336-337, 380-384
Barbie, Klaus 133-134, 161
Bartou, Louis 302
Bauer, Otto 34-35
Bayly, Christopher 25
Begin, Menachem 328
Bellezza, Simone 70
Ben Bella, Ahmed 328
Ben Gurion, David 240
Beorn, Waitman 179
Berdychowska, Bogumiła 92
Bergman, David 371
Berkhoff, Karel 316
Bhabha, Homi 25
Biden, Joe 346
Bisanz, Alfred 175, 178, 181
Blumenthal, Ralph 155
Boll, Bernd 216
Bos, Chandra 203
Brandon, Ray 171, 214
Brezhnev, Leonid 69-70, 230
Brown, Kate 74
Bruder, Franziska 210-211
Bul'ba Borovets', Taras 312
Bulgakov, Mikhail 379
Bunak, Viktor V. 261, 263, 267
Burds, Jeffrey 145, 150, 162, 187, 218
Bush, George H. W. 140, 161
Bykau, Vasil 200
Canovan, Margaret 27
Carynnyk, Marco 216, 316
Celmiņš, Gustavs 211

Chalev, Avner 195
Chernenko, Konstantin 69
Chervak, Bohdan 115
Chubar', Vlas 105, 106
Churchill, Winston 198-199, 351
Codreanu, Corneliu Zelea 211
Conason, Joe 145-149, 155-156, 158-160, 163
Connor, Walker 53
D'Annunzio, Gabriele 325
Danyk, Boris 246
de Gaulle, Charles 198, 328
Demjanjuk, John 142, 149
Denikin, Anton 46, 366
Derikh 183
Dietsch, Johan 88, 129, 191
Dimant, Frank 242
Dmowski, Roman 47
Dobzhansky, Theodosius 262-264, 286-287
Dontsov, Dmytro 30, 120, 213, 244, 265-270, 272-273, 277, 285, 291-295, 325
Doroshenko, Dmytro 37, 42
Dovzhenko, Oleksandr 56
Dreyer, Nicolas 353, 354
Drobovych, Anton 337-338
Duda, Andrzej 380
Dudaev, Dzhokhdar 339
Dudko, Oksana 342
Dulić, Tomislav 299
Ďurčanský, Ferdinand 313-314
Dworczyk Michał 377
Eichmann, Adolf 293
Eisenhower, Dwight D. 292
Engman, Max 361
Erlacher, Trevor 266
Essen, Hugo von 371
Fairey, Jack 24
Fallersleben von, Hoffman Heinrich August 33

Farrell, Brian P. 24
Fedorenko, Fedor 143, 149
Fichte, Johann Gottlieb 32
Filipchenko, Yurii 261-263
Fischer, Fritz 45
Foxman, Abraham H. 241
Franco, Francisco 20, 136, 139, 171, 219, 284, 291, 294, 311, 328
Frank, Hans 178, 279
Frei, Norbert 376
Friedrich Karl of Hesse 39
Fujiwara, Aya 224
Gerner, Kristian 379
Giedroyc, Jerzy 91-92
Ginzburg, Olha 113
Gladstone, William 78
Gobineau, Arthur de 289
Goebbels, Joseph 213, 266, 372
Golczewski, Frank 185, 265
Gorbachev, Mikhail 53, 71-72, 81, 374
Gorinov, Aleksei 370
Gramsci, Antonio 86
Grass, Günther 206
Griffin, Roger 209, 298
Grod, Paul 231, 233
Günther, Hans F. K. 213, 266-268, 289
Haidamacha, Andrii 101, 228
Hallin, Lena 349
Hayes, Carlton 209
Hazony, Yoram 27-28
Henlein, Konrad 325
Herder, Johan Gottfried 25-26, 28, 30
Herzner, Hans-Albrecht 174
Heydrich, Reinhard 64
Himka, John-Paul 193, 218, 225, 233, 237-238, 270, 298, 367
Himmler, Heinrich 63, 180

Hirsch, Francine 54, 263
Hitler, Adolf 28, 63, 136, 156, 170-171, 180, 189, 213, 216-217, 219, 223, 225, 247, 259, 266, 270, 284, 298, 311, 328, 342, 347, 354-357, 370
Hlinka, Andrej 211
Holovakha, Yehen 97
Holtzman, Elizabeth 162
Holub, Oleksandr 170
Hrabovs'kyi, Serhii 202-203
Hrushevs'kyi, Mykhailo 31-32, 56
Hryhor"ev Nykyfor 47
Hryn'okh, Ivan 138, 140, 175
Hrytsak, Yaroslav 130, 249
Hunchak, Taras 152-153, 155, 158, 217, 225, 300, 316-317
Il'in, Ivan 365-366
Ilchuk, Yuliya 77
Ivan III 362
Jaspers, Karl 375-377
Kaczyński, Jarosław 242
Kaczyński, Lech 244
Kaganovich, Lazar 104, 203
Kai-Shek, Chang 20, 139, 291
Kal'ba, Myroslav 182, 187, 190
Kaltenbrunner, Matthias 84
Kamusella, Tomasz 378
Kantor, Moshe 195
Karatnycky, Adrian 334-335
Karlsson, Klas-Göran 73, 87, 101
Kas'ianov, Heorhyi 98
Katchanovski, Ivan 94
Kedourie, Elie 26, 29
Kharkiv "Khmara", Viktor 174, 176
Khataevich, Mendel' 105-106
Khmel'nyts'kyi, Bohdan 90
Khvylovyi, Mykola 56, 61
Kiryukhin, Denys 361

Kliachkivs'kyi, Dmytro ("Klym Savur) 184, 244, 312
Klychko, Vitalii 112
Koch, Erich 66
Kohut, Andrii 113
Kohut, Zenon 234-235
Kokodniak, Iziaslav 188
Koldzins'kyi, Mykhailo 365
Kolesnychenko, Vadym 110-111
Kolodzins'kyi, Mykhailo 30, 76, 275-278, 281, 295, 303, 305-306, 309-310, 324
Konovalets', Yevhen 58, 90, 171, 213, 271, 275, 276
Kosakivs'kyi, Mykola 145-148
Kosior, Stanislav 105-106
Kostomarov, Mykola 31
Kosyk, Volodymyr 225, 317
Kozhevnikiv, Petro 326
Krasovskii, Anton 371-372
Kravchenko, Volodymyr 376
Kravchuk, Leonid 72, 78, 81-83, 97-98, 122, 384
Krüger, Hans 146, 156-157
Krutsyk, Roman 197-198
Kubiiovych, Volodymyr 64, 279, 288, 299
Kuchma, Leonid 95, 98, 102, 109
Kul'chyts'kyi, Stanislav 97
Kupchinsky, Roman 144, 149-152, 155, 158
Kuropas, Myron 240
Kurylo, Taras 276, 324-325
Kuzio, Taras 23, 55, 73, 107, 315, 328, 355
Kvit, Serhii 113
Langewische, Dieter 50, 85, 384
Lapid, Joseph "Tommy" 195-197
Lapidus, Izrail 202-203
LaRouche, Lyndon 168
Laval, Pierre 234

Lavrov, Sergei 343, 369-370
Lawrence, Douglas R. 357
Lebed', Mykola 19-20, 89, 91, 133-141, 143-146, 148-164, 172-173, 178, 181-182, 184, 194, 278, 304, 315
Leggewie, Claus 326
Lemkin, Raphael 341
Lenin, Vladimir 39, 51, 52, 74, 87, 227, 344, 365-367
Lenkavs'kyi, Stepan 217, 280-281, 310
Levytskyj, Marco 233, 235, 237, 240
Liashko, Oleh 114
Linde, Ann 349
Linkiewicz, Olga 257
Linnas, Karl 143
Lopatyns'kyi, Yurii 170
Losiev, Ihor 230, 245
Lozynskyj, Askold 237-238
Luburić, Vjekoslav 317-318
Luciuk, Lubomyr 233, 352
Luciw, Daria 233-234
Ludendorff, Erich 347
Luk''ianenko, Levko 105
Lukashenka, Aliaksandr 350
Lundborg, Herman 258, 266
Luts'kyi, Oleksandr 184
Lypa, Yurii 76, 272-274, 295, 365
Lysiak-Rudnyts'kyi, Ivan 330-331
MacLean, Hector 268
Makletsov, Aleksandr 259-260, 264
Malcolm X (Malcolm Little) 328
Mandela, Nelson 328
Markov, Sergei 372
Markus, Vasyl 299
Marples, David 94, 210-211, 225, 227, 232-235, 237, 245

Martin, Terry 51, 55, 59, 62, 75
Martynets' Volodymyr 214, 274, 276, 302
Marx, Karl 85
Matiushenko, Borys 260, 264, 271
Matla, Zinovyi 59, 159
Mayer, Arno 49
Mazepa, Ivan 90
McBride, Jared 215
McKee, Billy 328
Medinskii, Vladimir 367-368
Medvedev, Dmitrii 350
Mel'nyk, Andrii 59, 136, 171, 213-216, 274, 277-279, 305, 381-383
Mendel, Meron 382
Michnik, Adam 83
Mihailović, Draža 328
Mikhnovs'kyi, Mykola 36, 120, 264-265, 272
Miljan, Goran 299
Mill, John Stuart 26-27
Molotov, Viacheslav 105, 106
Morawiecki, Mateusz 378
Motyka, Grzegorz 220
Motyl, Alexander J. 121-122, 249, 302, 316, 320-321, 324, 326-327, 329, 334-335, 339-340, 352, 354-355
Mussolini, Benito 136, 171, 203, 213, 219, 266, 275, 284, 298, 302, 311, 328
Nalyvaichenko, Valentyn 101, 104
Nasser, Gamal Abdel 203
Naval'nyi, Aleksei 374
Nietzsche, Friedrich 265
Niinistö, Sauli 349
Nikitinskii, Leonid 362, 377
Nilsson, Göran B. 86

INDEX 459

Nolte, Ernst 209, 298
Nyshchuk, Evhen 124
Oberländer, Theodore 174
Obryn'ba, Nikolai 201, 202
Olesnycky, Nestor L. 156
Olszanski, Tadeusz. A. 107
Orly, Pylyp 90
Ovsiannikova, Marina 373, 375, 377
Pahiria, Oleksandr 328
Patryliak, Ivan 113, 328
Pavelić, Ante 136, 171, 211, 215, 217, 219, 275, 284, 311, 314
Pavlov, Aleksei 372
Pavlovs'kyi, Oleksii 30
Pavlyshyn, Luka Stepanovych 178
Payne, Stanley 298
Pelikh 183
Petliura, Symon 43, 45-48, 58, 90, 261, 338
Petrash, Stepan 117-118
Petrenko, Olena 273
Petruccelli, David 215
Petrushevych, Ievhen 46
Petryshyn, Roman 233
Pidhornyi, Mykola 69, 75-76, 78
Pieracki, Bronisław 135, 212, 302
Piłsudski, Jozef 47, 58-59,
Plav"iuk, Mykola 84
Plewa-Törnquist, Barbara 34
Pobihushchyi-Ren, Ievhen 182, 190-191
Podilsky, Taras 233
Poroshenko, Petro 17, 123, 128-129, 299, 334-335, 354, 358, 382-384
Portnikov, Vitaly 122
Posivnych, Mykola 182, 187, 191
Posokhov, Parmen 201
Postyshev, Pavel 105-106

Potichnyj, Petro 170, 239
Przydacz, Marcin 382
Putin, Vladimir 130, 235, 329-330, 339, 342-346, 348, 350-351, 354-357, 359-367, 369, 372- 378
Quisling, Vidkun 234
Rafeenko, Volodymyr 120
Rasevych, Vasyl 130
Reardon, Jenny 263, 287
Rebet, Lev 59, 159
Reichardt, Sven 308, 331
Rezmer, Waldemar 127
Riabchuk, Mykola 118-119, 122, 248, 327
Ribbentrop, Joachim von 171, 214
Rivlin, Reuben 126
Rodino, Peter W 144-145
Romanyshyn, Oleh 328
Rosenbaum, Willhelm 146
Rosenberg, Alfred 171, 213, 266, 325
Roshchin, Aleksei 374
Rositzke, Harry 163
Rossoliński-Liebe, Grzegorz 130, 336
Rothberg, Michael 240
Sanborn, Joshua 36, 51
Sands, Philippe 358
Sang, Aun 203, 328
Sapiehin, Andrii O. 261
Savaryn, Petro 233
Savitskii (Savits'kyi), Peter 365-366
Scholz, Olaf 350
Schopenhauer, Arthur 269
Schultz, Bruno 195
Semotiuk, Andriy J. 238-239
Senyk, Omelian 136
Serbyn, Roman 232-233

Sergeitsev, Timofei 369
Shapiro, Anatolii 195
Shcherbyts'kyi, Volodymyr 69, 82
Shelest, Petro 76, 78
Shemelev, Ivan 366
Sheptytsk'yi, Andrei 300
Sher, Neal M. 143
Shevchenko, Taras 31
Shkandrij, Myroslav 273
Shpak, Alina 123, 301
Shukhevych, Roman 19, 90, 109, 114, 125, 133, 137, 165-170, 172-178, 181-182, 184-192, 194- 206, 218-221, 223, 229, 231, 237, 242, 244, 248, 252, 280-281, 310, 328, 380
Shukhevych, Yurii 114, 167, 192, 203, 246
Sima, Horia 314
Simon'ian, Margarita 371
Skoropads'kyi, Pavlo 41-43, 338
Skrypnyk, Mykola 55, 61
Slezkine, Yuri 51
Smotrich, Bezalel 380
Snyder, Timothy 28, 210, 222, 245
Sobiński, Stanisław 172
Soldatenko, Valerii 109, 113
Sorel, Georges 266
Stakhiv, Yevhen 140
Stalin, Iosif 52, 60, 67-68, 70, 71, 86, 105, 106, 117, 223, 355, 365, 367
Stepaniak, Mykhailo 185
Stern, Avraham 328
Stets'ko, Yaroslav 20, 30, 120, 135, 136, 138, 153, 155, 166, 171, 198, 213, 216-217, 219, 221, 223, 225-226, 275-286,

291-295, 309-311, 313, 316-319, 321, 323-325, 328, 330
Stets'ko, Yaroslava (Slava) 166, 226, 341
Stiazhkina, Olena 120
Strauss, Franz-Josef 293
Struve, Kai 64, 284
Stsibors'kyi, Mykola 136, 278, 304-305, 325
Subtelny, Orest 23, 227
Sukhovers'kyi, Mykola 272
Suny, Ronald Grigor 54-55
Swyripa, Frances 224
Sych, Oleksandr 112
Sydor, Vasyl 184
Symonenko, Petro 111, 170
Szálasi, Ferenc 211, 234
Ther, Philipp 84
Tiahnibok, Oleh 246
Tikhonov, Mykola 69
Tiso, Jozef 211, 217, 234, 291, 313-314
Tokaev, Kasym-Zhomart 364
Tolstoi, Lev 379
Turchynov, Oleksandr 112
Turda, Marius 256
Tymoshenko, Yuliia 108, 207
Umland, Andreas 329, 340
Veidlinger, Jeffrey 45
Velychenko, Stephen 239-240
V"iatrovych, Volodymyr 81, 99-102, 104-105, 109- 110, 113, 116, 123, 125, 127- 129, 191-194, 196, 198- 201, 228, 319, 336-337
Vitrenko, Natalia 168
Vynnychenko, Volodymyr 37, 43, 47
Walcott, Derek 25
Washington, George 188, 350, 352

Waszczykowski, Witold 127, 380
Way, Lucan 122
Weindling, Paul 256
Weiner, Amir 65
Weiss-Wendt, Anton 358
Weiss, Ahron 237
Weitzman, Mark 241
Wilhelm II 39, 42
Willems, Bastiaan 336
Wilson, Andrew 83, 95, 120
Wilson, Woodrow 51
Wojnowski, Zbigniew 78
Yakimchuk, Liuba 120
Yakhymovych, Hryhoryi 76
Yanchuk, Oleh' 188, 237
Yaniv, Volodymyr 187
Yanukovych, Viktor 17, 108-113, 165, 167, 169-170, 192, 207, 241, 251, 300, 341- 343
Yasynevych, Yaryna 101, 125, 128
Yatseniuk, Arsenii 112
Yekelchyk, Serhiy 23, 130
Yeltsin, Boris 366
Yendyk, Rostislav 267, 269, 273, 287 291, 295
Yermolenko, Volodymyr 356
Yevtushenko, Yevgenii 376
Yukhnovs'kyi, Ihor' 102, 227
Yushchenko, Kateryna 226
Yushchenko, Viktor 19, 20, 81, 92, 95, 99, 102-104, 108-109, 123, 126, 129, 165-170, 191-192, 195-198, 207, 226-232, 241-246, 250-252, 318, 327, 340-341, 382-384
Zabuzhko, Oksana 378
Zaitsev, Oleksandr 171, 210, 297, 301-302, 306-307, 312, 317-318, 321, 324, 326

Zakharova, Mariia 349
Zaluzhny, Ivan 117-118
Zelens'kyi, Volodymyr 21, 331, 334-338, 345-346, 350-352, 357, 369, 380, 382-384
Zhirinovskii, Vladimir 359
Ziuganov, Gennadii 359
Zvarych, Roman 226

Places

Alberta 211, 224, 232-234
Auschwitz 158, 195, 293
Australia 89, 103, 160, 288
Austria 139, 221
Austro-Hungarian empire 27, 31, 33, 35, 43
Bakhmach 204
Balkan peninsula 257
Baltic Sea 350
Baltic states 75-76, 101, 377
Bamberg 353
Bandera Avenue (*Prospekt Bandery*) 116
Baranovichi 183
Barovka 187
Bavaria 293
Belarus 72, 82, 88, 96, 137, 176-182, 185-188, 190, 199-201, 203-204, 219, 229, 346, 353, 360
Belgium 268
Bergen-Belsen 158
Berlin 41, 136, 172, 219-220, 284-285, 311
Bessarabia 23, 39, 78
Białystok 180
Biarezina 199, 201
Bolivia 134
Bosnia-Herzegovina 95
Brailiv 175
Brazil 121, 288
Brest-Litovsk 40, 42
Brussels 249
Bucha 370, 378
Buh 42
Bulgaria 257
Burma 203
Cairo 150

Canada 20, 89, 103, 121, 139, 160, 222, 224-225, 231-234, 239, 242, 274, 277-288, 291, 336, 357
Carpathian Mountains 67, 189, 371
Caspian Sea 44, 64, 76, 216, 266, 295
Caucasus 23, 36, 44, 77, 264
Chernivtsi 272
Chechnya 37, 371
Chernihiv 345, 365
Chernihiv oblast 96, 346
Chernobyl 71, 352
China 291, 379
Courland 39
Crimea 23, 37, 94, 112, 118, 120, 122, 251, 354, 363, 374
Croatia 215, 217, 295, 299, 305, 321, 327
Curzon line 220
Czech Republic 357
Czechoslovakia 50, 76, 172, 256, 257, 259, 276, 324
Dachau 158
Dagestan 264
Danube 44, 65, 76, 216, 266, 295
Danzig 325
Dnipro 40, 42, 46, 62, 68,
Dnipropetrovs'k 62, 69, 115, 177
Dnister 42
Don Republic 46
Donbas 117-118, 122-124, 241, 357
Donets'k oblast' 94-95, 241, 343
Donetsk 38, 62, 68, 112, 120, 122, 251
Donetsk People's Republic 364
Donskoi Monastery 366

INDEX 463

Drohobycz 236
Dzvina 199, 201
Eastern Europe 74, 153, 163, 171, 211, 214, 236, 249, 255, 257-258, 270, 279, 324
Eastern Ukraine 169, 359, 367
Egypt 203
England 77, 203, 268
Eritrea 360
Estonia 37, 39
Europe 21, 23, 31, 35, 63, 108, 136, 166, 171, 203, 246, 249, 256, 258, 264, 267, 277, 279, 284, 294, 298, 311, 325, 327-328, 333, 347, 349, 379
European Union 22, 107, 111, 125, 127, 169, 246-248, 252, 380
Finland 39, 77, 348-349, 361, 377
Fiume 325
France 32, 198, 247, 268, 327
Frankfurt am Main 293
Frankfurt an der Oder 176
Galicia 23, 33, 35, 43, 47-48, 66-67, 72-73, 75, 89, 96, 100, 118, 124, 172, 175, 184-185, 205, 212, 220, 236, 244, 250, 251, 280, 285, 300, 312-322, 324, 331, 396
Georgia 362-363, 371, 377
Germany 20, 26, 28, 121, 133, 136, 139, 145, 155, 157, 159, 161, 163, 169, 171, 177, 185-186, 189, 198-199, 204, 214-215, 217, 219, 221, 245- 247, 257, 268- 270, 284-286, 288, 302, 315-316, 321, 325, 327, 331, 350, 375, 377, 379, 381-382
Gorodishche 183
Great Britain 27, 160, 198, 288

Greece 31, 127, 257
Habsburg empire 18, 22, 43, 96,
Hague, the 368
Hamburg 185
Hungary 47, 211, 257, 276
Imperial Germany 39
India 121
Ireland 357
Israel 21, 107, 125-126, 197, 229, 240, 382
Italy 171, 275, 302
Izium 370
Jasenovać 317
Jerusalem 145, 196
Kamianets'-Podil's'kyi 45
Kamians'ke 68
Katerynoslav 40
Kazakh ASSR 60
Kazakhstan 74, 377
Kharkiv 38, 46, 56, 69, 169, 260, 343, 345, 377
Kharkiv oblast 346
Kherson 38, 363, 377
Kherson oblast 38, 364
Khmel'nyts'kyi 45
Kholm 32, 279
Kolomyja 236
Konotop 204
Krakow 173-174, 215, 279-280, 299, 304-305, 310, 381
Kreschatyk 46
Krynitza 146
Kuban 41
Kyiv (Kiev) 40, 42, 46, 48-49, 103, 105, 107-108, 113, 116, 121, 123, 161, 167, 197, 229, 261, 301, 342, 345, 346, 351, 354, 356, 372, 379, 382
Kyiv oblast 346
L'viv (Lwów) 74, 99, 101, 110, 123, 130, 136, 171-172, 175,

178, 182, 187, 195, 210, 213, 216, 218, 221, 236, 244, 247, 249, 265, 279, 283, 297, 310, 321, 325, 381
Latvia 211, 350, 357
Lebanon 95
Lemberg 265
Lemko Region 64
Leningrad 261
Lepel 177, 201, 202
Lithuania 23, 39, 59, 88, 92, 350, 357
Livonia 30, 39
Ljubljana 259
London 150
Lubelsczcyzna 44
Lublin 279
Luhansk 38, 112, 122
Luhansk oblast 343, 364
Luhansk People's Republic 364
Luts'k 123
Lyon 134
Macedonia 127
Mahileu 177
Mariupol 367
Melitopol 265
Memel 325
Minsk 91, 203, 261
Moldova 88, 92, 346, 363
Montreal 213
Moscow 38, 56, 71-72, 95, 96, 149, 151, 159, 197, 199, 217, 238, 247, 249, 261, 280, 311, 363, 366, 367, 370, 372, 380
Moscow Avenue (*Moskovs'kyi Prospekt*) 116
Munich 89, 138, 150, 163, 173, 221, 243, 288, 291, 293, 362, 363, 381
Musovy 362
Naliboki forest 183

Nemyriv 262
Neuhammer 174, 176-177
New Jersey 246
New York 20, 89, 133, 135, 140, 145, 150, 158, 237, 286
Nordic states 257
North America 141, 143, 149, 222, 225, 252
North Caucasus 370
North Korea 360
North-western Europe 266
Nowy Sacz 44
Nuremberg 199, 234
Odesa 261, 342-343, 365, 373
Ohio 142
Oslo 358
Ostrówki 322
Ottawa 94, 103, 337
Paraguay 288
Paris 45, 91, 225, 274
Pereiaslavl 67, 77
Peru 288
Petrograd 28, 261
Philadelphia 187
Pittsburgh 162
Pochatovo 183
Podlachia 280
Podolia 45
Podols'k 262
Poland 18, 21, 23, 31, 39, 46-50, 57-59, 62, 77, 85, 91-92, 102-103, 107, 125-126, 128, 133, 135, 145, 156, 161, 172, 212, 214, 217, 222, 229, 236, 239, 242-243, 245-247, 252, 256-257, 264, 271, 277, 304, 324, 350, 353, 355, 357, 380, 382
Poland, Kingdom of 39
Polissia 137, 181, 244
Poltava 69, 177, 264
Prague 58, 172, 259, 276, 285

INDEX 465

Proskuriv 45, 175
Prussia 23, 39, 379
Rabka 133
Radyme 175
Ravensbrück 153
Riga 49, 58, 271
Rivne 45, 66
Romania 66, 211, 256-258, 271-272, 324
Romanov empire 43
Rome 135, 275, 278, 304, 310
Rostov-na-Donu 41
Rotterdam 276
Rus' 30, 32, 129 356, 362
Russia 18, 21, 23, 30-31, 33, 35, 37, 46, 48, 53, 72-73, 77-78, 82, 87-88, 91, 94, 96, 112, 122, 180, 191, 197, 229, 248-249, 260-262, 329-330, 333, 338-348, 350, 352, 354-357, 359-364, 366-375, 377-379, 383
Saargebiet 325
Sachsenhausen 136, 153, 155, 158, 220, 291, 317-318, 321
Scandinavia 268
Scotland 77
Serbia 83
Severodonets'k 95, 121
Sian 36, 42, 44, 264
Siberia 70, 74, 77, 370
Silesia 23, 174, 176-177
Slovakia 102, 211, 217
Sobibór 142
South America 343
Soviet Union 18, 53, 54, 59, 63, 71, 73, 76-77, 82, 97, 102, 109, 124-125, 133, 137, 139, 156-157, 163, 173-174, 185-186, 198, 214-215, 224, 231, 243, 251, 279, 283, 295, 321, 338, 347, 364
Spain 139, 291, 294
Spandau 219
St Petersburg 260, 364
Stalingrad 138, 181, 194, 219, 285
Stanislaviv (Stanisławów) 46, 236
Stryj 236
Sumy 96
Sweden 258-259, 349
Syria 360
Taganrog, 65
Taiwan 20, 139, 379
Tanzania 95
Tarnopol 236
Tauria guberniia 265
Ternopil 175, 218
Tisza 371
Toronto 93, 234, 352
Transcarpathia 23, 67, 276
Transnistria 23, 66
Treblinka 143
Tunisia 288
Turivka 264
Turkestan 37, 54,
Turkey 121, 377
Ukraine 18-19, 21-24, 30-32, 34, 36, 38-39, 42-44, 46, 48-51, 55-58, 61-63, 66-67, 70-73, 75, 78-79, 81-85, 87-88, 90-99, 101-107, 109-110, 112, 118-129, 131, 135-141, 143, 151-152, 156, 158-160, 163, 165-166, 168-169, 172, 180, 185, 187, 189, 191, 195-198, 204-205, 208, 210, 214-217, 219, 221-222, 225-229, 231, 233, 236-242, 244-246, 248-252, 256, 259, 260-262, 264-267, 274, 278, 280, 284-285,

292, 295, 298-301, 303, 306, 311, 319, 323, 326, 327, 333-337, 339-340, 342-349, 352-354, 356-357, 359-363, 365-366, 368-373, 375, 378-384
United Baltic Duchy 39
United States 20, 89, 108, 121, 139, 142, 145, 148, 150, 152, 160, 163, 241, 288, 291-293, 348, 360, 379
Ural region 49
USSR 50, 52, 70, 82, 95, 106, 139, 140, 143, 161, 215, 227, 256, 262, 280, 324, 362
Uzbekistan 95
Venezuela 288
Versailles 44
Vienna 41, 172, 177, 265
Vilnius 59, 92
Vinnytsia 45, 175-176, 218, 229
Vinnytsia oblast' 262
Vitebsk 177, 204
Volga region 49
Volhynia 45, 67, 100, 137, 181-183, 185, 205, 236, 239, 244, 280, 285, 296, 312, 327, 331, 355
Warsaw 48, 126, 127, 279, 347-348, 382
Washington, D.C. 348
Weimar 329
West End Avenue 160
West Ukraine 18, 72, 84, 135-136, 138-139, 221-222, 232, 236, 238, 284, 311, 326
West Ukrainian People's Republic 43
Western Europe 88, 141
Winnipeg 274
Wola Ostrowiecka 322
Yatra 183

Yatry 183
Yavoriv 175
Yonkers 133, 145, 226
Yugoslavia 50, 143, 215, 302
Yuzivka 38
Zakopane 133, 145-146, 148-150, 156, 158, 163, 173
Zapol'e 183
Zaporizhzhia 62, 124, 364
Zatareshch 183
Zatop'e 183
Zazhokhe 183
Zbruch 35, 57, 60, 65, 75, 79, 116
Zellenbau 136
Zhytomyr 40, 45, 136
Zolochiv 175, 218

SOVIET AND POST-SOVIET POLITICS AND SOCIETY
Edited by Dr. Andreas Umland | ISSN 1614-3515

1 *Андреас Умланд (ред.)* | Воплощение Европейской конвенции по правам человека в России. Философские, юридические и эмпирические исследования | ISBN 3-89821-387-0

2 *Christian Wipperfürth* | Russland – ein vertrauenswürdiger Partner? Grundlagen, Hintergründe und Praxis gegenwärtiger russischer Außenpolitik | Mit einem Vorwort von Heinz Timmermann | ISBN 3-89821-401-X

3 *Manja Hussner* | Die Übernahme internationalen Rechts in die russische und deutsche Rechtsordnung. Eine vergleichende Analyse zur Völkerrechtsfreundlichkeit der Verfassungen der Russländischen Föderation und der Bundesrepublik Deutschland | Mit einem Vorwort von Rainer Arnold | ISBN 3-89821-438-9

4 *Matthew Tejada* | Bulgaria's Democratic Consolidation and the Kozloduy Nuclear Power Plant (KNPP). The Unattainability of Closure | With a foreword by Richard J. Crampton | ISBN 3-89821-439-7

5 *Марк Григорьевич Меерович* | Квадратные метры, определяющие сознание. Государственная жилищная политика в СССР. 1921 – 1941 гг | ISBN 3-89821-474-5

6 *Andrei P. Tsygankov, Pavel A.Tsygankov (Eds.)* | New Directions in Russian International Studies | ISBN 3-89821-422-2

7 *Марк Григорьевич Меерович* | Как власть народ к труду приучала. Жилище в СССР – средство управления людьми. 1917 – 1941 гг. | С предисловием Елены Осокиной | ISBN 3-89821-495-8

8 *David J. Galbreath* | Nation-Building and Minority Politics in Post-Socialist States. Interests, Influence and Identities in Estonia and Latvia | With a foreword by David J. Smith | ISBN 3-89821-467-2

9 *Алексей Юрьевич Безугольный* | Народы Кавказа в Вооруженных силах СССР в годы Великой Отечественной войны 1941-1945 гг. | С предисловием Николая Бугая | ISBN 3-89821-475-3

10 *Вячеслав Лихачев и Владимир Прибыловский (ред.)* | Русское Национальное Единство, 1990-2000. В 2-х томах | ISBN 3-89821-523-7

11 *Николай Бугай (ред.)* | Народы стран Балтии в условиях сталинизма (1940-е – 1950-е годы). Документированная история | ISBN 3-89821-525-3

12 *Ingmar Bredies (Hrsg.)* | Zur Anatomie der Orange Revolution in der Ukraine. Wechsel des Elitenregimes oder Triumph des Parlamentarismus? | ISBN 3-89821-524-5

13 *Anastasia V. Mitrofanova* | The Politicization of Russian Orthodoxy. Actors and Ideas | With a foreword by William C. Gay | ISBN 3-89821-481-8

14 *Nathan D. Larson* | Alexander Solzhenitsyn and the Russo-Jewish Question | ISBN 3-89821-483-4

15 *Guido Houben* | Kulturpolitik und Ethnizität. Staatliche Kunstförderung im Russland der neunziger Jahre | Mit einem Vorwort von Gert Weisskirchen | ISBN 3-89821-542-3

16 *Leonid Luks* | Der russische „Sonderweg"? Aufsätze zur neuesten Geschichte Russlands im europäischen Kontext | ISBN 3-89821-496-6

17 *Евгений Мороз* | История «Мёртвой воды» – от страшной сказки к большой политике. Политическое неоязычество в постсоветской России | ISBN 3-89821-551-2

18 *Александр Верховский и Галина Кожевникова (ред.)* | Этническая и религиозная интолерантность в российских СМИ. Результаты мониторинга 2001-2004 гг. | ISBN 3-89821-569-5

19 *Christian Ganzer* | Sowjetisches Erbe und ukrainische Nation. Das Museum der Geschichte des Zaporoger Kosakentums auf der Insel Chortycja | Mit einem Vorwort von Frank Golczewski | ISBN 3-89821-504-0

20 *Эльза-Баир Гучинова* | Помнить нельзя забыть. Антропология депортационной травмы калмыков | С предисловием Кэролайн Хамфри | ISBN 3-89821-506-7

21 *Юлия Лидерман* | Мотивы «проверки» и «испытания» в постсоветской культуре. Советское прошлое в российском кинематографе 1990-х годов | С предисловием Евгения Марголита | ISBN 3-89821-511-3

22 *Tanya Lokshina, Ray Thomas, Mary Mayer (Eds.)* | The Imposition of a Fake Political Settlement in the Northern Caucasus. The 2003 Chechen Presidential Election | ISBN 3-89821-436-2

23 *Timothy McCajor Hall, Rosie Read (Eds.)* | Changes in the Heart of Europe. Recent Ethnographies of Czechs, Slovaks, Roma, and Sorbs | With an afterword by Zdeněk Salzmann | ISBN 3-89821-606-3

24 *Christian Autengruber* | Die politischen Parteien in Bulgarien und Rumänien. Eine vergleichende Analyse seit Beginn der 90er Jahre | Mit einem Vorwort von Dorothée de Nève | ISBN 3-89821-476-1

25 *Annette Freyberg-Inan with Radu Cristescu* | The Ghosts in Our Classrooms, or: John Dewey Meets Ceauşescu. The Promise and the Failures of Civic Education in Romania | ISBN 3-89821-416-8

26 *John B. Dunlop* | The 2002 Dubrovka and 2004 Beslan Hostage Crises. A Critique of Russian Counter-Terrorism | With a foreword by Donald N. Jensen | ISBN 3-89821-608-X

27 *Peter Koller* | Das touristische Potenzial von Kam''janec'–Podil's'kyj. Eine fremdenverkehrsgeographische Untersuchung der Zukunftsperspektiven und Maßnahmenplanung zur Destinationsentwicklung des „ukrainischen Rothenburg" | Mit einem Vorwort von Kristiane Klemm | ISBN 3-89821-640-3

28 *Françoise Daucé, Elisabeth Sieca-Kozlowski (Eds.)* | Dedovshchina in the Post-Soviet Military. Hazing of Russian Army Conscripts in a Comparative Perspective | With a foreword by Dale Herspring | ISBN 3-89821-616-0

29 *Florian Strasser* | Zivilgesellschaftliche Einflüsse auf die Orange Revolution. Die gewaltlose Massenbewegung und die ukrainische Wahlkrise 2004 | Mit einem Vorwort von Egbert Jahn | ISBN 3-89821-648-9

30 *Rebecca S. Katz* | The Georgian Regime Crisis of 2003-2004. A Case Study in Post-Soviet Media Representation of Politics, Crime and Corruption | ISBN 3-89821-413-3

31 *Vladimir Kantor* | Willkür oder Freiheit. Beiträge zur russischen Geschichtsphilosophie | Ediert von Dagmar Herrmann sowie mit einem Vorwort versehen von Leonid Luks | ISBN 3-89821-589-X

32 *Laura A. Victoir* | The Russian Land Estate Today. A Case Study of Cultural Politics in Post-Soviet Russia | With a foreword by Priscilla Roosevelt | ISBN 3-89821-426-5

33 *Ivan Katchanovski* | Cleft Countries. Regional Political Divisions and Cultures in Post-Soviet Ukraine and Moldova| With a foreword by Francis Fukuyama | ISBN 3-89821-558-X

34 *Florian Mühlfried* | Postsowjetische Feiern. Das Georgische Bankett im Wandel | Mit einem Vorwort von Kevin Tuite | ISBN 3-89821-601-2

35 *Roger Griffin, Werner Loh, Andreas Umland (Eds.)* | Fascism Past and Present, West and East. An International Debate on Concepts and Cases in the Comparative Study of the Extreme Right | With an afterword by Walter Laqueur | ISBN 3-89821-674-8

36 *Sebastian Schlegel* | Der „Weiße Archipel". Sowjetische Atomstädte 1945-1991 | Mit einem Geleitwort von Thomas Bohn | ISBN 3-89821-679-9

37 *Vyacheslav Likhachev* | Political Anti-Semitism in Post-Soviet Russia. Actors and Ideas in 1991-2003 | Edited and translated from Russian by Eugene Veklerov | ISBN 3-89821-529-6

38 *Josette Baer (Ed.)* | Preparing Liberty in Central Europe. Political Texts from the Spring of Nations 1848 to the Spring of Prague 1968 | With a foreword by Zdeněk V. David | ISBN 3-89821-546-6

39 *Михаил Лукьянов* | Российский консерватизм и реформа, 1907-1914 | С предисловием Марка Д. Стейнберга | ISBN 3-89821-503-2

40 *Nicola Melloni* | Market Without Economy. The 1998 Russian Financial Crisis | With a foreword by Eiji Furukawa | ISBN 3-89821-407-9

41 *Dmitrij Chmelnizki* | Die Architektur Stalins | Bd. 1: Studien zu Ideologie und Stil | Bd. 2: Bilddokumentation | Mit einem Vorwort von Bruno Flierl | ISBN 3-89821-515-6

42 *Katja Yafimava* | Post-Soviet Russian-Belarussian Relationships. The Role of Gas Transit Pipelines | With a foreword by Jonathan P. Stern | ISBN 3-89821-655-1

43 *Boris Chavkin* | Verflechtungen der deutschen und russischen Zeitgeschichte. Aufsätze und Archivfunde zu den Beziehungen Deutschlands und der Sowjetunion von 1917 bis 1991 | Ediert von Markus Edlinger sowie mit einem Vorwort versehen von Leonid Luks | ISBN 3-89821-756-6

44 *Anastasija Grynenko in Zusammenarbeit mit Claudia Dathe* | Die Terminologie des Gerichtswesens der Ukraine und Deutschlands im Vergleich. Eine übersetzungswissenschaftliche Analyse juristischer Fachbegriffe im Deutschen, Ukrainischen und Russischen | Mit einem Vorwort von Ulrich Hartmann | ISBN 3-89821-691-8

45 *Anton Burkov* | The Impact of the European Convention on Human Rights on Russian Law. Legislation and Application in 1996-2006 | With a foreword by Françoise Hampson | ISBN 978-3-89821-639-5

46 *Stina Torjesen, Indra Overland (Eds.)* | International Election Observers in Post-Soviet Azerbaijan. Geopolitical Pawns or Agents of Change? | ISBN 978-3-89821-743-9

47 *Taras Kuzio* | Ukraine – Crimea – Russia. Triangle of Conflict | ISBN 978-3-89821-761-3

48 *Claudia Šabić* | „Ich erinnere mich nicht, aber L'viv!" Zur Funktion kultureller Faktoren für die Institutionalisierung und Entwicklung einer ukrainischen Region | Mit einem Vorwort von Melanie Tatur | ISBN 978-3-89821-752-1

49　*Marlies Bilz* | Tatarstan in der Transformation. Nationaler Diskurs und Politische Praxis 1988-1994 | Mit einem Vorwort von Frank Golczewski | ISBN 978-3-89821-722-4

50　*Марлен Ларюэль (ред.)* | Современные интерпретации русского национализма | ISBN 978-3-89821-795-8

51　*Sonja Schüler* | Die ethnische Dimension der Armut. Roma im postsozialistischen Rumänien | Mit einem Vorwort von Anton Sterbling | ISBN 978-3-89821-776-7

52　*Галина Кожевникова* | Радикальный национализм в России и противодействие ему. Сборник докладов Центра «Сова» за 2004-2007 гг. | С предисловием Александра Верховского | ISBN 978-3-89821-721-7

53　*Галина Кожевникова и Владимир Прибыловский* | Российская власть в биографиях I. Высшие должностные лица РФ в 2004 г. | ISBN 978-3-89821-796-5

54　*Галина Кожевникова и Владимир Прибыловский* | Российская власть в биографиях II. Члены Правительства РФ в 2004 г. | ISBN 978-3-89821-797-2

55　*Галина Кожевникова и Владимир Прибыловский* | Российская власть в биографиях III. Руководители федеральных служб и агентств РФ в 2004 г.| ISBN 978-3-89821-798-9

56　*Ileana Petroniu* | Privatisierung in Transformationsökonomien. Determinanten der Restrukturierungs-Bereitschaft am Beispiel Polens, Rumäniens und der Ukraine | Mit einem Vorwort von Rainer W. Schäfer | ISBN 978-3-89821-790-3

57　*Christian Wipperfürth* | Russland und seine GUS-Nachbarn. Hintergründe, aktuelle Entwicklungen und Konflikte in einer ressourcenreichen Region| ISBN 978-3-89821-801-6

58　*Togzhan Kassenova* | From Antagonism to Partnership. The Uneasy Path of the U.S.-Russian Cooperative Threat Reduction | With a foreword by Christoph Bluth | ISBN 978-3-89821-707-1

59　*Alexander Höllwerth* | Das sakrale eurasische Imperium des Aleksandr Dugin. Eine Diskursanalyse zum postsowjetischen russischen Rechtsextremismus | Mit einem Vorwort von Dirk Uffelmann | ISBN 978-3-89821-813-9

60　*Олег Рябов* | «Россия-Матушка». Национализм, гендер и война в России XX века | С предисловием Елены Гощило | ISBN 978-3-89821-487-2

61　*Ivan Maistrenko* | Borot'bism. A Chapter in the History of the Ukrainian Revolution | With a new Introduction by Chris Ford | Translated by George S. N. Luckyj with the assistance of Ivan L. Rudnytsky | Second, Revised and Expanded Edition ISBN 978-3-8382-1107-7

62　*Maryna Romanets* | Anamorphosic Texts and Reconfigured Visions. Improvised Traditions in Contemporary Ukrainian and Irish Literature | ISBN 978-3-89821-576-3

63　*Paul D'Anieri and Taras Kuzio (Eds.)* | Aspects of the Orange Revolution I. Democratization and Elections in Post-Communist Ukraine | ISBN 978-3-89821-698-2

64　*Bohdan Harasymiw in collaboration with Oleh S. Ilnytzkyj (Eds.)* | Aspects of the Orange Revolution II. Information and Manipulation Strategies in the 2004 Ukrainian Presidential Elections | ISBN 978-3-89821-699-9

65　*Ingmar Bredies, Andreas Umland and Valentin Yakushik (Eds.)* | Aspects of the Orange Revolution III. The Context and Dynamics of the 2004 Ukrainian Presidential Elections | ISBN 978-3-89821-803-0

66　*Ingmar Bredies, Andreas Umland and Valentin Yakushik (Eds.)* | Aspects of the Orange Revolution IV. Foreign Assistance and Civic Action in the 2004 Ukrainian Presidential Elections | ISBN 978-3-89821-808-5

67　*Ingmar Bredies, Andreas Umland and Valentin Yakushik (Eds.)* | Aspects of the Orange Revolution V. Institutional Observation Reports on the 2004 Ukrainian Presidential Elections | ISBN 978-3-89821-809-2

68　*Taras Kuzio (Ed.)* | Aspects of the Orange Revolution VI. Post-Communist Democratic Revolutions in Comparative Perspective | ISBN 978-3-89821-820-7

69　*Tim Bohse* | Autoritarismus statt Selbstverwaltung. Die Transformation der kommunalen Politik in der Stadt Kaliningrad 1990-2005 | Mit einem Geleitwort von Stefan Troebst | ISBN 978-3-89821-782-8

70　*David Rupp* | Die Rußländische Föderation und die russischsprachige Minderheit in Lettland. Eine Fallstudie zur Anwaltspolitik Moskaus gegenüber den russophonen Minderheiten im „Nahen Ausland" von 1991 bis 2002 | Mit einem Vorwort von Helmut Wagner | ISBN 978-3-89821-778-1

71　*Taras Kuzio* | Theoretical and Comparative Perspectives on Nationalism. New Directions in Cross-Cultural and Post-Communist Studies | With a foreword by Paul Robert Magocsi | ISBN 978-3-89821-815-3

72　*Christine Teichmann* | Die Hochschultransformation im heutigen Osteuropa. Kontinuität und Wandel bei der Entwicklung des postkommunistischen Universitätswesens | Mit einem Vorwort von Oskar Anweiler | ISBN 978-3-89821-842-9

73　*Julia Kusznir* | Der politische Einfluss von Wirtschaftseliten in russischen Regionen. Eine Analyse am Beispiel der Erdöl- und Erdgasindustrie, 1992-2005 | Mit einem Vorwort von Wolfgang Eichwede | ISBN 978-3-89821-821-4

74 *Alena Vysotskaya* | Russland, Belarus und die EU-Osterweiterung. Zur Minderheitenfrage und zum Problem der Freizügigkeit des Personenverkehrs | Mit einem Vorwort von Katlijn Malfliet | ISBN 978-3-89821-822-1

75 *Heiko Pleines (Hrsg.)* | Corporate Governance in post-sozialistischen Volkswirtschaften | ISBN 978-3-89821-766-8

76 *Stefan Ihrig* | Wer sind die Moldawier? Rumänismus versus Moldowanismus in Historiographie und Schulbüchern der Republik Moldova, 1991-2006 | Mit einem Vorwort von Holm Sundhaussen | ISBN 978-3-89821-466-7

77 *Galina Kozhevnikova in collaboration with Alexander Verkhovsky and Eugene Veklerov* | Ultra-Nationalism and Hate Crimes in Contemporary Russia. The 2004-2006 Annual Reports of Moscow's SOVA Center | With a foreword by Stephen D. Shenfield | ISBN 978-3-89821-868-9

78 *Florian Küchler* | The Role of the European Union in Moldova's Transnistria Conflict | With a foreword by Christopher Hill | ISBN 978-3-89821-850-4

79 *Bernd Rechel* | The Long Way Back to Europe. Minority Protection in Bulgaria | With a foreword by Richard Crampton | ISBN 978-3-89821-863-4

80 *Peter W. Rodgers* | Nation, Region and History in Post-Communist Transitions. Identity Politics in Ukraine, 1991-2006 | With a foreword by Vera Tolz | ISBN 978-3-89821-903-7

81 *Stephanie Solywoda* | The Life and Work of Semen L. Frank. A Study of Russian Religious Philosophy | With a foreword by Philip Walters | ISBN 978-3-89821-457-5

82 *Vera Sokolova* | Cultural Politics of Ethnicity. Discourses on Roma in Communist Czechoslovakia | ISBN 978-3-89821-864-1

83 *Natalya Shevchik Ketenci* | Kazakhstani Enterprises in Transition. The Role of Historical Regional Development in Kazakhstan's Post-Soviet Economic Transformation | ISBN 978-3-89821-831-3

84 *Martin Malek, Anna Schor-Tschudnowskaja (Hgg.)* | Europa im Tschetschenienkrieg. Zwischen politischer Ohnmacht und Gleichgültigkeit | Mit einem Vorwort von Lipchan Basajewa | ISBN 978-3-89821-676-0

85 *Stefan Meister* | Das postsowjetische Universitätswesen zwischen nationalem und internationalem Wandel. Die Entwicklung der regionalen Hochschule in Russland als Gradmesser der Systemtransformation | Mit einem Vorwort von Joan DeBardeleben | ISBN 978-3-89821-891-7

86 *Konstantin Sheiko in collaboration with Stephen Brown* | Nationalist Imaginings of the Russian Past. Anatolii Fomenko and the Rise of Alternative History in Post-Communist Russia | With a foreword by Donald Ostrowski | ISBN 978-3-89821-915-0

87 *Sabine Jenni* | Wie stark ist das „Einige Russland"? Zur Parteibindung der Eliten und zum Wahlerfolg der Machtpartei im Dezember 2007 | Mit einem Vorwort von Klaus Armingeon | ISBN 978-3-89821-961-7

88 *Thomas Borén* | Meeting-Places of Transformation. Urban Identity, Spatial Representations and Local Politics in Post-Soviet St Petersburg | ISBN 978-3-89821-739-2

89 *Aygul Ashirova* | Stalinismus und Stalin-Kult in Zentralasien. Turkmenistan 1924-1953 | Mit einem Vorwort von Leonid Luks | ISBN 978-3-89821-987-7

90 *Leonid Luks* | Freiheit oder imperiale Größe? Essays zu einem russischen Dilemma | ISBN 978-3-8382-0011-8

91 *Christopher Gilley* | The 'Change of Signposts' in the Ukrainian Emigration. A Contribution to the History of Sovietophilism in the 1920s | With a foreword by Frank Golczewski | ISBN 978-3-89821-965-5

92 *Philipp Casula, Jeronim Perovic (Eds.)* | Identities and Politics During the Putin Presidency. The Discursive Foundations of Russia's Stability | With a foreword by Heiko Haumann | ISBN 978-3-8382-0015-6

93 *Marcel Viëtor* | Europa und die Frage nach seinen Grenzen im Osten. Zur Konstruktion ‚europäischer Identität' in Geschichte und Gegenwart | Mit einem Vorwort von Albrecht Lehmann | ISBN 978-3-8382-0045-3

94 *Ben Hellman, Andrei Rogachevskii* | Filming the Unfilmable. Casper Wrede's 'One Day in the Life of Ivan Denisovich' | Second, Revised and Expanded Edition | ISBN 978-3-8382-0044-6

95 *Eva Fuchslocher* | Vaterland, Sprache, Glaube. Orthodoxie und Nationenbildung am Beispiel Georgiens | Mit einem Vorwort von Christina von Braun | ISBN 978-3-89821-884-9

96 *Vladimir Kantor* | Das Westlertum und der Weg Russlands. Zur Entwicklung der russischen Literatur und Philosophie | Ediert von Dagmar Herrmann | Mit einem Beitrag von Nikolaus Lobkowicz | ISBN 978-3-8382-0102-3

97 *Kamran Musayev* | Die postsowjetische Transformation im Baltikum und Südkaukasus. Eine vergleichende Untersuchung der politischen Entwicklung Lettlands und Aserbaidschans 1985-2009 | Mit einem Vorwort von Leonid Luks | Ediert von Sandro Henschel | ISBN 978-3-8382-0103-0

98 *Tatiana Zhurzhenko* | Borderlands into Bordered Lands. Geopolitics of Identity in Post-Soviet Ukraine | With a foreword by Dieter Segert | ISBN 978-3-8382-0042-2

99 *Кирилл Галушко, Лидия Смола (ред.)* | Пределы падения – варианты украинского будущего. Аналитико-прогностические исследования | ISBN 978-3-8382-0148-1

100 *Michael Minkenberg (Ed.)* | Historical Legacies and the Radical Right in Post-Cold War Central and Eastern Europe | With an afterword by Sabrina P. Ramet | ISBN 978-3-8382-0124-5

101 *David-Emil Wickström* | Rocking St. Petersburg. Transcultural Flows and Identity Politics in the St. Petersburg Popular Music Scene | With a foreword by Yngvar B. Steinholt | Second, Revised and Expanded Edition | ISBN 978-3-8382-0100-9

102 *Eva Zabka* | Eine neue „Zeit der Wirren"? Der spät- und postsowjetische Systemwandel 1985-2000 im Spiegel russischer gesellschaftspolitischer Diskurse | Mit einem Vorwort von Margareta Mommsen | ISBN 978-3-8382-0161-0

103 *Ulrike Ziemer* | Ethnic Belonging, Gender and Cultural Practices. Youth Identitites in Contemporary Russia | With a foreword by Anoop Nayak | ISBN 978-3-8382-0152-8

104 *Ksenia Chepikova* | ‚Einiges Russland' - eine zweite KPdSU? Aspekte der Identitätskonstruktion einer postsowjetischen „Partei der Macht" | Mit einem Vorwort von Torsten Oppelland | ISBN 978-3-8382-0311-9

105 *Леонид Люкс* | Западничество или евразийство? Демократия или идеократия? Сборник статей об исторических дилеммах России | С предисловием Владимира Кантора | ISBN 978-3-8382-0211-2

106 *Anna Dost* | Das russische Verfassungsrecht auf dem Weg zum Föderalismus und zurück. Zum Konflikt von Rechtsnormen und -wirklichkeit in der Russländischen Föderation von 1991 bis 2009 | Mit einem Vorwort von Alexander Blankenagel | ISBN 978-3-8382-0292-1

107 *Philipp Herzog* | Sozialistische Völkerfreundschaft, nationaler Widerstand oder harmloser Zeitvertreib? Zur politischen Funktion der Volkskunst im sowjetischen Estland | Mit einem Vorwort von Andreas Kappeler | ISBN 978-3-8382-0216-7

108 *Marlène Laruelle (Ed.)* | Russian Nationalism, Foreign Policy, and Identity Debates in Putin's Russia. New Ideological Patterns after the Orange Revolution | ISBN 978-3-8382-0325-6

109 *Michail Logvinov* | Russlands Kampf gegen den internationalen Terrorismus. Eine kritische Bestandsaufnahme des Bekämpfungsansatzes | Mit einem Geleitwort von Hans-Henning Schröder und einem Vorwort von Eckhard Jesse | ISBN 978-3-8382-0329-4

110 *John B. Dunlop* | The Moscow Bombings of September 1999. Examinations of Russian Terrorist Attacks at the Onset of Vladimir Putin's Rule | Second, Revised and Expanded Edition | ISBN 978-3-8382-0388-1

111 *Андрей А. Ковалёв* | Свидетельство из-за кулис российской политики I. Можно ли делать добро из зла? (Воспоминания и размышления о последних советских и первых послесоветских годах) | With a foreword by Peter Reddaway | ISBN 978-3-8382-0302-7

112 *Андрей А. Ковалёв* | Свидетельство из-за кулис российской политики II. Угроза для себя и окружающих (Наблюдения и предостережения относительно происходящего после 2000 г.) | ISBN 978-3-8382-0303-4

113 *Bernd Kappenberg* | Zeichen setzen für Europa. Der Gebrauch europäischer lateinischer Sonderzeichen in der deutschen Öffentlichkeit | Mit einem Vorwort von Peter Schlobinski | ISBN 978-3-89821-749-1

114 *Ivo Mijnssen* | The Quest for an Ideal Youth in Putin's Russia I. Back to Our Future! History, Modernity, and Patriotism according to Nashi, 2005-2013 | With a foreword by Jeronim Perović | Second, Revised and Expanded Edition | ISBN 978-3-8382-0368-3

115 *Jussi Lassila* | The Quest for an Ideal Youth in Putin's Russia II. The Search for Distinctive Conformism in the Political Communication of Nashi, 2005-2009 | With a foreword by Kirill Postoutenko | Second, Revised and Expanded Edition | ISBN 978-3-8382-0415-2

116 *Valerio Trabandt* | Neue Nachbarn, gute Nachbarschaft? Die EU als internationaler Akteur am Beispiel ihrer Demokratieförderung in Belarus und der Ukraine 2004-2009 | Mit einem Vorwort von Jutta Joachim | ISBN 978-3-8382-0437-6

117 *Fabian Pfeiffer* | Estlands Außen- und Sicherheitspolitik I. Der estnische Atlantizismus nach der wiedererlangten Unabhängigkeit 1991-2004 | Mit einem Vorwort von Helmut Hubel | ISBN 978-3-8382-0127-6

118 *Jana Podßuweit* | Estlands Außen- und Sicherheitspolitik II. Handlungsoptionen eines Kleinstaates im Rahmen seiner EU-Mitgliedschaft (2004-2008) | Mit einem Vorwort von Helmut Hubel | ISBN 978-3-8382-0440-6

119 *Karin Pointner* | Estlands Außen- und Sicherheitspolitik III. Eine gedächtnispolitische Analyse estnischer Entwicklungskooperation 2006-2010 | Mit einem Vorwort von Karin Liebhart | ISBN 978-3-8382-0435-2

120 *Ruslana Vovk* | Die Offenheit der ukrainischen Verfassung für das Völkerrecht und die europäische Integration | Mit einem Vorwort von Alexander Blankenagel | ISBN 978-3-8382-0481-9

121 *Mykhaylo Banakh* | Die Relevanz der Zivilgesellschaft bei den postkommunistischen Transformationsprozessen in mittel- und osteuropäischen Ländern. Das Beispiel der spät- und postsowjetischen Ukraine 1986-2009 | Mit einem Vorwort von Gerhard Simon | ISBN 978-3-8382-0499-4

122 *Michael Moser* | Language Policy and the Discourse on Languages in Ukraine under President Viktor Yanukovych (25 February 2010–28 October 2012) | ISBN 978-3-8382-0497-0 (Paperback edition) | ISBN 978-3-8382-0507-6 (Hardcover edition)

123 *Nicole Krome* | Russischer Netzwerkkapitalismus Restrukturierungsprozesse in der Russischen Föderation am Beispiel des Luftfahrtunternehmens „Aviastar" | Mit einem Vorwort von Petra Stykow | ISBN 978-3-8382-0534-2

124 *David R. Marples* | 'Our Glorious Past'. Lukashenka's Belarus and the Great Patriotic War | ISBN 978-3-8382-0574-8 (Paperback edition) | ISBN 978-3-8382-0675-2 (Hardcover edition)

125 *Ulf Walther* | Russlands „neuer Adel". Die Macht des Geheimdienstes von Gorbatschow bis Putin | Mit einem Vorwort von Hans-Georg Wieck | ISBN 978-3-8382-0584-7

126 *Simon Geissbühler (Hrsg.)* | Kiew – Revolution 3.0. Der Euromaidan 2013/14 und die Zukunftsperspektiven der Ukraine | ISBN 978-3-8382-0581-6 (Paperback edition) | ISBN 978-3-8382-0681-3 (Hardcover edition)

127 *Andrey Makarychev* | Russia and the EU in a Multipolar World. Discourses, Identities, Norms | With a foreword by Klaus Segbers | ISBN 978-3-8382-0629-5

128 *Roland Scharff* | Kasachstan als postsowjetischer Wohlfahrtsstaat. Die Transformation des sozialen Schutzsystems | Mit einem Vorwort von Joachim Ahrens | ISBN 978-3-8382-0622-6

129 *Katja Grupp* | Bild Lücke Deutschland. Kaliningrader Studierende sprechen über Deutschland | Mit einem Vorwort von Martin Schulz | ISBN 978-3-8382-0552-6

130 *Konstantin Sheiko, Stephen Brown* | History as Therapy. Alternative History and Nationalist Imaginings in Russia, 1991-2014 | ISBN 978-3-8382-0665-3

131 *Elisa Kriza* | Alexander Solzhenitsyn: Cold War Icon, Gulag Author, Russian Nationalist? A Study of the Western Reception of his Literary Writings, Historical Interpretations, and Political Ideas | With a foreword by Andrei Rogatchevski | ISBN 978-3-8382-0589-2 (Paperback edition) | ISBN 978-3-8382-0690-5 (Hardcover edition)

132 *Serghei Golunov* | The Elephant in the Room. Corruption and Cheating in Russian Universities | ISBN 978-3-8382-0570-0

133 *Manja Hussner, Rainer Arnold (Hgg.)* | Verfassungsgerichtsbarkeit in Zentralasien I. Sammlung von Verfassungstexten | ISBN 978-3-8382-0595-3

134 *Nikolay Mitrokhin* | Die „Russische Partei". Die Bewegung der russischen Nationalisten in der UdSSR 1953-1985 | Aus dem Russischen übertragen von einem Übersetzerteam unter der Leitung von Larisa Schippel | ISBN 978-3-8382-0024-8

135 *Manja Hussner, Rainer Arnold (Hgg.)* | Verfassungsgerichtsbarkeit in Zentralasien II. Sammlung von Verfassungstexten | ISBN 978-3-8382-0597-7

136 *Manfred Zeller* | Das sowjetische Fieber. Fußballfans im poststalinistischen Vielvölkerreich | Mit einem Vorwort von Nikolaus Katzer | ISBN 978-3-8382-0757-5

137 *Kristin Schreiter* | Stellung und Entwicklungspotential zivilgesellschaftlicher Gruppen in Russland. Menschenrechtsorganisationen im Vergleich | ISBN 978-3-8382-0673-8

138 *David R. Marples, Frederick V. Mills (Eds.)* | Ukraine's Euromaidan. Analyses of a Civil Revolution | ISBN 978-3-8382-0660-8

139 *Bernd Kappenberg* | Setting Signs for Europe. Why Diacritics Matter for European Integration | With a foreword by Peter Schlobinski | ISBN 978-3-8382-0663-9

140 *René Lenz* | Internationalisierung, Kooperation und Transfer. Externe bildungspolitische Akteure in der Russischen Föderation | Mit einem Vorwort von Frank Ettrich | ISBN 978-3-8382-0751-3

141 *Juri Plusnin, Yana Zausaeva, Natalia Zhidkevich, Artemy Pozanenko* | Wandering Workers. Mores, Behavior, Way of Life, and Political Status of Domestic Russian Labor Migrants | Translated by Julia Kazantseva | ISBN 978-3-8382-0653-0

142 *David J. Smith (Eds.)* | Latvia – A Work in Progress? 100 Years of State- and Nation-Building | ISBN 978-3-8382-0648-6

143 *Инна Чувычкина (ред.)* | Экспортные нефте- и газопроводы на постсоветском пространстве. Анализ трубопроводной политики в свете теории международных отношений | ISBN 978-3-8382-0822-0

144 *Johann Zajaczkowski* | Russland – eine pragmatische Großmacht? Eine rollentheoretische Untersuchung russischer Außenpolitik am Beispiel der Zusammenarbeit mit den USA nach 9/11 und des Georgienkrieges von 2008 | Mit einem Vorwort von Siegfried Schieder | ISBN 978-3-8382-0837-4

145 *Boris Popivanov* | Changing Images of the Left in Bulgaria. The Challenge of Post-Communism in the Early 21st Century | ISBN 978-3-8382-0667-7

146 *Lenka Krátká* | A History of the Czechoslovak Ocean Shipping Company 1948-1989. How a Small, Landlocked Country Ran Maritime Business During the Cold War | ISBN 978-3-8382-0666-0

147 *Alexander Sergunin* | Explaining Russian Foreign Policy Behavior. Theory and Practice | ISBN 978-3-8382-0752-0

148 *Darya Malyutina* | Migrant Friendships in a Super-Diverse City. Russian-Speakers and their Social Relationships in London in the 21st Century | With a foreword by Claire Dwyer | ISBN 978-3-8382-0652-3

149 *Alexander Sergunin, Valery Konyshev* | Russia in the Arctic. Hard or Soft Power? | ISBN 978-3-8382-0753-7

150 *John J. Maresca* | Helsinki Revisited. A Key U.S. Negotiator's Memoirs on the Development of the CSCE into the OSCE | With a foreword by Hafiz Pashayev | ISBN 978-3-8382-0852-7

151 *Jardar Østbø* | The New Third Rome. Readings of a Russian Nationalist Myth | With a foreword by Pål Kolstø | ISBN 978-3-8382-0870-1

152 *Simon Kordonsky* | Socio-Economic Foundations of the Russian Post-Soviet Regime. The Resource-Based Economy and Estate-Based Social Structure of Contemporary Russia | With a foreword by Svetlana Barsukova | ISBN 978-3-8382-0775-9

153 *Duncan Leitch* | Assisting Reform in Post-Communist Ukraine 2000–2012. The Illusions of Donors and the Disillusion of Beneficiaries | With a foreword by Kataryna Wolczuk | ISBN 978-3-8382-0844-2

154 *Abel Polese* | Limits of a Post-Soviet State. How Informality Replaces, Renegotiates, and Reshapes Governance in Contemporary Ukraine | With a foreword by Colin Williams | ISBN 978-3-8382-0845-9

155 *Mikhail Suslov (Ed.)* | Digital Orthodoxy in the Post-Soviet World. The Russian Orthodox Church and Web 2.0 | With a foreword by Father Cyril Hovorun | ISBN 978-3-8382-0871-8

156 *Leonid Luks* | Zwei „Sonderwege"? Russisch-deutsche Parallelen und Kontraste (1917-2014). Vergleichende Essays | ISBN 978-3-8382-0823-7

157 *Vladimir V. Karacharovskiy, Ovsey I. Shkaratan, Gordey A. Yastrebov* | Towards a New Russian Work Culture. Can Western Companies and Expatriates Change Russian Society? | With a foreword by Elena N. Danilova | Translated by Julia Kazantseva | ISBN 978-3-8382-0902-9

158 *Edmund Griffiths* | Aleksandr Prokhanov and Post-Soviet Esotericism | ISBN 978-3-8382-0963-0

159 *Timm Beichelt, Susann Worschech (Eds.)* | Transnational Ukraine? Networks and Ties that Influence(d) Contemporary Ukraine | ISBN 978-3-8382-0944-9

160 *Mieste Hotopp-Riecke* | Die Tataren der Krim zwischen Assimilation und Selbstbehauptung. Der Aufbau des krimtatarischen Bildungswesens nach Deportation und Heimkehr (1990-2005) | Mit einem Vorwort von Swetlana Czerwonnaja | ISBN 978-3-89821-940-2

161 *Olga Bertelsen (Ed.)* | Revolution and War in Contemporary Ukraine. The Challenge of Change | ISBN 978-3-8382-1016-2

162 *Natalya Ryabinska* | Ukraine's Post-Communist Mass Media. Between Capture and Commercialization | With a foreword by Marta Dyczok | ISBN 978-3-8382-1011-7

163 *Alexandra Cotofana, James M. Nyce (Eds.)* | Religion and Magic in Socialist and Post-Socialist Contexts. Historic and Ethnographic Case Studies of Orthodoxy, Heterodoxy, and Alternative Spirituality | With a foreword by Patrick L. Michelson | ISBN 978-3-8382-0989-0

164 *Nozima Akhrarkhodjaeva* | The Instrumentalisation of Mass Media in Electoral Authoritarian Regimes. Evidence from Russia's Presidential Election Campaigns of 2000 and 2008 | ISBN 978-3-8382-1013-1

165 *Yulia Krasheninnikova* | Informal Healthcare in Contemporary Russia. Sociographic Essays on the Post-Soviet Infrastructure for Alternative Healing Practices | ISBN 978-3-8382-0970-8

166 *Peter Kaiser* | Das Schachbrett der Macht. Die Handlungsspielräume eines sowjetischen Funktionärs unter Stalin am Beispiel des Generalsekretärs des Komsomol Aleksandr Kosarev (1929-1938) | Mit einem Vorwort von Dietmar Neutatz | ISBN 978-3-8382-1052-0

167 *Oksana Kim* | The Effects and Implications of Kazakhstan's Adoption of International Financial Reporting Standards. A Resource Dependence Perspective | With a foreword by Svetlana Vlady | ISBN 978-3-8382-0987-6

168 *Anna Sanina* | Patriotic Education in Contemporary Russia. Sociological Studies in the Making of the Post-Soviet Citizen | With a foreword by Anna Oldfield | ISBN 978-3-8382-0993-7

169 *Rudolf Wolters* | Spezialist in Sibirien Faksimile der 1933 erschienenen ersten Ausgabe | Mit einem Vorwort von Dmitrij Chmelnizki | ISBN 978-3-8382-0515-1

170 *Michal Vít, Magdalena M. Baran (Eds.)* | Transregional versus National Perspectives on Contemporary Central European History. Studies on the Building of Nation-States and Their Cooperation in the 20th and 21st Century | With a foreword by Petr Vágner | ISBN 978-3-8382-1015-5

171 *Philip Gamaghelyan* | Conflict Resolution Beyond the International Relations Paradigm. Evolving Designs as a Transformative Practice in Nagorno-Karabakh and Syria | With a foreword by Susan Allen | ISBN 978-3-8382-1057-5

172 *Maria Shagina* | Joining a Prestigious Club. Cooperation with Europarties and Its Impact on Party Development in Georgia, Moldova, and Ukraine 2004–2015 | With a foreword by Kataryna Wolczuk | ISBN 978-3-8382-1084-1

173 *Alexandra Cotofana, James M. Nyce (Eds.)* | Religion and Magic in Socialist and Post-Socialist Contexts II. Baltic, Eastern European, and Post-USSR Case Studies | With a foreword by Anita Stasulane | ISBN 978-3-8382-0990-6

174 *Barbara Kunz* | Kind Words, Cruise Missiles, and Everything in Between. The Use of Power Resources in U.S. Policies towards Poland, Ukraine, and Belarus 1989–2008 | With a foreword by William Hill | ISBN 978-3-8382-1065-0

175 *Eduard Klein* | Bildungskorruption in Russland und der Ukraine. Eine komparative Analyse der Performanz staatlicher Antikorruptionsmaßnahmen im Hochschulsektor am Beispiel universitärer Aufnahmeprüfungen | Mit einem Vorwort von Heiko Pleines | ISBN 978-3-8382-0995-1

176 *Markus Soldner* | Politischer Kapitalismus im postsowjetischen Russland. Die politische, wirtschaftliche und mediale Transformation in den 1990er Jahren | Mit einem Vorwort von Wolfgang Ismayr | ISBN 978-3-8382-1222-7

177 *Anton Oleinik* | Building Ukraine from Within. A Sociological, Institutional, and Economic Analysis of a Nation-State in the Making | ISBN 978-3-8382-1150-3

178 *Peter Rollberg, Marlene Laruelle (Eds.)* | Mass Media in the Post-Soviet World. Market Forces, State Actors, and Political Manipulation in the Informational Environment after Communism | ISBN 978-3-8382-1116-9

179 *Mikhail Minakov* | Development and Dystopia. Studies in Post-Soviet Ukraine and Eastern Europe | With a foreword by Alexander Etkind | ISBN 978-3-8382-1112-1

180 *Aijan Sharshenova* | The European Union's Democracy Promotion in Central Asia. A Study of Political Interests, Influence, and Development in Kazakhstan and Kyrgyzstan in 2007–2013 | With a foreword by Gordon Crawford | ISBN 978-3-8382-1151-0

181 *Andrey Makarychev, Alexandra Yatsyk (Eds.)* | Boris Nemtsov and Russian Politics. Power and Resistance | With a foreword by Zhanna Nemtsova | ISBN 978-3-8382-1122-0

182 *Sophie Falsini* | The Euromaidan's Effect on Civil Society. Why and How Ukrainian Social Capital Increased after the Revolution of Dignity | With a foreword by Susann Worschech | ISBN 978-3-8382-1131-2

183 *Valentyna Romanova, Andreas Umland (Eds.)* | Ukraine's Decentralization. Challenges and Implications of the Local Governance Reform after the Euromaidan Revolution | ISBN 978-3-8382-1162-6

184 *Leonid Luks* | A Fateful Triangle. Essays on Contemporary Russian, German and Polish History | ISBN 978-3-8382-1143-5

185 *John B. Dunlop* | The February 2015 Assassination of Boris Nemtsov and the Flawed Trial of his Alleged Killers. An Exploration of Russia's "Crime of the 21st Century" | ISBN 978-3-8382-1188-6

186 *Vasile Rotaru* | Russia, the EU, and the Eastern Partnership. Building Bridges or Digging Trenches? | ISBN 978-3-8382-1134-3

187 *Marina Lebedeva* | Russian Studies of International Relations. From the Soviet Past to the Post-Cold-War Present | With a foreword by Andrei P. Tsygankov | ISBN 978-3-8382-0851-0

188 *Tomasz Stępniewski, George Soroka (Eds.)* | Ukraine after Maidan. Revisiting Domestic and Regional Security | ISBN 978-3-8382-1075-9

189 *Petar Cholakov* | Ethnic Entrepreneurs Unmasked. Political Institutions and Ethnic Conflicts in Contemporary Bulgaria | ISBN 978-3-8382-1189-3

190 *A. Salem, G. Hazeldine, D. Morgan (Eds.)* | Higher Education in Post-Communist States. Comparative and Sociological Perspectives | ISBN 978-3-8382-1183-1

191 *Igor Torbakov* | After Empire. Nationalist Imagination and Symbolic Politics in Russia and Eurasia in the Twentieth and Twenty-First Century | With a foreword by Serhii Plokhy | ISBN 978-3-8382-1217-3

192 *Aleksandr Burakovskiy* | Jewish-Ukrainian Relations in Late and Post-Soviet Ukraine. Articles, Lectures and Essays from 1986 to 2016 | ISBN 978-3-8382-1210-4

193 *Natalia Shapovalova, Olga Burlyuk (Eds.)* | Civil Society in Post-Euromaidan Ukraine. From Revolution to Consolidation | With a foreword by Richard Youngs | ISBN 978-3-8382-1216-6

194 *Franz Preissler* | Positionsverteidigung, Imperialismus oder Irredentismus? Russland und die „Russischsprachigen", 1991–2015 | ISBN 978-3-8382-1262-3

195 *Marian Madeła* | Der Reformprozess in der Ukraine 2014-2017. Eine Fallstudie zur Reform der öffentlichen Verwaltung | Mit einem Vorwort von Martin Malek | ISBN 978-3-8382-1266-1

196 *Anke Giesen* | „Wie kann denn der Sieger ein Verbrecher sein?" Eine diskursanalytische Untersuchung der russlandweiten Debatte über Konzept und Verstaatlichungsprozess der Lagergedenkstätte „Perm'-36" im Ural | ISBN 978-3-8382-1284-5

197 *Victoria Leukavets* | The Integration Policies of Belarus and Ukraine vis-à-vis the EU and Russia. A Comparative Analysis Through the Prism of a Two-Level Game Approach | ISBN 978-3-8382-1247-0

198 *Oksana Kim* | The Development and Challenges of Russian Corporate Governance I. The Roles and Functions of Boards of Directors | With a foreword by Sheila M. Puffer | ISBN 978-3-8382-1287-6

199 *Thomas D. Grant* | International Law and the Post-Soviet Space I. Essays on Chechnya and the Baltic States | With a foreword by Stephen M. Schwebel | ISBN 978-3-8382-1279-1

200 *Thomas D. Grant* | International Law and the Post-Soviet Space II. Essays on Ukraine, Intervention, and Non-Proliferation | ISBN 978-3-8382-1280-7

201 *Slavomír Michálek, Michal Štefansky* | The Age of Fear. The Cold War and Its Influence on Czechoslovakia 1945–1968 | ISBN 978-3-8382-1285-2

202 *Iulia-Sabina Joja* | Romania's Strategic Culture 1990–2014. Continuity and Change in a Post-Communist Country's Evolution of National Interests and Security Policies | With a foreword by Heiko Biehl | ISBN 978-3-8382-1286-9

203 *Andrei Rogatchevski, Yngvar B. Steinholt, Arve Hansen, David-Emil Wickström* | War of Songs. Popular Music and Recent Russia-Ukraine Relations | With a foreword by Artemy Troitsky | ISBN 978-3-8382-1173-2

204 *Maria Lipman (Ed.)* | Russian Voices on Post-Crimea Russia. An Almanac of Counterpoint Essays from 2015–2018 | ISBN 978-3-8382-1251-7

205 *Ksenia Maksimovtsova* | Language Conflicts in Contemporary Estonia, Latvia, and Ukraine. A Comparative Exploration of Discourses in Post-Soviet Russian-Language Digital Media | With a foreword by Ammon Cheskin | ISBN 978-3-8382-1282-1

206 *Michal Vít* | The EU's Impact on Identity Formation in East-Central Europe between 2004 and 2013. Perceptions of the Nation and Europe in Political Parties of the Czech Republic, Poland, and Slovakia | With a foreword by Andrea Pető | ISBN 978-3-8382-1275-3

207 *Per A. Rudling* | Tarnished Heroes. The Organization of Ukrainian Nationalists in the Memory Politics of Post-Soviet Ukraine | ISBN 978-3-8382-0999-9

208 *Kaja Gadowska, Peter Solomon (Eds.)* | Legal Change in Post-Communist States. Progress, Reversions, Explanations | ISBN 978-3-8382-1312-5

209 *Paweł Kowal, Georges Mink, Iwona Reichardt (Eds.)* | Three Revolutions: Mobilization and Change in Contemporary Ukraine I. Theoretical Aspects and Analyses on Religion, Memory, and Identity | ISBN 978-3-8382-1321-7

210 *Paweł Kowal, Georges Mink, Adam Reichardt, Iwona Reichardt (Eds.)* | Three Revolutions: Mobilization and Change in Contemporary Ukraine II. An Oral History of the Revolution on Granite, Orange Revolution, and Revolution of Dignity | ISBN 978-3-8382-1323-1

211 *Li Bennich-Björkman, Sergiy Kurbatov (Eds.)* | When the Future Came. The Collapse of the USSR and the Emergence of National Memory in Post-Soviet History Textbooks | ISBN 978-3-8382-1335-4

212 *Olga R. Gulina* | Migration as a (Geo-)Political Challenge in the Post-Soviet Space. Border Regimes, Policy Choices, Visa Agendas | With a foreword by Nils Muižnieks | ISBN 978-3-8382-1338-5

213 *Sanna Turoma, Kaarina Aitamurto, Slobodanka Vladiv-Glover (Eds.)* | Religion, Expression, and Patriotism in Russia. Essays on Post-Soviet Society and the State. ISBN 978-3-8382-1346-0

214 *Vasif Huseynov* | Geopolitical Rivalries in the "Common Neighborhood". Russia's Conflict with the West, Soft Power, and Neoclassical Realism | With a foreword by Nicholas Ross Smith | ISBN 978-3-8382-1277-7

215 *Mikhail Suslov* | Geopolitical Imagination. Ideology and Utopia in Post-Soviet Russia | With a foreword by Mark Bassin | ISBN 978-3-8382-1361-3

216 *Alexander Etkind, Mikhail Minakov (Eds.)* | Ideology after Union. Political Doctrines, Discourses, and Debates in Post-Soviet Societies | ISBN 978-3-8382-1388-0

217 *Jakob Mischke, Oleksandr Zabirko (Hgg.)* | Protestbewegungen im langen Schatten des Kreml. Aufbruch und Resignation in Russland und der Ukraine | ISBN 978-3-8382-0926-5

218 *Oksana Huss* | How Corruption and Anti-Corruption Policies Sustain Hybrid Regimes. Strategies of Political Domination under Ukraine's Presidents in 1994-2014 | With a foreword by Tobias Debiel and Andrea Gawrich | ISBN 978-3-8382-1430-6

219 *Dmitry Travin, Vladimir Gel'man, Otar Marganiya* | The Russian Path. Ideas, Interests, Institutions, Illusions | With a foreword by Vladimir Ryzhkov | ISBN 978-3-8382-1421-4

220 *Gergana Dimova* | Political Uncertainty. A Comparative Exploration | With a foreword by Todor Yalamov and Rumena Filipova | ISBN 978-3-8382-1385-9

221 *Torben Waschke* | Russland in Transition. Geopolitik zwischen Raum, Identität und Machtinteressen | Mit einem Vorwort von Andreas Dittmann | ISBN 978-3-8382-1480-1

222 *Steven Jobbitt, Zsolt Bottlik, Marton Berki (Eds.)* | Power and Identity in the Post-Soviet Realm. Geographies of Ethnicity and Nationality after 1991 | ISBN 978-3-8382-1399-6

223 *Daria Buteiko* | Erinnerungsort. Ort des Gedenkens, der Erholung oder der Einkehr? Kommunismus-Erinnerung am Beispiel der Gedenkstätte Berliner Mauer sowie des Soloveckij-Klosters und -Museumsparks | ISBN 978-3-8382-1367-5

224 *Olga Bertelsen (Ed.)* | Russian Active Measures. Yesterday, Today, Tomorrow | With a foreword by Jan Goldman | ISBN 978-3-8382-1529-7

225 *David Mandel* | "Optimizing" Higher Education in Russia. University Teachers and their Union "Universitetskaya solidarnost'" | ISBN 978-3-8382-1519-8

226 *Mikhail Minakov, Gwendolyn Sasse, Daria Isachenko (Eds.)* | Post-Soviet Secessionism. Nation-Building and State-Failure after Communism | ISBN 978-3-8382-1538-9

227 *Jakob Hauter (Ed.)* | Civil War? Interstate War? Hybrid War? Dimensions and Interpretations of the Donbas Conflict in 2014–2020 | With a foreword by Andrew Wilson | ISBN 978-3-8382-1383-5

228 *Tima T. Moldogaziev, Gene A. Brewer, J. Edward Kellough (Eds.)* | Public Policy and Politics in Georgia. Lessons from Post-Soviet Transition | With a foreword by Dan Durning | ISBN 978-3-8382-1535-8

229 *Oxana Schmies (Ed.)* | NATO's Enlargement and Russia. A Strategic Challenge in the Past and Future | With a foreword by Vladimir Kara-Murza | ISBN 978-3-8382-1478-8

230 *Christopher Ford* | Ukapisme – Une Gauche perdue. Le marxisme anti-colonial dans la révolution ukrainienne 1917-1925 | Avec une préface de Vincent Présumey | ISBN 978-3-8382-0899-2

231 *Anna Kutkina* | Between Lenin and Bandera. Decommunization and Multivocality in Post-Euromaidan Ukraine | With a foreword by Juri Mykkänen | ISBN 978-3-8382-1506-8

232 *Lincoln E. Flake* | Defending the Faith. The Russian Orthodox Church and the Demise of Religious Pluralism | With a foreword by Peter Martland | ISBN 978-3-8382-1378-1

233 *Nikoloz Samkharadze* | Russia's Recognition of the Independence of Abkhazia and South Ossetia. Analysis of a Deviant Case in Moscow's Foreign Policy | With a foreword by Neil MacFarlane | ISBN 978-3-8382-1414-6

234 *Arve Hansen* | Urban Protest. A Spatial Perspective on Kyiv, Minsk, and Moscow | With a foreword by Julie Wilhelmsen | ISBN 978-3-8382-1495-5

235 *Eleonora Narvselius, Julie Fedor (Eds.)* | Diversity in the East-Central European Borderlands. Memories, Cityscapes, People | ISBN 978-3-8382-1523-5

236 *Regina Elsner* | The Russian Orthodox Church and Modernity. A Historical and Theological Investigation into Eastern Christianity between Unity and Plurality | With a foreword by Mikhail Suslov | ISBN 978-3-8382-1568-6

237 *Bo Petersson* | The Putin Predicament. Problems of Legitimacy and Succession in Russia | With a foreword by J. Paul Goode | ISBN 978-3-8382-1050-6

238 *Jonathan Otto Pohl* | The Years of Great Silence. The Deportation, Special Settlement, and Mobilization into the Labor Army of Ethnic Germans in the USSR, 1941–1955 | ISBN 978-3-8382-1630-7

239 *Mikhail Minakov (Ed.)* | Inventing Majorities. Ideological Creativity in Post-Soviet Societies | ISBN 978-3-8382-1641-6

240 *Robert M. Cutler* | Soviet and Post-Soviet Foreign Policies I. East-South Relations and the Political Economy of the Communist Bloc, 1971–1991 | With a foreword by Roger E. Kanet | ISBN 978-3-8382-1654-6

241 *Izabella Agardi* | On the Verge of History. Life Stories of Rural Women from Serbia, Romania, and Hungary, 1920–2020 | With a foreword by Andrea Pető | ISBN 978-3-8382-1602-7

242 *Sebastian Schäffer (Ed.)* | Ukraine in Central and Eastern Europe. Kyiv's Foreign Affairs and the International Relations of the Post-Communist Region | With a foreword by Pavlo Klimkin and Andreas Umland| ISBN 978-3-8382-1615-7

243 *Volodymyr Dubrovskyi, Kalman Mizsei, Mychailo Wynnyckyj (Eds.)* | Eight Years after the Revolution of Dignity. What Has Changed in Ukraine during 2013–2021? | With a foreword by Yaroslav Hrytsak | ISBN 978-3-8382-1560-0

244 *Rumena Filipova* | Constructing the Limits of Europe Identity and Foreign Policy in Poland, Bulgaria, and Russia since 1989 | With forewords by Harald Wydra and Gergana Yankova-Dimova | ISBN 978-3-8382-1649-2

245 *Oleksandra Keudel* | How Patronal Networks Shape Opportunities for Local Citizen Participation in a Hybrid Regime A Comparative Analysis of Five Cities in Ukraine | With a foreword by Sabine Kropp | ISBN 978-3-8382-1671-3

246 *Jan Claas Behrends, Thomas Lindenberger, Pavel Kolar (Eds.)* | Violence after Stalin Institutions, Practices, and Everyday Life in the Soviet Bloc 1953–1989 | ISBN 978-3-8382-1637-9

247 *Leonid Luks* | Macht und Ohnmacht der Utopien Essays zur Geschichte Russlands im 20. und 21. Jahrhundert | ISBN 978-3-8382-1677-5

248 *Iuliia Barshadska* | Brüssel zwischen Kyjiw und Moskau Das auswärtige Handeln der Europäischen Union im ukrainisch-russischen Konflikt 2014-2019 | Mit einem Vorwort von Olaf Leiße | ISBN 978-3-8382-1667-6

249 *Valentyna Romanova* | Decentralisation and Multilevel Elections in Ukraine Reform Dynamics and Party Politics in 2010–2021 | With a foreword by Kimitaka Matsuzato | ISBN 978-3-8382-1700-0

250 *Alexander Motyl* | National Questions. Theoretical Reflections on Nations and Nationalism in Eastern Europe | ISBN 978-3-8382-1675-1

251 *Marc Dietrich* | A Cosmopolitan Model for Peacebuilding. The Ukrainian Cases of Crimea and the Donbas | With a foreword by Rémi Baudouï | ISBN 978-3-8382-1687-4

252 *Eduard Baidaus* | An Unsettled Nation. Moldova in the Geopolitics of Russia, Romania, and Ukraine | With forewords by John-Paul Himka and David R. Marples | ISBN 978-3-8382-1582-2

253 *Igor Okunev, Petr Oskolkov (Eds.)* | Transforming the Administrative Matryoshka. The Reform of Autonomous Okrugs in the Russian Federation, 2003–2008 | With a foreword by Vladimir Zorin | ISBN 978-3-8382-1721-5

254 *Winfried Schneider-Deters* | Ukraine's Fateful Years 2013–2019. Vol. I: The Popular Uprising in Winter 2013/2014 | ISBN 978-3-8382-1725-3

255 *Winfried Schneider-Deters* | Ukraine's Fateful Years 2013–2019. Vol. II: The Annexation of Crimea and the War in Donbas | ISBN 978-3-8382-1726-0

256 *Robert M. Cutler* | Soviet and Post-Soviet Russian Foreign Policies II. East-West Relations in Europe and the Political Economy of the Communist Bloc, 1971–1991 | With a foreword by Roger E. Kanet | ISBN 978-3-8382-1727-7

257 *Robert M. Cutler* | Soviet and Post-Soviet Russian Foreign Policies III. East-West Relations in Europe and Eurasia in the Post-Cold War Transition, 1991–2001 | With a foreword by Roger E. Kanet | ISBN 978-3-8382-1728-4

258 *Paweł Kowal, Iwona Reichardt, Kateryna Pryshchepa (Eds.)* | Three Revolutions: Mobilization and Change in Contemporary Ukraine III. Archival Records and Historical Sources on the 1990 Revolution on Granite | ISBN 978-3-8382-1376-7

259 *Mikhail Minakov (Ed.)* | Philosophy Unchained. Developments in Post-Soviet Philosophical Thought. | With a foreword by Christopher Donohue | ISBN 978-3-8382-1768-0

260 *David Dalton* | The Ukrainian Oligarchy After the Euromaidan. How Ukraine's Political Economy Regime Survived the Crisis | With a foreword by Andrew Wilson | ISBN 978-3-8382-1740-6

261 *Andreas Heinemann-Grüder (Ed.)* | Who Are the Fighters? Irregular Armed Groups in the Russian-Ukrainian War in 2014–2015 | ISBN 978-3-8382-1777-2

262 *Taras Kuzio (Ed.)* | Russian Disinformation and Western Scholarship. Bias and Prejudice in Journalistic, Expert, and Academic Analyses of East European, Russian and Eurasian Affairs | ISBN 978-3-8382-1685-0

263 *Darius Furmonavicius* | LithuaniaTransforms the West. Lithuania's Liberation from Soviet Occupation and the Enlargement of NATO (1988–2022) | With a foreword by Vytautas Landsbergis | ISBN 978-3-8382-1779-6

264 *Dirk Dalberg* | Politisches Denken im tschechoslowakischen Dissens. Egon Bondy, Miroslav Kusý, Milan Šimečka und Petr Uhl (1968-1989) | ISBN 978-3-8382-1318-7

265 *Леонид Люкс* | К столетию «философского парохода». Мыслители «первой» русской эмиграции о русской революции и о тоталитарных соблазнах XX века | ISBN 978-3-8382-1775-8

266 *Daviti Mtchedlishvili* | The EU and the South Caucasus. European Neighborhood Policies between Eclecticism and Pragmatism, 1991-2021 | With a foreword by Nicholas Ross Smith | ISBN 978-3-8382-1735-2

267 *Bohdan Harasymiw* | Post-Euromaidan Ukraine. Domestic Power Struggles and War of National Survival in 2014–2022 | ISBN 978-3-8382-1798-7

268 *Nadiia Koval, Denys Tereshchenko (Eds.)* | Russian Cultural Diplomacy under Putin. Rossotrudnichestvo, the "Russkiy Mir" Foundation, and the Gorchakov Fund in 2007–2022 | ISBN 978-3-8382-1801-4

269 *Izabela Kazejak* | Jews in Post-War Wrocław and L'viv. Official Policies and Local Responses in Comparative Perspective, 1945-1970s | ISBN 978-3-8382-1802-1

270 *Jakob Hauter* | Russia's Overlooked Invasion. The Causes of the 2014 Outbreak of War in Ukraine's Donbas | With a foreword by Hiroaki Kuromiya | ISBN 978-3-8382-1803-8

271 *Anton Shekhovtsov* | Russian Political Warfare. Essays on Kremlin Propaganda in Europe and the Neighbourhood, 2020-2023 | With a foreword by Nathalie Loiseau | ISBN 978-3-8382-1821-2

272 *Андреа Пето* | Насилие и Молчание. Красная армия в Венгрии во Второй Мировой войне | ISBN 978-3-8382-1636-2

273 *Winfried Schneider-Deters* | Russia's War in Ukraine. Debates on Peace, Fascism, and War Crimes, 2022–2023 | With a foreword by Klaus Gestwa | ISBN 978-3-8382-1876-5

ibidem.eu